MW01097634

Encyclopedia of Detail in Contemporary Residential Architecture

Virginia McLeod

Laurence King Publishing

Published in 2010 by
Laurence King Publishing Ltd
361–373 City Road
London
EC1V 1LR
e-mail: enquiries@laurenceking.com
www.laurenceking.com

A catalogue record for this book is
available from the British Library

ISBN: 978 1 85669 692 0

Designed by Hamish Muir
Illustrations by Advanced Illustrations
Limited
Picture research by Sophia Gibb
Technical research by Vic Brand

Printed in China

Foreword

The *Encyclopedia of Detail in Contemporary Residential Architecture* reveals a completely new approach to the representation of architectural construction details. The book presents 100 of the best recent architect-designed houses from around the world, which together represent the many diverse methods of contemporary design and construction. However, rather than presenting each house as a discrete project, here, over 700 construction details have been grouped together by type in order to illustrate, and give an overall view of, the ways in which the key elements of houses are constructed.

Construction details are as vital a part of residential architecture as its external form and interior layout. Whether so subtle as to be invisible or revealed as extraordinarily complex, the construction details determine the quality and character of the building. Good detailing entails exercising the utmost care and attention at the junctions between materials, between the different elements of a building and where a material changes direction. Through details, the myriad parts that make up a building come together to form a whole – joints, connections, seams, openings and surfaces are transformed, via a combination of technology and invention, into a building.

The construction details also act as one of the most challenging intellectual and technical exercises for any architect, producing, as they must, a series of what are essentially graphic representations of every single junction and connection in a building. Almost exclusively made up of two-dimensional representations (horizontal and vertical sectional drawings), the challenge resides in the architect's ability to imagine the most complex of junctions, assemblies and components in three dimensions – as they will actually be built on site – and transfer them on to paper, or on to a screen, in two dimensions, employing the conventional drawn representations that have been used in the construction industry for decades, even centuries.

Primarily, of course, construction details were originally drawn to be used by builders, engineers and other participants in the building process in order to construct the building. Here, they have been gathered together and arranged to provide a guide to the inner workings of 100 of the most inspiring examples of contemporary residential architecture. This book brings to the reader what has, until now, been hidden behind the facade, what had previously remained invisible. These details provide not only an 'x-ray' of the houses presented, but an insight into the cognitive processes of the architects who brought the houses into being.

It is my sincere hope that these 100 projects and 730 construction details reveal the diversity, experimental spirit and architectural excellence in each of the finished buildings. They not only inspire, but also help us to understand the thought that went into the making of the buildings and perhaps the technical problems that were solved along the way.

Virginia McLeod

How to Use the Book

The book has been arranged in two main sections. The Directory of Houses at the front of the book acts as an introduction to each of the 100 houses and provides an overall picture of the creative and technical diversity in contemporary residential architecture of recent years. Here, each house is represented by colour photographs and a brief explanatory text. The houses have been grouped together by material type so that concrete houses, glass houses, masonry houses, steel houses and timber houses by different architects in diverse locations can be viewed together. The Directory can also be used as a reference point for the construction details. Each introduction includes the reference number for each detail from that house which appears in the second, and main, part of the book. The prefix number refers to the chapter – 1 for Walls, 2 for Floors, 3 for Windows, 4 for Doors, 5 for Roofs, 6 for Stairs and 7 for Landscape details. The suffix number refers to the location of the detail within the chapter. For example, the reference 3.021 in the introduction to Chenchow Little Architects' Freshwater House on page 32, refers to the twenty-first detail, likewise numbered 3.021 in the Window Details chapter.

In the second, and main, part of the book, the construction details have been arranged into seven chapters according to type. The types, or chapters – Walls, Floors, Windows, Doors, Roofs, Stairs and Landscape details – together provide, in one location, an in-depth picture of how windows, or roofs, for example, are detailed by different architects for different designs. Each detail includes a page number in square brackets to refer the reader back to the Directory of Houses at the front of the book, in order to see the architectural context of the detail. For example, construction detail 3.021 on page 141 by Chenchow Little Architects includes in the title the number [32]. This refers back to page 32 where the introductory text and photographs for Chenchow Little Architects' Freshwater House can be found.

Finally, the Project Credits at the end of the book provide additional information about the people involved in the creation of each house. This also includes a reference number in square brackets to refer the reader back to the Directory of Houses at the front of the book.

Notes

US and Metric Measurements
Dimensions have been provided by the architects in metric and converted to US measurements, except in case of projects in the US, where dimensions have been converted to metric.

Terminology
An attempt has been made to standardize terminology to aid understanding across readerships, for example 'wood' is generally referred to as 'timber' and 'aluminum' as 'aluminium'. However, materials or processes that are peculiar to a country, region or architectural practice that have no direct correspondence are presented in the original.

Scale
Detail drawings are presented at conventional architectural scales, typically 1:2, 1:5, 1:10 and 1:20.

Contents

Directory of Houses

Concrete Houses

Simon Walker Architects
Dane House, Caherdaniel, County Kerry, Ireland

Correia Ragazzi Arquitectos
Casa no Gerês, Vieira do Minho, Portugal

This private house, on a mountainside overlooking the sea in County Kerry, is located in the far southwest of Ireland. The site is located at the top of a valley which sweeps westward down from Ireland's tallest mountains, to the sea. The scale of the structure is influenced by the nearby barn buildings, which revealed the possibility of large living spaces not normally found in traditional farm cottages. But to accommodate such a large space it was necessary to make the structure recede into the landscape, and indeed to disappear completely when approached from certain aspects. The prevailing contours are modified to align with the primary structural bays and levels of the house, which is set down into an excavated pocket in the hillside. The trabeated colonnade structure is cast in concrete, and acts as an aqueduct to channel the prodigious amounts of rainwater away from the building. The roof, which is set below the level of the approach road and is the first visible indication of the house, is also concrete, and blends seamlessly with the rest of the structure.

Floors **2.059 2.062 2.065**
Windows **3.072**
Roofs **5.049 5.144**

This project involved the reconstruction and augmentation of a ruin into a weekend retreat on a beautiful, densely wooded site on the banks of the Cávado River in northern Portugal. The programme was for a house for a couple and their child, guest accommodation preferably located away from the house, as well as storage for waterski equipment that would include a shower and bathroom. The habitable area of the new house had to be no larger than the area of the existing ruin. The solution to this constraint was to place the house at right angles to the slope to create an optimum relationship to the site, especially the river, while at the same time avoiding damaging any of the existing trees which are protected under a conservation order. Private spaces such as the bedrooms are embedded in the site away from the river, while the shared spaces, including the living room, dining room and kitchen emerge with large expanses of glazing to embrace the landscape. The ruin has been restored to accommodate the waterski store and second bathroom.

Floors **2.020 2.029**
Windows **3.053 3.095**
Doors **4.073**
Roofs **5.084**

Alphaville
Hall House 1, Otsu, Shiga, Japan

Matharoo Associates
Dilip Sanghvi Residence, Surat, Gujarat, India

Ensamble Studio
Hemeroscopium House, Madrid, Spain

This small house in a residential district of Shiga was designed for a couple who required a parking space, billiard room, dining-kitchen, and bedroom with bathroom. These spaces are contained in one open space that changes its height according to the slope of the front road. The inclined volume is bent at an angle of 70 degrees to fit into the irregular shape of the site, with the gap between the first and the second floors becoming a terrace that lets plenty of natural light into the interior via the glass bathroom. In spite of the closed nature of the interior, the sloped roof provides the inhabitants with an outlook over the surrounding roofscape. To realize the complex pentagonal plan and folded roof, a monocoque structural system was adopted with 150 mm (6 inch) thick concrete walls and a 180 mm (7 inch) thick concrete roof. The system includes a water repellent coating allowing rain to run off directly into underground drains, without the need for gutters, and reinforcing the clean geometry of the house.

Walls **1.004**
Floors **2.006**
Windows **3.062**
Doors **4.060 4.099**
Roofs **5.134**
Stairs **6.011**

This house for a diamond merchant involved a complex programme that required the careful separation of family, social and private spaces. Separate areas for business activities, guest accommodation, social and entertainment spaces are tied together in a busy urban setting. The complex geometry of the site is used as a cue to develop the architecture so that all areas of the house open out onto a tranquil and private green space. The house can be entered from two sides, through large, custom-designed entrance doorways that open into the entrance hallway. These two separate entrances act as a connecting space, opening on one side into the family areas and on the other into the formal spaces that are distinguished by the skewed concrete and travertine box. At one end of the passage is the family prayer room with the study above, giving religion and intellect their due prominence. The dwelling utilizes the concept of a precious jewel through the use of contrasting materials, especially the concrete walls poured in stone casts and the translucent onyx wall.

Walls **1.060**
Windows **3.060 3.061 3.116**
Roofs **5.046**

The Hemeroscopium House features massive structural elements disposed in a way that provokes a sense of incredulity or even wonder that gravity has not intervened to compromise the structural integrity of this unique building. Seven pre-cast concrete beams are piled up to generate a helix that originates from a central stable support. The composition then moves upwards in a sequence that becomes lighter as the structure grows, culminating in structural equilibrium. This is expressed visually with the apparently precarious placement of a 20 ton granite block which acts as a counterweight to the entire structure. The apparent simplicity of the structural system did in fact required complex calculations to take into account the necessary reinforcement, as well as the pre-stressing and post-tensioning of the steel reinforcement in the concrete beams. This extraordinary structure took a full year to engineer but only seven days to build due to the prefabrication of all of the main elements as well as a rigorously coordinated on site assembly procedure.

Walls **1.076**
Windows **3.008 3.009 3.122**
Roofs **5.039 5.040 5.160**

Agence Michel Tortel
Mikado House, Saint Maximin la Sainte Baume,
Provence, France

Morphogenesis
N85 Residence, New Delhi, India

Barclay & Crousse Architecture
Casa O, Cañete Province, Peru

The site's position shelters it from the worst effects of the mistral and gives it a panoramic view of the Verdon mountains. The house is designed along three main themes. Firstly, the creation of windows onto the landscape, framing views which range from the intimate to the grand scale. Secondly, the integration of the building into the site – the house makes use of three plateaus which form extensions to the natural rock outcrops. Finally, the house is designed around the sensory experience of its spaces and destinations. Based on the paths taken by each individual, the spaces reveal a series of visual surprises which change from day to day as they frame the changing natural landscape. The final arrangement of volumes was established via 'virtual walks' through the house. The result appears chaotic, but in fact every line and alignment is justified by the perspective it creates or the landscape it highlights. In the absence of a regular grid, detailed work on the structural design removed the need for intermediate columns and allows continuous architectural lines.

Floors **2.069 2.072 2.088**
Windows **3.135**
Doors **4.089 4.118**
Roofs **5.120**
Stairs **6.022 6.023**

This family home creates its own terrain, a veritable oasis, within its inscribed territory. Lush landscaping is contrasted with crisp, clear planes of stone, wood and concrete, which are simply striated or set in interlocking patterns. Transparency is achieved through the combination of glass, water, reflection, and modulated lighting. The house is a home for three generations of a family and their many visitors. The building is split into three levels – the private domain of the bedrooms and breakfast room, the shared inter-generational spaces such as the family room, kitchen and dining areas, and the fluid public domain of the lobby and living spaces. Moving through the house, it is immediately clear that the central space is the fulcrum of the project. The ceiling is dotted by circular skylights with an interior garden below, a green sanctuary within the house. A lap pool fed by harvested rainwater runs the length of the terrace on the second floor. Environmental design plays an integral role in achieving a network of green and open spaces.

Floors **2.014 2.015**
Windows **3.033**
Doors **4.065 4.110**
Roofs **5.047 5.141**
Stairs **6.013**

The O House is located in a densely populated private beach community. The design creates living spaces that relate directly to newly created exterior spaces without relying on a direct relationship to the nearby beach and without compromising privacy. The site is surrounded by a street, an alleyway, an adjacent house and the beach. These boundaries have given rise to a precinct in which open and closed spaces are arranged to create a self-contained interior living environment. A grid is used to create two solid volumes intercalated with two voids. The solids – the main bedroom and service area on the first floor, and the bedrooms on the lower level have a direct relationship with the most important open and closed public spaces of the dwelling. These are the terrace facing the sea, the living room, the exterior dining area, and the open terrace on the lower level. Water, the most precious element in the desert, flows through the house, in two distinct planes – a reflecting pool on the patio and the swimming pool on the terrace facing the sea.

Walls **1.062 1.063 1.065**
Doors **4.035 4.054 4.119 4.120**

Pezo von Ellrichshausen Architects
Poli House, Coliumo Peninsula, Tomé, Chile

Kotaro Ide / ARTechnic architects
Shell House, Kitasuku, Nagano, Japan

O'Donnell + Tuomey Architects
The Sleeping Giant – Killiney House, Killiney, County Dublin, Ireland

The house is located on the Coliumo Peninsula south of Santiago. The compact form is positioned as close as possible to the cliff edge to intensify the drama of the sea view and of the vertical cliff face where the sea explodes against the rocks below. The interior is divided into three platforms spread over a dramatic triple-height volume. The building functions both as a summer house and a cultural centre, hosting activities such as reunions, workshops and exhibitions. As a result, the interior must mediate between being very public and being intimate and informal. To achieve this, the service functions such as the vertical circulation, kitchen and bathrooms are situated inside a thick perimeter zone that acts as a buffer. For public functions the furniture can be stored inside this perimeter, freeing the space for multiple activities. The entire structure was built with handmade concrete, using untreated wooden frames. The same battered frames were used to wrap the interior and to build sliding panels that function both as doors and security shutters.

Walls **1.018 1.073**
Floors **2.043 2.044**
Windows **3.115**
Doors **4.009**
Roofs **5.108**

The architectural concept behind this family holiday house places it on a densely wooded site around a large fir tree at the centre of the plot, with a row of pine trees as the main view. To embrace the random location of the trees, a shell structure with three-dimensionally curved surfaces was created, with a C-shaped section to surround the fir tree and a J-shaped plan that moves around the trees. The structure is made from two white cylindrical masses with curved cut-outs to create glazed openings. The top of the oval shaped section thickens by 350 mm (1.1 feet) and its width continuously increases up to 750 mm (2.5 feet) at the sides to meet the structural requirements. The floor is built above the ground, with the lower half of the shell protruding towards the exterior to support the two large terraces. The curved plan is disposed over two levels. On the ground floor a generous master bedroom suite sits on one side of the courtyard, with the living, dining and kitchen areas on the other. Upstairs, three bedrooms enjoy views over the courtyard and landscape beyond.

Walls **1.046 1.047**
Roofs **5.068**
Stairs **6.038 6.058**

The site is high on a hill in Killiney with a view southwards towards Dublin Bay. The house is built into the rocky outcrops of granite that characterize the site in a series of split levels. The plan form is angled into the shape of the site to provide optimum views of the sea, and to bring sunshine into the house at all times of the day. The interlocking rooms step over the rocky site, providing a variety of views. The building is a reinforced concrete construction with solid granite outer walls forming a base, and lime render on the walls above. The most distinctive and challenging aspect of the design is the faceted concrete roof which is inspired by the granite rock formation around it. The roof is anchored by an exposed in-situ concrete chimney and rests on lines of slender steel columns. The concrete has been left exposed on the interior to provide a tent-like ceiling which reflects light throughout the day. The roof floats clear of the internal walls, with a series of glazed clerestories allowing daylight and views to penetrate into the depths of the house.

Windows **3.041 3.042 3.043**
Roofs **5.018 5.019 5.078**

Stam Architecten
Two Apartments, Antwerp, Belgium

Kallos Turin
Casa Zorzal, Maldonado, Uruguay

Charles Pictet Architecte
Villa Frontenex, Geneva, Switzerland

The house is located in the suburbs of Antwerp on a rectangular site bordered on both sides by terraced family houses. Instead of organizing another traditional one-family programme on two levels, the client chose to build two compact apartments, one on each level. The street level apartment reflects the footprint of the neighbouring properties and functions as a rental unit. The dividing wall between this and the entrance to the second space is designed as a thick wall containing storage and sanitary functions for both apartments. The first floor apartment is orientated towards the rear garden. Introverted spaces at the front accommodate bedrooms which are protected by aluminium louvres in front of a transparent glass skin. The main spaces are executed in carefully finished cast in-situ concrete which is announced by the mass of the concrete entrance stair. Smooth cast ceilings and floors are contrasted with dark oak furniture elements which are arranged as islands to create minimal divisions in the larger space.

Floors **2.001 2.002**
Windows **3.044**
Roofs **5.069**

Casa Zorzal is one of 13 seasonal vacation homes on the Villalagos Estate on the coast of Uruguay near Punta del Este. The architecture of each home on the estate consists of simple abstracted forms inserted into the hills and manipulated to address the specific topography and views. Casa Zorzal takes advantage of its sloped site with a series of volumes and terraces that flow down the site, culminating in a two-storey building overlooking the dramatic southeast view to the ocean. The glazed upper storey houses the main living spaces and opens to a light-filled pool pavilion and courtyard garden on one side and a viewing deck on the other. The building simultaneously shelters the courtyard, pool and pool pavilion from the wind and provides views from the courtyard through the double glazing to the landscape beyond. Local South American materials and building technologies have been used throughout – walls of stucco and frameless glass, poured concrete floors, Brazilian lapacho hardwood and Uruguayan black granite form the basis of the material palette.

Walls **1.026**
Floors **2.079**
Windows **3.096**
Doors **4.059 4.109**
Roofs **5.022 5.023 5.130**
Stairs **6.007 6.008**

Located on the outskirts of Geneva, the neighbourhood in which Villa Frontenex is situated is characterized by dignified manor houses dating from the 18th and 19th centuries. The site itself was once a small farm and still features a collection of stone farm buildings. The grandest of them, the orangery, has been used as the starting point for the creation of a contemporary family home. The orangery has been transformed into an expansive open-plan living, dining and kitchen space featuring a long wall of angled south facing glazing. The rear stone wall of the orangery has been punctured to create a link to the new part of the house which contains, over two above-ground levels and a basement, the rest of the functions of a family home. First floor bedrooms and the ground floor master suite are arranged around a grand staircase, allowing each room to enjoy expansive views across the landscape. Monolithic cast in-situ concrete has been used throughout the new building, its integral colour chosen to match that of the stone of the orangery.

Windows **3.074 3.075 3.076 3.077**
Doors **4.094**
Roofs **5.087**

Mount Fuji Architects Studio
Rainy Sunny House, Tokyo, Japan

Pierre Minassian Architecte
Biscuit House, Lyon, France

The site strategy for this house involved placing two single-storey triangular blocks diagonally across the rectangular site to create two residual outdoor courts: one a public space leading to the entrance, and the other of a more private character in the form of a garden. Internally, a double-height living room rises to a level ridge on the centre line of the site, dividing two symmetrical triangular soffits that fall away to opposite corners. Upstairs, a closet, bathroom and study with its own external balcony, overlook the double living space below. Externally, the beautifully crafted timber parquetry that is used extensively for the floors, walls and ceilings, extends out into the courtyard garden that features a single specimen tree. Other than the glazed wall that opens onto the garden, only two windows break the continuity of the finely detailed external concrete skin. This was cast using a zigzag formwork of shiplapped plywood. The resulting textured surface creates a weatherproof skin that combats a climate with considerable rainfall.

Walls **1.066**
Floors **2.056**
Windows **3.024 3.025**
Doors **4.083**

The house is located in a small village near Lyon on a very steep slope facing an open landscape. The building, a simple rectangular prism, is embedded in the slope of the terrain and is composed over two floors, both of which have direct access to the garden. All materials used for the structure are natural and untreated – concrete is used for the envelope and the floors, steel for the columns and window frames, and untreated iroko for the external curtain. This screen of timber 'biscuits' which gives the house its name, was hand made by the architect and required more than 200 hours of work. The timber screen has two main functions. It integrates the house with the landscape where local houses are built in beige stone, as well as reducing the impact of solar gain in the bedrooms on the upper floor. The ground floor is lined with full height windows allowing the living spaces to connect directly with the landscape. A suspended staircase, without risers, allows maximum natural daylight to penetrate the depths of the house and gives uninterrupted views.

Floors **2.068**
Roofs **5.103**
Stairs **6.041 6.061 6.062**

Lee + Mundwiler Architects
The Coconut House, Los Angeles, California, USA

Innovarchi
Gold Coast House, Queensland, Australia

Cassion Castle Architects
Twofold House, London, England, UK

This is an infill project tightly built onto a small site in a densely populated neighbourhood in Los Angeles. Along a busy thoroughfare, the familiar typology of 'home' is introduced – a traditional pitched roof, windows to the street and a chimney. A linear approach from the street leads to the point of arrival, situated at the core of the house where a courtyard takes centre stage, bringing light, air and nature into the living spaces. The predominantly white palette illuminates the inner core of the dwelling, enhancing light coming through from the skylight and the louvred courtyard. The facade of dark fibre-core panels with natural timber veneer emulates the tough shell of a coconut. This maintenance-free exterior will eliminate the use of petroleum products, such as paints and sealers, for many years to come. Further sustainable features, such as passive solar energy, active cross ventilation, recycled cementitous wood particle-board fencing and eco-resin panels, together with drought tolerant landscaping, feature throughout the project.

Windows **3.050 3.103**
Doors **4.002 4.003 4.121**
Roofs **5.045**
Stairs **6.067**

This house was designed as a sleek, hard edged glass box, the brief for which was 'a fishbowl with somewhere to get dressed'. On a sloping site facing the distant coastline, two pavilions are separated by a central entry platform. Living spaces are on the upper level, with an art gallery, studio and guest suite below. On the glazed upper level, large sliding panels and hinged walls modulate the internal space. Floor to ceiling glass doors across the length of the verandah dramatically open up the interior to the views. Designed for the sub-tropical climate, passive climatic control principals were employed to reduce energy consumption. Extensive cross ventilation from north to south is facilitated by the operable glass facades. The narrow plan and large areas of shaded glass maximize indirect daylight penetration. The heavy base acts as a cooling device for the upper floor in summer and as a warming device in the relatively mild winter, when the lower level is heated and the dark concrete slab on the upper floor is exposed to direct sunlight.

Windows **3.034 3.035 3.121**
Roofs **5.020 5.021**

The house is located on a very constrained site in an industrial alleyway, parallel to a busy shopping street. The clients, two industrial designers, required a place to live and work that could offer a sanctuary from the bustling city. The building is designed to minimize views out, to create a sense of shelter from the outside world. The studio and living spaces are arranged as two interlocking L-shaped forms, with a balcony overlooking the studio carved out of the bedroom wall. From the street the building is expressed as a foreign object 'wedged' into the existing terrace in a series of block-like forms and carved out spaces. The street facade is designed as an elegant double-height glass box overhanging an anti fly-poster painted ground floor entrance, which is set back to create a threshold onto the alley. When the doors and windows are closed, the building is shielded from the outside entirely, with light filtering in from the north facing clerestory window and a lightwell. The interior is crystalline white, providing a blank canvas for the interplay of light and shadow.

Windows **3.108**
Doors **4.006 4.007 4.008**
Roofs **5.033 5.060 5.138**

David Nossiter Architects
Kitsbury Road House, Hertfordshire, England, UK

Tony Fretton Architects
The Courtyard House, London, England, UK

Atelier Tekuto + Masahiro Ikeda
Lucky Drops, Tokyo, Japan

The site is a dwelling forming part of a Victorian terraced house. Whilst the front of the terrace remains largely original, various additions had been made to the rear. The architect sought to unify the house and to define the relationship between the house and the garden. The reworked rear elevation is comprised of a simple flat roof with the ground becoming a continuous plane that steps up as it wanders towards the rear of the house, rising each time a space changes in function. On entering the house, long views of the garden are reinforced by an uninterrupted stone worktop that runs the length of the party wall and emerges into the garden, where it becomes an external counter and seating area. The whole of this zone is top lit via continuous roof lights. Folding surfaces are a recurring theme – a stone worktop folds to emphasize the tactile realization of its corner, while laminated plywood shelves fold around surfaces and frame views, connecting spaces.

Walls **1.092**
Floors **2.021 2.022 2.050**
Windows **3.113**
Doors **4.084**
Roofs **5.026 5.027**
Landscape **7.007**

The house occupies a narrow site in Chelsea, which begins at the main street beneath an apartment building, continues between tall windowless walls and ends at another street to the rear. For the clients, the attraction of the site was its capacity to give a long continuous space on the ground floor for living, entertaining and displaying art. This is realized as a series of places of different characters, arranged around sources of light and outlook. The entrance and garage are placed on either side of the apartment building foyer. Diffused daylight comes into the entrance through etched glass windows onto the street. Here, a stair leads to a guest bedroom, playroom and spa in the basement. Beyond the entrance are a glazed open-air courtyard and stone stair rising to the first floor. The living room, a few steps down from the entrance, features a fireplace and a glazed wall with views into a courtyard garden. The first floor is arranged in three sections. In the centre is a courtyard with a glass floor, with a library on one side, and on the other the children's rooms.

Floors **2.036**
Doors **4.043 4.044**
Roofs **5.013 5.014 5.099 5.150**
Stairs **6.005 6.006**

This house, on a small plot, even by Tokyo standards, takes advantage of the site characteristics by utilizing the entire width, which is just 3.2 metres (10.5 feet), to maximize interior space. A light emitting and transmitting pitched glass shell shelters the majority of the interior spaces which, out of necessity, are placed below ground. The floors are constructed from expanded metal, letting maximum amounts of sunlight penetrate deep into the house. The primary living spaces are buried underground. Conventional earth-retaining work using concrete was rejected in favour of a simplified system of steel plates with anticorrosive, heat-insulating and waterproof treatments, painted white throughout to further increase the penetration of natural light. The name 'Lucky Drops', refers to a traditional Japanese saying, the English equivalent for which is 'saving the best for last'. Throughout the design and construction of this house, every effort has been made to live up to this sentiment, turning this leftover plot of land into a place for comfortable living.

Walls **1.059**
Floors **2.026 2.028**
Roofs **5.034**
Stairs **6.015**

Steven Holl Architects
Swiss Embassy Residence, Washington, D.C., USA

dRMM (de Rijke Marsh Morgan Architects)
Sliding House, Suffolk, England, UK

MacGabhann Architects
Tuath na Mara, Lough Swilly, County Donegal, Ireland

This scheme was placed first in a competition between ten Swiss-American architectural teams to design a replacement for the Washington, D.C. residence of the Swiss Ambassador. It is a private house as well as a cultural gathering place on which the standards and self-image of its country are measured. Sited on a hill with a direct view through the trees to the Washington monument in the distance, the concept is derived from a diagonal line of overlapping spaces drawn through a cruciform courtyard plan. Official arrival and ceremonial spaces are connected along this diagonal line on the first level, while private living quarters are on the level above. Materials are charcoal coloured concrete trimmed in local slate and sandblasted structural glass planks. Constructed according to the Swiss 'Minergie Standard', the south facades use passive solar energy. The existing natural landscape has been clarified with new walkways and trees, while the plateau of the residence defines an arrival square and a reception courtyard.

Walls **1.016 1.048**
Windows **3.026 3.027 3.112**
Doors **4.077**
Landscape **7.014**

The brief for this unusual residence was for a house where the owners could grow food, entertain friends and enjoy the landscape. An appreciation of vernacular farm buildings shared by architect and client led to the design of three apparently conventional timber 'sheds'. The linear arrangement includes three programmes – house, garage and annexe. The garage is pulled off axis to create a courtyard between the three. The composition is further defined by material and colour – red rubber membrane, glass and red-and-black stained larch. Almost shockingly, the separated forms can be transformed by a 20 ton mobile enclosure which traverses the site, creating combinations of enclosure, open-air living and attractive framing of views. This is an autonomous structure constructed from steel, timber, insulation and unstained larch and runs along recessed railway tracks. Movement is powered by hidden electric motors on wheels integrated into the wall thickness. The tracks can be extended in the future should the client wish to build a swimming pool, which may need occasional shelter.

Walls **1.008 1.022 1.067**
Floors **2.054**
Roofs **5.028**

This project concerns itself with the specifics of the site and putting the personal and particular above the powerful and the public. The site is hidden from the road and is accessed from high ground, where the first experience is of an elevated view of the site and the sea beyond. Therefore the importance of the roof, or fifth facade, dictated a metal zinc cladding which is used for both the walls and roof. The plan is inspired by traditional narrow cottages and contains three sleeping cells and auxiliary spaces in the middle, with two living areas, one at each end, connected by a library. The roof of both living areas is flipped and directed in opposite directions towards particular points in the landscape. Both living areas are fully glazed. By way of contrast, the sloped slit windows of the bedrooms act as a counterpoint to the absolute horizontal of the ocean horizon. The roof rainwater is drained by gargoyles, making one aware of the elements even in the lightest of showers, thus reinforcing the connection between inhabitant and nature.

Walls **1.045**
Floors **2.089**
Windows **3.012 3.013 3.139**
Roofs **5.064 5.065**

Powerhouse Company
Villa 1, Veluwezoom, The Netherlands

Public
Rattlesnake Creek House, Missoula, Montana, USA

The villa is orientated towards views of woodland terrain with half of the programme pushed below ground to meet local zoning regulations. This creates a clear dichotomy in the spatial experience of the house – a glass box above ground where built-in furniture elements alone divide the space, and a basement below where spaces are carved out of the mass. The Y plan arrangement is the result of the optimal configuration of the programme towards the sun and views. A study, library and music room in the northeast wing are shaped by the nut-wood central furniture piece containing the stair and a WC. The kitchen is defined by a full height slate-clad island in the southeast wing, while the living room, patio and studio in the west wing are defined by concrete blade walls. Counteracting the extreme openness of the ground floor, the basement level shelters the most intimate spaces including the master bedroom, stair and bathroom in one wing, two guest rooms, a patio, and a vaulted closet-corridor in another, with the third wing containing the garage.

Walls **1.053 1.054 1.090**
Floors **2.045**
Doors **4.049**
Roofs **5.110 5.157 5.158**

The six acre (2.4 hectare) site is bisected by Rattlesnake Creek, a wide shallow creek that flows year round and lies at the foot of a densely wooded mountain range. The house is sited on the bank amid pine trees and native grasses. The clients are a working couple with a love of nature and simple spaces. The programme was not the driving force behind the project. Besides the usual requirement of rooms for eating, living, and sleeping, the nature of these spaces is dictated by the site itself and the creek. All of the spaces within the house have individual relationships to the outdoors which creates a narrow but long sliver of building that is either compartmentalized with sliding walls or is left as one volume. The soft, colourful rooms are composed of a collage of cabinets and panels, which in turn are surrounded by the more austere exterior materials that shield the delicate interior of the house while welcoming in the landscape. The outer shell is board-formed concrete that stops short of the metal pan roof, allowing it to float on a band of light glazing.

Walls **1.051 1.052**
Doors **4.133**
Roofs **5.082 5.143 5.159**
Stairs **6.043**
Landscape **7.013**

Studio Longheu
Casa C, Vicenza, Italy

Hawkes Architecture
Crossway, Staplehurst, Kent, England, UK

Paulo David with Luz Ramalho
Casa Funchal, Madeira, Portugal

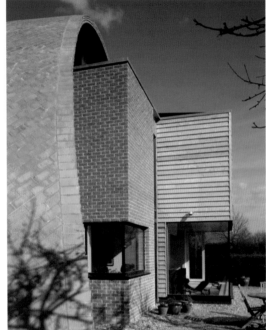

This house near Vicenza is embedded in a context of rich environmental and natural elements whose character it seeks to interpret and enhance. The first influential element is a stone wall embedded in the ground that follows the sloping course of the site and emerges as a base standing out from the white mass of the building. Its task is to delimit and include, to leave a trace of the site's history, while merging with the house to become a part of the present. It is a house that is sensitive to the landscape, sometimes framing particular views and sometimes opening up completely. The interpretation of inside and outside is enhanced in the living areas which are extended by terraces and loggias, and by flush door and window frames. Connected to the living area by an inclined roof, the bedroom wing is distinguished by dark wood cladding. The house offers its inhabitants the pleasure of different atmospheres: cosy in the small study or light and spacious in the swimming pool, where a sunken covered area embraces the spectacular view.

Walls **1.049**
Windows **3.045**
Doors **4.087**
Roofs **5.106 5.152**
Stairs **6.003 6.004**

Crossway feels rooted in its context, its arched form helping to minimize its mass. The arch gives the effect of the landscape being lifted up, with timber framed structures quietly slotted beneath. The colour and texture of local clay bricks and tiles along with locally grown cedar help instill a sense of familiarity in the Kent countryside. The vaulted arch is only 120 millimetres (5 inches) thick yet supports 300 millimetres (12 inches) of site spoil seeded with meadow plants from a nearby nature reserve. Built using clay dug and hand made nearby, the porous clay tiles naturally regulate humidity and the vast thermal mass regulates the temperature of the internal spaces. Heat recovery ventilation, triple glazing and high insulation minimize the energy needs of the house. Newspapers, car tyres and crushed bottles used in the lime mortar and in the polished ground floor are but a few of the recycled materials used. Pioneering energy systems generate electricity and store thermal energy. On-site waste treatment and rainwater harvesting are also in place.

Walls **1.025 1.075 1.094**
Windows **3.063 3.064 3.092**
Doors **4.062**
Roofs **5.129**
Stairs **6.036**

The orthogonal form of this house contrasts with the irregular shape of the plot which acts as a plateau from which to gaze out to sea. The section through the building sets up a dialogue with the site which is reinforced by a slot in the upper floor that fragments the volume, creating two 'bulges' resting on the main volume below. This box, which is at the same level as the plateau, defines the living spaces which extend out into the landscape. A central volume houses the kitchen, bathrooms and storage and defines the vertical and horizontal circulation. The two volumes on the upper level contain the bedrooms and have the character of watchtowers that monitor the seascape. The rough black skin that clads the exterior is a combination of a bonding agent with selected and sorted basalt particles. The chromatic uniformity is continued to the flat roof, where volcanic ash is used. In contrast, the interior surfaces are flat and white, allowing natural light to flood the interior.

Walls **1.030**
Floors **2.055**
Doors **4.017 4.018 4.129**
Roofs **5.091 5.133**
Stairs **6.028**

Haddow Partnership
Higher Farm, Blandford, Dorset, England, UK

Steffen Leisner, Ali Jeevanjee, Phillip Trigas
1+3=1 House, Venice, California, USA

Hamiltons
Holmewood House, Buckinghamshire, England, UK

This house is partly built into the ground, respecting the contours of the landscape and moulding itself into the hillside with the retained mature hedgerow as a backdrop. The structure embraces a contemporary aesthetic both externally and internally, and utilizes natural and sustainable materials as well as energy and resource saving techniques, throughout. Red-brown facing bricks are used as a solid base to the building, contrasted with coloured render to the upper ground level and glazed panels above. The main roof supports of powder-coated galvanized steel anchor the roof to the ground at the point where the land drops away and serve to tie the over sailing roof back to the main structure. The oak-clad circular stair tower features a balcony constructed of galvanized checker plate, powder-coated support struts and a stainless steel balustrade. Elsewhere, galvanized steel is used as internal bracing, wind posts and isolated structural members. The form of the roof references Dutch barn structures, which helps to unify the grouping of farm buildings.

Floors **2.064**
Doors **4.053**
Roofs **5.113**
Stairs **6.024**

The 1+3=1 House is located in a dense residential neighbourhood in Venice Beach. The clients work primarily from home and required a modest home office and a detached art studio. The principal programmatic objective was to maximize space while retaining an existing bungalow. A 'subtractive' design strategy generated the maximum volume permitted by zoning laws, then a series of strategic volumetric operations were undertaken to achieve both the client requirements and architectural goals. Five on-site parking spaces had to be provided, which led to the creation of courtyards that double as parking. The geometries of the master suite and the art studio resulted from cantilevering the buildings above the parking spaces to incorporate more usable space. One wing contains an office on the ground level, with a dedicated entry from the garden and a meditation room above. The other wing houses the living room on the ground level and the master suite upstairs. The living room features large expanses of glazing that connect the interior to the courtyard.

Floors **2.061**
Windows **3.065 3.102**
Roofs **5.008 5.009 5.128**
Stairs **6.053**

Holmewood, a new house on a private estate, nestles into the magnificent Chiltern Hills. The brief called for a home, but also a place to entertain, and a neutral foil for furniture and art. Principal rooms should be flooded with daylight, with external walls that could open up and embrace the surrounding landscape. The resulting single storey building appears as an effortless, elegant intervention. The project integrates mature trees, helping to create a building whose overall form appears as an integral part of the gently undulating landscape. An axial sequence of spaces link the entrance hall to the principal reception rooms arranged along the glazed south facing elevation. The building is ordered around a covered central courtyard with a glazed roof. A swimming pool in the central courtyard, together with retracting walls connecting the principal reception rooms, provide flexibility to accommodate a variety of functions within the house. The graceful curve of the heavily insulated grass covered roof acts as a unifying feature floating above the house.

Walls **1.112**
Floors **2.071**
Roofs **5.015 5.016 5.017**
Stairs **6.012**
Landscape **7.016**

Stephenson Bell Architects
House 780, Manchester, England, UK

Waro Kishi + K. Associates Architects
Hakata House, Fukuoka, Fukuoka Prefecture, Japan

ODOS Architects
House in Wicklow, County Wicklow, Ireland

The client's brief was to provide a high quality contemporary dwelling that would take advantage of the site's topography, with its gentle gradient and stunning views. The building is formed by two blocks, set at different levels, one of which incorporates a double height living space. The entrance is via two bridges, one concrete vehicle bridge into the upper level garage, and the lightweight steel and glass pedestrian bridge. The main stair descends into the double height space, and towards the corridor leading to the bedroom, bathroom, gym and study wing. All rooms utilize full height and width glazing, with sliding doors that provide views and access to the landscape. The double height living space is dominated by five metre (16.4 foot) tall glazing, with its external oak louvres at high level, and the chimney structure that penetrates the roof. The kitchen is adjacent to the living space, and provides numerous views through it, and back up towards the road and bridges. The two spaces can be separated by a full height sliding oak door.

Walls **1.079**
Windows **3.110**
Doors **4.026 4.027 4.078 4.117**
Roofs **5.062**

This house was built in a dense residential area of Fukuoka. The only possibility for a green outlook for this L-shaped, planar building was a small slot of space that forms the new courtyard in the three-level stairwell on the northwest corner of the site. The courtyard, which links the three above-ground floors, acts as a *Tsuboniwa* (Japanese courtyard garden) for the Japanese style room on the ground floor, while at the same time performing its central function as a landscape seen from the glazed wall of the first floor dining room. Bamboo was selected for this garden, acting as both a traditional element of Japanese gardens, and as contemporary architectural planting. While functioning as an urban residence in a high-density district, the ground floor might best be described as a closed, introspective space. The rooftop garden above, however, is in stark contrast, being so open as to be almost completely exposed. The inclusion of these two outdoor spaces, the courtyard and the rooftop garden, ensures the building's success as an urban residence.

Windows **3.017 3.054 3.055 3.056 3.057 3.093**

This bold sculptural house sits at the foot of a steep escarpment in the Wicklow Hills. Accommodation is comprised of a two-car garage, boiler room, WC and utility at ground floor level and open plan living, kitchen, dining areas with three bedrooms, study and family bathroom on the first floor. The building is entered at first floor level via an external stair. On entering, a hallway leads to the open plan living, kitchen and dining areas. These are contained within a propped cantilevered volume, which hovers above the landscape. A forest of red columns has been inserted below the cantilever. These columns 'guard' a pedestrian route, which leads under the cantilever to the rear garden and living room deck at first floor level. The entry hall has been conceived as an internal street, the dimensions of which widen to embrace the more public aspects of the plan, and diminish along the points of entry to private bedrooms and bathrooms. The roof is peppered with skylights to let in views of the steep escarpment, sky and foliage to the rear of the house.

Walls **1.013 1.029 1.116**
Windows **3.039**
Doors **4.086**
Roofs **5.105**

Hertl Architekten
Krammer House, Waidhofen an der Ybbs, Austria

Javier Artadi Arquitecto
Las Arenas Beach House, Lima, Peru

Studio d'ARC Architects
Live / Work Studio II, Pittsburgh, Pennsylvania, USA

The River Ybbs defines one of the site edges on which an old house was to be adapted and enlarged to create a new family residence. While a small garden exists between the building and the edge of the river, the river had never before been the focus of the site. In the new design, the existing lower level has been retained and rendered in white. A new upper level, clad in anthracite-coloured roofing shingles that are typical to the area, has been added and now offers panoramic views of the river from both expansive glazed openings and a large deck. The arrangement of the programme has been inverted so that private spaces such as bedrooms, bathrooms and a library occupy the lower level. Meanwhile shared spaces, including the open plan living and dining spaces as well as the kitchen, are located on the upper level to take advantage of natural light and views. In addition, an existing basement level offers cellar and storage space. Walls and floors of concrete with white painted ceilings lend a monastic calm to the interiors.

Walls **1.040 1.041**
Floors **2.018**
Roofs **5.096**

The project is a small house located near a beach 100 kilometres (62 miles) south of Lima. Conceptually, the project explores the expansion of the typical activities that take place in a beach house. The architects have created a box-like container, a unifying space that features the living-dining room with its associated terrace and swimming pool as the centrepiece, along with diverse elements and spaces that allow multiple options for the use of the space. Architecturally, the rectangular prism has been strategically cut and hollowed out to achieve sun control, to frame views and to create private outdoor living spaces. In addition, the box has been suspended over the lawn to create a sense of visual weightlessness. Private spaces such as the bedrooms, kitchen and bathrooms surround the main living spaces. On the main level, the kitchen and the master bedroom are both connected visually to the terrace and swimming pool and, by extension, with the desert coast of Peru. A small lower level, buried in the site, accommodates two smaller bedrooms and a TV room.

Windows **3.083**
Doors **4.055 4.056 4.057 4.112**
Stairs **6.030**
Landscape **7.004**

This project explores how a region's past can influence the form and use of a vacant city building site. An empty infill lot in Pittsburgh's historic South Side neighbourhood was selected to test this idea. Built as both a home and studio for two architects, this project contains the programmatic needs of a modest studio, living, dining, kitchen, bedroom, garage, basement and two gardens. One garden is an extension of the living space and the other is a roof terrace. The sequence of the building exists between two parallel masonry bearing walls while three large glazed surfaces organize the interior spaces. The large second floor window above the street collects western light and allows it to travel deep within the interior. A horizontal, sliding roof window acts as a central focus of the interior, while a large window on the east elevation connects the living spaces to the ground level garden. The building materials, in particular steel and glass, are used as references to the past industrial character of the area.

Walls **1.011**
Floors **2.052**
Windows **3.114**
Doors **4.101**
Roofs **5.006 5.007 5.054**
Stairs **6.050**

BmasC Arquitectos
Mayo House, Avila, Spain

Western Design Architects
The Moat House, Shaftesbury, Dorset, England, UK

de Blacam and Meagher Architects
Morna Valley Residence, Ibiza, Spain

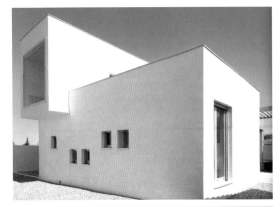

The building is located on a flat site amongst the bush and pine Moragaña that surrounds it. The building is shaped as a set of two pure rectangular forms, one on top of the other, which reference the straw bales that cover the surrounding plains in August. The prismatic configuration is reflected in the floor plan, which is designed in three bands on the ground floor. The living room, the hall with the stairway to the floor above, the kitchen and the three bedrooms and two bathrooms are on the ground floor. The first floor is a continuous and diaphanous space which leads to the living room below by means of a cut out which emphasizes the intersection of the two levels. A linear exterior wall delineates the house from the surrounding trees, and serves as a containing influence. The resulting courtyard creates a shady respite from the summer sun.

Walls **1.110**
Floors **2.011 2.012**
Doors **4.045**
Roofs **5.001 5.002**

The Moat House is located in a semi-rural setting on the edge of a small village. The concept was to frame the living accommodation to maximize views across the countryside which resulted in a simple box form with a wall of glass. To the north, an enclosed entrance courtyard was formed, as well as a side terrace leading to the expansive rear southern terrace. The ground floor living area is open plan, with a central hallway and staircase. The second floor contains four bedrooms, a study and three bathrooms, whilst a further flight of stairs leads to a second floor observatory. A moat in the entrance courtyard wraps around three sides of the house, with bridges and stepping-stones giving access. From within the living room the moat is visible through a curved glass corner window, a glazed screen behind the fireplace and the glazed southern corner. External facing materials include white render, iroko timber and slate paving, with powder-coated aluminium window frames. Simple plastered walls and stone flooring are used internally.

Walls **1.027**
Floors **2.016 2.017**
Windows **3.069 3.070 3.071**
Doors **4.071**
Roofs **5.122 5.124**
Stairs **6.020 6.021**

The house is located on a south facing slope of the hills facing the Morna Valley in the centre of the island of Ibiza and is the principal residence on an estate which has a second smaller guest house. Ibiza has a unique form of indigenous architecture based on cubes and their repetition, with houses located in groupings on terraced land. Important houses feature porticos to indicate entry, and for drying crops. Almost the entire island is terraced with dry stone walls and planted with almond, olive and algarroba trees. This site consisted of overgrown terraces with one particularly large terrace on which the house could be placed. The house is based on a 3.6 metre (12 foot) cube in plan and section, constructed from reinforced concrete columns and beams, infilled with pre-cast beams and terracotta ceramic blocks. Walls finished in stucco, contrasted with the expanses of aluminium-framed glass, take in views of the landscape while white-painted walls and floors of white marble and limestone help to keep the house cool in the hot, dry climate.

Walls **1.021**
Floors **2.023 2.067**
Doors **4.050 4.092**
Roofs **5.011 5.012 5.136**

McBride Charles Ryan
The Dome House, Melbourne, Victoria, Australia

Tzannes Associates
Parsley Bay Residence, Sydney, New South Wales, Australia

diederendirrix
Villa PPML, Venlo, The Netherlands

The client is an artist with a large family and circle of friends who often stay over. The site features a large oak tree and an adjacent Victorian house on a hill-top that terminates in tennis courts. The response began with the idea of a garden through the centre of the house and a plan that features a central living area with ancillary rooms on either side. The unusual container for this arrangement emerged as a dome in the form of an incomplete puzzle, with the superimposition of dome and rectilinear plan resulting in a great variety of domestic interior spaces. Externally, the dome form is subtracted just enough to hold the original form, so that the object after subtraction is greater and more intriguing than if it had remained whole. Associated elements such as the integrated letterbox, seats, sheds, fence and lights are expressed as markers of outdoor space. Internal spaces are divided and colour coded between two categories – the exterior (main living area) and within the dome (bleached white).

Walls **1.100**
Doors **4.038**
Roofs **5.010 5.097**
Stairs **6.052**
Landscape **7.001 7.008 7.011**

This is a new family residence on a waterside site fronting onto Sydney Harbour. Significant view axes along the length of the site were established to define circulation paths. The section was designed with expanding and contracting volumes to determine public and private, internal and external space. An open courtyard area with a significant staircase is located at the heart of the site. The residence spans three levels and extends over almost the full length of the site. A double height formal living space opens to the courtyard via fully retracting steel doors and shutters, expanding the living space across the full width of the site. A curved wet edge pool with dark tiling acts as an interface between the harbour and the residence which presents itself to the harbour with a formal and dramatic two-storey loggia framed by columns incorporating operable fabric sunscreen blinds. The main harbourfront room consists of an open plan kitchen, living and dining space while private bedrooms and family circulation areas occupy the upper two levels.

Windows **3.081 3.132**
Doors **4.001 4.028 4.029**
Roofs **5.123**

Villa PPML is situated on a multiple-housing site whose urban plan was designed by West 8. The urban plan specified particular conditions that each architect had to conform to, including that the living room floor had to be at least 80 centimetres (2.6 feet) above ground level. This has been achieved through the introduction of a split-level arrangement in which the office space and master bedroom are raised half a floor, creating space on the ground level to extend the entranceway. The dramatic overhang which dominates the front facade houses a parking space and the entrance to the basement beneath. The facade incorporates two different sizes of bricks which have been placed randomly across the surface. Except for the main entrance all the window openings are detailed with hidden frames, resulting in brick surfaces punctuated by sharply defined openings. In contrast with the front and side facades, the south elevation is totally glazed. On the upper floor the glass is protected by vertical louvres while on the ground floor an overhang shades the living room.

Walls **1.017 1.115**
Floors **2.027**
Windows **3.010 3.011**
Doors **4.074**
Roofs **5.085**
Stairs **6.018**

Boyd Cody Architects
Richmond Place House, Dublin, Ireland

Robert Seymour & Associates
The Riverhouse, Dartmouth, Devon, England, UK

Johnston Marklee & Associates
Hill House, Los Angeles, California, USA

The house is located close to the city centre, on a small infill corner site. The accommodation consists of two bedrooms, two bathrooms, kitchen, utility and living-dining area, all set over three levels. At two storeys the house is in character with adjacent terrace houses and forms a bookend to Richmond Place. Triangular in shape and with a pronounced curve along the street, the house adopts the site boundary line along its north and south elevations and aligns with the adjacent terrace to the east and west. The resultant form is carved twice to make two compressed entrance spaces, one to the front and a smaller one at the rear. The house exploits its section to create a series of interconnected but separate spaces of varying height and dimension. The main bedroom opens out into the roof-lit stairwell, connecting with the living room and kitchen below. The kitchen is placed at the entry level and overlooks the living space across the worktop, with storage units opening into the living room. Externally the house is faced entirely in brick, referencing the neighbouring houses.

Windows **3.001 3.002**
Doors **4.004 4.005 4.107 4.108**
Roofs **5.059 5.066 5.135**

Sandwiched between traditional riverside houses, the new Riverhouse hugs the bank of the River Dart in a designated Area of Outstanding Natural Beauty (AONB), in the historic town of Dartmouth. Contemporary in its design, the award winning property, which replaces an earlier timber framed building, addresses sustainability and the threat of rising sea levels and is brimming with state-of-the-art technology. Water from the river is used as a heat source and grey water is stored for toilet and washing facilities. A one metre (three feet) high wall wraps around the site, appearing as a triple glazed balustrade in places, while the barrel-vaulted copper roof floats above a glass slit which washes calming daylight into the living areas below. Balconies, terraces and flowing courtyards are complemented by sedum planted roofs and external staircases. Glass floors and folding glass doors dissolve the transition between internal and external space. Despite the challenge of an 18 metre (59 foot) high cliff, the site-generated architectural forms have maximized natural daylight, views and internal and external spaces.

Walls **1.080**
Floors **2.034 2.035 2.053**
Windows **3.097**
Roofs **5.115 5.151**

The Hill House was designed for a steeply sloping site that offers panoramic views from Rustic and Sullivan Canyons to Santa Monica Bay. Hillside ordinances, building codes, coastal regulations, and design review boards have imposed restrictions on hillside construction, however the Hill House sets a new precedent by liberating itself from these restraints, transforming stringent criteria into a sculptural and efficient design that seamlessly engages with the surrounding site. The massing of the house results from two criteria – to maximize the volume allowed by the zoning requirements, and to minimize contact with the natural terrain. Literally interpreting the zoning laws as building form, the house adopts the maximum zoning envelope as its form. The skin of the building is covered in an elastomeric, cementitious exterior coating that requires no control joints. The embedded lavender colour of the coating was sampled from local eucalyptus bark, reinforcing the house's connection to the site from which its form is derived.

Walls **1.042 1.044**
Floors **2.038 2.039**
Windows **3.107 3.140**
Doors **4.091**

Keith Williams Architects
The Long House, London, England, UK

Glas Architects
The Nail Houses, London, England, UK

Ibarra Rosano Design Architects
Winter Residence, Tucson, Arizona, USA

This family house in a St. Johns Wood conservation area replaces two former dwellings separated by a vacant plot which together occupied part of a triangular site. The long low house comprises living and dining spaces, a top-lit subterranean lap pool, four bedrooms, a guest and maid's wing and garage. The new house has been conceived as a 'secret dwelling', introverted and screened from the outside world. Much of the new house is single storey, with its flank to the mews formed by the rebuilt single storey garden boundary wall, surmounted by a clerestory glazed strip and zinc vault forming the garden wing. The much smaller upper portions of the house are formed of simple blank facades, one in white render and one in stock brick, which have been deployed along the top of the wall, echoing the volumes of the earlier buildings. To the garden side the elevations open out toward the garden in a freer and more transparent way, beginning to dissolve the relationship between inside and out.

Floors **2.060 2.082**
Doors **4.068 4.069 4.070**
Roofs **5.035 5.044 5.140**
Stairs **6.070 6.071**

The mass of these two new semi-detached houses is defined by polished masonry blocks for the front face and coarse split-face blocks to the remaining sides. In contrast to the exterior, the inside is defined by planar elements and high spaces filled with natural light. The mass of masonry is carved out at ground level, revealing the space inside. The recesses are lined with stained plywood. At the rear, the timber lining is seen again at ground level, and above in window boxes projecting from the bedrooms. Internally the major space is a dramatic double height living and dining room with open plan kitchen. A mezzanine projects into the double height room and acts as a transitional space between the public areas below and the private bedrooms above. A roof light above the stair further accentuates the height, while open stair treads allow light from above to filter down to the ground floor. The first floor contains two bedrooms and a shared bathroom. The windows are colour coded to identify each house – red on the left and yellow on the right.

Walls **1.077 1.109**
Floors **2.074 2.075**
Windows **3.085 3.100 3.138**
Doors **4.113**
Roofs **5.077 5.102**

The Winter Residence project began as a transformation of an existing house. The interior was rejuvenated by bouncing natural light throughout the building and removing the fireplace that bisected the main living areas. The opening for the chimney became a large skylight that fills the living spaces with daylight. Applying the same principle, a wall between the master dressing room and bathroom was removed to make a large, bright space for dressing and bathing. The original seldom-used entrance was decommissioned, and the side entry became the primary entrance, with a dramatic concrete and beach-pebble parking plaza and views of the city lights, exterior deck and long cantilevered concrete bench. The creation of several small courtyards and patios throughout the house give a feeling of connection to the exterior while providing shelter and privacy. The area adjacent to the study and guest room have become a serene courtyard with a fountain, a small square of grass, a single tree, and a horizontal opening that frames Tucson's skyline.

Floors **2.019**
Doors **4.106**
Roofs **5.041 5.042**
Stairs **6.066**
Landscape **7.005**

Donovan Hill
Z House, Brisbane, Queensland, Australia

Designworkshop: SA
Igoda View House, East London, South Africa

Jun Aoki & Associates
J House, Tokyo, Japan

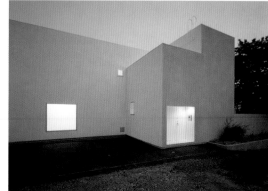

A north sloping site has been cut to position a brick shell as a retaining element embedded against a hill. The hot climate is dealt with by relying on building orientation, thermal mass and cross ventilation. Intensive shade planting, festooned creepers and protective trellising are heaped into the composition to further finesse the building's environmental performance. In this way, naturally weathering materials, picturesque openings and the contrived landscape are combined to suggest a ruin. The overscaled portal, which is a feature of the approach elevation, captures views within its frame – fragmented hillsides, parts of the interior and the clambering vegetation. The fenestration is treated as a series of 'holes in the wall' rather than 'windows in the room' and occupants are encouraged to transform the space, opening or closing it to change the experience of the interior. Interior spaces, including those for cooking, washing and resting, are defined by opportunities to capture natural light, reactivity to landscape and climate, the adjustability of openings and by sensuous materials.

Walls **1.012**
Floors **2.008**
Windows **3.082**
Roofs **5.003 5.004 5.147**

Having discovered a magnificent site on the Eastern Cape, overlooking the Igoda River with views of the Indian Ocean, the UK-based client decided to build his holiday home there. A winding driveway terminates in a landscaped forecourt alongside a rough brick courtyard wall. The brief was for a house that could also function as three independent living spaces made up of a primary house and two guest suites. The main house, situated between the two side wings, is a double height volume, solid at the upper level, and open below. The three parts are arranged around a courtyard, with the fourth side defined by a linear pool. Each wing opens either to the courtyard, or towards the sea. Privacy is provided by sliding timber screens to the courtyard, and the wings are articulated with overhangs and openings towards focused views. The limited palette of material makes reference to the simple Eastern Cape vernacular, with rough common-brick walls, white, bagged brickwork and shuttered concrete. The attached glass canopies and slatted screens add delicacy and sophistication.

Floors **2.031**
Doors **4.058**
Roofs **5.024 5.025 5.080 5.127 5.148**
Stairs **6.069**

The site is in a residential area close to downtown Tokyo. An existing mature cherry tree is central to the design which unites the tree, the house and a workshop. Everything in the house, from the structural grid, to the openings between rooms, the joinery and the wall panelling, is based on the geometry of a square. This, in turn, is based on the client's extensive art collection which includes paintings of different sizes, but all of which are square. The position and the size of the openings between each room are determined by interior viewpoints and by partial views of the cherry tree and the sky, in order to bring a different environment to each room. The same shape and finish is used for all of the openings to encourage the perception of simple, white surfaces that will become a neutral background for the paintings. Rooms that have been sized to accommodate the vagaries in the programme are arranged to form an unusual Y-shaped volume.

Windows **3.091**
Doors **4.030 4.031**
Roofs **5.032 5.053**
Stairs **6.035**
Landscape **7.009**

Steel Houses

Barton Myers Associates
Bekins Residence, Santa Barbara, California, USA

Scott Tallon Walker Architects
Fastnet House, Kinsale, County Cork, Ireland

Situated on a property in the Santa Barbara hillside area with ocean views, this residence is designed on a single level for a family of four. Conceived as a luxurious warehouse for living, the plan includes a large kitchen, dining and living room, each opening onto a covered porch. A long partition wall separates three bedrooms, bathrooms, pantry, media room, storage and a courtyard from the shared living spaces. A north facing courtyard serves as a quiet oasis and Zen garden, while the kitchen's eastern patio is designed as the family's outdoor dining and barbecue area. Exposed concrete floors and structural steel give the design a simple, industrial aesthetic. Building materials are accented by a muted palette of finishes and colours derived from the surrounding landscape. A covered porch and terrace are the home's focal point, allowing the main living space to completely open to the landscape beyond by means of motorized, overhead doors. Operable, north facing clerestory windows negated the need for air conditioning by taking advantage of ocean breezes.

Walls **1.007**
Windows **3.058 3.099 3.118**
Doors **4.036 4.047 4.095 4.096 4.097 4.100**

This site enjoys quite magnificent views over Kinsale Harbour and is the location for a house whose brief was to provide open, glazed living spaces with views towards Kinsale, four bedrooms and separate guest accommodation accessible both from the main house and from the outside. Also required were a swimming pool, a games room and a barbeque area. Approximately half of the programme is conventionally located in the visible two-storey structure, which relates to the form of the existing house. The balance is sunk into the ground and the habitable rooms achieve natural light and ventilation through narrow slot windows in the terrace and parking area retaining walls. All rooms are accessed off the upper or lower circulation halls. The external finishes include painted steel framework, floor to ceiling glazing, grass roof, cedar cladding and random stone walling to match the colour of the existing on-site rock. The living and kitchen areas enjoy maximum views through three metre (10 foot) high floor-to-ceiling windows which are all flush with the floor level.

Walls **1.083 1.084 1.085 1.108 1.113 1.114 1.118**
Floors **2.063 2.086 2.090**
Windows **3.105 3.120**
Doors **4.130 4.132**
Stairs **6.014**

Tonkin Zulaikha Greer
Hastings Parade House, Bondi, New South Wales,
Australia

Peter L. Gluck and Partners, Architects
Inverted Guest House, Lake George, New York, USA

Frank Harmon Architect
Low Country Residence, Mount Pleasant, South Carolina,
USA

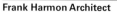

Over the years, this 1930s Bondi house had become somewhat built out by its neighbours. The house was in need of another storey and complete reconfiguration of the interior to take advantage of its magnificent views. Originally, the house had sat on a headland, overlooking Bondi Beach in one direction and the Tasman Sea the other. The intention of the redesign was to restore that privilege. Beneath sawtooth roof forms, three angled walls march towards Bondi Beach while another turns toward Hastings Parade and the ocean. Beach and ocean views are now seen from every new room, and daylight flows throughout. Internal materials are based on a beach theme taking advantage of the abundance of natural light. The joinery lining the stair is 'sea foam' coloured polyurethane, and the white walls give a reflective open-air shimmer to the space. Timber floors and trim are reminiscent of boat finishes and natural stone glistens like the Bondi sand. Materials surfaces are untreated, with minimal detail, expressed in their natural state.

Floors **2.047 2.048**
Windows **3.106 3.136**
Doors **4.088 4.114**
Roofs **5.093 5.121**

The Inverted Guest House is part of a summer family retreat on Lake George, New York. The unusual programmatic requirements – two private guest suites and a large storage area for furniture, cars and equipment – dictated the form of the building. The site is located deep in the woods behind a ridge that separates the guest house from the main house and the lake. The sloping site provided the impetus for the architectural solution. The one-storey storage area acts as a datum with two-storey living spaces flanking it on either end. Large aeroplane hangar doors allow the storage space to be opened to the landscape or closed when not in use. The plans of the apartments are the inverse of each other with one glass-enclosed living room located above and the other below. The upper apartment acts as a gatehouse to the complex, overlooking the entrance to the site.

Walls **1.071**
Windows **3.022 3.023 3.051**
Doors **4.066 4.098**
Roofs **5.048 5.100**
Stairs **6.029**

The house was designed to tread lightly on its lush site, and to evoke the feeling of living outdoors. The long, one-room-deep floor plan creates a slender footprint and gives each room views of Shem Creek. Approaching the house under a canopy of moss-draped oak trees, the view of the marsh – replete with blue herons and water lilies – appears like an element in a Japanese painting. The brief included two challenges: to prioritize views while protecting the house from the hot climate and for the house to be able to withstand hurricane-strength winds and the accompanying debris. The programme called for a large living room and kitchen, a guest room, workshop, large screened porch, and a lap pool. The floor plan positions the bedrooms on opposite ends of the central, loft-like living, dining and kitchen area, beneath a single shed roof. To capitalize on the view, a large glass wall fronts the southwest side of the house which is protected from excessive summer heat gain by a series of hinged perforated-metal screens that also allow cooling breezes to enter the house.

Walls **1.058**
Floors **2.040**
Windows **3.037**
Doors **4.093**
Roofs **5.058 5.079**

Touraine Richmond Architects
One Window House, Los Angeles, California, USA

Shuhei Endo Architect Institute
Rooftecture S, Kobe, Hyogo, Japan

Kengo Kuma & Associates
Steel House, Tokyo, Japan

This house is the second unit on a property zoned for two dwellings. By going up instead of out in response to increasing densities in this urban neighbourhood, the house has views of the city and mountains from the top floor bedroom and deck. The house is zoned to create a seamless flow from front to back gardens through the ground level living space. By rotating the pattern, the tectonic relationships between the floating element and the wrapped volume that perches on top, are expressed. The house is built using a combined steel and wood frame, with aluminium framed doors and one window to complete the envelope. Interior finishes include sanded oriented strand board, diamond-polished concrete and solid-surface plastics. Heating and cooling loads are almost non-existent in the coastal microclimate – the large glazed walls on the ground floor are shaded with mylar curtains paired with a white polyester velvet to reflect direct solar gain and insulate against heat loss. The landscape is designed exclusively with native plants to minimize watering.

Walls **1.072 1.087**
Floors **2.073**
Windows **3.131**
Roofs **5.070**
Stairs **6.055**

Rooftecture S, a small residence for a couple, clings onto a steep inclination that faces the Setonaikai National Park, and is bordered by a Y-intersection at the base of a hill, in a relatively old residential zone developed in tiered platforms. The main area of architectural investigation was to solve the problem of the considerable slope across the site, which ranges from five to eight metres (16 to 26 feet), not to mention the limited site area on which it would be possible to build. The solution is an artificial ground plane supported on a set of five piles, as well as the roof and walls that enclose the internal spaces. On the second floor, the roof and the floor (which is the artificial ground that continues onto the northern terrace) capture the existing stone retaining wall and use it as an inner wall. The development of the metal shingle board-clad combined roof and wall is at the heart of this design. It dramatizes the natural slope of the land, reinforces the geometry of the tight triangular site and defines the spatial quality of this unusual house.

Windows **3.029 3.030 3.031 3.125**
Stairs **6.048 6.056**

This house is distinguished by having no beams or columns of any kind. Instead, 3.2 millimetre (0.1 inch) thick corrugated steel plates have been used to create an entirely open monocoque structure that, it could be argued, resembles a freight car. The client, a devoted fan of railway cars since childhood, needed a home for his collection of several thousand model trains. Fitting into the L-shaped site, the house looks as if a freight train has recently come to a halt. The structure was originally designed using the conventional arrangement of structure and skin. However the concept of the freight train led to the use of a singular system of bent steel plates. The crimped steel has been left in its original metallic state, without any applied finish to further reinforce the presence of the steel. Arranged over three levels, the main level accommodates a garage as well as an open plan kitchen, dining and living space complete with display space for the model trains. The lower level contains a traditional tatami room and a study, while the first floor houses the master suite.

Walls **1.057**
Floors **2.037**
Windows **3.104**
Roofs **5.043**

TNA Architects
Stage House, Karuizawa, Nagano, Japan

Koffi & Diabaté Architectes
Villa Talon, Cotonou, Benin

WPA
Weese Young Residence, Cedar Key, Florida, USA

The site is located half an hour from central Karuizawa on a large sloping private plot. The house is situated away from the road to avoid being overlooked by neighbouring properties and is arranged as a stage or platform that follows the downwards slope of the site. The roof appears to grow out of the site, with its trajectory in dramatic opposition to the slope. The cladding used for both the roof and exterior walls echoes the black bark of the surrounding trees. On the long elevations, windows are kept to a minimum in order to maintain privacy, however the principal double height elevation facing the forest features expansive full height glass to the sleeping mezzanine and a covered open terrace below that accommodates a jacuzzi. The ground floor accommodates the living, dining, kitchen, sunroom and terrace. Essentially one contiguous space, the functions are delineated by 900 millimetre (3 foot) high steps in the timber floor the width of the building. These 'stages' are used to allow a sense of privacy even when other 'stages' are occupied by other inhabitants.

Walls **1.078**
Windows **3.067 3.078 3.079 3.080 3.133 3.134**
Doors **4.046 4.079**

This house, located in a dense urban neighbourhood in the centre of Cotonou, attempts to reconciliate the practical qualities of a city house with the benefits of a traditional villa. All of the main rooms are organized around the garden and swimming pool. Exterior terraces, which constitute the principal living spaces, are the typical arrangement in tropical African cities. The plan reflects the cultural need to clearly separate the public from the private, domestic functions, which in this case has resulted in over a third of the floor space being dedicated to service functions. The floating cantilevered aluminium roof protects the main living spaces from the sun and shades the terrace floor from direct exposure, therefore lowering the inside temperature by a few degrees while regulating the intensity of the natural light. The main living spaces benefit from cross ventilation through atria and large bay windows. The entire house is protected with a ventilated facade, using both red terracotta large format tiles and resin coated timber panels.

Walls **1.056**
Doors **4.010 4.012 4.080**
Stairs **6.031**

The site is situated on the gulf coast of Florida adjacent to a national wildlife refuge and the house acts as an escape from the harsh Chicago winters. The vertical form is a response to the climate, the site and to the Dade County building code, which requires structures to be built to withstand hurricane-strength winds. The lowest level of the house is 5.5 metres (18 feet) above grade and 6 metres (20 feet) above the mean high water line. The structure is an off-site-fabricated system of steel frames welded in segments and bolted together on site. At ground level, a large two-storey opening provides an entrance and a view of the marsh beyond, interrupting the opaque and translucent surfaces of the house. The land side of the house contains the more pragmatic functions including the stair tower, utility tower, storage, kitchen and bathrooms. The water side is framed by the grid with large glass sliding panels. Interior spaces are as tall as they are wide, providing high ceilings and excellent ventilation, and feature a collection of natural timbers, graphic linoleum and glass tiles.

Walls **1.015 1.028 1.088 1.089**
Doors **4.014 4.015 4.016**
Roofs **5.109**
Stairs **6.051**

Blank Studio
Xeros Residence, Phoenix, Arizona, USA

Arjaan de Feyter
Zoersel House, Antwerp, Belgium

Peter Stutchbury Architecture
Avalon House, Avalon, New South Wales, Australia

The Xeros residence is positioned on the upward slope of a double lot facing the North Phoenix mountain preserve. The house includes a two-storey design studio with a single storey residence above. The path to the studio requires that guests pass behind a mesh screen and descend a short flight of stairs into a mesh-enclosed forecourt. A stainless steel water feature leads down the steps and terminates at a reflecting pool. To access the residence, visitors ascend an exterior steel staircase to an upper level balcony before entering the living, dining and kitchen area. From the living area, a central gallery leads to the cantilevered master bedroom suite and media room which is completely glazed on the north facade to enjoy the mountain views. The primary building material is exposed steel which is used as structure, cladding and shading. The environmentally responsive building is solid where it faces the intense western afternoon sun, while the more exposed facades to the south and east are shielded by woven metal shade mesh.

Walls **1.009 1.010 1.096**
Floors **2.080**
Windows **3.084 3.117**
Doors **4.039 4.040 4.041**
Roofs **5.098**

This original Bauhaus building was designed in 1969 as a case study prototype. The original plans show a villa arranged as a perfect grid of nine squares with a steel skeleton and a half-open ground floor with a central core. The domestic functions were clustered on the upper floor, and on the ground floor were an entrance hall, staircase, storeroom and open carport. Over the years the house had been converted and extended unrecognizably. In 2005, architect Arjaan de Feyter bought the house in 2005 which by that time was in total decay and ready for demolition. The original first floor layout was retained and the ground floor extended to include a workspace. The house was stripped to its steel skeleton which had to be restored. The aluminium sandwich panels and the original timber windows, now double glazed, were then fitted back into the renovated skeleton. The problem of cold bridges characteristic of steel skeletons, was resolved by a quick-drying two-component resin which was sprayed onto all the beams and pillars in contact with the outside air.

Windows **3.101 3.111**
Doors **4.011 4.013**
Stairs **6.063**

Located on steep, east facing land on the Northern Beaches of Sydney, the site was difficult to access and prone to slippage. However, the project was an opportunity to produce a low cost building that would satisfy the client's faith in architecture. The approach was to initiate a prefabricated building using steel as the primary structure. Both primary and secondary components, such as the Meccano-like set of parts that took two days to assemble, epitomize the architectural approach. The north and south facades were treated with obvious functional, industrial, and thus economical, fixtures and fittings. A skillion roof connects the building to the site while high level glazing gives the roof a lightness that sits at ease with the surrounding tree canopy. The main living space, which was designed using standardized components, sits lightly among the treetops, while downstairs, bedrooms and bathrooms are quietened by major shifts in scale and reductions in light. The outcome is a palette of varied experiences using a minimum of architectural tools.

Walls **1.082**
Floors **2.081**
Windows **3.046 3.047**
Doors **4.051**
Roofs **5.057**
Stairs **6.060**

Safdie Rabines Architects
Artist Bridge Studio, San Diego, California, USA

Timber Houses

Troppo Architects
Buttfield Town House, Adelaide, South Australia,
Australia

This project is a studio for two artists wishing to create a
new workspace while minimizing the impact of any new
construction on the natural landscape of their property.
The studio is located to the rear of the house, connecting
it to a beautiful portion of the site which, prior to the
addition, had not been accessible. To create the studio
and library without disturbing the surrounding area, the
studio was conceived of as a 'bridge' spanning a small
dry creek bed adjacent to the house, providing the
opportunity to experience the 'canyon' from the best of
all possible locations, both in and above it. The bridge is
supported on two concrete piers on either side of the
creek bed and is spanned with two trusses made of top
and bottom glulam chords with steel cross members.
Due to its positioning, the structure maintains a rare
lightness, and when viewed from the exterior, appears
to levitate above the land. On the interior, a pair of
oversized sliding doors on either side open to allow for
an interaction with the elements, adding to the feeling
of suspension while capturing ocean breezes.

Walls **1.033 1.034**
Floors **2.070**
Doors **4.081 4.085**
Roofs **5.111**

Located on a leafy terrace adjacent to the city's prized
Park Lands, the Town House is an urban retreat that
engages with its environment and wholeheartedly
embraces ecologically sustainable design principles.
Solar-passive design for winter warming and summer
cooling, carefully selected fixtures and fittings,
photovoltaic power panels, basement rainwater tanks
and stormwater detention ensure that the Town House is
energy efficient and water conservative. Roof forms and
orientations embrace the northern sun whilst obviating
glare to neighbours and the street. Materials and their
few applied finishes are selected with an eye to low
embodied energy, low maintenance, low life cycle cost
and, especially, to ageing gracefully. Natural materials
include rammed earth, local stone, natural finish metals,
and Australian hardwoods. The house is built over four
levels, but fits within its two-storey context in height and
scale. The primary living area and bedroom wrap around
a tranquil private garden. Other areas open to the Park
Lands and smaller courtyards.

Walls **1.050 1.081 1.093 1.105 1.106**
Roofs **5.055 5.117 5.118 5.137**
Stairs **6.001 6.002**

Lahz Nimmo Architects
Casuarina Ultimate Beach House, Casuarina Beach, New South Wales, Australia

Skene Catling de la Peña Architects
The Dairy House, Castle Cary, Somerset, England, UK

The Miller Hull Partnership
Chuckanut Drive Residence, Bellingham, Washington, USA

The design has a simple strategy – that of an open, breezy, relaxed living pavilion juxtaposed with a two-storey shuttered timber sleeping box. The concept is a piece of driftwood sitting in the sand (sleeping) and a floating jetty (living). The house includes a series of external spaces surrounding the living pavilion that can be inhabited in differing ways depending on the time of day and time of year. The living pavilion is connected to the sleeping box by a double height breezeway which acts as an entry and sheltered deck area. The sleeping box is clad in shiplapped Australian hardwood boards with a natural stain finish and has a series of shutters and timber louvres allowing it to be opened up or closed down depending on the occupant's requirements. The street side of the house acts as the formal public interface, housing car parking and presenting a closed protective face to this western orientation. There is also a second and more interactive street – the beach. Here the house opens up like a viewing platform.

Walls **1.099 1.103 1.104**
Windows **3.038 3.068**
Doors **4.024 4.025**
Roofs **5.090**

This project is the result of the conversion of a former dairy into a family house with a small pool. The original building was re-planned, with lean-to sheds removed and an extension added to create a total of five bedrooms, three bathrooms and a more generous circulation space. The extension houses two wet rooms, while layered oak and laminated glass produce an eerie, filtered light. The way the light moves around the house over the course of the day draws the user through it. In the morning, low light floods the east of the house and by midday, the overhead sun streams through the roof light slot, penetrating through to the ground floor. Timber for the construction was coppiced from the estate and was planked and dried in the storage barns. The method of drying in which raw planks are separated to allow air circulation became the generator of the logic and aesthetic of the extension. The spaced external timber screen increases in depth towards the base of the house to reinforce a sense of weight and rustication.

Floors **2.066 2.076 2.078**
Windows **3.098**
Roofs **5.101 5.119 5.131 5.132**
Stairs **6.009 6.010**

This 130 square metre (1,400 square foot) main house and guest house with garage is located on a heavily wooded cliff site with views out over the San Juan Islands of Washington State. The plan is orientated to major views south down the coastline and west out to the islands, while being careful to stay outside of the drip line of the Douglas fir trees that dominate the site. Large overhangs protect glazing and provide shelter. The concept marries a long gently sloping roof form containing the kitchen, entry and studio with a vertical tower containing the living room and master bedroom above. A separate guest house is also located on the site. Key materials include expressed wood and glulam framing, concrete and wood floors, high efficiency exterior metal-clad timber windows, standing seam metal roofs and a combination of painted cedar siding and natural coloured cement board siding.

Walls **1.038 1.120**
Windows **3.124**
Doors **4.061 4.123 4.124 4.125**
Roofs **5.029 5.030**
Stairs **6.042 6.068**

John Onken Architects
Dolphin Cottage, Cowes, Isle of Wight, England, UK

Jackson Clements Burrows Architects
Edward River House, Deniliquin, New South Wales, Australia

Chenchow Little Architects
Freshwater House, Sydney, New South Wales, Australia

This project is a replacement for the client's existing two-storey house in the heart of Cowes, Isle of Wight, an area which features a rich mixture of boat sheds, cottages, terraces and detached houses. The clients were keen to add a substantial modern house to their site within this mixed context. The design of the project started by re-interpreting the organization of the large site into a definite 'front' and 'rear,' creating clearer territories for entry, parking and recreation spaces. The ground floor was then seen as a group of transparent spaces balanced between the two halves of the site. Each ground floor room has its own sister space outside. The upper bedroom floor was then added as a more private structure with carefully placed openings to special views. The contrast of the closed, heavy 'shed' above the lighter ground floor was exaggerated using textured and stained Thermowood cladding. The single storey section of the garage and entry also featured timber cladding to create a building resembling a fence, allowing it to become a background to the main living spaces.

Walls **1.019 1.020 1.086**
Roofs **5.061 5.114 5.149**
Stairs **6.033**
Landscape **7.012**

This farmhouse explores an interpretation of historic farm buildings in the local area which are typically constructed of timber frames and corrugated iron cladding. The two-storey structure is linked to a water tank tower which identifies its position amongst the red gums on the riverbank. The plan is arranged within a regular grid of exposed structural timber columns and externally, hardwood timber purlins are revealed to the inside face of the corrugated iron cladding. Extensive areas of external and internal western red cedar doors, windows and cladding accentuate the contrast with concrete, steel and corrugated iron. Internally, the pragmatic aspects of the farmhouse programme such as a boot room, laundry, garage and workshop, are located on the ground floor, while the living areas are located on the first floor to take advantage of elevated views to the river. Timber has been used extensively throughout the internal spaces which engage with the surrounding landscape and define an aesthetic which reflects the informal lifestyle associated with farming.

Walls **1.039 1.111**
Windows **3.018 3.019 3.090**
Doors **4.075**

The Freshwater House overlooks the beach in a northern suburb of Sydney. The client required large outdoor spaces and expansive views. The resulting building is made up of three distinct parts – a podium base, a garden/living space, and a screened bedroom volume. The podium is introverted, concealing a recessed entry vestibule and garage within the natural topography of the site, and is clad with vertical timber battens which extend to the ground floor to form a balustrade. The living level above is open and expansive, in contrast to the contained basement below. Sandwiched between the upper and lower volumes, the living space is conceived as one fluid horizontal landscaped space. The immateriality of this level is further heightened by the material choice, with highly reflective chrome and black mirror contrasting with the colour and texture of weathered timber in cabinetry and exterior balustrading. The top bedroom level floats above the landscaped living level and is veiled with custom-made external bi-folding shutters in anodized dark bronze.

Walls **1.005 1.006 1.097 1.098**
Windows **3.020 3.021**
Roofs **5.056**
Landscape **7.015**

Hampson Williams
Glass and Timber Houses, London, England, UK

Alison Brooks Architects
Herringbone Houses, London, England, UK

Studio Bednarski
Hesmondhalgh House, London, England, UK

These two houses are located on the site of some former joinery workshops and are bounded on all sides by the rear gardens of Victorian terraces. The brief called for ground floor spaces with uninterrupted open plan living visually linked to the external landscape, with more cellular bedroom spaces above. Each dwelling has been arranged around an inward looking double-height glazed courtyard. At ground floor the courtyard affords long views through each house, connecting the courtyard with the living spaces and the private gardens beyond. The original perception of greenness from neighbouring properties has been maintained by landscaping all levels, including extensive green roofscapes. Engineered timber beams and joists form the principle framing technology, with site fabricated timber-framed wall panels dressed in vertical western red cedar boarding for the external walls. Internally the extensive use of timber continues with Douglas fir being used for the courtyard glazing frames and sliding doors and for the expressed suspended staircase.

Walls **1.069 1.070**
Floors **2.030 2.083 2.084**
Windows **3.126 3.127 3.128 3.129**
Roofs **5.086 5.095**
Stairs **6.025 6.026 6.027**

The Herringbone Houses are two 400 square metre (4,305 square feet) houses with integrated landscape located in a wooded site overlooking the South London Bowls Club. Named 'Herringbone Houses' for the unique patterning of the timber facades, each open plan house is composed of two surfaces of herringbone timber and graphite render that extend from exterior to interior to form walls, floors, external decking and fences. These planes interlock and fold inward at the centre of the house to create a double height entrance hall open to the sky. The ground floor living spaces open directly onto series of terraces and decks. The first floor bedrooms are accessed from a gallery space and library, with a balcony offering views down into the living space. Across the facade all materials, including the timber, render and glazing, are in the same plane in order to further enhance the buildings' abstract planar quality. Elements of the timber cladding are prefabricated making the installation cost equivalent to standard weatherboard cladding.

Windows **3.004 3.005 3.137**
Roofs **5.083**
Stairs **6.017 6.047**

Built in a confined and overlooked urban context of rear gardens, the design was informed by the lightness of garden pavilions and the elegance of traditional Japanese architecture. The aim of the design, while strongly dictated by the planning authorities, was to create a light structure, intertwined, as much as possible, with the garden, into one uplifting and comfortable family living environment. A large flowing open plan living space is located at the lower level from where there is direct access to the external paved patio, while the bedrooms are located at the entrance level. The house features a double volume living space crossed by a bridge that links the children's area, set at the far end of the house, with the parents' quarters located near the entrance. Over fifty per cent of the house's floor area is below ground level, including a sunken, terraced garden. Playful symmetrical stairs lead from the living level to bedrooms, one for the children and one for the parents and guests. Plenty of wall space was created to cater for the owner's large collection of books and art.

Walls **1.035 1.036 1.037 1.095 1.107**
Floors **2.085**
Windows **3.052**
Doors **4.032 4.033 4.115**
Roofs **5.063**

MELD Architecture with Vicky Thornton
House in Tarn et Garonne, Saint Amans de Pellagal,
Tarn et Garonne, France

Go Hasegawa & Associates
Forest House, Karuizawa, Nagano, Japan

Room 11
Kingston House, Kingston, Tasmania, Australia

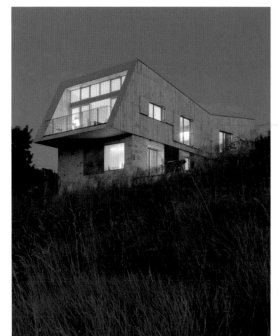

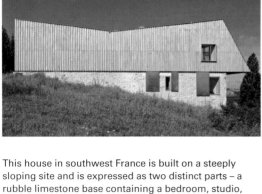

This house in southwest France is built on a steeply sloping site and is expressed as two distinct parts – a rubble limestone base containing a bedroom, studio, shower and utility rooms and, above, the main living and bedroom spaces enclosed in a chestnut-clad timber frame. The upper level responds to the approach, landscape and surrounding views. At one end, the high roof of the front porch, angled to look along the access road, slopes down towards the centre of the plan where a top-lit staircase is located, before rising up over the main living area with its expansive views out across the countryside. The angled returns to the cantilevered living terrace reveal views of the valley and distant hilltop town while concealing adjacent houses. Vernacular materials and elements include rubble stone walls, timber shuttered windows and sliding galvanized steel doors. Here the timber shutters close flush with the walls to continue the board-on-board rhythm of the chestnut cladding, giving strong vertical shadow lines which complement the heavy modelling of the rubble stone.

Walls **1.031 1.032 1.061**
Doors **4.020 4.021 4.127**
Stairs **6.057**

This tiny weekend house is situated in a forest near the famous mountain resort area of Karuizawa, two hours by car from Tokyo. The form of the house is a rectangular plan, surmounted by a simple gable roof. The exterior walls and roof are clad in black corrugated sheet. Under the roof, all of the rooms are double height, taking into their volume the gabled ceiling. Skylights in the roof bring views of the forest into the house. A stair tucked between a bedroom and the study at one short end of the house climbs up to a small viewing balcony on the roof. Climbing the staircase, the beauty and warmth of the timber panelled gable ceilings are especially apparent. The translucent surface of the ceiling brings the special effects of changing light and swaying tree shadows into each room. In the living room, the ceiling is made up of sliced thin maple sheets adhered to clear acrylic board hung on a wooden framework. Through the use of transparent and translucent surfaces, the changing light and seasons of the forest are brought to bear in every room.

Walls **1.023**
Windows **3.089**
Doors **4.042**
Roofs **5.052 5.067 5.153**
Stairs **6.034**

Careful observation of the site – a large sun warmed mass of rock with a view of distant Mount Wellington – led to the conclusion that the house should embody the experience of contemplation and groundedness that the site inspired. The interior of the house is a human orientated habitat that highlights the joy of the transition of light across the surrounding landform. The exterior has been finished in dark stained timber to allow it to recede into its wooded site. Voids sliced through the building strengthen the connection to the immediate site and allow views through to the distant mountain. The linear volumes have been arranged to promote particular vistas – east to the river, north to the mountain, and south to the rock shelf. The voids that open up between the volumes have been used to pull the landscape into the heart of the house. Here, deciduous species add a seasonal progression to the building, the various changes in colour and texture affecting the emotional and experiential qualities of the interior of the house throughout the year.

Walls **1.117**
Floors **2.046**
Doors **4.067**
Roofs **5.081 5.116**
Stairs **6.040**

EZZO
Leça House, Leça da Palmeira, Portugal

Avanti Architects
Long View, Henley-on-Thames, Oxfordshire, UK

Marlon Blackwell Architect
L-Stack House, Fayetteville, Arkansas, USA

This sophisticated little house is located on an unassuming site in the streets surrounding the marina and docks, and in close proximity to the beach, in Leça da Palmeira. An existing building, little more than a timber hut, was refurbished and extended vertically to create a comfortable family home. The ground floor was reconfigured to create an open living and dining space on one side, and on the other a garage, kitchen and small patio garden. An open-tread timber stair from the living room leads up to the entirely new first floor that accommodates two children's bedrooms and the master bedroom, all with access to an expansive roof terrace. The new first floor structure draws inspiration from historic dockside buildings nearby and is framed in steel, with expansive glazing shielded by black, horizontal timber battens. These protect the interior from solar gain, and maintain the privacy of the occupants. The super graphics that identify the house from the exterior are based on the numbering and signage systems used in the timber storage sheds at the nearby docks.

Floors **2.004 2.005**
Doors **4.082**
Roofs **5.094 5.125 5.126**
Stairs **6.039 6.064**

The brief for Long View was for a contemporary family house with a flexible living, dining and kitchen area, a space for music making, four bedrooms, a workshop for piano repair, a small study, and ample storage and service spaces. Natural daylight was a priority as well as a fluid relationship between indoors and outdoors. The aim was to create a composition that complements an adjacent listed building in terms of form and materials, while having a clear identity of its own. The narrow site dictated a longitudinal form arranged down, rather than along, the contours. The pinwheel plan and precise layout were designed to take maximum advantage of the southern outlook, several fine existing trees and some existing natural features including an old Victorian rockery. The structure consists of a steel frame on a concrete ground slab, with timber cladding to blockwork back-up walls and a blue-black engineering brick for the plinth and selected panels. The roofscape echoes the sloping site and gently suggests the image of a raised piano lid.

Walls **1.002 1.003 1.091**
Floors **2.003**
Windows **3.040 3.123**
Doors **4.034 4.128**
Roofs **5.089 5.155 5.156**

The L-Stack House responds to the urban grid, the modest scale of existing houses and the presence of a dry creek bed that traverses the site, through a strategy of bridging and stacking of forms. The resulting scheme is an 'L' configuration that subdivides the interior programme and the site into private and public entities, with a glass-enclosed stairway connecting the two boxes. The ground floor is organized as a linear open plan with connecting terraces adjacent to the creek. Throughout the house, windows and skylights provide controlled views, illumination, a sense of privacy, and opportunities to observe the dynamic nature of the creek. The stairway penetrates the underbelly of the second floor where private spaces are more discreet and cellular, however, all spaces open onto a hall that serves as common family space. The exterior cladding is a unique rainscreen system articulated with rot-resistant Brazilian redwood which is stacked and screwed on the flat to create a horizontal louvred effect on the long walls.

Floors **2.041 2.042 2.077**
Windows **3.014 3.015**
Doors **4.103 4.104**
Roofs **5.072**
Stairs **6.032**

Marsh Cashman Koolloos Architects
Maroubra House, Sydney, New South Wales, Australia

Architectus
North Shore House, Auckland, New Zealand

Bercy Chen Studio
Peninsula House, Austin, Texas, USA

The Maroubra House is an alterations and additions project. The brief was to renovate an existing single storey dwelling on a site that enjoys views towards the beach. The challenge was to connect all levels and to open internal spaces to the outdoor areas. The house follows the contours of the site and responds to its context in form and texture. The renovated house provides a more effective response to the environment with better access to sunlight and ventilation, opening to the north while maintaining privacy. The lower spaces at the entry level were refurbished to form a study and guest rooms alongside the main entry, which was relocated to sit in line with the central staircase. The lowest level was extended to make a double garage and storage area. The roof became the forecourt to the house via a relocated entry stair. The main living level, at the right hand side of the dwelling, is a large double height space that contains the lounge, dining and kitchen activities and extends through glazed walls at each end to the garden to the north and the views to the south.

Walls **1.101**
Windows **3.066 3.086**
Doors **4.063 4.102**
Roofs **5.031 5.076 5.139**

The site for this family house abuts a reserve on one side and an unoccupied site on the other, and falls from the street down to the sea. The house inevitably follows the site, while endeavouring to enrich the journey by providing places to stop along the way and different pathways both inside and out. A two-bay wide structure on four levels is stretched along the site, with the degree of enclosure varying to provide a courtyard and terraces within the overall form. The inevitability of the movement towards the water view is resisted by the courtyard. Here, the living spaces are organized around this covered outdoor room, providing protection from the weather, while allowing the view to be enjoyed through the living space. Walls in the long direction are generally solid, and project beyond the laminated beam structure to contain cabinetry, protect openings and allow slotted and incised views that contrast with those offered by the simply glazed crosswalls. The roof is a plane of gravel populated by timber-clad roof lights that both emit and admit light.

Windows **3.109**
Doors **4.064 4.111**
Roofs **5.092 5.146**
Stairs **6.049**
Landscape **7.010**

The house occupies a dramatic site with lake frontage and views of Mount Bonnell. Through the use of glass, steel, natural light and sophisticated detailing, an existing 1980s house has been adapted to better unite the house with the lake and the mountain beyond. The bones of the original structure were retained, while completely reorganizing the layout. New Brazilian hardwood cladding and a copper roof were used on the exterior to give the volume new clean lines and a bold presence. A slatted timber solarium with the same slope of the roof was added, along with a triangular pool that extends out to the boathouse and the lake. The interior architectural strategy relies on opening up the space and bringing in natural light. Reflective and translucent materials such as acrylic panels, etched glass and mirrors create a subtle reflection of light and the motion of water throughout the interior. The ground floor has been opened up to create a panoramic view of the lake, while the former attic has been transformed to house the children's bedrooms and shared play space.

Floors **2.051**
Doors **4.105 4.122**
Roofs **5.107**
Landscape **7.002 7.003 7.006**

Welsh + Major
Pitt Street House, Sydney, New South Wales, Australia

Bates Masi + Architects
Noyack Creek Residence, Noyack, New York, USA

Jun Igarashi Architects
Rectangle of Light, Sapporo, Hokkaido, Japan

The house is part of Fitzroy Terrace, an important example of Georgian domestic architecture in Sydney. Behind the front facade, the house has been significantly altered over the years. The latest alteration involved a significant rebuild and extension of the rear terrace wing and the construction of a new studio around the original masonry outhouse. The rear of the house was dismantled, with the salvaged timbers graded, assessed, and stored on site to be re-used for the new rear facade. The rear wing envelope was determined by folding up the roof plane to create a larger bedroom and balcony over the rear living spaces. The form of the new studio building was determined by extruding the profile of the old outhouse in one direction, and extending the roof in another direction to achieve a usable floor plate. Using salvaged timber meant that the final configuration of the cladding could not be determined until construction had commenced, allowing 'chance' (or at least a series of circumstances not readily anticipated) to play a part in determining the architectural outcome.

Walls **1.014**
Windows **3.016 3.048 3.049**
Stairs **6.044 6.045**

The client, an actor from New York, sought a place for relaxation and entertaining set on a deep, narrow site fronting Noyack Creek. The design of the house was predetermined by the restrictions imposed by the site's wetlands and narrow dimensions, and allowed just enough space to accommodate the programme, including the client's request for a symbiosis between the exterior and interior living spaces. All of the living spaces are organized along a timber decked linear path so that interior and exterior uses alternate in succession, separated by glass walls. The walls enclosing these spaces are panels of perforated Skatelite, a natural resin composite commonly used for lining skateboard ramps, which allows light and air into the building while protecting it from solar gain. The glass western facade allows every room to overlook the creek and summer sunsets. These windows are supplemented by light from a clerestory in the second storey that brings sunlight through a double height atrium to the kitchen at the core of the house.

Walls **1.055**
Doors **4.048 4.126**
Stairs **6.016 6.046**

Located in the north of Sapporo, this small site is contained on three sides by adjacent buildings and on the fourth by a poplar forest. Planning regulations dictated that buildings must be set back from the tree line, resulting in a buildable area of only 40 square metres (430 square feet). The house is arranged vertically in order to accommodate the brief for a couple and their two children. The plan has been split into one large, and one small area. The small area has been ingeniously arranged to accommodate the main stair, as well as a number of secondary spaces and functions inserted into the split levels as they rise upwards, including bathrooms and study areas. The remaining larger space accommodates the main family spaces. The large double height open living area and kitchen has been sunk 600 mm (2 feet) underground to help combat the harsh winters. The house contains no conventional windows. Instead, openings are covered with fibre plastic boarding to let light in. The effect created is of an entirely interior world for the occupants to inhabit.

Walls **1.102**
Floors **2.049**
Windows **3.059**
Doors **4.076 4.116**
Stairs **6.037**

Bercy Chen Studio
Riverview Gardens, Austin, Texas, USA

Rowan Opat Architects
Courtyard House, Somers, Victoria, Australia

Terry Pawson Architects
The Tall House, London, England, UK

Riverview Gardens is a series of three identical houses inspired by a dramatic waterfall near Austin. Rainwater is directed to the end of each house and falls three storeys in a sheet to form a dramatic water feature which is then collected in a shared pond. The plan of each house is stretched on an axis towards the river to frame the primary view, while creating semi-private outdoor spaces between the houses. A series of glass and vegetative screens divide the main spaces on each floor, creating a filter between public spaces facing the lake and private spaces. The houses are monolithic on the east and west, contrasted with fully glazed facades to the north and south allowing uninterrupted views of the lake. The minimized footprint ensures large shared gardens with dramatic Brazilian hardwood walls. A shared central courtyard serves as part of the circulation, and is framed entirely by clear glass walls to allow views through the interior rooms and out to the lake. The roofs of the houses have been designed as occupiable outdoor rooms with translucent panels to ensure privacy.

Walls **1.064 1.119**
Windows **3.006 3.007**
Doors **4.019 4.072**
Stairs **6.065**

The client's brief was for a low maintenance home to accommodate an expanding family with regular guests. Located in a semi-rural context, the house is designed to function independently of mains water, gas, sewerage and electricity. The depth of the plan, height of ceilings, circulation of air, catchment of heat and controlling of direct natural light are refined to optimize the passive solar effectiveness. While the external walls are lightweight, the fireplace and floor create an effective thermal mass. The need to avoid internal overshadowing resolved itself by arranging the buildings in a square. The spaces in-between then grew into outdoor living areas. The result is a house comprised of outdoor spaces that are an extension of living areas, the interplay of which form verandahs, porticos, catwalks and breezeways. The roofscape directly responds to the interior functions, monumental over the living spaces and low slung over sleeping areas. Darker external colours integrate the house into the shadows of the surrounding bushland.

Walls **1.074**
Floors **2.057**
Doors **4.022 4.023**
Roofs **5.104**
Stairs **6.059**

Built adjacent to a mature oak tree, the house is made predominantly of timber and brick. The main organizing element of the house is the principal stair that sits centrally in the plan, becoming both conduit and separator between the living spaces that face the garden and the more private bedrooms that are contained in the oak clad tower. This tower element derives its scale from the heights of the buildings along Arthur Road and the proximity of the mature oak tree that marks the corner of the site. This timber tower also takes its material cues from the oak tree and other properties in the vicinity, some of which have expressed timber framed elements on their facades. The simplicity of the plan combined with an interlocking three-dimensional geometry, has produced a rich internal spatial sequence where sunlight penetrates into every corner of the building. The house has been carefully designed for sculpture and paintings to be displayed, without feeling like an art gallery – the house resolutely remains a private domestic space.

Walls **1.043**
Windows **3.073**
Roofs **5.071 5.088**
Stairs **6.054**

OFIS Arhitekti
Alpine Hut, Bohinj Lake, Slovenia

ARTEC Architekten
Holiday House, Bocksdorf, Burgenland, Austria

A-Piste Arkkitehdit
Villa O, Inkoo, Finland

The Alpine Hut is situated in a small village in Triglav National Park, Slovenia, with very strict rules governing construction and architectural design. The site had been purchased with permission to build a generic project. Without wanting to apply for a new permit, the client wanted to improve the design to suit his family, to build in sustainable factors, and to reposition the openings toward the views. Materials, including stone, timber columns and facade patterns, are inspired by traditional precedents in the area. The rational interior organization is arranged around a central staircase that travels up around the fireplace. On the top floor are three bedrooms and a bathroom with sauna, while the ground floor is an open plan space which includes the kitchen, dining and living rooms, with storage under the staircase. Inside, window sills double as sofas with views towards the mountains. A large corner window is positioned towards the sun so that on sunny days in winter no heating is required. The upper floor is pushed over the ground floor, providing shade in summer.

Floors **2.024 2.025**
Roofs **5.073 5.074 5.075**

The site for this simple weekend retreat for two people extends from a quiet road over the rise of a ridge and benefits from a magnificent southwesterly view from the sloping hillside deep into Styria. The amount of space is modest – one large room for the owners and another smaller room for guests. Each area, separated by a buffer zone, has its own bathroom and glazing to the southwest. The space in between the rooms can be annexed or closed off. A large terrace consists of two elevated covered surfaces that provide outdoor living spaces sheltered from the elements, and hovering above the sloping meadow. The roof's considerable overhang also blocks the sun in summer, thus preventing the overheating of the interior spaces. The prefabricated timber building is linked to an underground level by a small storage space of cast-in-place concrete, as well as by individual columns.

Walls **1.068**
Floors **2.007 2.013**
Windows **3.028 3.036 3.119**
Doors **4.131**
Roofs **5.112 5.142**

Villa O is a holiday house in the Inkoo archipelago on the south coast of Finland. The site lies on a rocky promontory where the villa looks out towards the sea through the pine trees. Using traditional materials and modern prefabrication technology, the massing of the villa follows the colours and forms of the landscape. The terraces cut into the main volume blur the border between inside and outside to create views from each room, via covered outdoor spaces, of the landscape and the sea. The long rectangular plan has its highest part towards the north, where the mezzanine master bedroom sits above the living area. Ancillary functions such as bathrooms and service areas are placed on the west side of the circulation spine. The open kitchen and the traditional Japanese furo bath are linked to one of two stone cores. The facade of untreated aspen has been left to weather into a silvery grey. Deliberately simple details such as the sturdy waxed timber window frames, the modest materials and classical furniture emphasize the role of the landscape in the interior space.

Walls **1.001**
Windows **3.032**
Doors **4.037**
Roofs **5.005**
Stairs **6.019**

Thaler Thaler Architekten
Z House, Vienna, Austria

Tham & Videgård Arkitekter
Archipelago House, Stockholm archipelago, Sweden

Saunders Architecture
Villa Storingavika, Bergen, Norway

This suburban site in Vienna is notable for its triangular form and its location at the junction of two roads. The elongated site shape, combined with Vienna's building regulations, have created a narrow, angular construction envelope. In order to take advantage of spectacular city views and to leave most of the site as landscaped space, the building area was reduced to a minimum, while increasing the volume to accommodate the programme. This generated a form that gives the impression of a monolithic tower. The bedrooms on the upper floor have access to a balcony offering panoramic views over the city, while sheltering the terrace on the ground floor below. The building is a prefabricated timber structure, set on a concrete cellar, with natural cement panels used for the cladding. As few panels as possible have been used, with waste panels used to form linear bands across the facade. A red concrete wall, stretching from the cellar to the upper floor, is the background for a transparent staircase that separates the service areas from the living areas.

Floors **2.032 2.033**
Windows **3.087**
Roofs **5.037 5.038 5.154**

This house is situated in the dramatic landscape of the Stockholm archipelago, well known as the location for the holiday homes of Stockholm residents. The starting point for the design was the establishment of a direct relation to the dramatic archipelago landscape. This has been achieved using the architectural device of a simple frame on a timber platform. Conceived as a lightweight structure in timber and glass, the horizontal character of the black-stained timber exterior cladding relates visually to the verticals of tall mature pine trees and the mirrored surface of the Baltic Sea. The geometry of the plan is generated by the specifics of the site – the house is placed carefully onto the flat surface between two rocky outcrops and turns simultaneously towards the sun in the south and towards the sea in the west. With the smaller private spaces placed towards the rear of the plan, the social areas of the house stand out as an open platform crisscrossed by sliding glass. The stepped layout also creates a series of exterior living spaces sheltered from the prevailing winds.

Walls **1.024**
Floors **2.058 2.087**
Windows **3.088 3.094 3.130**
Roofs **5.036 5.050 5.145**

Overlooking breathtaking fjords and a stretch of Norway's west coast archipelago, Villa Storingavika is a robust yet refined house from which to appreciate the delicate coastline and sometimes rugged climate. It is a pale timber volume enrobed in a crisp, pleated dark timber exterior. The brief called for an upper level with generous open plan living rooms and a master suite, with a lower level to accommodate the children and a small self-contained apartment. The primary aim was to create more open space than the small site seemed to offer, by reclaiming as much outdoor space as possible. Concrete stairs link an upper outdoor terrace with a lower lawn, thus utilizing all of the natural terrain. On both storeys, the utility and service rooms are located along the northern side of the house, while the living areas open out to the south and the view to the sea via large floor-to-ceiling windows. Emerging from the landscape-bound volume of the house is a lightweight outdoor room in the form of a cantilevered balcony anchored by three circular steel columns.

Floors **2.009 2.010**
Windows **3.003**
Doors **4.052 4.090**
Roofs **5.051**

Directory of Construction Details

**1.001
Glass External Wall
Detail 1:10**

A-Piste Arkkitehdit
Villa O [39]

1 Triple glazing of 6
  mm (1/4 inch), 4 mm
  (1/8 inch) and 6 mm
  (1/4 inch) glass panes
2 250 x 80 mm (10 x
  3 1/8 inch) laminated
  timber window
  frames
3 180 x 20 mm (7 1/16 x
  3/4 inch) timber
  capping
4 15 mm (5/8 inch)
  Siberian larch
  flooring with brushed
  and waxed oiled
  finish
5 22 mm (7/8 inch)
  chipboard

6 45 x 260 mm (1 3/4 x
  10 1/4 inch) end joist
7 100 mm (4 inch)
  impact-sound
  insulation
8 22 x 100 mm (7/8 x 4
  inch) boarding
9 13 mm (1/2 inch)
  plasterboard
10 100 mm (4 inch)
  reinforced concrete
  slab with underfloor
  heating
11 100 + 50 mm (4 + 2
  inch) thermal
  insulation
12 300 mm (12 inch)
  crushed stone
13 360 x 80 mm (14 x
  3 1/8 inch) laminated
  timber sill
14 80 mm (3 1/8 inch)
  thermal insulation
15 125 mm (4 9/10 inch)
  concrete blockwork

16 50 x 50 mm (2 x 2
  inch) timber blocking
17 33 x 90 mm (1 1/3 x
  3 1/2 inch) finger
  jointed, untreated
  aspen boarding
18 Ventilation gap

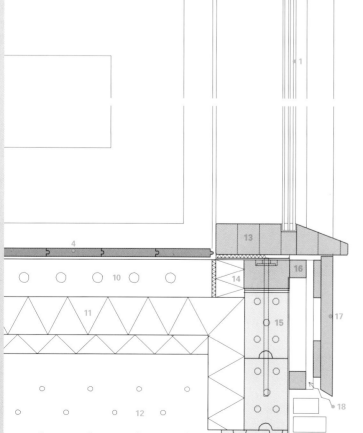

**1.002
Wall Section Detail 1:10**

Avanti Architects
Long View [35]

1 65 x 22 mm (2 1/2 x 7/8
  inch) tongue and
  groove
  weatherboards
  secret fixed to
  counter battens
2 40 x 60 mm (1 5/8 x
  2 3/8 inch) horizontal
  counter battens
3 90 x 60 mm (3 1/2 x
  2 3/8 inch) vertical
  battens
4 Breather membrane
5 12 mm (1/2 inch)
  weather bonded and
  proofed plywood
  bracing
6 12.5 mm (1/2 inch)
  plasterboard taped
  and skimmed
7 160 x 160 mm (6 1/4 x
  6 1/4 inch) steel
  column shown
  dotted
8 Vapour control layer
9 150 mm (6 inch)
  insulation between
  studding
10 Insect mesh
11 3 mm (1/8 inch)
  folded polyester
  powder-coated
  aluminium flashing
  to gap
12 150 x 50 mm (6 x 2
  inch) timber stud
  frame
13 50 x 75 mm (2 x 3
  inch) horizontal
  counter battens
14 Facing brick
15 Wall cavity vent hole
16 Flashing from
  structural timber wall
  to angle across cavity
  to ventholes

**1.003
Wall Plan Detail 1:10**

Avanti Architects
Long View [35]

1 Two layers of 12.5
  mm (1/2 inch)
  plasterboard
2 150 mm (6 inch)
  insulation between
  studding
3 150 x 50 mm (6 x 2
  inch) timber stud
  frame
4 160 x 160 mm (6 1/4 x
  6 1/4 inch) steel
  column with 80 mm

(3 1/8 inch) insulation
  infill
5 50 mm (2 inch) metal
  stud frame to fix
  internal lining to
  services void
6 Vapour control layer
  fixed over timber
  studs and horizontal
  counter battens
7 Breather membrane
8 12 mm (1/2 inch)
  weather bonded and
  proofed plywood
  bracing
9 90 x 60 mm (3 1/2 x
  2 3/8 inch) vertical
  battens provide

ventilation to wall
  cavity space
10 40 x 60 mm (1 5/8 x
  2 3/8 inch) horizontal
  counter battens
11 65 x 22 mm (2 1/2 x 7/8
  inch) tongue and
  groove weather
  boards secret fixed
  vertically to
  horizontal counter
  battens
12 20 mm (3/4 inch)
  Celotex insulation
13 3 mm (1/8 inch)
  folded polyester
  powder-coated
  aluminium flashing

to door jamb
14 Double glazed
  aluminium window

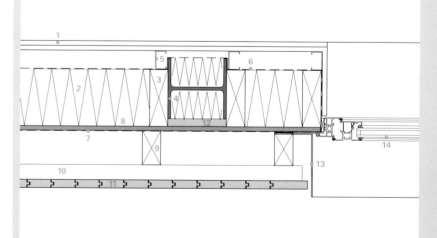

1.004
Terrace Balustrade
Detail 1:10

Alphaville
Hall House 1 [07]

1 75 x 30 x 2 mm (3 x 1¹/₅ x ¹/₁₂ inch) stainless steel top rail
2 265 x 70 x 5 mm (10²/₅ x 2³/₄ x ³/₁₆ inch C-shaped polycarbonate cover panel
3 100 x 50 x 5 mm (4 x 2 x ³/₁₆ inch) hot-dip galvanized steel gusset plate
4 4.5 mm (³/₁₆ inch) hot-dip galvanized steel plate flashing
5 Fair-faced concrete floor with water repellent paint finish
6 Fair-faced concrete exterior wall with osmosis liquid waterproofing paint finish

1.005
Wall Detail 1:10

Chenchow Little
Architects
Freshwater House [32]

1 Drainage cell
2 Membrane
3 Geotextile fabric
4 Concrete slab and beam
5 50 x 50 mm (2 x 2 inch) galvanized steel frame to garage door
6 50 x 50 mm (2 x 2 inch) horizontal timber battens
7 Sarking
8 90 x 40 mm (3¹/₂ x 1⁵/₈ inch) vertical timber battens
9 Fibre cement sheeting made ready for painting internally and at external edges
10 200 mm (8 inch) wide stainless steel grate with integral drain
11 Garage area

1.006
External Wall Detail 1:10

Chenchow Little
Architects
Freshwater House [32]

1 Colorbond sheet metal capping
2 Colorbond Kliplok profile sheet metal roof
3 Insulation
4 Timber roof battens
5 150 x 50 mm (6 x 2 inch) timber rafters at 600 mm (23²/₃ inch) centres
6 Painted plasterboard ceiling lining
7 Fabricated steel fascia beam
8 Steel angle
9 150 x 50 mm (6 x 2 inch) timber rafters
10 Vertically mounted Custom Orb wall sheeting
11 Sarking
12 12 mm (¹/₂ inch) plasterboard wall lining, paint finished
13 100 x 50 mm (4 x 2 inch) timber stud framing with insulation in between
14 Craftwood skirting with painted finish
15 Tiled floor
16 Screed
17 Fabricated steel beam
18 Concrete slab and beam
19 Fabricated steel beam
20 Fabricated steel beam
21 Steel beam
22 Horizontally mounted Custom Orb wall sheeting
23 Aluminium angle
24 Membrane and flashing
25 Waterproof membrane
26 Concrete block retaining wall
27 Cavity
28 Brickwork wall
29 Concrete interior wall

1.007
External Wall Detail 1:10

Barton Myers Associates
Bekins Residence [25]

1 Roofing membrane on plywood layer
2 Plywood
3 Galvanized steel scupper
4 Timber joists
5 Building insulation
6 Gypsum wall board
7 Galvanized steel chain
8 Cement plaster
9 Plywood panel
10 Insulation
11 Structural concrete slab
12 Moisture barrier
13 Continuous void form
14 Concrete splash block
15 Concrete paving
16 Galvanized steel flashing
17 Aluminium weep hole
18 Grade beam
19 Concrete caisson beyond

1.008
Window Sliding Wall Detail 1:10

dRMM (de Rijke Marsh Morgan Architects)
Sliding House [14]

1 Primary portal frames welded together
2 Portal frame steel connector
3 Timber frame to aperture
4 Membrane to reveal of sliding wall window apertures
5 Inward opening tilt-and-turn double glazed window
6 Larch rainscreen cladding
7 Aluminium trim to membrane
8 Portal frame steel connector
9 Double glazed unit
10 Waterproof membrane
11 Oriented strand board sheathing
12 Full-fill insulation between timber studs
13 Tongue and groove internal cladding
14 185 x 50 mm (7¼ x 2 inch) timber stud frame
15 Glasshouse fixed back to steel section within timber floor zone
16 Mezzanine floor level
17 Oak flooring on
18 200 x 100 mm (8 x 4 inch) rectangular hollow section to receive glass fixing bracket
19 200 x 60 mm (8 x 2³/₈ inch) timber joist
20 Two layers of 12.5 mm (½ inch) plasterboard
21 Oak floor as edging
22 Nylon brush air seal

battens

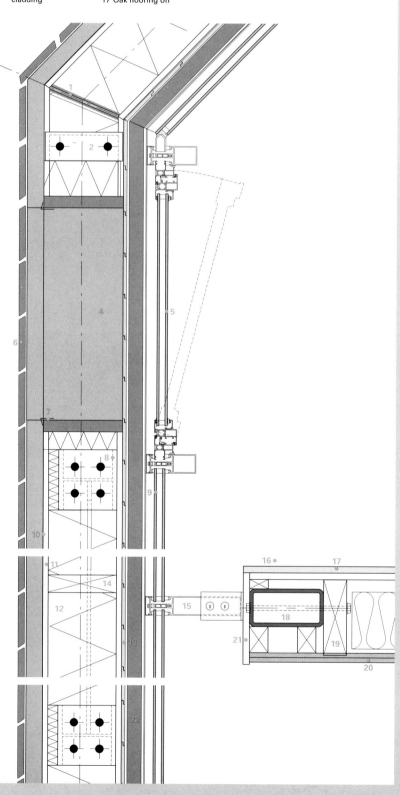

1.009
Basement Wall Detail
1:10

Blank Studio
Xeros Residence [29]

1 Stainless steel
flashing behind
aluminium wall
panels extending
into shower pan
beneath grating
flange
2 20 gauge
standing-seam metal
cladding on
self-healing
waterproof
membrane on 12.5
mm (1/2 inch) exterior
plywood
3 Steel framing
4 225 x 12.5 mm (9 x
1/2 inch) framing and
hangers
5 12.5 mm (1/2 inch)
reveal

6 150 mm (6 inch)
structural steel studs
at 600 mm (24 inch)
centres with batt
insulation between
7 12.5 mm (1/2 inch)
plaster on 12.5 mm
(1/2 inch) interior
finish cement board
8 Flashing and silicone
sealant behind metal
cladding at glass
9 12.5 mm (1/2 inch)
laminated glazing
tape and clear
silicone
10 5 mm (3/16 inch)
unfinished steel plate
blind fastened to 150
mm (6 inch) steel
stud framing
11 Subsurface trench
drain
12 200 mm (8 inch) thick
concrete stem wall

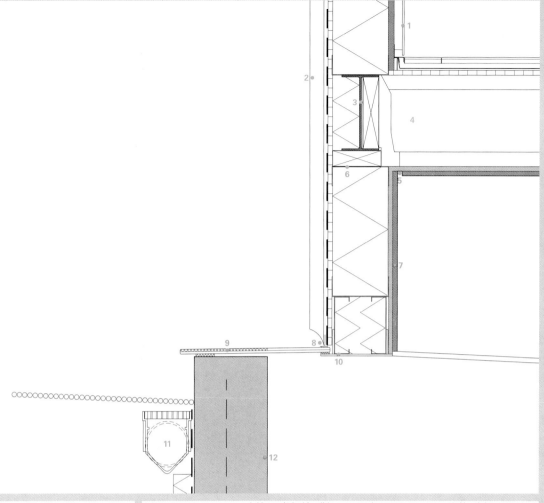

1.010
Basement Wall Footing
Detail 1:10

Blank Studio
Xeros Residence [29]

1 50 mm (2 inch) rigid
insulation over
waterproof coating
2 200 mm (8 inch) thick

concrete stem wall
3 Fabric filter over 100
mm (4 inch) tile in
washed gravel
4 100 mm (4 inch) floor
reveal with washed
gravel to match site
5 100 mm (4 inch)
polished concrete
slab on grade, on 100
mm (4 inch)

aggregate base
course
6 Reinforced concrete
footing

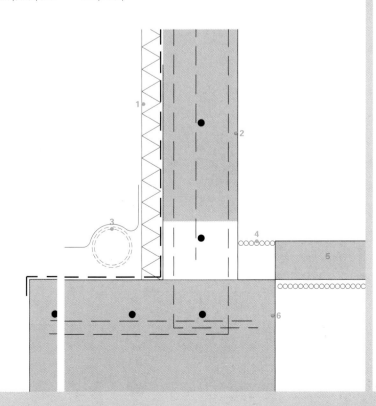

1.011
Exterior Wall Plan Detail
1:10

Studio d'ARC Architects
Live / Work Studio II [19]

1 Duratherm window
system
2 3 mm (1/8 inch)
weathered steel plate

3 23 mm (1 inch) solid
maple jamb
4 50 x 150 mm (2 x 6
inch) stud framing
5 Timber blocking
6 Vapour barrier
7 18 gauge corrugated,
weathered, steel
sheet fixed with
stainless steel screws
with neoprene metal

washers
8 Building felt
9 20 mm (3/4 inch)
exterior grade
plywood sheathing
10 Batt insulation
11 15 mm (5/8 inch)
gypsum board
12 100 mm (4 inch)
diameter galvanized
downspout

13 Aluminium reveal
14 18 gauge weathered
steel angle
15 200 mm (8 inch)
concrete masonry
unit
16 Insulating inserts
17 Neighbouring
structure

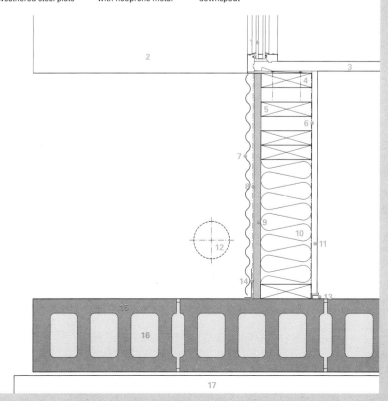

1.012
External Wall Detail 1:20

Donovan Hill
Z House [24]

1 Glazing tape and
structural silicone
over aluminium
T-section
2 Roll formed steel
C-channel purlin
3 9mm (3/8 inch) blue
coloured backed
toughened glass
over fibre-cement
sheeting
4 Painted finish on
square set
plasterboard
5 Termite proof pine
timber frame
6 Copper sheet
flashing
7 Aluminium sliding
window guide
8 Copper sheet
window hood
9 25 x 25 mm (1 x 1
inch) clear sealed
New Guinea
rosewood outrigger
at 500 mm (20 inch)
centres
10 120 x 45 mm (43/4 x
13/4 inch) clear sealed
New Guinea
rosewood top rail
with brush seal
11 Hardwood timber
packer
12 9 mm (3/8 inch)
toughened glass
13 Clear sealed New
Guinea rosewood
window frame
14 Flexible polymer
render
15 50 x 70 mm (2 x 23/4
inch) clear sealed
New Guinea
rosewood bottom rail
with brush seal
16 Mixture of 86 x 19
mm (33/8 x 3/4 inch)
and 42 x 19 mm (15/8
x 3/4 inch) clear
sealed spotted gum
hardwood timber
flooring
17 Core-filled concrete
blockwork
18 Stainless steel mesh
termite barrier
19 Bitumen coated
waterproof
membrane
20 Concrete retaining
wall
21 Subsurface drainage
22 Concrete foundation

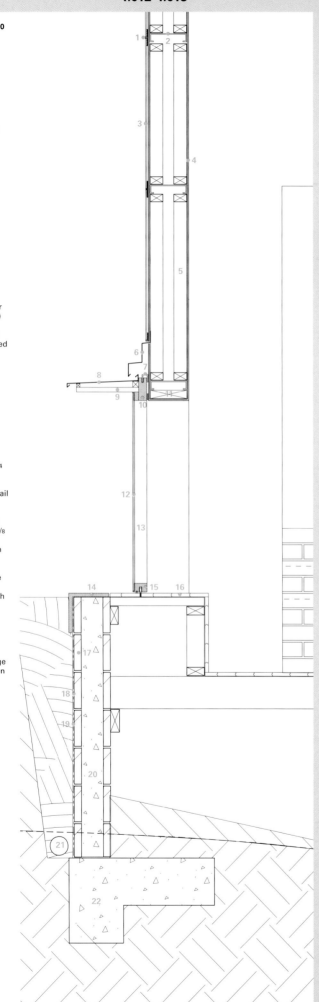

1.013
**External Wall Plan Detail
1:10**

ODOS Architects
House in Wicklow [18]

1 Two layers of 80 mm
(31/8 inch) Thermo
Hemp insulation
2 Full height treated
hardwood timber
cladding panels
secret fixed to 25 x
50 mm (1 x 2 inch)
treated horizontal
counter battens on
35 x 50 mm (13/8 x 2
inch) treated vertical
battens on breather
membrane. Panel
frame of 110 x 44 mm
(43/8 x 13/4 inch)
treated softwood
timber studs at 400
mm (16 inch) centres
with horizontal
noggins at 800 mm
(32 inch) centres
3 Ventilated cavity
4 12.5 mm (1/2 inch)
plasterboard,
skimmed and painted
5 Recessed brush seals
6 Full-height insulated
timber door with
stainless steel drips
top and bottom,
made of secret-fixed
treated hardwood
timber cladding to
match external
cladding, with 13 mm
(1/2 inch) marine
grade plywood on
treated softwood
timber carcassing.
Insulation in core
with a vapour control
layer internally and a
damp proof course
externally
7 Internal balustrade of
toughened and
laminated safety
glass
8 Recessed hardwood
timber frame
9 Pressed metal
powder-coated sill on
damp proof course
fixed into recess of
treated hardwood
timber bottom rail
10 Full-height, clear
double glazed fixed
unit comprised of 8
mm (1/3 inch)
toughened glass
outer pane, 12 mm
(1/2 inch) air gap and
8 mm (1/3 inch) clear
toughened inner
pane in a recessed
treated hardwood
timber frame. All
joints between glass
panes to be silicone
sealed and bonded

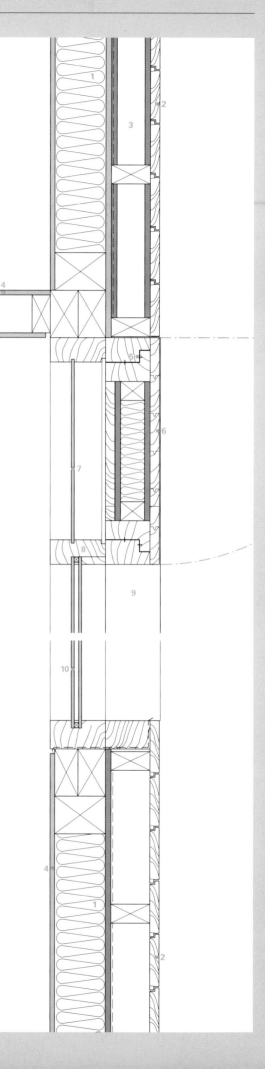

1.014
External Wall and Roof
Detail 1:10

Welsh + Major
Pitt Street House [37]

1 16 mm (5/8 inch) diameter mild steel balustrade trim
2 Folded galvanized mild steel flashing
3 Timber boarding on 40 x 25 mm (15/8 x 1 inch) timber battens
4 16 mm (5/8 inch) Firecheck board on substrate
5 200 mm (8 inch) insulation
6 10 mm (3/8 inch) plasterboard lining
7 100 x 100 mm (8 x 8 inch) square hollow section
8 180 x 20 mm (71/8 x 3/4 inch) timber barge board
9 200 x 85 mm (8 x 33/8 inch) window head frame
10 Painted timber handrail
11 Painted, timber framed, glazed sliding door
12 Line of sliding flyscreen door (in closed position)
13 200 x 85 mm (8 x 33/8 inch) window sill
14 19 x 32 mm (3/4 x 11/4 inch) dressed timber bead
15 16 mm (5/8 inch) diameter mild steel roof support rod
16 Fibre cement sheet with acrylic render
17 Sarking
18 200 x 75 mm (8 x 3 inch) parallel flange channel
19 10 mm (3/8 inch) plasterboard lining
20 Insulation
21 Existing weatherboarding
22 30 x 25 mm (11/8 x 1 inch) dividing bead
23 New timber weatherboarding to match existing
24 Fibre cement sheet with acrylic render
25 Salvaged timber boards

1.015
Corrugated Metal Wall
Detail 1:10

WPA
Weese Young Residence [28]

1 Lite-ply wall lining
2 Insulation
3 Corrugated zincalume on timber battens on waterproof membrane on plywood
4 Painted square hollow section column
5 Head flashing
6 Aluminium sliding window
7 Sill flashing
8 Poplar base and skirting
9 Vertical grain pine on plywood subfloor
10 Engineered timber joist
11 Timber edge beam
12 Insulation
13 Painted exterior grade plywood
14 Painted rectangular hollow section beam
15 Painted cementitious panels on waterproof membrane on plywood sheathing
16 Timber stud frame

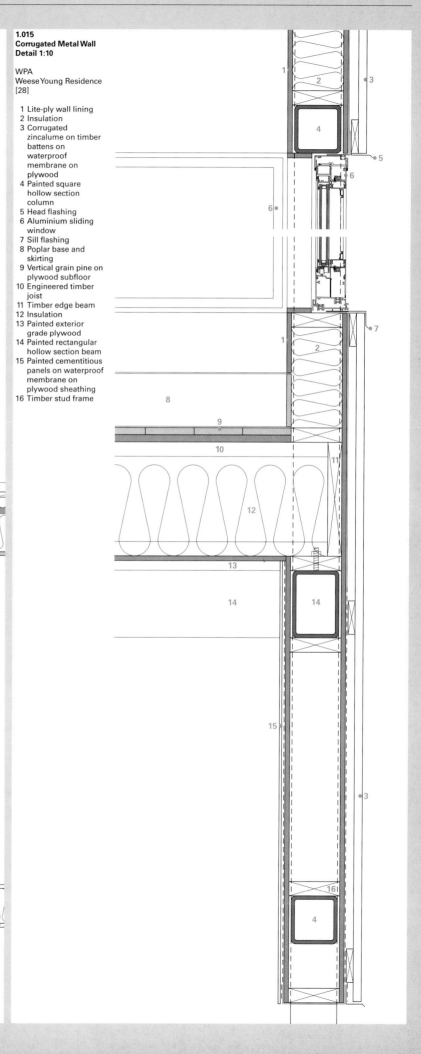

1.016
External Wall and Sliding Doors at Balcony Plan Detail 1:10

Steven Holl Architects
Swiss Embassy
Residence [14]

1 Channel glass
2 Edge of concrete
3 Steel column
4 Concrete balcony parapet
5 Aluminium door with fixed translucent insulated glass unit
6 Steel substructure
7 3 mm (1/8 inch) stainless steel window box
8 Light alcove above
9 Opening for sunshade above
10 Line of edge above
11 Aluminium sliding door
12 Compressible neoprene gasket
13 Timber blocking
14 Batt insulation
15 25 mm (1 inch) clear insulated glass unit
16 Waterproofing layer
17 Two layers 15 mm (5/8 inch) gypsum wall board
18 Vapour barrier

1.017
External Wall Detail 1:10

Diederendirrix
Villa PPML [21]

1 Exterior brickwork to cavity wall
2 Insulation
3 Cast lime and sand stone blocks to interior of cavity wall
4 10 mm (2/5 inch) stucco interior wall
5 20 x 35 mm (3/4 x 1 1/3 inch) aluminium corner profile
6 Trowelled floor finish
7 Cement screed
8 Insulation layer
9 Cast in-situ reinforced concrete floor slab
10 Stucco ceiling finish
11 Cast in-situ reinforced concrete wall
12 Stucco wall finish

1.018
External Wall Detail 1:20

Pezo von Ellrichshausen Architects
Poli House [09]

1 150 mm (6 inch) reinforced concrete wall
2 25 x 100 mm (1 x 4 inch) pine board
3 30 mm (1 1/4 inch) polystyrene thermal insulation
4 25 x 100 mm (1 x 4 inch) recycled pine board
5 Fixed double glazing

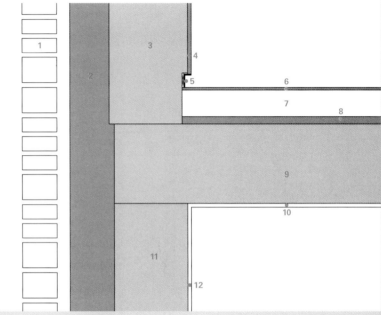
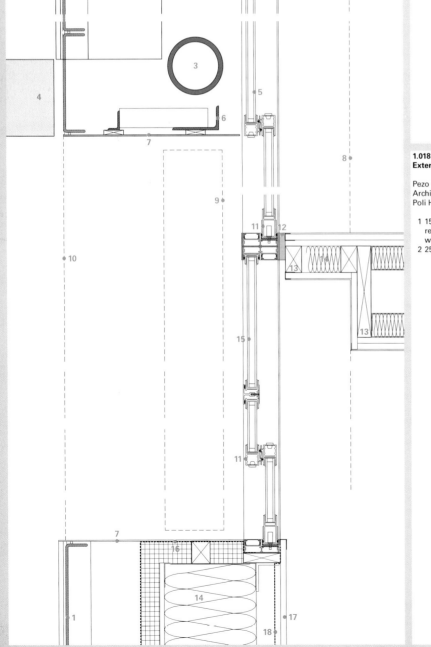
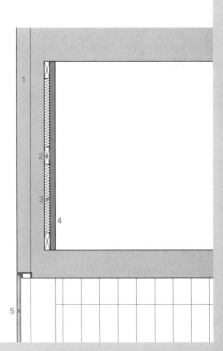

1.019
External Wall Detail 1:10

John Onken Architects
Dolphin Cottage [32]

1 Vertical Thermowood board cladding with open joints pinned to battens
2 38 x 45 mm (1½ x 1¾ inch) treated softwood horizontal battens at 600 mm (24 inch) vertical centres over breather membrane
3 100 mm (4 inch) external blockwork
4 100 mm (4 inch) Dritherm full-fill cavity batt insulation
5 100 mm (4 inch) medium density internal blockwork
6 15 mm (⅝ inch) plaster with paint finish
7 75 mm (3 inch) high tile skirting set flush with plaster with reveal joint above
8 Tile floor finish over 75 mm (3 inch) reinforced screed with underfloor heating pipes
9 100 mm (4 inch) rigid floor insulation with sheet damp proof membrane above
10 Beam and block floor structure with ventilated void below
11 Damp proof course
12 Sand-cement render to base of wall
13 Solid grouting to cavity at ground level
14 Concrete strip foundation

1.020
External Wall Detail at First Floor Overhang 1:10

John Onken Architects
Dolphin Cottage [32]

1 Vertical timber board cladding
2 Plywood sheathing and breather membrane
3 Fibreglass batt insulation
4 Painted skirting board
5 21 mm (⅘ inch) tongue and groove floor decking
6 300 mm (12 inch) deep truss-joist floor framing
7 Vertical board cladding returns under soffit
8 300 mm (12 inch) overall blockwork wall with insulated steel lintel in cavity
9 Render finish to external blockwork
10 Bell-cast drip edge
11 Double glazed, softwood framed window, paint finish
12 External render returns into window reveal
13 Cedar window sill to match cladding
14 Damp proof course
15 Sand-cement to base of wall
16 Rigid insulation
17 Solid grouting behind insulation
18 Tile floor finish over 75 mm (3 inch) reinforced screed with underfloor heating pipes
19 100 mm (4 inch) rigid floor insulation with sheet damp proof membrane above
20 Beam and block floor structure with ventilated void below
21 Concrete strip foundation

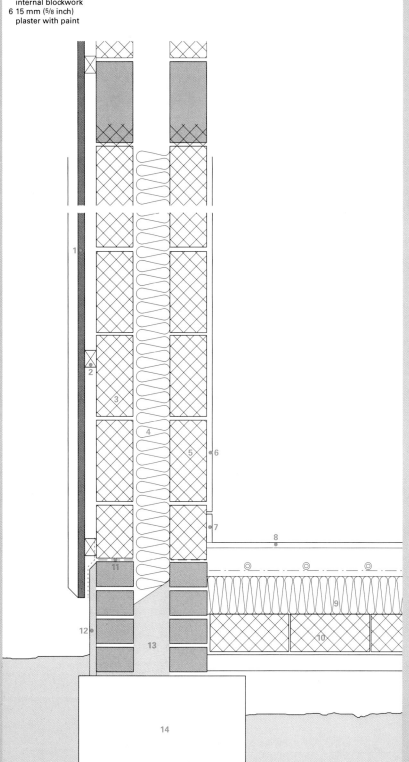

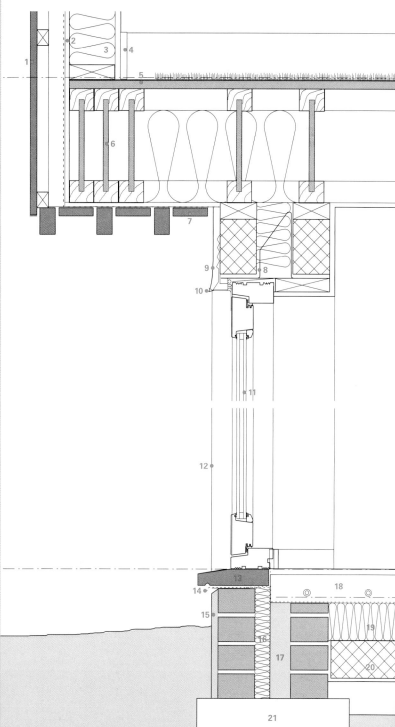

**1.021
External Wall and
Footing Detail 1:20**

de Blacam and Meagher
Architects
Morna Valley Residence
[20]

1 Reinforced concrete
 pad foundation
2 Reinforced concrete
 ground beam
3 250 x 250 mm (10 x
 10 inch) reinforced
 concrete column
4 Hardcore
5 Hollow concrete
 block
6 Concrete screed
7 Terracotta blocks
8 Cement render
9 Rigid insulation
10 Screed with
 embedded services
11 Rigid insulation
12 Damp proof
 membrane
13 Levelling screed
14 Sand and cement
 bedding mortar
15 600 x 400 x 20 mm
 (24 x 16 x 3/4 inch)
 white Ibiza marble
 tile
16 100 x 20 mm (4 x 3/4
 inch) white Ibiza
 marble skirting flush
 with render
17 White painted plaster

**1.022
Sliding Wall Track
Mechanism Detail 1:20**

dRMM (de Rijke Marsh
Morgan Architects)
Sliding House [14]

1 Larch rainscreen
 cladding
2 Membrane
3 Tongue and groove
 internal cladding
4 Full-fill insulation
 between timber
 studs
5 Double glazed
 conservatory formed
 of curtain walling
 system
6 150 x 75 mm (6 x 3
 inch) rolled steel
 channel
7 Two 12 volt DC
 batteries
8 Electric motor and
 gearbox
9 Chain driven steel
 wheel
10 Concealed gutters
11 Aluminium box
 section with bottom
 transom of curtain
 wall concealed in
 floor
12 Quartzite paved
 flooring on mortar
 bed
13 Zone of underground
 heating
14 50 mm (2 inch)
 diameter duct drain
 leading to perforated
 pipe land drain
15 Concrete slab
16 300 mm (12 inch) CP
 Cordek Cellcore
17 Concrete pile
18 Grassed area

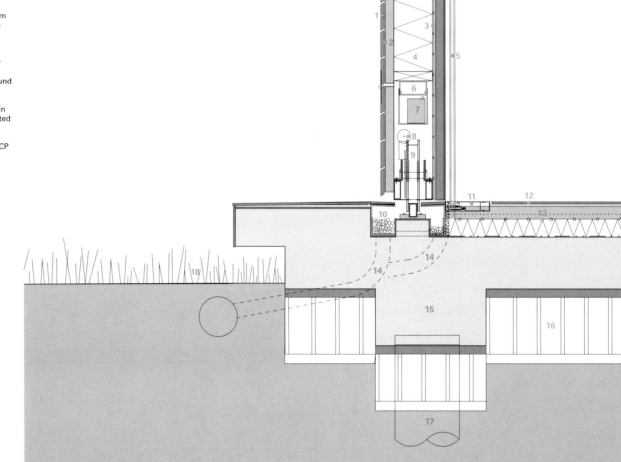

1.023
Corner Wall Detail 1:5

Go Hasegawa &
Associates
Forest House [34]

1 25 x 25 mm (1 x 1
   inch) narrow-pitch
   galvanized-
   aluminium coated
   corner angle
2 Narrow-pitch
   galvanized-
   aluminium coated
   corrugated sheet
   external wall
3 10 x 30 mm (3/8 x 1 1/5

inch) firring strips at
455 mm (18 1/4 inch)
centres
4 12 mm (1/2 inch)
   structural plywood
5 120 x 120 mm (4 3/4 x
   4 3/4 inch) column
6 12 mm (1/2 inch)
   structural plywood
   and 5.5 mm (1/4 inch)
   plywood interior wall
   with oil stain clear
   lacquer finish

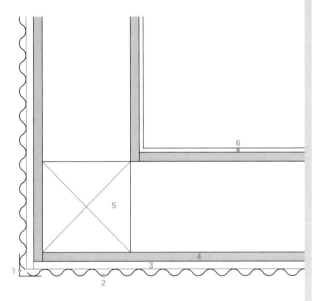

1.024
Facade Detail 1:10

Tham & Videgård
Arkitekter
Archipelago House [40]

1 18 mm (7/10 inch)
   plywood cladding
   screwed to 45 x 45
   mm (1 3/4 x 1 3/4 inch)
   and 22 x 22 mm (9/10
   x 9/10 inch) battens at
   200 mm (8 inch)
   centres
2 Moisture diffusing
   windproof building
   paper

3 45 mm (1 3/4 inch)
   rockwool insulation
4 Vapour barrier
5 23 x 95 mm (9/10 x
   3 3/4 inch) dovetailed
   timber boarding
6 150mm (6 inch)
   Rockwool insulation
7 45 x 45 mm (1 3/4 x
   1 3/4 inch) timber
   battens
8 50 x 135 mm (2 x 5 1/4
   inch) vertical post
9 22 x 120 mm (7/8 x
   4 3/4 inch) floorboards
10 Vapour barrier
11 45 x 220 mm (1 3/4 x
   8 5/8 inch) timber

beam
12 20 x 160 mm (3/4 x
   6 1/4 inch) dovetailed
   timber boards
13 220 mm (8 5/8 inch)
   Rockwool insulation

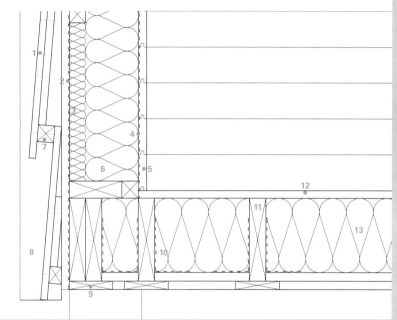

1.025
Vault Base Detail 1:20

Hawkes Architecture
Crossway [16]

1 Native wildflower
   meadow using seeds
   from a nearby nature
   reserve
2 Gravel drainage zone
3 Kaycel Super-plus
   Graphite insulation
4 Kaycel Super-plus

Graphite insulation
5 Clay tile timbrel
   vaulted arch
6 Kaycel Super-plus
   Graphite insulation
7 Reinforced concrete
   slab
8 Crushed glass bottle
   and resin polished
   flooring
9 Kaycel Super-plus
   Graphite insulation
10 Visqueen
   Ecomembrane damp

proof membrane
bonded to Bituthene
self-adhesive damp
proof membrane
11 Crushed bottle eco
   sand blinding
12 Cordek Cellcore
   anti-heave layer
13 Concrete pile
   foundation
14 Black rubber EPDM
   (ethylene propylene
   dieme monomer)
   waterproofing

15 Perforated pipe
   perimeter land drain

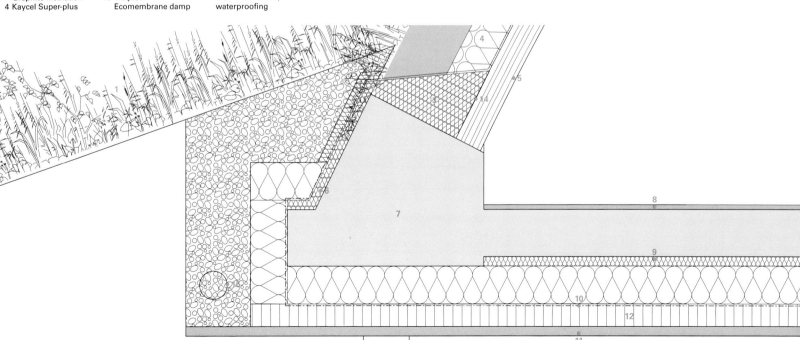

1.026
External Wall at Reflecting Pool Detail 1:5

Kallos Turin
Casa Zorzal [10]

1 Brick wall
2 Waterproof mortar
3 'Tarquini' integrated plaster
4 25 mm (1 inch) polystyrene insulation
5 3 mm (1/8 inch) plaster skim coat, paint finished
6 Cement mortar
7 20 x 15 mm (3/4 x 5/8 inch) aluminium channel plaster bead
8 45 mm (13/4 inch) pigmented cement screed
9 Underfloor heating
10 Ballast layer of gravel
11 Reinforced concrete
12 400 mm (16 inch) deep water
13 'Aquavation' render
14 Pebbles

1.027
External Wall Plan Detail 1:5

Western Design Architects
The Moat House [20]

1 Colour coordinating unplasticised polyvinyl chloride movement bead
2 20 mm (3/4 inch) polymer reinforced through colour render
3 Renderlath panel with stainless steel mesh
4 25 x 50 mm (1 x 2 inch) vertical timber batten
5 12 mm (1/2 inch) plywood
6 50 x 100 mm (2 x 4 inch) vertical timber stud
7 50 mm (2 inch) cavity
8 50 mm (2 inch) cavity insulation
9 100 mm (4 inch) glass fibre quilt between treated timber frame
10 12.5 mm (1/2 inch) plasterboard and skim plaster coat

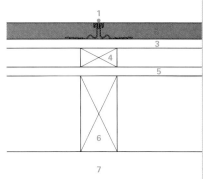

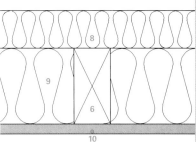

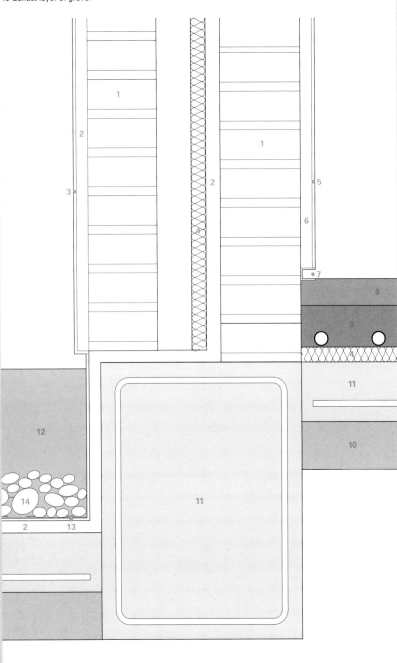

1.028
Polycarbonate Wall Detail 1:10

WPA
Weese Young Residence [28]

1 Polycarbonate panels
2 Extruded aluminium hardware
3 Painted square hollow section column
4 Timber stud frame

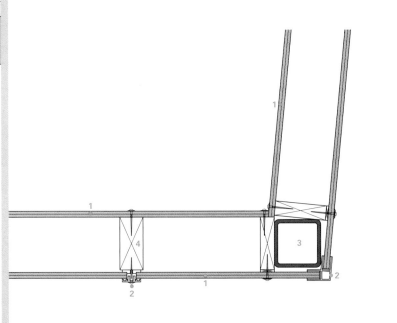

1.029
External Wall Detail
1:10

ODOS Architects
House in Wicklow [18]

1 Fire-rated 4.8kg granular surfaced polyester reinforced modified bitumen high performance membrane, fully torch bonded
2 Fibreboard faced composite insulation
3 18 mm (7/10 inch) marine grade plywood
4 Structural timber joist
5 18 mm (7/10 inch) marine grade plywood
6 Steel beam
7 Canopy above entrance porch to be continuation of roof and parapet structure and finishes
8 Recessed hardwood timber frame
9 Recessed hardwood timber liner to reveal
10 Shadow gap
11 12.5 mm (1/2 inch) plasterboard ceiling, skimmed and painted
12 Finish to reveal to match external facade
13 22 mm (4/5 inch) full height treated hardwood timber cladding panels secret fixed to 25 x 50 mm (1 x 2 inch) treated horizontal counter battens on 35 x 50 mm (13/8 x 2 inch) treated vertical battens on breather membrane. Panel frame of 110 x 44 mm (43/8 x 13/4 inch) treated softwood timber studs at 400 mm (16 inch) centres with horizontal noggins at 800 mm (32 inch) centres
14 12 mm (1/2 inch) marine grade plywood on treated softwood carcass
15 Insulation core with vapour control layer to internal face and damp proof course to external face
16 Finish to be 150 mm (6 inch) fair-faced powerfloated reinforced white concrete to match stairs
17 Damp proof membrane
18 Timber sill with anodized aluminium drip profile
19 Recessed hardwood timber frame
20 Recessed hardwood timber liner to reveal
21 Damp proof course
22 Polished concrete screed on 59 mm (23/8 inch) powerfloated in-situ concrete screed, screed contains underfloor heating conduits on vapour control layer with taped overlaps at all junctions. 50 mm (2 inch) Kingspan insulation on solid concrete block and plank ceiling spanning between steel beams
23 Structural steel beam

1.030
External Wall Detail 1:10

Paulo David with Luz Ramalho
Casa Funchal [16]

1 Layer of black volcanic pebbles
2 Geotextile blanket
3 Two layers of 40 mm (15/8 inch) insulation
4 Two layers of waterproof membrane
5 Concrete screed
6 Concrete roof slab
7 Zinc capping to parapet wall
8 Concrete extended from inner layer to cover block wall
9 Monomass render system to external wall
10 150 mm (6 inch) concrete block wall
11 Air cavity
12 30 mm (11/8 inch) insulation
13 Fine plaster lining to concrete block wall
14 Ground drainage
15 Hardwood skirting
16 Polyurethane floor with protective layer
17 Underfloor heating system
18 Underfloor heating
19 Concrete floor slab
20 Flashing
21 High capacity drainage layer
22 Delta drain layer
23 Bituminous paint
24 Compacted pebble layer

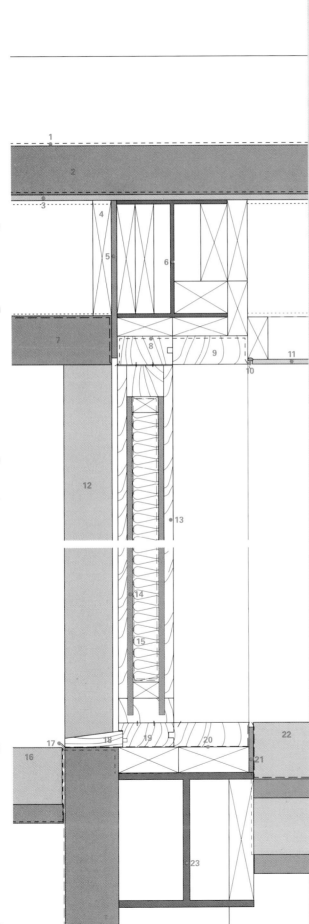

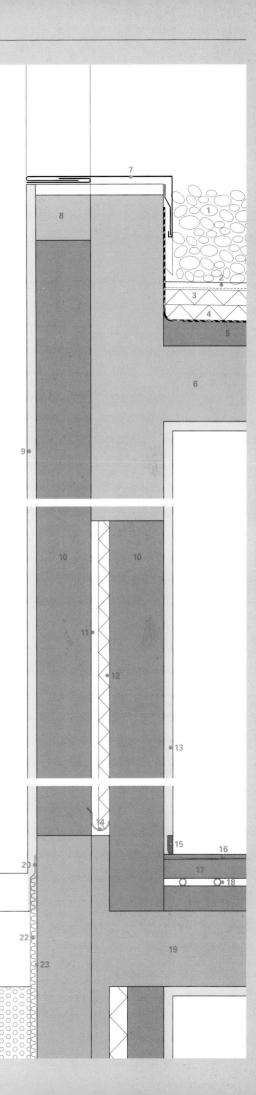

1.031
Wall Detail at Ground Floor 1:10

MELD Architecture with Vicky Thornton
House in Tarn et Garonne [34]

1 Bespoke double glazed oak framed window
2 Laminated pine board
3 Sealed oak window frame
4 Expanded polystyrene full-fill cavity insulation
5 Limestone rubble wall
6 Damp proof membrane
7 Expanded polystyrene full-fill cavity insulation
8 Dense concrete blockwork
9 Lime render
10 Polished screed floor
11 Exterior concrete paving
12 Mixed pebbles to drainage channel
13 Damp proof membrane
14 Dense concrete blockwork
15 Damp proof membrane

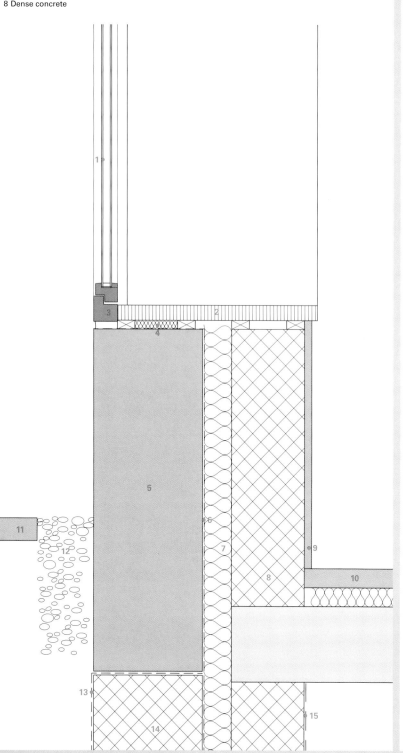

1.032
Wall Detail at First Floor 1:10

MELD Architecture with Vicky Thornton
House in Tarn et Garonne [34]

1 Bespoke double glazed oak framed window
2 Galvanized flashing
3 Chestnut timber sill
4 Polished screed floor
5 125 mm (5 inch) wide board on untreated chestnut cladding
6 Breather membrane
7 Treated softwood wall plate
8 Cast concrete lintel
9 Expanded polystyrene full-fill cavity insulation
10 Pre-cast concrete lintel
11 Lime render
12 Lime mortar
13 Expanded polystyrene full-fill cavity insulation
14 Laminated pine board

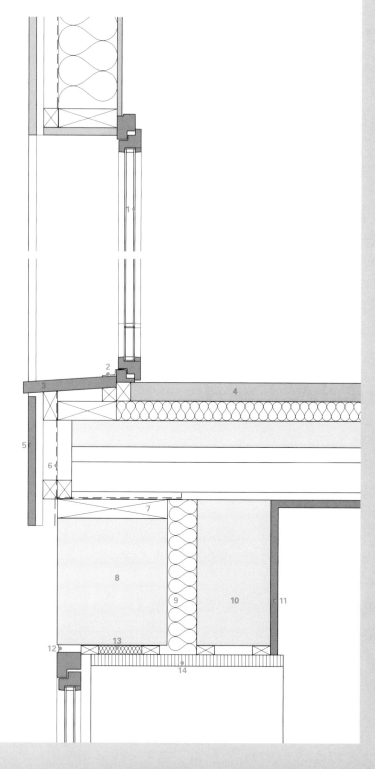

1.033
Wall Section at Bridge
Detail 1:20

Safdie Rabines
Architects
Artist Bridge Studio [30]

1 Sheet metal parapet
 capping
2 Galvanized metal
 flashing
3 Base flashing
4 Built-up roof
 membrane on
 plywood roof
 sheathing
5 350 x 150 mm (14 x 6
 inch) glulam beam
6 Insulation
7 15 mm (5/8 inch)
 gypsum board
 ceiling
8 15 mm (5/8 inch)
 gypsum wallboard
9 Insulation
10 Trespa high
 performance exterior
 cladding panels
11 Building paper
12 Structural plywood
 sheathing
13 Hardwood floor
14 Plywood floor
 sheathing
15 Insulation
16 Two layers of
 gypsum board
17 22 mm (7/8 inch)
 plaster over metal
 lath
18 Glulam beam
 connection plate to
 concrete footing

1.034
Wall Section at Bridge
Detail 1:20

Safdie Rabines
Architects
Artist Bridge Studio [30]

1 350 x 150 mm (14 x 6
 inch) glulam beam
2 Galvanized metal
 flashing
3 Sheet metal parapet
 capping
4 Base flashing
5 Built-up roof
 membrane on
 plywood roof
 sheathing
6 Insulation
7 Roll-down shade
 screen
8 15 mm (5/8 inch)
 gypsum board
 ceiling
9 Double glazed sliding
 doors

10 Prefinished metal
 drip
11 240 x 40 mm (9 1/2 x
 1 5/8 inch) timber joist
12 Sliding door track
 flush with hardwood
 floor
13 Hardwood floor
14 Plywood floor
 sheathing
15 Two layers of
 gypsum board
16 22 mm (7/8 inch)
 plaster over metal
 lath

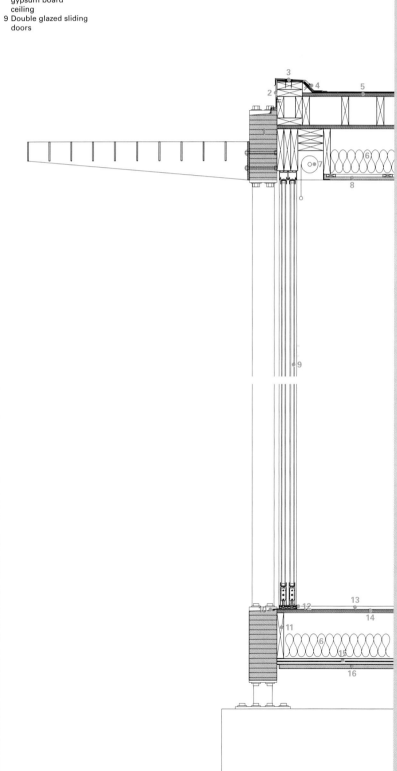

1.035
Typical Stud Wall Detail
1:2

Studio Bednarski
Hesmondhalgh House
[33]

1 3 mm (1/8 inch)
   plaster skim coat
2 12.5 mm (1/2 inch)
   gypsum wallboard
3 Expamet plaster stop
   bead
4 Painted softwood
   skirting board
5 100 x 50 mm (4 x 2
   inch) timber stud
6 Floor finish bonded
   onto subfloor
7 19 mm (3/4 inch)
   plywood subfloor

1.036
External Wall Detail 1:10

Studio Bednarski
Hesmondhalgh House
[33]

1 Pre-patinated copper
   fascia
2 Pre-patinated copper
   drip
3 Silicone joint
4 100 x 50 mm (4 x 2
   inch) mild steel
   rectangular hollow
   section steel beam
5 Vapour barrier
6 200 x 50 mm (8 x 2
   Inch) hardwood
   frame
7 Two layers 12.5 mm
   (1/2 inch)
   plasterboard
8 Fixed double glazed
   safety glass
9 200 x 80 mm (8 x 3 1/8
   inch) hardwood
   transom
10 Timber window sill
11 Square section
    timber finishing bead
12 Window frame
13 Timber window sill
14 Fixed double glazed
    safety glass in
    hardwood door
15 Aluminium drip
    profile
16 225 x 75 mm (9 x 3
    inch) hardwood
    threshold
17 Rigid insulation
18 Timber floor
19 Screed with
    underfloor heating
    coils
20 Insulation
21 Tanking
22 Concrete ground slab
23 1200 x 600 mm (48 x
    24 inch) raised
    paving slabs with 10
    mm (3/8 inch) gaps on
    paving slab support
24 80 mm (3 1/8 inch)
    permeable block
25 Bedding grit

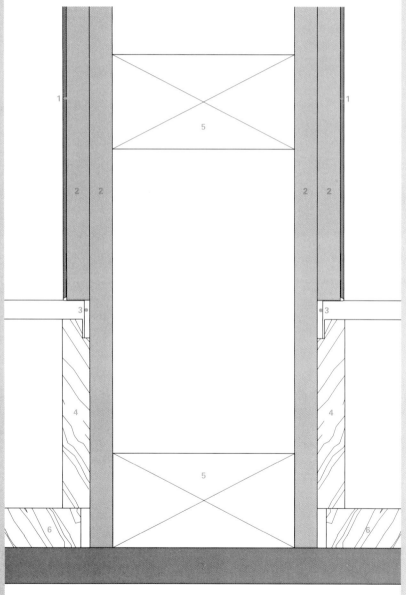

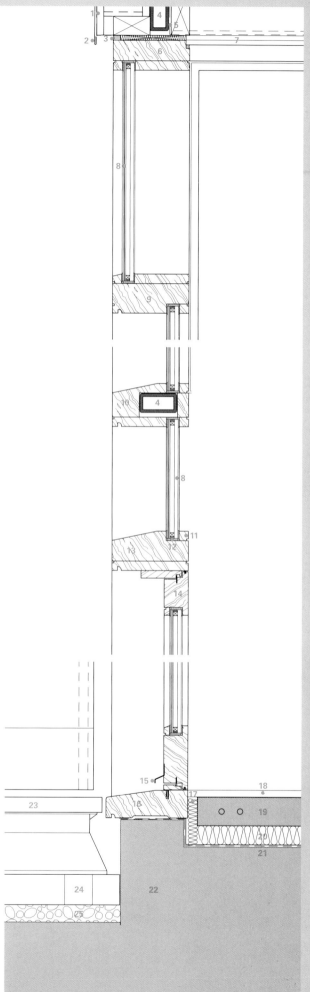

1.037
Stud Wall With Door Jamb Detail 1:2

Studio Bednarski
Hesmondhalgh House
[33]

1 3 mm (1/8 inch) plaster skim coat
2 12.5 mm (1/2 inch) thick gypsum wallboard
3 Expamet plaster stop bead
4 100 x 50 mm (4 x 2 inch) timber stud frame

5 154 x 50 mm (6 1/8 x 2 inch) timber door jamb

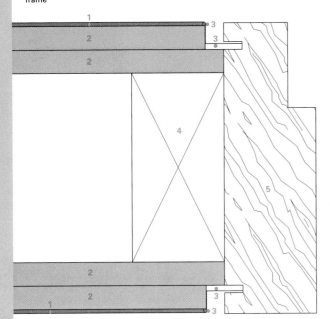

1.038
Corner Post Detail 1:5

The Miller Hull
Partnership
Chuckanut Drive
Residence [31]

1 Aluminium clad timber windows
2 Aluminium window jamb
3 Timber window jamb
4 Self-adhered membrane
5 Mullion cover
6 115 x 115 mm (4 1/2 x 4 1/2 inch) square

hollow section steel corner post
7 Pre-painted cedar battens
8 Aluminium corner clip
9 12 mm (1/2 inch) plywood packing
10 Timber trim
11 Insulated glazing

1.039
Wall and Sun Shade Section Detail 1:10

Jackson Clements
Burrows Architects
Edward River House
[32]

1 266 x 110 mm (10 1/2 x 4 3/8 inch) laminated timber structural column
2 Air space

3 Vertical corrugated metal wall cladding
4 Horizontal corrugated metal wall cladding
5 Insulation fill between studs
6 13 mm (1/2 inch) internal plasterboard wall lining
7 120 x 45 mm (4 3/4 x 1 3/4 inch) expressed rough sawn timber girt
8 100 x 100 mm (4 x 4

inch) steel shelf angle
9 6 mm (1/4 inch) folded aluminium sun shade
10 6 mm (1/4 inch) folded aluminium fixing bracket
11 Flashing
12 90 x 40 mm (3 1/2 x 1 5/8 inch) pine stud frame
13 10 mm (3/8 inch) zincaneal shadowline

stopping angle
14 140 x 40 mm (5 1/2 x 1 5/8 inch) cedar window head
15 10 mm (3/8 inch) fixed float glass
16 Bracket bolted to structural beam
17 140 x 40 mm (5 1/2 x 1 5/8 inch) cedar window jamb

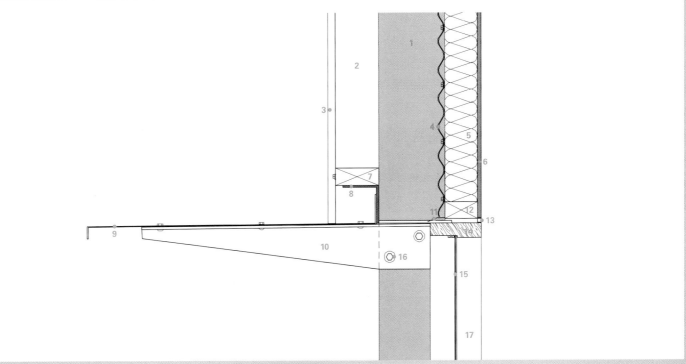

1.040
Wall Section Detail 1:20

Hertl Architekten
Krammer House [19]

 1 Double glazing unit
 2 Glassfibre reinforced
   plastic channel
 3 60 mm (2³/8 inch)
   floor screed with
   integrated heating
   and sealed finish
 4 Foil layer
 5 25 mm (1 inch)
   impact sound
   insulation
 6 Cement concrete fill
 7 Foil on 15 mm (5/8
   inch) oriented strand
   board
 8 240 mm (9¹/2 inch)
   timber beams with
   insulation in between
 9 20 mm (³/4 inch)
   plasterboard ceiling
10 15 mm (5/8 inch)
   oriented strand
   board
11 Eternit clapboard
   cladding
12 Waterproof
   membrane
13 Circular concrete grid
14 Plaster
15 Reinforced concrete
   header beam
16 Existing wall
17 Plaster flush with
   window frame
18 Insulated glass
   window
19 Aluminium
   profile sill
20 Existing ceiling

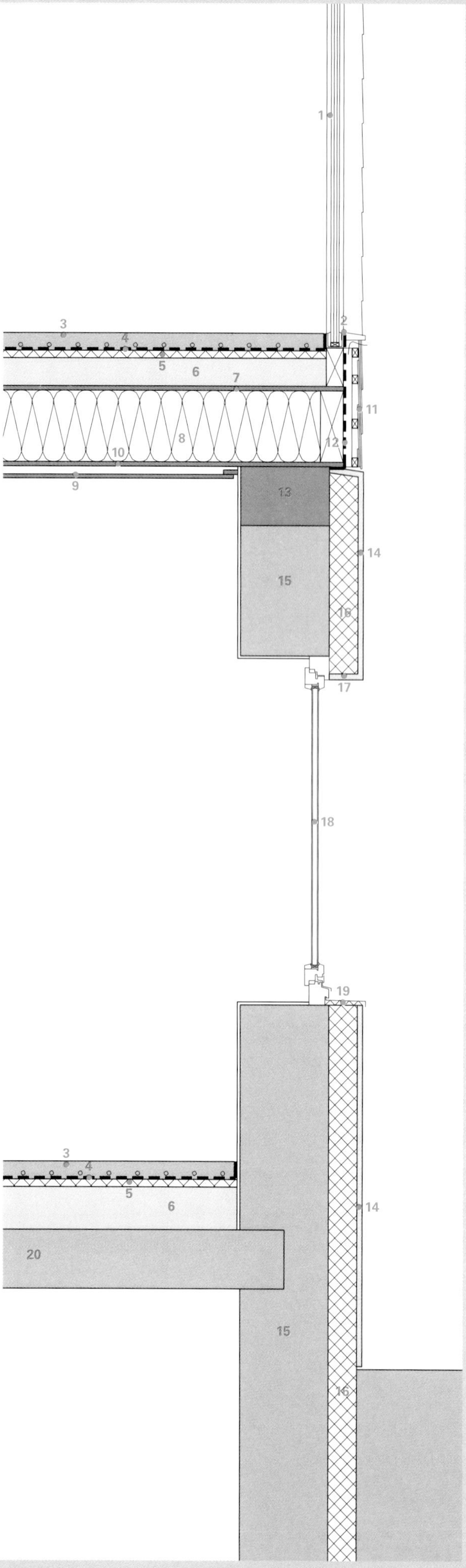

1.041
**External Wall and Roof
Parapet Detail 1:20**

Hertl Architekten
Krammer House [19]

 1 Reinforced concrete
   exterior wall
 2 35 mm (1³/8 inch)
   timber deck on
   substructure
 3 EPDM (ethylene
   propylene dieme
   monomer) foil
 4 22 mm (7/8 inch)
   oriented strand
   board
 5 200 mm (8 inch)
   timber beams with
   insulation in between
 6 15 mm (5/8 inch)
   gypsum plasterboard
 7 15 mm (5/8 inch)
   oriented strand
   board
 8 Vapour barrier
 9 Timber beam
10 Circular concrete grid
11 Existing wall
12 Plaster
13 Existing masonry
   wall
14 60 mm (2¹/3 inch)
   floor screed with
   integral heating and
   sealed finish
15 Foil layer
16 25 mm (1 inch)
   impact sound
   insulation
17 Cement concrete fill
18 Existing ceiling

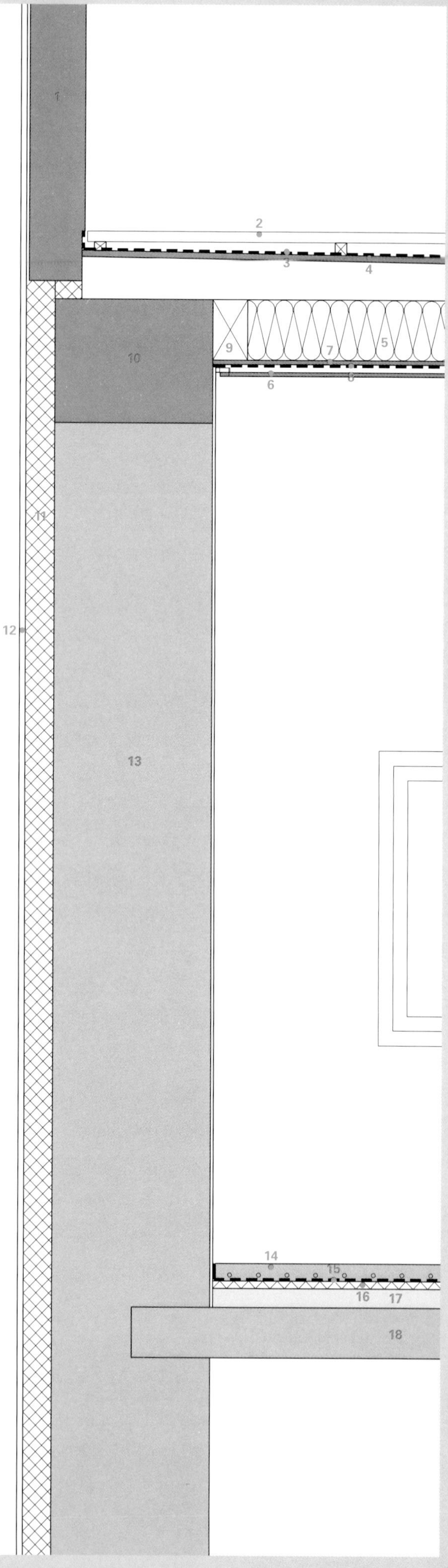

1.042
Wall Plan Details 1:10

Johnston Marklee &
Associates
Hill House [22]

1 Superflex waterproof
   layer
2 12 mm ($1/2$ inch)
   plywood substrate
3 50 x 200 mm (2 x 8
   inch) studs at 400
   mm (16 inch) centres
4 50 x 150 mm (2 x 6
   inch) studs at 400
   mm (16 inch) centres
5 Batt insulation
6 Concrete retaining
   wall
7 Rigid insulation
8 Metal Z-channel at
   600 mm (24 inch)
   centres
9 Firring strips
10 Vapour barrier
11 16 mm ($5/8$ inch)
   gypsum board
12 Waterproof
   membrane
13 Compacted soil base

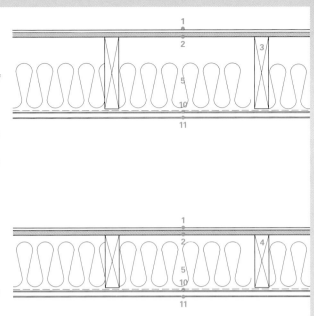

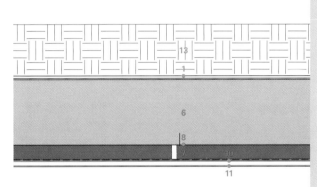

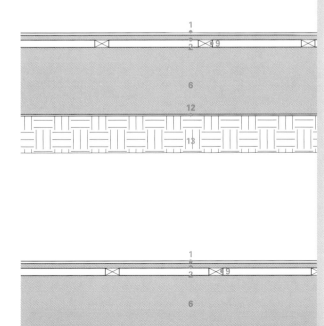

1.043
Timber Facade Detail
1:10

Terry Pawson Architects
The Tall House [38]

1 12.5 mm ($1/2$ inch)
   plasterboard and
   skim coat
2 125 mm ($49/10$ inch)
   mineral wool
   insulation
3 Ventilated cavity
4 20 mm ($3/4$ inch) thick
   unseasoned English
   oak cladding boards
   set out at 150 mm (6
   inch) centres
5 Breather membrane
   dressed over ply and
   stainless steel angle
6 Varnished 83 x 20
   mm ($31/4$ x $3/4$ inch)
   oak strip floorboards
   nailed to 25 x 50 mm
   (1 x 2 inch) softwood
   battens
7 32 x 25 mm ($51/10$ x 1
   inch) stainless steel
   angle welded to
   frame
8 130 x 20 mm ($31/4$ x
   $3/4$ inch) oak window
   surround
9 Double glazed sealed
   window unit
   comprised of 10 mm
   ($2/5$ inch) outer glass
   pane, 12 mm ($1/2$
   inch) air gap and 6
   mm ($1/4$ inch) inner
   glass pane, silicone
   bonded into frame
10 160 x 30 mm ($63/10$ x
   $11/5$ inch) oak window
   sill
11 Stainless steel angle
   as drip
12 12 mm ($1/2$ inch)
   plywood sheathing

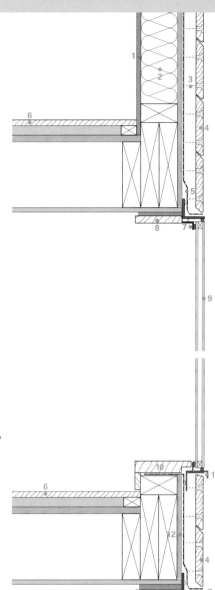

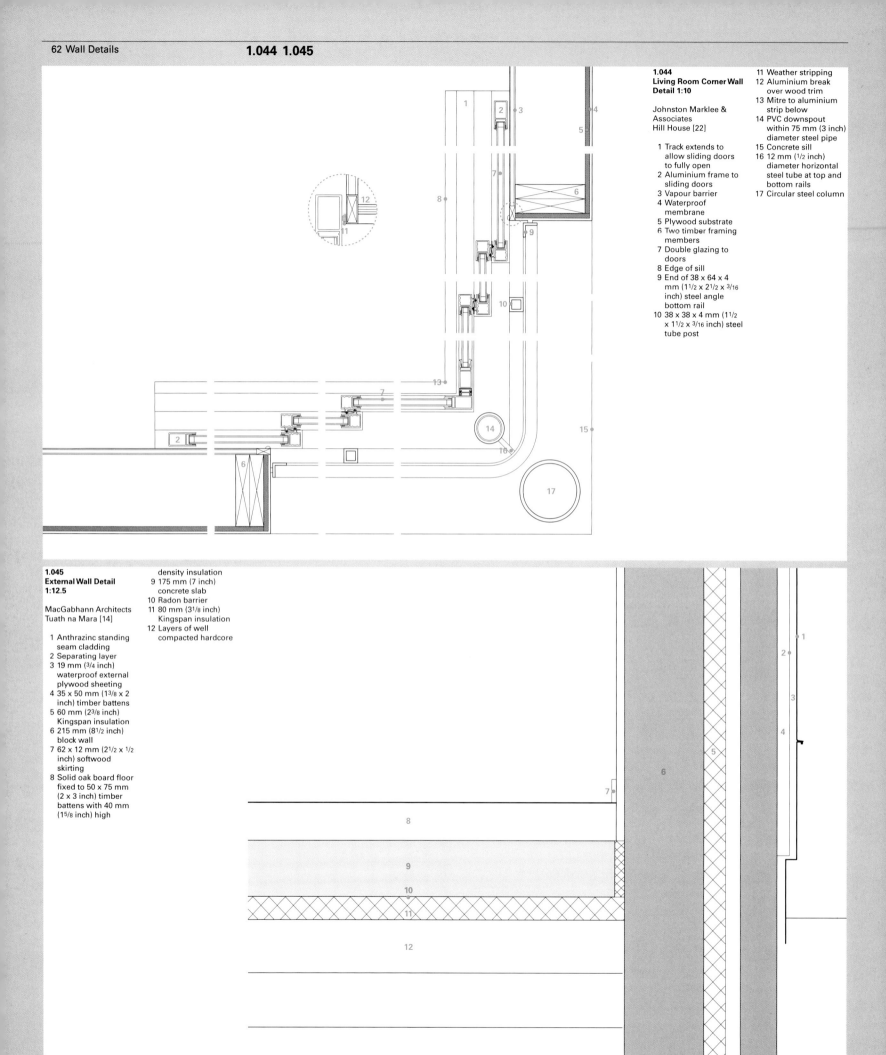

1.044
Living Room Corner Wall Detail 1:10

Johnston Marklee & Associates
Hill House [22]

1 Track extends to allow sliding doors to fully open
2 Aluminium frame to sliding doors
3 Vapour barrier
4 Waterproof membrane
5 Plywood substrate
6 Two timber framing members
7 Double glazing to doors
8 Edge of sill
9 End of 38 x 64 x 4 mm ($1^{1}/2$ x $2^{1}/2$ x $3/16$ inch) steel angle bottom rail
10 38 x 38 x 4 mm ($1^{1}/2$ x $1^{1}/2$ x $3/16$ inch) steel tube post
11 Weather stripping
12 Aluminium break over wood trim
13 Mitre to aluminium strip below
14 PVC downspout within 75 mm (3 inch) diameter steel pipe
15 Concrete sill
16 12 mm ($1/2$ inch) diameter horizontal steel tube at top and bottom rails
17 Circular steel column

1.045
External Wall Detail 1:12.5

MacGabhann Architects
Tuath na Mara [14]

1 Anthrazinc standing seam cladding
2 Separating layer
3 19 mm ($3/4$ inch) waterproof external plywood sheeting
4 35 x 50 mm ($1^{3}/8$ x 2 inch) timber battens
5 60 mm ($2^{3}/8$ inch) Kingspan insulation
6 215 mm ($8^{1}/2$ inch) block wall
7 62 x 12 mm ($2^{1}/2$ x $1/2$ inch) softwood skirting
8 Solid oak board floor fixed to 50 x 75 mm (2 x 3 inch) timber battens with 40 mm ($1^{5}/8$ inch) high density insulation
9 175 mm (7 inch) concrete slab
10 Radon barrier
11 80 mm ($3^{1}/8$ inch) Kingspan insulation
12 Layers of well compacted hardcore

1.046
Bathroom Wall Detail
1:10

Kotaro Ide / ARTechnic
architects
Shell House [09]

1 Hard urethane foam
   insulation
2 Screw fixing
3 Waterproof
   membrane
4 Mortar finish on
   metal lathes
5 Tiled wall
6 Styrofoam with FRP
   (Fibre Reinforced

Polymer) outer layer
7 Hard urethane foam
   insulation
8 Concrete structural
   wall
9 Styrofoam with FRP
   (Fibre Reinforced
   Polymer) outer layer
10 Veneer
11 Concrete structural
   wall

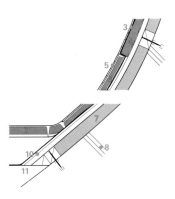

1.047
Wall Ventilation Slit
Detail 1:10

Kotaro Ide / ARTechnic
architects
Shell House [09]

1 Hard urethane foam
   insulation
2 Plywood substrate
3 Double layer of
   water-resistant
   plasterboard with
   skim plastered finish
4 Firring strips
5 Screw fixings
6 Exhaust air duct

7 Ventilation chamber
8 Plastered wall finish
9 Condensation-
   resistant felt
10 Fluorescent light
   fitting
11 Acrylic light cover
12 Clip to hold acrylic
   lamp cover in place
13 Concrete structural
   wall
14 Closet space
15 Closet door

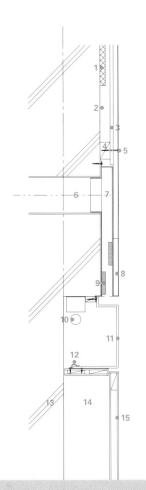

1.048
Wall Section Detail 1:10

Steven Holl Architects
Swiss Embassy
Residence [14]

1 Stainless steel
   flashing and formed
   drip
2 Plywood
3 Timber blocking
4 Welded steel for
   curtain wall support
5 15 mm (9/16 inch)
   welded steel curtain
   wall support
6 Insect screen
7 Anchor bolts
8 Channel glass
   perimeter frame
   assembly
9 Waterproof layer
10 Stainless steel
   flashing
11 50 mm (2 inch) rigid
   insulation
12 Channel glass

13 Concrete parapet
14 Gravel margin
15 Green roof assembly
16 12 mm (1/2 inch)
   exterior grade
   plywood sheathing
17 Steel plate anchored
   to concrete slab
18 Ceiling
19 Two layers 15 mm
   (5/8 inch) gypsum
   wall board
20 Welded steel support
   for sliding door
21 Vapour barrier
22 Corner bead
23 Aluminium sliding
   door
24 Stainless steel
   cover-panel to
   roller-blind recess
25 Stainless steel
   ventilation screen
26 Curtain wall support
   welded and bolted to
   substructure
27 Recessed roller blind

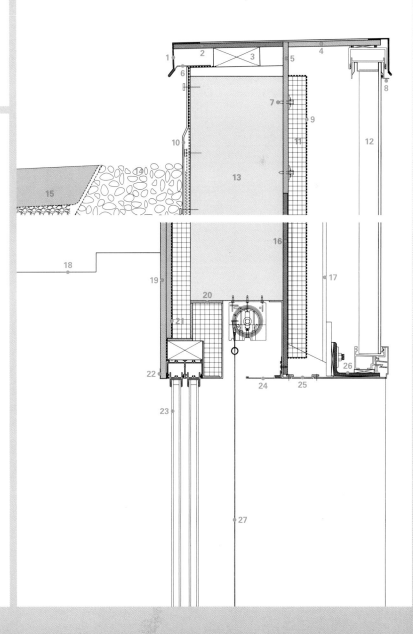

1.049
Wall Detail 1:15

Vittorio Longheu
Casa C [16]

1 30 mm (1¼ inch)
external render
2 200 mm (8 inch) brick
wall
3 10 mm (3/8 inch)
render coat
4 40 mm (15/8 inch)
polystyrene
insulating board
5 80 mm (31/8 inch)
brick
6 20 mm (3/4 inch)
plaster
7 Tile flooring
8 Mortar laying bed
9 Concrete bed for
laying underfloor
heating
10 Fine concrete layer of
Foamcem for laying
of water and

electrical services
11 Formwork for in-situ
concrete
12 Concrete bed
13 Gravel bed
14 Ventilation pipe
15 Ventilation stone grid
with 10 mm (3/8 inch)
diameter holes
16 Stone skirting
17 200 x 200 mm (8 x 8
inch) concrete socle
18 Natural stone
flooring
19 Concrete bed
20 Waterproof layer
21 Earth back-fill
22 Concrete foundation
23 100 mm (4 inch) lean
concrete

1.050
Wall at Ground Floor
Detail 1:10

Troppo Architects
Buttfield Town House
[30]

1 Galvanized
half-round gutter
with brackets at 1000
mm (40 inch) centres
2 150 x 42 mm (6 x 15/8
inch) hardwood
purlin fixed to rafter
by joist hanger
3 145 x 32 mm (53/4 x
11/4 inch) hardwood
fascia
4 Polycarb corrugated
roof sheeting
5 50 x 50 mm (2 x 2
inch) angle purlin
welded to square
hollow section strut
6 50 x 50 mm (2 x 2
inch) square hollow

section fixed to cleat
7 170 x 42 mm (63/4 x
13/4 inch) hardwood
handrail with arris to
top edges and rebate
underside to receive
plate
8 89 x 89 mm (31/2 x
31/2 inch) expressed
square hollow
section column with
6 mm (1/4 inch) cap
and cleat to top
9 Galvanized capping
10 Cleat welded to
square hollow
section corner posts
11 Galvanized Miniorb
U-trim
12 Hardwood decking
on 35 x 35 mm (13/8 x
13/8 inch) slats at 450
mm (18 inch) centres
13 Zincal tray on 18 mm
(3/4 inch) marine ply,
folded at end to form
lip

14 200 x 50 mm (8 x 2
inch) laminated
veneer lumber
bearer
15 Aluminium flashing
to match window
frame
16 Nominal fall
17 150 x 50 mm (6 x 2
inch) laminated
veneer lumber joists
at 450 mm (18 inch)
centres
18 Plaster edge stop to
form shadow gap

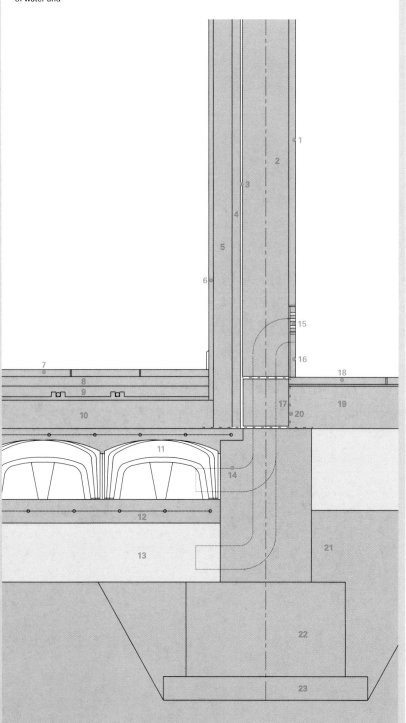

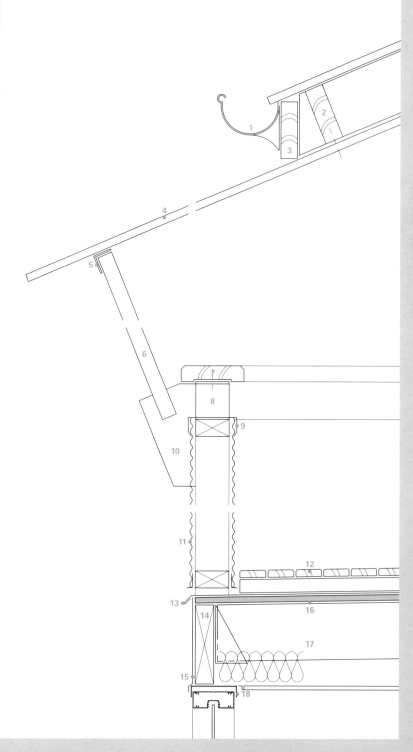

1.051
Stud Wall at Change in
Floor Level Detail 1:10

Public
Rattlesnake Creek
House [15]

1 Wall lining from
   veneered plywood
   on timber stud
   framing
2 Wall lining from
   veneered plywood
   on timber stud
   framing
3 10 mm (3/8 inch)
   plywood reveal
4 150 x 50 mm (6 x 2
   inch) timber blocking
5 Stone tile set on
   mortar bed
6 Reinforced concrete
   floor slab
7 150 x 50 mm (6 x 2
   inch) timber stud and
   sole plates

1.052
Wood Panels at Exterior
Concrete Wall Detail
1:20

Public
Rattlesnake Creek
House [15]

1 Fixed double glazing
   unit
2 200 x 50 mm (8 x 2
   inch) ledger with joist
   hanger
3 Exterior concrete
   wall
4 10 mm (3/8 inch)
   plywood
5 Timber framing to
   veneered wall lining
   with paint finish
6 20 mm (3/4 inch)
   gypsum board with
   fine wood veneer
   wall lining
7 200 x 50 mm (8 x 2
   inch) timber joist
8 Double layer of 50 x
   100 mm (2 x 4 inch)
   timber framing
9 Hardwood flooring
10 Rigid insulation
11 Concrete floor slab

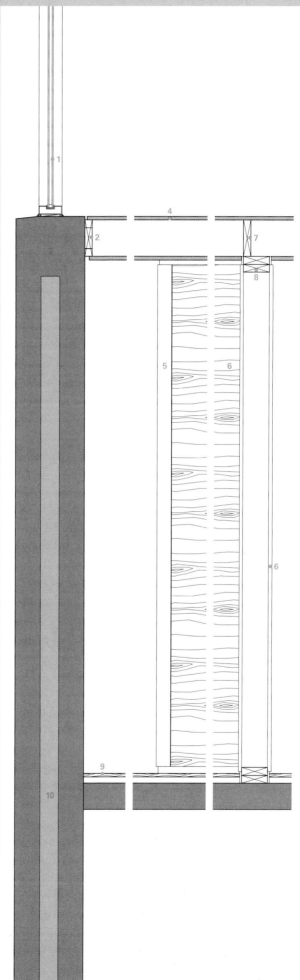

1.053
External Wall 'Waterfall' Detail (Upper Part) 1:5

Powerhouse Company
Villa 1 [15]

1 Timber structure
2 Insulation
3 100 mm (4 inch) IPE structure
4 18 mm (3/4 inch) waterproof bonded plywood
5 Stotherm classic exterior wall system insulation
6 100 x 40 mm (4 x 1 5/8 inch) timber stud
7 60 mm (2 3/8 inch) diameter drain pipe
8 140 x 60 mm (5 1/2 x 2 3/8 inch) steel channel
9 800 x 800 x 20 mm (32 x 32 x 3/4 inch) travertine panels glued to multiplex boarding
10 Powder-coated aluminium profile
11 10 mm (3/8 inch) Stotherm classic on 30 mm (1 1/5 inch) insulation

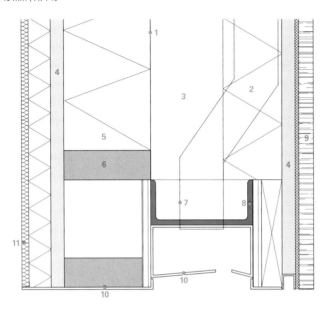

1.054
External Wall 'Waterfall' Detail (Lower Part) 1:5

Powerhouse Company
Villa 1 [15]

1 Powder-coated aluminium capping
2 White stone bed
3 Damp proof membrane
4 18 mm (3/4 inch) timber base for forming gutter
5 140 x 60 mm (5 1/2 x 2 3/8 inch) steel channel as gutter
6 10 mm (3/8 inch) Stotherm classic external wall system on 30 mm (1 1/5 inch) insulation
7 18 mm (3/4 inch) waterproof bonded plywood multiplex boarding
8 90 x 40 mm (3 1/2 x 1 5/8 inch) timber framing
9 100 mm (4 inch) drain pipe
10 800 x 800 x 20 mm (32 x 32 x 3/4 inch) travertine panels glued to multiplex boarding
11 10 mm (3/8 inch) Stotherm classic on 30 mm (1 1/5 inch) insulation

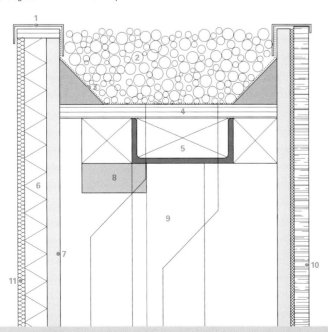

1.055
Exterior Wall and Footing Detail 1:10

Bates Masi + Architects
Noyack Creek Residence [37]

1 Aluminium capping with integral drip profile
2 Cladding fastened onto framing
3 Pressure treated timber flooring
4 50 x 250 mm (2 x 10 inch) timber joists at 400 mm (16 inch) centres
5 50 x 100 mm (2 x 4 inch) timber wall framing
6 50 x 250 mm (2 x 10 inch) timber ledger lag-bolted into framing
7 Continuous rebar at top of foundation wall
8 50 x 100 mm (2 x 4 inch) timber wall framing bolted to precast concrete wall at 400 mm (16 inch) centres with two 12 mm (1/2 inch) acrylic ties top and bottom
9 50 mm (2 inch) layer of 12 mm (1/2 inch) crushed bluestone gravel
10 200 mm (8 inch) precast concrete wall
11 Vertical rebar at 1200 mm (48 inch) centres to full height of wall and horizontal rebar at 600 mm (24 inch) centres
12 Rebar at 1200 mm (48 inch) centres locking footing to foundation
13 250 x 500 mm (10 x 20 inch) poured concrete footing set on undisturbed soil
14 Framing below grade to have green wood preservative applied to all sides and ends

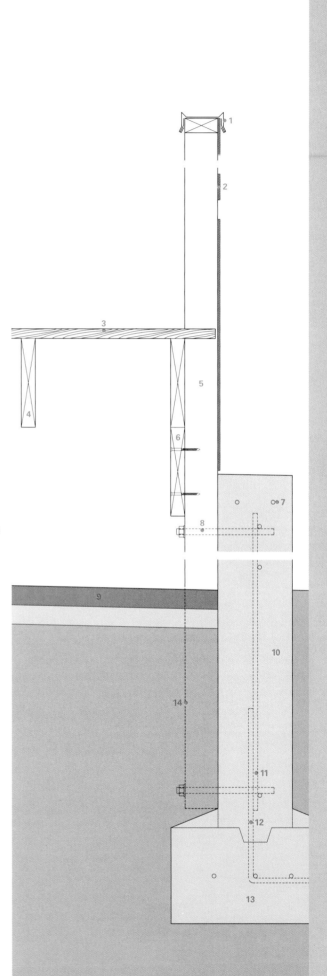

1.056
External Wall Detail 1:10

Koffi & Diabaté
Architectes
Villa Talon [28]

1 Parapet wall
2 Aluminium L-section support to terracotta tiles
3 Sloped concrete for rainwater drainage
4 Reinforced concrete roof slab
5 External wall cladding from terracotta tiles
6 Plasterboard with skim coat painted suspended ceiling
7 Roller shutter
8 Reinforced concrete beam
9 Steel support for veneered plywood soffit lining to roller shutter recess
10 Veneered plywood soffit lining to roller shutter recess
11 Roller shutter guide rail
12 Aluminium framed sliding glass door
13 Travertine tiled floor
14 Concrete floor slab
15 Aluminium frame to sliding glass doors
16 Travertine sill
17 Reinforced concrete footing wall
18 Cantilevered travertine stair tread
19 Circular concrete tread support
20 Concrete pavers laid on ground surface

1.057
External Wall Detail 1:10

Kengo Kuma & Associates
Steel House [27]

1 3.2 mm (1/8 inch) thick hot dip galvanized vertical steel-plate structure seen in elevation
2 Steel bracing for polycarbonate 'Lume' wall
3 3.2 mm (1/8 inch) hot dip galvanized vertical steel-plate structure seen in section
4 20 mm (3/4 inch) hard urethane spray foam insulation
5 40 mm (13/5 inch) hollow polycarbonate sheeting to form Takiron 'Lume' wall system
6 Fluorescent light fitting
7 40 x 40 mm (15/8 x 15/8 inch) steel L-angle
8 Steel support angle
9 Removable inspection panel in flooring from 14 mm (1/2 inch) thick oak
10 45 x 45 mm (13/4 x 13/4 inch) timber blocking
11 Underfloor storage heater panel
12 12 mm (1/2 inch) plywood
13 Steel support angle
14 40 mm (13/5 inch) hard urethane spray foam insulation
15 16 mm (2/3 inch) steel plate
16 2.3 mm (1/10 inch) steel plate
17 2.3 mm (1/10 inch) steel plate
18 Levelling mortar
19 Hot dip galvanized double-nut bolt embedded in external concrete wall
20 Reinforced external concrete wall
21 50 mm (2 inch) glass wool insulation
22 12.5 mm (1/2 inch) plasterboard

permanent concrete formwork

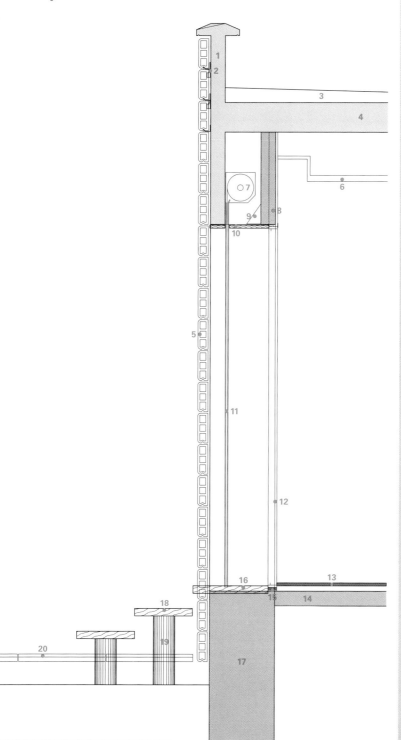

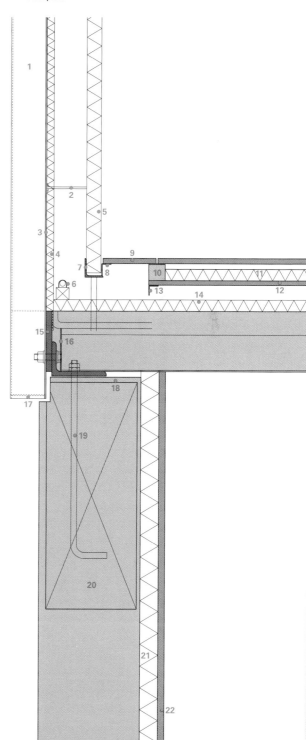

1.058
Glazed Wall Detail 1:5

Frank Harmon Architect
Low Country Residence
[26]

1 Double glazing
2 Storefront window
  frame
3 152 x 200 mm (6 x 8
  inch) universal steel
  beam
4 Through bolt
  connection
5 50 x 100 mm (2 x 4
  inch) timber blocking
6 Metal closure piece
7 152 x 100 mm (6 x 4
  inch) steel L-angle
8 Steel counterweight
9 16 gauge perforated
  steel channels
10 Folding screen frame
11 50 mm (2 inch) steel
  tube

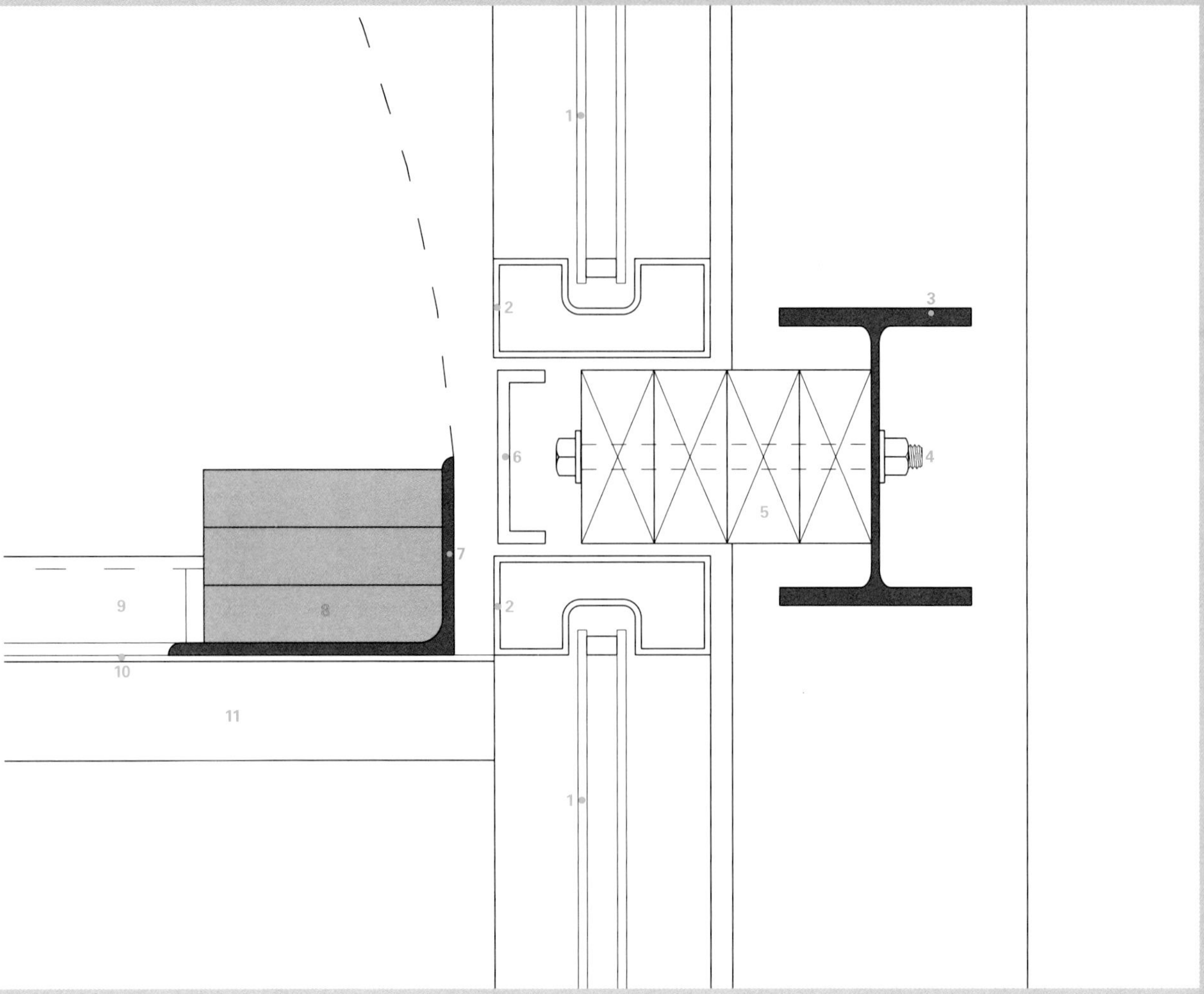

1.059
**External Wall Base Detail
1:5**

Atelier Tekuto +
Masahiro Ikeda
Lucky Drops [13]

1 Insulation
2 Fibre reinforced
  plastic sheeting
3 31 x 31 mm (1¼ x
  1¼ inch) steel square
  hollow section
  framing
4 40 x 40 mm (1⅝ x
  1⅝ inch) steel angle
5 32 mm (1¼ inch)
  diameter circular
  steel column with oil
  paint finish
6 50 x 50 mm (2 x 2
  inch) steel section
7 32 mm (1¼ inch)
  diameter circular
  steel column with oil
  paint finish
8 Flashing
9 Galvanized, coloured
  steel sheet cladding
10 Fibre reinforced
  plastic sheeting
11 Timber packer
12 75 x 75 mm (3 x 3
  inch) steel angle
13 Sheet piling
14 Waterproof paper
15 Steel H-section with
  oil paint finish
16 Steel nut with oil
  paint finish
17 60 x 19 mm (2⅓ x ¾
  inch) steel plate
18 Gravel bed
19 Soil

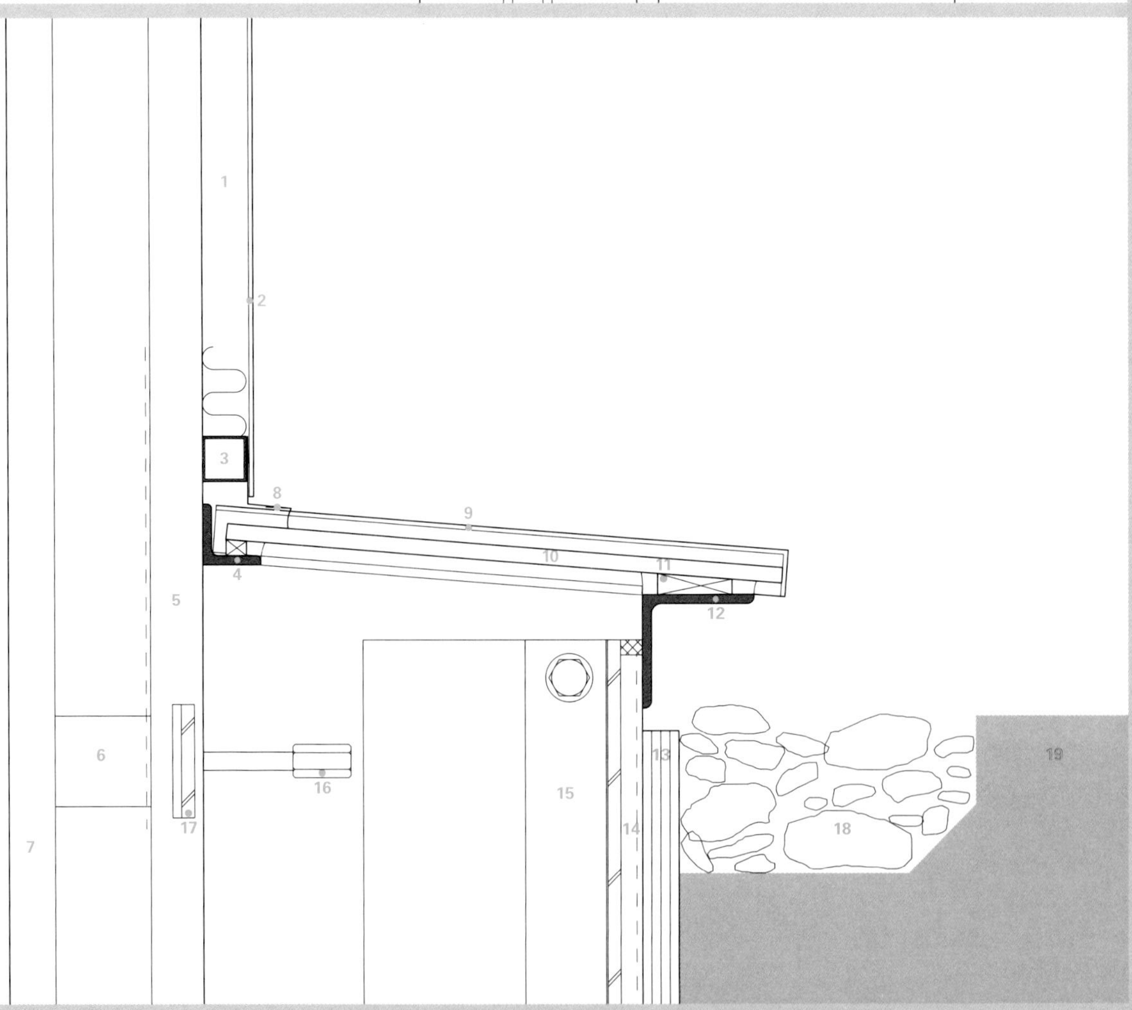

1.060
External Wall Detail 1:10

Matharoo Associates
Dilip Sanghvi Residence
[07]

1 Aluminium window
   frame
2 Aluminium window
   sill
3 20 mm (3/4 inch)
   flame granite
   cladding on 185 mm
   (71/4 inch) thick
   concrete wall
4 25 mm (1 inch)
   internal plasterboard
   wall lining
5 Groove filled with
   clear silicone
6 25 mm (1 inch)
   internal plasterboard
   wall lining
7 20 mm (3/4 inch)
   flame granite
   cladding on 185 mm

(71/4 inch) concrete
wall
8 15 mm (5/8 inch)
   skirting, surface flush
   with plaster line
9 20 mm (3/4 inch)
   marble flooring
10 20 mm (3/4 inch)
   smooth granite top
   sloping 10 mm (3/8
   inch) towards
   channel
11 50 x 50 mm (2 x 2
   inch) channel sloping
   towards drainpipe
12 150 mm (6 inch)
   reinforced concrete
   floor slab
13 Air conditioning
   plenum
14 Trap door for air
   conditioning
15 15 x 15 mm (5/8 x 5/8
   inch) drip mould
16 Steel framing
17 185 mm (71/2 inch)
   core concrete wall

18 Lintels, jamb and sill
   clad in flame granite

1.061
**Wall Detail at First Floor
1:10**

MELD Architecture with
Vicky Thornton
House in Tarn et
Garonne [34]

1 Bespoke double
   glazed oak framed
   window
2 50 mm (2 inch) solid
   oak window seat and
   reveals
3 Oak window
   surround
4 125 mm (5 inch) wide
   board on untreated
   chestnut cladding
5 Mineral wool
   insulation between
   timber studs
6 14 mm (5/8 inch)
   oriented strand
   board on softwood
   frame

7 Polished screed floor
   over underfloor
   heating, on concrete,
   terracotta pot and
   concrete beam
8 Breather membrane
9 Cast concrete lintel,
   with imprint of
   rough-sawn timber
   shuttering
10 Expanded
   polystyrene full-fill
   cavity insulation
11 Pre-cast concrete
   lintel
12 Lime render
13 Expanded
   polystyrene full-fill
   cavity insulation
14 Laminated pine
   board

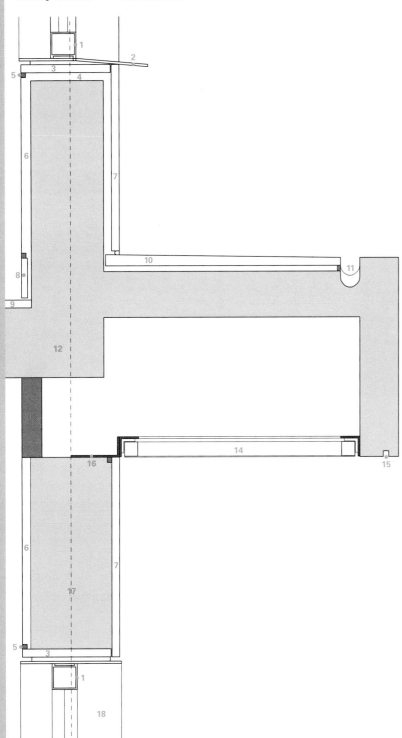

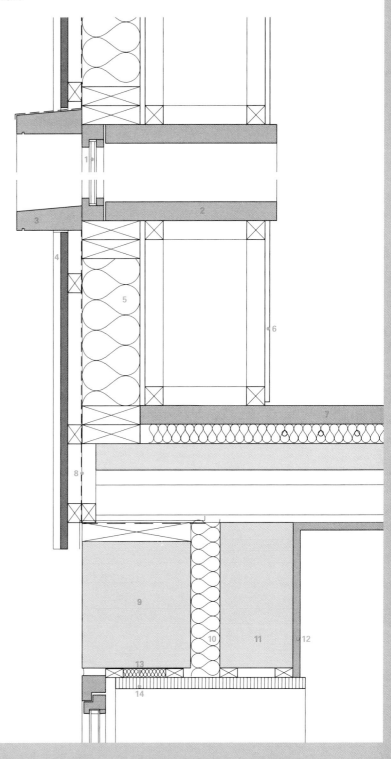

1.062
Inclined Wall Plan Detail
1:20

Barclay & Crousse
Architecture
Casa O [08]

1 25 x 25 mm (1 x 1
  inch) Sombra
  tumbled marble
  mosaic tiles
2 Bed of decorative
  pebbles
3 25 x 25 mm (1 x 1
  inch) Sombra
  tumbled marble
  mosaic tiles

4 Translucent tiles
5 Circular concrete
  column
6 Grass
7 100 mm (4 inch) high
  stone border

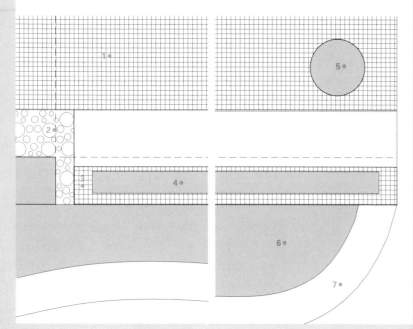

1.064
**External Wall and Floor
Junction Detail 1:10**

Bercy Chen Studio
Riverview Gardens [38]

1 150 x 6 mm (6 x $\frac{1}{4}$
  inch) steel end plate
  with drip edge
2 16 mm ($\frac{5}{8}$ inch)
  double polygal on
  two layers bubble
  wrap on 50 x 100 mm
  (2 x 4 inch) timber
  stud framing
3 8 mm ($\frac{3}{8}$ inch)
  polygal on two layers
  bubble wrap
4 Flashing with drip
  edge
5 Tapered rigid
  insulation on 30 mm
  (1$\frac{1}{5}$ inch) plywood
6 Batt insulation
7 Metal channel joist
8 15 mm ($\frac{5}{8}$ inch)
  gypsum ceiling
9 Perimeter flange
  channel
10 6 mm ($\frac{1}{4}$ inch) steel
  plate with drip edge
11 25 mm (1 inch)
  double glazed fixed
  window
12 6 mm ($\frac{1}{4}$ inch) steel
  sill with drip edge
13 16 mm ($\frac{5}{8}$ inch)
  polygal on two layers
  bubble wrap on 50 x
  100 mm (2 x 4 inch)
  timber stud framing

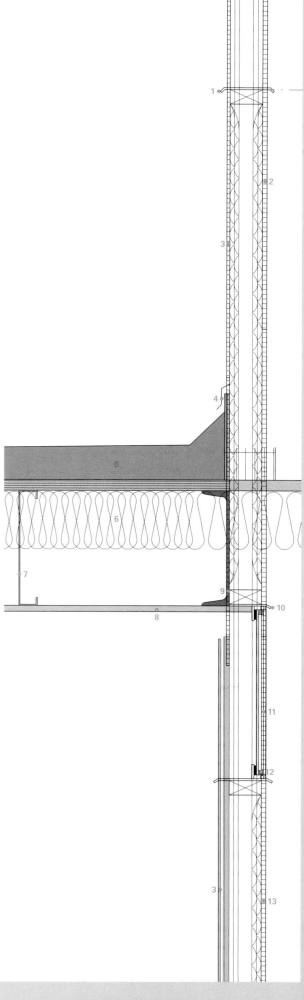

1.063
**Inclined Wall Section
Detail 1:20**

Barclay & Crousse
Architecture
Casa O [08]

1 Fluorescent light
  covered with opaque
  glass
2 25 x 25 mm (1 x 1
  inch) Sombra
  tumbled marble
  mosaic tiles to
  surface of inclined
  wall
3 Inclined concrete

parapet
4 Bed of loose pebbles
5 25 x 25 mm (1 x 1
  inch) Sombra
  tumbled marble
  mosaic tiles to
  surface of inclined
  wall

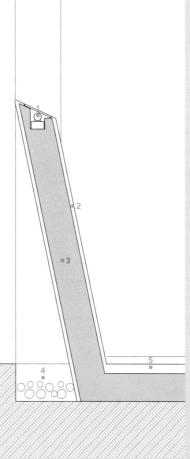

1.065
Top Edge to Inclined Wall Detail 1:5

Barclay & Crousse
Architecture
Casa O [08]

1 25 x 25 mm (1 x 1 inch) Sombra tumbled marble mosaic tiles
2 Translucent glass light cover
3 Fluorescent light fitting
4 25 x 25 mm (1 x 1 inch) Sombra

tumbled marble mosaic tiles
5 Inclined concrete parapet

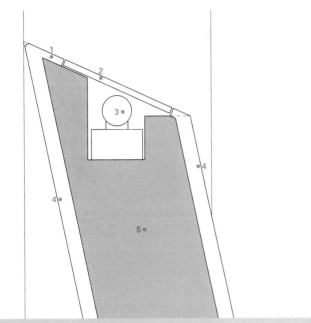

1.066
Wall Section Detail 1:10

Mount Fuji Architects Studio
Rainy Sunny House [11]

1 Trowelled mortar exterior wall finish
2 Waterproof membrane coating
3 Trowelled concrete
4 Concrete poured with larch-faced plywood shuttering
5 Hardwood herringbone timber interior wall lining

6 Plywood substrate
7 Timber framing

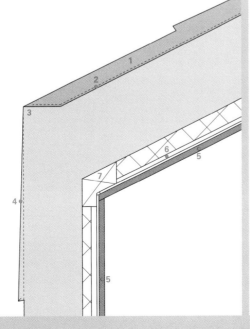

1.067
Garage Wall Detail 1:12.5

dRMM (de Rijke Marsh Morgan Architects)
Sliding House [14]

1 Larch rainscreen cladding
2 Portal frame
3 Full-fill insulation between timber studs
4 Oriented strand board internal sheeting
5 Henderson standard wheel unit for

top-hung timber door concealed behind cladding
6 Oriented strand board internal sheeting

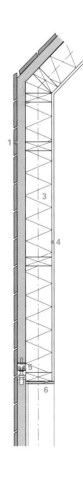

1.068
Wall Plan Detail 1:10

ARTEC Architekten
Holiday House [39]

1 16 mm (5/8 inch)
plywood board on
100 mm (4 inch)
construction timber
and insulation with
15 mm (5/8 inch)
oriented strand
board, moisture
barrier and 6 mm (1/4
inch) birch plywood
board
2 Exterior

3 Thermionic radiator
4 20 mm (9/10 inch)
birch plywood wall
lining
5 Natural anodized
aluminium plate
glued to 15 mm (5/8
inch) birch plywood
board on 80 mm (31/8
inch) construction
timber and insulation
and 15 mm (5/8 inch)
birch plywood board
6 Sliding timber door

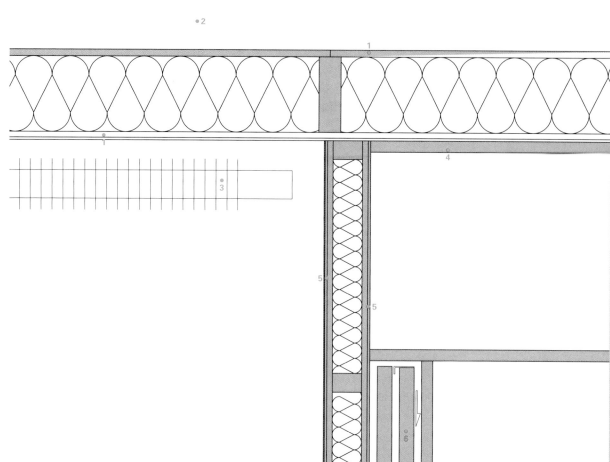

1.069
**Typical External Wall
Detail 1:5**

Hampson Williams
Glass and Timber
Houses [33]

1 18 mm (7/10 inch)
tongue and groove
Canadian western
red cedar cladding
impregnated with
non-com exterior fire
retardant
2 Ventilation zone on
34 x 34 mm (13/8 x
13/8 inch) tanalised
timber battens
impregnated with
non-com exterior fire
retardant
3 12 mm (1/2 inch)
pre-drilled and
screwed tongue and
groove Versapanel
4 150 mm (6 inch)
Kingspan insulation

retardant
2 Ventilation zone on
comprised of two 75
mm (3 inch) layers
5 Vapour control layer
6 25 mm (1 inch) taper
edged plasterboard
taped and skimmed
comprised of two
12.5 mm (1/2 inch)
layers
7 150 x 50 mm (6 x 2
inch) tanalised
timber studs

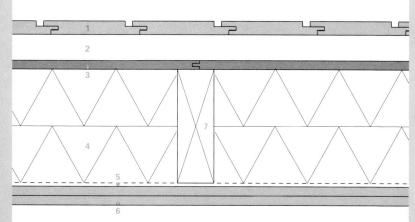

1.070
External Wall Detail 1:5

Hampson Williams
Glass and Timber
Houses [33]

1 18 mm (7/10 inch)
tongue and groove
Canadian western
red cedar cladding
impregnated with
non-com exterior fire
retardant

2 12 mm (1/2 inch)
tongue and groove
Versapanel
pre-drilled and
screwed
3 80 x 50 mm (31/8 x 2
inch) tanalised
timber studs
4 80 mm (31/8 inch)
Kingspan insulation
5 Vapour control layer
6 25 mm (1 inch) taper
edged plasterboard
taped and skimmed

comprised of two
12.5 mm (1/2 inch)
layers

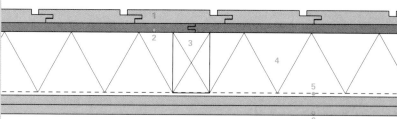

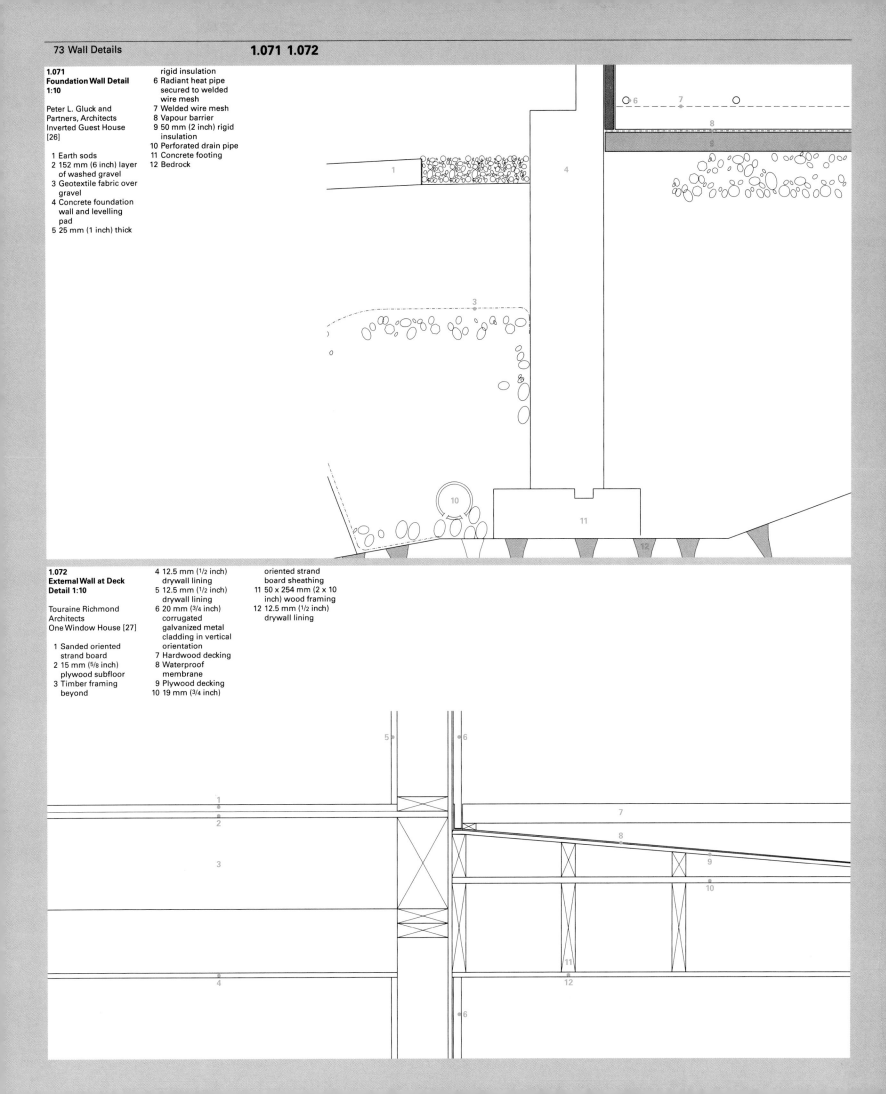

1.071
Foundation Wall Detail
1:10

Peter L. Gluck and
Partners, Architects
Inverted Guest House
[26]

1 Earth sods
2 152 mm (6 inch) layer
 of washed gravel
3 Geotextile fabric over
 gravel
4 Concrete foundation
 wall and levelling
 pad
5 25 mm (1 inch) thick

rigid insulation
6 Radiant heat pipe
 secured to welded
 wire mesh
7 Welded wire mesh
8 Vapour barrier
9 50 mm (2 inch) rigid
 insulation
10 Perforated drain pipe
11 Concrete footing
12 Bedrock

1.072
External Wall at Deck
Detail 1:10

Touraine Richmond
Architects
One Window House [27]

1 Sanded oriented
 strand board
2 15 mm (5/8 inch)
 plywood subfloor
3 Timber framing
 beyond

4 12.5 mm (1/2 inch)
 drywall lining
5 12.5 mm (1/2 inch)
 drywall lining
6 20 mm (3/4 inch)
 corrugated
 galvanized metal
 cladding in vertical
 orientation
7 Hardwood decking
8 Waterproof
 membrane
9 Plywood decking
10 19 mm (3/4 inch)

oriented strand
board sheathing
11 50 x 254 mm (2 x 10
 inch) wood framing
12 12.5 mm (1/2 inch)
 drywall lining

1.073
External Wall With Sliding Shutter Detail 1:20

Pezo von Ellrichshausen Architects
Poli House [09]

1 150 mm (6 inch) reinforced concrete wall
2 30 mm (1 1/4 inch) polystyrene thermal insulation
3 25 x 100 mm (1 x 4 inch) recycled pine board
4 25 x 100 mm (1 x 4 inch) pine battens
5 30 mm (1 1/4 inch) timber rail for shutter
6 25 x 100 mm (1 x 4 inch) recycled pine board shutter
7 Double glazing of 8 mm (3/8 inch) glass, 10 mm (3/8 inch) air gap and 6 mm (1/4 inch) glass

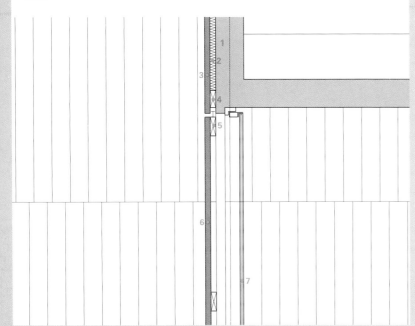

1.074
External Corner Wall Detail 1:10

Rowan Opat Architects
Courtyard House [38]

1 Indigenous hardwood radial sawn timber deck shown beyond
2 Timber mullion cover plate with paint finish
3 Silicone bead
4 Timber mullion with paint finish
5 Timber glazing bead with paint finish
6 High performance glazing
7 Board and batten radial sawn timber cladding with paint finish
8 Board and batten radial sawn timber cladding with paint finish
9 Timber frame
10 Internal plaster lining with paint finish
11 Heating panel

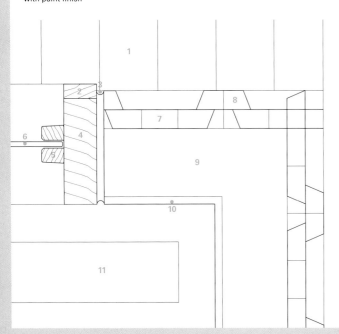

1.075
External Wall Detail 1:10

Hawkes Architecture
Crossway [16]

1 Waterproof plywood
2 English cedar weatherboard
3 Panelvent vapour permeable sheathing board
4 Warmcell recycled newspaper insulation
5 Wood fibre web infill insulation
6 Joist
7 Plasterboard fixed on Dupont Energain thermal mass board
8 Timber framed triple glazed window with interstitial blinds
9 Treated softwood battens and counter battens
10 Toughened glass external glass pane concealing louvre blind in glazing cavity
11 Toughened glass argon-filled double glazed unit
12 Timber framed triple glazed window with interstitial blinds
13 Aluminium and polyurethane insulation capping to all timber framed windows
14 Tescon airtightness tape
15 Painted environmentally friendly medium density fibreboard window sill
16 Waterproof plywood
17 Joist
18 Painted plasterboard
19 Painted timber skirting board
20 Solid bamboo flooring
21 Weatherdeck boarding
22 Isonat flax and lambswool acoustic insulation
23 Plywood sheathing board
24 Expanded foam insulation
25 Aluminium capping
26 Toughened glass argon-filled triple glazing
27 Painted timber window frame
28 Aluminium window sill
29 Internorm Generation timber window frame
30 Painted environmentally friendly medium density fibreboard window sill
31 Levelling shim
32 Waterproof plywood
33 Thermalite blockwork plinth
34 Painted cementitious board
35 Gravel strip
36 Warmcell recycled newspaper insulation
37 Panelvent vapour-permeable sheathingboard
38 Tyvek Enercor wall membrane

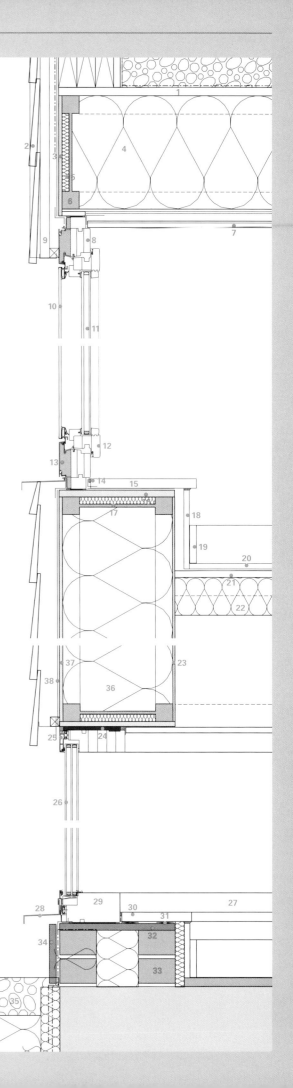

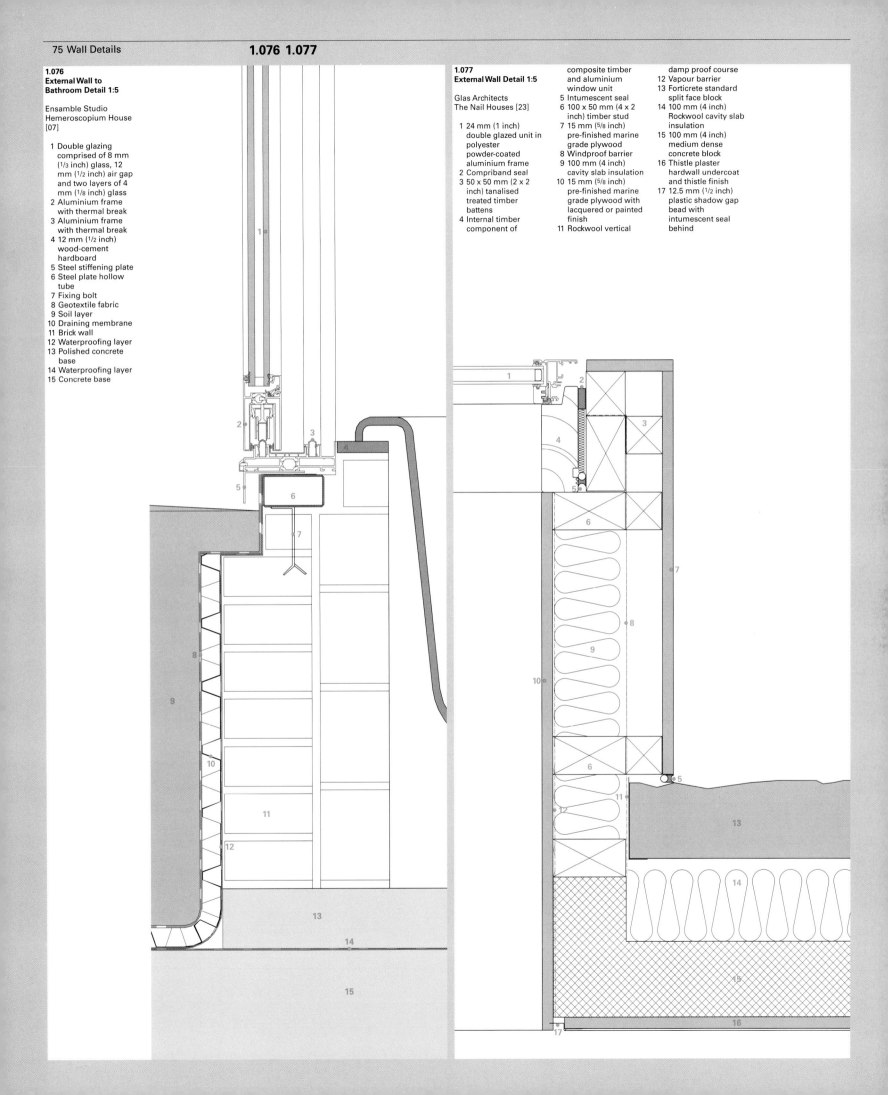

1.076
**External Wall to
Bathroom Detail 1:5**

Ensamble Studio
Hemeroscopium House
[07]

1 Double glazing
   comprised of 8 mm
   (1/3 inch) glass, 12
   mm (1/2 inch) air gap
   and two layers of 4
   mm (1/8 inch) glass
2 Aluminium frame
   with thermal break
3 Aluminium frame
   with thermal break
4 12 mm (1/2 inch)
   wood-cement
   hardboard
5 Steel stiffening plate
6 Steel plate hollow
   tube
7 Fixing bolt
8 Geotextile fabric
9 Soil layer
10 Draining membrane
11 Brick wall
12 Waterproofing layer
13 Polished concrete
   base
14 Waterproofing layer
15 Concrete base

1.077
External Wall Detail 1:5

Glas Architects
The Nail Houses [23]

1 24 mm (1 inch)
   double glazed unit in
   polyester
   powder-coated
   aluminium frame
2 Compriband seal
3 50 x 50 mm (2 x 2
   inch) tanalised
   treated timber
   battens
4 Internal timber
   component of
   composite timber
   and aluminium
   window unit
5 Intumescent seal
6 100 x 50 mm (4 x 2
   inch) timber stud
7 15 mm (5/8 inch)
   pre-finished marine
   grade plywood
8 Windproof barrier
9 100 mm (4 inch)
   cavity slab insulation
10 15 mm (5/8 inch)
   pre-finished marine
   grade plywood with
   lacquered or painted
   finish
11 Rockwool vertical
   damp proof course
12 Vapour barrier
13 Forticrete standard
   split face block
14 100 mm (4 inch)
   Rockwool cavity slab
   insulation
15 100 mm (4 inch)
   medium dense
   concrete block
16 Thistle plaster
   hardwall undercoat
   and thistle finish
17 12.5 mm (1/2 inch)
   plastic shadow gap
   bead with
   intumescent seal
   behind

1.078
Wall Detail 1:5

TNA Architects
Stage House [28]

1 105 x 105 mm (4 1/8
  inch) timber stud
2 12.5 mm (1/2 inch)
  plasterboard wall
  lining with acrylic
  emulsion paint finish
3 Rigid foam insulation
4 Galvanized coloured

steel sheet exterior
cladding
5 Urethane foam spray
  finish
6 Galvanized coloured
  steel sheet to reveal
7 Hinge to concealed
  door panel
8 Galvanized coloured
  steel sheet to
  concealed door panel

1.079
Limestone External Wall
Detail 1:5

Stephenson Bell
Architects
House 780 [18]

1 Two layers 12 mm
  (1/2 inch)
  plasterboard with
  skim finish
2 100 mm (4 inch)
  blockwork
3 Damp proof course
  cavity tray
4 Limestone rainscreen
  with insect mesh at
  base of wall
5 Weep hole
6 Extruded aluminium
  trim
7 Liquid membrane
  dressed over damp
  proof membrane
8 Damp proof
  membrane turned up

side of slab and
terminated in
blockwork joint
9 20 mm (3/4 inch)
  limestone flooring
10 Concrete screed
11 Underfloor heating
   with insulation
12 Concrete slab
13 Perimeter insulation
   to prevent cold
   bridge
14 Black granite bonded
   to blockwork
15 Weak mix concrete
   fill to terminate 225
   mm (8 7/8 inch) below
   damp proof course
   level
16 Insulation through
   floor construction
17 Sand blinding

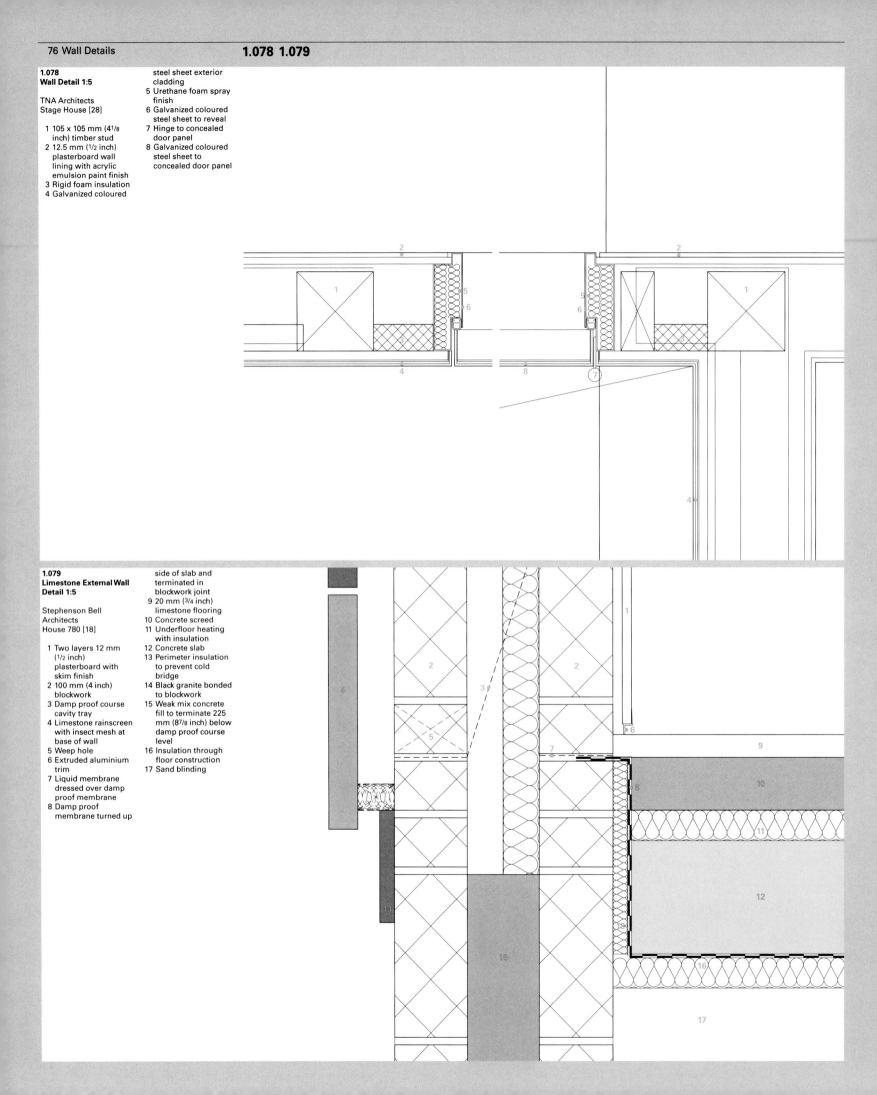

1.080
Internal Corner Wall Detail 1:10

Robert Seymour & Associates
The Riverhouse [22]

1 100 mm (4 inch) thick blockwork outer leaf with 100 mm (4 inch) cavity incorporating 60 mm (2³/8 inch) insulation boards to inside face of 100mm (4 inch) blockwork inner leaf with nominal 20 mm (³/4 inch) StoRend silicone through colour render internal finish
2 Insulated vertical damp proof course
3 20 mm (³/4 inch) StoRend flex coat silicone render applied to eternit bluclad board using mesh between board and blockwork to avoid cracking. Bluclad boards fixed to 48 mm (2 inch) C-section studs. 50 mm (2 inch) acoustic partition roll fixed between studs

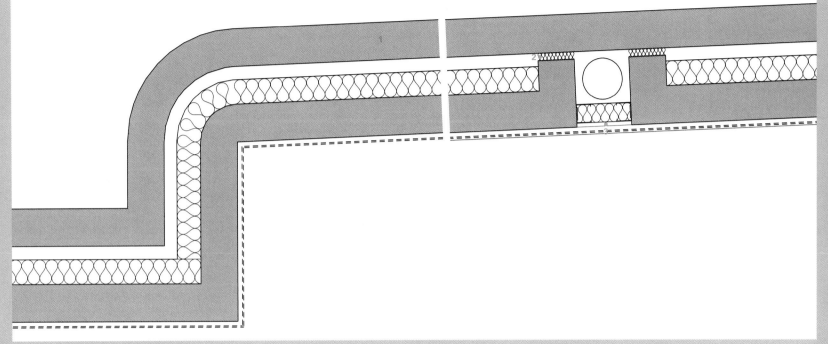

1.081
Entry Wall Plan Detail 1:10

Troppo Architects
Buttfield Town House [30]

1 190 mm (7¹/2 inch) concrete blockwork
2 10 mm (³/8 inch) select pre-colour render
3 Clear glazing
4 15 mm (5/8 inch) anodized aluminium glazing channel with silicone sealant
5 Rammed earth wall
6 Compressed foam sealant strip
7 25 x 25 mm (1 x 1 inch) aluminium angle trim to match frame
8 Nominal 30 mm (1¹/5 inch) arrissed corner to rammed earth wall
9 Anodized aluminium door frame
10 Solid door core

1.082
External Wall Detail 1:10

Peter Stutchbury Architecture
Avalon House [29]

1 150 x 100 x 5 mm (6 x 4 x 1/5 inch) galvanized rectangular hollow section steel column
2 Awning window constructed from 40 x 40 x 5 mm (15/8 x 15/8 x 1/5 inch) galvanized steel angle frame with clear glazed infill
3 40 x 5 mm (15/8 x 1/5 inch) galvanized steel glazing bar welded to topside of window sill
4 Rondo shadowline
5 90 x 40 mm (3¹/2 x 15/8 inch) timber stud
6 125 x 75 x 6 mm (5 x 3 x 1/4 inch) galvanized steel angle window sill
7 9 mm (³/8 inch) plasterboard wall lining
8 Polythene wool batt insulation
9 Sarking behind cladding shown dotted
10 Galvanized steel flat sheet cladding on timber studs with edges overlapped by 150 mm (6 inch) and joints sealed with silicone bead
11 Rondo shadowline and black Sikaflex to floorboard joint
12 90 x 40 mm (3¹/2 x 15/8 inch) timber sole plate
13 200 x 100 mm (8 x 4 inch) galvanized universal beam bolted to galvanized steel cleat
14 150 x 10 mm (6 x 2/5 inch) galvanized steel cleat welded to 150 x 100 mm (6 x 4 inch) rectangular hollow section column
15 25 mm (1 inch) tongue and groove hardwood floorboards
16 18 mm (³/4 inch) structural plywood fixed to joists and bearers
17 Galvanized steel floor purlin bolted to cleat
18 Firring channels spaced to suit size of ceiling panels
19 9 mm (³/8 inch) plywood ceiling panels

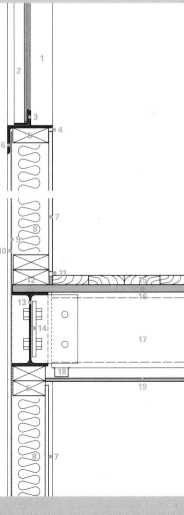

1.083
External Wall Detail 1:10

Scott Tallon Walker
Architects
Fastnet House [25]

1 Powder-coated
aluminium closer
plate
2 Mastic joint
3 Galvanized and
painted parallel
flange channel
4 Timber fillet
5 Gravel drainage bed
6 Aluminium border
trim to retain
extensive sedum
blanket
7 Roofing membrane
8 Tapered insulation
on marine ply
9 Galvanized and
painted mild steel
plate to form rebate
10 Universal beam
11 Mild steel angle
welded to universal
beam
12 Shallow profiled
metal decking
13 Mineral fibre quilt
insulation
14 Galvanized and
painted mild steel
plate welded to
universal beam
15 Ceiling hanger
16 Painted skim finish to
plasterboard
17 Motorized roller blind
18 Mastic joint
19 Solid cedar window
frame
20 Aluminium drip
profile
21 Insulation to cavity
22 Marine ply
23 Untreated secret
fixed shiplapped
cedar panelling
24 Softwood grounds
25 Copper sheeting on
marine ply
26 Sloped timber fillet
27 Insulation
28 Square hollow
section
29 Mild steel plate
welded to square
hollow section
30 Untreated cedar
soffit boarding secret
fixed to grounds
31 Untreated secret
fixed shiplapped
cedar panelling
32 Untreated secret
fixed shiplapped
cedar panelling
33 Hardwood door
frame
34 Solid cedar door sill
35 Weather seal
36 Floor pivot bearing
37 Insulation strip
38 Concrete cobble sett
paving
39 Sand bedding
40 Perimeter insulation
strip
41 Limestone tiling
42 Sand-cement screed
43 Heating pipework
support and spacer
44 Underfloor heating
pipes
45 Reinforced concrete
floor slab

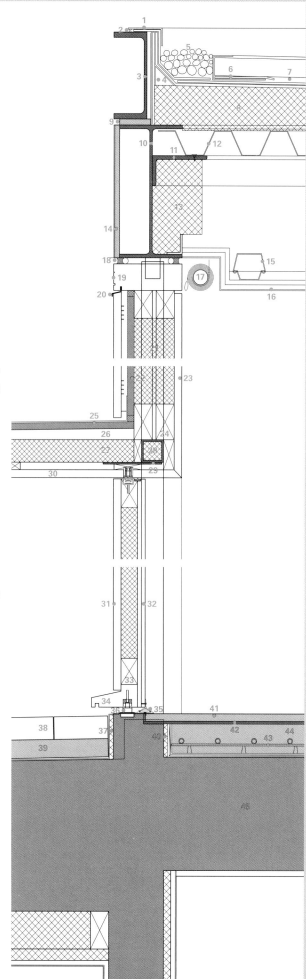

1.084
Wall Detail 1:10

Scott Tallon Walker
Architects
Fastnet House [25]

1 Powder-coated
aluminium closer
plate
2 Roofing membrane
3 Gravel drainage bed
to form border
around sedum green
roof
4 Extensive sedam
blanket
5 Roofing membrane
6 Tapered insulation
on marine ply
7 Timber fillet
8 Galvanized and
painted parallel
flange channel
9 Mild steel angle
welded to universal
beam to support
decking
10 Universal beam
11 Shallow profiled
metal decking
12 Mineral fibre
insulation
13 Galvanized and
painted mild steel
plate welded to
universal beam
14 Timber framing
15 Painted skim finish to
suspended
plasterboard ceiling
16 Painted skim finish
on plasterboard
17 Insulated
plasterboard
18 Vapour barrier
19 Insulation
20 Shiplapped
untreated cedar
cladding secret fixed
to marine ply
21 Painted skirting
22 Limestone tiled floor
on bedding
23 Sand-cement screed
topping
24 Reinforced concrete
floor slab
25 Mastic seal
26 Concrete cobble
paving
27 Weathering
membrane
28 Sand bedding

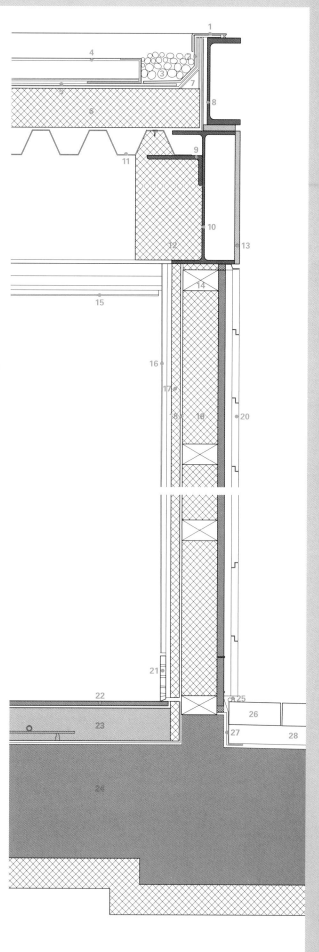

1.085
Exterior Wall Detail 1:20

Scott Tallon Walker
Architects
Fastnet House [25]

1 Parapet in
  background
2 Extensive sedum
  roof
3 Aluminium border
  trim to retain
  extensive sedum
  blanket
4 Roofing membrane
5 Tapered timber fillets
6 Timber joists
7 Moisture resistant
  plasterboard lining
8 Gravel drainage bed
9 Powder-coated
  aluminium coping
10 Roofing membrane
  on marine ply
11 Concrete block wall
12 Top of stone cladding

13 Mastic sealant
14 Galvanized mild steel
  frame
15 Motorized awning
16 Galvanized mild steel
  frame
17 Self coloured render
18 Self coloured render
19 Slate lining
20 Blockwork wall
21 Slate counter
22 Gas supply line to
  barbeque
23 Sand-cement screed
24 Reinforced concrete
  floor slab
25 Blockwork wall
26 Self coloured render
27 Slate skirting
28 Baseplate to steel
  frame
29 Limestone open
  jointed paving
30 Pedestal to raised
  floor system

1.086
Balustrade Detail 1:5

John Onken Architects
Dolphin Cottage [32]

1 42 mm (1 5/8 inch)
  diameter oak
  handrail
2 Satin stainless steel
  bracket clamps
3 12 mm (1/2 inch)
  toughened clear
  glass balustrade,
  drilled for handrail
  fixings and polished
  both sides
4 Carpeting to conceal
  steel backplate
5 4 mm (1/8 inch)
  structural silicone
  and packing both
  sides of glass
6 21 mm (7/8 inch)
  tongue and groove
  floor decking
7 6 mm (1/4 inch) mild

steel plate secured to
floor structure and
drilled and tapped
for bolts
8 Hard rubber glass
  setting blocks
9 300 mm (12 inch)
  deep truss-joist floor
  framing
10 6 mm (1/4 inch)
  primed and painted
  continuous mild steel
  clamping plate
11 Countersunk
  hex-head bolts
  through hardwood
  spacers
12 Plasterboard ceiling
  with stop bead to
  form reveal joint

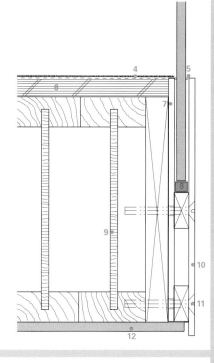

1.087
External Wall Detail 1:10

Touraine Richmond
Architects
One Window House [27]

1 20 mm (3/4 inch)
  corrugated
  galvanized metal
  cladding
2 Waterproof
  membrane
3 50 mm (2 inch)
  plywood sheathing
4 Aluminium window
  header with drip
5 12.5 mm (1/2 inch)

tempered glass
6 12.5 mm (1/2 inch)
  drywall lining
7 Sanded oriented
  strand board
8 15 mm (5/8 inch)
  plywood subfloor
9 Timber framing
  beyond
10 12.5 mm (1/2 inch)
  drywall ceiling

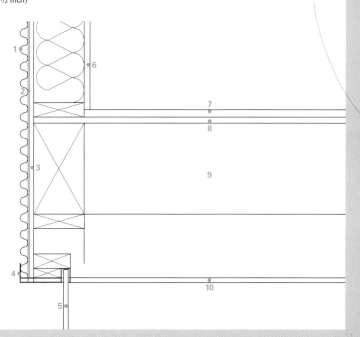

1.088
Bathroom Wall Detail
1:10

WPA
Weese Young Residence
[28]

1 Quartz countertop
2 Sill flashing
3 Mirror on plywood
4 Corrugated
zincalume on timber
battens on
waterproof
membrane on
plywood
5 Insulation
6 Lighting fixture
7 White porcelain
wall-hung sink
8 Pre-finished colour
plywood
9 Glass tiles to wall
10 Insulation
11 Poplar base and
skirting
12 Marmoleum on
plywood subfloor
13 Engineered timber
joist
14 Insulation
15 Painted rectangular
hollow section beam
16 Exterior grade
plywood
17 Timber stud frame

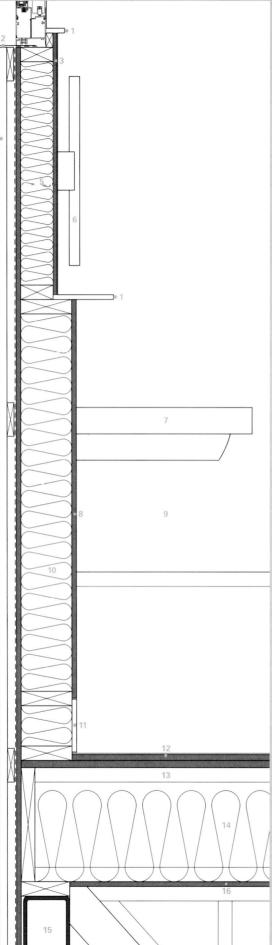

1.089
Wall With Shelving
Detail 1:10

WPA
Weese Young Residence
[28]

1 Pre-finished colour
plywood
2 Birch plywood
3 Marmoleum flooring
on plywood subfloor
4 Poplar base and
skirting
5 Timber stud frame
6 Vertical grain pine on
plywood subfloor
7 Engineered timber
joist
8 Insulation
9 Painted exterior
grade plywood
10 Timber top plate
11 Painted rectangular
hollow section beam

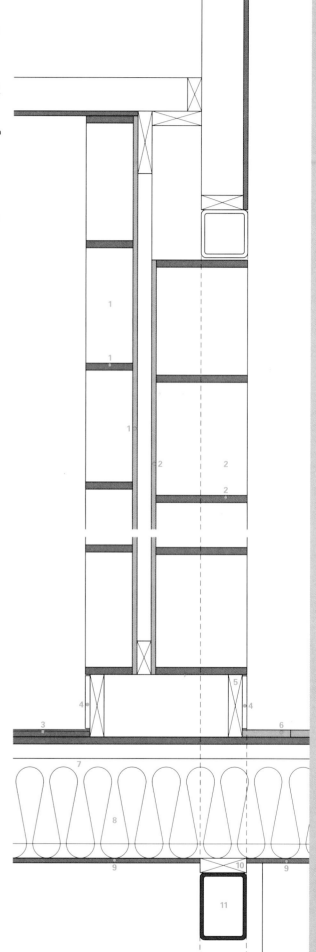

1.090
**External Wall Corner
Detail 1:5**

Powerhouse Company
Villa 1 [15]

1 800 x 800 x 20 mm
(32 x 32 x 3/4 inch)
travertine stone
panels
2 Travertine glued to
multiplex boarding
3 18 mm (3/4 inch)
waterproof multiplex
boarding
4 180 x 67 mm (7 x 25/8
inch) timber stud

5 60 mm (23/8 inch)
timber strut and rails
6 12 mm (1/2 inch)
cement fibre sheath
7 30 mm (11/4 inch)
insulation
8 10 mm (3/8 inch)
StoTherm classic
external wall
insulation system
9 Aluminium stucco
stop
10 3 mm (1/8 inch)
polyurethane floor
finish
11 50 mm (2 inch)
concrete floor laid to
fall

12 80 mm (31/8 inch)
pressure-proof
insulation
13 139 x 54 mm (51/2 x
21/8 inch) timber rails
14 Concrete slab
15 110 mm (43/8 inch)
diameter water
drainage pipe
16 Aluminium channel

1.091
Wall Plan Detail 1:10

Avanti Architects
Long View [35]

1 150 mm (6 inch)
insulation between
timber studs
2 150 x 50 mm (6 x 2
inch) timber stud
frame
3 Steel column
4 Vapour control layer
fixed over timber
studs and horizontal
counter battens
5 50 x 75 mm (2 x 3

inch) horizontal
counter battens and
services void
6 12.5 mm (1/2 inch)
plasterboard taped
and skimmed
7 65 x 22 mm (21/2 x 7/8
inch) tongue and
groove
weatherboards
secret fixed vertically
to horizontal counter
battens
8 40 x 60 mm (15/8 x
23/8 inch) horizontal
counter battens
9 Breather membrane
10 12 mm (1/2 inch)

weather bonded and
proofed plywood
bracing
11 20 mm (3/4 inch)
Celotex insulation
12 90 x 60 mm (31/2 x
23/8 inch) vertical
batten

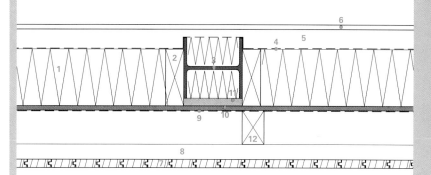

1.092
External Wall Detail 1:5

David Nossiter
Architects
Kitsbury Road House
[13]

1 12.5 mm (1/2 inch)
plasterboard with
vapour barrier
2 Insulation
3 25 x 25 mm (1 x 1
inch) timber battens
to hold insulation in
place
4 100 x 50 mm (4 x 2
inch) timber stud

5 100 x 100 mm (4 x 4
inch) square steel
section
6 Masonry party wall

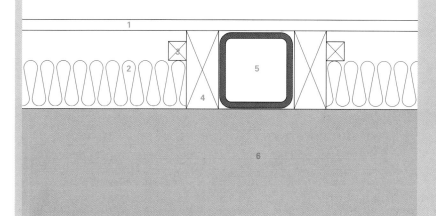

1.093
External Wall Detail 1:10

Troppo Architects
Buttfield Town House
[30]

1 200 x 45 mm (8 x 1¾ inch) laminated veneer lumber beam
2 Galvanized flashing
3 Galvanized profiled roof sheeting to minimum 1degree fall
4 90 x 45 mm (3½ x 1¾ inch) purlins to fall
5 70 x 35 mm (2¾ x 1⅜ inch) ceiling joists with insulation infill
6 12.5 mm (½ inch) plasterboard ceiling and wall lining with paint finish
7 Square hollow section column
8 Tongue and groove floorboards
9 35 x 42 mm (1⅜ x 1⅝ inch) batten at 450 mm (18 inch) centres
10 Concrete slab
11 90 x 190 mm (3½ x 7½ inch) blockwork
12 Galvanized flashing cap to parapet
13 90 x 190 mm (3½ x 7½ inch) blockwork, tied to studwork with select bagged finish
14 10 mm (⅜ inch) pre-coloured render
15 Sisalation to overlap damp proof membrane
16 Two sole plates for lining fixing
17 Damp proof membrane
18 Rebate as required
19 210 mm (8¼ inch) concrete wall

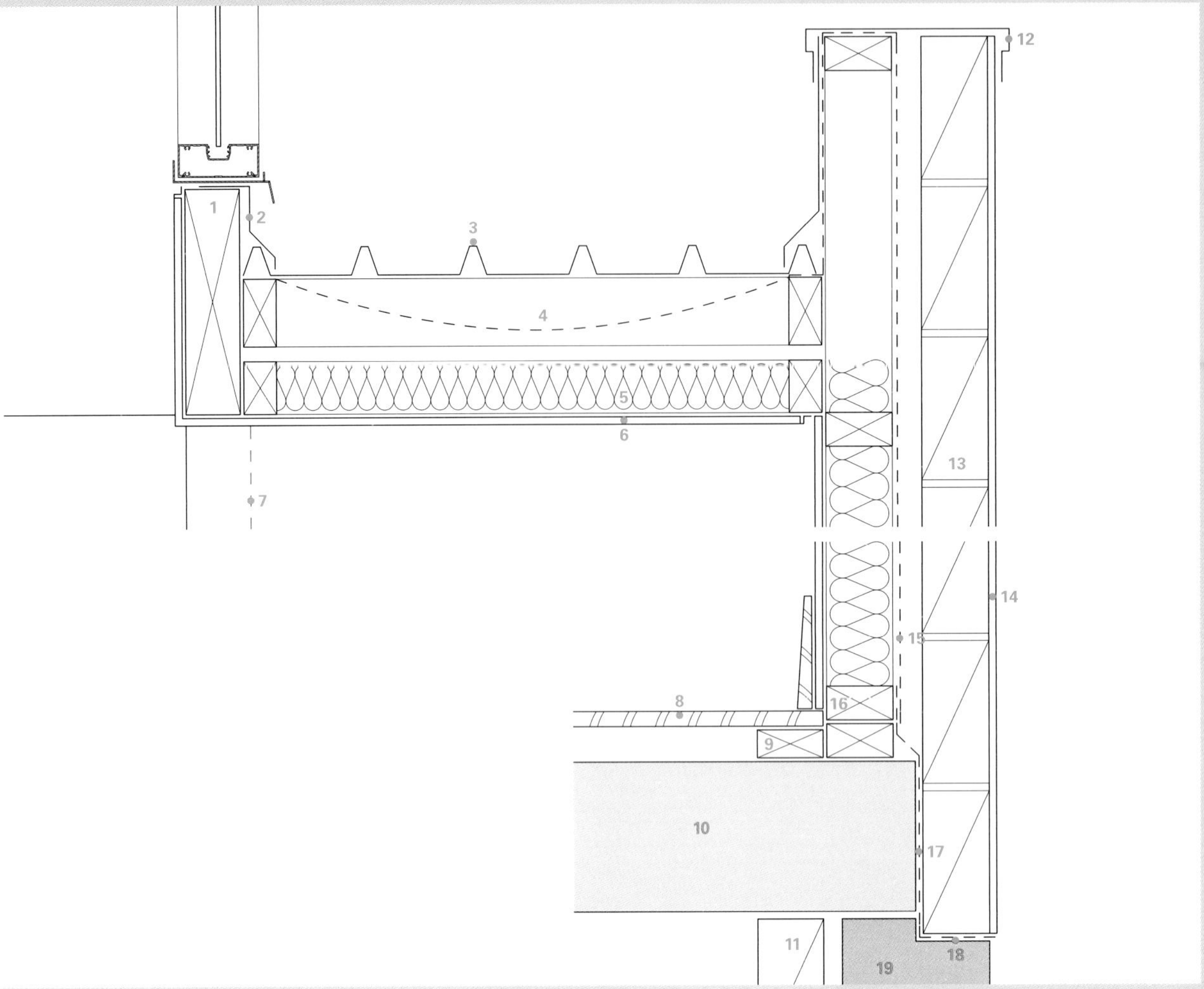

1.094
Wall Base at Foundation Detail 1:10

Hawkes Architecture
Crossway [16]

1 Panelvent vapour-permeable sheathing board
2 Warmcell recycled newspaper insulation
3 Service cavity behind kitchen units
4 Red brick with lime mortar using crushed bottle sand
5 Kitchen carcass units made from plywood
6 Thermalite blockwork plinth
7 Celotex cavity insulation
8 External stone paving
9 Crushed bottle eco sand
10 Crushed recycled concrete sub-base
11 Clay subsoil
12 Gravel drainage strip
13 Kaycel Super-plus Graphite insulation
14 Visqueen Ecomembrane damp proof membrane bonded to bituthene self-adhesive damp proof membrane
15 Kaycel Super-plus Graphite insulation
16 Reinforced concrete slab
17 Kaycel Super-plus Graphite insulation
18 Cordek Cellcore anti-heave layer
19 Crushed bottle eco sand blinding
20 Foil backed Celotex insulation
21 Lafarge Aquaboard waterproof plasterboard

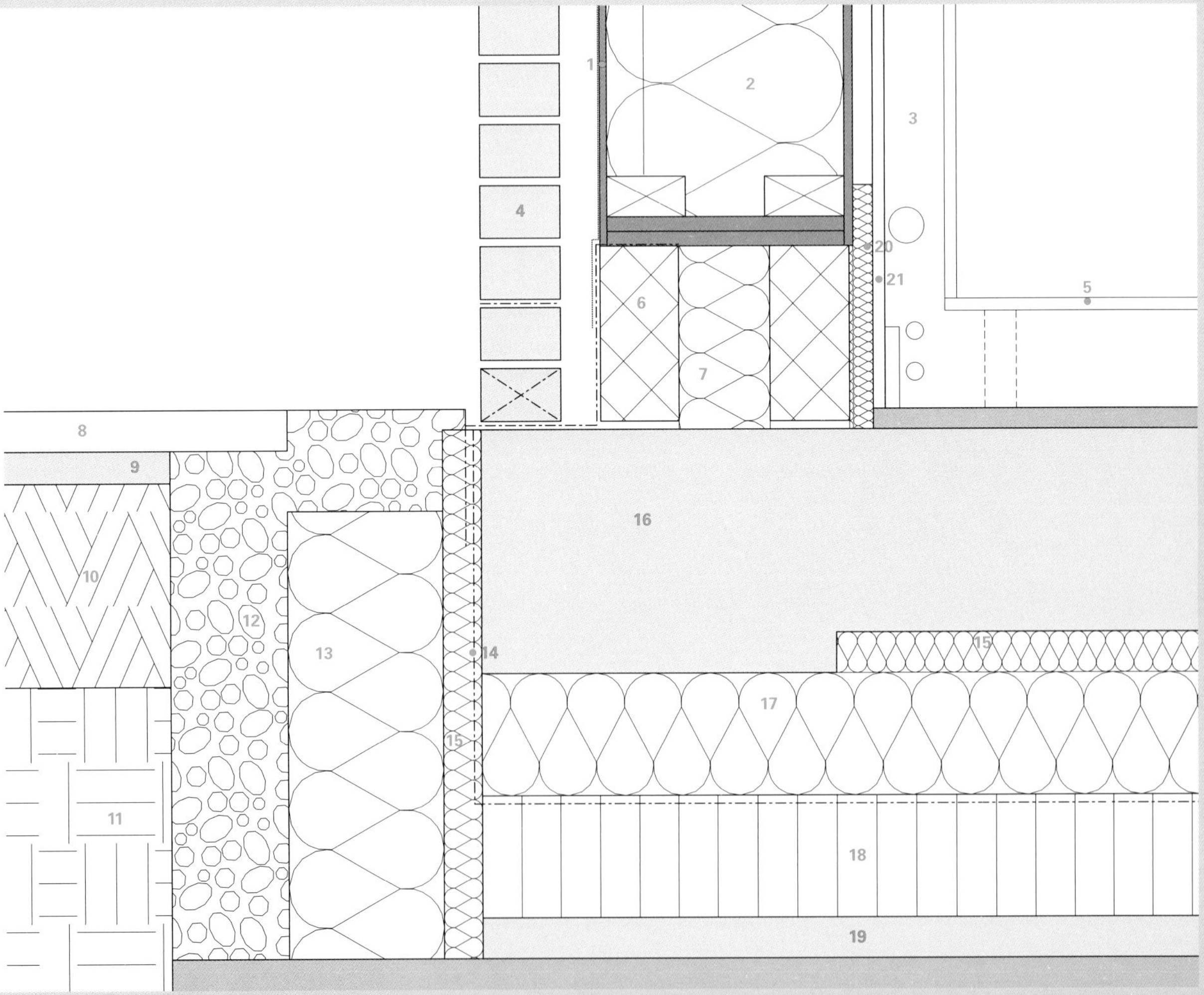

1.095
Blockwork Wall With
Door Jamb Detail 1:2

Studio Bednarski
Hesmondhalgh House
[33]

1 3 mm (1/8 inch) skim
  coat
2 11 mm (3/8 inch)
  gypsum thistle
  hardwall plaster
3 Expamet plaster stop
  bead
4 Concealed screw
  fixing between
  timber packing and
  door jamb
5 Timber packing
6 126 x 50 mm (5 x 2
  inch) door jamb
7 Blockwork

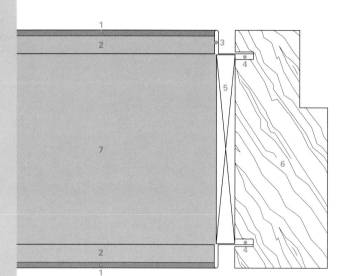

1.096
Glass Wall Detail 1:10

Blank Studio
Xeros Residence [29]

1 16 mm (5/8 inch)
  painted gypsum
  board on 75 x 16 mm
  (3 x 5/8 inch) steel
  studs with acoustical
  batts
2 6 mm (1/4 inch)
  translucent tempered
  glass
3 Flitch plates with 12.5
  mm (1/2 inch) angle
  to support glazing
4 Veneered plywood
  floor, epoxy adhered
  to 12.5 mm (1/2 inch)
  plywood sheathing
5 275 x 22 mm (11 x 7/8
  inch) framing and
  hangers

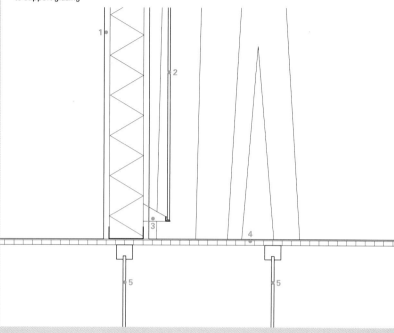

1.097
Wall Detail 1:5

Chenchow Little
Architects
Freshwater House [32]

1 Core-filled reinforced
  concrete block wall
2 50 x 50 mm (2 x 2
  inch) horizontal
  timber battens
3 90 x 40 mm (31/2 x
  15/8 inch) timber
  battens alternated
  with 40 x 40 mm (15/8
  x 15/8 inch) battens
4 100 x 59 mm (4 x 2
  inch) timber frame
5 Anodized black
  aluminium angle
6 Waterproofed joint
7 Compressed
  fibre-cement
  sheeting with
  exterior grade
  polyurethane finish
8 Tile floor
9 Stainless steel grate
  and integrated drain

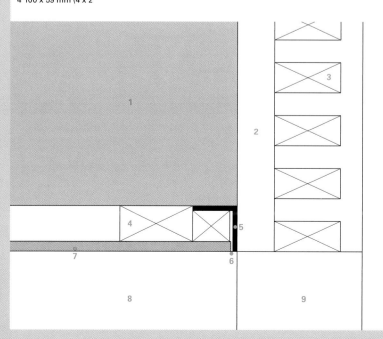

1.098
Wall Detail 1:10

Chenchow Little
Architects
Freshwater House [32]

1 Reinforced concrete
  beam
2 50 x 50 mm (2 x 2
  inch) horizontal
  timber battens
3 90 x 40 mm (31/2 x
  15/8 inch) vertical
  timber battens
4 60 x 60 mm (23/8 x
  23/8 inch) anodized
  black aluminium
  angle
5 Timber packing
6 Fibre-cement
  sheeting with
  exterior grade
  polyurethane finish
7 90 x 40 mm (31/2 x
  15/8 inch) vertical
  timber battens
8 Tiled floor
9 Screed
10 Concrete slab and
   beam
11 Stainless steel grate
12 Integrated drain

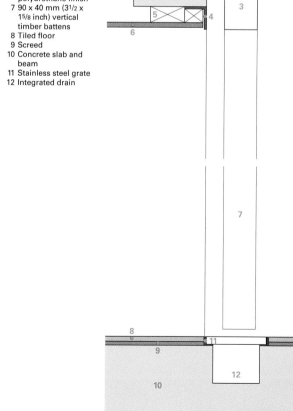

1.099
Timber Screen Wall
Detail 1:10

Lahz Nimmo Architects
Casuarina Ultimate
Beach House [31]

1 Dressed hardwood studs with stain finish
2 35 mm (1 3/8 inch) belt-sanded recycled blue gum hardwood stain-finished prior to fixing and countersunk screw fixed
3 Lighting unit
4 Folded Colorbond flashing
5 18 mm (3/4 inch) compressed fibre cement sheet
6 Flashing lapped over roof membrane
7 Butynol roof

membrane on plywood substrate
8 20 mm (3/4 inch) thick finger-jointed dressed hardwood trim secret fixed to 20 mm (3/4 inch) thick timber spacers with paint finish
9 200 x 75 mm (8 x 3 inch) parallel flange channel
10 Rafters fixed between beams to fall of roofing
11 Insulation
12 Plasterboard ceiling fixed using packing wedges
13 Aluminium framed sliding glass door with bottom roller

1.100
Copper Dome Wall
Detail 1:20

McBride Charles Ryan
The Dome House [21]

1 Timber battens
2 Timber battens
3 Insulation
4 Roof battens on timber box beam
5 Copper sheeting on two layers of 8 mm (1/3 inch) plywood substrate
6 Cavity with vapour permeable sarking

and stained timber battens
7 Timber plate
8 Bedding sand
9 Concrete slab and strip footing
10 Blinding concrete
11 Stones on stainless steel grate welded to 50 x 50 mm (2 x 2 inch) stainless steel angles. Stainless steel angles required along sump edges
12 150 mm (6 inch) diameter PVC pipe
13 Prefabricated sump, 500 mm (20 inch)

diameter semi-circular PVC pipe 4000 mm (160 inch) in length and heat-fused at ends

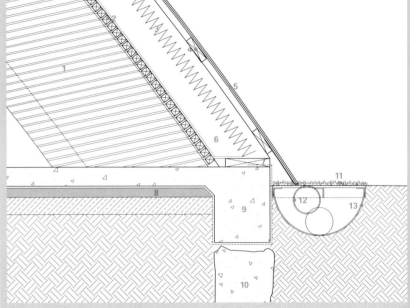

1.101
Attic Level Wall Plan
Detail 1:10

Marsh Cashman
Koolloos Architects
Maroubra House [36]

1 Hardwood timber floor decking
2 Hardwood timber panelling
3 Vapour barrier
4 Insulation
5 Timber stud
6 Continuous 50 x 50 mm (2 x 2 inch) aluminium angle

7 Timber corner bead
8 Compressed fibre cement sheet
9 Motorized blinds shown dotted
10 New steel column
11 Timber window

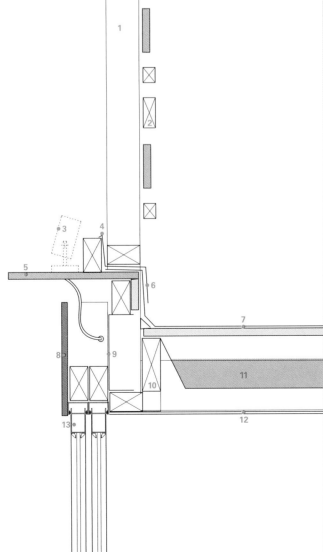

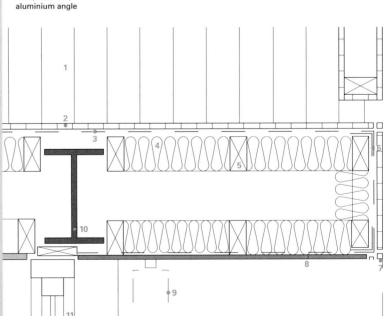

1.102
Wall Detail
1:10

Jun Igarashi Architects
Rectangle of Light [37]

1 12.5 mm (1/2 inch)
   plasterboard with
   vinyl cloth finish
2 12.5 mm (1/2 inch)
   composite panel with
   vinyl cloth finish
3 105 x 105 mm (4 x 4
   inch) timber stud
4 50 x 105 mm (2 x 4
   inch) timber stud
5 105 x 105 mm (4 x 4
   inch) timber end
   piece cut at 45
   degrees

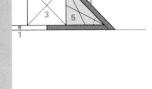
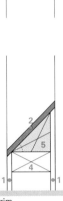

1.103
Garage Batten Wall
Detail 1:10

Lahz Nimmo Architects
Casuarina Ultimate
Beach House [31]

1 6 mm (1/4 inch)
   compressed fibre
   cement sheet with
   joints taped and set
   for paint finish
2 Building paper
3 120 x 20 mm (43/4 x
   3/4 inch) hardwood
   boards shiplapped
   with joints secret
   nailed and stain
   finished
4 20 mm (3/4 inch)
   recycled blue gum
   hardwood reveal at
   head notched around
   studs
5 Line of timber board
   cladding beyond
6 Exposed timber stud

frame with stain
finish
7 35 mm (13/8 inch)
   recycled blue gum
   timber battens, screw
   fixed with stainless
   steel screws and
   stain finished
8 Concrete slab steel
   trowel finished with
   coloured oxide finish
   to garage
9 Waterproof
   membrane on 50
   mm (2 inch) sand bed
10 Zinc folded termite
   proof flashing
11 Steel trowel trim coat
   finish to exposed
   face of concrete
12 Concrete paver on
   sand bed

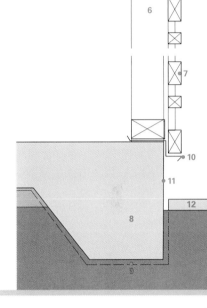

1.104
External Wall Detail 1:10

Lahz Nimmo Architects
Casuarina Ultimate
Beach House [31]

1 Timber roof purlins
2 Ceiling battens fixed
   on spacers to purlins
   at 600 mm (24 inch)
   centres
3 10 mm (3/8 inch)
   timber veneer fixed
   to ceiling battens.
   Joints covered with
   half-round timber
   bead from 20 mm (3/4
   inch) diameter dowel
4 20 mm (3/4 inch)
   diameter dowel
   stopping bead
5 Final timber purlin
   extended to close off
   ceiling space
6 Insulation
7 Corrugated sheet
   steel Colorbond
   roofing
8 Profiled eaves closer
9 Timber fascia purlin
10 Enviroflo gutter
11 13 mm (1/2 inch)
   plasterboard with 10
   mm (3/8 inch) shadow
   gap
12 Z flashing over
   glazing adaptor to
   tuck under fascia
   purlin
13 Anodized aluminium
   glazing adaptor for 6
   mm (1/4 inch) glass,
   screw fixed to fascia
   purlin
14 Timber mid-support,
   shown dotted, fixed
   to beam and fascia
   purlin
15 Translucent
   laminated glass
16 20 mm (3/4 inch)

dressed edge trim
17 Thickened render
   flush with top plate
18 Steel plate with bolt
   connection
19 Blocking piece fixed
   to beam and notched
   for mid-support
20 140 x 35 mm (51/2 x
   13/8 inch) hardwood
   beam
21 25 x 25 x 5 mm (1 x 1
   x 1/5 inch) galvanized
   mild steel angle
   compressible seal to
   glazing, screw fixed
   to glazing adaptor
   and mid-support with
   separator between
   aluminium and steel
22 Cleat connection
   with bolt
23 Galvanized steel stub
   column
24 200 mm (8 inch)
   reinforced blockwork,
   rendered externally
   and plastered
   internally

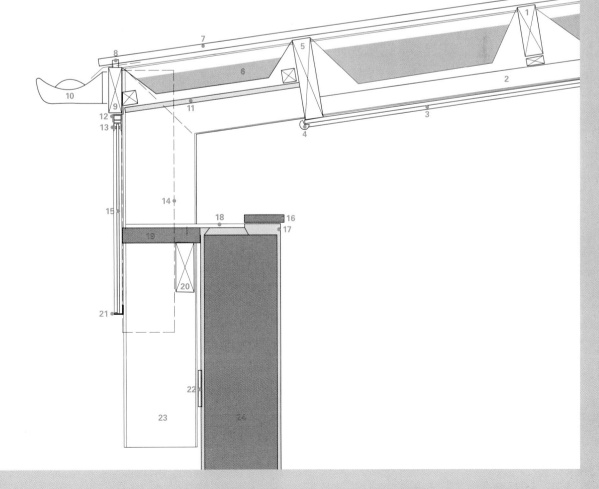

1.105
Interior Balustrade
Detail 1:10

Troppo Architects
Buttfield Town House
[30]

1 140 x 42 mm (5¹/₂ x
  1⁵/₈ inch) hardwood
  handrail with arris to
  top edges and rebate
  to underside to
  receive plate
2 90 x 42 mm (3¹/₂ x
  1⁵/₈ inch) hardwood
  rail fixed to bracket
  and countersunk
  fixed through to
  underside of handrail
3 Plasterboard on 90
  mm (3¹/₂ inch) stud
  frame
4 Stainless steel spider
  bracket
5 Glazing panel
6 35 x 35 mm (1³/₈ x

1³/₈ inch) square
hollow section with
paint finish
7 Hardwood nosing
8 Tongue and groove
  floorboards on 19
  mm (³/₄ inch)
  structural floor
  substrate
9 200 x 50 mm (8 x 2
  inch) laminated
  veneer lumber joist
  at 450 mm (18 inch)
  centres
10 300 x 90 mm (12 x
  3¹/₂ inch) parallel
  flange channel
  bearer with paint
  finish
11 Acoustic insulation

1.106
Exterior Balustrade
Detail 1:10

Troppo Architects
Buttfield Town House
[30]

1 140 x 42 mm (5¹/₂ x
  1⁵/₈ inch) hardwood
  handrail with arris to
  top edges and rebate
  underside to receive
  plate
2 90 x 42 mm (3¹/₂ x
  1⁵/₈ inch) hardwood
  rail, fixed to bracket
  and countersunk
  fixed through to
  underside of handrail
3 6 mm (¹/₄ inch) cleat
  welded to baluster
4 8 mm (³/₈ inch)
  profiled mild steel
  baluster with paint
  finish
5 3 mm (¹/₈ inch)

stainless steel cables
with nylon ferrules
6 90 x 42 mm (3¹/₂ x
  1⁵/₈ inch) hardwood
  footrail, with 3mm
  (¹/₈ inch) arris to top
  edges and spliced to
  cleat at ends and
  fixed by four M8
  bolts
7 6 mm (¹/₄ inch) mild
  steel cleat
8 Hardwood decking
9 6 mm (¹/₄ inch) cleat
  parallel flange
  channel
10 200 x 50 mm (8 x 2
  inch) laminated
  veneer lumber joist
  at 450 mm (18 inch)
  centres
11 300 x 90 mm (12 x
  3¹/₂ inch) parallel
  flange channel
  bearer with paint
  finish

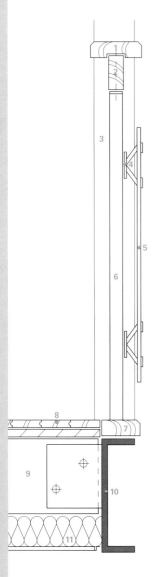

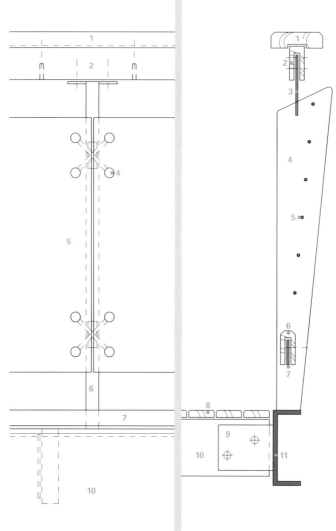

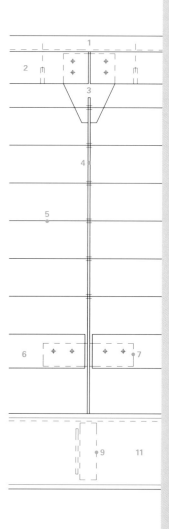

1.107
Typical Blockwork Wall
Detail 1:2

Studio Bednarski
Hesmondhalgh House
[33]

1 3 mm (1/8 inch) skim
   coat
2 11 mm (3/8 inch)
   gypsum thistle
   hardwall plaster
3 Expamet plaster stop
   bead
4 Painted softwood
   skirting board
5 Floor finish bonded
   onto screed
6 75 mm (3 inch)
   heated screed
7 Polythene slip layer
8 Concrete blockwork

1.108
External Wall Detail 1:20

Scott Tallon Walker
Architects
Fastnet House [25]

1 Line of parapet in
   background
2 Extensive sedum
   blanket
3 Gravel drainage bed
4 Roofing membrane
5 Concrete block wall
6 Powder-coated
   aluminium coping
7 Cedar battens secret
   fixed to vertical
   bearer
8 Self coloured render
9 Timber door frame
10 Solid core door
11 Block wall in
   background
12 Sand-cement screed
13 Weather seal
14 Reinforced concrete
   floor slab
15 Limestone
   open-jointed paving
16 Pedestal to support
   limestone paving

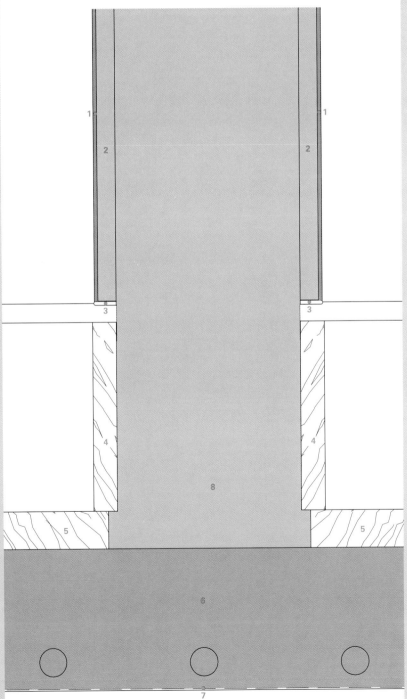

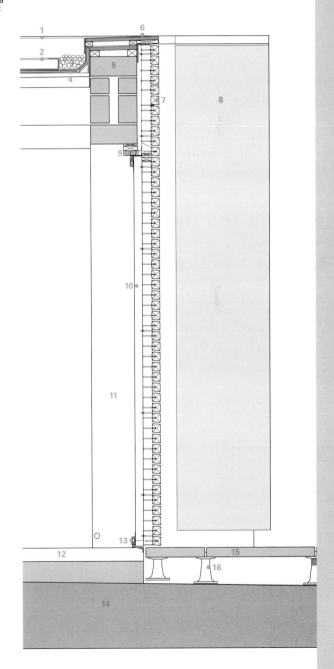

1.109
Wall Detail 1:10

Glas Architects
The Nail Houses [23]

1 440 x 102.5 x 102.5
   mm (17 1/2 x 4 x 4
   inch) Forticrete
   polished Medici
   block, Bellini colour
   to front elevation,
   split face block in
   pewter colour to side
   and rear elevations
2 Full-filled cavity
   insulation
3 100 mm (4 inch)
   lightweight concrete
   block above ground
   level
4 Thistle hard wall
   plaster undercoat
   and thistle finish
5 Pre-formed cavity
   tray with stop-ends
6 Weep holes

7 Air brick with
   adjustable telescopic
   vents with damp
   proof course to joint
   under in outer leaf
8 12.5 mm (1/2 inch)
   plastic shadow gap
   bead with
   intumescent seal
   behind
9 100 mm (4 inch)
   medium density
   fibreboard skirting
   with intumescent
   seal behind floor
   junction
10 15 mm (5/8 inch)
   engineered timber
   floorboards
11 12 mm (1/2 inch)
   plywood
12 Underfloor heating
   cables
13 60 mm (2 3/8 inch)
   Rockwool duct slab
   insulation
14 60 mm (2 3/8 inch)

Rockwool flexi
   insulation
15 Vapour control layer
16 Beam and block floor
17 Damp proof course
   to return vertically
   into blockwork
18 440 x 215 x 115 mm
   (17 1/2 x 8 1/2 x 4 1/2
   inch) Celcon
   foundation block
19 Insulation in cavity to
   overlap by 150 mm
   (6 inch)
20 440 x 215 x 330 mm
   (17 1/2 x 8 1/2 x 13 1/4
   inch) Celcon
   foundation block
21 170 mm (6 3/4 inch)
   ventilation void
22 Sand blinding over
   damp proof course
23 Compacted soil
24 Concrete foundation

1.110
Kitchen and Bathroom
Tiled Wall Detail 1:10

BmasC Arquitectos
Mayo House [20]

1 300 x 300 mm (12 x
   12 inch) tiles
2 Cement mortar
3 Double air brick
4 Plastered wall finish
5 Stoneware floor
6 Polythene waterproof
   coating
7 Suspended ground
   floor
8 Moisture barrier skin
9 Gravel stratum

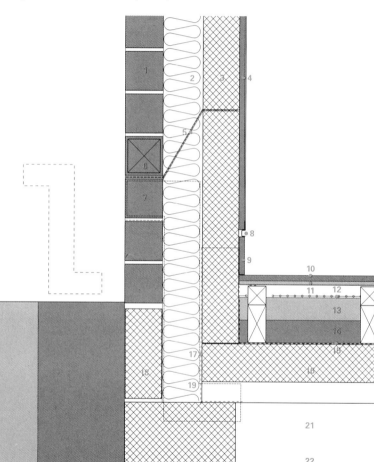

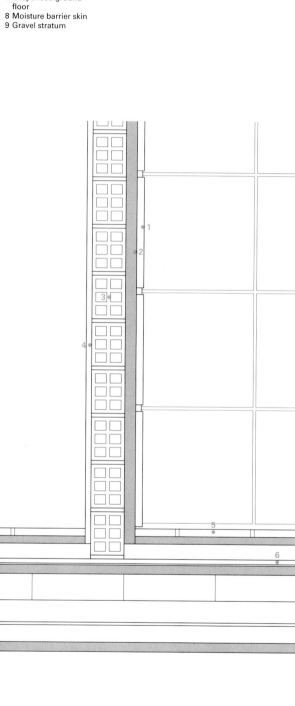

1.111
Wall and Sun Shade
Plan Detail 1:10

Jackson Clements
Burrows Architects
Edward River House
[32]

1 6 mm (1/4 inch)
   folded aluminium
   sun shade
2 Vertical corrugated
   metal wall cladding

3 Air space
4 10 mm (3/8 inch) fixed
   float glass
5 140 x 40 mm (51/2 x
   15/8 inch) cedar
   window sill
6 6 mm (1/4 inch)
   folded aluminium
   fixing bracket for
   supporting sun
   shade, shown dotted
7 266 x 110 mm (101/2 x
   43/8 inch) laminated
   timber structural

column
8 Bracket bolted to
   structural beam
9 140 x 40 mm (51/2 x
   15/8 inch) cedar
   window jamb
10 Cedar infill panel

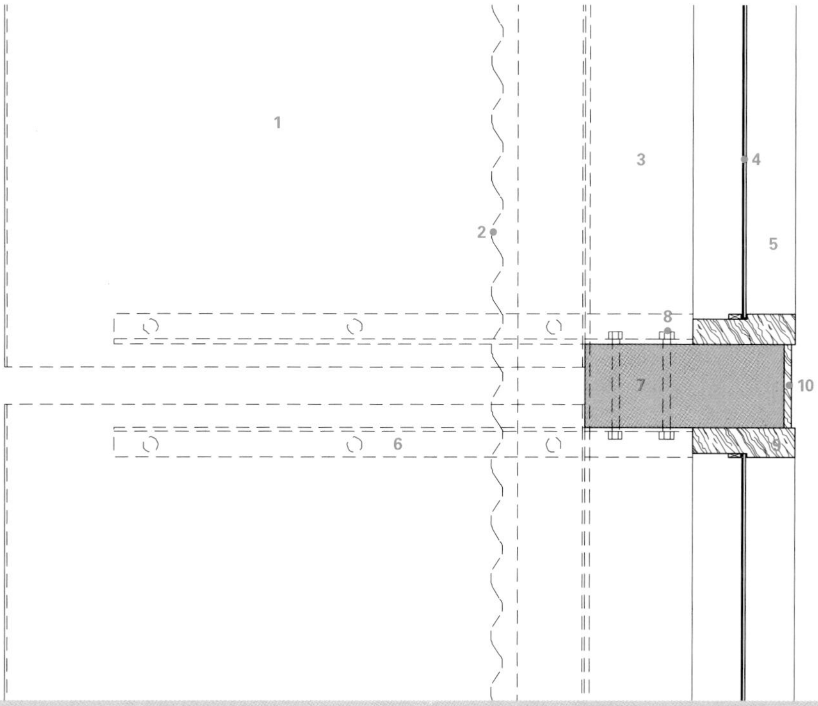

1.112
Terrace Interface Detail
1:10

Hamiltons
Holmewood House [17]

1 30 mm (11/5 inch)
   travertine paving
2 150 mm (6 inch)
   bedding and
   concrete slab
3 Gravel fill
4 Glazed sliding door
5 Stainless steel grille
   to drainage channel
6 Stainless steel
   drainage channel
   with insert channel
   laid to fall
7 Anodized aluminium
   window bottom
   frame
8 Support angle for
   stainless steel sill
9 100 mm (4 inch)
   insulation
10 Waterproofing
   membrane
11 Continuous steel
   angle
12 Linear aluminium
   trench heater grille
13 Convector heating
   elements
14 Structural concrete
   wall to undercroft
15 Damp proofing

membrane
16 Insulation fill
17 30 mm (11/5 inch)
   limestone paving on
   50 mm (2 inch) thick
   sand-cement
   bedding
18 100 mm (4 inch)
   cement screed with
   underfloor heating
19 100 mm (4 inch) thick
   insulation
20 Damp proof
   membrane
21 Concrete slab on
   metal decking

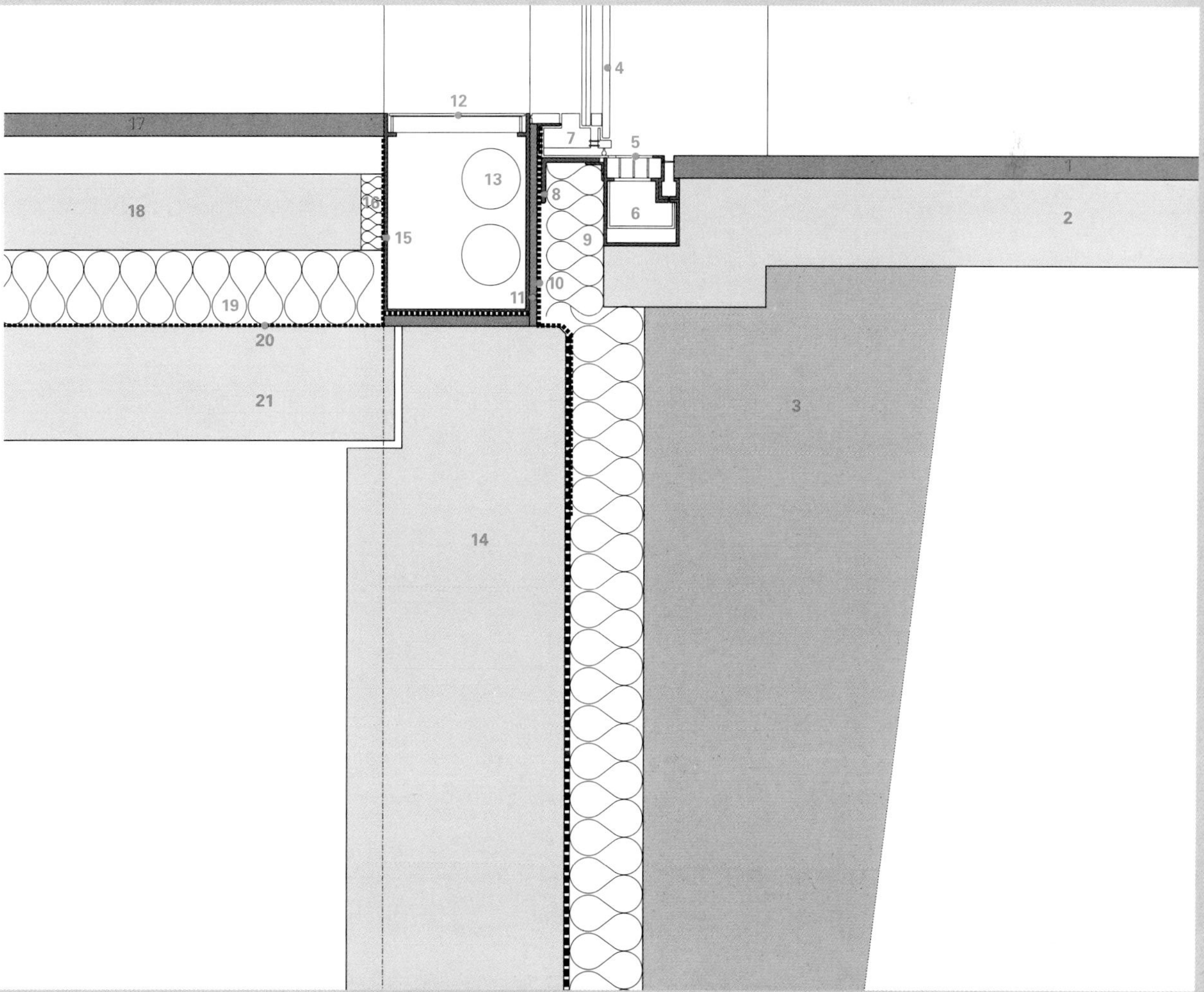

1.113 1.114

1.113
External Wall Detail 1:20

Scott Tallon Walker
Architects
Fastnet House [25]

1 Line of top of parapet
2 Extensive sedum
 blanket
3 Aluminium border
 trim to retain
 extensive sedum
 blanket
4 Painted mild steel
 angle
5 Galvanized and
 painted parallel
 flange channel
6 Insulation
7 Marine ply
8 Shallow profiled
 metal decking
9 Mild steel angle in
 background
10 Mechanical supply
 duct

11 Downlighter
12 Painted skim coat to
 suspended
 plasterboard ceiling
13 Ceiling hanger
14 Roller blind
15 Mineral fibre
 insulation
16 Universal beam
17 Parallel flange
 channel in
 background
18 Thermally broken
 aluminium frame
19 Thermally broken
 double glazed unit
20 Skirting in
 background
21 Solid oak wide plank
 timber floor
22 Underfloor heating
23 Sand-cement screed
 topping on
 separating layer
24 Reinforced concrete
 floor slab
25 Insulation

26 Galvanized and
 painted mild steel
 plate welded to
 universal beam
27 Untreated secret
 fixed shiplapped
 cedar panelling
28 Painted skim finish to
 suspended
 plasterboard ceiling
29 Curtain
30 Aluminium and
 timber thermally
 broken composite
 window system
31 Carpet on underlay
32 Trench heater
33 Insulation
34 Reinforced concrete
 floor slab
35 Concrete cobble
 paving laid to fall
36 Sand bedding
37 Hardcore fill
38 Insulation

1.114
External Wall Detail 1:10

Scott Tallon Walker
Architects
Fastnet House [25]

1 Concrete cobble
 paving
2 Sand bedding
3 Reinforced concrete
 roof slab laid to fall
4 Stainless steel
 uprights with
 tensioned cable to
 form guarding
5 Slate packers
6 Random rubble stone
 wall
7 Air cavity with
 reflective insulation
8 Insulation
9 Painted skim finish
 on suspended
 plasterboard ceiling
10 Solid oak panelling
11 Motorized roller blind
12 Stone relieving angle
 with galvanized
 finish
13 Stone slip fixed and
 bonded to underside
 of angle
14 Thermally broken
 aluminium opening
 vent
15 Solid oak panelling
16 Thermally broken
 double glazed unit
17 Stone sill
18 Solid oak panelling
19 Painted skim finish
20 Insulation
21 Reinforced concrete
 wall
22 Insulation
23 Damp proof course
24 Stone paving
25 Painted timber
 skirting
26 Carpet on underlay
27 Sand cement screed
28 Insulation

1.115
Glass Wall Detail 1:10

diederendirrix
Villa PPML [21]

1 Cast in-situ reinforced concrete floor slab
2 Stucco skim coat ceiling finish
3 20 x 20 mm (3/4 x 3/4 inch) aluminium U-profile glazing section
4 Fixed glazing
5 20 x 30 mm (3/4 x 1 1/5 inch) aluminium profile glazing section
6 Fasteners for U-profile glazing section
7 Trowel finish to floor
8 Base for U-profile fasteners
9 Cement screed
10 12.5 mm (1/2 inch) gypsum board
11 Exterior grade stucco to external wall
12 Cast in-situ reinforced concrete floor slab
13 Timber framing for mounting gypsum board
14 Corner bead stucco protector
15 Stucco soffit lining
16 Steel column
17 12.5 mm (1/2 inch) gypsum board
18 Insulation between timber slats
19 Timber framing for mounting gypsum board
20 67 x 139 mm (2 2/3 x 5 1/2 inch) timber door frame
21 Insulated double glazing

1.116
External Wall Detail 1:10

ODOS Architects
House in Wicklow [18]

1 Profiled metal drip
2 Fire-rated 4.8kg granular surfaced polyester reinforced APP modified bitumen high performance membrane, fully torch bonded
3 Packing timbers
4 Vapour barrier
5 Silicone based paint finish to external walls on cement based mineral render on insulation system
6 Steel beam
7 12.5 mm (1/2 inch) plasterboard, skimmed and painted
8 Two layers of 80 mm (3 1/8 inch) Thermo Hemp insulation
9 12 mm (1/2 inch) softwood skirting, painted square edge, set flush with a 10 mm (3/8 inch) shadow gap to wall finish
10 70 mm (2 3/4 inch) ground and polished concrete screed on 59 mm (2 3/8 inch) powerfloated in-situ concrete screed containing underfloor heating conduits on vapour control layer with taped overlaps at all junctions
11 Perimeter insulation
12 50 mm (2 inch) insulation on solid block and plank ceiling spanning between steel beams
13 Packing timbers
14 Structural steel beam

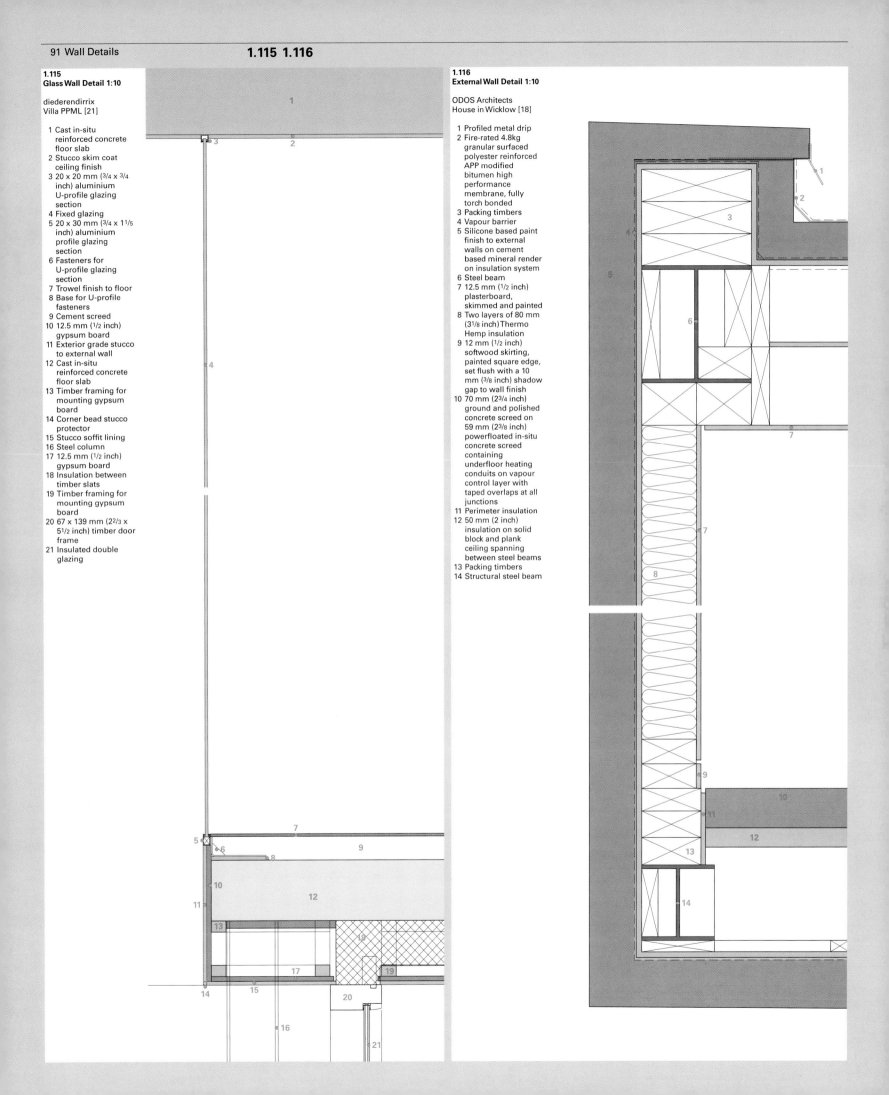

1.117
External Wall Detail 1:10

Room 11
Kingston House [34]

1 Crushed rock
  drainage layer,
  minimum 300 mm
  (11⁴/5 inch) wide
2 Core-filled concrete
  block wall
3 Concrete fill to
  concrete blocks
4 Bituminous
  waterproof
  membrane tanking
5 Timber batten fixed
  to concrete block wall
6 Celery top pine
  cladding
7 In-situ concrete wall
  with rough sawn
  timber formwork
8 Top soil
9 Steel reinforcement
  at 400 mm (15³/4

inch) centres
10 Waterproof seal to
  concrete wall
11 20 mm (³/4 inch) blue
  metal stone drainage
  layer
12 120 mm (4³/4 inch)
  minimum thickness
  concrete slab laid to
  fall to 70 mm (2³/4
  inch) edge with
  reinforcing bars at
  400 mm (15³/4 inch)
  centres into footing
13 Damp proof
  membrane
14 Rock edge
15 300 x 600 mm (11⁴/5 x
  23⁷/5 inch) concrete
  footing
16 Agricultural drain

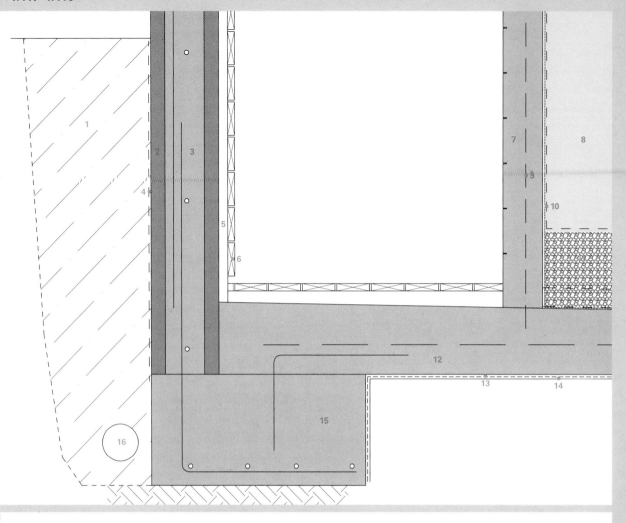

1.118
Wall Detail 1:10

Scott Tallon Walker
Architects
Fastnet House [25]

1 Reinforced concrete
  roof slab
2 Insulation
3 Ceiling hangers
4 Painted skim finish
  on moisture resistant
  plasterboard
5 Ceiling support
  fixings
6 Powder-coated slot
  diffuser
7 Slot diffuser frame
8 Mechanical supply
  duct
9 Painted skim finish
  on moisture resistant
  plasterboard
10 Mastic sealant
11 Concrete block wall
12 Plaster finish

13 Hanger to suspended
  ceiling frame
14 Channel to
  suspended ceiling
  frame
15 Closer channel to
  suspended ceiling
  frame
16 Cedar battens secret
  fixed to bearer
17 Vertical timber bearer
18 Tiled skirting
19 Tiled floor
20 Sand-cement topping
  with underfloor
  heating
21 Perimeter insulation
  strip
22 Grounds
23 Secret fixed cedar
  timber lining to
  sauna

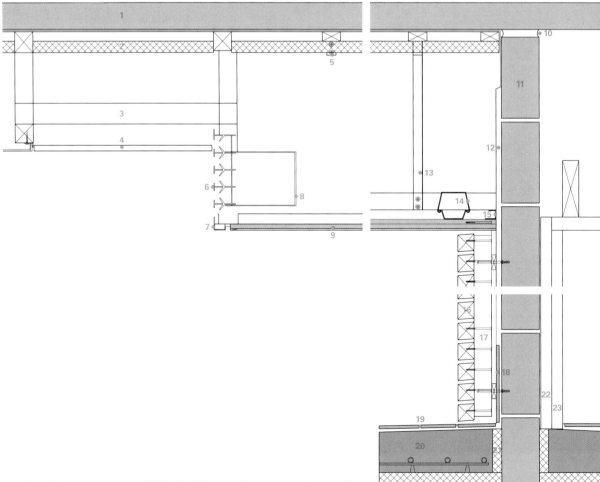

1.119
Patio Wall Detail 1:5

Bercy Chen Studio
Riverview Gardens [38]

1 8 mm (3/8 inch)
polygal on two layers
bubble wrap
2 16 mm (2/3 inch)
polygal on two layers
of bubble wrap on 50
x 100 mm (2 x 4 inch)
timber stud framing
3 20 mm (3/4 inch)
Indian sandstone
flooring
4 28 mm (11/10 inch)
plywood subfloor
5 Structural steel
channel
6 20 mm (3/4 inch)
plywood blocking
Ramset-fastened to
steel
7 Structural steel joist
8 Shear tab

9 Fibreglass pan
wrapped 50 mm (2
inch) minimum
above surface of
sandstone
10 20 mm (3/4 inch) thick
Indian sandstone
flooring
11 Fibreglass pan under
sandstone

1.120
Section and Plan Detail
of Beam Hanger 1:5

The Miller Hull
Partnership
Chuckanut Drive
Residence [31]

1 12 mm (1/2 inch)
plywood sheathing
2 115 x 40 mm (41/2 x
15/8 inch) timber stud
3 Cement board
cladding over
building paper on 8
mm (3/8 inch) firring
4 12 mm (1/2 inch)
painted gypsum
board wall lining
5 Timber skirting
6 20 mm (3/4 inch)
timber floor
7 12 mm (1/2 inch)
sound board
8 20 mm (3/4 inch)
plywood

9 130 x 340 mm (51/8 x
131/2 inch) glulam
beam
10 Joists bolted to
painted steel joist
hangers by three 12
mm (1/2 inch)
diameter bolts
11 Pre-finished metal
drip to match
windows
12 Timber trim
13 Aluminium clad
windows
14 200 x 75 mm (8 x 3
inch) timber joists
15 Prefinished metal
column wrap
16 150 x 150 mm (6 x 6
inch) timber post
17 Beam hangers
18 Self-adhered
membrane

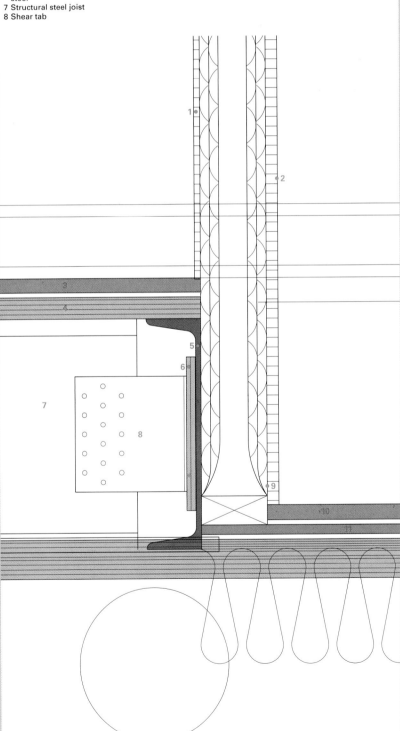

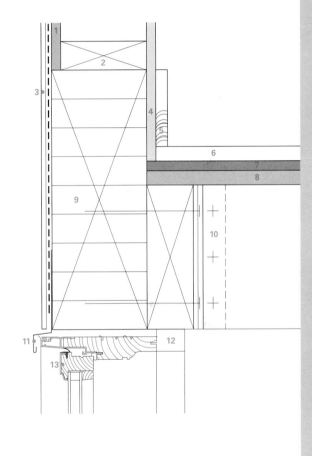

2 Floor Details

2.001 2.002

2.001
Floor Detail 1:10

Stam Architecten
Two Apartments [10]

1 Column beyond
2 Architectonic
  reinforced concrete
3 Polyurethane floor
  finish
4 Screed
5 Underfloor heating
6 Insulation
7 Reinforced concrete
  floor
8 Prefabricated
  concrete floor
  construction
9 Flashing
10 Brickwork pier

2.002
Floor Detail 1:10

Stam Architecten
Two Apartments [10]

1 Column beyond
2 Interior skin of
  brickwork
3 Insulation
4 Architectonic
  reinforced concrete
5 Plaster finish to sill
  and interior wall
  surface
6 Timber skirting
  board
7 Polyurethane floor
  finish
8 Concrete screed
9 Underfloor heating
10 Concrete downturn
  beam
11 Prefabricated
  concrete floor
  construction
12 L-shaped steel profile
  to window head

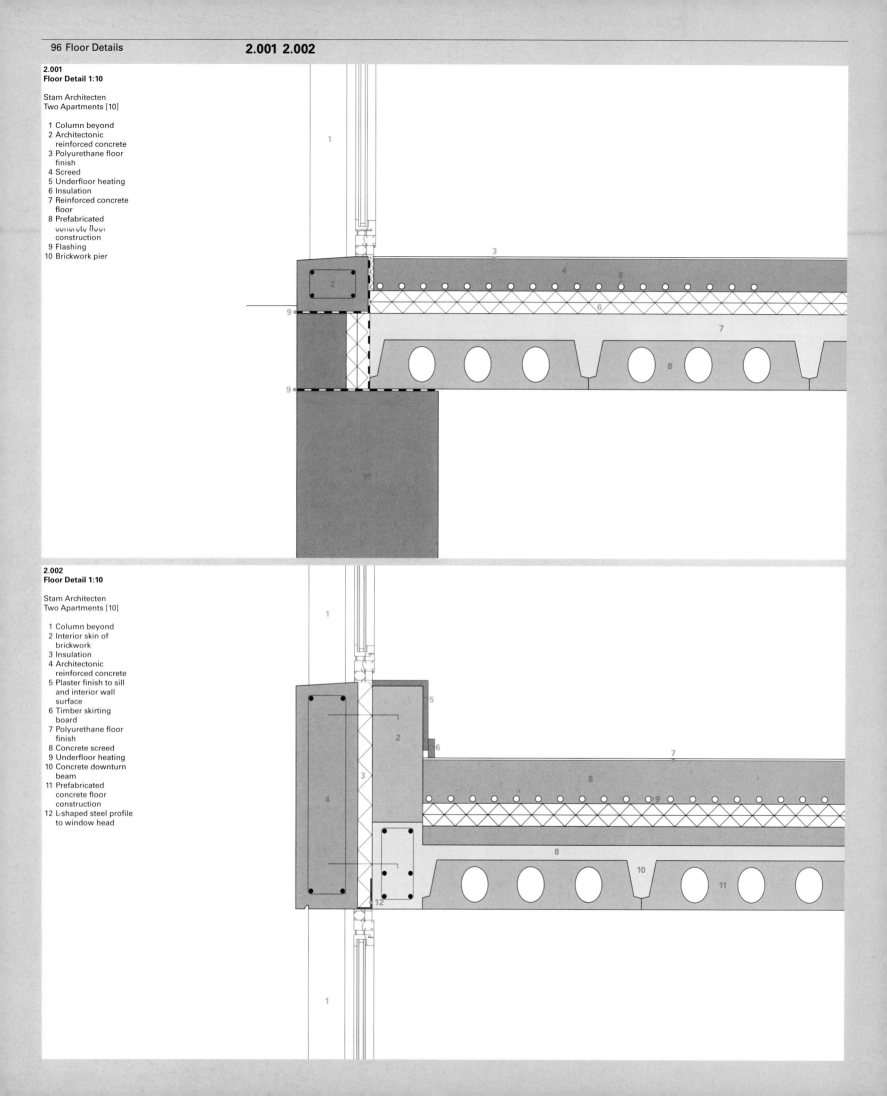

2.003
Footing Detail 1:10

Avanti Architects
Long View [35]

1 65 x 22 mm (2³/8 x ⁷/8 inch) tongue and groove weatherboards secret fixed vertically to horizontal counter battens
2 50 x 75 mm (2 x 3 inch) horizontal counter battens
3 90 x 60 mm (3¹/2 x 2³/8 inch) vertical battens
4 Breather membrane
5 12 mm (¹/2 inch) weather bonded and proofed plywood bracing
6 Insect mesh fixed to underside
7 Polyester

powder-coated heavy grade aluminium flashing
8 12.5 mm (¹/2 inch) plasterboard taped and skimmed
9 Vapour control layer fixed over timber studs and horizontal counter battens
10 150 mm (6 inch) insulation between timber studs
11 Timber skirting board
12 Tongue and groove parquet floor on 2 mm (¹/12 inch) non-woven fabric for tension reduction
13 22 mm (⁷/8 inch) aquapanel board on 30 mm (1¹/5 inch) pre-formed foam boards with heating pipes and radiation coating

14 50 mm (2 inch) insulation of extruded rigid foam on 8 mm (¹/3 inch) hard fibreboard
15 30 mm (1¹/4 inch) lightweight screed on 10 mm (³/8 inch) bituminous sheeting
16 225 mm (8⁷/8 inch) reinforced concrete slab
17 150 mm (6 inch) void
18 Horizontal damp proof course
19 215 mm (8¹/2 inch) blockwork
20 Two treated timber soleplates
21 Wall cavity vent hole
22 Fair-faced brickwork
23 Selected topsoil
24 Woven geofabric protects rock fill from soil ingress
25 Free-flowing granulated rock fill

26 100 mm (4 inch) diameter slotted drains to discharge to soaker pit
27 Free-flowing granulated rock fill
28 Foundation strip

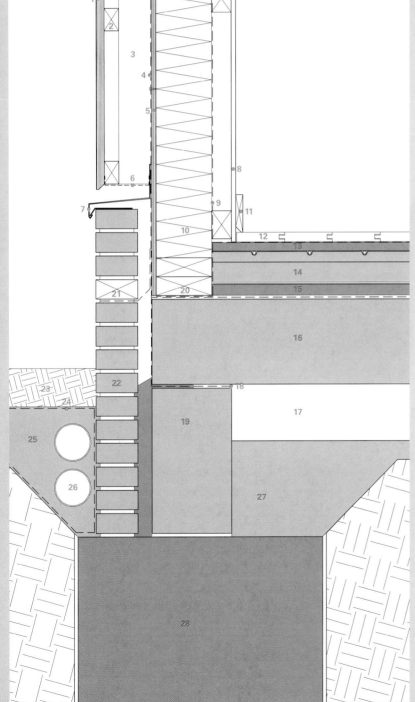

2.004
Footing and Floor Detail 1:10

EZZO
Leça House [35]

1 40 x 50 mm (1⁵/8 x 2 inch) timber profile on battens painted with polyurethane paint
2 10 mm (³/8 inch) waterproof medium density fibreboard painted with polyurethane paint
3 Double glazing unit

4 40 mm (1³/5 inch) polystyrene thermal insulation
5 Open timber frame painted with polyurethane paint
6 Timber profile
7 170 x 22 mm (6³/4 x ⁷/8 inch) pine wood flooring
8 10 mm (³/8 inch) steel bar for horizontal fixing structure
9 10 mm (³/8 inch) steel bar for vertical fixing structure
10 Drywall lining
11 Cement screed

12 Concrete rubble-work below threshold
13 Waterproof PVC screen
14 Concrete slab
15 Adjustment layer
16 40 mm (1³/5 inch) polystyrene thermal insulation
17 Concrete rubble fill
18 170 mm (6⁷/10 inch) concrete slab
19 Waterproof PVC screen
20 Stainless steel fixing bolts
21 Reinforced concrete

22 Existing granite wall

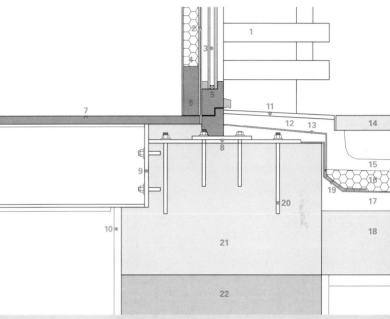

2.005
Floor and Wall Detail 1:10

EZZO
Leça House [35]

1 110 mm (4³/8 inch) brick wall skin
2 40 mm (1⁵/8 inch) thermal insulation
3 Sanded plaster
4 PVC screen
5 Treated pine floorboards
6 5 mm (¹/5 inch) steel bar for horizontal fixing structure

7 10 mm (³/8 inch) steel bar for fixing structure
8 40 x 40 mm (1⁵/8 x 1⁵/8 inch) steel angle
9 10 mm (³/8 inch) steel bar for vertical fixing structure
10 Stainless steel fixing screws
11 Reinforced concrete slab
12 Sanded plaster
13 Existing granite wall

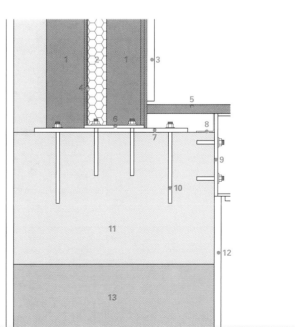

2.006
Floor Detail 1:10

Alphaville
Hall House 1 [07]

1 440 x 660 x 10 mm
(17 1/3 x 26 x 3/8 inch)
floor tiles
2 9 mm (3/8 inch)
structural plywood
3 12 mm (1/2 inch) floor
heating panel
4 12 mm (1/2 inch) layer
of structural plywood
5 50 mm (2 inch)
polystyrene foam
floor insulation
6 Fair-faced concrete
floor
7 50 mm (2 inch)
polystyrene foam
insulation

2.007
Floor Detail 1:10

ARTEC Architekten
Holiday House [39]

1 20 x 20 mm (3/4 x 3/4
inch) aluminium
bracket
2 72 mm (2 7/8 inch)
diameter zinced steel
thermionic radiator
3 Perforated sheet
metal
4 35 x 50 x 50 mm (1 3/8
x 2 x 2 inch) GRP
(glass reinforced
plastic) profile
5 27 x 92 mm (1 x 3 5/8
inch) timber slats on
two 60 x 60 mm (2 3/8
x 2 3/8 inch) scantling
screw-fixed, on two
10 mm (3/8 inch)
rubber strip on
Sarnafil T glued to
100 mm (4 inch) solid
wood board
6 I-section steel beam

2.008
Floor Detail 1:10

Donovan Hill
Z House [24]

1 9mm (3/8 inch)
toughened glass
2 Bi-fold door
hardware
3 Dressed spotted gum
hardwood timber
door frame
4 Dressed spotted gum
hardwood timber
fascia clear finished
5 Dressed spotted gum
hardwood timber
frame
6 9 mm (3/8 inch)
toughened glass
window
7 80mm (3 inch)
coloured concrete
topping slab
8 Reinforced concrete
structural slab
9 Silicone sealant
timber and backing
rod
10 Waterproof
membrane in
concrete bed
11 9mm (3/8 inch) fixed
toughened glass
12 70 x 45 mm (2 3/4 x
1 3/4 inch) dressed
spotted gum
hardwood timber
studs
13 Spotted gum
hardwood timber
decking
14 70 x 45 mm (2 3/4 x
1 3/4 inch) dressed
spotted gum
hardwood timber
joists
15 Dressed spotted gum
hardwood timber
frame
16 Nambucca
river-stones ballast
17 70 x 45 mm (2 3/4 x
1 3/4 inch) dressed
spotted gum
hardwood timber
bottom plate
18 Stainless steel
endless thread
19 Aluminium angle
(waterproofing)
20 Bitumen coated
waterproof
membrane
21 Face brickwork
biscuits
22 Precast concrete
ceiling panels as
permanent formwork
23 Reinforced core-filled
face brickwork

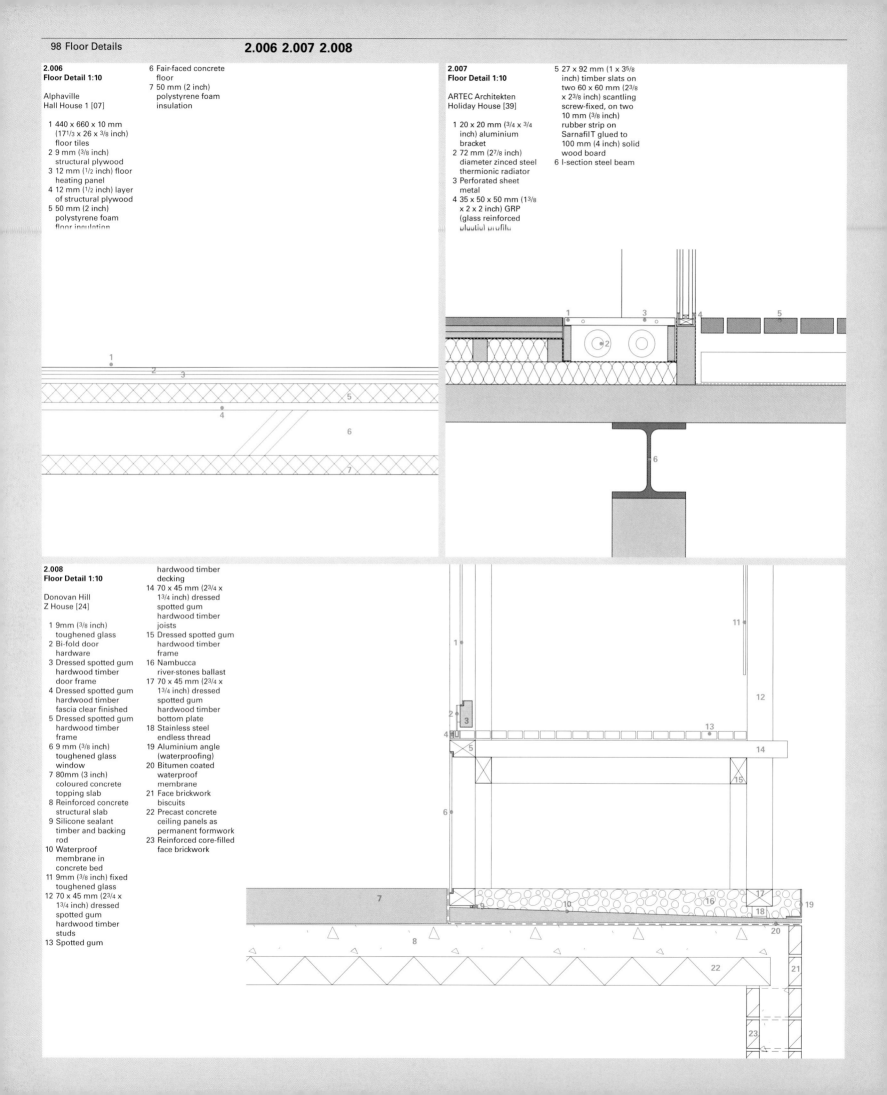

2.009
Floor Detail 1:10

Saunders Architecture
Villa Storingavika [40]

1 Canadian cedar
  cladding
2 50 x 50 mm (2 x 2
  inch) vertical battens
3 9 mm (1/3 inch)
  waterproof gyprock
  boarding
4 13 mm (1/2 inch)
  gyprock boarding
5 50 x 150 mm (2 x 6
  inch) bottom plate
6 21 mm (4/5 inch) oak
  timber floor
7 Water based
  underfloor heating
8 Subflooring

9 350 mm (13 3/4 inch)
  engineered floor
  joists
10 Bolt fixings
11 9 mm (1/3 inch)
  gyprock boarding
12 50 x 304 mm (2 x 12
  inch) edge boarding
13 Steel beam shoes
14 Spruce overlap
  cladding, stained
  black
15 25 mm (1 inch)
  timber battens
16 25 x 304 mm (1 x 12
  inch) edge boards

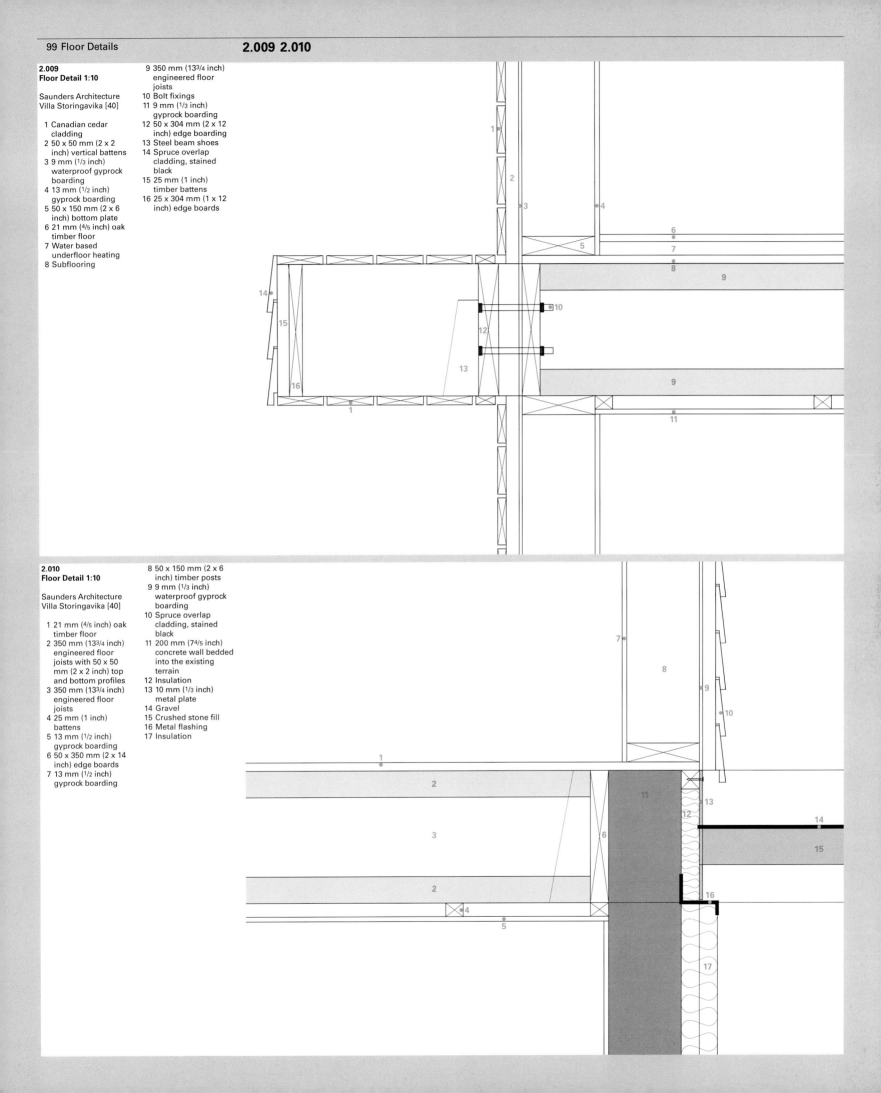

2.010
Floor Detail 1:10

Saunders Architecture
Villa Storingavika [40]

1 21 mm (4/5 inch) oak
  timber floor
2 350 mm (13 3/4 inch)
  engineered floor
  joists with 50 x 50
  mm (2 x 2 inch) top
  and bottom profiles
3 350 mm (13 3/4 inch)
  engineered floor
  joists
4 25 mm (1 inch)
  battens
5 13 mm (1/2 inch)
  gyprock boarding
6 50 x 350 mm (2 x 14
  inch) edge boards
7 13 mm (1/2 inch)
  gyprock boarding

8 50 x 150 mm (2 x 6
  inch) timber posts
9 9 mm (1/3 inch)
  waterproof gyprock
  boarding
10 Spruce overlap
  cladding, stained
  black
11 200 mm (7 4/5 inch)
  concrete wall bedded
  into the existing
  terrain
12 Insulation
13 10 mm (1/3 inch)
  metal plate
14 Gravel
15 Crushed stone fill
16 Metal flashing
17 Insulation

2.011
Mezzanine Floor Detail
1:10

BmasC Arquitectos
Mayo House [20]

1 Double air brick wall
   substructure
2 Rendered plaster
   finish to wall
3 Aluminium profile
   handrail capping
   anchored at both
   ends
4 Tempered glass
   balustrade
5 Aluminium channel
   profile to take glass
   balustrade anchored
   at both ends
6 Reinforced concrete
   edge beam
7 Timber skirting
8 Timber flooring
9 Timber battens
10 Semi-resistant joist

and small vaulted
slab
11 Coating

2.012
Floor and Footing Detail
1:10

BmasC Arquitectos
Mayo House [20]

1 Galvanized steel
   sheet
2 Interior plastered
   wall surface
3 Insulation
4 Perforated brick
5 Polythene waterproof
   coating
6 Double air brick
7 Steel fixings
8 Stoneware skirting
9 Stoneware flooring
10 Separation slip
11 Suspended ground
    floor
12 150 mm (6 inch)
    galvanized steel
    sheet
13 External tiled
    sidewalk

14 Reinforced concrete
   foundation
15 Moisture barrier skin
   over gravel stratum
16 Moisture barrier skin
17 150 mm (6 inch)
   porous concrete
   drainage tube
18 Base concrete
19 Blinding concrete

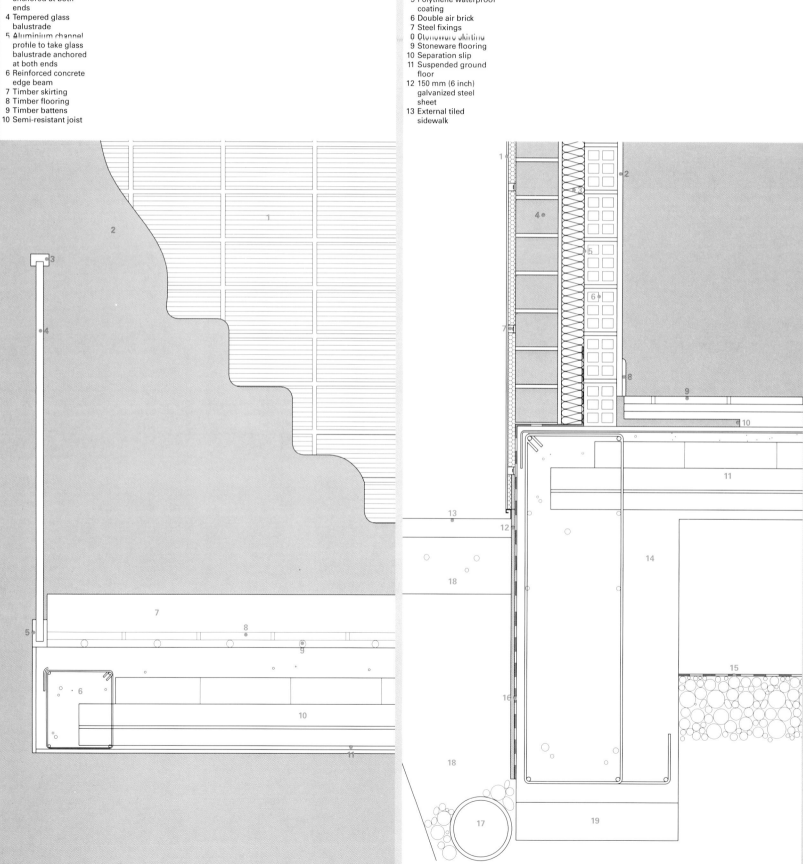

2.013
Floor Detail 1:10

ARTEC Architekten
Holiday House [39]

1 15 mm (5/8 inch)
    oriented strand
    board
2 27 x 92 mm (1 x 35/8
    inch) timber slats on
    two 60 x 60 mm (23/8
    x 23/8 inch) scantling
    screw-fixed, on two
    10 mm (3/8 inch)
    rubber strip on
    SarnafilT glued to
    100 mm (4 inch) solid
    wood board
3 280 x 30 mm (11 x 1
    1/5 inch) timber cover
    plate to terrace end
4 Steel edge plate
5 Metal bracket
6 Aluminium terminal
    strip
7 Moisture barrier lug

8 22 mm (7/8 inch)
    parquet birch floor
    glued to two layers
    16 mm (5/8 inch)
    placing boards on
    moisture barrier, 60 x
    120 mm (23/8 x 43/4
    inch) battens with
    120mm (43/4 inch)
    insulation between,
    on 100 mm (4 inch)
    solid wood floor
9 60 x 145 mm (23/8 x
    57/10 inch) bearer
10 220 x 220 mm (85/8 x
    85/8 inch) timber wall
    plate
11 Glued inserts
12 200 mm (8 inch)
    concrete wall
13 Bituminous sheeting

2.014
Terrace Floor and
Balustrade Detail 1:10

Morphogenesis
N85 Residence [08]

1 125 x 250 mm (5 x 10
    inch) hardwood
    member
2 80 x 18 mm (31/8 x 3/4
    inch) hardwood
    beading
3 12 mm (1/2 inch) thick
    toughened glass with
    ceramic frit
4 60 x 100 mm (23/8 x 4
    inch) teak wood block
    screwed to timber
    deck
5 External grade
    timber deck
6 Timber battens and
    counter battens
7 Cement concrete bed
8 20 mm (3/4 inch) thick
    external timber

9 25 x 25 mm (1 x 1
    inch) framework

2.015
Terrace Floor and
Balustrade Detail 1:10

Morphogenesis
N85 Residence [08]

1 40 x 40 x 6 mm (15/8
    x 15/8 x 1/4 inch)
    square hollow
    section column with
    10 mm (3/8 inch) teak
    panelling to all sides
2 Stainless steel nut
    and bolt with 25 mm
    (1 inch) head to
    support glass
3 12 mm (1/2 inch) thick
    toughened glass with
    ceramic frit
4 Four 6 mm (1/4 inch)
    thick tension wires
    attached to verticals
5 60 x 60 mm (23/8 x
    23/8 inch) snap plate
    on base plate
    screw-fixed to wood

block
6 Teak wood block
    anchored to cement
    concrete bed
7 50 x 30 mm (2 x 11/5
    inch) timber
    framework
8 Timber battens and
    counter battens
9 Cement topped
    concrete bed
10 20 mm (3/4 inch) thick
    external grade
    timber cladding
11 25 x 25 mm (1 x 1
    inch) timber
    framework
12 Reinforced concrete
    floor slab

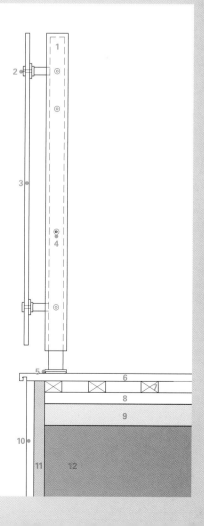

2.016
Internal and External
Floor Detail 1:10

Western Design
Architects
The Moat House [20]

1 Double glazed
thermally broken
aluminium frame
screen
2 Sill bedded on
gap-filling foam
sealant
3 Polyester
powder-coated
aluminium sill, with
ends of extrusion
capped at works
before fitting
4 Membrane to be
lapped under door
sill
5 25 x 100 mm (1 x 4
inch) treated timber
decking to bridge
6 50 x 50 mm (2 x 2
inch) treated timber
bearers at 400 mm
(16 inch) centres
7 Single ply membrane
bonded to concrete
base
8 100 mm (4 inch)
concrete base
9 Slate slabs on 50 mm
(2 inch) sand bedding
10 Permeable fill well
compacted in layers
11 Membrane dressed
down face of
concrete slab
12 100 mm (4 inch)
dense concrete block
13 Damp proof course
14 25 mm (1 inch) thick
insulation to floor
perimeter
15 Black rubber
expansion bead to
edge of floor

16 25 mm (1 inch) floor
covering
17 75 mm (3 inch) floor
screed incorporating
underfloor heating
18 75 mm (3 inch) floor
insulation
19 150 mm (6 inch)
concrete beam and
block floor

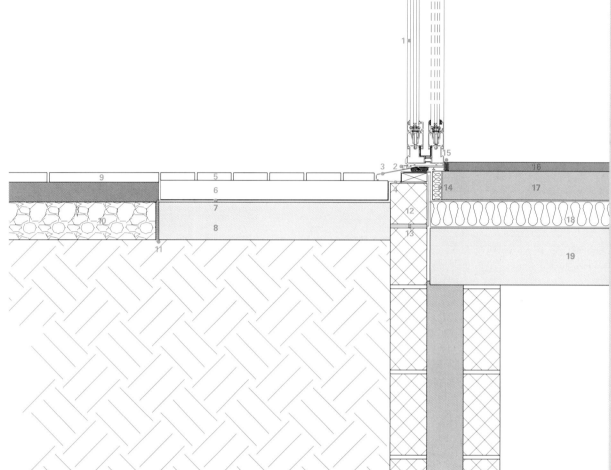

2.017
Internal and External
Floor Detail 1:10

Western Design
Architects
The Moat House [20]

1 Glass balustrade to
height of 1100 mm
(44 inches) above
finish floor level of
deck
2 Powder-coated
thermally broken
aluminium window
frame
3 Sill bedded on
gap-filling foam
sealant
4 25 x 100 mm (1 x 4
inch) treated timber
decking on 25 x 50
mm (1 x 2 inch)
treated timber
battens at 400 mm
(16 inch) centres
5 'P' trapped gully
outlets equally
spaced along
balcony
6 Single ply membrane
dressed down
behind glass
balustrade
7 25 mm (1 inch) thick
exterior quality
plywood shot-fired to
steelwork
8 White powder-coated
galvanized steel
apron to balustrade
configuration with
countersunk
stainless steel fixings
in uniform
connections
9 200 x 90 mm (8 x 3$^1/_2$
inch) parallel flange
channel
10 20 mm ($^3/_4$ inch)
polymer reinforced

through colour
render
11 Renderlath panel
with stainless steel
mesh
12 Treated timber
battens
13 White soffit
ventilators at 900
mm (36 inch) centres
14 Powder-coated
pressed aluminium
flashing and drip
15 204 x 146 mm (8 x
5$^3/_4$ inch) universal
beam at 900 mm (36
inch) centres
16 Timber blocking
piece
17 Black rubber
expansion bead to
edge of floor
18 25 mm (1 inch) floor
covering
19 25 mm (1 inch) thick
insulation to floor
perimeter
20 75 mm (3 inch)
screed incorporating
underfloor heating
21 203 x 203 mm (8 x 8
inch) universal
column
22 125 mm (5 inch) thick
insulation
23 50 mm (2 inch) floor
insulation
24 150 mm (6 inch)
concrete beam and
block floor
25 12.5 mm ($^1/_2$ inch)
plasterboard ceiling
26 Ceiling edge
insulation, to
minimize cold bridge,
between 50 x 50 mm
(2 x 2 inch) timber
ceiling battens
27 Roller blind in recess

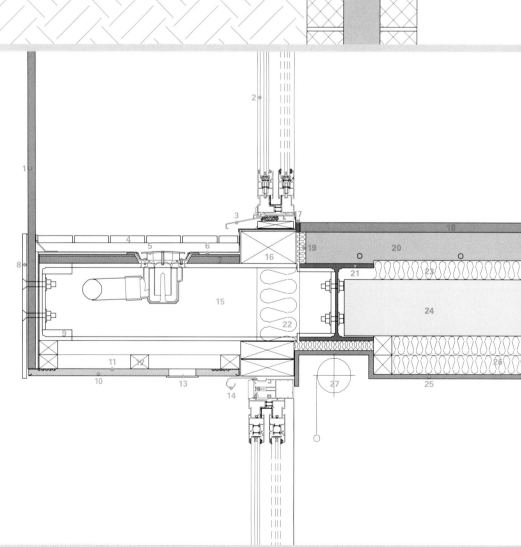

2.018
Floor Detail 1:20

Hertl Architekten
Krammer House [19]

1 60 mm (2³/8 inch) heating floor screed with sealed finish
2 Foil layer
3 25 mm (1 inch) impact sound insulation
4 Cement concrete fill
5 15 mm (⁵/8 inch) oriented strand board
6 240 mm (9¹/2 inch) timber beams with insulation between
7 22 mm (⁷/8 inch) oriented strand board on wind barrier
8 Timber battens
9 Eternit fixed to timber battens and counter battens
10 Plaster wall finish
11 Reinforced concrete beam
12 Rigid insulation
13 Existing masonry wall
14 540 x 50 mm (21¹/2 x 2 inch) timber joists with insulation between
15 Insulation
16 Oriented strand board
17 20 mm (³/4 inch) plasterboard ceiling
18 Reinforced concrete steps
19 Acoustic insulation

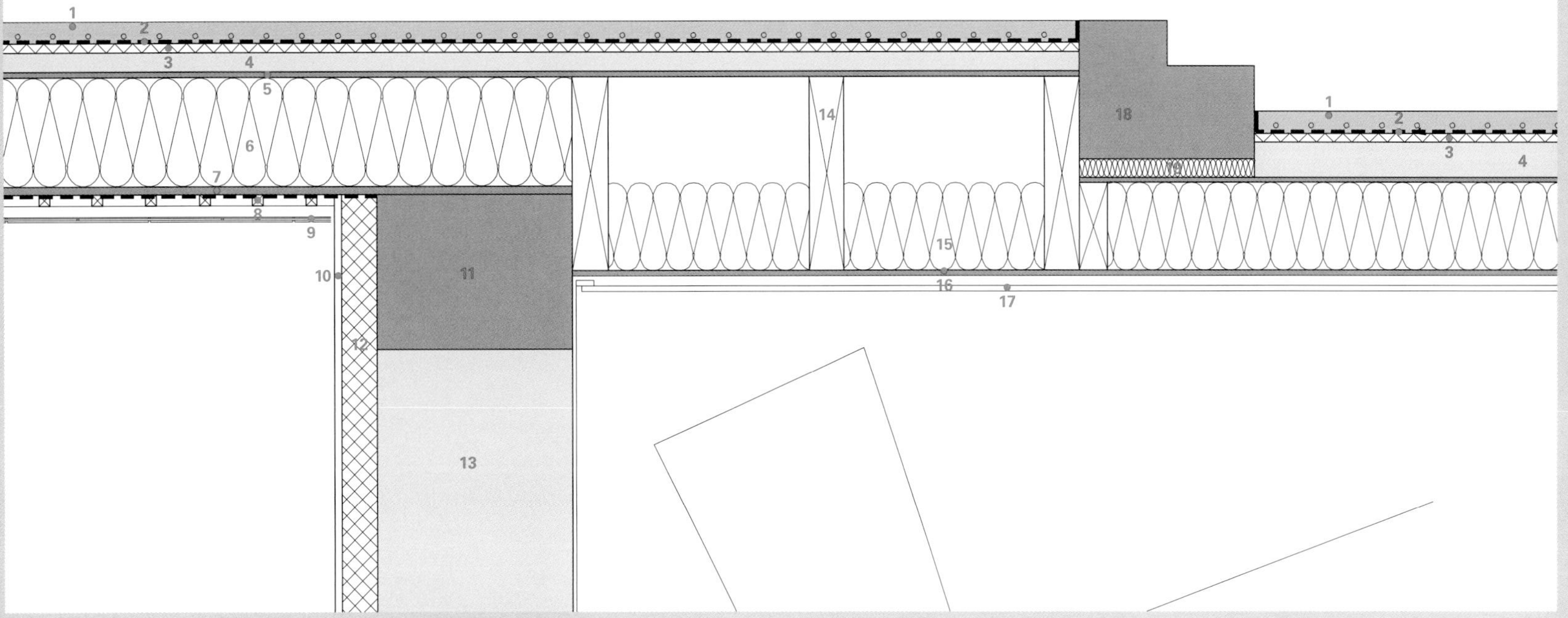

2.019
Footing Detail 1:20

Ibarra Rosano Design Architects
Winter Residence [23]

1 Track channels spaced 12.5 mm (¹/2 inch) apart
2 125 x 125 x 8 mm (5 x 5 x ⁵/16 inch) angle mitred and welded at corners
3 100 mm (4 inch) x 12.5 mm (¹/2 inch) diameter HSA (High Strength Austenitic) steel bolts at 400 mm (16 inch) centres
4 Diagonal bottom steel reinforcing bar
5 125 mm (5 inch) thick reinforced concrete slab
6 200 mm (8 inch) CMU (concrete masonry unit) wall with reinforcing bars at 600 mm (24 inch) centres with solid grouting
7 Geotextile fabric
8 Pea gravel
9 Stucco finish with waterproofing below grade
10 Engineered back fill
11 100 mm (4 inch) diameter PVC drain pipe
12 Reinforcing bars at 400 mm (16 inch) centres, with 750 mm (30 inch) overlaps with vertical reinforcing
13 Continuous reinforcing bars

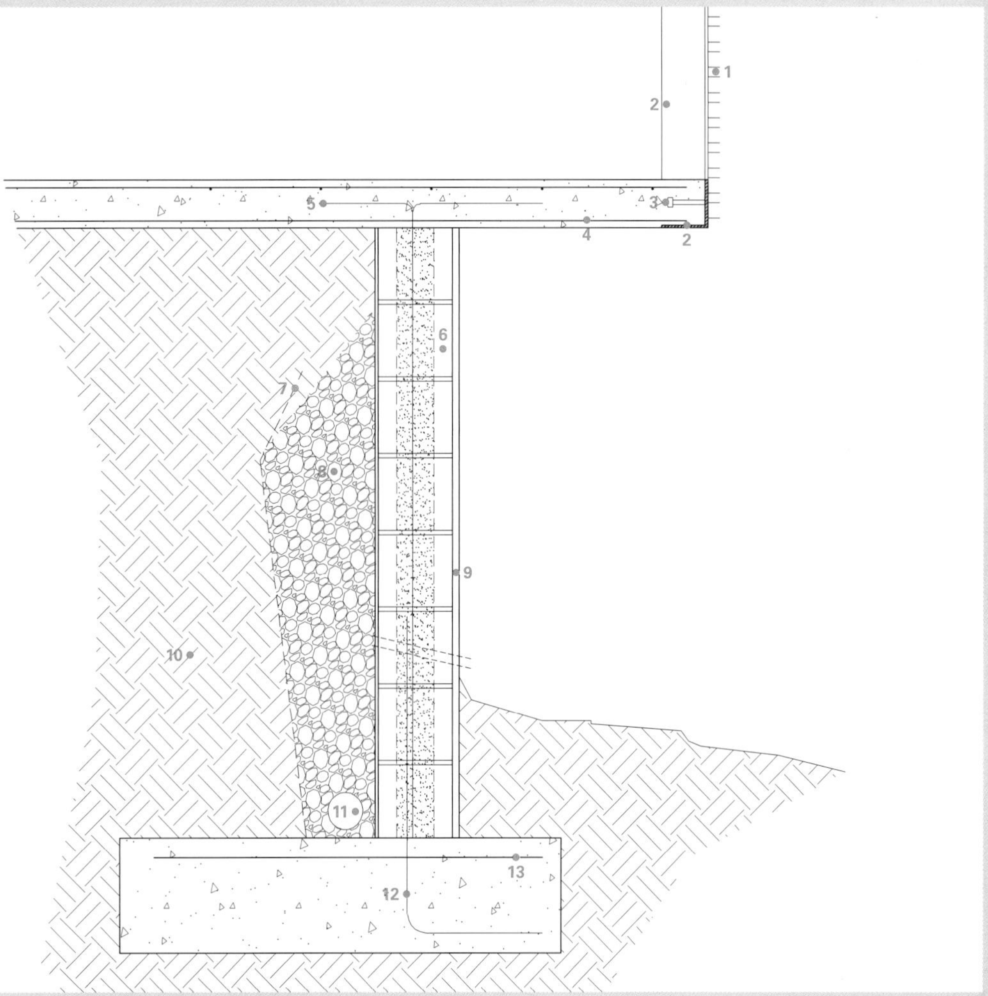

2.020
Floor and Footing Detail
1:5

Correia Ragazzi
Arquitectos
Casa no Gerês [06]

1 Double glazing
comprised of 10 mm
($2/5$ inch) glass, 8 mm
($3/10$ inch) air gap and
6 mm ($1/4$ inch) glass
2 Aluminium window
frame
3 Aluminium window
sub-frame
4 35 x 15 mm ($13/8$ x $5/8$

inch) aluminium
channel
5 Resin based flooring
6 Screed
7 Filling
8 Bitumen membrane
9 Insulation
10 Tempered concrete
11 20 x 20 mm ($3/4$ x $3/4$
inch) aluminium
angle
12 Isolation barrier
13 Gravel bed
14 Drainage pipe
15 Sand layer

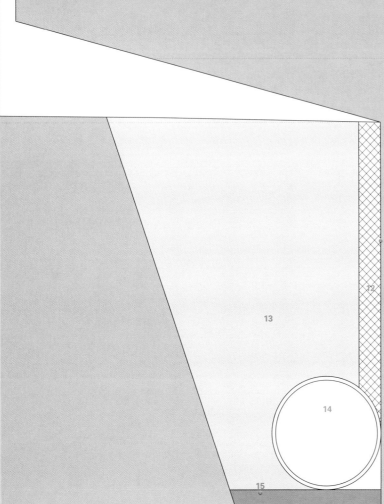

2.021
Floor Detail 1:10

David Nossiter
Architects
Kitsbury Road House
[13]

1 Timber floor
2 Timber joists
3 Timber upstand to
match floor
4 Brushed metal edge
bead
5 Insulation
6 Vapour barrier
7 Underfloor heating
pipes within screed

8 Sand and cement
screed on separating
layer
9 Basalt flooring
10 Damp proof
membrane
11 20 mm ($3/4$ inch)
insulation as
movement joint
12 Reinforced concrete
slab
13 150 mm (6 inch) well
compacted and
regularized hardcore
14 Existing footing

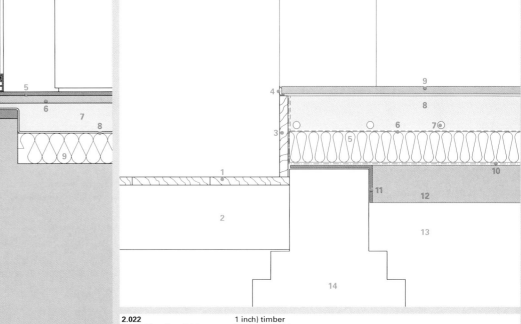

2.022
Stone Floor Detail 1:5

David Nossiter
Architects
Kitsbury Road House
[13]

1 12.5 mm ($1/2$ inch)
plasterboard
2 Vapour barrier
3 50 mm (2 inch)
insulation
4 25 mm (1 inch)
insulation
5 100 x 50 mm (4 x 2
inch) timber studs
with 25 x 25 mm (1 x

1 inch) timber
battens to hold
insulation in place
6 Basalt flooring
7 Sand and cement
screed on separating
layer
8 Underfloor heating
pipes within screed
9 Vapour barrier
10 Insulation
11 Damp proof
membrane
12 Reinforced concrete
slab with 150 mm (6
inch) well compacted
and regularized
hardcore below

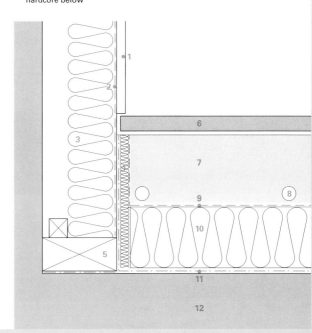

2.023
**External Wall and
Footing Detail 1:10**

de Blacam and Meagher
Architects
Morna Valley Residence
[20]

1 Sand and cement
  render
2 120 mm (4³/4 inch)
  terracotta blocks
3 Extruded polystyrene
  insulation
4 Cavity
5 60 mm (2³/8 inch)
  terracotta blocks
6 100 x 20 mm (4 x ³/4
  inch) white Ibiza
  marble skirting
7 600 x 400 x 20 mm
  (24 x 16 x ³/4 inch)
  white Ibiza marble
  tile
8 20 mm (³/4 inch) sand
  and cement bedding

  mortar
9 80 mm (3¹/8 inch)
  screed with
  underfloor heating
10 Extruded polystyrene
  insulation
11 Damp proof
  membrane
12 Reinforced concrete
  slab
13 Damp proof course
14 Blinding
15 Hardcore fill
16 Reinforced concrete
  pad foundation
17 Filled hollow
  concrete blockwork

2.024
Floor Detail 1:33

OFIS Arhitekti
Alpine Hut [39]

1 200 x 200 mm (8 x 8
  inch) larch pillar
2 Window
3 Larch window board
4 Timber window
  frame and sill
5 Larch timber deck
6 200 x 200 mm (8 x 8
  inch) larch beam
7 Cement render
8 100 mm (4 x 4 inch)
  insulation

9 Tiled flooring on
  rigid insulation
10 Reinforced concrete
  floor slab
11 Reinforced concrete
  wall and foundation
12 Damp proof
  membrane
13 Soil backfill
14 Drainage pipe

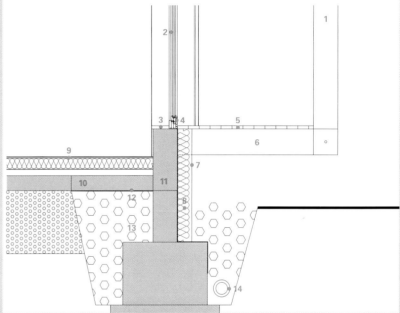

2.025
Floor Detail 1:33

OFIS Arhitekti
Alpine Hut [39]

1 200 x 200 mm (8 x 8
  inch) larch column
  with integral
  drainage
2 Double glazing
3 Brushed and oiled
  oak parquet flooring
4 Timber bearer
5 Timber window
  frame and sill
6 Larch fascia on
  battens

7 80 mm (3¹/8 inch)
  insulation
8 Larch cladding to
  facade
9 Reinforced concrete
  floor slab
10 20 mm (³/4 inch)
  timber cladding on
  thermal insulation
11 200 mm (8 inch) clay
  brick wall with
  thermal insulation
12 Natural local stone
  cladding

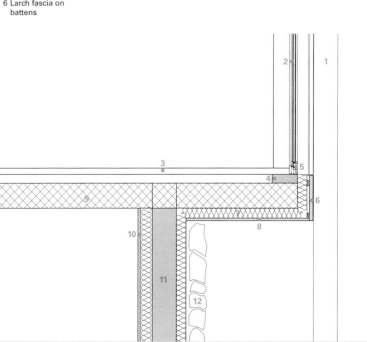

2.026
Floor Detail 1:5

Atelier Tekuto +
Masahiro Ikeda
Lucky Drops [13]

1 Steel stylopodium oil paint finish
2 60 x 19 mm (2¹/₃ x ³/₄ inch) steel plate
3 Steel nut with oil paint finish
4 Top flange to steel H-section
5 10 mm (³/₈ inch) porcelain floor tiles
6 5.5 mm (¹/₄ inch) plywood underlayment
7 12 mm (¹/₂ inch) electric panel heating
8 20 mm (³/₄ inch) particle board
9 36 x 45 mm (1³/₈ x 1³/₄ inch) timber floor joist
10 25 mm (1 inch) timber laminated sheet pile
11 200 x 100 mm (8 x 4 inch) steel beam
12 12 mm (¹/₂ inch) steel plate
13 Self-adhesive waterproofing sheet
14 Bentonaite solution
15 25 mm (1 inch) thick styrofoam insulation
16 25 mm (1 inch) thick gravel
17 60 mm (2³/₈ inch) crushed stone
18 Space for drain pipe

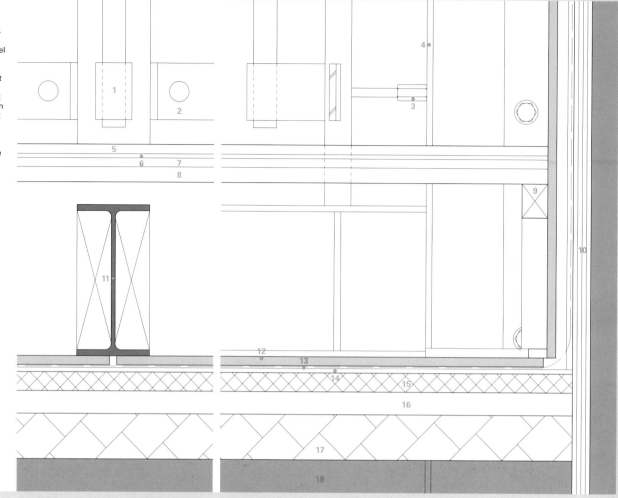

2.027
Terrace and Balustrade Detail 1:10

diederendirrix
Villa PPML [21]

1 115 mm (4¹/₂ inch) diameter steel column
2 Trowelled floor finish
3 Cement screed with underfloor heating
4 Cast in-situ reinforced concrete floor slab
5 Insulated double glazing
6 Insulation
7 Floor grate in gutter at sliding door openings only
8 Rainwater drainage through concrete terrace plateau
9 Cold bridge insulation
10 Rainwater drainage connection to stand pipe
11 Cast in-situ reinforced concrete wall
12 Air duct for delivery to heating system
13 Timber framing for mounting exterior stucco ceiling-lining
14 Brickwork to exterior of cavity wall
15 Void in prefabricated concrete terrace
16 Prefabricated concrete terrace plateau with non-slip surface
17 Suspended ceiling hangers
18 Timber fillets for attaching suspended ceiling
19 Fibre reinforced cementitious board with applied stucco
plateau for rainwater drainage connection
20 100 x 50 mm (4 x 2 inch) galvanized and painted steel angle
21 400 mm (15³/₄ inch) steel flat bar capping to end of terrace
22 Welded steel flat bars for attaching steel plate to prefabricated concrete terrace plateau
23 Cast in-situ fasteners for mounting
finish
balustrade
24 Galvanized and painted 150 mm (6 inch) steel plate balustrade support
25 Galvanized and painted 45 mm (1³/₄ inch) steel flat bar balustrade upright

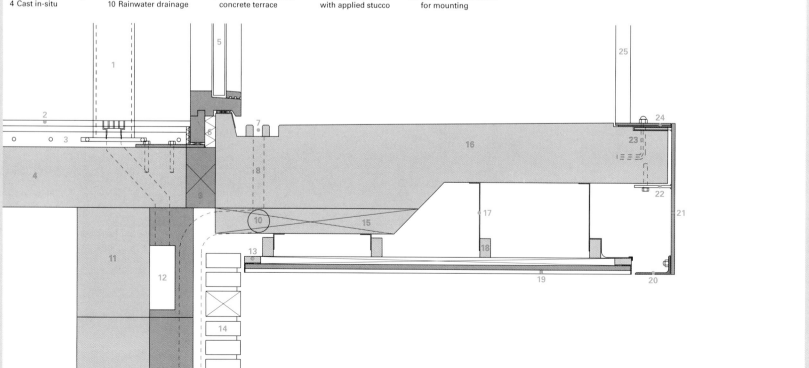

2.028
Floor Detail 1:2

Atelier Tekuto +
Masahiro Ikeda
Lucky Drops [13]

1 Expanding metal
 with oil paint finish
2 60 x 19 mm (2³/8 x ³/4
 inch) steel beam
3 Steel shopwork
 metal edge
4 Mitred steel corner

2.029
Floor Detail 1:5

Correia Ragazzi
Arquitectos
Casa no Gerês [06]

1 Aluminium sliding
 door frame
2 Line of wall beyond
3 Double glazing
 comprised of 10 mm
 (²/5 inch) glass, 8 mm
 (³/10 inch) air gap and
 6 mm (¹/4 inch) glass
4 Cantilevered
 aluminium framed
 floor construction
5 70 x 35 mm (2³/4 x 1
 ³/8 inch) aluminium
 channel
6 Silicone seal
7 Concrete screed fill
8 Drip groove
9 Resin based flooring
10 Screed
11 Filling
12 Bitumen membrane
13 40 mm (1¹/2 inch)
 Roofmate insulation
14 Tempered concrete

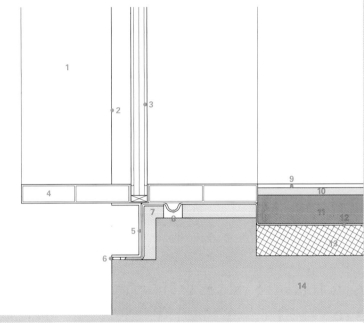

2.030
Floor Detail 1:5

Hampson Williams
Glass and Timber
Houses [33]

1 18 mm (7/10 inch)
 flooring finish
2 22 mm (7/8 inch)
 tongue and groove
 boards
3 50 mm (2 inch)
 proprietary
 underfloor heating
 insulation units
4 34 x 34 mm (1³/8 x
 1³/8 inch) tanalised
 timber battens
5 241 mm (9¹/2 inch)
 deep joists
6 100 mm (4 inch)
 Gypsum Isowool
 insulation
7 12.5 mm (¹/2 inch)
 taper edged
 plasterboard jointed
 and skimmed

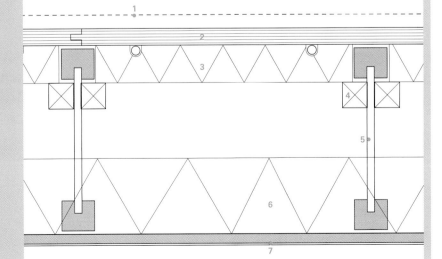

2.031
**External Floor Detail
1:10**

Designworkshop: SA
Igoda View House [24]

1 12 mm (¹/2 inch)
 armour plate glass
 grouted into stainless
 steel channel
2 50 x 110 mm (2 x 4³/8
 inch) purpose made
 stainless steel
 channel, epoxy fixed
 between support
 channels
3 25 x 100 mm (1 x 4
 inch) decking boards
 with 3 mm (1/8 inch)
 gap between boards
4 260 x 90 mm (10¹/4 x
 3¹/2) channel fixed to
 main beam and
 cantilevered at the
 ends
5 38 x 76 mm (1¹/2 x 3
 inch) continuous
 channel welded to
 100 x 50 mm (4 x 2
 inch) parallel flange
 channel to form
 internal gutter
6 Purpose made
 brackets welded to
 channel at joist
 centres
7 Galvanized rainwater
 spout
8 Parallel flange
 channel to form
 internal gutter
9 100 x 50 mm (4 x 2
 inch) timber bearer
 to support gutter
10 150 x 50 mm (6 x 2
 inch) timber joist
11 Waterproof
 membrane torch
 fixed to top side of
 shutter board
12 18 mm (³/4 inch)
 shutter board fixed to
 joists at maximum
 250 mm (10 inch)
 centres with 50 mm
 (2 inch) stainless steel
 countersunk screws
13 100 mm (4 inch) ipe
 timber joists bolted
 to flanges
14 12 mm (¹/2 inch)
 marine plywood
 fixed to joists at
 maximum 250 mm
 (10 inch) centres with
 40 mm (1⁵/8 inch)
 screws
15 203 x 133 mm (8 x
 5¹/4 inch) parallel
 flange I-section
 bolted to upper and
 lower support beams

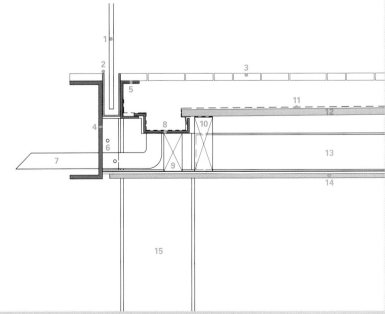

2.032 2.033 2.034 2.035

2.032
Internal and External Floor Detail 1:10

ThalerThaler Architekten
Z House [40]

1 16 mm (2/3 inch) laminated timber face to door with paint finish
2 Thermal insulation with vapour barrier to core of timber door
3 8 mm (1/3 inch) fibre cement sheeting
4 Steel angle
5 Weather strip to bottom of door
6 Soft impact sound insulation
7 Laminated timber beam
8 13 mm (1/2 inch) oak parquet flooring
9 70 mm (23/4 inch) floated cement screed
10 50 mm (2 inch) impact sound insulation
11 Reinforced concrete floor slab
12 Precast concrete step
13 100 mm (4 inch) gravel layer
14 Sealing layer
15 Compacted earth
16 80 mm (31/8 inch) thermal insulation

2.033
Floor Detail 1:10

ThalerThaler Architekten
Z House [40]

1 Sun-screen roller blind
2 Sheet aluminium capping
3 30 x 120 mm (11/5 x 43/4 inch) larch boards to balcony
4 Timber counter battens
5 Sealing layer
6 8 mm (1/3 inch) fibre cement sheeting
7 30 x 80 mm (11/5 x 31/8 inch) timber battens
8 Laminated timber beam
9 Rainwater gutter
10 8 mm (1/3 inch) fibre cement sheeting
11 Double glazing unit
12 Softwood door frame with paint finish
13 Softwood door frame with paint finish
14 13 mm (1/2 inch) oak parquet flooring
15 70 mm (23/4 inch) floated cement screed
16 16 mm (2/3 inch) oriented strand board
17 Soft impact sound insulation
18 20 mm (3/4 inch) thermal insulation
19 16 mm (2/3 inch) oriented strand board
20 Batt insulation
21 12.5 mm (1/2 inch) plasterboard on open boarding
22 8 mm (1/3 inch) fibre cement sheeting beyond
23 Softwood door frame with paint finish

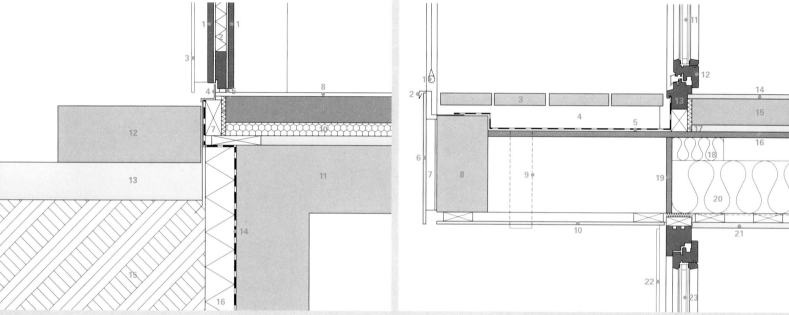

2.034
Floor Detail 1:10

Robert Seymour & Associates
The Riverhouse [22]

1 Oiled oak boarding on insect mesh on 38 mm (11/2 inch) treated softwood battens on breather membrane, fixed back to 18 mm (3/4 inch) waterproof bonded plywood fixed to 150 x 50 mm (6 x 2 inch) treated softwood vertical studs at 450 mm (18 inch) centres
2 Insulation between studs
3 12.5 mm (1/2 inch) plasterboard and skim on vapour control layer
4 150 x 15 mm (6 x 5/8 inch) medium density fibreboard skirting fixed to 50 x 50 mm (2 x 2 inch) treated softwood battens
5 Insect mesh
6 260 x 90 mm (101/4 x 31/2 inch) galvanized and painted parallel flange channel
7 Eternit board to soffit fixed to 50 x 50 mm (2 x 2 inch) treated softwood framing
8 Polyester powder-coated doors with sealed double glazing units
9 8 mm (1/3 inch) solid oak flooring on 18 mm (3/4 inch) plywood on 35 x 50 mm (13/8 x 2 inch) treated softwood battens with extruded polystyrene insulation with pre-routed channels incorporating underfloor heating
10 20 mm (3/4 inch) resin self-levelling screed on 100 mm (4 inch) blockwork floor spanning between concrete beam floor system
11 12.5 mm (1/2 inch) plasterboard and skim ceiling system suspended by strap angle sections
12 Damp proof course

2.035
Floor and Footing Detail 1:10

Robert Seymour & Associates
The Riverhouse [22]

1 Polyester powder-coated doors with sealed double glazing units
2 Bridge beyond
3 260 x 90 mm (101/4 x 31/2 inch) galvanized and sprayed parallel flange channel with 90 x 10 mm (31/2 x 3/8 inch) galvanized and powder-coated mild steel upstand
4 Single ply membrane on fleece lining, adhesive fixed to radon damp proof membrane bonded to concrete slab
5 Green slates with natural riven finish and sawn edge, to be laid on nominal 5 mm (1/5 inch) grey fluid cement based adhesive
6 600 x 400 x 15 mm (24 x 16 x 5/8 inch) thick green slates with natural riven finish with 4 mm (1/6 inch) joint laid on 75 mm (3 inch) screed
7 Underfloor heating system clipped to 75 mm (3 inch) rigid foam insulation on radon membrane bonded to 20 mm (3/4 inch) resin bonded screed on beam and block floor
8 Damp proof membrane taped over steelwork and dressed into door threshold

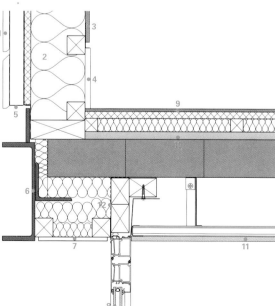

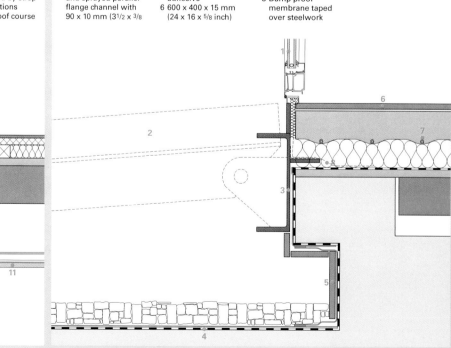

2.036
Glazed Floor Detail 1:10

Tony Fretton Architects
The Courtyard House
[13]

1 Double glazed aluminium sliding doors
2 Double glazed aluminium sliding door beyond
3 Outer frame to sliding door
4 75 x 75 mm (2⁹/₁₀ x 2⁹/₁₀ inch) steel angle frame upstand to support aluminium glazing
5 Stainless steel skirting
6 30 mm (1¹/₅ inch) hardwood flooring
7 75 mm (2⁹/₁₀ inch) foil faced rigid insulation
8 Steel floor beam
9 Steel connecting plate welded between flanges of steel beam
10 Exterior component of fire-rated walk-on double glazed floor unit with screen printed carborundum antislip finish
11 Interior component of fire-rated walk-on double glazed floor unit antislip finish
12 Stainless steel gutter with removable perforated stainless steel cover
13 Mild steel edge frame to double glazed units
14 Mild steel support angle to provide fall to glass
15 100 x 100 mm (4 x 4 inch) rectangular hollow section secondary steel
16 Mild steel support bracket
17 Painted plasterboard lining to roof light steelwork
18 Recessed light fitting
19 Approximate position of primary steelwork shown dotted
 beams to glazed roof light

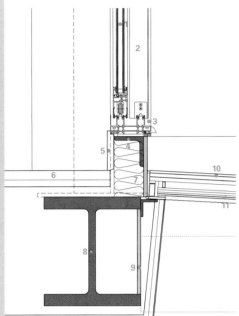

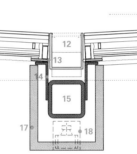
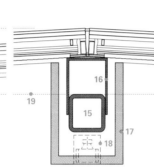
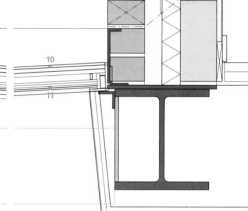

2.037
Floor Detail 1:5

Kengo Kuma & Associates
Steel House [27]

1 14 mm (¹/₂ inch) thick solid oak flooring
2 12 mm (¹/₂ inch) plywood
3 Steel support angle
4 40 mm (1³/₅ inch) styrofoam insulation
5 Removable inspection panel in flooring from 14 mm (¹/₂ inch) thick oak
6 Steel support angle
7 Stainless steel anchor bolt
8 40 x 40 mm (1⁵/₈ x 1⁵/₈ inch) steel L-angle
9 40 mm (1³/₅ inch) hollow polycarbonate sheeting to form Takiron 'Lume' wall system
10 Steel bracing for polycarbonate 'Lume' wall
11 20 mm (³/₄ inch) hard urethane spray foam insulation
12 3.2 mm (¹/₈ inch) hot dip galvanized vertical steel plate structure seen in section
13 3.2 mm (¹/₈ inch) hot dip galvanized vertical steel plate structure seen in elevation
14 Fluorescent light fitting
15 Fluorescent light transformer
16 160 mm (6¹/₃ inch) reinforced concrete floor slab
17 2.3 mm (¹/₁₀ inch) steel plate permanent concrete formwork
18 16 mm (²/₃ inch) reinforcing metal washer
19 75 x 75 mm (3 x 3 inch) steel angle
20 Mild steel bolt

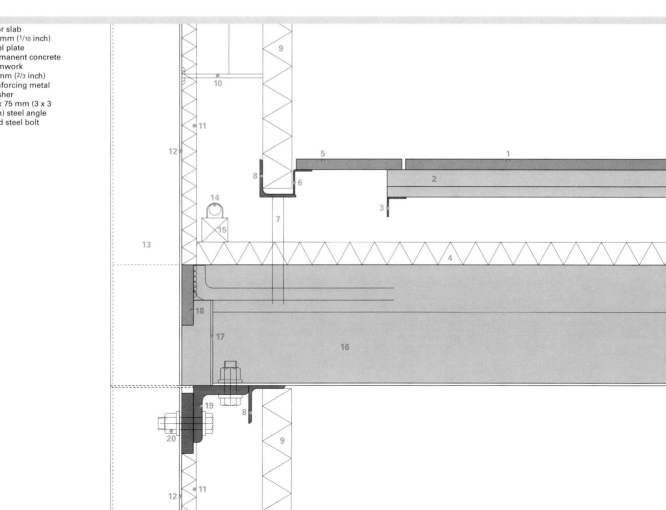

2.038
Floor Section Details
1:10

Johnston Marklee &
Associates
Hill House [22]

1 90 mm (3¹/2 inch)
poured concrete
2 50 mm (2 inch)
corrugated metal
deck
3 Top flange of beam
4 Timber nailer bolted
to bottom flange of
beam
5 Firring at 600 mm (24
inch) centres
6 16 mm (⁵/8 inch)
gypsum board
7 Hardwood floor
8 20 mm (³/4 inch)
plywood substrate
9 50 x 300 mm (2 x 12
inch) timber joists
10 Batt insulation
11 12 mm (¹/2 inch)
plywood substrate
12 Waterproof layer
13 Concrete slab on
grade
14 50 mm (2 inch) sand
bed
15 6 mm (¹/4 inch)
polyethylene film
16 Compacted soil base

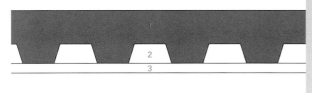

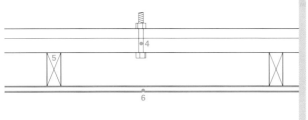

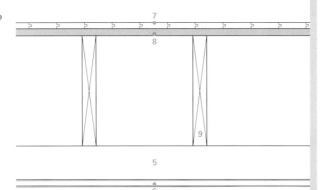

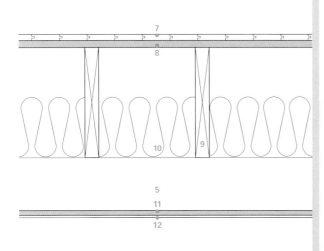

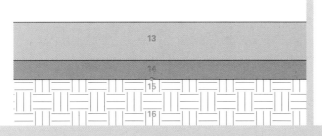

2.039
Cross and Longitudinal
Floor Section Details
1:10

Johnston Marklee &
Associates
Hill House [22]

1 Waterproof layer
2 15 mm (⁵/8 inch)
plywood substrate
3 Timber firring
elements at 610 mm
(24 inch) centres
4 19 mm (³/4 inch)
plywood
5 Two 254 mm (10
inch) timber joists
6 Batt insulation
7 Vapour barrier
8 15 mm (⁵/8 inch)
gypsum board lining

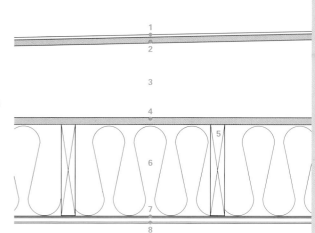

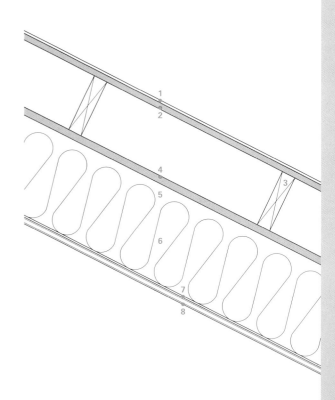

2.040
Internal and External
Floor Detail 1:5

Frank Harmon Architect
Low Country Residence
[26]

1 Double glazing unit
2 Storefront glazing
 frame
3 Flashing
4 Timber nailer
5 Air supply register
6 25 mm (1 inch)
 plywood sheathing
7 30 mm (1¼ inch)
 timber decking
8 Treated 50 x 240 mm
 (2 x 9 ⅖ inch) timber
 bearer
9 Two 50 x 300 mm (2
 x 11⅘ inch) timber
 floor beams
10 Batt insulation
11 6 mm (3/16 inch)
 galvanized steel plate

12 Treated 50 x 300 mm
 (2 x 11⅘ inch)
 continuous timber
 plate
13 15 mm (⅝ inch)
 anchor bolts at 1220
 mm (48 inch) centres
 with 150 mm (6
 inches) embedded in
 bond beam
14 Grout
15 Continuous
 reinforcing bar to
 grouted cavity
16 200 mm (8 inch)
 concrete bond beam
17 Water-based latex
 formulated
 waterproofing finish
18 200 mm (8 inch) thick
 concrete masonry
 unit wall with
 reinforcing bars at
 810 mm (32 inch)
 centres

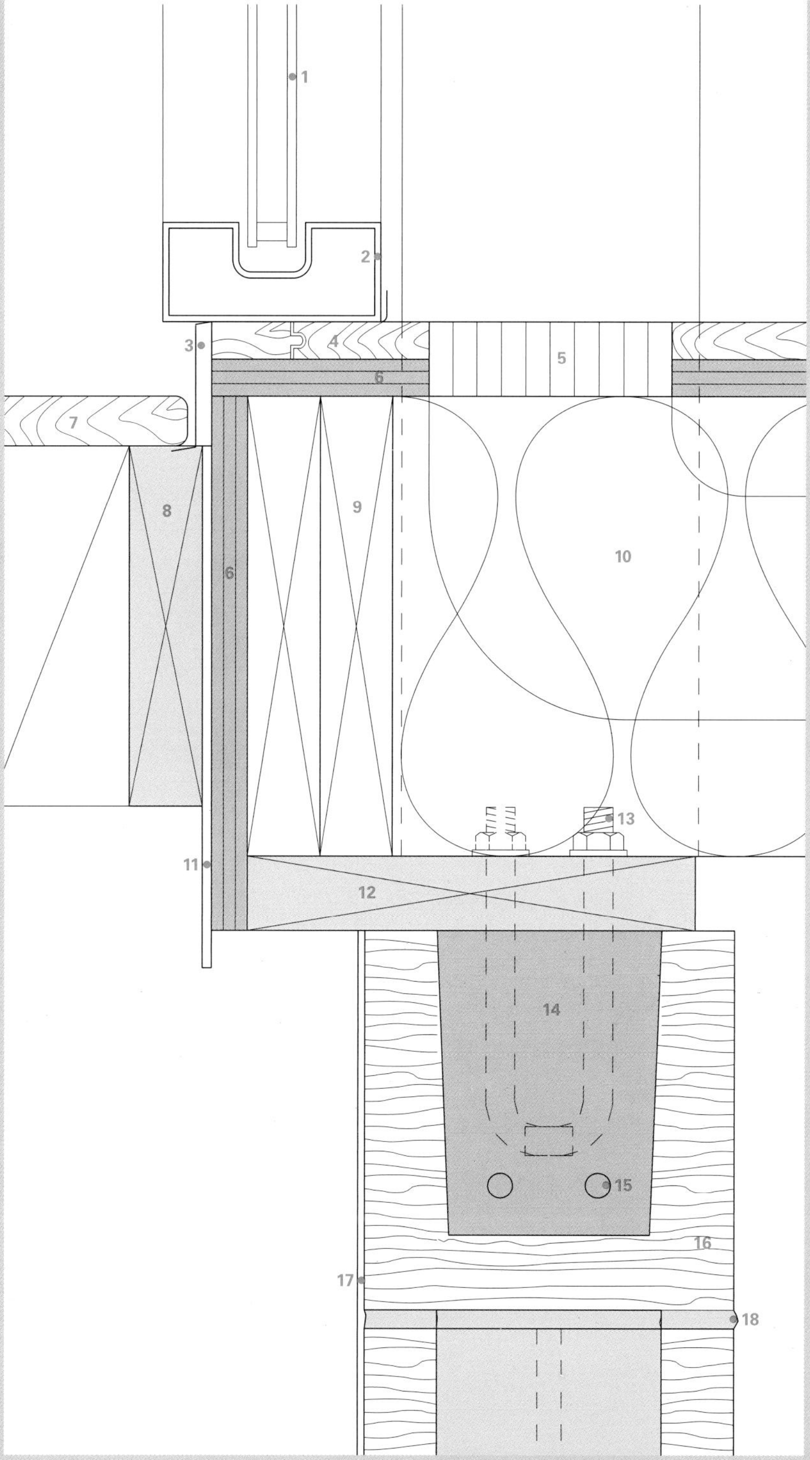

2.041
Interior Floor Detail at
Bridge 1:10

Marlon Blackwell
Architect
L-Stack House [35]

1 40 mm (1¾ inch)
 wide Brazilian
 redwood rainscreen
 screw fixed to
 battens at minimum
 800 mm (32 inch)
 centres with a 20 mm
 (¾ inch) gap
 vertically between
 each strip
2 EPDM (ethylene
 propylene dieme
 monomer) weather
 barrier for rainscreen
 application at wall
 substrate
3 Five ply waterproof
 exterior grade
 fir-faced plywood
 sheathing
4 Soy-based foam
 insulation
5 12 mm (½ inch)
 gypsum board with
 paint finish
6 25 x 100 mm (1 x 4
 inch) baseboard,
 grouted and painted

7 90 mm (3½ inch)
 tongue and groove
 Brazilian teak strip
 flooring over 20 mm
 (¾ inch) oriented
 strand board
 subfloor
8 50 x 150 mm (2 x 6
 inch) timber blocking
9 Soy-based foam
 insulation
10 19 mm (¾ inch)
 plywood sheathing
11 Joist hanger
12 50 x 150 mm (2 x 6
 inch) treated timber
 blocking
13 50 mm (2 inch)

vented soffit
14 400 mm (16 inch)
 open-web floor joist
15 Metal soffit panel
 over 12 mm (½ inch)
 plywood sheathing
16 Steel beam
17 Drip flashing along
 bottom of sheathing
 substrate
18 Two layers of 50 x
 100 mm (2 x 4 inch)
 treated timber studs
 on the flat at 812 mm
 (32 inch) centres

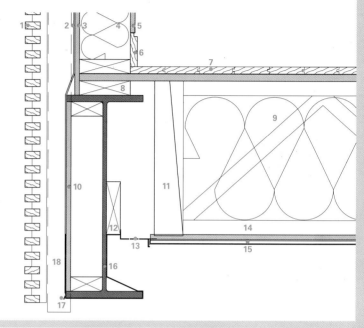

2.042
Exterior and Interior
Floor Detail 1:10

Marlon Blackwell
Architect
L-Stack House [35]

1 25 mm (1 inch)
 flamed black granite
 tiles over mortar bed
 on concrete slab at
 entrance porch and
 steps
2 100 mm (4 inch)
 structural concrete
 slab with thickened
 edge

3 Clean gravel over
 compacted fill
4 Custom shaped
 Brazilian teak
 threshold
5 44 mm (1¾ inch)
 thick solid core
 painted timber door
6 6 mm (¼ inch)
 painted steel plate at
 top and sides of
 windows and doors
7 25 x 150 mm (1 x 6
 inch) tongue and
 groove Brazilian teak
 strip flooring over
 timber sub-floor
8 Oriented strand

board tongue and
 groove 19 mm (¾
 inch) subfloor
9 50 x 100 mm (2 x 4
 inch) timber blocking
10 Concrete stem wall
11 Soy-based foam
 insulation between
 floor joists
12 350 mm (14 inch)
 floor joist at 400 mm
 (16 inch) centres
13 203 mm (8 inch)
 prefinished metal
 soffit panel over 19
 mm (¾ inch)
 plywood sheathing
14 25 mm (1 inch) rigid

perimeter insulation
15 Painted bituminous
 waterproof coating
 on side of concrete
 wall

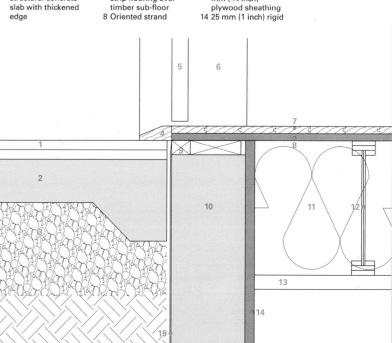

2.043
**Interior Timber Ceiling
and Terrace Balustrade
Detail 1:20**

Pezo von Ellrichshausen
Architects
Poli House [09]

1 Fixed double glazing
2 Aluminium frame
3 150 mm (6 inch) thick
  reinforced concrete
  slab
4 50 x 100 mm (2 x 4
  inch) pine bearers
5 25 x 100 mm (1 x 4
  inch) pine boards to

ceiling
6 20 x 20 mm (³/4 x ³/4
  inch) square hollow
  section steel
  balustrade painted
  white
7 30 mm (1¹/4 inch)
  mortar bed with
  water repellent
  coating
8 160 to 120 mm (6¹/4
  to 4³/4 inch)
  insulating concrete
  laid to fall
9 Steel roof structure
10 5 mm (¹/5 inch)
  bituminous sealing
  layer

11 Fixed double glazing

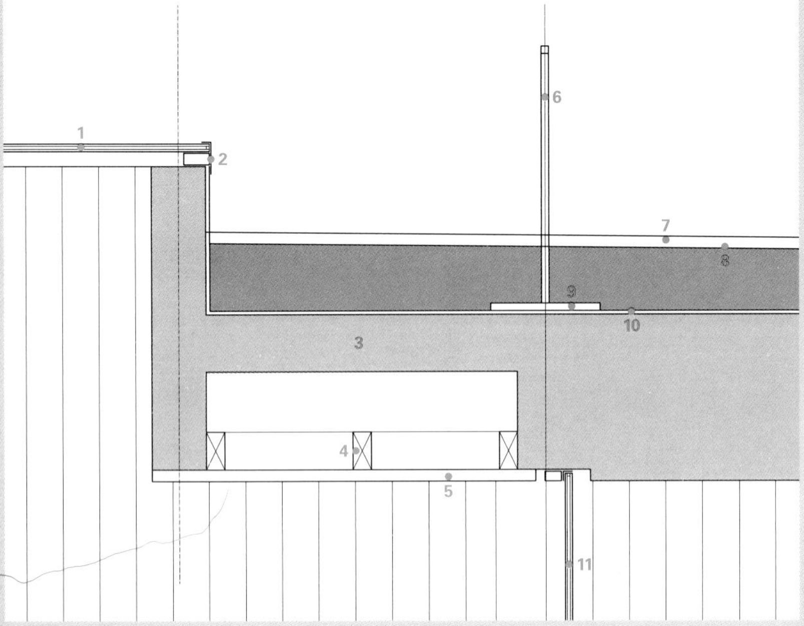

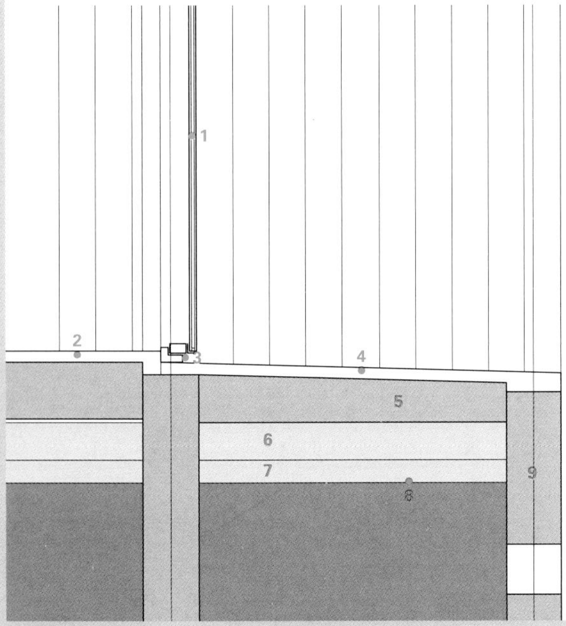

2.045
Floor Detail 1:10

Powerhouse Company
Villa 1 [15]

1 Glazing of 10 mm (³/8
  inch), 15 mm (⁵/8
  inch) and 8 mm (³/8
  inch) glass panels
2 3 mm (¹/8 inch) white
  polyurethane floor
3 50 mm (2 inch)
  concrete screed
4 50 x 30 x 5 mm (2 x
  1¹/4 x ¹/5 inch)
  aluminium angles
5 50 x 50 mm (2 x 2
  inch) timber blocking
6 Condensation
  channel
7 139 x 67 mm (5¹/2 x
  2³/4 inch) timber
  blocking
8 150 mm (6 inch)
  structural concrete
9 90 x 90 mm (3¹/2 x

3¹/2 inch) steel angle
10 100 mm (4 inch)
  insulation
11 250 mm (10 inch)
  concrete floor
12 250 x 250 x 25 mm
  (10 x 10 x 1 inch)
  stainless steel angle
  to support terrace
  floor
13 150 mm (6 inch) hard
  insulation
14 250 mm (10 inch)
  basement concrete
  wall
15 Rigid insulation

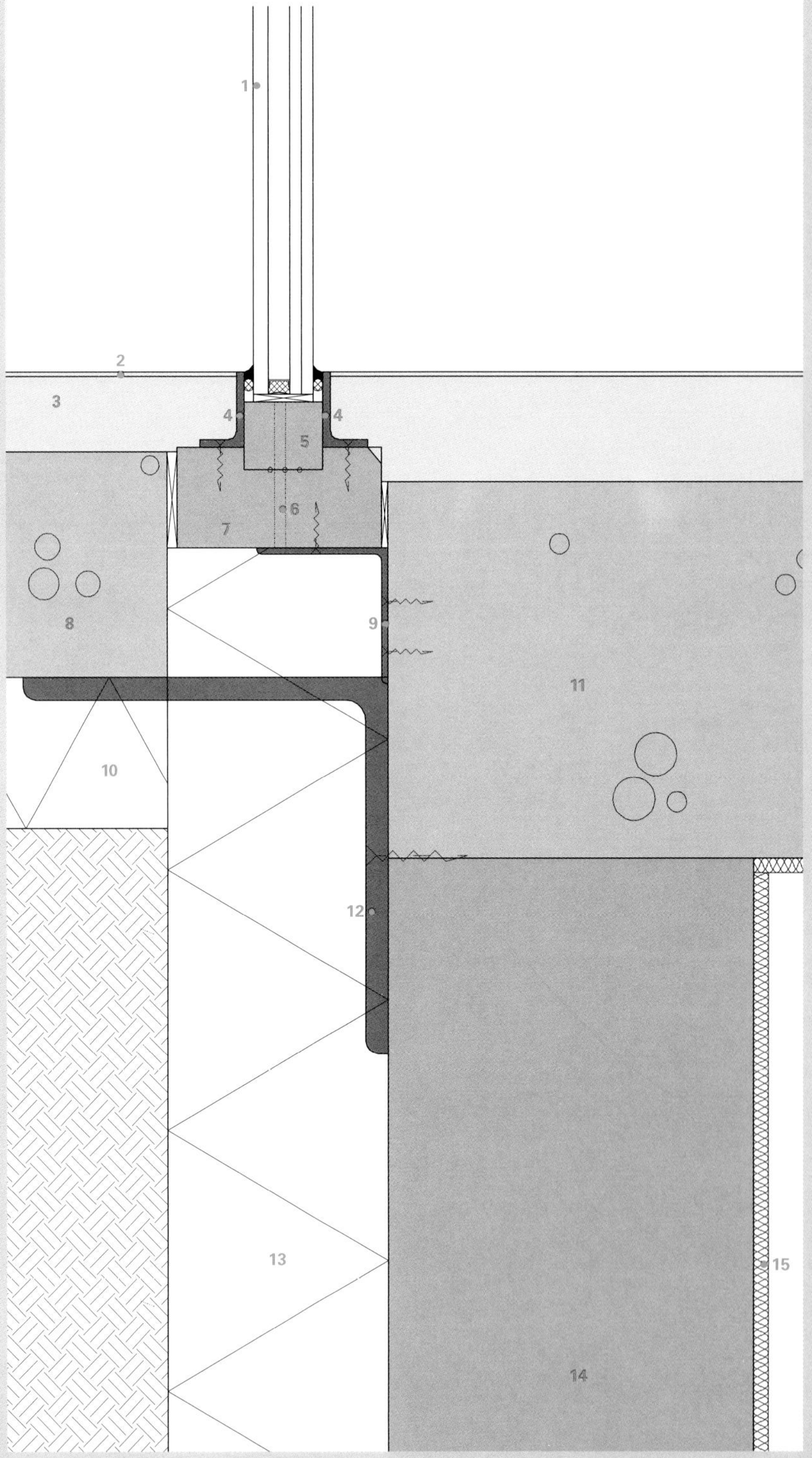

2.044
Balcony Floor Detail 1:20

Pezo von Ellrichshausen
Architects
Poli House [09]

1 Fixed double glazing
2 30 mm (1¹/5 inch)
  mortar bed
3 Aluminium window
  frame to fixed
  glazing
4 30 mm (1¹/5 inch)
  mortar bed
5 140 mm (5¹/2 inch)
  reinforced concrete
  slab

6 100 mm (4 inch)
  gravel bed
7 60 mm (2³/8 inch)
  consolidated soil
  layer
8 5 mm (¹/5 inch)
  sealing layer
9 150 mm (6 inch)
  reinforced concrete
  wall

2.046
Floor Detail 1:10

Room 11
Kingston House [34]

1 90 x 90 mm (3¹/₂ x 3¹/₂ inch) square hollow section welded to cast in plate, and where possible welded to beam below before pouring concrete slab
2 10 mm (³/₈ inch) Colorbond steel flashing to cover plywood
3 150 mm (6 inch) thick concrete slab allowing 70 mm (2³/₄ inch) cover over reinforcing
4 150 x 75 mm (6 x 3 inch) parallel flange channel

5 12 mm (¹/₂ inch) smooth stained boral evolution plywood, smooth over timber battens
6 180 mm (7¹/₈ inch) universal beam
7 12 mm (¹/₂ inch) smooth boral evolution plywood attached to underside of concrete slab via suspended 30 mm (1¹/₅ inch) aluminium firring channels with 50 mm (2 inch) bulk insulation
8 140 x 140 mm (5¹/₂ x 5¹/₂ inch) square hollow section steel column
9 250 x 250 x 10 mm (10 x 10 x ³/₈ inch) steel plate
10 Two 12 mm (¹/₂ inch) diameter steel ties, 300 mm (12 inch)

long and with 75 mm (3 inch) hook, set into concrete
11 450 mm (18 inch) diameter bored pier to rock

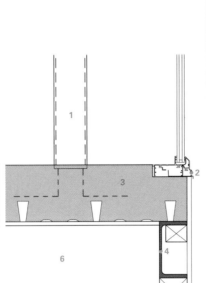

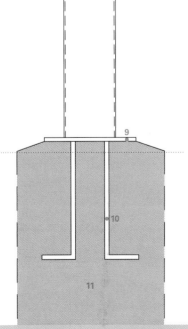

2.047
Internal and External Floor Detail 1:10

Tonkin Zulaikha Greer Hastings Parade House [26]

1 Timber framed glazed door
2 Existing reinforced concrete slab with existing timber floor
3 Universal beam with galvanized finish
4 66 x 19 mm (2³/₅ x ³/₄ inch) hardwood timber decking

continued to cover beam to fit flush with hardwood fascia
5 Mild steel joist hanger
6 140 x 45 mm (5¹/₂ x 1³/₄ inch) hardwood joists at 450 mm (18 inch) centres with fixed cleats spanning from existing wall to beam
7 Corrugated zincalume roof sheeting with fall fixed to suspended firring channels from joists

8 Outline of 50 mm (2 inch) half round zincalume gutter

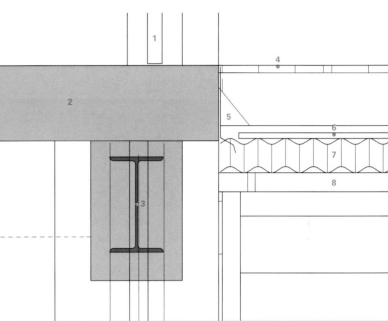

2.048
External Floor Detail 1:10

Tonkin Zulaikha Greer Hastings Parade House [26]

1 66 x 19 mm (2³/₅ x ³/₄ inch) hardwood timber decking continued to cover beam to fit flush with hardwood fascia
2 140 x 45 mm (5¹/₂ x 1³/₄ inch) hardwood joists at 450 mm (18 inch) centres with

fixed cleats spanning from existing wall to beam
3 Corrugated zincalume roof sheeting with fall fixed to suspended firring channels from joists
4 Outline of 50 mm (2 inch) diameter half round zincalume gutter
5 Glass balustrade fixed in 10 mm (³/₈ inch) fabricated steel plate supporter
6 2 x 10 mm (¹/₁₆ x ³/₈

inch) steel plate with galvanized finish continuously welded to beam for glass balustrade support
7 Steel cleat
8 Flashing
9 Timber packing
10 20 mm (³/₄ inch) hardwood fascia fitted flush with column and to cover all exposed sides of beam
11 Universal steel beam with galvanized finish
12 Outline of 150 x 150

mm (6 x 6 inch) hardwood column

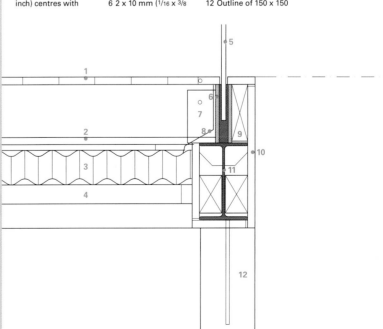

2.049
Floor Landing Detail
1:10

Jun Igarashi
Rectangle of Light [37]

1 2 mm (1/16 inch) tile
  on 24 mm (1 inch)
  structural plywood
2 Timber frame
3 105 x 105 mm (4 x 4
  inch) timber
4 20 x 20 mm (3/4 x 3/4

inch) timber battens
5 12.5 mm (1/2 inch)
  plasterboard
6 Plaster edge beading
  to form shadow gap
7 Desk top in natural
  finished spotted
  laurel
8 9.5 mm (3/8 inch)
  solid conifer plywood
  weatherboarding on
  battens with
  decay-resistant paint
  finish

9 Timber battens
10 Waterproof paper
11 Polyethylene film
12 12 mm (1/2 inch)
   insulation board
13 100 mm (4 inch)
   glass wool insulation

2.050
Interior and Exterior
Floor Detail 1:5

David Nossiter
Architects
Kitsbury Road House
[13]

1 Aluminium thermally
  broken window with
  flush threshold strip
  and continuous
  packer beneath damp
  proof membrane
2 Silicone sealant
3 Basalt flooring
4 Sand and cement
  screed on separating
  layer
5 Underfloor heating
  pipes within screed
6 Vapour barrier
7 Insulation
8 Damp proof
  membrane
9 Reinforced concrete
  slab and ground
  beam
10 100 x 75 mm (4 x 3
   inch) aluminium
   section
11 Profiled and treated
   timber decking,
   minimum 10 mm (4
   inch) wide with 7 mm
   (1/4 inch) gap
   between boards
12 Decking on 100 x 50
   mm (4 x 2 inch)
   battens at 450 mm
   (18 inch) centres
13 Uni-shims raised
   floor system on
   spacer feet
14 Steel drainage grille
15 Concrete coping with
   drip
16 10 mm (3/8 inch)
   protection board
17 Pre-cast concrete
   drainage channel on

concrete bed with
minimum 150 mm (6
inch) clear depth
18 Gravel topping on
   well compacted
   hardcore
19 Geotextile
   membrane

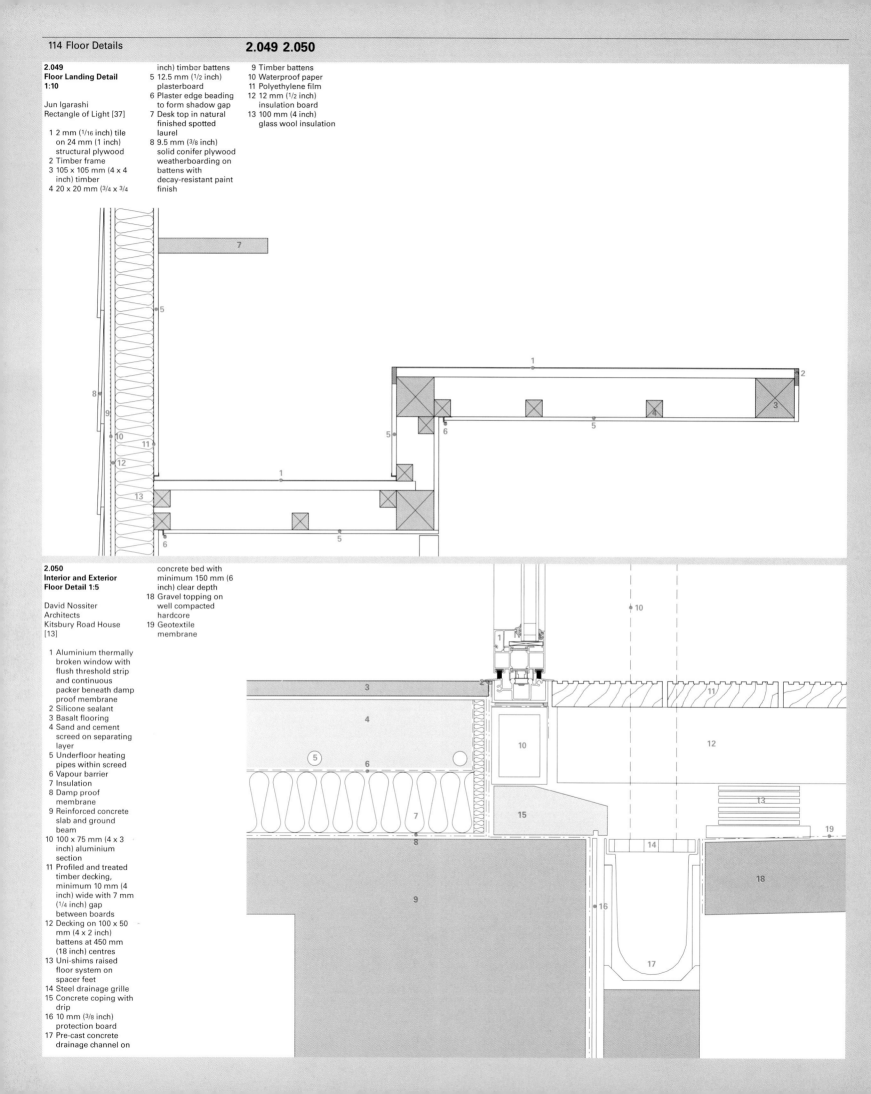

2.051
Floor Detail 1:20

Bercy Chen Studio
Peninsula House [36]

1 12 mm (1 inch)
 insulated, tempered,
 tinted, low-E glass
2 Column beyond
3 Sloped lawn laid to
 drain
4 12.5 x 600 mm (1/2 x
 24 inch) wide
 travertine tile on 6
 mm (1/4 inch) mud
 bed, sealed between
 tile and steel with tan

silicone
5 Continuous 12.5 x
 150 mm (1/2 x 6 inch)
 steel plate with 18
 mm (7/10 inch) steel
 plate overhang from
 outside face of
 foundation attached
 to topping slab
6 Stem wall continuing
 at concrete slab
 overpour
7 12.5 x 600 x 600 mm
 (1/2 x 24 x 24 inch)
 travertine tile on 6
 mm (1/4 inch) mud
 bed
8 Topping slab as

needed attached to
 existing foundation
9 Existing foundation
 at porch with existing
 overpour

2.052
Glass Floor Detail 1:5

Studio d'ARC Architects
Live / Work Studio II [19]

1 12.5 mm (1/2 inch)
 tempered glass
2 25 mm (1 inch)
 laminated glass floor
3 Neoprene pad
4 75 x 50 x 6 mm (3 x 2
 x 1/4 inch) steel angle
5 375 x 90 mm (15 x
 35/8 inch) rolled steel
 channel
6 20 mm (3/4 inch)
 diameter bolts

beyond
7 10 mm (3/8 inch) steel
 beyond

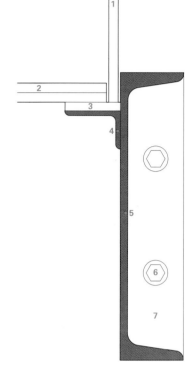

2.053
Floor Detail 1:10

Robert Seymour &
Associates
The Riverhouse [22]

1 15 mm (5/8 inch)
 toughened glass
 balustrade with
 bevelled edges set
 within mild steel
 clamping flats
2 Gunned silicone
 formed to chamfered
 exposed edge
3 90 x 10 mm (31/2 x 3/8
 inch) galvanized and
 sprayed mild steel
 flat upstand
4 260 x 90 mm (101/4 x
 31/2 inch) galvanized
 and powder-coated
 parallel flange
 channel
5 100 x 75 mm (4 x 3
 inch) galvanized and
 sprayed rolled steel
 angle
6 Line of mild steel
 upstand beyond
7 Hardwood decking
 on treated timber
 bearers
8 152 x 75 mm (6 x 3
 inch) galvanized
 T-section
9 10 mm (3/8 inch) rigid
 insulation
10 260 x 90 mm (101/4 x
 31/2 inch) galvanized
 and sprayed parallel
 flange channel with
 90 x 10 mm (31/2 x 3/8
 inch) galvanized and
 powder-coated mild
 steel upstand
11 Line of external
 render face
12 Polyester
 powder-coated doors
 with sealed double

glazing units
13 8 mm (3/16 inch) solid
 oak flooring on 18
 mm (3/4 inch)
 waterproof plywood
 on 35 mm (13/8 inch)
 thick medium density
 extruded polystyrene
 insulation, routed for
 underfloor heating
 system between 35 x
 50 mm (13/8 x 2 inch)
 treated softwood
 battens
14 20 mm (3/4 inch) resin
 self-levelling screed
 on 100 mm (4 inch)
 blockwork floor
 spanning between
 concrete beam floor
 system
15 12.5 mm (1/2 inch)
 plasterboard and
 skim ceiling system
 suspended by strap
 angle sections from
 primary support
 channel
16 Line of internal
 render face

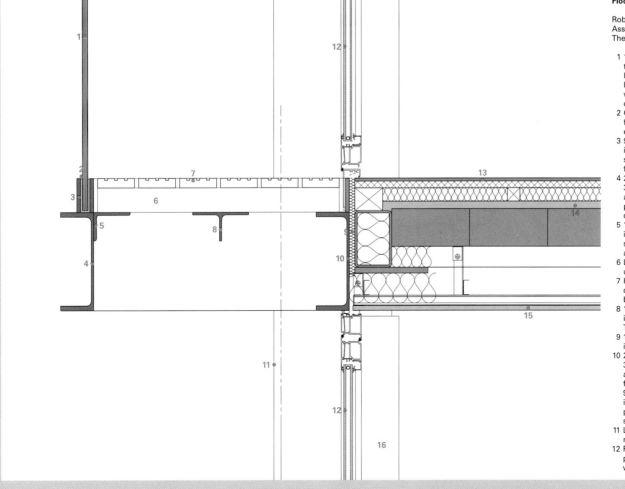

2.054
Garage Floor Detail 1:20

dRMM (de Rijke Marsh
Morgan Architects)
Sliding House [14]

1 Membrane on 12 mm
  (1/2 inch) oriented
  strand board to
  sliding door
2 Steel roller fixed to
  guide rail
3 Concealed gutters
4 300 mm (12 inch)
  Cordex cellcore
  expanded
  polystyrene

  insulation
5 Concrete slab
6 Gap between
  separated concrete
  slabs
7 Floating concrete
  garage slab
8 Concrete pile
9 Void space below
  slab
10 Grass

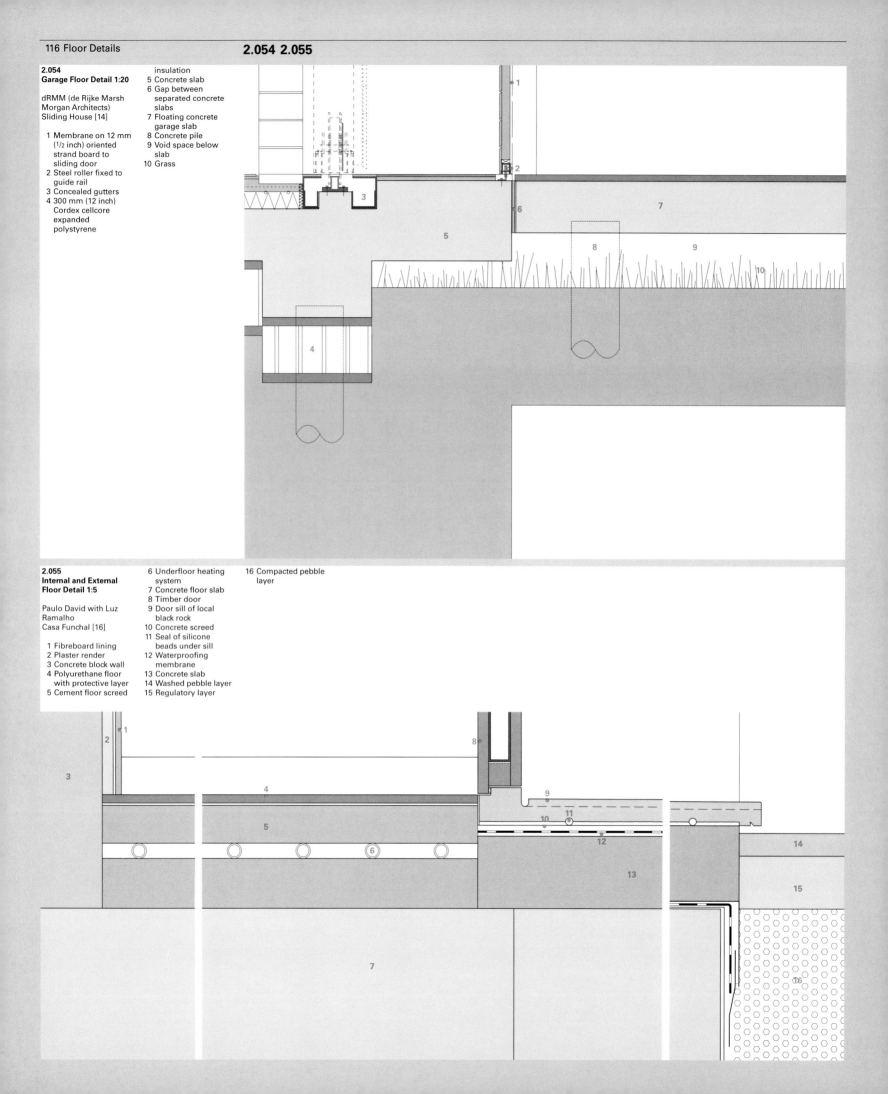

2.055
**Internal and External
Floor Detail 1:5**

Paulo David with Luz
Ramalho
Casa Funchal [16]

1 Fibreboard lining
2 Plaster render
3 Concrete block wall
4 Polyurethane floor
  with protective layer
5 Cement floor screed

6 Underfloor heating
  system
7 Concrete floor slab
8 Timber door
9 Door sill of local
  black rock
10 Concrete screed
11 Seal of silicone
  beads under sill
12 Waterproofing
  membrane
13 Concrete slab
14 Washed pebble layer
15 Regulatory layer

16 Compacted pebble
  layer

2.056
Catwalk Floor
Balustrade Detail 1:10

Mount Fuji Architects
Studio
Rainy Sunny House [11]

1 16 mm (5/8 inch) steel
  plate flooring
2 Australian cypress
  herringbone timber
  flooring
3 75 x 75 x 6 mm (3 x 3
  x 1/4 inch) steel angle
4 Timber shuttered
  concrete
5 40 x 55 mm (11/2 x

2 1/8 inch) oak
  handrail
6 32 x 19 mm (11/4 x 3/4
  inch) flat steel bar
  handrail structure
7 32 x 16 mm (11/4 x 5/8
  inch) flat steel bar
  balustrade upright
8 16 mm (5/8 inch)
  diameter steel rail

2.057
Floor Detail 1:10

Rowan Opat Architects
Courtyard House [38]

1 Glazing
2 Sashless double
  hung glazing seal
3 Timber mullion cover
  plate with paint finish
4 Timber sill with paint
  finish
5 Internal plasterboard
  lining with paint
  finish
6 Timber framing
7 Board and batten

radial sawn timber
cladding with paint
finish
8 Board and batten
  radial sawn timber
  cladding with paint
  finish
9 Indigenous
  hardwood radial
  sawn timber deck
  shown beyond
10 Timber deck joists
11 Concrete footings
12 Subfloor area

2.058
Floor Detail 1:10

Tham & Videgård
Arkitekter
Archipelago House [40]

1 Double glazing
  comprised of 6 mm
  (1/4 inch) glass, 15
  mm (5/8 inch) air
  space and 6 mm (1/4
  inch) glass
2 Timber frame to
  sliding glass window
3 55 x 205 mm (21/8 x
  81/8 inch) timber sill
4 Black silicone sealant
5 45 x 120 mm (13/4 x
  43/4 inch) timber
  decking
6 45 x 220 mm (13/4 x
  85/8 inch) timber
  beam
7 Metal fixing plate for
  joist to beam
  connection

8 45 x 220 mm (13/4 x
  85/8 inch) beam
9 Vapour barrier
10 20 x 160 mm (3/4 x
  61/4 inch) dovetailed
  timber boards
11 220 mm (85/8 inch)
  Rockwool insulation
12 Dovetailed timber
  boarding with
  serrated face and
  treated with cuprinol
13 22 x 120 mm (7/8 x
  43/4 inch) junction
  cover board
14 Air cavity
15 100 mm (4 inch)
  gravel bed

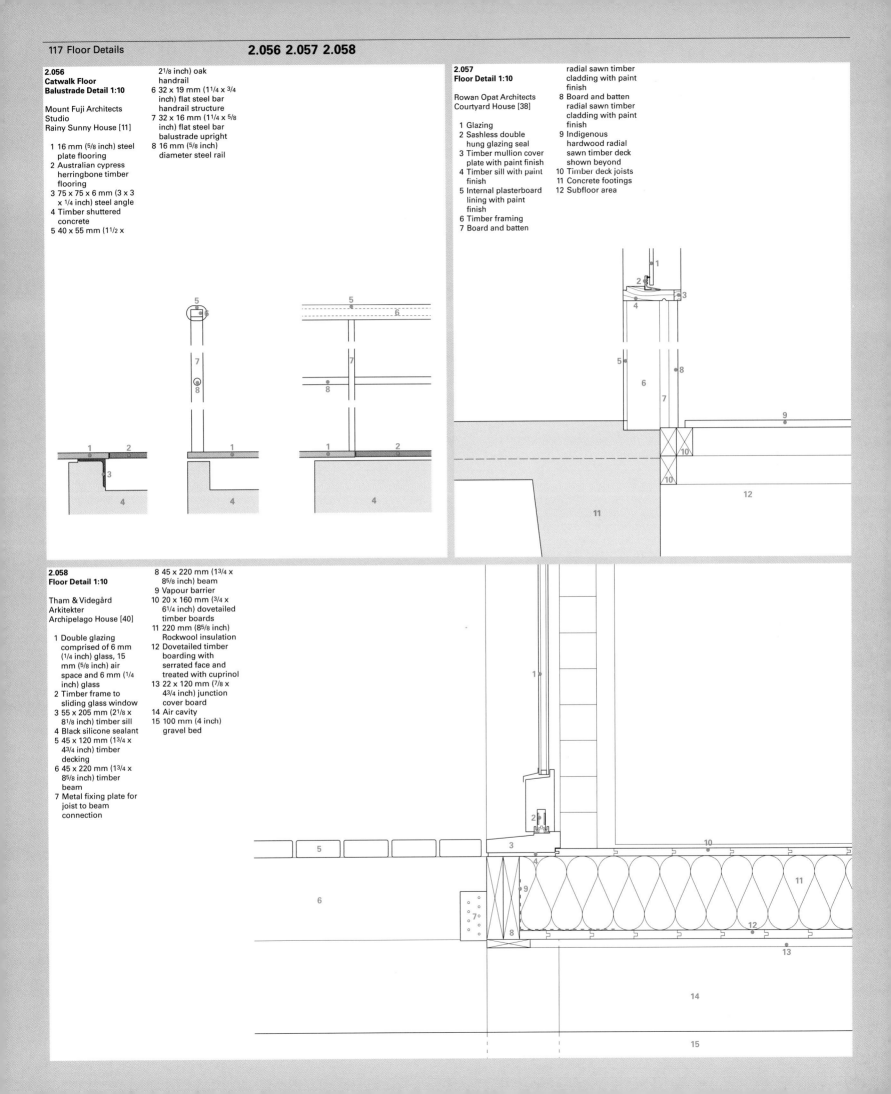

2.059
Floor Detail 1:10

Simon Walker Architects
Dane House [06]

1 Laminated double
glazed unit
comprised of 8.4 mm
($1/3$ inch) glass, 12
mm ($1/2$ inch) air gap
and 8.4 mm ($1/3$ inch)
glass
2 Solid iroko jamb and
frame to pivot door
with linseed oil finish
to interior and
exterior left bare
3 Solid iroko track
housing to sliding
door
4 20 mm ($3/4$ inch) thick
solid Irish oak
floorboards with
white oil finish
5 18 mm ($7/10$ inch)
waterproof plywood

subfloor
6 175 x 50 mm ($6^9/10$ x
2 inch) treated timber
joists
7 Trimmer joist
8 100 x 50 mm (4 x 2
inch) suspended
timber frame
9 1.5 mm ($1/16$ inch)
mill-finish aluminium
panel on 18 mm ($7/10$
inch) waterproof
plywood
10 100 x 50 mm (4 x 2
inch) suspended
timber ceiling joists
11 Fibreglass quilt
insulation
12 18 mm ($7/10$ inch)
birch multiply ceiling
panels
13 Proprietary
aluminium vent grille
14 100 x 75 mm (4 x 3
inch) treated timber
head
15 18 mm ($7/10$ inch)

solid iroko surround
to bathroom window
16 12 mm ($1/2$ inch) birch
multiply architrave to
bathroom window
17 Solid iroko frame to
bathroom window
18 50 mm (2 inch) solid
iroko casement
window
19 Laminated double
glazed unit
comprised of 8.4 mm
($1/3$ inch) glass, 12
mm ($1/2$ inch) air gap
and 8.4 mm ($1/3$ inch)
glass

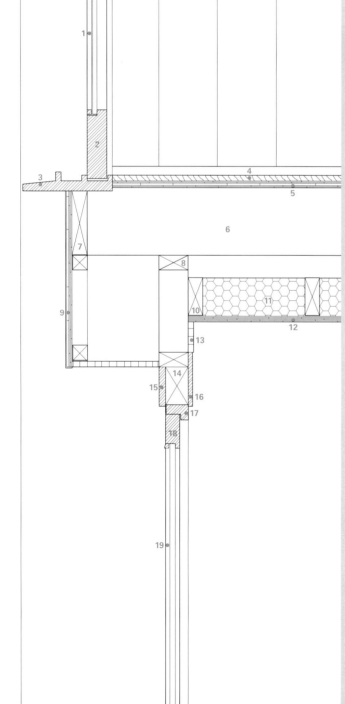

2.060
Floor and Window Seat
Detail 1:20

Keith Williams Architects
The Long House [23]

1 Double glazed
window unit
2 Oiled hardwood
cladding to sill and
fascia
3 Osma underfloor
heating panels on
softwood battens
4 Reinforced concrete
slab
5 100 mm (4 inch)

self-coloured
external insulated
render system
6 Powder-coated
aluminium angle to
fix transom to
reinforced concrete
slab
7 10 mm ($3/8$ inch)
shadow gap to
floor–wall junction
formed with
polyester
powder-coated
aluminium bead
8 20 mm ($3/4$ inch) oak
floor finish, secret
fixed on 18 mm ($3/4$

inch) flooring grade
chipboard screwed to
battens
9 12.5 mm ($1/2$ inch)
skimmed
plasterboard ceiling
10 Powder-coated
aluminium double
glazed window unit

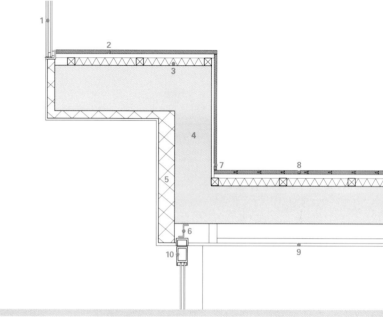

2.061
Floor Detail 1:10

Steffen Leisner, Ali
Jeevanjee, Phillip Trigas
1+3=1 House [17]

1 Gypsum wallboard
2 Batt insulation
3 Plywood lining
4 Timber framing
5 Neoprene strip and
sealant
6 Lightweight concrete
topping slab with
matt finish acrylic
floor polish
7 Hydronic radiant

floor heating system
8 Asphalt paper
9 Acoustical underlay
10 Two layers of
structural plywood
decking
11 Existing timber beam
12 J-Mold sealant and
backer rod
13 Laminated veneer
lumber beam
14 Laminated veneer
lumber edge piece
15 Hot rolled steel angle
joist hanger
16 Laminated veneer
lumber joist

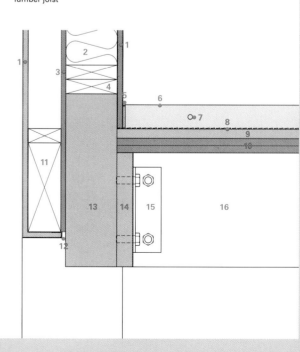

2.062
Floor Detail 1:10

Simon Walker Architects
Dane House [06]

1 Laminated double
   glazed unit
   comprised of 8.4 mm
   (1/3 inch) glass, 12
   mm (1/2 inch) air gap
   and 8.4 mm (1/3 inch)
   glass
2 Solid iroko frame to
   bedroom door
3 Solid iroko sill
   section
4 18 mm (7/10 inch)
   solid iroko frame to
   bedroom door
5 18 mm (7/10 inch)
   birch multiply
   architrave to
   bedroom door
6 50 x 50 mm (2 x 2
   inch) treated timber
   upstand to bedroom

door
7 20 mm (3/4 inch) thick
   solid Irish oak
   floorboards with
   white oil finish
8 100 mm (4 inch) rigid
   foam insulation
9 225 x 50 mm (8 4/5 x 2
   inch) treated timber
   trimmer joist
10 20 x 20 x 1.5 mm (3/4
   x 3/4 x 1/16 inch) mill
   finish aluminium
   frame
11 Proprietary
   aluminium vent grille
   to undercroft
12 Natural sandstone
   paver to exterior
13 Reinforced concrete
   floor slab
14 Line of existing
   ground level

2.063
Internal Floor and
Balcony Detail 1:10

Scott Tallon Walker
Architects
Fastnet House [25]

1 Wide plank oak
   flooring on marine
   ply
2 Sand-cement screed
   with underfloor
   heating
3 Reinforced concrete
   floor slab
4 Closer angle
5 Reflective insulation
6 Shiplapped cedar
   soffit boarding
7 Aluminium capping
8 Thermally broken
   double glazed unit
9 Painted skim finish to
   suspended
   plasterboard ceiling
10 Transom support
11 Aluminium and
   timber thermally-
   broken composite
   window system

12 Powder-coated
   aluminium mullion in
   background
13 Thermally broken
   double glazed unit
14 Galvanized and
   painted parallel
   flange channel
15 Tensile cable to
   balcony guarding
16 Mild steel angle
17 Powder-coated
   aluminium transom
18 Thermal break to
   transom
19 Iroko decking with
   pencil rounded
   edges
20 Timber
   counterbatten
21 Back to back
   galvanized and
   painted mild steel
   angles
22 Rigid insulation
23 Universal steel
   bearer

2.064
First Floor and Glazed Awning Detail 1:10

Haddow Partnership
Higher Farm [17]

1 Single clear glass panel to be bonded between external window and internal steelwork column with clear sealant
2 Powder-coated aluminium window section
3 Insulated sill
4 Insulated sill
5 Damp proof course
6 Glazed roof section
7 Lead flashing
8 50mm (2 inch) insulation
9 100 x 250 mm (4 x 10 inch) timber framing to glazed roof
10 102.5 mm (4 inch) facing brickwork
11 Insulated lintel
12 Insulated lintel
13 125 mm (5 inch) blockwork
14 12.5 mm (1/2 inch) internal plaster
15 32 mm (11/4 inch) Internal timber oak floor
16 Two layers of 50 mm (2 inch) screed
17 100 mm (4 inch) insulation
18 12.5 mm (1/2 inch) internal plaster
19 100x 150 mm (4 inch x 6 inch) rectangular hollow section steel tube
20 150 x 150 mm (6 x 6 inch) square hollow section steel tube
21 100 x 20 mm (4 x 3/4 inch) oak skirting
22 Powder-coated aluminium window
23 12.5 mm (1/2 inch) internal plaster

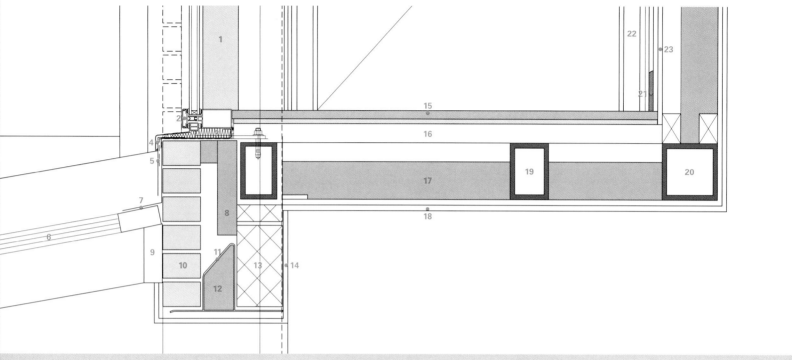

2.065
Floor Detail 1:10

Simon Walker Architects
Dane House [06]

1 Laminated double glazed unit comprised of 8.4 mm (1/3 inch) glass, 12 mm (1/2 inch) air gap and 8.4 mm (1/3 inch) glass
2 Solid iroko jamb and frame to pivot door with linseed oil finish to interior and exterior left bare
3 Solid iroko sill
4 25 x 25 x 3 mm (1 x 1 x 1/16 inch) cold rolled stainless steel angle
5 20 mm (3/4 inch) thick solid Irish oak floorboards with white oil finish
6 18 mm (7/10 inch) waterproof plywood subfloor
7 175 x 40 mm (69/10 x 15/8 inch) treated timber joists
8 Double trimmer joists
9 Skim finish ceiling on 12.5 mm (1/2 inch) plasterboard
10 Sliding door hardware
11 Plaster ceiling returned
12 40 mm (13/5 inch) laminated birch multiply sliding door
13 100 x 60 mm (4 x 23/8 inch) tanalised timber decking
14 Tanalised timber sleeper joists
15 30 mm (11/5 inch) asphalt roof covering on sanded roll underlay
16 18 mm (7/10 inch) waterproof plywood deck
17 175 x 40 mm (69/10 x 15/8 inch) treated timber joists
18 Fibreglass quilt insulation
19 Skim finish ceiling on 12.5 mm (1/2 inch) plasterboard

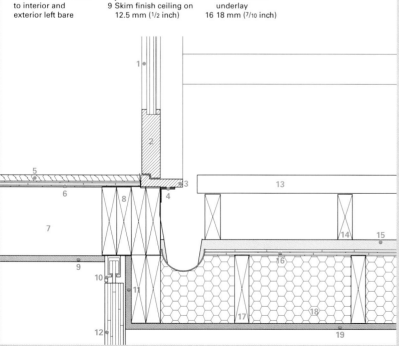

2.066
Floor Detail 1:10

Skene Catling de la Peña Architects
The Dairy House [31]

1 Waney edge timber board
2 Compriband seal
3 Laminated glass block
4 Euroseal gasket
5 Drainage channel filled with pebbles
6 Timber packer
7 Lead cover to trench
8 Light fitting
9 18 mm (7/10 inch) formed plywood trench
10 Concrete and slate slabs
11 Fibreglass
12 Timber firring pieces
13 65 mm (21/2 inch) screed with underfloor heating
14 65 mm (21/2 inch) rigid insulation
15 Concrete pit

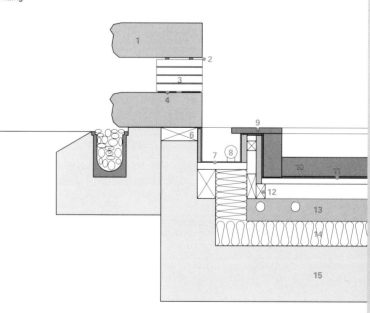

2.067
Floor Detail 1:20

de Blacam and Meagher
Architects
Morna Valley Residence
[20]

1 600 x 400 x 20 mm
  (24 x 16 x 3/4 inch)
  white Ibiza marble
  tile
2 20 mm (3/4 inch) sand
  and cement bedding
  mortar
3 80 mm (3 1/8 inch)
  screed with
  underfloor heating

system
4 Extruded polystyrene
  insulation
5 Structural screed
6 Reinforced concrete
7 Terracotta arch panel

2.068
Floor Detail 1:20

Pierre Minassian
Architecte
Biscuit House [11]

1 Stainless steel cable
2 Iroko wood slats
3 Double glazed fixed
  window
4 Steel column
5 Suspended plaster
  ceiling
6 Stainless steel angle
7 Silicone seal
8 Concrete floor slab

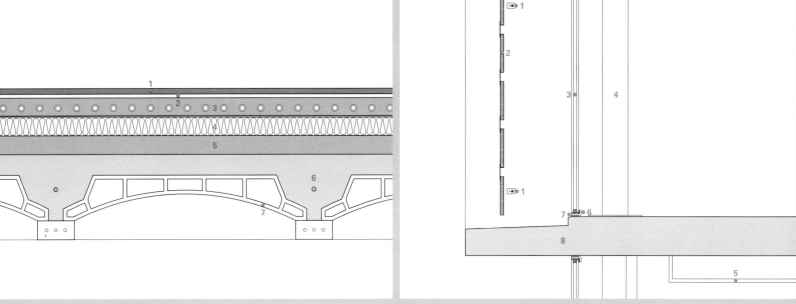

2.069
Terrace Floor Detail 1:10

Agence Michel Tortel
Mikado House [08]

1 Reinforced concrete
  wall and floor
2 Reinforced concrete
  balcony floor slab
3 Itauba timber
  decking
4 Timber battens
5 Adjustable point
  support to timber
  battens
6 External insulation
7 Waterproofing

membrane
8 Internal insulation
9 18 mm (3/4 inch)
  skimmed and painted
  plasterboard wall
  and ceiling lining

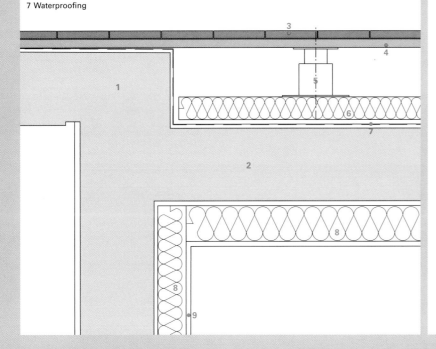

2.070
Floor Detail 1:10

Safdie Rabines
Architects
Artist Bridge Studio [30]

1 Trespa high
  performance exterior
  cladding panels
2 Building paper
3 Structural plywood
  sheathing and
  substrate for Trespa
  panels
4 Wall insulation
5 15 mm (5/8 inch)
  gypsum wallboard

interior lining
6 140 x 40 mm (5 1/2 x
  15/8 inch) timber stud
7 Prefinished metal
  drip groove
8 Continuous sealant
9 Hardwood timber
  floor
10 Structural plywood
  sheathing floor
  substrate
11 240 x 40 mm (9 1/2 x
  15/8 inch) timber joist
12 350 x 150 mm (14 x 6
  inch) glulam beam
13 Insulation
14 Two layers
  gypsum-board

ceiling lining
15 22 mm (7/8 inch)
  plaster over metal
  lath
16 Backer rod and
  sealant
17 Glulam beam
  connection plate to
  concrete footing

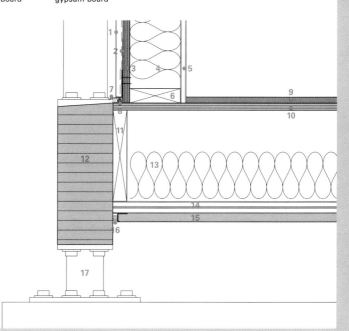

2.071
Floor Detail 1:20

Hamiltons
Holmewood House [17]

 1 Anodized aluminium
   internal and external
   louvres to plantroom
 2 215 mm (8¹/2 inch)
   thick blockwork wall
 3 Paint finish
 4 30 mm (1¹/5 inch)
   travertine paving
 5 Bedding and
   concrete sub base
 6 Travertine strip
 7 Gravel fill
 8 Concrete strip
   support for drainage
   channel
 9 Stainless steel grille
   above drainage
   channel
10 Drainage channel
11 Powder-coated steel
   angle
12 Insulation
13 Cement screed floor
   to plantroom
14 Insulation and
   polystyrene fill
15 Concrete on metal
   decking suspended

slab
16 Waterproofing
   membrane
17 100 mm (4 inch)
   insulation
18 Waterproofing
   membrane
19 Structural concrete
   slab

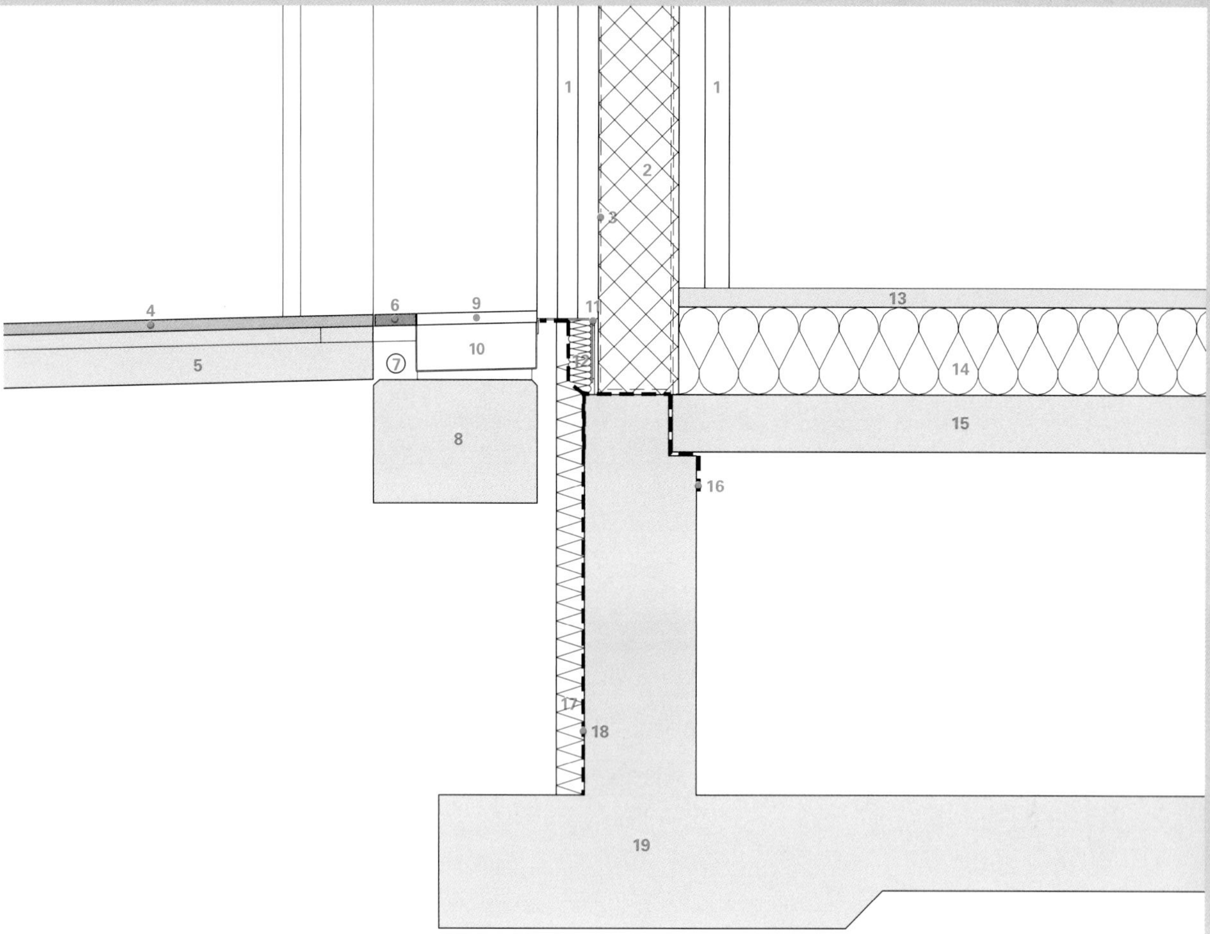

2.072
Floor and Inclined Wall
Detail 1:10

Agence Michel Tortel
Mikado House [08]

 1 Itauba timber floor
 2 Timber battens
 3 Concrete floor slab
   and beam
 4 Inclined wall in 18
   mm (3/4 inch) plaster
   with steel channels

and internal
insulation
 5 Ventilation ducts
 6 False ceiling with
   upstand forming
   cladding to beam
 7 Linear fluorescent
   tube lighting
 8 13 mm (1/2 inch)
   plasterboard ceiling

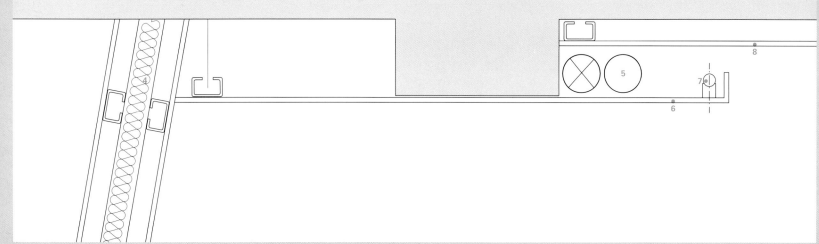

2.073
Floor Detail 1:10

Touraine Richmond
Architects
One Window House [27]

1 140 mm (5 1/2 inch)
   batt insulation
2 25 mm (1 inch)
   drywall lining
3 25 mm (1 inch)
   oriented strand
   board sheathing
4 20 mm (7/8 inch)
   corrugated metal
   siding
5 Timber decking

6 Waterproof
   membrane
7 Air gap
8 25 mm (1 inch)
   oriented strand
   board sheathing
9 Batt insulation
10 25 mm (1 inch)
   drywall lining
11 130 x 420 mm (5 1/8 x
   16 5/8 inch) wood
   framing
12 50 x 235 mm (2 x 9 1/2
   inch) wood framing
   beyond
13 25 mm (1 inch)
   oriented strand
   board sheathing

14 19 mm (3/4 inch)
   sanded and stained
   oriented strand
   board finished floor

2.074
Floor Detail 1:5

Glas Architects
The Nail Houses [23]

1 4 mm (1/6 inch)
   rubber flooring
2 24 mm (1 inch)
   plywood sheathing
3 Underfloor heating
   cables
4 60 mm (2 3/8 inch)
   Rockwool duct slab
   insulation
5 60 mm (2 3/8 inch)
   Rockwool flexible
   insulation

6 Vapour control layer
7 Beam and block floor
8 Air space below
   ground floor
9 50 x 50 mm (2 x 2
   inch) timber batten
10 50 x 100 mm (2 x 4
   inch) timber battens
   at 400 mm (16 inch)
   centres

2.075
Floor Detail 1:5

Glas Architects
The Nail Houses [23]

1 10 mm (3/8 inch)
   rubber flooring
2 12 mm (3/8 inch)
   plywood
3 Underfloor heating
   cables
4 60 mm (2 3/8 inch)
   Rockwool duct slab
   insulation
5 60 mm (2 3/8 inch)
   Rockwool flexi
   insulation
6 50 x 50 mm (2 x 2
   inch) timber batten
7 50 x 100 mm (2 x 4
   inch) timber batten at
   400 mm (16 inch)
   centres
8 Vapour control layer
9 Beam and block floor
10 Air space below
   ground floor
11 Intumescent seal
12 Internal timber
   component of
   composite timber
   and aluminium
   window unit

13 24 mm (1 inch)
   double glazed
   window unit in
   polyester
   powder-coated
   aluminium frame
14 Compriband seal
15 Grip surface finish
   treatment
16 Damp proof
   membrane
17 100 mm (4 inch)
   concrete slab
18 50 mm (2 inch)
   hardcore
19 Ground fill

2.076
Floor Detail 1:10

Skene Catling de la Peña
Architects
The Dairy House [31]

1 Bronze-clad timber
   door set
2 20 mm (3/4 inch) slate
   flooring
3 Floor spring
4 65 mm (21/2 inch)
   screed with
   underfloor heating
5 65 mm (21/2 inch)
   rigid insulation
6 Concrete slab and

upstand
7 Drainage brickslot
   channel
8 Cut stone wall
9 Timber framed,
   double glazed doors

2.077
Decking Detail 1:10

Marlon Blackwell
Architect
L-Stack House [35]

1 25 x 152 mm (1 x 6
   inch) Brazilian teak
   decking attached to
   timber sleepers with
   concealed screws
2 50 x 100 mm (2 x 4
   inch) treated timber
   sleepers at 406 mm
   (16 inch) centres
3 25 x 85 mm (31/3 x 6
   inch) Brazilian teak

board
4 Sloped concrete pad
   and concrete stem
   wall
5 Free-draining gravel
   over compacted soil
6 150 mm (6 inch)
   perforated drain

2.078
Floor Detail 1:10

Skene Catling de la Peña
Architects
The Dairy House [31]

1 Concrete and slate
   slabs
2 Fibreglass
3 25 mm (1 inch)
   plywood
4 Timber firring pieces
5 65 mm (21/2 inch)
   screed with
   underfloor heating
6 65 mm (21/2 inch)
   rigid insulation

7 Concrete pit
8 Rubber pad
9 89 x 152 mm (31/2 x 6
   inch) steel beam
10 25 mm (1 inch)
   plywood support to
   slab
11 12.5 mm (1/2 inch)
   plasterboard
   skimmed and painted
12 18 mm (3/4 inch)
   painted medium
   density fibreboard
   shelves
13 30 mm (11/8 inch)
   thermaboard
14 100 mm (4 inch)
   blockwork

2.079
External Terrace Floor at
Pool Detail 1:5

Kallos Turin
Casa Zorzal [10]

1 Ballast layer
2 45 mm (13/4 inch)
   pigmented cement
   screed
3 5 x 20 mm (1/5 x 3/4
   inch) stainless steel
   flat section
4 Water to pool

5 Waterproof mortar
6 'Aquavation' render
7 Reinforced concrete
   retaining wall
8 Subsoil

2.080
Terrace Floor Detail 1:10

Blank Studio
Xeros Residence [29]

1 Steel column
2 Open area beneath
   guardrail beyond
3 50 mm (2 inch) thick
   x 4 mm (3/16 inch)
   width welded steel
   bar grating
4 Stretched wire mesh
   shade screen

5 Steel beam
6 Structural steel plate
   to bolted frame
   connection
7 Steel beam

2.082
**Interior and Exterior
Floor Detail 1:20**

Keith Williams Architects
The Long House [23]

1 Powder-coated
   double glazed
   aluminium sliding
   unit
2 32 mm (1 1/4 inch)
   Pietro Lauro stone
   slabs
3 Adjustable supports
   for stone slabs
4 Caltite reinforced
   concrete slab
5 Structural aluminium
   transom
6 Perimeter heating
   element under
   anodized finished
   grille
7 20 mm (3/4 inch) oiled
   oak solid timber strip
   flooring bonded to

sand and cement
screed
8 Sand and cement
   screed to required
   level
9 Water based
   underfloor heating
10 Rigid polystyrene
   insulation with
   preformed pockets
   for pipe location
11 50 mm (2 inch) sand
   blinding
12 50 mm (2 inch) sand
   blinding

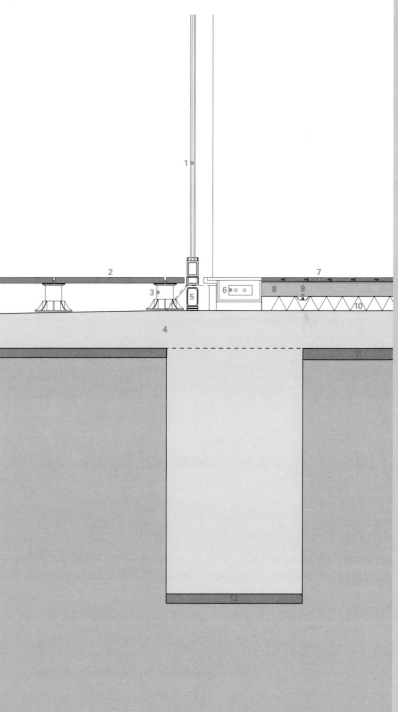

2.081
Floor Detail 1:10

Peter Stutchbury
Architecture
Avalon House [29]

1 Galvanized steel
   flat-sheet cladding
   on timber studs with
   edges overlapped by
   150 mm (6 inch) and
   joints sealed with
   silicone bead
2 Sarking behind
   cladding shown
   dotted
3 Plasterboard wall
   lining
4 Polyester wool batt
   insulation
5 90 x 40 mm (3 1/2 x
   1 5/8 inch) timber sole
   plate
6 Rondo shadowline
   and black Sikaflex to
   floorboard joint
7 200 x 100 mm (8 x 4
   inch) galvanized
   universal beam
   bolted to galvanized
   steel cleat
8 150 x 10 mm (6 x 2/5
   inch) galvanized steel

cleat welded to 150 x
100 mm (6 x 4 inch)
rectangular hollow
section column
9 25 mm (1 inch)
   tongue and groove
   hardwood
   floorboards
10 18 mm (3/4 inch)
   structural plywood
   fixed to joists and
   bearers
11 Galvanized steel floor
   purlin bolted to cleat
12 Firring channels fixed
   to beam
13 90 x 40 mm (3 1/2 x
   1 5/8 inch) timber stud
   frame
14 9 mm (3/8 inch)
   plywood ceiling
   panels

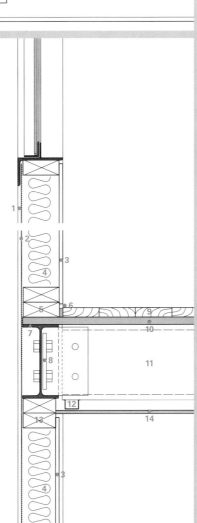

2.083
Upper Floor Detail to
Link Bridge 1:10

Hampson Williams
Glass and Timber
Houses [33]

1 18 mm (7/10 inch)
tongue and groove
Canadian western
red cedar cladding
impregnated with
non-com exterior fire

retardant
2 12 mm (1/2 inch)
cementitous
exterior-grade lining
panel
3 25 mm (1 inch)
taper-edged
plasterboard, taped
and skimmed,
comprised of two
12.5 mm (1/2 inch)
thick layers
4 150 x 50mm (6 x 2
inch) tanalised

softwood structural
timber section
5 15 mm (3/5 inch) mild
steel angle with
integral drip detail
6 50 x 10 mm (2 x 2/5
inch) steel plate
7 37 x 37 mm (11/2 x
11/2 inch)
powder-coated
aluminium angle
8 28 mm (11/10 inch)
argon-filled
toughened and

laminated offset
sliding double glazed
unit
9 145 x 70 mm (57/10 x
23/4 inch) Douglas fir
sliding door system
10 Douglas fir subframe
11 Compressible seal
12 25 mm (1 inch) taper
edged plasterboard
taped and skimmed
comprised of two
12.5 mm (1/2 inch)
thick layers

13 240 x 90 mm (91/2 x
31/2 inch) glulam
beam
14 18 mm (7/10 inch)
thick engineered
bamboo floating
floor
15 50 mm (2 inch)
proprietary
underfloor heating
insulation units
16 100 mm (4 inch)
mineral wool
insulation

17 Single layer of 12.5
mm (1/2 inch)
plasterboard
18 Compressible seal
19 28 mm (11/10 inch)
argon-filled
toughened and
laminated offset
double glazed unit
20 Douglas fir subframe

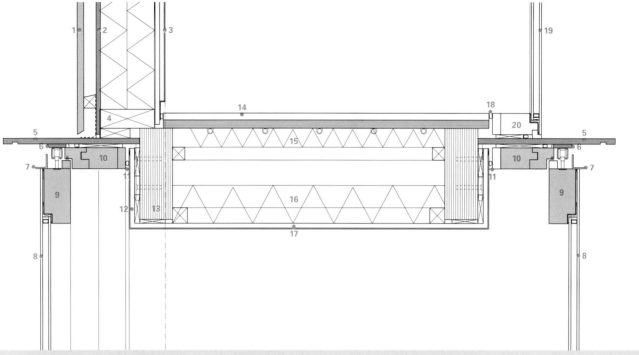

2.084
Lower Floor Detail to
Link Bridge 1:10

Hampson Williams
Glass and Timber
Houses [33]

1 28 mm (11/10 inch)
argon-filled
toughened and
laminated offset
double glazed unit
2 145 x 70 mm (57/10 x

23/4 inch) Douglas fir
sliding door system
3 3 mm (1/10 inch) black
powder-coated mild
steel plate
4 Douglas fir subframe
5 125 x 100 mm (5 x 4
inch) steel angle
6 18 mm (7/10 inch)
tongue and groove
Canadian western
red cedar cladding
impregnated with
non-com exterior fire

retardant
7 36 x 24 mm (12/5 x 1
inch) tapered
continuous larch
batten
8 8 mm (1/3 inch)
cementitous exterior
grade lining panel
9 240 x 90 mm (91/2 x
31/2 inch) glulam
beam
10 18 mm (7/10 inch)
engineered bamboo
floating floor

11 Multi-layered
thermal insulation
12 100 mm (4 inch)
mineral wool
insulation
13 13 mm (1 inch)
cementitous
exterior-grade lining
panel
14 150 x 22 mm (6 x 4/5
inch) massaranduba
timber decking

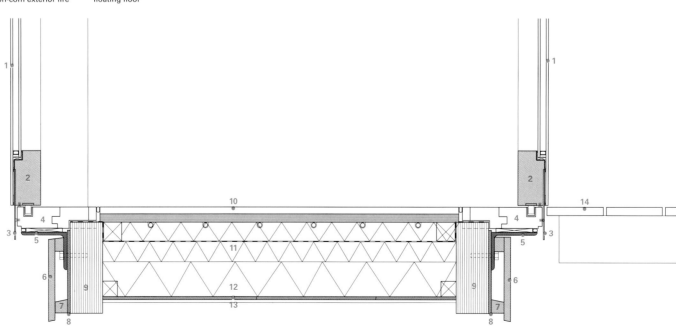

2.085
Bridge and Glass
Balustrade Detail 1:10

Studio Bednarski
Hesmondhalgh House
[33]

1 12.4 mm (1/2 inch)
  laminated toughened
  glass balustrade
2 Oak floor
3 Compressible strip
4 High modulous
  sealant
5 Epoxy sulphide
  compound
6 M16 stainless steel
  countersunk bolts at
  500 mm (20 inch)
  centres
7 Nut pre-welded to
  steel plate
8 Continuous 12 mm
  (1/2 inch) thick mild
  steel plate welded to
  rolled steel joist
9 Continuous 12 mm
  (1/2 inch) thick mild
  steel plate
10 Medium density
   fibreboard facing
11 305 x 102 mm (12 x 4
   inch) universal beam
12 Cut-outs in cross
   universal beam for
   services as required

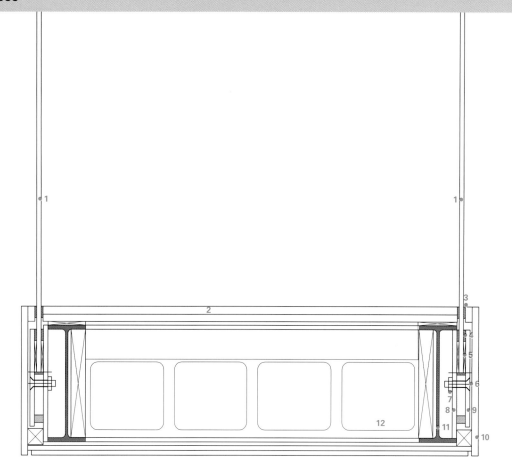

2.086
Floor and Footing Detail
1:20

Scott Tallon Walker
Architects
Fastnet House [25]

1 Profiled tiled edging
  to swimming pool
2 Concealed drainage
  channel
3 Swimming pool
  cover
4 Tiled finish to
  swimming pool wall
5 Ozone treated water
6 Aluminium frame
  with tiled finish to
  hide drum
7 Motorized drum to
  swimming pool
  cover
8 Tiled floor
9 Sand-cement screed
  topping with
  underfloor heating
10 Insulation
11 Insulation
12 Reinforced concrete
   floor slab
13 Damp proof
   membrane with
   radon barrier
14 Insulation
15 Plaster finish
16 Concrete blockwork
   wall
17 Painted skirting
18 Carpet on underlay
19 Sand-cement screed
   topping with
   underfloor heating
20 Insulation
21 Reinforced concrete
   floor slab

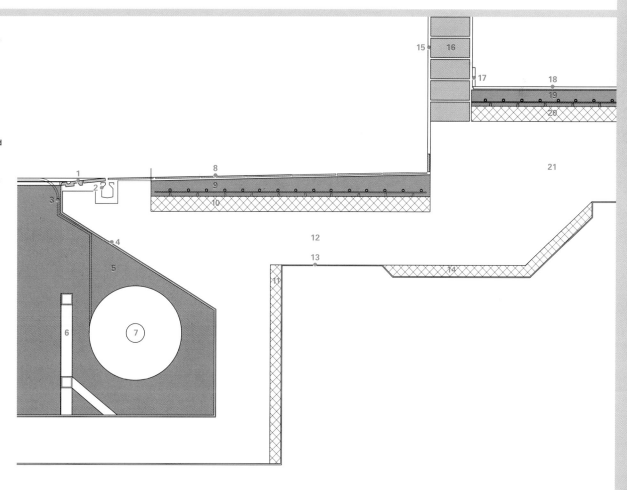

2.087
Floor Detail 1:10

Tham & Videgård
Arkitekter
Archipelago House [40]

1 Timber profile
2 Glass balustrade
3 Floor finish
4 Screed
5 Underfloor heating
6 Insulation
7 Concrete

8 Prefabricated
  concrete floor
  construction
9 Bolt for fixing
  U-shaped profile to
  concrete
10 U-shaped profile to
  take glass balustrade
11 Concrete staircase

2.088
**Internal and External
Floor Detail 1:20**

Agence Michel Tortel
Mikado House [08]

1 210 mm (8¹/₄ inch)
  diameter structural
  steel column with
  welded baseplate
  fixed into concrete
  slab
2 Tiled finish to

concrete stair
3 Internal floating
  polished concrete
  floor screed
4 Insulation and
  underfloor heating
5 Concrete slab and
  beam
6 Internal floating
  polished concrete
  floor screed

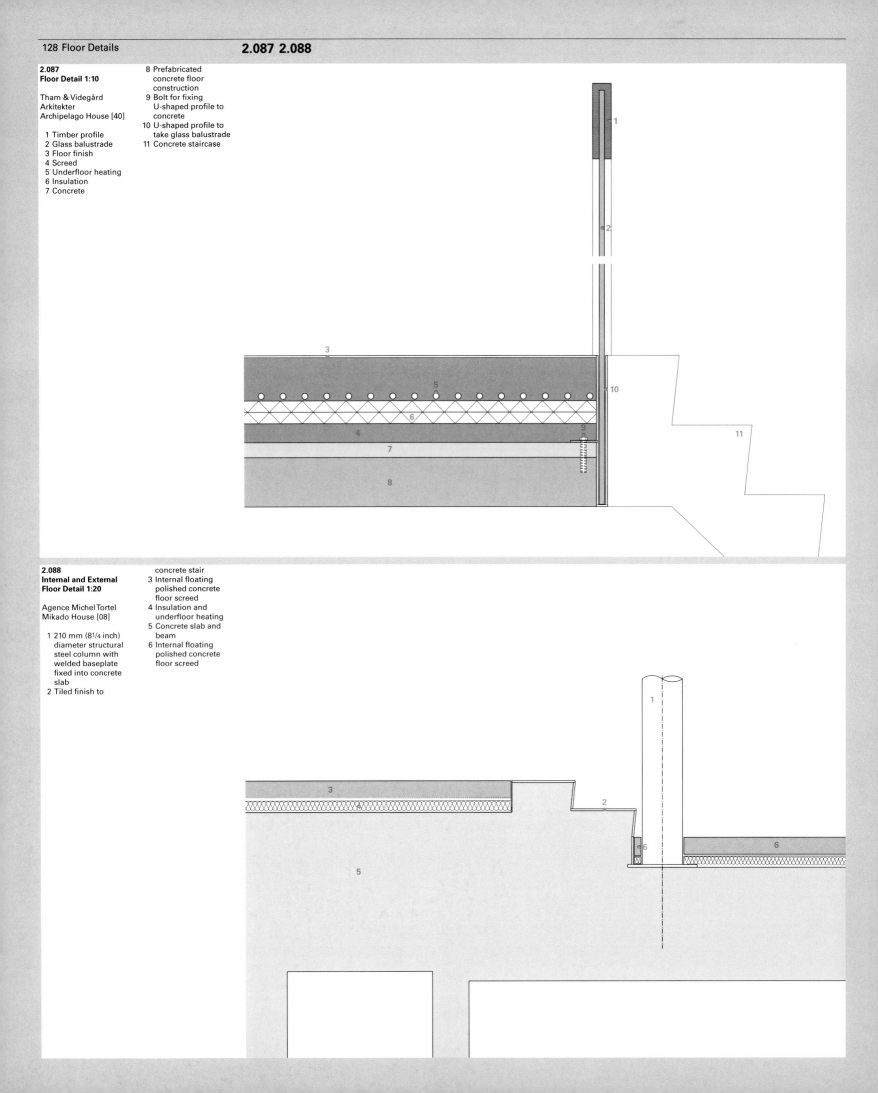

2.089
Living Room Floor
Detail 1:10

MacGabhann Architects
Tuath na Mara [14]

1 Aluminium capping
  piece to powder-
  coated aluminium
  curtain wall glazing
2 Drip profile to
  anthrazinc sill
3 Anthrazinc standing
seam cladding
4 100 mm (4 inch)
  block wall
5 40 mm (1 5/8 inch)
  cavity
6 60 mm (2 7/8 inch)
  Kingspan insulation
7 215 mm (8 1/2 inch)
  block wall
8 Solid oak board floor
  fixed to 50 x 75 mm
  (2 x 3 inch) timber
  battens with 40 mm
  (1 5/8 inch) high
density insulation
9 175 mm (6 7/8 inch)
  concrete slab
10 Radon barrier
11 80 mm (3 1/8 inch)
  Kingspan insulation
12 Layers of well
  compacted hardcore

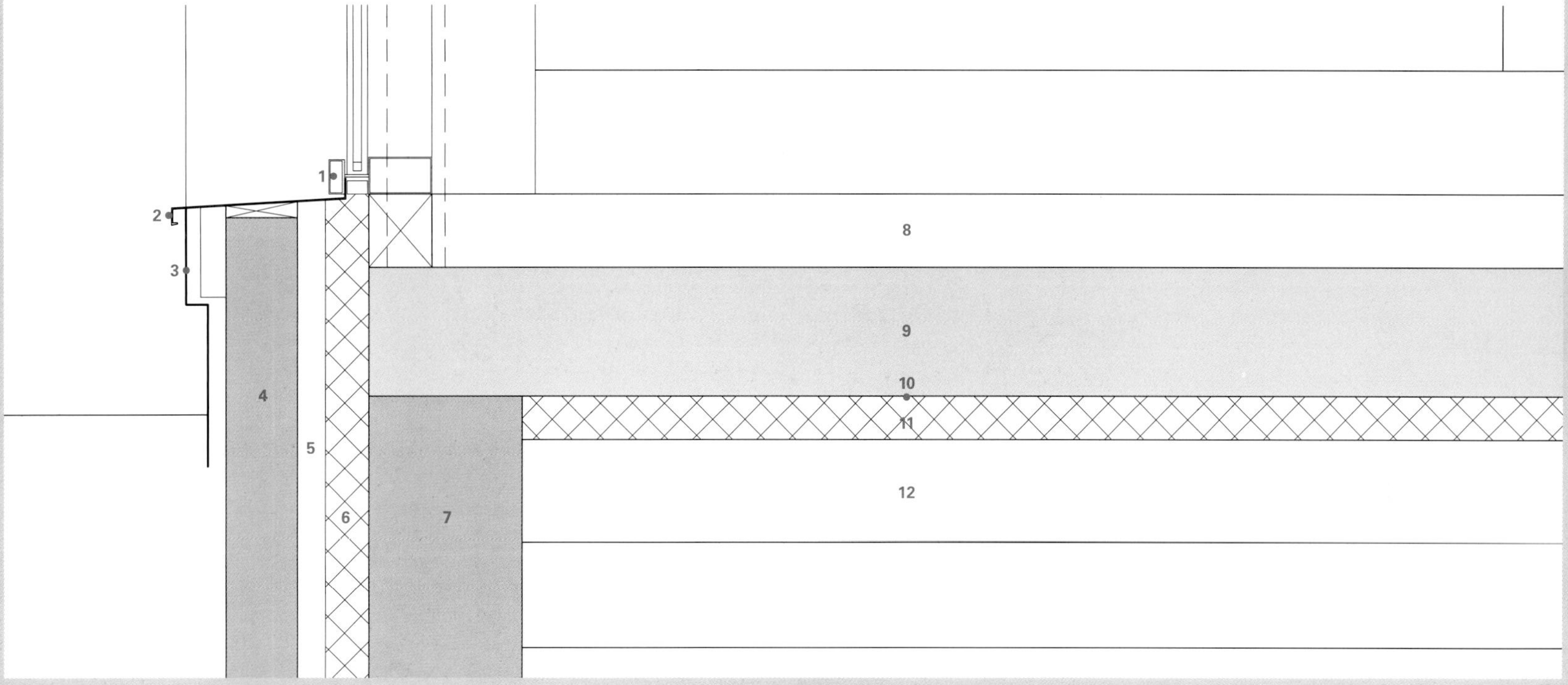

2.090
Floor Detail 1:5

Scott Tallon Walker
Architects
Fastnet House [25]

1 Wide plank oak
  flooring
2 Marine ply
3 Sand-cement screed
  with underfloor
  heating
4 Insulation barrier
5 Reinforced concrete
  floor slab
6 Mastic joint
7 Restraint angle
8 Transom support
  fixings
9 Transom base plate
10 Strip insulation
11 Aluminium pressing
12 Pedestals to support
  limestone paving
13 Limestone open joint
  paving
14 Powder-coated
  aluminium mullion in
  background
15 Thermally broken
  double glazed unit
16 Galvanized and
  painted parallel
  flange channel
17 Tensile cable to
  balcony guarding

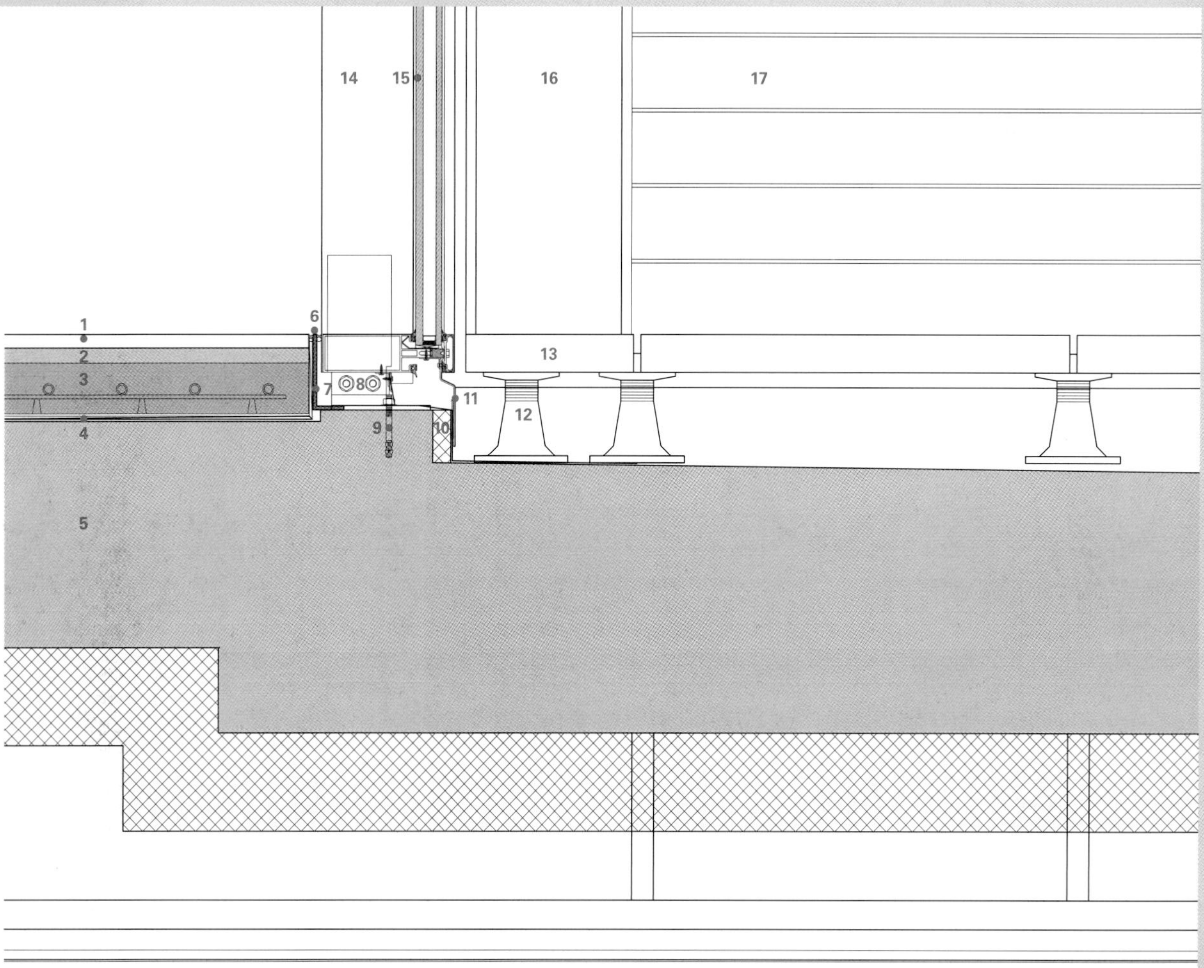

3 Window Details

3.001
Window Detail 1:5

Boyd Cody Architects
Richmond Place House
[22]

1 Continuous
 perimeter mastic seal
 to match brickwork
2 Bronze satin
 anodized aluminium
 window frame
3 Double glazed unit
4 6 mm (1/4 inch) reveal
5 6 mm (1/4 inch)
 insulation behind
 plasterboard

6 External single skin
 brick wall
7 Vertical damp proof
 course lapped
 around corner and
 clamped into frame
8 Rigid insulation to
 cavity
9 Reinforced concrete
 structural wall
10 18 mm (7/10 inch)
 veneered plywood
 internal wall lining
11 25 x 50 mm (1 x 2
 inch) softwood
 battens

3.002
Window Detail 1:5

Boyd Cody Architects
Richmond Place House
[22]

1 Continuous
 perimeter mastic seal
 to match brickwork
2 Bronze satin
 anodized aluminium
 window frame
3 Double glazed unit
4 6 mm (1/4 inch) reveal
 formed with expamet
 plaster stop bead
5 Insulation packing

behind plasterboard
6 External single skin
 brick wall
7 Rigid insulation to
 cavity
8 Vertical damp proof
 course lapped
 around corner and
 clamped into frame
9 Reinforced concrete
 structural wall
10 25 x 50 mm (1 x 2
 inch) softwood
 battens
11 Plasterboard internal
 wall lining with paint
 finish

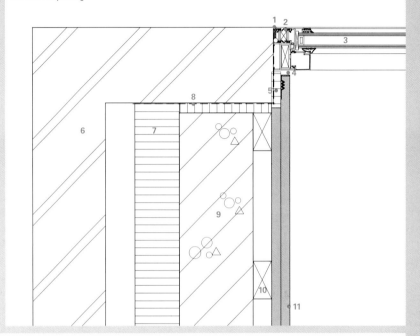

3.003
Window Detail 1:20

Saunders Architecture
Villa Storingavika [40]

1 9 mm (1/3 inch)
 gyprock boarding
2 Laminated timber
 post
3 Glass sliding door
4 Canadian cedar
 cladding
5 900 mm (352/5 inch)

high laminated glass
 railing on terrace
6 Terrace boards,
 stained black
7 Spruce overlap
 cladding, stained
 black
8 Timber door jamb
9 Timber door jamb
 spacer
10 50 x 150 mm (2 x 6
 inch) posts
11 Canadian cedar
 cladding

12 13 mm (1/2 inch)
 waterproof gyprock
13 9 mm (1/3 inch)
 gyprock boarding
14 Interior plasterboard
 wall

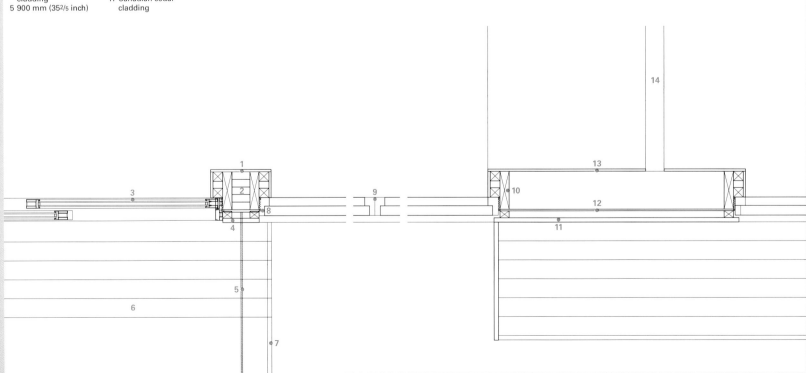

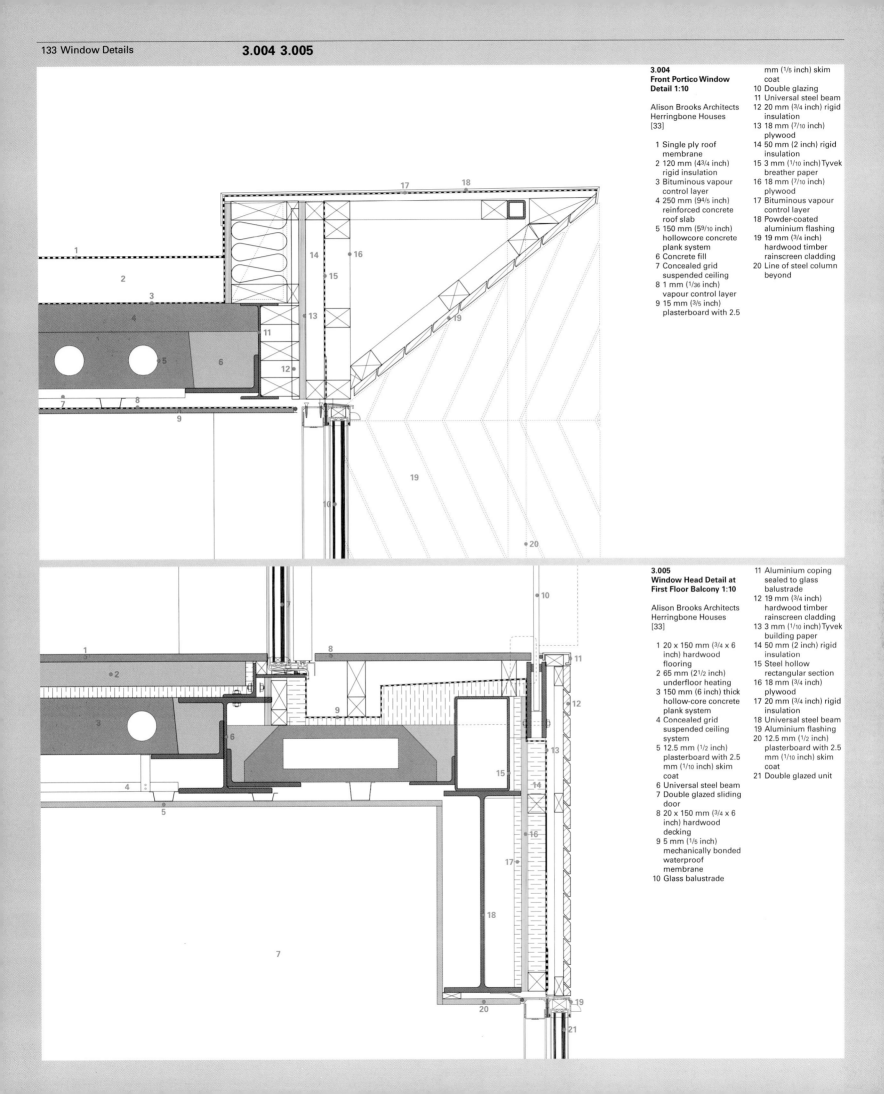

3.004
Front Portico Window Detail 1:10

Alison Brooks Architects
Herringbone Houses
[33]

1 Single ply roof membrane
2 120 mm (4³/₄ inch) rigid insulation
3 Bituminous vapour control layer
4 250 mm (9⁴/₅ inch) reinforced concrete roof slab
5 150 mm (5⁹/₁₀ inch) hollowcore concrete plank system
6 Concrete fill
7 Concealed grid suspended ceiling
8 1 mm (¹/₃₆ inch) vapour control layer
9 15 mm (³/₅ inch) plasterboard with 2.5 mm (¹/₅ inch) skim coat
10 Double glazing
11 Universal steel beam
12 20 mm (³/₄ inch) rigid insulation
13 18 mm (⁷/₁₀ inch) plywood
14 50 mm (2 inch) rigid insulation
15 3 mm (¹/₁₀ inch) Tyvek breather paper
16 18 mm (⁷/₁₀ inch) plywood
17 Bituminous vapour control layer
18 Powder-coated aluminium flashing
19 19 mm (³/₄ inch) hardwood timber rainscreen cladding
20 Line of steel column beyond

3.005
Window Head Detail at First Floor Balcony 1:10

Alison Brooks Architects
Herringbone Houses
[33]

1 20 x 150 mm (³/₄ x 6 inch) hardwood flooring
2 65 mm (2¹/₂ inch) underfloor heating
3 150 mm (6 inch) thick hollow-core concrete plank system
4 Concealed grid suspended ceiling system
5 12.5 mm (¹/₂ inch) plasterboard with 2.5 mm (¹/₁₀ inch) skim coat
6 Universal steel beam
7 Double glazed sliding door
8 20 x 150 mm (³/₄ x 6 inch) hardwood decking
9 5 mm (¹/₅ inch) mechanically bonded waterproof membrane
10 Glass balustrade
11 Aluminium coping sealed to glass balustrade
12 19 mm (³/₄ inch) hardwood timber rainscreen cladding
13 3 mm (¹/₁₀ inch) Tyvek building paper
14 50 mm (2 inch) rigid insulation
15 Steel hollow rectangular section
16 18 mm (³/₄ inch) plywood
17 20 mm (³/₄ inch) rigid insulation
18 Universal steel beam
19 Aluminium flashing
20 12.5 mm (¹/₂ inch) plasterboard with 2.5 mm (¹/₁₀ inch) skim coat
21 Double glazed unit

3.006
Typical Fixed Glazing
Detail 1:5

Bercy Chen Studio
Riverview Gardens [38]

1 Structural silicone
  with backing rod
2 6 mm (1/4 inch) steel
  bar
3 25 mm (1 inch)
  double glazed
  window fixed to
  angle with 6 mm (1/4
  inch) butyl tape
4 16 mm (5/8 inch)
  gypsum board
  ceiling
5 25 mm (1 inch)
  double glazed
  window
6 20 mm (3/4 inch)
  Indian sandstone
  flooring
7 28 mm (1 1/10 inch)
  plywood subfloor
8 Structural steel
  channel
9 20 mm (3/4 inch)
  plywood blocking
  ramset fastened to
  steel channel
10 Shear tab
11 Metal joist

3.007
Fixed Glazing to Powder
Room Detail 1:10

Bercy Chen Studio
Riverview Gardens [38]

1 Timber powder room
  door
2 10 mm (3/8 inch) steel
  work surface
3 20 mm (3/4 inch)
  medium density
  fibreboard millwork
  with conversion
  varnish
4 25 mm (1 inch)
  double glazed fixed
  window
5 Steel angle
6 6 mm (1/4 inch)
  painted hardiplank
  panels on 20 mm (3/4
  inch) firring battens
  on 12 mm (1/2 inch)
  plywood
7 20 mm (3/4 inch)

medium density
fibreboard millwork
with conversion
varnish finish
8 12 mm (1/2 inch)
  plywood
9 Closet door
10 50 x 100 mm (2 x 4
   inch) timber framing
11 25 mm (1 inch)
   frosted double glazed
   fixed window

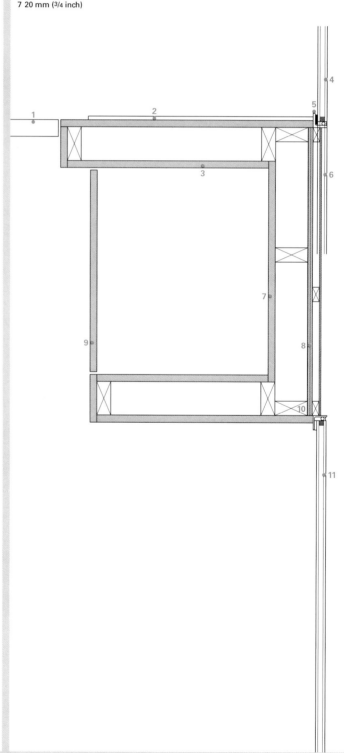

3.008
Ground Floor Window Detail 1:5

Ensamble Studio
Hemeroscopium House
[07]

1 Floor mounted radiator
2 Double glazing comprised of 8 mm (1/3 inch) glass, 12 mm (1/2 inch) air gap and two layers of 4 mm (1/8 inch) glass
3 Steel plate U-profile anchor piece
4 Steel plate stiffener
5 Steel plate hollow rectangular section
6 Steel plate stiffener
7 Waterproofing, PVC membrane and geotextile fabric
8 Precast concrete floor slab
9 Expanded polystyrene foam insulation

3.009
Window Detail 1:5

Ensamble Studio
Hemeroscopium House
[07]

1 Floor mounted radiator
2 Double glazing comprised of 8 mm (1/3 inch) glass, 12 mm (1/2 inch) air gap and two layers of 4 mm (1/8 inch) glass
3 U-profile steel anchor
4 Steel plate stiffener angle
5 Steel beam
6 19 mm (3/4 inch) cement bonded chipboard between steel channels
7 Waterproof membrane
8 40 mm (13/5 inch) Rockwool thermal and acoustic insulation
9 50 mm (2 inch) thick concrete compression slab
10 200 mm (8 inch) thick hollow-core precast concrete slab
11 7 mm (1/4 inch) thick neoprene membrane
12 Steel L-profile
13 40 mm (13/5 inch) Rockwool thermal and acoustic insulation
14 7.5 mm (3/10 inch) plasterboard
15 7.5 mm (3/10 inch) plasterboard
16 Steel place anchor piece
17 Steel place anchor piece
18 Steel plate stiffener
19 Steel plate stiffener
20 15 x 20 mm (3/5 x 3/4 inch) glazing bead

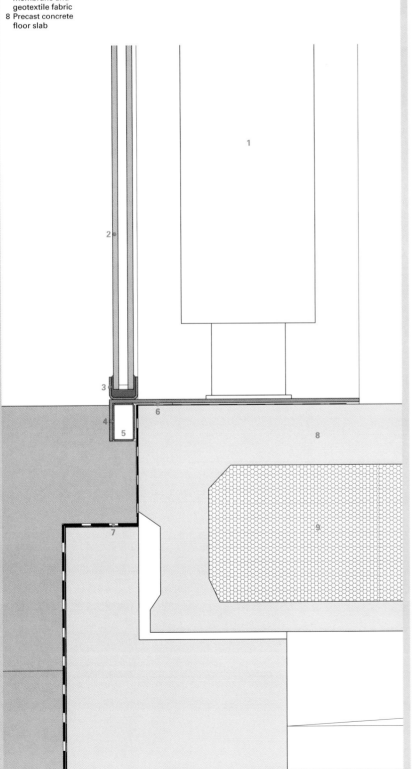

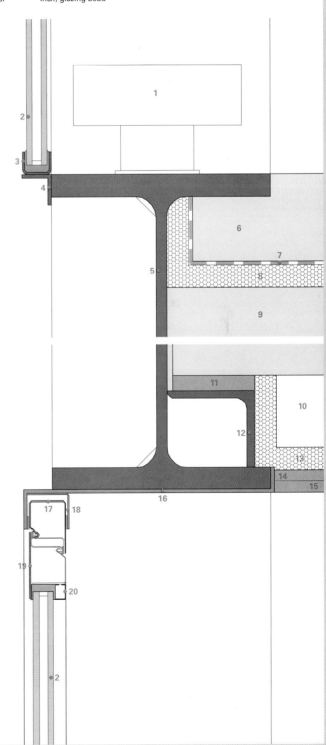

3.010
Window Detail 1:5

diederendirrix
Villa PPML [21]

1 Brickwork to exterior of cavity wall
2 Insulation
3 Water resistant layer
4 Cement fill to base of cavity wall
5 Steel plate for mounting blockwork wall
6 Welded steel facade support
7 Fastener for steel console
8 Reinforced concrete wall
9 Stucco finish to interior wall
10 Timber framing
11 Timber packer
12 67 x 139 mm (2²/3 x 5¹/2 inch) timber window frame
13 Aluminium stucco profile
14 Timber glazing bead
15 Welded steel facade support
16 Line of timber window reveal beyond
17 Insulated double glazing
18 Roller blind
19 Water resistant medium density fibreboard window reveal
20 Water resistant medium density fibreboard window reveal
21 Water resistant medium density fibreboard window sill
22 Folded steel sill drip flashing
23 Continuous water resistant plywood mounting strip
24 Timber support for drip flashing
25 67 x 139 mm (2²/3 x 5¹/2 inch) timber window frame

3.011
Window Detail 1:5

diederendirrix
Villa PPML [21]

1 Brickwork to exterior of cavity wall
2 Water resistant layer
3 Insulation
4 Cement fill to base of cavity wall
5 Steel plate for mounting blockwork wall
6 Fastener for steel console
7 Stucco finish to interior wall
8 Timber framing
9 Timber packer
10 67 x 139 mm (2²/3 x 5¹/2 inch) timber window frame
11 Welded steel facade support
12 Galvanized and painted steel flat bar welded to steel facade support
13 54 x 90 mm (2¹/8 x 3¹/2 inch) timber casement window with insulated double glazing
14 Roller blind
15 Stucco corner profile
16 Water resistant medium density fibreboard window reveal
17 Insulated double glazing
18 54 x 90 mm (2¹/8 x 3¹/2 inch) timber casement window frame
19 Water resistant medium density fibreboard window sill
20 Caulking
21 Stucco finish to interior wall
22 67 x 139 mm (2²/3 x 5¹/2 inch) timber window frame
23 Timber packer
24 Timber mounting strip
25 Cast in-situ reinforced concrete wall
26 Folded steel drip sill flashing
27 Continuous water resistant plywood mounting strip
28 Water resistant sheathing

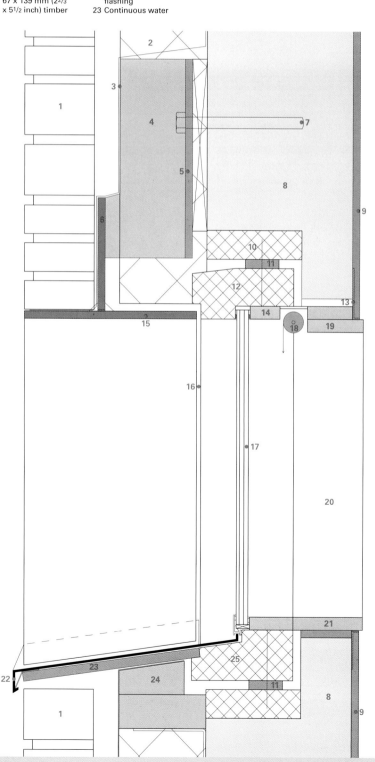

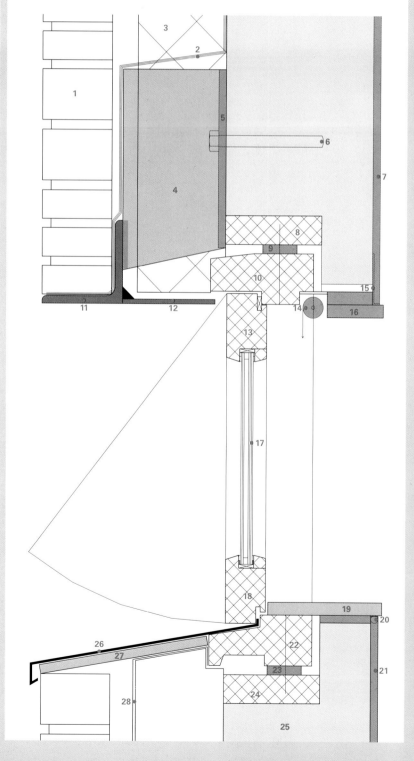

3.012
Bay Window Head Detail
1:10

MacGabhann Architects
Tuath na Mara [14]

1 Anthra-zinc standing
   seam cladding
2 150 mm (6 inch)
   wide, 100 mm (4
   inch) deep pressed
   metal gutter
3 Anthra-zinc standing
   seam cladding
4 Separating layer
5 19 mm (^{3}/$_4$ inch)
   weather bonded and
   proofed external
   plywood sheeting
6 50 x 50 mm (2 x 2
   inch) timber battens
7 225 x 44 mm (9 x 1^3/$_4$
   inch) timber joists at
   400 mm (16 inch)
   centres
8 140 mm (5^1/$_2$ inch)

Kingspan
Thermapitch
insulation
9 Vapour barrier
10 12.5 mm (^{1}/$_2$ inch)
   plasterboard lining
11 Masonry concrete
   blocks
12 Reinforced concrete
   lintel
13 Steel frame structure
14 Powder-coated
   aluminium window
   frame

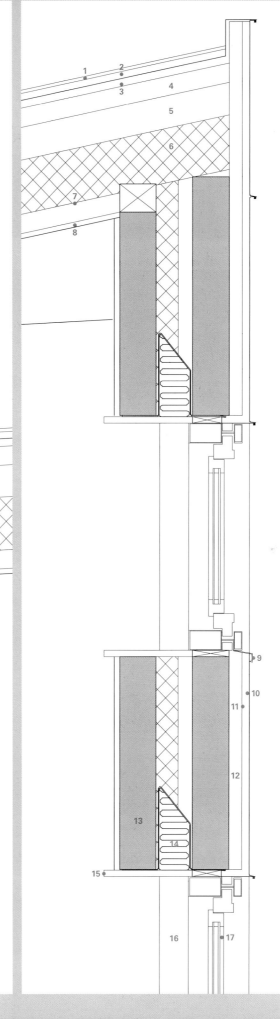

3.013
Bedroom Window Detail
1:10

MacGabhann Architects
Tuath na Mara [14]

1 Anthra-zinc standing
   seam cladding
2 Separating layer
3 19 mm (^{3}/$_4$ inch)
   weather bonded and
   proofed external
   plywood sheeting
4 50 x 50 mm (2 x 2
   inch) timber battens
5 225 x 44 mm (9 x 1^3/$_4$
   inch) timber joists at
   400 mm (16 inch)
   centres
6 140 mm (5^1/$_2$ inch)
   Kingspan
   Thermapitch
   insulation
7 Vapour barrier
8 12.5 mm (^{1}/$_2$ inch)
   plasterboard lining
9 Anthra-zinc sill
   flashing
10 Separating layer
11 19 mm (^{3}/$_4$ inch)
   weather bonded and
   proofed external
   plywood sheeting
12 35 x 50 mm (1^3/$_8$ x 2
   inch) sub-
   construction timber
   battens
13 100 mm (4 inch)
   block wall
14 Steel lintel
15 250 x 20 mm (10 x ^{3}/$_4$
   inch) solid red deal
   timber boards at
   head and sill
16 80 x 80 mm (3^1/$_8$ x
   3^1/$_8$ inch) steel posts
   to support lintels to
   every internal wall
17 Powder-coated
   aluminium
   curtain-wall double
   glazing

3.014
Window Section Detail
1:10

Marlon Blackwell
Architect
L-Stack House [35]

1 Soy-based foam
  insulation
2 Exterior grade
  waterproof fir-faced
  plywood sheathing
3 12 mm (1/2 inch)
  painted gypsum
  board interior lining
4 EPDM (ethylene
  propylene dieme
  monomer) weather
  barrier for rainscreen
  application at wall
  substrate
5 40 mm (13/4 inch)
  wide Brazilian
  redwood rainscreen
  screw-fixed to
  custom routed 50 x

100 mm (2 x 4 inch)
battens at minimum
800 mm (32 inch)
centres with a 20 mm
(3/4 inch) gap
vertically between
each strip
6 40 x 300 mm (13/4 x
  117/8 inch) laminated
  veneer lumber with
  two spacers as
  window header
7 Weather barrier
  wrapped over timber
  fillet
8 150 x 90 x 8 mm (6 x
  31/2 x 5/16 inch) angle
  frame continued
  around head, jambs
  and sill to windows
9 Sealant and backer
  rod
10 6 mm (1/4 inch) shim
11 Aluminium
  storefront window
  system
12 Clear, insulated low-E

glass
13 Two timber sill plates

3.015
Bay Window Detail 1:10

Marlon Blackwell
Architect
L-Stack House [35]

1 40 mm (13/4 inch)
  wide Brazilian
  redwood rainscreen
  screw-fixed to
  battens at minimum
  800 mm (32 inch)
  centres with a 20 mm
  (3/4 inch) gap
  vertically between
  each strip
2 12 mm (1/2 inch) thick
  painted gypsum-
  board wall lining
3 Exterior grade
  waterproof fir-faced
  plywood sheathing
4 40 x 300 mm (13/4 x
  117/8 inch) laminated
  veneer lumber with
  two spacers as

window header
5 10 mm (3/8 inch)
  J-mold reveal
6 6 mm (1/4 inch)
  painted steel 'box'
  bay window
7 EPDM (ethylene
  propylene dieme
  monomer) roofing
  membrane
8 Aluminium window
  with casement
9 Fabric-upholstered
  tufted foam cushion
10 20 mm (3/4 inch)
  plywood base for
  cushion
11 Clear double glazed
  window unit

3.016
Window Head and Sill
Detail 1:10

Welsh + Major
Pitt Street House [37]

1 160 x 35 mm (6¼ x 1⅜ inch) painted timber handrail capping
2 Salvaged timber boards
3 Acrylic render
4 Fibre cement sheet cladding
5 Sarking
6 90 x 40 mm (3½ x 1⅝ inch) stud framing
7 Painted, timber framed, glazed sliding door
8 Dressed timber sill
9 Bottom roller mechanism and track
10 Timber decking on 40

x 25 mm (1½ x 1 inch) timber battens
11 Waterproof membrane
12 Fibre cement sheet deck substrate
13 150 x 75 mm (6 x 3 inch) parallel flange channel
14 Salvaged timber boards
15 2 mm (1/12 inch) folded galvanized mild steel hood
16 Track for bi-fold sliding door system
17 Dressed timber trim to conceal retractable flyscreen mechanism
18 130 x 40 mm (5⅛ x 1⅝ inch) timber joists
19 100 mm (4 inch) insulation between joists
20 Timber boarding
21 Painted, timber

framed, glazed bi-fold door
22 Line of timber trim beyond
23 Salvaged brick pavers
24 Flashing over cavity, upturned behind sill
25 Timber boarding on 50 x 50 mm (2 x 2 inch) battens
26 Concrete slab

3.017
Bay Window With
Shoji Screen Section
Detail 1:10

Waro Kishi + K. Associates Architects
Hakata House [18]

1 27 x 40 mm (1/16 x 1⅝ inch) timber louvres at 50 mm (2 inch) centres
2 150 x 150 mm (6 x 6 inch) universal steel beam
3 Steel bolt
4 Traditional Japanese plaster wall finish
5 Two 50 x 50 mm (2 x 2 inch) steel columns at 300 mm (11⅘ inch) centres
6 Caulking
7 Traditional Japanese plaster finish to reinforced concrete

wall
8 65 x 65 mm (2½ x 2½ inch) stainless steel angle
9 6 x 100 mm (¼ x 4 inch) steel brackets at 300 mm (11⅘ inch) centres
10 6 x 125 mm (¼ x 5 inch) steel bracket
11 Timber plaster stop bead
12 Traditional Japanese plaster wall finish
13 Aluminium ventilation grille
14 Reveal joint and shadow gap
15 150 x 150 mm (6 x 6 inch) universal steel beam
16 Reinforced concrete wall

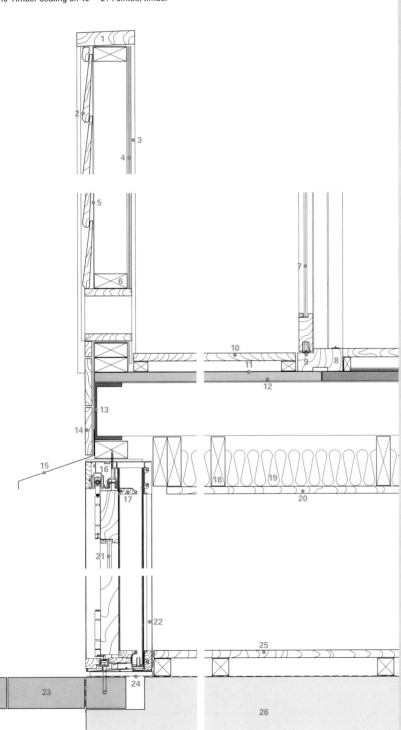

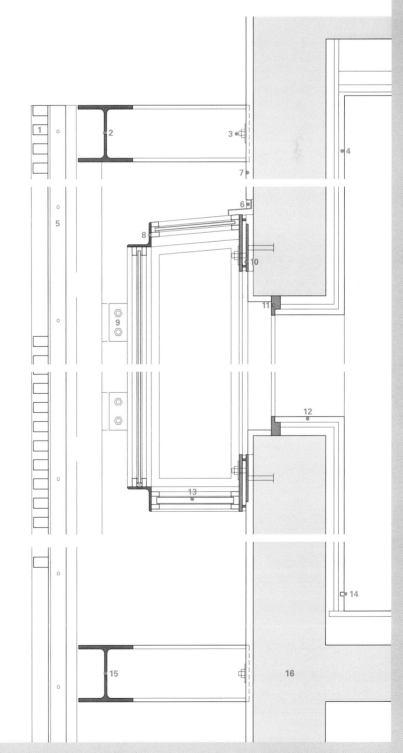

3.018
Window Jamb and
Concrete Panel Junction
Detail 1:10

Jackson Clements
Burrows Architects
Edward River House
[32]

1 140 x 40 mm (5$\frac{1}{2}$ x 1$\frac{5}{8}$ inch) cedar window sill
2 10 mm ($\frac{3}{8}$ inch) fixed float glass
3 140 x 40 mm (5$\frac{1}{2}$ x 1$\frac{5}{8}$ inch) cedar window jamb
4 Silicone weather seal
5 Flashing
6 10 mm ($\frac{3}{8}$ inch) zincaneal shadowline stopping angle
7 Exposed aggregate polished concrete floor
8 Exposed 180 mm (7$\frac{1}{8}$ inch) pre-cast concrete panel
9 13 mm ($\frac{1}{2}$ inch) internal plasterboard wall lining

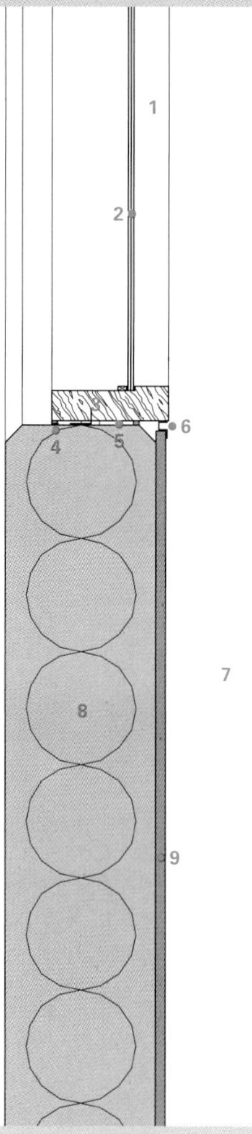

3.019
Corner Window and
Column Junction Detail
1:10

Jackson Clements
Burrows Architects
Edward River House
[32]

1 266 x 110 mm (10$\frac{1}{2}$ x 4$\frac{3}{8}$ inch) laminated timber structural column
2 Flashing
3 140 x 40 mm (5$\frac{1}{2}$ x 1$\frac{5}{8}$ inch) cedar window jamb
4 140 x 40 mm (5$\frac{1}{2}$ x 1$\frac{5}{8}$ inch) cedar window sill
5 100 x 40 mm (4 x 1$\frac{5}{8}$ inch) cedar sliding window with 10 mm ($\frac{3}{8}$ inch) fixed float glass
6 100 x 40 mm (4 x 1$\frac{5}{8}$ inch) cedar sliding window with fly-wire
7 140 x 19 mm (5$\frac{1}{2}$ x $\frac{3}{4}$ inch) spotted gum polished timber floorboards
8 Proprietary glass louvre system

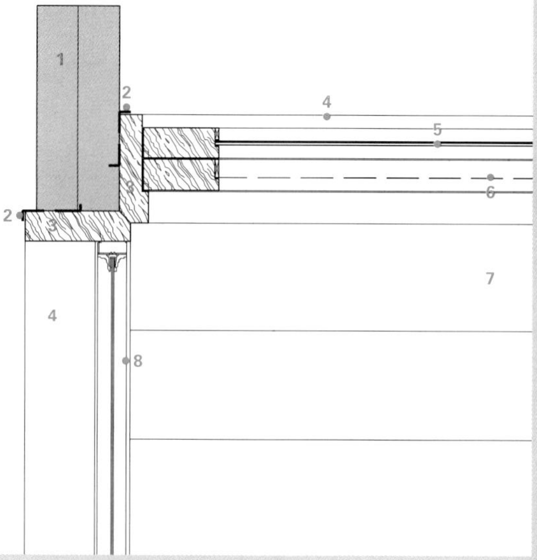

3.020
Window Detail 1:10

Chenchow Little
Architects
Freshwater House [32]

1 Fabricated steel beam
2 Louvre shutters
3 Fibre cement sheeting
4 External metal corner angle to plasterboard edge
5 Timber packer
6 Aluminium sliding doors, with aluminium section isolated from
incompatible metals
7 Timber packers
8 Curtain track
9 Plasterboard with painted finish
10 Steel column
11 Tiled floor
12 Screed
13 Concrete slab and beam
14 Aluminium door track and sill
15 Membrane
16 Stainless steel grate
17 Integrated drain
18 Geotextile fabric
19 Drainage cell
20 Membrane
21 Landscaping bed

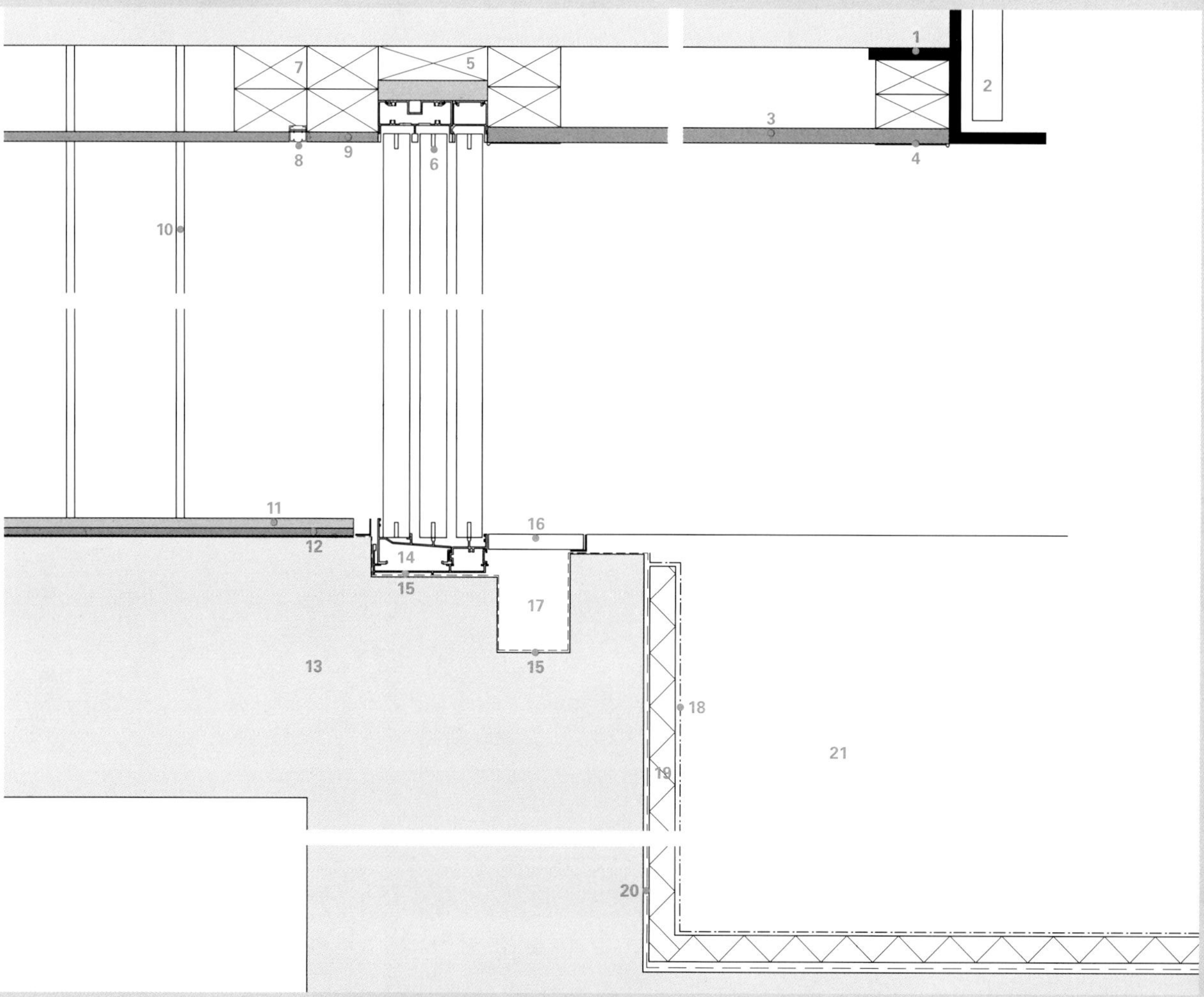

3.021
Window Detail 1:10

Chenchow Little
Architects
Freshwater House [32]

1 Colorbond sheet
  metal capping
2 Fabricated steel
  fascia beam
3 Kliplok roof sheeting
4 Insulation
5 Timber roof battens
6 150 x 50 mm (6 x 2
  inch) timber rafter
7 Timber packer
8 Timber packer
9 Suspended
  plasterboard ceiling
  system with paint
  finish
10 Curtain track
11 Aluminium sliding
  doors with
  aluminium section
  isolated from

incompatible metals
12 Tiled floor
13 Screed
14 Flexible joint
15 Aluminium door
  track and sub sill
16 Stainless steel grate
17 Integrated drain
18 Membrane
19 Frameless glass
  balustrade
20 Fabricated steel
  fascia beam
21 Steel plate
22 Electric motor
23 Louvre shutters
24 Top track of louvre
  shutter system
25 Pulley system
26 Hanger bolt
27 Bottom track of
  louvre shutter
  system
28 Aluminium
  balustrade support

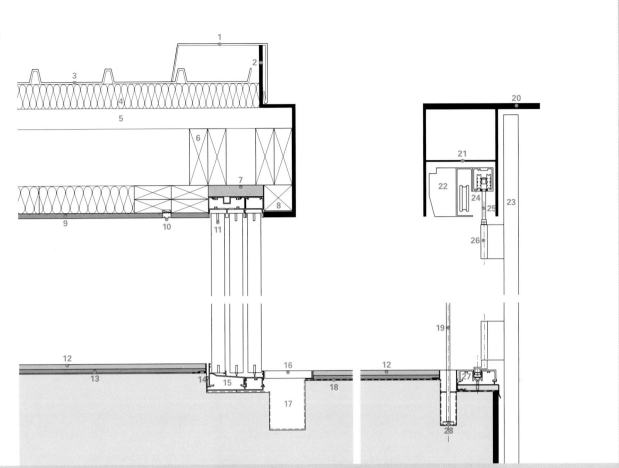

3.022
**Window Jamb at
Shutter Detail 1:5**

Peter L. Gluck and
Partners, Architects
Inverted Guest House
[26]

1 Gypsum wall board
2 Timber stud wall
  with insulation
  between studs
3 Plywood blocking
4 Double glazed timber
  sliding window
5 Timber window jamb
6 Insect screen

7 Sealant with rod
  backing
8 Flat seam copper
  cladding
9 Moisture barrier
10 Plywood
11 Heavy duty knuckle
  hinge
12 Bi-fold door
13 Cedar girt
14 Copper cladding
15 Bi-fold door in open
  position

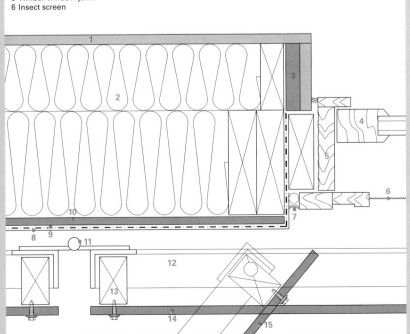

3.023
**Window Jamb At
Shutter Detail 1:5**

Peter L. Gluck and
Partners, Architects
Inverted Guest House
[26]

1 Gypsum wall board
2 Timber stud wall
  with insulation
  between studs
3 Plywood blocking
4 Timber window jamb
5 Double glazed timber
  sliding window
6 Sealant with rod

backing
7 Steel framed door
8 Copper cladding
9 Carrier track with
  roller
10 Copper flashing
11 Cedar girt
12 Moisture barrier
13 Plywood

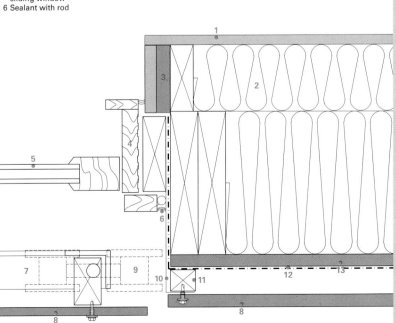

3.024
Window Plan Detail 1:5

Mount Fuji Architects
Studio
Rainy Sunny House [11]

1 40 x 55 mm (1^1/$_2$ x
  2^1/$_8$ inch) oak
  handrail
2 32 x 19 mm (1^1/$_4$ x ^{3}/$_4$
  inch) flat steel bar
3 19 mm (^{3}/$_4$ inch)
  diameter steel bar
4 5 mm (^{1}/$_5$ inch) float
  glass double glazed
  window
5 200 x 22 mm (8 x ^{7}/$_8$

inch) flat steel bar
6 32 x 16 mm (1^1/$_4$ x ^{5}/$_8$
  inch) flat steel bar
7 2.3 mm (^{1}/$_8$ inch)
  steel plate
8 Window screen

3.025
**Window Section Detail
1:5**

Mount Fuji Architects
Studio
Rainy Sunny House [11]

1 Hardwood
  herringbone parquet
  interior wall lining
2 27 x 27 x 3 mm (1 x 1
  x ^{1}/$_8$ inch) aluminium
  angle
3 5 mm (^{1}/$_5$ inch) float
  glass
4 25 x 16 mm (1x ^{5}/$_8$
  inch) flat steel bar

5 190 x 19 mm (7^1/$_2$ x
  ^{3}/$_4$ inch) flat steel bar
6 Australian cypress
  hardwood
7 Hardwood
  herringbone parquet
  flooring
8 Fibre reinforced
  plastic waterproofing
  layer
9 400 x 100 x 16 mm
  (16 x 4 x ^{5}/$_8$ inch) flat
  steel bar
10 Mortar layer
11 Reinforced concrete
  floor slab

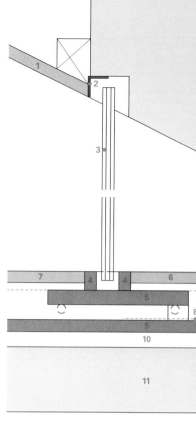

3.026
Window Sill Detail 1:5

Steven Holl Architects
Swiss Embassy
Residence [14]

1 25 mm (1 inch) clear
  insulated glass unit
2 Top-hinged in-swing
  aluminium window
3 Stainless steel sill
4 50 x 25 mm (2 x 1
  inch) rectangular
  hollow steel
  substructure
5 Waterproofing layer
6 Timber blocking

7 Rigid insulation
8 Vapour barrier
9 Two layers 15 mm
  (^{5}/$_8$ inch) gypsum
  wall board
10 Insulation
11 12 mm (^{1}/$_2$ inch)
  plywood sheathing
12 Curtain wall support
  welded and bolted to
  substructure
13 Sealant with backer
  rod
14 Channel glass
  perimeter frame
15 Channel glass

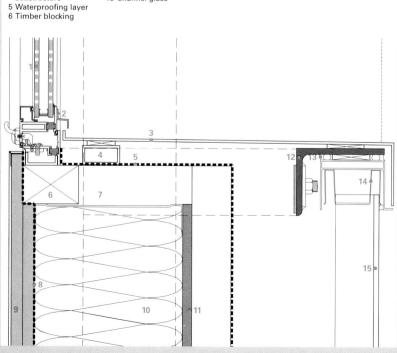

3.027
**Bedroom Window Detail
1:5**

Steven Holl Architects
Swiss Embassy
Residence [14]

1 Translucent insulated
  glass unit
2 Fixed aluminium
  glazed window
3 Compressible
  neoprene
4 Timber blocking
5 15 mm (^{5}/$_8$ inch)
  gypsum wall board
6 50 mm (2 inch) batt

insulation
7 200 mm (8 inch)
  concrete masonry
  unit
8 Steel firring channel

3.028
Window Detail 1:10

ARTEC Architekten
Holiday House [39]

1 15 mm (5/8 inch)
   plywood board on
   100 mm (4 inch
   construction timber
   and insulation with
   15 mm (5/8 inch)
   oriented strand
   board, moisture
   barrier and 6 mm (1/4
   inch) birch plywood
   board
2 Timber hung window

3 15 mm (5/8 inch)
   plywood board
   window reveal
4 Timber sill
5 200 mm (8 inch)
   insulation

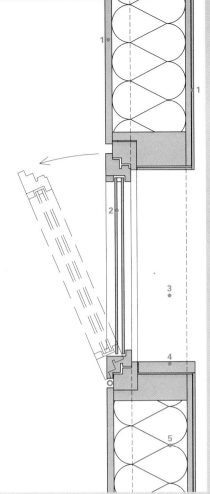

3.029
Fixed Glass Frame
Section Detail 1:10

Shuhei Endo Architect
Institute
Rooftecture S [27]

1 Stainless steel
   profiled sheet as wall
   cladding with 30 mm
   (1 1/5 inch) urethane
   foam insulation
2 Galvanized steel
   internal lining
3 100 x 100 mm (4 x 4
   inch) square hollow
   section column
4 125 x 90 x 7 mm (5 x
   3 1/2 x 1/4 inch) hot dip
   zinc-aluminium alloy
   coated steel angle
5 Double glazed fixed
   window with 8 mm
   (5/16 inch) glass, 6
   mm (1/4 inch) air gap
   and 8 mm (5/16 inch)

glass
6 15 mm (1/5 inch)
   timber floorboards
7 Timber joist
8 Galvanized steel
   flashing with sealant
   to cladding
9 40 x 40 x 5 mm (1 1/2
   x 1 1/2 x 1/5 inch) hot
   dip zinc-aluminium
   steel channel
10 Timber blocking
11 30 x 200 mm (1 1/5 x 8
   inch) steel beam
12 Profiled galvanized
   steel cladding with
   applied waterproof
   membrane
13 12 mm (1/2 inch)
   waterproofed veneer
   board
14 Galvalume edge and
   drip profile
15 Corrugated
   galvanized steel
   eaves soffit

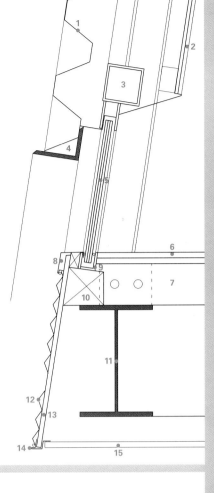

3.030
Fixed Glass Frame Plan
Detail 1:10

Shuhei Endo Architect
Institute
Rooftecture S [27]

1 Square steel section
   with paint finish
2 Aluminium sash
   window
3 100 x 100 mm (4 x 4
   inch) steel beam
4 Timber frame with
   oil stain finish
5 Aluminium window
   sash

6 Stainless steel angle
7 Double glazed fixed
   window with 6 mm
   (1/4 inch) air gap
8 Sealant with backer
   rod
9 Stainless steel
   profiled sheet wall
   cladding with 30 mm
   (1 1/5 inch) urethane
   foam insulation
10 12 mm (1/2 inch)
   plasterboard wall
   lining

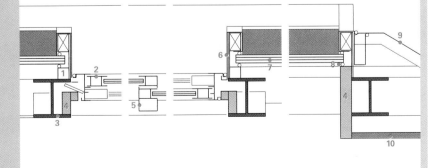

3.031
Aluminium Window
Section Detail 1:10

Shuhei Endo Architect
Institute
Rooftecture S [27]

1 Stainless steel
   profiled sheet roof
   cladding
2 100 x 50 mm (4 x 2
   inch) metal stud
   frame
3 Stainless steel
   profiled sheet wall
   cladding with 30 mm
   (1 1/5 inch) urethane

foam insulation
4 Timber framing with
   oil stain finish
5 Aluminium window
   frame
6 Double glazed fixed
   window
7 Timber framing with
   oil stain finish
8 Timber framing with
   oil stain finish
9 Timber sill with
   stainless steel
   flashing and formed
   drip turned in to
   cladding sheet

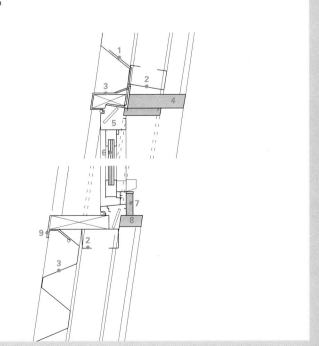

3.032
Window Detail 1:10

A-Piste Arkkitehdit
Villa O [39]

1 Triple glazing of 6 mm (1/4 inch), 4 mm (1/8 inch) and 6 mm (1/4 inch) glass panes
2 Flagstone exterior surface
3 Silicone seal
4 130 mm (51/8 inch) façade masonry
5 30 mm (11/4 inch) ventilated cavity
6 25 mm (1 inch) weathershield
7 125 mm (5 inch) mineral wool insulation
8 Crushed stone fill
9 Waterproof bituminous membrane
10 15 mm (5/8 inch)

Siberian larch flooring, brushed and wax oiled
11 100 mm (4 inch) reinforced concrete slab with underfloor heating
12 Two layers of 50 mm (2 inch) thermal insulation
13 300 mm (12 inch) crushed stone
14 125 mm (5 inch) concrete blockwork
15 125 mm (5 inch) thermal insulation
16 200 mm (79/10 inch) concrete blockwork

3.033
Full Height Window Detail 1:20

Morphogenesis
N85 Residence [08]

1 External grade ipe timber slat cladding
2 External grade ipe timber slat cladding
3 Timber framework
4 Reinforced concrete lintel
5 12 mm (1/2 inch) thick plaster
6 4 mm (1/8 inch) thick timber veneer false ceiling
7 4 mm (1/8 inch) thick timber veneer cladding
8 140 x 85 mm (51/2 x 31/3 inch) hardwood frame
9 60 x 125 mm (21/3 x 5 inch) timber stile

10 Timber louvres
11 Timber veneer cladding
12 Hardwood flooring
13 130 mm (51/2 inch) thick cement bed
14 Stone edge strip
15 External grade timber cladding
16 Waterproofing
17 External grade ipe timber slat cladding
18 External grade ipe timber slat cladding

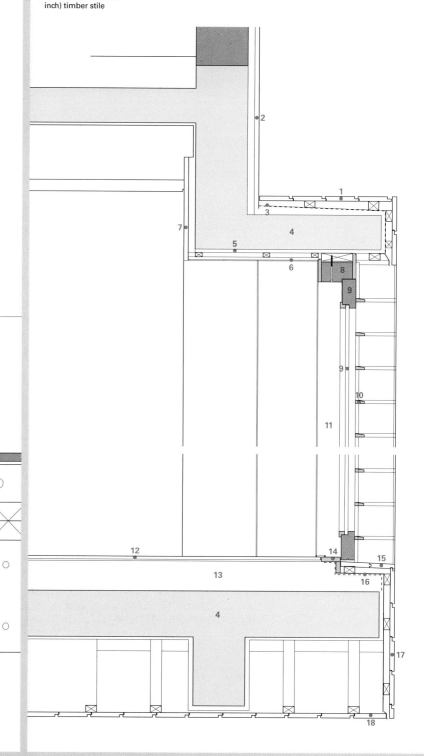

3.034
Window Section and
Plan Detail 1:5

Innovarchi
Gold Coast House [12]

1 Clear anodized
  aluminium extrusion
  (upper part)
2 Clear anodized
  aluminium extrusion
  (lower part)
3 Painted plasterboard
  ceiling
4 Performance
  laminated fixed
  frameless glazing
5 Clear anodized
  aluminium sill
6 Sealed concrete floor
  finish
7 Concrete topping
  slab
8 Clear anodized
  aluminium extrusion
  (mullion)

9 Performance
  laminated fixed
  frameless glazing

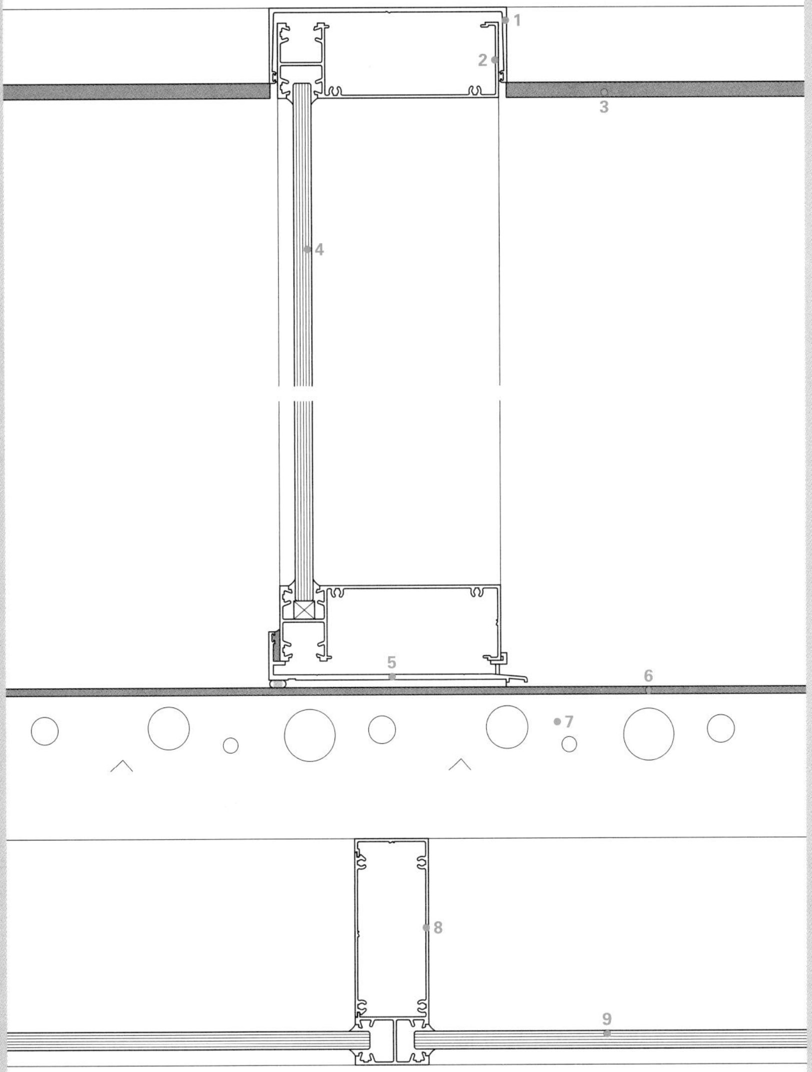

3.035
Louvred Window
Section and Plan Detail
1:5

Innovarchi
Gold Coast House [12]

1 Painted steel mullion
2 Clear glass louvred
  window with plastic
  clip mechanism
3 Clear glass louvred
  window in closed
  position
4 Clear anodized
  window frame (sill)
5 Sealed concrete floor
  finish
6 Painted steel mullion
7 Clear glass louvred
  window
8 Performance
  laminated frameless
  fixed glazing

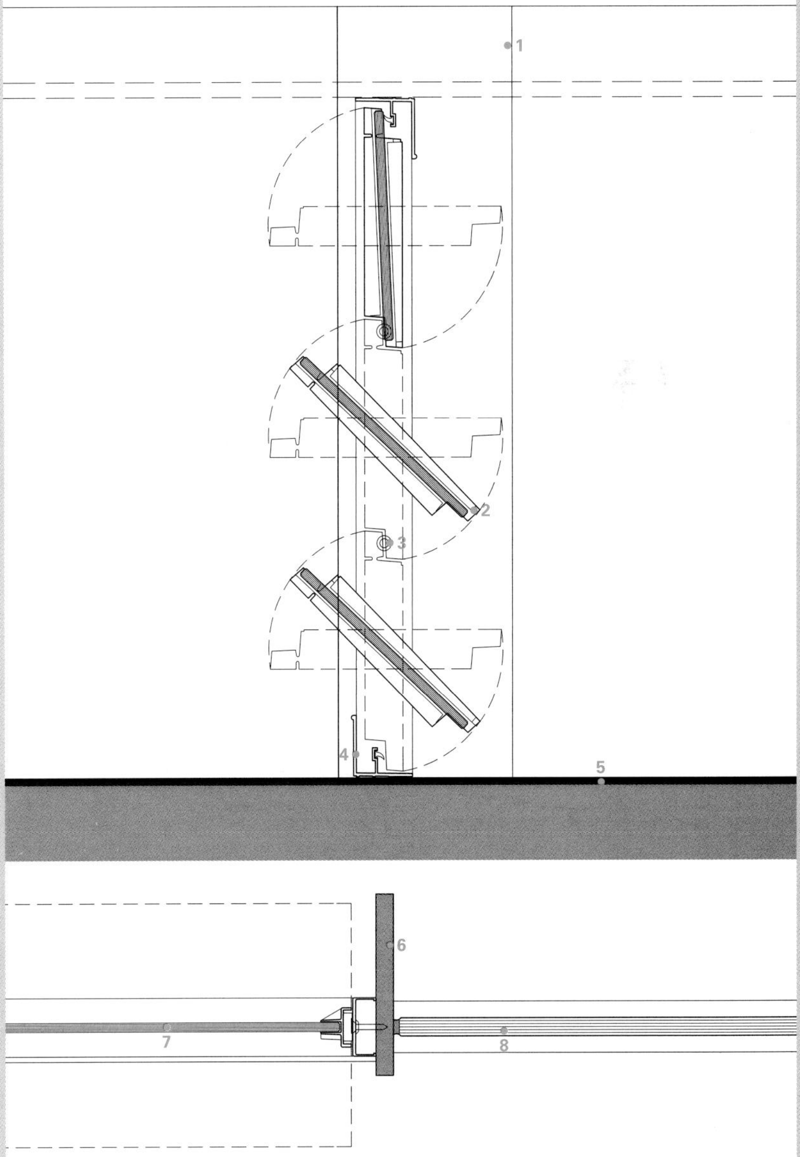

3.036
Window Detail 1:20

ARTEC Architekten
Holiday House [39]

1 20 mm (3/4 inch)
   timber roof decking
2 100 mm (4 inch)
   insulation
3 Steel I-beam
4 200 x 30 mm (8 x 1 1/5
   inch) timber board
5 108 mm (4 1/4 inch)
   solid timber boarding
6 35 x 50 x 50 mm (1 3/8
   x 2 x 2 inch) glass
   reinforced plastic
   profile
7 Double glazing
8 Shim
9 280 x 30 mm (11 x
   1 1/5 inch) timber
   fascia
10 Insect screen
11 Stainless steel cable
12 400 x 80 mm (16 x

3 1/8 inch) timber
   balustrade
13 20 x 20 mm (3/4 x 3/4
   inch) aluminium
   bracket
14 72 mm (2 7/8 inch)
   diameter zinced steel
   thermionic radiator
15 Perforated sheet
   metal
16 35 x 50 x 50 mm (1 3/8
   x 2 x 2 inch) glass
   reinforced plastic
   profile
17 I-section steel beam
18 27 x 92 mm (1 x 3 5/8
   inch) timber decking
19 108 mm (4 1/4 inch)
   solid timber boarding
20 280 x 30 mm (11 x
   1 1/5 inch) timber
   fascia
21 Assembly bracket
22 Membrane layer
23 Edge plate

3.037
Window Detail 1:5

Frank Harmon Architect
Low Country Residence
[26]

1 Double glazing unit
2 Storefront window
   framing system
3 Metal flashing
4 Hardwood timber sill
5 50 x 180 mm (2 x
   7 1/12 inch) timber sill
   plate
6 12 mm (1/2 inch)
   Hardipanel cladding
   system
7 Batt insulation
8 25 mm (1 inch)
   plywood sheathing
9 50 x 180 mm (2 x
   7 1/12 inch) timber
   wall framing
10 Line of mechanical
   air supply duct
11 50 x 150 mm (2 x 6
   inch) tongue and
   groove timber
   decking
12 50 x 100 mm (2 x 4
   inch) timber blocking
13 Universal steel beam
14 50 x 240 mm (2 x 9 1/2
   inch) double timber
   beam
15 25 x 150 mm (1 x 6
   inch) tongue and
   groove timber ceiling
16 50 x 100 mm (2 x 4
   inch) timber window
   header
17 Metal closure piece

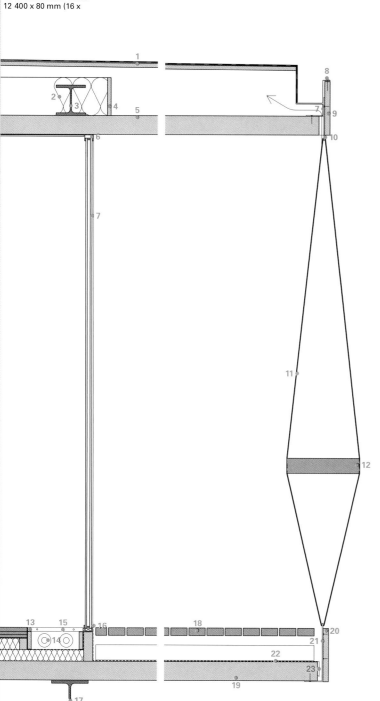

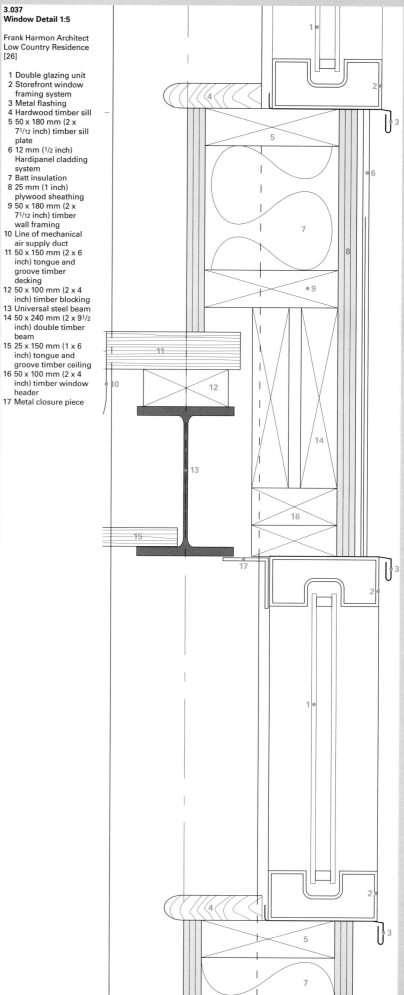

3.038
Louvred Window Detail
1:10

Lahz Nimmo Architects
Casuarina Ultimate
Beach House [31]

1 Building paper
2 Painted fibre cement
   ceiling
3 Translucent
   toughened glass
   blade louvres with
   black clip fasteners
4 120 x 20 mm (4³/₄ x
   ³/₄ inch) hardwood
   boards shiplapped
   with joints secret
   nailed and stain
   finished
5 Fibre cement sheet
   to wall beyond
6 Dressed exposed
   hardwood nogging
7 35 x 60 mm (1³/₈ x
   2³/₈ inch) recycled
   blue gum timber
   battens, screw fixed
   to stud frame with
   stainless steel screws
   and stain finished
8 Sill at 700 mm (28
   inch) from finish
   floor level to main
   bath area
9 Carry tiles to bath
   into reveal
10 Waterproof
   membrane
11 Two part folded steel
   flashing with
   minimum 150 mm (6
   inch) overlap and lap
   under fibre cement at
   sides
12 Tiles to bath
13 Mortar bed
14 6 mm (¹/₄ inch) fibre
   cement sheet
   substrate
15 Sharp even finish to
   exposed edge of
   folded steel flashing

3.039
Fixed Glazing Detail 1:10

ODOS Architects
House in Wicklow [18]

1 Profiled metal drip
2 Fire-rated 4.8kg
   granular surfaced
   polyester reinforced
   modified bitumen
   high performance
   membrane, fully
   torch bonded
3 Steel beam
4 Silicone based paint
   finish to external
   walls on cement-
   based mineral render
   and insulation
   system
5 Vapour barrier
6 Pull down black-out
   blind recessed into
   ceiling with a secret
   fixed softwood
   access panel painted
   to match ceiling
7 12.5 mm (¹/₂ inch)
   plasterboard,
   skimmed and painted
8 Recessed hardwood
   timber frames with
   treated hardwood
   timber packing piece
9 Finish to reveal to
   match external
   facade
10 Full height, clear
   double glazed fixed
   unit comprised of 8
   mm (¹/₃ inch)
   toughened glass
   outer pane, 12 mm
   (¹/₂ inch) air gap and
   8 mm (¹/₃ inch) clear
   toughened inner
   pane in a recessed
   treated hardwood
   timber frame. All
   joints between glass
   panes to be silicone
   sealed and bonded
11 Carpet on 70 mm
   (2³/₄ inch)
   power-floated in-situ
   concrete screed,
   screed contains
   underfloor heating
   conduits on vapour
   control layer with
   taped overlaps at all
   junctions. 50 mm (2
   inch) Kingspan
   insulation on solid
   concrete block and
   plank ceiling
   spanning between
   steel beams
12 Damp proof course
13 Pressed metal
   powder-coated sill on
   damp proof course
   fixed into recess of
   treated hardwood
   timber bottom rail

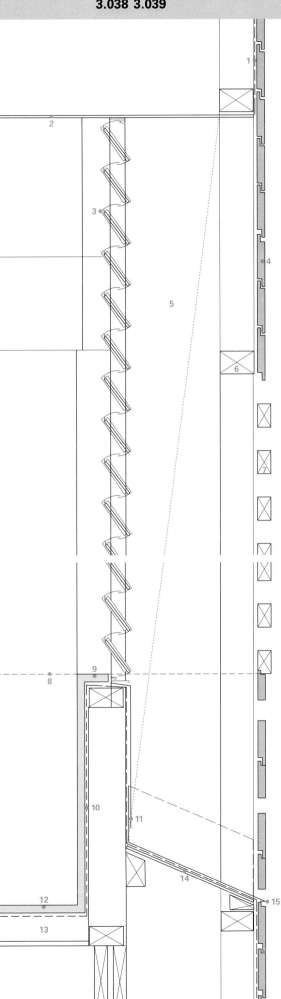

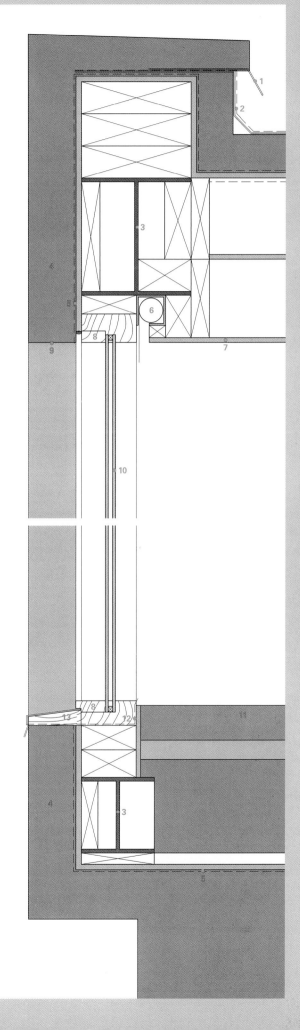

3.040
Bay Window Detail 1:20

Avanti Architects
Long View [35]

1 Two 250 x 50 mm (10 x 2 inch) timber beams, shown dotted below window sill, blocked and braced
2 65 x 22 mm (2 1/2 x 7/8 inch) tongue and groove

weatherboards secret fixed vertically to horizontal counter-battens
3 100 x 50 mm (4 x 2 inch) timber stud frame with two layers of 12 mm (1/2 inch) plywood bracing externally and 12.5 mm (1/2 inch) plasterboard over 12 mm (1/2 inch) plywood bracing

over vapour control layer internally
4 Schuco aluminium operable windows
5 Two layers of 12.5 mm (1/2 inch) plasterboard
6 Waterproof membrane
7 150 mm (6 inch) insulation between studding
8 150 x 50 mm (6 x 2 inch) timber stud

frame
9 90 x 60 mm (3 1/2 x 2 3/8 inch) vertical battens provide ventilation to wall cavity space

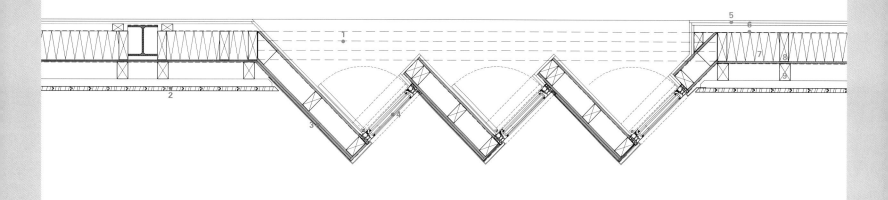

3.041
Study Window Plan Detail 1:10

O'Donnell +Tuomey Architects
The Sleeping Giant – Killiney House [09]

1 Galvanized steel brackets at 450 mm (18 inch) centres built into blockwork and fixed to wall
2 Recessed mastic pointing
3 Timber packers
4 195 x 70 mm (7 3/4 x

2 3/4 inch) iroko frame
5 Recessed transparent silicone mastic pointing
6 95 x 70 mm (3 3/4 x 2 3/4 inch) Iroko sash
7 Glazing bead
8 Double glazing
9 195 x 70 mm (7 3/4 x 2 3/4 inch) iroko mullion

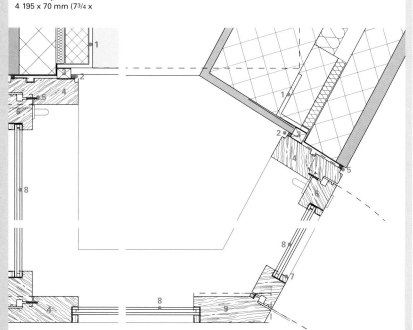

3.042
Clerestory Window Detail 1:10

O'Donnell +Tuomey Architects
The Sleeping Giant – Killiney House [09]

1 Mastic
2 Anti-capillary groove
3 Timber packer
4 Damp proof course
5 Iroko window frame
6 Glazing bead
7 Double glazed fixed window
8 Continuous iroko sill fixed through timber to steel bracket
9 Iroko extension piece to sill
10 Timber bearer
11 Bitumen damp proof course bonded to the vertical vapour barrier

12 Damp proof membrane
13 0.8 gauge terne-coated stainless steel cover flashing
14 1.5 mm (1/16 inch) thick homogeneous PVC-P membrane on 19 mm (3/4 inch) thick waterproof plywood deck on softwood firrings on 50 x 200 mm (2 x 8 inch) joists
15 Concrete beam
16 70 mm (2 3/4 inch) insulation
17 Painted rough sand-cement render
18 Softwood firrings
19 Insulation on vapour barrier behind iroko boarding

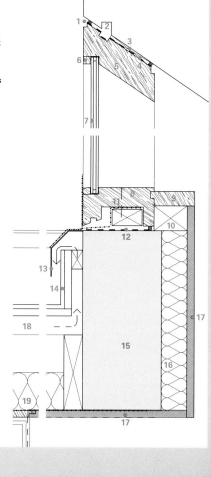

3.043
Clerestory Window Plan
Detail 1:10

O'Donnell + Tuomey
Architects
The Sleeping Giant –
Killiney House [09]

1 Blockwork wall
2 Galvanized steel
 brackets at 450 mm
 (18 inch) centres built
 into blockwork and
 fixed to wall
3 50 mm (2 inch)
 insulation
4 340 x 70 mm (13½ x
 2¾ inch) iroko frame
5 Damp proof course
6 Glazing bead
7 Double glazing
8 195 x 70 mm (7¾ x
 2¾ inch) iroko frame
9 Concrete wall
10 100 mm (4 inch) thick
 granite external leaf

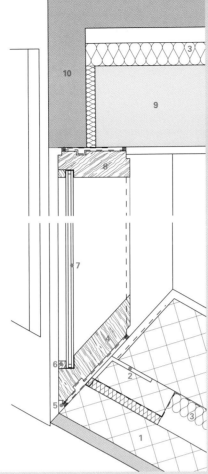

3.044
Window Plan Detail 1:5

Stam Architecten
Two Apartments [10]

1 Window frame
2 Steel T-profile column
3 Aluminium cladding
4 Fixing bolts
5 Architectonic
 reinforced concrete
 floor
6 Double glazing unit

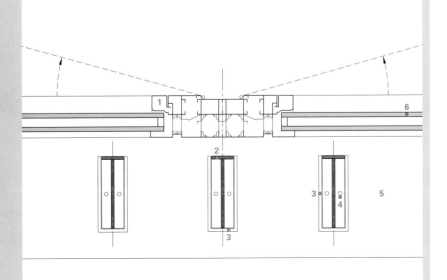

3.045
Window and Blind
Detail 1:10

Vittorio Longheu
Casa C [16]

1 Two layers of 12 mm
 (½ inch)
 plasterboard
2 Heat insulation
3 100 mm (4 inch)
 insulated panel
4 Steel angle
5 Sliding rail
6 Zinc sheet box to
 house roller blinds
7 Roller blind
8 Stone covering
9 Steel rectangular
 hollow section
10 Metal reveal lining
11 Brush guides to roller
 blind
12 Guides for roller
 blind
13 Unbreaking double
 glazed window unit
14 Sliding track for
 window unit
15 Drain
16 Metal frame of
 glazed window unit

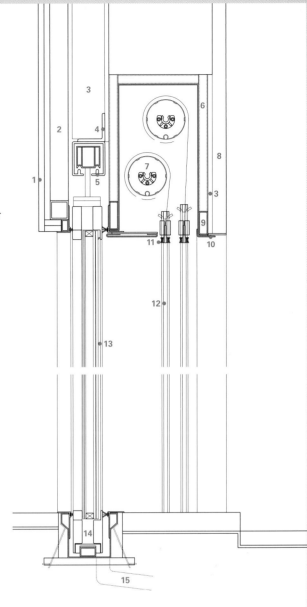

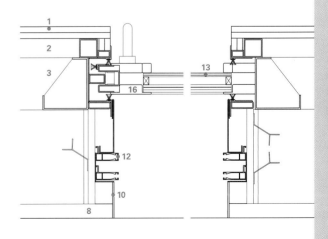

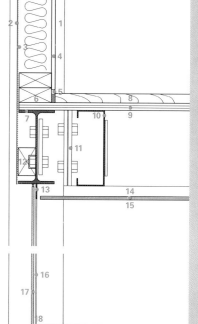

3.046
Louvred Window Detail
1:10

Peter Stutchbury
Architecture
Avalon House [29]

1 Glass and timber framed louvre system
2 Upper floor
3 25 mm (1 inch) hardwood tongue and groove floorboards
4 Black Sikaflex to floorboard joint
5 100 x 45 mm (4 x 1³/₄ inch) aluminium sill
6 18 mm (7/10 inch) structural plywood fixed to floor purlins
7 200 mm (8 inch) galvanized steel floor purlins
8 Galvanized steel bolts
9 Galvanized steel connection plates to columns and beams
10 Galvanized steel cleat for bolted floor purlin connection
11 9 mm (3/8 inch) plywood ceiling panels
12 Curtain track set in recess
13 200 mm (8 inch) galvanized universal steel bearer
14 Galvanized steel flat sheet cladding
15 Aluminium weather seal to timber framed glass louvres when in closed position
16 Plywood ceiling panel fixed after curtain track has been installed, allowing for 10 mm (3/8 inch) shadowline
17 150 x 100 x 5 mm (6 x 4 x 1/5 inch) galvanized rectangular hollow section steel column

3.047
Fixed Window Detail
1:10

Peter Stutchbury
Architecture
Avalon House [29]

1 150 x 100 x 5 mm (6 x 4 x 1/5 inch) galvanized rectangular hollow section steel column
2 Galvanized steel flat sheet cladding on timber studs with edges overlapped by 150 mm (6 inch) and joints sealed with silicone bead
3 Sarking behind cladding shown dotted
4 Plasterboard wall lining
5 Rondo shadowline and black Sikaflex to floorboard joint
6 90 x 40 mm (3¹/₂ x 1⁵/₈ inch) timber sole plate
7 200 x 100 mm (8 x 4 inch) galvanized universal beam bolted to galvanized steel cleat
8 25 mm (1 inch) tongue and groove hardwood floorboards
9 18 mm (3/4 inch) structural plywood fixed to joists and bearers
10 200 x 75 mm (8 x 3 inch) galvanized steel channel as floor purlin and bolted to cleat
11 Galvanized steel connection plates bolt beams to columns
12 Timber fixing blocks
13 40 x 5 mm (1⁵/₈ x 1/5 inch) galvanized steel glazing bar welded to underside of beam
14 Firring channels fixed to beam
15 9 mm (3/8 inch) plywood ceiling panels fixed to firring channels
16 40 x 5 mm (1⁵/₈ x 1/5 inch) galvanized steel glazing bar welded to side of column
17 Fixed clear glazed panel
18 Rondo shadowline and black Sikaflex to floorboard joint

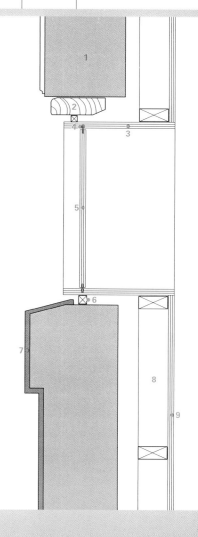

3.048
Clerestory Window
Detail 1:10

Welsh + Major
Pitt Street House [37]

1 Folded zincalume flashing
2 220 x 20 mm (8³/₄ x ³/₄ inch) painted timber fascia
3 Custom Orb zincalume roof sheet
4 150 mm (6 inch) insulation
5 Fixed glazing
6 2 mm (¹/₁₂ inch) folded galvanized hood
7 150 x 75 mm (6 x 3 inch) parallel flange channel
8 Line of sliding flyscreen door beyond
9 Painted, timber framed, glazed sliding door

3.049
Existing Window Detail
1:10

Welsh + Major
Pitt Street House [37]

1 Existing brickwork
2 Existing weathered timber lintel
3 15 mm (5/8 inch) cross-direction grade ply box
4 Timber dowel pins
5 15 mm (5/8 inch) ply pivoting blade
6 25 x 25 mm (1 x 1 inch) timber packing
7 Existing ashlar render
8 80 x 35 mm (3¹/₄ x 1³/₈ inch) internal timber stud frame
9 15 mm (5/8 inch) plywood lining

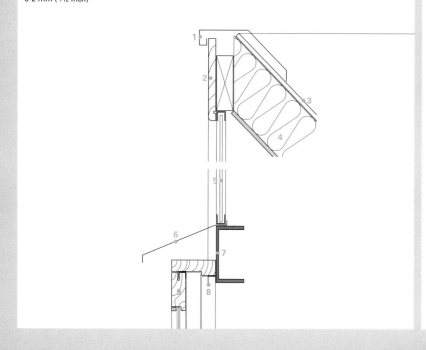

3.050
Kitchen Box Window
Detail 1:5

Lee + Mundwiler
Architects
The Coconut House [12]

1 Phenolic resin wood
  veneer panels
2 Vertical timber
  battens
3 Weather resistant
  barrier, vapour
  permeable building
  paper
4 Plywood sheathing
5 140 x 350 mm (5¹/₂ x
  14 inch) timber beam
6 15 mm (⁵/₈ inch)
  gypsum board
7 24 gauge metal
  flashing
8 Continuous caulking
9 20 mm (³/₄ inch)
  hardwood casing to
  top, sides and sill, cut

as shown and
painted
10 Awning, or fixed
   window with cut
   nailing strip off every
   100 mm (4 inch) with
   remaining material
   inserted through
   slots in hardwood
   casing
11 Metal reveal
   moulding
12 Timber top plate
13 Batt insulation
14 Kitchen cabinets

3.051
Window Head Detail 1:5

Peter L. Gluck and
Partners, Architects
Inverted Guest House
[26]

1 Moisture barrier
2 Corrugated copper
  cladding
3 Plywood wall
  structure
4 Gypsum white board
5 Copper flashing with
  formed drip
6 Steel clip angle
7 Bi-fold track
8 Boxed timber and ply
  header
9 Plywood wall
  structure
10 Sealant with rod
   backing
11 Steel L-angle
12 Aluminium sliding
   track

13 Steel frame with
   cedar girts
14 Insect screen
15 Double glazed sliding
   timber windows

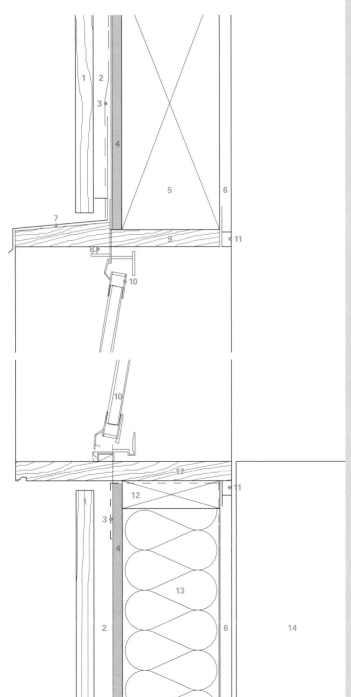

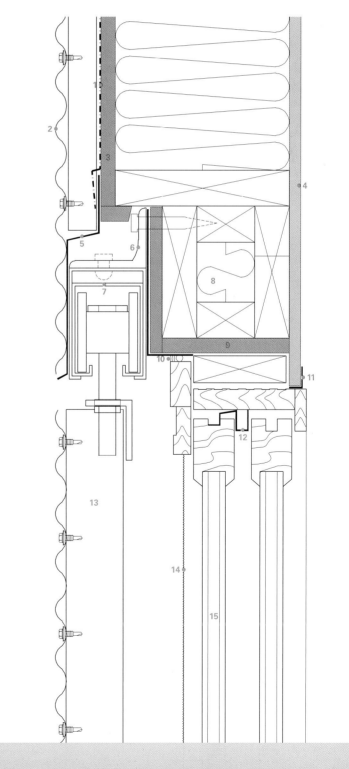

3.052
**Kitchen Window Detail
1:10**

Studio Bednarski
Hesmondhalgh House
[33]

1 30 to 40 mm (1¼ to
  1⅝ inch) size pebble
  border
2 Extra layer capping
  sheet at border
3 Pre-patinated copper
  capping and facing
4 18 mm (¾ inch)
  weather bonded and
  proofed plywood
5 90 mm (3½ inch)
  insulation
6 500 gauge vapour
  barrier
7 18 mm (¾ inch)
  weather bonded and
  proofed plywood
8 152 x 152 x 37 mm (6
  x 6 x 1½ inch)

universal beam
9 25 mm (1 inch)
  weather bonded and
  proofed plywood
  fascia
10 Pre-patinated copper
  fascia and drip
11 Fixed double glazed
  hardwood window
12 200 x 75 mm (8 x 3
  inch) hardwood sill
13 Two layers 12.5 mm
  (½ inch)
  plasterboard
14 500 gauge vapour
  barrier
15 Timber stair tread
16 Timber stair fixing
17 Two layers 18 mm
  (¾ inch) weather
  bonded and proofed
  plywood
18 Insulation
19 100 x 50 mm (4 x 2
  inch) timber stud
  frame
20 100 x 50 mm (4 x 2

inch) mild steel
rectangular hollow
section steel beam

3.053
Window Detail 1:2

Correia Ragazzi
Arquitectos
Casa no Gerês [06]

1 10 mm (⅜ inch)
  plywood
2 Timber edging
3 60 x 60 mm (2⅜ x
  2⅜ inch) aluminium
  angle bracket
4 Stone
5 Mastic sealant
6 Hinge
7 Rubber backstop
8 60 x 8 mm (2⅜ x ⅜
  inch) steel flat bar
9 25 x 25 mm (1 x 1
  inch) steel angle
  bracket
10 Lead wedge
11 Transparent silicone
  seal
12 Vertical timber
  window shutter

13 Double glazing
  comprised of 5 mm
  (⅕ inch) glass, 10
  mm (⅜ inch) air gap
  and 5 mm (⅕ inch)
  glass
14 Window fastener
15 20 x 5 mm (¾ x ⅕
  inch) steel flat bar
16 60 x 60 mm (2⅜ x
  2⅜ inch) aluminium
  angle bracket
17 Shelf
18 Metallic shelf bracket

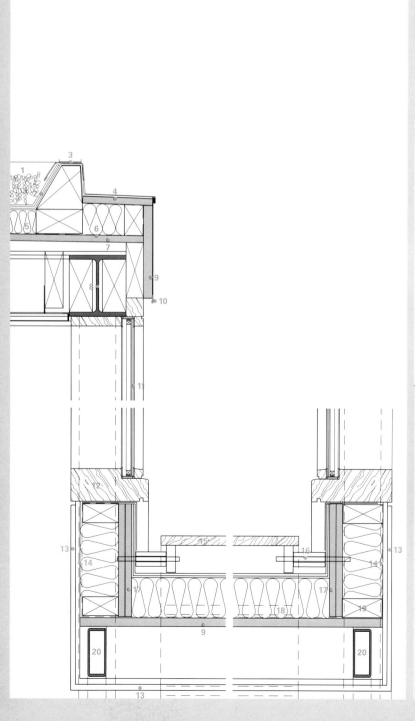

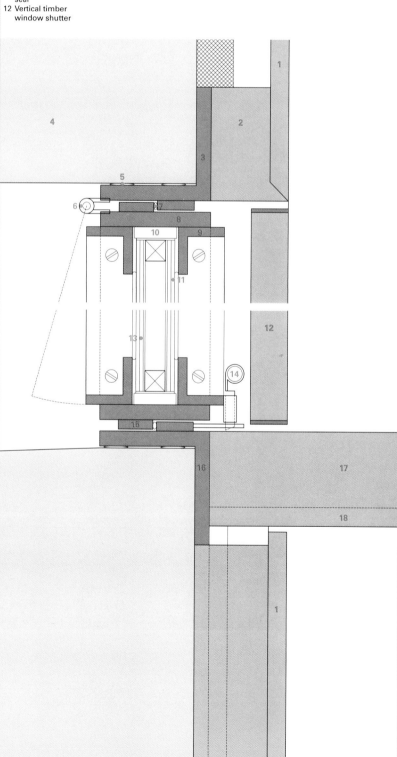

3.054
Window Detail 1:5

Waro Kishi + K.
Associates Architects
Hakata House [18]

1 Caulking
2 Screen door
3 Sliding door with
  heat resistant glass
4 Aluminium sash
  frame
5 Anchor rod
6 Reinforced concrete
7 Timber casing
8 Timber door jamb
9 Timber column
10 Traditional Japanese
  plaster finish to wall

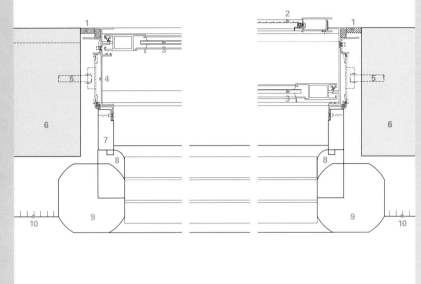

3.055
Window Detail 1:5

Waro Kishi + K.
Associates Architects
Hakata House [18]

1 Traditional Japanese
  plaster wall finish
2 Reinforced concrete
  wall structure
3 Timber door jamb
4 Single hung window
  with shoji screen
5 Timber stop

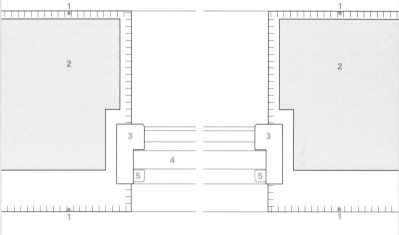

3.056
Window Detail 1:5

Waro Kishi + K.
Associates Architects
Hakata House [18]

1 Reinforced concrete
2 Anchor rod
3 Caulking
4 Screen door
5 Sliding door
6 Timber door stile
7 Timber casing
8 Aluminium drip
  profile
9 Aluminium sash
  frame
10 Anchor rod
11 Waterproof boarding
12 Timber casing
13 Traditional Japanese
  plaster wall finish
14 Timber column
15 Timber lintel and
  upper track to shoji
  screen
16 Timber lintel and
  lower track to shoji
  screen
17 Timber blocking
18 Tatami flooring
19 Plywood lining
20 Timber joist

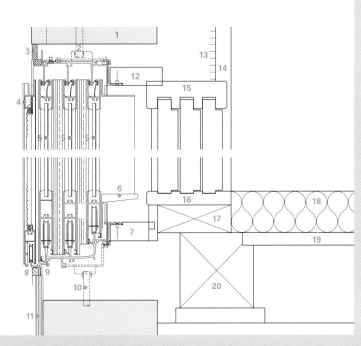

3.057
Window Detail 1:5

Waro Kishi + K.
Associates Architects
Hakata House [18]

1 Traditional Japanese
  plaster wall finish
2 Timber window head
3 Waterproof plywood
4 Insert anchor
5 Caulking
6 Aluminium flashing
7 Polished wire glass
8 Steel angle
9 Caulking
10 Traditional Japanese
  plaster wall finish
11 Timber plaster stop
  bead
12 Timber plaster stop
  bead
13 Single hung window
  with shoji screen
14 Timber window sill

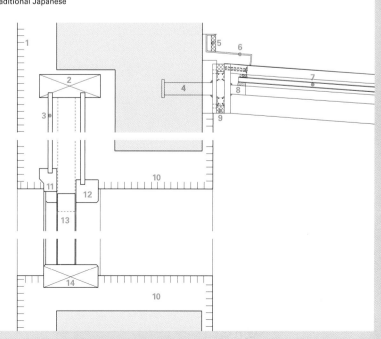

3.058
Clerestory Window Sill
Detail 1:2

Barton Myers Associates
Bekins Residence [25]

1 Glazing
2 Steel angle
3 Galvanized steel
   flashing
4 Aluminium glazing
   bead
5 Sealant
6 Sliding glass door
7 Insect screen
8 Exterior
9 Interior

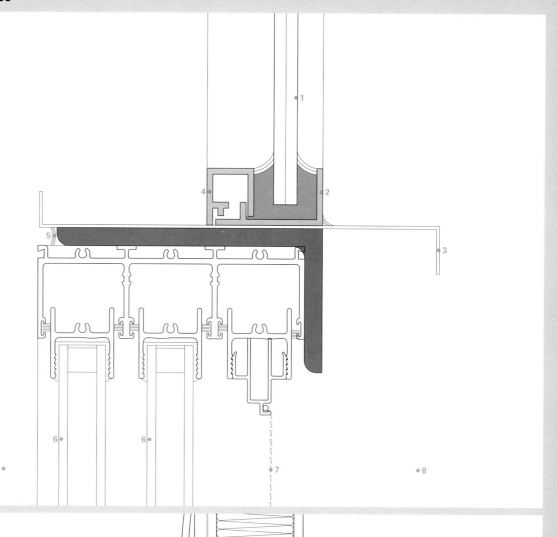

3.059
Window Plan and
Section Detail 1:5

Jun Igarashi Architects
Rectangle of Light [37]

1 100 mm (4 inch)
   glass wool insulation
2 9.5 mm (3/8 inch)
   solid conifer plywood
   weatherboarding on
   battens with
   decay-resistant paint
   finish
3 Waterproof paper
4 12 mm (1/2 inch)
   insulation board
5 Galvanized and
   aluminium coated
   steel sheet flashing
6 105 x 50 mm (4 x 2
   inch) timber stud
7 12.5 mm (1/2 inch)
   plasterboard with
   vinyl cloth
   polyethylene film

8 Polyethylene film
9 105 x 30 mm (4 x 1 1/5
   inch) timber stud
10 Timber window
    frame
11 Timber sash
12 Double glazed
    window unit
13 Timber stopper
14 Handle
15 Hinge
16 Caulking
17 Steel plate
18 Timber window
    frame

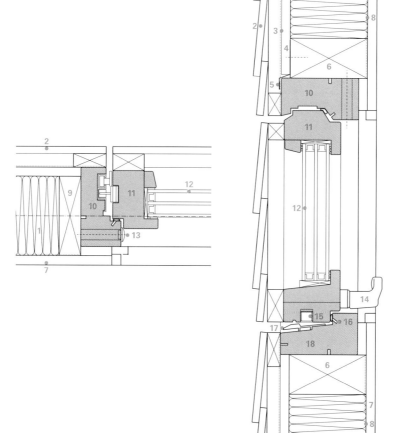

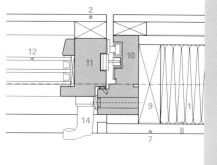

3.060
Window Detail 1:10

Matharoo Associates
Dilip Sanghvi Residence
[07]

1 25 mm (1 inch) thick
 internal plaster
 (ground floor only)
2 20 mm (3/4 inch) thick
 white travertine
 cladding
3 185 mm (71/4 inch)
 concrete wall
4 Interior
5 Window frame
6 Aluminium window
 frame
7 Wood finish concrete
 wall
8 Sill projection
9 Exterior
10 8 mm (5/8 inch)
 groove filled with
 clear silicone
11 Structural column

12 25 mm (1 inch) thick
 smooth-finish
 internal plaster
 surface
13 225 mm (9 inch) thick
 wood-finish exposed
 concrete wall

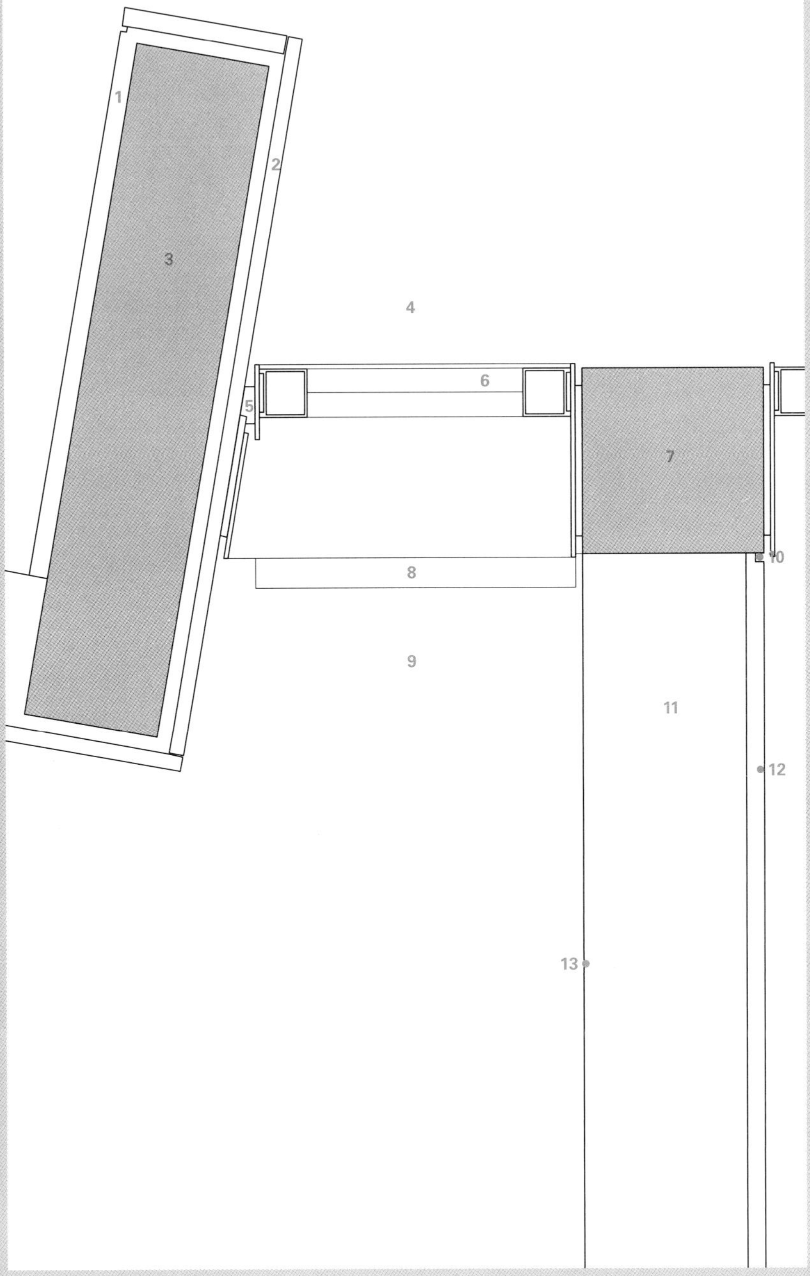

3.061
**Louvred Window Detail
1:2**

Matharoo Associates
Dilip Sanghvi Residence
[07]

1 Ply finish to concrete
 ceiling
2 Groove filled with
 silicone sealant
3 Sliding door track
 fixed to ceiling
4 Sliding door track
 and roller assembly
5 12 x 25 mm (1/2 x 1
 inch) stainless steel
 rod
6 Rectangular hollow
 section stainless
 steel vertical member
7 19 mm (3/4 inch) thick
 teak slat fixed to 12 x
 12 mm (1/2 x 1/2 inch)
 stainless steel rod
 and 20 mm (3/4 inch)

 diameter stainless
 steel pipe
8 12 x 25 mm (1/2 x 1
 inch) bottom rail
 stainless steel rod
9 Floor guide

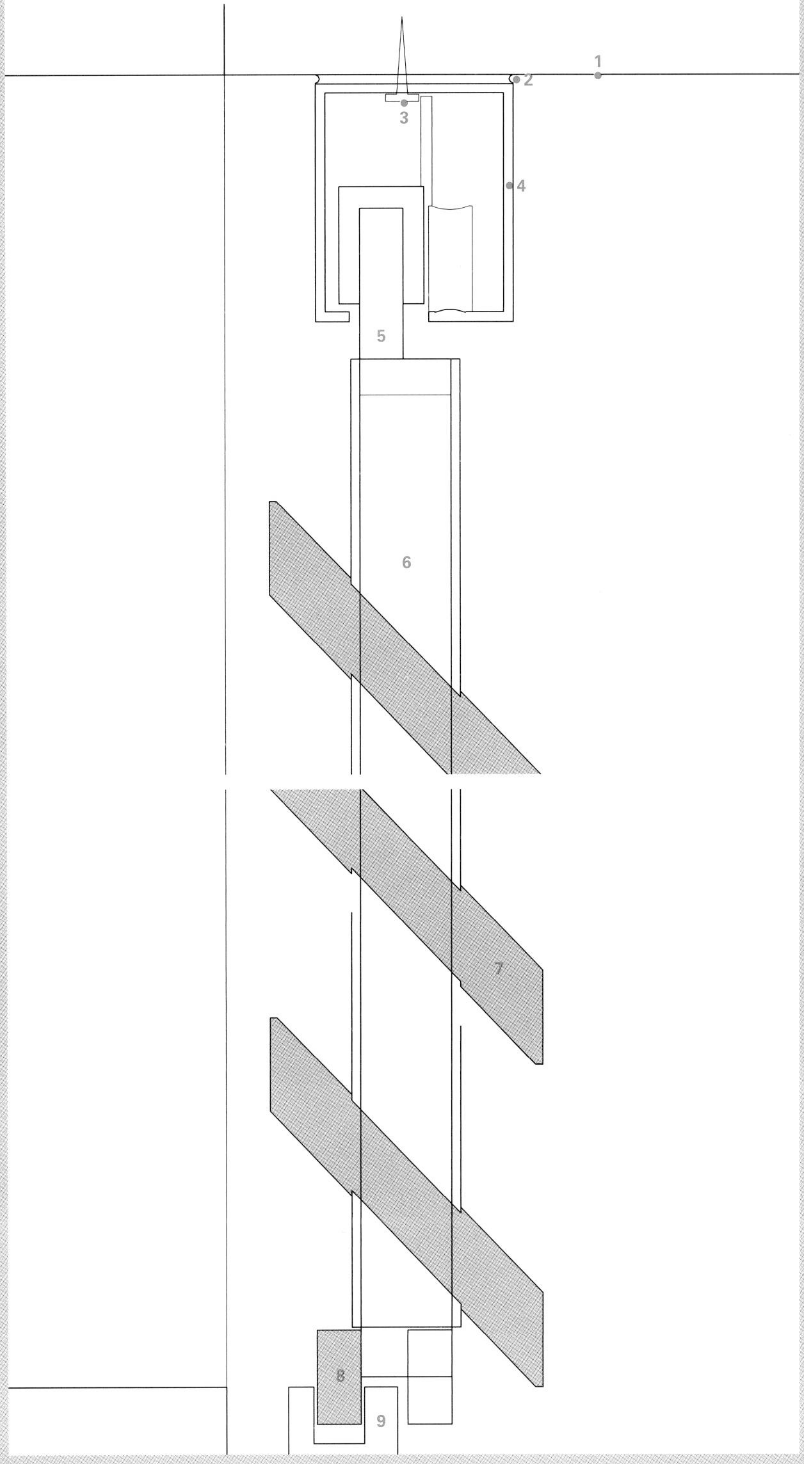

3.062
Window and Skylight
Detail 1:10

Alphaville
Hall House 1 [07]

1 Fair-faced concrete
roof with osmosis
liquid waterproofing
paint finish
2 40 x 20 x 2 mm (13/5
x 3/4 x 1/12 inch)
aluminium angle
sash
3 50 mm (2 inch)
urethane foam
insulation
4 9.5 mm (3/8 inch)
plasterboard with
emulsion paint finish
fixed to 70 x 30 mm
(23/4 x 11/5 inch)
timber substrate
framing
5 80 x 50 mm (31/8 x 2
inch) timber end

piece with emulsion
paint finish
6 10 mm (3/8 inch) float
glass
7 Structural glazing
sealant
8 2 mm (1/12 inch)
stainless steel plate
sash
9 6 mm (1/4 inch) float
glass, 6 mm (1/4 inch)
air space, 6 mm (1/4
inch) float glass
10 25 mm (1 inch) glue
laminate timber
board with urethane
paint finish
11 40 x 2 mm (13/5 x 1/12
inch) stainless steel
flat bar sash
12 Fair-faced concrete
exterior wall with
osmosis liquid
waterproofing paint
finish

3.063
Window Head and Sill in
Timber Wall Detail 1:10

Hawkes Architecture
Crossway [16]

1 Clay tile timbrel
vaulted arch
2 Warmcell recycled
newspaper insulation
3 Painted waterproof
plywood fascia panel
to match colour of
window frame
4 Painted hardwood
cover architrave to
match colour of
window frame
5 Internorm Edition
Passiv timber framed
window
6 Wood fibre web infill
insulation
7 Joist
8 Waterproof plywood
9 Toughened glass

argon-filled triple
glazing
10 Aluminium window
sill
11 Internorm Edition
Passiv timber framed
window
12 Painted
environmentally
friendly medium
density fibreboard
window sill
13 Tescon airtightness
tape
14 Painted plasterboard

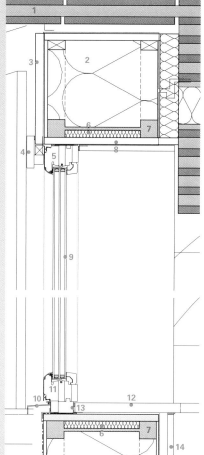

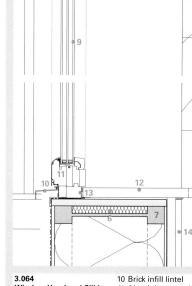

3.064
Window Head and Sill in
Timber Wall Detail 1:10

Hawkes Architecture
Crossway (16)

1 Red brick with lime
mortar using crushed
bottle sand
2 Panelvent
vapour-permeable
sheathing board
3 Warmcell recycled
newspaper insulation
4 Painted plasterboard
5 Joist
6 Waterproof plywood
7 Wood fibre web infill
insulation
8 Internorm
Generation timber
window frame
9 Cavity tray bonded to
Tyvek Enercor
membrane

10 Brick infill lintel
11 Aluminium capping
12 Toughened glass
argon-filled triple
glazing
13 Aluminium window
sill
14 Internorm
Generation timber
window frame
15 Waterproof plywood
16 Painted
environmentally
friendly medium
density fibreboard
window sill

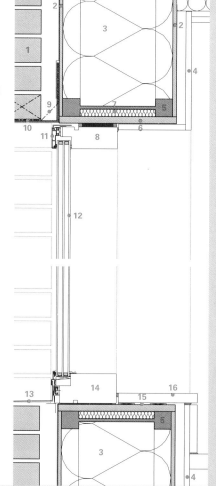

3.065
Aluminium Window
Detail 1:5

Steffen Leisner, Ali
Jeevanjee, Phillip Trigas
1+3=1 House [17]

1 Lightweight concrete
topping slab with
matt finish acrylic
floor polish
2 Hydronic radiant
floor heating system
3 Asphalt paper
4 Acoustic underlay
5 Two layers structural
plywood decking
6 Laminated veneer
lumber joist
7 Hot rolled steel angle
joist hanger
8 Laminated veneer
lumber edge piece
9 Laminated veneer
lumber beam
10 Joist continued

through
11 Batt insulation
12 Timber blocking
13 Sealant with backer
rod
14 J-Mold sealant and
backer rod
15 Waterproofing layer
16 Plywood sheathing
17 Cement plaster with
smooth trowel finish
18 Insulated double
glazed window unit
19 Sealant with backer
rod
20 Neoprene strip and
sealant
21 Concrete slab
22 20 gauge metal
flashing

3.066
Mezzanine Window Sill
and Head Detail 1:5

Marsh Cashman
Koolloos Architects
Maroubra House [36]

1 Paint finished
plasterboard lining
2 Timber cladding
3 Timber framing as
required
4 Insulation
5 Plasterboard ceiling
lining
6 Timber clad wall
beyond
7 Anodized aluminium
framed sliding doors
8 Timber head to
match cladding
9 Mitred corner
10 Plasterboard clad
wall beyond
11 Timber sill to match
vertical cladding

12 Flashing, trimmed
neatly at visible
edges
13 Waterproof sarking
lining
14 Timber cladding
15 Insulation
16 Timber sill to match
vertical cladding

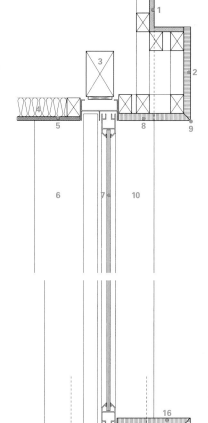

3.067
Window Detail 1:5

TNA Architects
Stage House [28]

1 Urethane foam spray
insulation
2 Galvanized coloured
sheet steel exterior
cladding
3 105 x 50 mm (4 1/8 x 2
inch) structural
timber header
4 Urethane foam spray
insulation
5 12.5 mm (1/2 inch)
plasterboard wall
lining with acrylic
emulsion paint finish
6 Bent steel plate to
soffit of window
reveal
7 Aluminium frame
8 Galvanized coloured
sheet steel

9 Timber skirting
board
10 Bent steel plate to sill
11 Aluminium frame
12 Concrete floor
structure
13 Rigid insulation foam

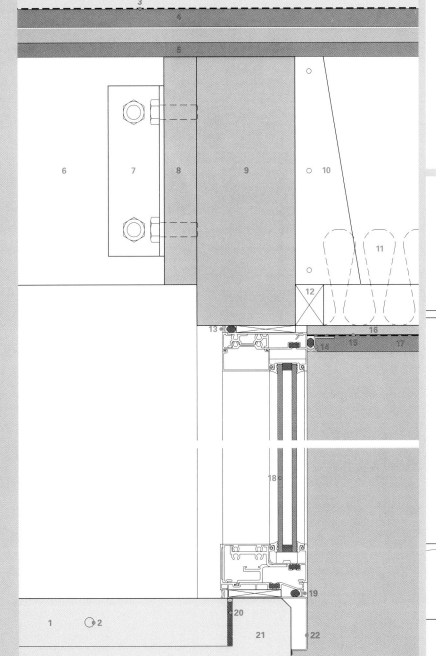

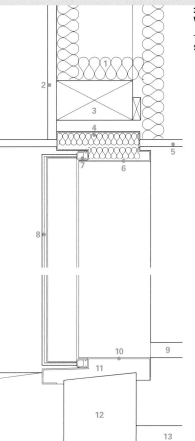

3.068
Hinged Shutter Detail
1:10

Lahz Nimmo Architects
Casuarina Ultimate
Beach House [31]

1 Building paper
2 Outline of wardrobe
joinery
3 120 x 20 mm (4³/₄ x
³/₄ inch) recycled
blue gum hardwood
boards shiplapped
with joints secret
nailed and stain
finished
4 Head flashing
5 20 mm (³/₄ inch) thick
hardwood board at
head and jamb.
Board to be 5 mm (¹/₅
inch) proud of
adjacent boards
6 Track trim to finish
flush with top of

opening
7 Sashless sliding
glazed unit
8 Hinged timber
shutter shown dotted
9 Anodized adjustable
sliding sashless
window system
10 Dressed hardwood to
match wardrobe with
beeswax finish
11 Profiled hardwood
sill
12 Sill flashing
13 13 mm (¹/₂ inch)
plasterboard lining

3.069
Louvre Window Head
Detail 1:10

Western Design
Architects
The Moat House [20]

1 20mm (³/₄ inch)
through colour
render
2 12.5 mm (¹/₂ inch)
plaster
3 100 mm (4 inch)
dense concrete
blockwork
4 Damp proof course
5 Foam insulation to

the void in lintel
6 Galvanized steel
lintel
7 7 mm (¹/₄ inch)
polysulphide bead
8 Top of frame tapered
for water run-off
9 50 x 175 mm (2 x 7
inch) western red
cedar sub-frame
10 Heavy duty stainless
steel hinges
11 Powder-coated
thermally broken
aluminium window
frame
12 50 x 150 mm (2 x 6
inch) western red

cedar frame
13 25 mm (1 inch) thick
western red cedar
louvres housed into
frame at 150 mm (6
inch) centres
14 Powder-coated
thermally broken
aluminium window
frame with 6 mm (¹/₄
inch) thick
self-cleaning high
performance clear
glass outer pane, 12
mm (¹/₂ inch)
argon-filled cavity, 6
mm (¹/₄ inch) thick
low-emissivity

coated glass inner
pane for thermal
control

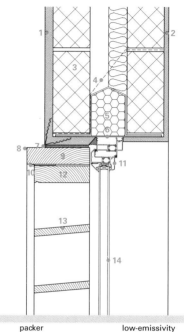

3.070
Louvre Window Sill
Detail 1:10

Western Design
Architects
The Moat House [20]

1 Powder-coated
thermally broken
aluminium window
frame with 6 mm (¹/₄
inch) thick
self-cleaning high
performance clear
glass outer pane, 12
mm (¹/₂ inch)
argon-filled cavity, 6

mm (¹/₄ inch) thick
low-emissivity
coated glass inner
pane for thermal
control
2 25 mm (1 inch) thick
western red cedar
louvres housed into
frame at 150 mm (6
inch) centres
3 50 x 150 mm (2 x 6
inch) western red
cedar frame
4 Powder-coated
thermally broken
aluminium window
frame
5 50 mm (2 inch)

western red cedar sill
6 8 mm (³/₈ inch) drip,
machined into cedar
frame
7 7 mm (¹/₄ inch)
polysulphide bead
8 20 mm (³/₄ inch)
through colour
render
9 100 mm (4 inch)
dense concrete
blockwork
10 50 mm (2 inch) cavity
11 12.5mm (¹/₂ inch)
plaster
12 25 mm (1 inch) thick
painted medium
density fibreboard

window sill
13 Cavity closer

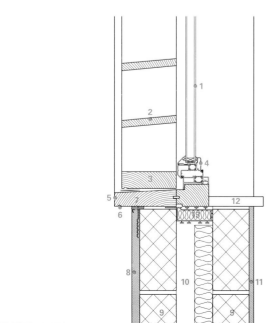

3.071
Corner Louvre Window
Jamb Detail 1:10

Western Design
Architects
The Moat House [20]

1 8 mm (³/₈ inch) drip,
machined into cedar
frame
2 50 x 175 mm (2 x 7
inch) western red
cedar sub-frame
3 50 x 150 mm (2 x 6
inch) western red
cedar frame
4 Treated timber

packer
5 Stainless steel
countersunk head
screws and
hardwood pellets
fixing sub-frame to
timber blocking
6 Powder-coated
thermally broken
aluminium window
frame with 6 mm (¹/₄
inch) thick self
cleaning high
performance clear
glass outer pane, 12
mm (¹/₂ inch)
argon-filled cavity, 6
mm (¹/₄ inch) thick

low-emissivity
coated glass inner
pane for thermal
control
7 Powder-coated
thermally broken
aluminium window
frame
8 100 mm (4 inch)
dense concrete
blockwork
9 12.5mm (¹/₂ inch)
plaster
10 50 x 150 mm (2 x 6
inch) western red
cedar louvre frame
11 Powder-coated
thermally broken

aluminium window
frame with 6 mm (¹/₄
inch) self
cleaning high
performance clear
glass outer pane, 12
mm (¹/₂ inch)
argon-filled cavity, 6
mm (¹/₄ inch) thick
low-emissivity
coated glass inner
pane for thermal
control
12 Powder-coated
thermally broken
aluminium window
frame

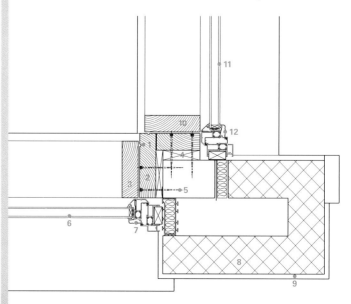

3.072
Window Detail 1:10

Simon Walker Architects
Dane House [06]

1 Laminated double
  glazed unit
  comprised of 8.4 mm
  (1/3 inch) glass, 12
  mm (1/2 inch) air gap
  and 8.4 mm (1/3 inch)
  glass
2 20 mm (3/4 inch) thick
  solid Irish oak
  floorboards with
  white oil finish
3 18 mm (7/10 inch)
  waterproof plywood
  subfloor
4 18 mm (7/10 inch)
  solid iroko finish to
  floor recess
5 225 x 50 mm (84/5 x 2
  inch) treated timber
  joists
6 Solid iroko sill

section with linseed
oil finish to interior
and exterior left bare
7 150 x 150 x 10 mm (6
  x 6 x 2/5 inch) steel
  universal angle to
  support fixed glazing
8 1.5 mm (1/16 inch)
  mill-finish aluminium
  panel on 18 mm (7/10
  inch) waterproof
  plywood
9 100 x 50 mm (4 x 2
  inch) suspended
  timber frame
10 Fibreglass quilt
  insulation
11 100 x 50 mm (4 x 2
  inch) suspended
  ceiling joists
12 18 mm (7/10 inch)
  birch multiply ceiling
  panels
13 Proprietary
  aluminium vent grille
14 18 mm (7/10 inch)
  solid iroko surround

to bathroom window
15 Solid iroko frame to
  bedroom door

3.073
Window Wall Detail 1:20

Terry Pawson Architects
The Tall House [38]

1 Planted roof system
2 Two-ply membrane
  on 12 mm (1/2 inch)
  curved plywood
3 125 mm (5 inch)
  Rockwool insulation
4 9 mm (3/8 inch)
  curved plasterboard
  ceiling
5 3 mm (1/8 inch)
  stainless steel plate
6 Stepped up layers of
  membrane
7 Insulation and
  plywood packer
8 90 x 90 mm (31/2 x
  31/2 inch) curved
  structural steel
9 75 x 50 mm (3 x 2
  inch) mild steel angle
10 Double-glazed sealed
  window unit
  comprised of 10 mm
  (2/5 inch) outer glass
  pane, 12 mm (1/2
  inch) air gap and 6
  mm (1/4 inch) inner
  glass pane, silicone
  bonded into frame
11 Stainless steel fascia
  surround
12 Stainless steel
  drainage angle and
  drip
13 Structural steel beam
  and lintel
14 12.5 mm (1/2 inch)
  plasterboard with
  skim coat
15 Double glazed sealed
  window unit
  comprised of 10 mm
  (2/5 inch) outer glass
  pane, 12 mm (1/2
  inch) air gap and 6
  mm (1/4 inch) inner
  glass pane, silicone
  bonded into frame
16 Stainless steel fascia
  surround
17 Sliding folding door
  rail
18 Sliding folding door
  system

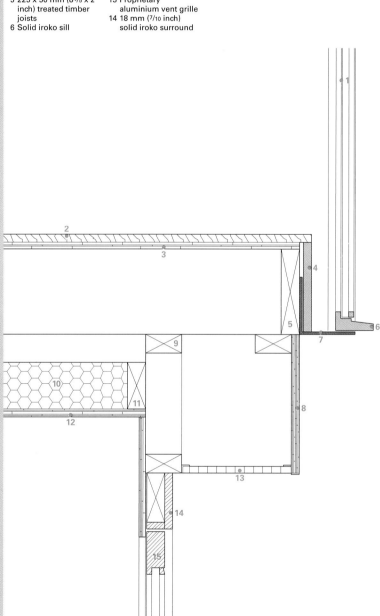

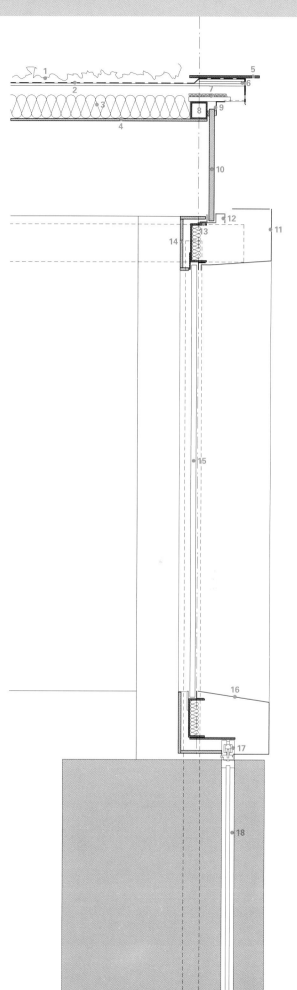

3.074
Window Detail 1:5

Charles Pictet
Architectes
Villa Frontenex [10]

1 Reinforced concrete
roof slab
2 30 mm (1 1/5 inch)
insulation
3 160 x 50 mm (6 3/10 x
2 inch) timber beam
4 Timber lintel
5 50 x 40 mm (2 x 1 5/8
inch) timber blocking
6 Double glazing
comprised of 8 mm
(1/3 inch) laminated
and tempered glass
7 45 mm (1 3/4 inch)
anodized aluminium
grid
8 Anodized aluminium
brackets
9 80 mm (3 1/8 inch)
screed with
underfloor heating
10 Metal brackets
11 Cement slope to
create 0 to 80 mm
(3 1/8 inch) incline
12 2 x 12.5mm (1/8 x 1/2
inch) plasterboard
ceiling
13 Steel angle
14 50 x 40 mm (2 x 1 5/8
inch) timber blocking

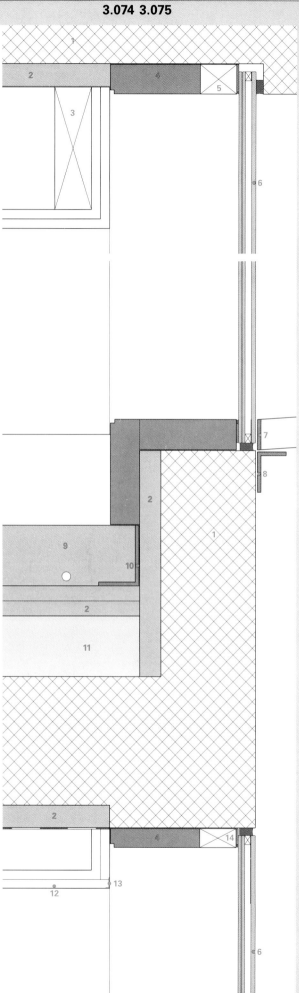

3.075
Window Detail 1:7.5

Charles Pictet
Architectes
Villa Frontenex [10]

1 200 mm (7 9/10 inch)
reinforced concrete
wall
2 120 mm (4 3/4 inch)
insulation
3 2 x 12.5mm (1/16 x 1/2
inch) plasterboard
4 Steel brackets
5 Silicone sealant
6 Double glazing
comprised of 8 mm
(1/3 inch) laminated
and tempered glass
7 80 mm (3 1/8 inch)
frame insulation
8 Steel brackets
9 Steel brackets
10 100 mm (3 9/10 inch)
metal capping

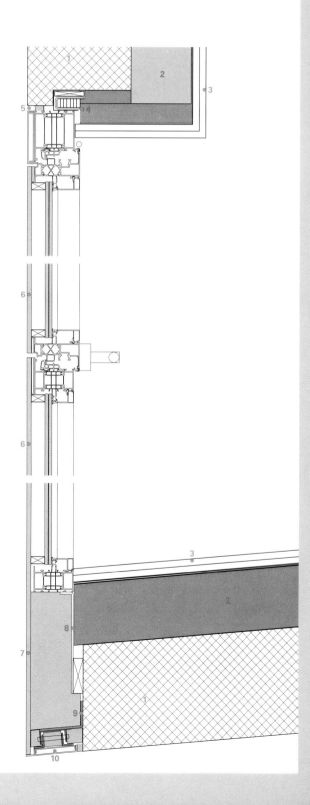

3.076
Window Detail 1:7.5

Charles Pictet
Architectes
Villa Frontenex [10]

1 Resin sealing layer
2 120 mm (4³/₄ inch)
  insulation
3 50 x 120 mm (2 x 4³/₄
  inch) timber joist
4 2 x 12.5 mm (¹/₁₆ x ¹/₂
  inch) plasterboard
5 200 mm (7⁹/₁₀ inch
  reinforced concrete
6 Steel brackets
7 Silicone sealant
8 100 mm (4 inch)
  external metal
  capping
9 Double glazing
  comprised of 8 mm
  (¹/₃ inch) laminated
  and tempered glass
10 Steel brackets
11 150 x 30 mm (6 x 1¹/₅

inch) timber packer
12 40 mm (1³/₅ inch)
  insulation
13 120 mm (4³/₄ inch)
  insulation
14 200 mm (7⁹/₁₀ inch)
  reinforced concrete
  wall

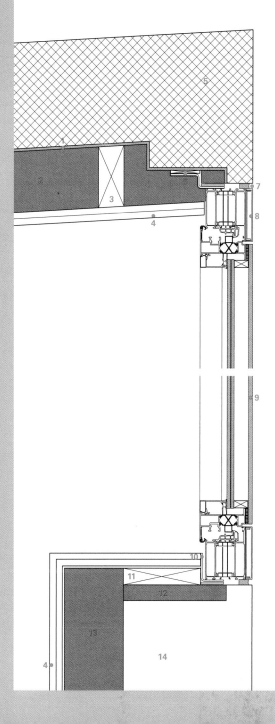

3.077
**Window and Shutter
Detail 1:20**

Charles Pictet
Architectes
Villa Frontenex [10]

1 Roof slates
2 30 x 50 mm (1¹/₅ x 2
  inch) timber lathes
3 45 x 50 mm (1³/₄ x 2
  inch counter lathes
4 2 x 6 mm (¹/₁₆ x ¹/₄
  inch) fibreboard
5 Aluminium gutter
6 Timber guard board
7 27 x 100 x 100 mm
  (1 x 4 x 4 inch)
  curved timber blocks
8 Roller blind
9 15 x 20 mm (³/₅ x ³/₄
  inch) timber beam
10 25 mm (¹/₂ inch) solid
  wood flooring
11 100 x 160 mm (4 x
  6³/₁₀ inch) timber
  joists with insulation
12 Vapour barrier
13 2 x 12.5 mm (¹/₁₆ x ¹/₂
  inch) plasterboard
14 180 x 280 mm (7¹/₁₆ x
  11 inch) timber beam
15 Steel brackets
16 Blind guide
17 Double glazing
18 Existing hook
19 Metal window frame
20 Timber mullion
21 Metal window frame
22 Metal bracket
23 Timber worktop
24 Timber joinery
25 Rough cast finish to
  masonry wall
26 Existing masonry
27 Convector heater
28 Concrete screed
29 80 mm (3¹/₈ inch)
  concrete screed
30 40 mm (1³/₅ inch)
  floor insulation
31 210 mm (8¹/₄ inch)
  reinforced concrete
  floor slab

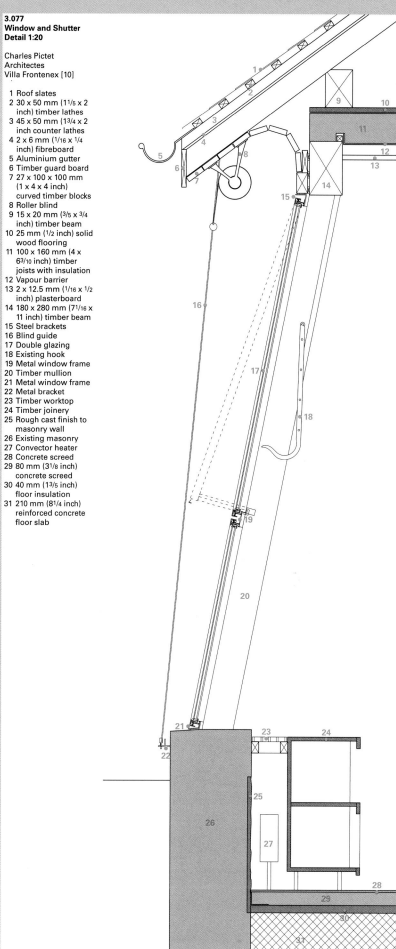

3.078
Window Plan Detail
1:5

TNA Architects
Stage House [28]

1 Timber beam
2 45 x 45 mm (1³/₄ x 1³/₄ inch) timber batten
3 Urethane foam spray insulation
4 Rigid foam insulation
5 105 x 50 mm (4¹/₈ x 2 inch) structural timber stud
6 Galvanized colour steel sheet exterior cladding
7 Timber framing
8 Steel window support
9 12.5 mm (1/2 inch) plasterboard wall lining with acrylic emulsion paint finish
10 Wire mesh insect screen
11 Double glazing comprised of 8 mm (1/3 inch) glass, 12 mm (1/2 inch) air gap and 8 mm (1/3 inch) glass
12 Steel window frame
13 Vapour permeable waterproof membrane

3.079
Window Section Detail
1:5

TNA Architects
Stage House [28]

1 Urethane foam spray insulation
2 Timber batten
3 Galvanized colour steel sheet exterior cladding
4 Timber header
5 Steel angle
6 Galvanized colour steel sheet soffit lining
7 Steel box section
8 Galvanized colour steel sheet window frame reveal
9 Steel window frame
10 Double glazing comprised of 8 mm (1/3 inch) glass, 12 mm (1/2 inch) air gap and 8 mm (1/3 inch) glass
11 Steel sill cover panel
12 Flashing
13 20 mm (3/4 inch) plywood substrate
14 Concrete floor structure

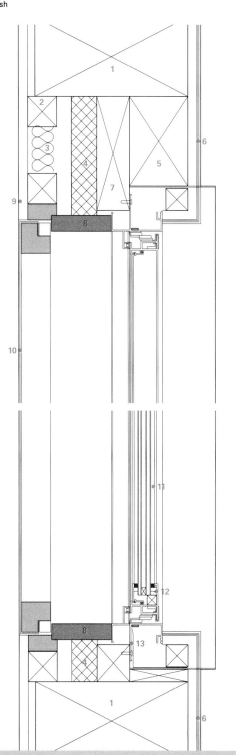

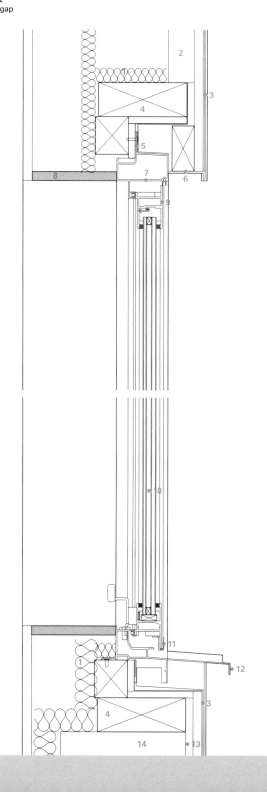

3.080
Window Section Detail
1:5

TNA Architects
Stage House [28]

1 9.5 mm (1/3 inch)
   plasterboard with
   acrylic insulating
   paint finish
2 Timber blocking for
   window support
3 Galvanized coloured
   sheet steel exterior
   cladding
4 Window frame
5 Wire mesh insect
   screen
6 Pinch block
7 Galvanized coloured
   sheet steel
8 Window handle and
   lock
9 Steel window sill
10 Flashing
11 Window blocking

12 20 mm (3/4 inch)
   plywood substrate
13 Galvanized coloured
   sheet steel exterior
   cladding
14 Urethane foam spray
   insulation

3.081
Double Hung Window
and Timber Shutters
Sectional Detail 1:10

Tzannes Associates
Parsley Bay Residence
[21]

1 Render coat
2 Concrete slab
3 Drip groove
4 Plasterboard ceiling
   on battens
5 Plasterboard
   shadowline trim
6 Timber framed
   double hung louvred
   shutter
7 Timber framed
   double hung window
8 Timber framed
   double hung louvred
   shutter in open
   position, shown
   dotted
9 Stone flooring

10 Screed
11 Brass angle
12 Flashing
13 Timber fascia
14 Timber sill
15 Timber framed fixed
   screen, concealed
   fixing at jamb and
   head
16 Sill flashing

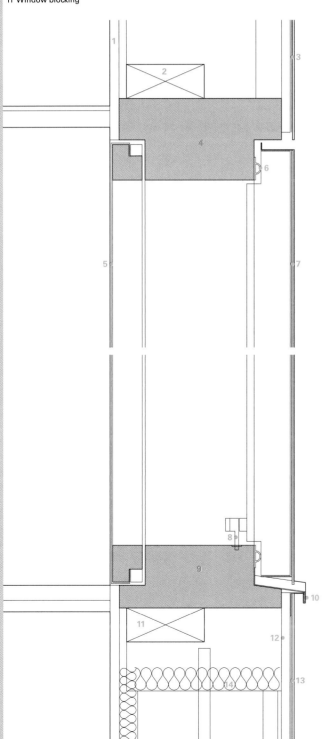

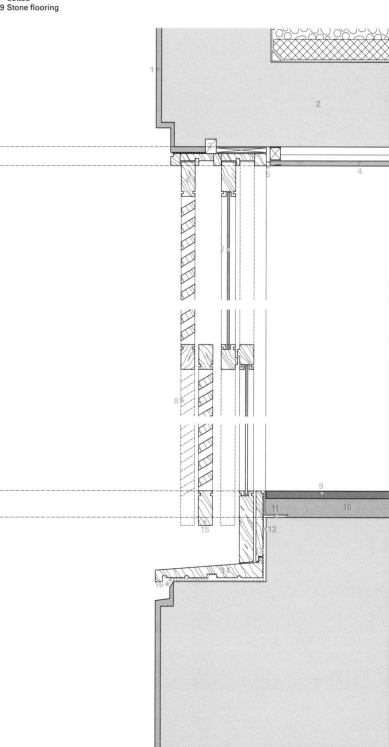

3.082
Window Detail 1:10

Donovan Hill
Z House [24]

1 Magnetic insect
screen to hopper
window opening
2 Dressed New Guinea
rosewood transom
3 9mm (3/8 inch)
toughened glass
4 Anodized aluminium
sill for hopper
window
5 Anodized aluminium
transom
6 Anodized aluminium
head
7 9 mm (3/8 inch) fixed
toughened glass
flush with aluminium
frame and fixed with
structural glazing
tape and silicone
sealant

8 Aluminium frame
bracket
9 Spotted gum
hardwood timber
flooring, clear sealed
10 Basement below
11 Cork to prevent
timber expansion
12 Reinforced core-filled
face brickwork
13 Aluminium flashing
and waterproofing

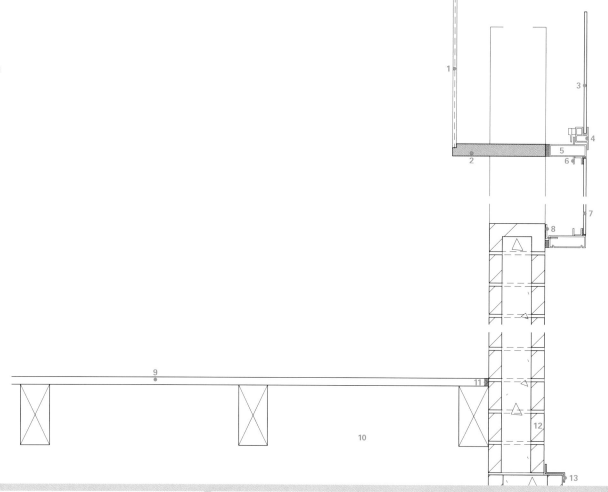

3.083
**Kitchen Window Detail
1:5**

Javier Artadi Arquitecto
Las Arenas Beach House
[19]

1 Silicone seal
2 6 mm (1/4 inch)
tempered clear glass
3 Aluminium profile
window frame
4 Socle for sliding door
with pulley and latch
5 Aluminium coloured
silicone
6 Aluminium frame for

fixed glass
7 Aluminium profile
window frame
8 Stainless steel
self-tapping screws
with plastic
blockhead
9 Aluminium top rail
for sliding door
10 Aluminium lower rail
for sliding door with
stainless steel
self-tapping screws
with plastic
blockhead

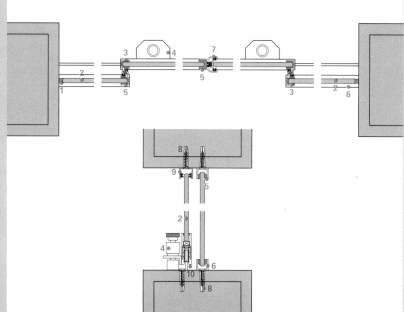

3.084
**Bathroom Skylight
Detail 1:10**

Blank Studio
Xeros Residence [29]

1 6 mm (1/4 inch)
laminated glazing,
set with glazing tape
and sealed with clear
silicone with a slope
of 12.5 mm (1/2 inch)
per 300 mm (12 inch)
to drain
2 Continuous bent
metal flashing
3 Two timber blocking

pieces with
condensation
channel
4 Membrane roof
system with rock
ballast to match site
5 300 mm (114/5 inch)
framing and hangers
6 Batt insulation
between joists
7 Painted 15.8 mm (5/8
inch) moisture-
resistant gypsum
board
8 Light-gauge steel hat
channels and hanger
wire for ceiling
support

9 Light-gauge metal
U-framing and
acoustic batt
insulation
10 Flitch plates with 12.5
mm (1/2 inch) angle
to support glazing
11 9.5 mm (3/8 inch)
translucent,
tempered glass
12 Lighting unit
13 18 mm (7/10 inch)
veneer plywood

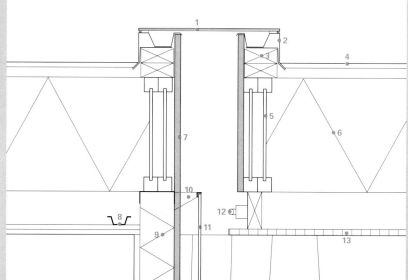

3.085
Window Plan Detail 1:5

Glas Architects
The Nail Houses [23]

1 440 x 102.5 x 102.5 mm (17½ x 4 x 4 inch) polished Medici block, Bellini colour to front elevation
2 Compriband seal
3 Full-filled cavity with Rockwool insulation
4 Intumescent seal
5 100 x 50 mm (4 x 2 inch) timber frame
6 100 mm (4 inch) medium dense concrete blockwork
7 Two layers of plaster finished, skimmed and painted with end stop bead at junction with medium density fibreboard
8 Internal timber component of composite timber and aluminium window unit
9 Insulated cavity

closer
10 Medium density fibreboard routed to form shadow gap
11 15 mm (5/8 inch) mitred medium density fibreboard sill, jamb and head on timber battens, painted and aligned to wall finish. All to have intumescent seal to junction with blockwork and timber packers
12 Medium density fibreboard edging
13 12 mm (1/2 inch) shadow gap
14 24 mm (1 inch) double glazed unit in polyester powder-coated aluminium frame
15 Polyester powder-coated aluminium pressed flashing to match window frames

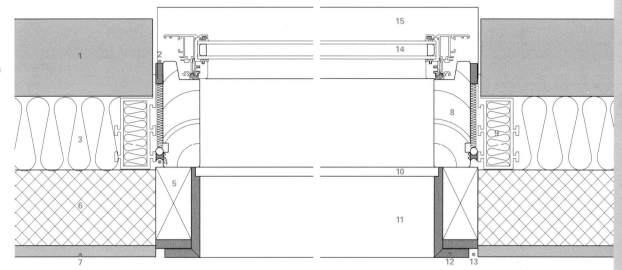

3.086
Mezzanine Window Jamb Detail 1:10

Marsh Cashman
Koolloos Architects
Maroubra House [36]

1 Plasterboard lining with paint finish
2 Steel column
3 Anodized aluminium framed sliding windows
4 Metal stud frame
5 Timber wall cladding
6 Anodized aluminium framing to sliding

windows
7 Timber frame
8 Insulation
9 Plasterboard lining with paint finish

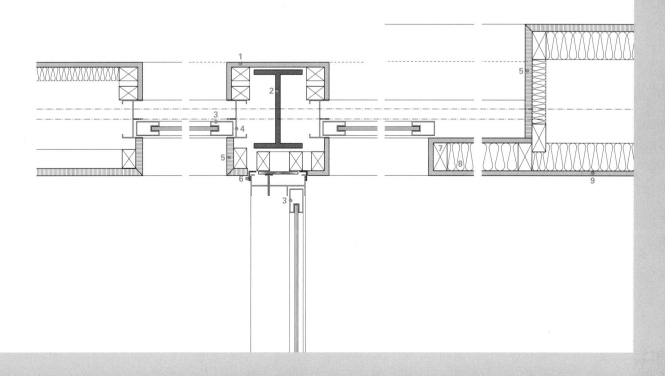

3.087
Window Detail 1:5

Thaler Thaler Architekten
Z House [40]

1 Double glazed
  window unit
2 Softwood window
  casement frame with
  paint finish
3 12.5 mm (1/2 inch)
  plasterboard on 40 x
  60 mm (13/5 x 23/8
  inch) timber battens
4 40 mm (13/5 inch)
  mineral wool
  insulation
5 Frame seal
6 Sheet aluminium
  covering
7 30 x 80 mm (11/5 x
  31/8 inch) timber
  battens
8 Laminated timber
  frame
9 Windproof paper
10 8 mm (1/3 inch) fibre
  cement sheeting
11 Thermal insulation
12 16 mm (2/3 inch)
  oriented strand
  board with vapour
  barrier

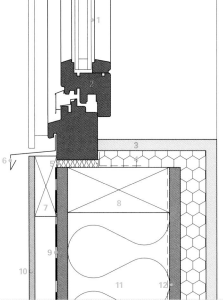

3.088
Window Detail 1:10

Tham & Videgård
Arkitekter
Archipelago House [40]

1 Double glazing
  comprised of 6 mm
  (1/4 inch) glass, 15
  mm (5/8 inch) air
  space and 6 mm (1/4
  inch) glass
2 Sheet aluminium sill
  capping
3 Timber sill
4 Track for sliding
  screen
5 20 x 160 mm (3/4 x
  61/4 inch) dovetailed
  timber boards
6 220 mm (85/8 inch)
  Rockwool insulation
7 45 x 220 mm (13/4 x
  85/8 inch) beam
8 Vapour barrier
9 22 x 120 mm (7/8 x
  43/4 inch) floorboards
10 200 x 200 mm (8 x 8
  inch) concrete plinth
11 45 x 90 mm (13/4 x
  31/2 inch) timber
  beam
12 45 x 120 mm (13/4 x
  43/4 inch) timber
  decking

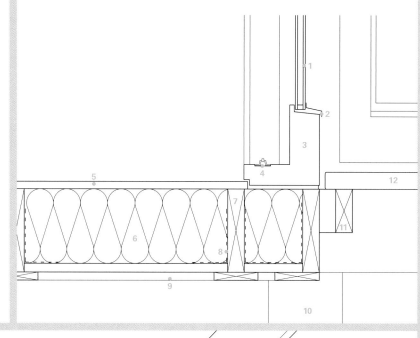

3.089
**Sliding Window Section
Detail 1:5**

Go Hasegawa &
Associates
Forest House [34]

1 105 x 150 mm (4 x 6
  inch) timber beam
2 9 mm (3/8 inch)
  plywood ceiling with
  oil stain clear lacquer
  finish
3 43 x 224 mm (17/10 x
  84/5 inch) Nyatoh
  window frame with
  oil stain clear lacquer
  finish
4 16 x 42 mm (3/5 x 12/3
  inch) rubber packing
5 10 x 22 mm (2/5 x 4/5
  inch) stainless steel
  upper rail of window
6 56 mm (21/4 inch)
  nyatoh framed sash
  window with oil stain
  clear lacquer finish
7 56 x 90 mm (21/4 x
  31/2 inch) nyatoh
  framed sash window
  with oil stain clear
  lacquer finish
8 Double glazing of 4
  mm (1/8 inch) float
  glass, 12 mm (1/2
  inch) air gap and 4
  mm (1/8 inch) float
  glass
9 Stainless steel mesh
  and 10 x 22 mm (2/5 x
  4/5 inch) nyatoh
  window frame
  screen with oil stain
  clear lacquer finish
10 12 mm (1/2 inch)
  maple flooring on 12
  mm (1/2 inch)
  structural plywood
11 10 x 20 mm (2/5 x 3/4
  inch) stainless steel
  bottom rail of
  window
12 55 x 55 mm (21/8 x
  21/8 inch) timber floor
  joists at 300 mm (12
  inch) centres
13 56 x 224 mm (21/4 x
  84/5 inch) nyatoh
  window frame with
  oil stain clear lacquer
  finish
14 3 mm (1/8 inch)
  aluminium flashing
15 Narrow-pitch
  galvanized
  aluminium coated
  corrugated sheet
  external wall

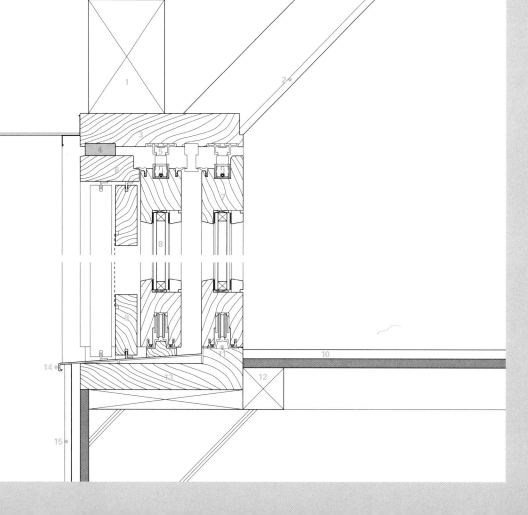

3.090
Corner Window and Column Junction Detail 1:10

Jackson Clements Burrows Architects Edward River House [32]

1 Horizontal corrugated metal wall cladding
2 90 x 40 mm (3$\frac{1}{2}$ x 1$\frac{5}{8}$ inch) pine stud frame
3 Insulation fill between studs
4 13 mm ($\frac{1}{2}$ inch)

internal plasterboard wall lining
5 10 mm ($\frac{3}{8}$ inch) zincaneal shadowline stopping angle
6 140 x 40 mm (5$\frac{1}{2}$ x 1$\frac{5}{8}$ inch) cedar window jamb
7 140 x 19 mm (5$\frac{1}{2}$ x $\frac{3}{4}$ inch) spotted gum polished timber floorboards
8 140 x 40 mm (5$\frac{1}{2}$ x 1$\frac{5}{8}$ inch) cedar window sill
9 100 x 40 mm (4 x 1$\frac{5}{8}$ inch) cedar sliding window with fly-wire

10 100 x 40 mm (4 x 1$\frac{5}{8}$ inch) cedar sliding window with 10 mm ($\frac{3}{8}$ inch) fixed float glass
11 Flashing
12 266 x 110 mm (10$\frac{1}{2}$ x 4$\frac{3}{8}$ inch) laminated timber structural column
13 Air space
14 120 x 45 mm (4$\frac{3}{4}$ x 1$\frac{3}{4}$ inch) expressed rough sawn timber girt
15 Vertical corrugated metal wall cladding

3.091
Window Detail 1:5

Jun Aoki & Associates J House [24]

1 Lysine sprayed wall cladding
2 20 mm ($\frac{3}{4}$ inch) mortar finish on metal lath
3 Waterproof seal
4 Aluminium window
5 Double glazed window of 6 mm ($\frac{1}{4}$ inch) glass, 6 mm ($\frac{1}{4}$ inch) air gap and 8 mm ($\frac{3}{8}$ inch) glass
6 60 x 27 mm (2$\frac{3}{8}$ x 1$\frac{1}{8}$ inch) cedar stud frame
7 20 x 40 mm ($\frac{3}{4}$ x 1$\frac{5}{8}$ inch) aluminium angle
8 12 mm ($\frac{1}{2}$ inch) plywood
9 9 mm ($\frac{3}{8}$ inch) plasterboard
10 Puttied mesh cloth
11 9 mm ($\frac{3}{8}$ inch) Japanese linden plywood with acrylic emulsion paint finish
12 12 mm ($\frac{1}{2}$ inch) Japanese linden plywood to form recess for roller blind
13 Roller blind concealed in recess

14 120 x 60 mm (4$\frac{3}{4}$ x 2$\frac{3}{8}$ inch) cedar stud frame
15 Accordion storage system for insect screen

3.092
Window Head Detail 1:10

Hawkes Architecture Crossway [16]

1 Native wildflower meadow using seeds from a nearby nature reserve
2 Clay tile finishing layer on cement mortar bonded to rubber EPDM (ethylene propylene dieme monomer) membrane
3 Black rubber EPDM (ethylene propylene dieme monomer) waterproofing
4 Cement mortar bonding between second and third layers of clay tiles
5 Clay tiles made from local clay to form timbrel vaulted arch
6 Waterproof plywood
7 Timber fillets forming arched profile of wall
8 Plywood sheathing
9 Foil backed Celotex insulation
10 Tyvek Enercor wall membrane
11 Untreated English

cedar finger-jointed timber cladding
12 Painted hardwood cover architrave to match colour of window frame
13 Toughened glass argon-filled triple glazing
14 Painted plasterboard
15 Wood fibre web infill insulation
16 Waterproof plywood
17 Joist
18 Gravel drainage strip
19 Clay subsoil contained within Geoweb soil stabilizing system
20 Geotextile filter membrane
21 Kaycel insulation
22 Foamglas recycled glass load-bearing insulation
23 Black rubber EPDM (ethylene propylene dieme monomer waterproofing)

3.093
Bay Window Plan Detail
1:10

Waro Kishi + K.
Associates Architects
Hakata House [18]

1 Reinforced concrete
  wall
2 Polished wire glass
3 6 x 65 mm (1/4 x 21/2
  inch) steel flat bar
4 Traditional Japanese
  plaster wall finish
5 Traditional Japanese
  plaster wall finish
6 Timber plaster stop

bead
7 Polished wire glass
8 Single hung window
  with shoji screen
9 Traditional Japanese
  plaster wall finish
10 65 x 65 mm (21/2 x
   21/2 inch) stainless
   steel angle

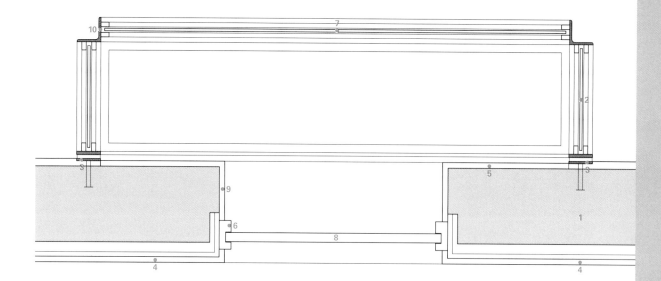

3.094
Window Detail 1:10

Tham & Videgård
Arkitekter
Archipelago House [40]

1 23 mm (7/8 inch)
  dovetailed wood
  layer with serrated
  facade
2 200 x 55 (8 x 21/8
  inch) timber door
  jamb

3 Double glazing
  comprised of 6 mm
  (1/4 inch) glass, 15
  mm (5/8 inch) air
  space and 6 mm (1/4
  inch) glass
4 23 mm (7/8 inch)
  dovetailed timber
  cladding
5 Three 45 x 120 mm
  (13/4 x 43/4 inch)
  timber studs
6 Two 45 x 120 mm
  (13/4 x 43/4 inch)

timber studs
7 18 mm (7/10 inch)
  plywood
8 51 x 300 mm (2 x 12
  inch) laminated
  timber boards
9 45 x 120 mm (13/4 x
  43/4 inch) timber
  decking
10 150 mm (6 inch)
   insulation
11 50 mm (2 inch)
   insulation
12 45 x 45 mm (13/4 x

13/4 inch) timber
  battens
13 18 mm (7/10 inch)
   plywood cladding
   screwed to 45 x 45
   mm (13/4 x 13/4 inch)
   and 22 x 22 mm (9/10
   x 9/10 inch) battens at
   200 mm (8 inch)
   centres
14 Two 45 x 150 mm
   (13/4 x 6 inch) timber
   studs
15 50 x 135 mm (2 x 51/4

inch) vertical post
16 56 x 315 mm (21/5 x
   122/5 inch) glulam
   timber beam

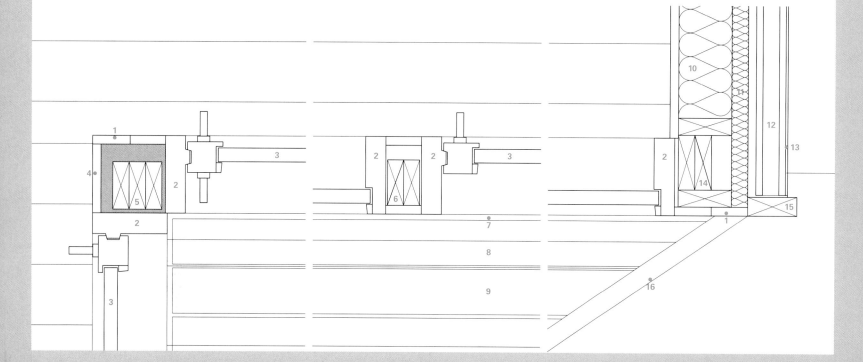

3.095
Window Plan Detail 1:2

Correia Ragazzi
Arquitectos
Casa no Gerês [06]

1 10mm (3/8 inch)
   plywood cladding
2 Window shutter
   hinge
3 Timber window
   shutter
4 Timber closure piece
5 60 x 60 mm (23/8 x
   23/8 inch) aluminium
   angle bracket
6 20 x 5 mm (3/4 x 1/5

inch) steel flat bar
7 Mastic
8 Stone wall
9 Rubber back stop
10 60 x 8 mm (23/8 x 3/10
   inch) steel flat bar
11 25 x 25 mm (1 x 1
   inch) steel angle
   bracket
12 Stainless steel hinge
13 25 x 25 mm (1 x 1
   inch) steel angle
   bracket
14 Screw fixing

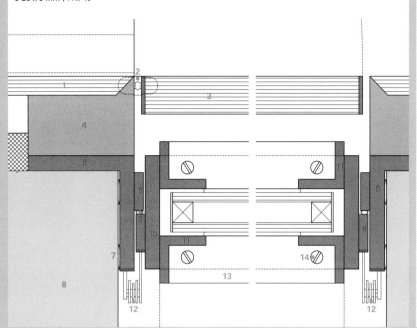

3.096
Window With Concealed
Lighting Detail 1:10

Kallos Turin
Casa Zorzal [10]

1 Reinforced concrete
   structure
2 3 mm (1/8 inch)
   plaster skim coat
   with paint finish
3 Sand and cement
   mortar
4 16 mm (5/8 inch)
   laminated glass
5 Aluminium channel
   frame

6 Concealed
   incandescent strip
   lighting
7 45 mm (13/4 inch)
   pigmented cement
   screed laid to fall to
   drain
8 Reinforced concrete
   slab
9 5 mm (1/5 inch)
   waterproof
   membrane
10 Levelling layer
11 Concrete filling
   forming slope to
   drainage
12 30 mm (11/4 inch)
   polystyrene

insulation
13 Vapour barrier
14 Brick wall

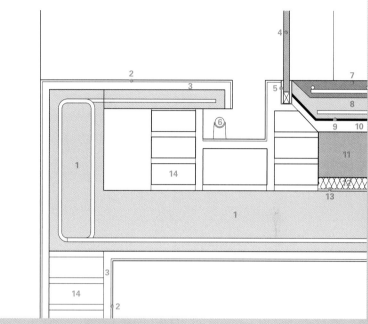

3.097
Window Head and Sill
Detail 1:10

Robert Seymour &
Associates
The Riverhouse [22]

1 Polyester
   powder-coated
   window system with
   sill dressed over 30
   mm (11/5 inch)
   upstand to parallel
   flange channel
2 Line of external
   render finish beyond
3 End of parallel flange

channel projects 5
mm (1/5 inch) beyond
face of render
4 230 x 75 mm (9 x 3
   inch) galvanized and
   sprayed parallel
   flange channel with
   welded end plates
   and mild steel
   upstand built into
   blockwork wall
   beyond
5 Full-fill insulation
6 Polyester
   powder-coated soffit
   trim
7 Line of internal
   render finish beyond

8 Damp proof course
   laid on 18 mm (3/4
   inch) waterproof
   bonded plywood on
   treated softwood
   studding
9 200 x 75 mm (8 x 3
   inch) galvanized and
   sprayed parallel
   flange channel with
   welded end plates
   built into blockwork
   wall beyond with 90
   x 10 mm (31/2 x 3/8
   inch) galvanized and
   sprayed mild steel
   flat downstand
10 Concealed automatic

blind fixed to 10 mm
(3/8 inch) painted
medium density
fibreboard lining

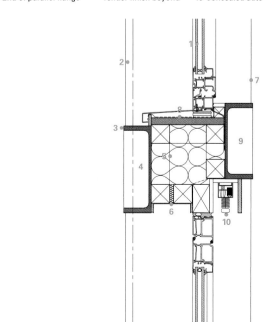

3.098
Fixed Window Detail
1:10

Skene Catling de la Peña
Architects
The Dairy House [31]

1 Fixed double glazed
   unit
2 Bronze clad timber
   door set
3 Folded steel plate
4 Steel angle
5 Painted aluminium
   trim to form shadow
   gap
6 Drainage channel

7 200 x 90 mm (8 x 31/5
   inch) steel channel
8 Timber studs with
   insulation between
9 12.5 mm (1/2 inch)
   plasterboard,
   plastered and
   painted
10 Render painted black
11 Fibreglass lining
12 Concrete pool wall

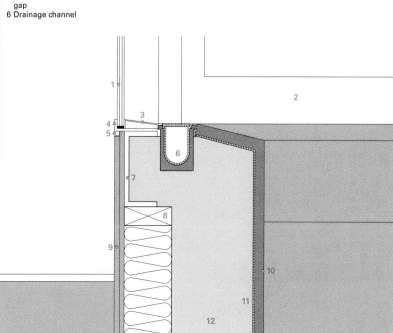

3.099
Window Detail 1:10

Barton Myers Associates
Bekins Residence [25]

1 Roofing membrane
  on plywood layer
2 Plywood
3 Building insulation
4 Timber joists
5 Gypsum wall board
6 Galvanized steel drip
7 Aluminium sliding
  door
8 Glazing
9 Cement plaster
10 Structural concrete
   slab
11 Galvanized steel
   flashing
12 Gravel
13 Moisture barrier
14 Continuous void
   form

3.100
**Window Section Detail
1:5**

Glas Architects
The Nail Houses [23]

1 Two layers of plaster,
  finished, skimmed
  and painted with end
  stop bead at junction
  with medium density
  fibreboard
2 100 mm (4 inch)
  medium dense
  concrete blockwork
3 Cavity full-filled with
  Rockwool insulation
4 440 x 102.5 x 102.5
  mm (17½ x 4 x 4
  inch) Forticrete
  polished Medici
  block, Bellini colour,
  to front elevation
5 Damp proof course
  formed over Catnic
  lintel and under

weep hole
6 Weep hole
7 12 mm (½ inch)
  shadow gap
8 100 x 50 mm (4 x 2
  inch) timber frame
9 Compriband seal
10 Medium density
   fibreboard routed to
   form shadow gap
11 24 mm (1 inch)
   double glazed unit in
   polyester
   powder-coated
   aluminium frame
12 15 mm (5/8 inch)
   mitred medium
   density fibreboard
   sill, jamb and head
   on timber battens,
   painted and aligned
   to wall finish.All to
   have intumescent
   seal to junction with
   blockwork and
   timber packers
13 Polyester

powder-coated
aluminium pressed
flashing to match
window frames
14 Insulated cavity
   closer

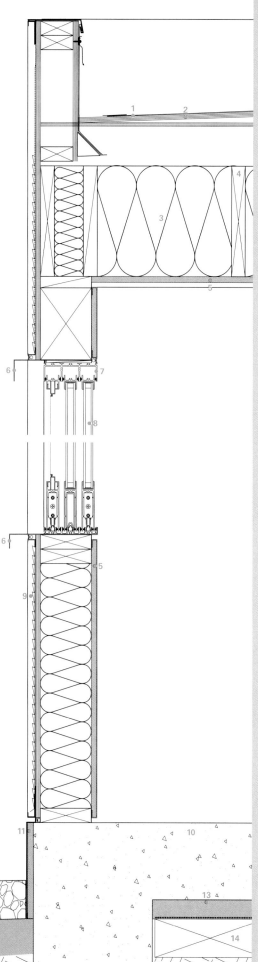

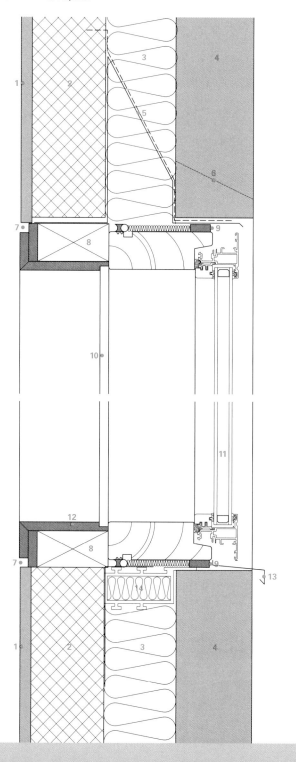

3.101
Sliding Door Detail 1:5

Arjaan de Feyter
Zoersel House [29]

1 100 mm (4 inch)
  concrete slab
2 10 x 70 mm (3/8 x 23/4
  inch) window frame
  fixing plug
3 140 x 140 mm (51/2 x
  51/2 inch) steel
  column
4 50 x 50 mm (2 x 2
  inch) steel angle to
  support concrete slab
5 Polyurethane foam
  insulation
6 3 x 40 mm (1/8 x 15/8
  inch) galvanized
  anchor brace at 400
  mm (153/4 inch)
  centres
7 Insulation infill
8 Ventilation grille
9 Medium density

fibreboard curtain
pelmet
10 Horizontal beam
11 Medium Density
  Fibreboard casing to
  support beam
12 Curtain enclosure
13 Aluminium frame to
  sliding glass door
14 Perforated steel
  angle for ventilation
15 50 x 50 mm (2 x 2
  inch) aluminium
  L-profile
16 280 x 100 mm (11 x 4
  inch) steel channel
17 Window insulation
  tape
18 Double glazed fixed
  window unit with 10
  mm (3/8 inch) glass,
  15 mm (5/8 inch) air
  gap and 10 mm (3/8
  inch) glass
19 Powder-coated
  aluminium door stop
20 Powder-coated

folded aluminium
profile with mosquito
net
21 Curtain
22 Concrete threshold
23 Rail for sliding insect
  screen
24 Rail for sliding
  window
25 Cement screed floor
  finish

3.102
**Aluminium Window
Detail 1:5**

Steffen Leisner, Ali
Jeevanjee, Phillip Trigas
1+3=1 House [17]

1 Cement plaster with
  smooth trowel finish
2 Plywood wall
  sheathing
3 Waterproofing layer
4 Batt insulation
5 Timber wall framing
6 Nail-on flange to
  aluminium window
7 Cement fibre board
8 Thinset mosaic glass
  tile
9 Sealant and backer
  rod
10 Aluminium window
  frame
11 Insulated double
  glazed window unit
12 Sealant with

backer rod
13 Sloping mortar bed
14 Waterproofing
  membrane
15 Drip edge on nail-on
  flange

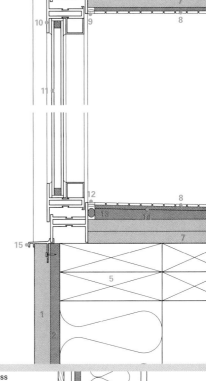

3.103
Window Detail 1:10

Lee + Mundwiler
Architects
The Coconut House [12]

1 Phenolic resin wood
  veneer panels
2 Vertical timber
  battens
3 Plywood sheathing
4 Batt insulation
5 15 mm (5/8 inch)
  drywall lining
6 Metal reveal
  moulding
7 15 mm (5/8 inch)
  painted medium
  density fibreboard
  baseboard
8 Hardwood floor
9 100 x 300 mm (4 x 12
  inch) timber beam
10 24 gauge metal drip
  edge
11 Metal top track to

receive window glass
12 Curtain tracks
13 15 mm (5/8 inch)
  drywall ceiling
14 20 mm (3/4 inch)
  laminated low-E
  security glass set in
  silicone at bottom
15 Hardwood floor
16 18 mm (7/10 inch)
  plywood floor
  sheeting
17 Concrete slab
  pedestal
18 Expansion joint
19 Concrete slab
20 Weather resistant
  barrier, vapour
  permeable building
  paper
21 Silicone seal

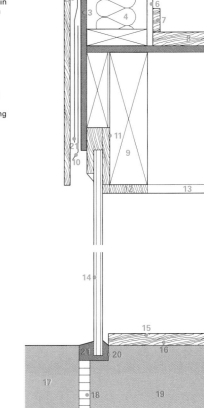

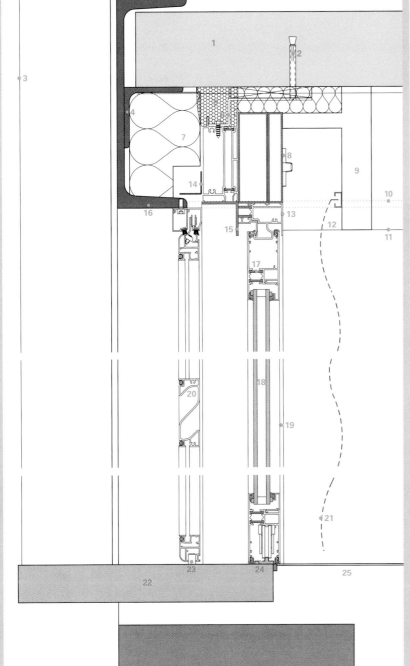

3.104
Window Detail 1:5

Kengo Kuma &
Associates
Steel House [27]

1 3.2 mm (1/8 inch) hot
dip galvanized
vertical steel-plate
structure seen in
elevation
2 20 mm (3/4 inch) hard
urethane spray foam
insulation
3 40 mm (13/5 inch)
hollow
polycarbonate
sheeting to form
Takiron 'Lume' wall
system
4 3.2 mm (1/8 inch) hot
dip galvanized
vertical steel-plate
structure seen in
section
5 16 mm (2/3 inch)

reinforcing metal
washer
6 40 x 40 mm (15/8 x
15/8 inch) steel
L-angle
7 Steel closer plate
8 3.2 mm (1/8 inch) hot
dip galvanized
vertical steel-plate
structure seen in
section
9 Silicone fill
10 125 x 45 mm (5 x 13/4
inch) hot dip
galvanized soffit
11 Silicone fill
12 Steel stiffening rod
13 50 x 50 mm (2 x 2
inch) aluminium
angle window frame
14 50 x 50 mm (2 x 2
inch) aluminium
angle to finish hollow
polycarbonate
sheeting 'Lume' wall
15 Sliding sun screen
16 Sliding aluminium-

framed double
glazing
17 2 mm (1/16 inch) hot
dip galvanized drip
profile and sill
18 125 x 45 mm (5 x 13/4
inch) hot dip
galvanized sill

3.105
Skylight Detail 1:20

Scott Tallon Walker
Architects
Fastnet House [25]

1 Existing concrete
blockwork wall
2 Powder-coated
aluminium pressing
3 Capping to roof light
4 Powder-coated
aluminium insulated
panel
5 Structural silicone
joint
6 Fixing plate to
transom support
7 Mullion bracket
8 Aluminium transom
9 Aluminium mullion
10 Thermally-broken
double glazed fixed
vent
11 Random rubble stone
wall

12 Reinforced concrete
wall
13 Reflective insulation
14 Painted skim coat on
plasterboard
15 Universal beam
16 Painted skim coat on
plasterboard
17 Insulation
18 Marine ply
19 Random rubble stone
wall
20 Drainage channel
21 Concrete cobble
paving
22 Reinforced concrete
roof slab
23 Reflective insulation
24 Painted skim coat on
plasterboard
25 Insulation
26 Painted plasterboard

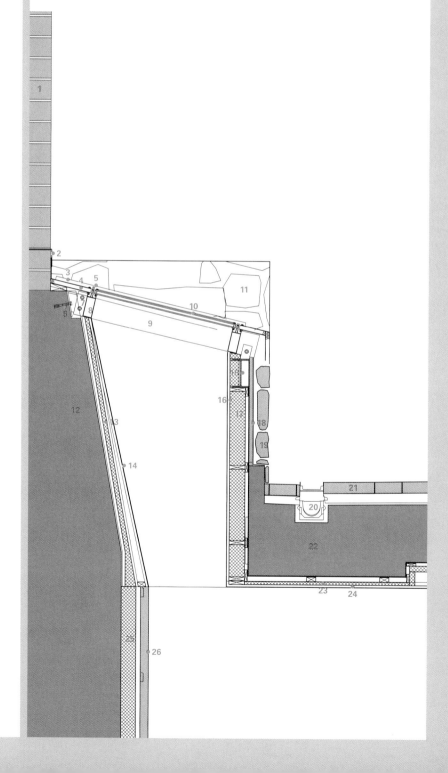

3.106
Clerestory Window Plan
Detail 1:10

Tonkin Zulaikha Greer
Hastings Parade House
[26]

1 Zinc flashing
2 Painted compressed
  fibre cement
3 89 x 89 x 5 mm (3 1/2
  x 3 1/2 x 1/4 inch)
  square hollow
  section column fixed
  to steel angle to
  concrete slab
4 Zinc wall cladding
  with horizontal
  standing seam fixed
  to plywood sheeting
5 19 mm (3/4 inch)
  plywood sheeting
  fixed to 90 mm (3 1/2
  inch) timber stud
  frame
6 13 mm (1/2 inch)

plasterboard fixed to
90 mm (3 1/2 inch)
timber stud frame,
paint finish
7 Outline of 90 x 90
  mm (3 1/2 x 3 1/2 inch)
  steel angle
  underneath, welded
  to square hollow
  section columns
  fixed to concrete slab
  shown dotted
8 Frameless double
  hung aluminium
  window
9 Outline of roof above
10 Triple 90 x 45 mm
   (3 1/2 x 1 3/4 inch)
   timber studs
11 100 x 75 mm (4 x 3
   inch) downpipe
12 89 x 89 x 5 mm (3 1/2
   x 3 1/2 x 1/4 inch)
   square hollow
   section column fixed
   to base plate and
   steel angle to

concrete slab
13 Outline of raked
   plasterboard ceiling
   above

3.107
Study Window Section
Detail 1:10

Johnston Marklee &
Associates
Hill House [22]

1 Waterproofing
  membrane
2 15 mm (5/8 inch)
  plywood substrate
3 Timber firring
  elements at 610 mm
  (24 inch) centres
4 Timber nailer
5 Universal steel beam
6 Joist hanger
7 50 x 254 mm (2 x 10
  inch) timber joists
8 15 mm (5/8 inch)
  gypsum board
  ceiling and wall
  lining
9 Timber framing
10 Plywood substrate
11 Metal reveal for drip
   stop
12 50 x 100 mm (2 x 4
   inch) firring at 400
   mm (16 inch) centres
13 Timber framing
14 Corner bead
15 Curtain track
16 Aluminium window
   frame
17 Double glazing unit
18 Window sill
19 75 x 75 x 10 mm (3 x
   3 x 3/8 inch) steel tube
20 Timber packer
21 Ripped 50 x 100 mm
   (2 x 4 inch) timber
   bearers at 300 mm
   (12 inch) centres

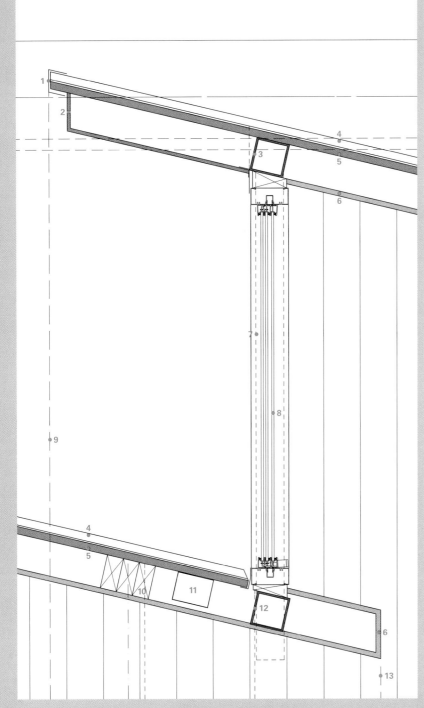

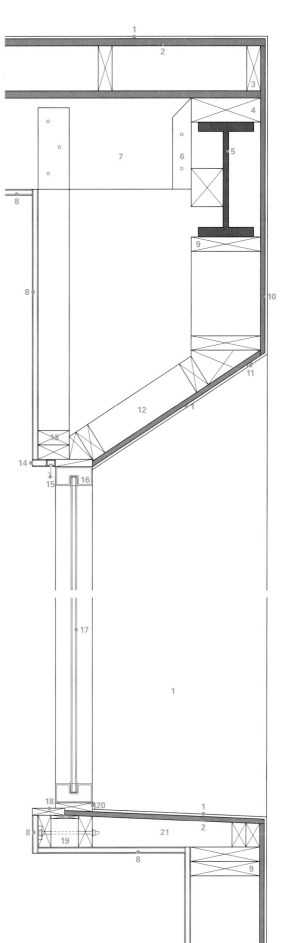

3.108
Full Height Glazing
Detail 1:10

Cassion Castle
Architects
Twofold House [12]

1 18 mm (7/10 inch) waterproof plywood
2 Glass reinforced plastic roof finish
3 50 x 250 mm (2 x 10 inch) timber joists
4 50 mm (2 inch) continuous ventilation between joists below firrings
5 200 mm (8 inch) insulation
6 200 x 200 mm (8 x 8 inch) rolled steel joist
7 Gutter laid to fall
8 Glass fibre roof nosing
9 20 mm (3/4 inch) sand and cement render

on breather membrane
10 12 mm (1/2 inch) glazing security tape
11 12 mm (1/2 inch) plasterboard with 25 mm (1 inch) rigid insulation backing
12 48 x 43 mm (17/8 x 15/8 inch) concealed sliding door track
13 Timber sliding door
14 Hardwood timber post
15 28 mm (11/8 inch) double glazed unit comprised of 6 mm (1/4 inch) Pilkington-K glass, 16 mm (5/8 inch) argon-filled spacer and 6 mm (1/4 inch) Optifloat glass
16 40 x 40 mm (15/8 x 15/8 inch) anodized aluminium angle
17 50 x 50 mm (2 x 2 inch) battens on 50 x

250 mm (2 x 10 inch) joists
18 15 mm (5/8 inch) Fireline plasterboard with 3 mm (1/8 inch) plaster skim coat
19 Concealed rainwater downpipe emptying into glass fibre tray
20 Hardwood timber decking
21 Glass fibre rainwater tray
22 150 x 150 mm (6 x 6 inch) rolled steel joist

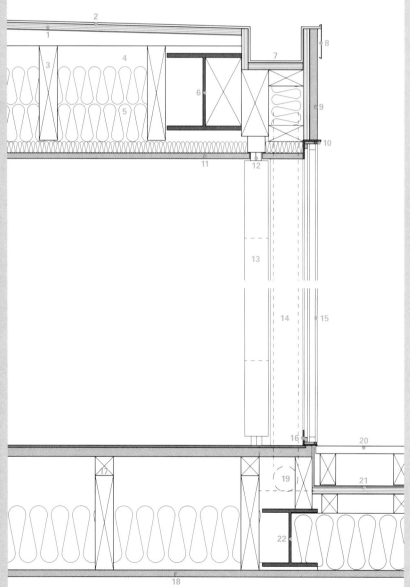

3.109
Window / Skylight
Detail 1:10

Architectus
North Shore House [36]

1 50 x 25 mm (2 x 1 inch) Lawson cypress duckboards on 50 mm (2 inch) wide timber firrings packed 10 mm (2/5 inch) off membrane with 10 x 50 mm (2/5 x 2 inch) packers at 600 mm (232/3 inch) centres
2 Membrane on 18 mm (7/10 inch) construction plywood screw fixed at 600 mm (232/3 inch) centres
3 25 mm (1 inch) timber fillet
4 25 x 50 mm (1 x 2 inch) timber batten
5 40 x 3 mm (11/2 x 1/8 inch) aluminium bar to terminate membrane
6 50 x 25 mm (2 x 1 inch) shaped Lawson cypress hit and miss battens screw fixed to 75 x 50 mm (3 x 2 inch) battens aligned with window mullions
7 Thermal insulation to cavity
8 9 mm (1/3 inch) hoop pine plywood lining screw fixed to framing
9 140 x 50 mm (51/2 x 2 inch) timber lintel
10 Safety glazing in anodized aluminium section with anodized aluminium

head flashing
11 9 mm (1/3 inch) hoop pine plywood lining screw fixed to framing with 10mm negative detail to vertical facing
12 20 to 30 mm (3/4 to 11/5 inch) pebbled roof over filter textile on 15 mm (5/8 inch) drainage cell over waterproof membrane
13 9 mm (1/3 inch) hoop pine plywood lining screw fixed to framing
14 15 mm (3/5 inch) slope up of ply at the last 150 mm (6 inches)
15 50 mm (2 inch) wide timber firrings on 50 x 250 mm (2 x 10 inch) timber roof beams
16 9 mm (1/3 inch) hoop pine plywood lining to inside of skylights
17 Greenstuf insulation
18 9 mm (1/3 inch) hoop pine plywood lining screw fixed to framing

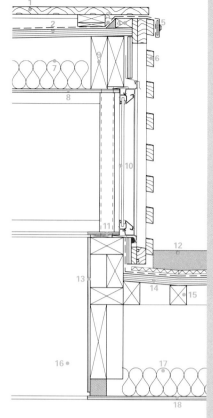

3.110
Window Head Detail 1:5

Stephenson Bell
Architects
House 780 [18]

1 75 mm (3 inch) insulation with waterproof render system
2 15 mm (3/8 inch) drainage cavity between insulation and blockwork wall
3 100 mm (4 inch) blockwork wall
4 50 mm (2 inch)

insulation
5 12 mm (1/2 inch) plasterboard with skim finish on dabs
6 Damp proof course
7 Steel ties
8 Insulated cavity closer
9 Sealant with backing rod
10 Powder-coated aluminium glazing system
11 Softwood packer with sealant and backing rod
12 Extruded aluminium trim

13 Double glazed window unit

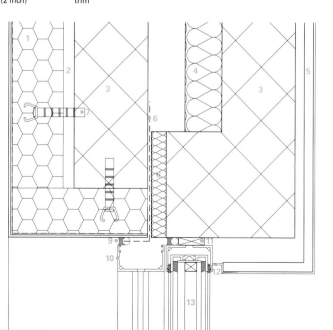

3.111
Corner Window Glazing
Detail 1:5

Arjaan de Feyter
Zoersel House [29]

1 140 x 60 mm (5^1/$_2$ x 2^3/$_8$ inch) steel channel section
2 Line of horizontal beam
3 Joint sealant
4 Double glazed fixed window unit with 10 mm (^{3}/$_8$ inch) glass, 15 mm (^{5}/$_8$ inch) air gap and 10 mm (^{3}/$_8$ inch) glass

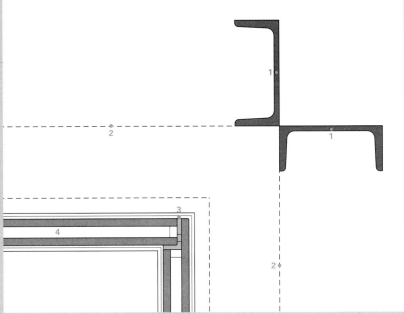

3.112
Study Window Detail 1:5

Steven Holl Architects
Swiss Embassy
Residence [14]

1 Channel glass
2 Channel glass above
3 25 x 25 mm (1 x 1 inch) steel angle welded to strut for stainless steel window box support
4 3 mm (^{1}/$_8$ inch) stainless steel window box
5 Waterproofing layer
6 Rigid insulation
7 12 mm (^{1}/$_2$ inch) plywood sheathing
8 Metal stud frame
9 Steel vertical substructure
10 Insulation
11 Vapour barrier
12 Two layers 15 mm (^{5}/$_8$ inch) gypsum wall board
13 Timber blocking
14 Top-hinged in-swing aluminium window
15 25 mm (1 inch) clear insulated glass unit
16 Corner bead
17 Concrete parapet

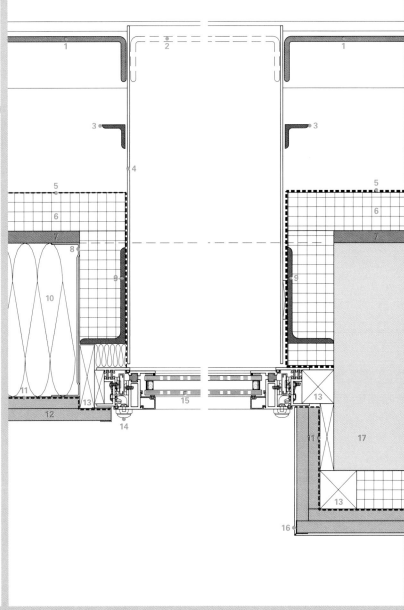

3.113
Window Jamb Detail 1:5

David Nossiter
Architects
Kitsbury Road House
[13]

1 50 mm (2 inch) insulation
2 25 x 25 mm (1 x 1 inch) timber battens to hold insulation in place
3 Stone splashback
4 100 x 50 mm (4 x 2 inch) timber studs
5 100 x 100 mm (4 x 4 inch) square hollow steel section
6 Damp proof course
7 Timber packer
8 Double glazed window from low-E toughened glass with 20 mm (^{3}/$_4$ inch) argon-filled gas cavity
9 Aluminium thermally broken window
10 Metal flashing with sealing compound at aluminium window and masonry wall
11 Render
12 Masonry wall

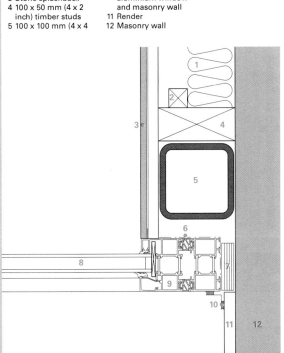

3.114
Fixed Window Detail 1:5

Studio d'ARC Architects
Live / Work Studio II [19]

1 Black asphalt shingle
2 Building felt
3 20 mm (3/4 inch)
   exterior grade
   plywood sheathing
4 Batt insulation
5 50 x 250 mm (2 x 10
   inch) timber joists
6 Aluminium reglet
7 Shim as required
8 Aluminium flashing
9 Duratherm window
   system
10 12.5 mm (1/2 inch)
   maple plywood
   sliding panel
11 Sealant with backer
   rod
12 Two 50 x 150 mm (2
   x 6 inch) timber studs
13 15 mm (5/8 inch)
   gypsum board
14 Vapour barrier

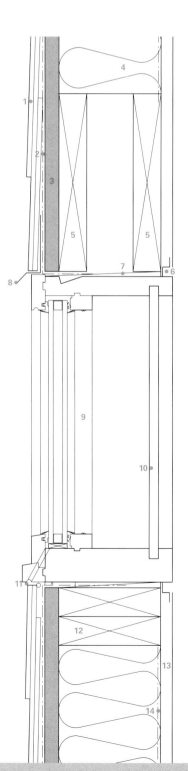

3.115
Window Detail 1:20

Pezo von Ellrichshausen
Architects
Poli House [09]

1 25 x 100 mm (1 x 4
   inch) recycled pine
   board
2 30 mm (11/4 inch)
   polystyrene thermal
   insulation
3 25 x 100 mm (1 x 4
   inch) pine boards
4 150 mm (6 inch)
   reinforced concrete
   wall
5 Black electro-painted
   aluminium frame
6 30 mm (11/4 inch)
   reveal for shutter
7 Double glazing
8 140 mm (51/2 inch)
   reinforced concrete
   slab
9 10 mm (3/8 inch)
   plywood sill painted
   white
10 Dotted line of shutter
   position

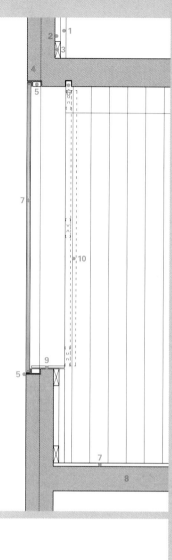

3.116
Window Detail 1:10

Matharoo Associates
Dilip Sanghvi Residence
[07]

1 20 mm (3/4 inch) thick
   flame granite stone
   cladding
2 20 mm (3/4 inch) thick
   mortar
3 185 mm (71/4 inch)
   core concrete wall
4 25 mm (1 inch) thick
   internal smooth
   plaster
5 8 mm (3/8 inch)
   groove filled with
   clear silicone
6 Hollow section
   window frame
7 Window sill
8 Window reveal liner
9 250 mm x 250 mm
   (10 x 10 inch)
   concrete column

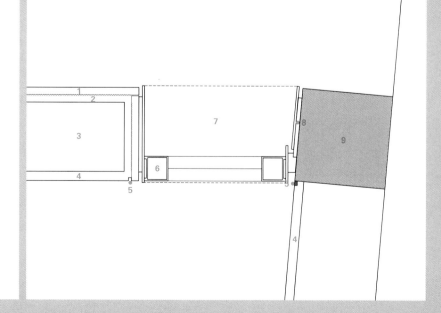

3.117
Skylight Jamb Detail
1:10

Blank Studio
Xeros Residence [29]

1 12.5 mm (1/2 inch)
   coloured laminated
   glass set with black
   silicone
2 Stretched wire mesh
   shade screen
3 22 gauge corrugated
   metal cladding on
   self-healing
   waterproof
   membrane on 12.5

mm (1/2 inch) exterior
plywood
4 140 mm (51/2 inch)
   steel I-beam column
5 6 mm (1/4 inch)
   translucent glass
6 16 gauge, cold-rolled
   steel plate sheet on
   12.5 mm (1/2 inch)
   plywood sheathing
7 Veneer plywood
   partition
8 Light-gauge metal
   U-framing
9 12.5 mm (1/2 inch)
   veneer plywood

3.118
Clerestory Window
Detail 1:5

Barton Myers Associates
Bekins Residence [25]

1 Roofing membrane
2 Gypsum roof board
3 Tapered insulation
4 Sealant
5 Galvanized steel
   fascia
6 Aluminium
   termination
7 Multi-purpose tape
8 Steel angle bracket
9 Rectangular hollow

section steel tube
10 Galvanized steel
    gutter
11 Fixed glazing
12 Galvanized steel deck

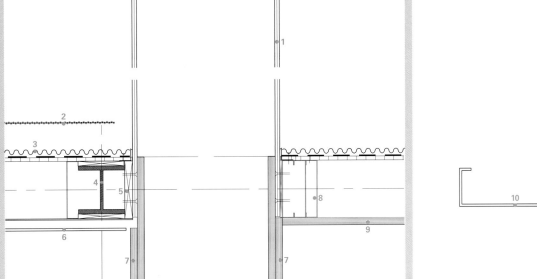

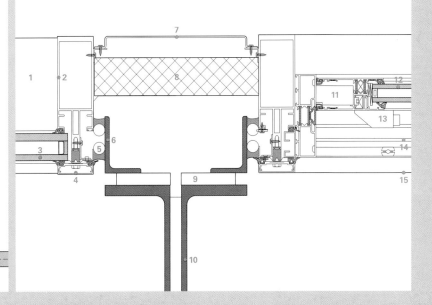

3.119
Window Detail 1:10

ARTEC Architekten
Holiday House [39]

1 Double glazed
   window unit
2 150 x 150 mm (6 x 6
   inch) timber bearer
3 150 x 100 mm (6 x 4
   inch) timber bearer
4 Gasket
5 20 x 30 x 5 mm (3/4 x
   11/8 x 1/5 inch)
   aluminium bracket
6 40 mm (15/8 inch)
   plywood sliding door

7 Perforated
   sheet-metal radiator
   cover

3.120
Window Detail 1:5

Scott Tallon Walker
Architects
Fastnet House [25]

1 Transom below
2 Aluminium
   powder-coated
   mullion
3 Thermally broken
   double glazed unit
4 Aluminium
   powder-coated
   capping
5 Backing rod to mastic
   sealant

6 Galvanized and
   painted mild steel
   angle welded to back
   of plate to form
   rebate with parallel
   flange channel
7 Powder-coated
   pressed aluminium
   panel to form
   internal lining
8 Cavity insulation
9 Galvanized and
   painted mild steel
   plate
10 Galvanized and
    painted back-to-back
    parallel flange
    channels separated

by mild steel plate
11 Aluminium
    powder-coated
    sliding door jamb
12 Thermally broken
    double glazed unit
13 Door stop
14 Sliding door track
    below
15 Line of capping
    below

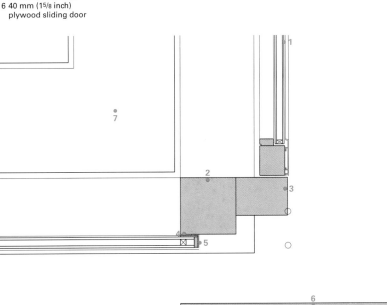

3.121
Window Section and
Plan Detail 1:5

Innovarchi
Gold Coast House [12]

1 Timber packer
2 Clear anodized
  window frame (head)
3 Painted plasterboard
  ceiling
4 Sashless double
  hung window
5 Painted steel mullion
6 Clear anodized
  window frame (sill)
7 Sealed concrete floor
  finish
8 Painted steel mullion
9 Sashless double
  hung window
10 Performance-
  laminated frameless
  fixed glazing

3.122
Window Detail 1:5

Ensamble Studio
Hemeroscopium House
[07]

1 Precast concrete
  beam
2 5 mm ($^1/_5$ inch) steel
  plate covering
3 Line of universal
  steel beam beyond
4 Universal steel beam
5 Steel L-profile
6 15 mm ($^3/_5$ inch) thick
  sheet plasterboard
7 15 mm ($^3/_5$ inch) thick
  sheet plasterboard
8 5 mm ($^1/_5$ inch) steel
  plate stiffener
9 Steel anchor piece
10 Silicone joint
11 Double glazing

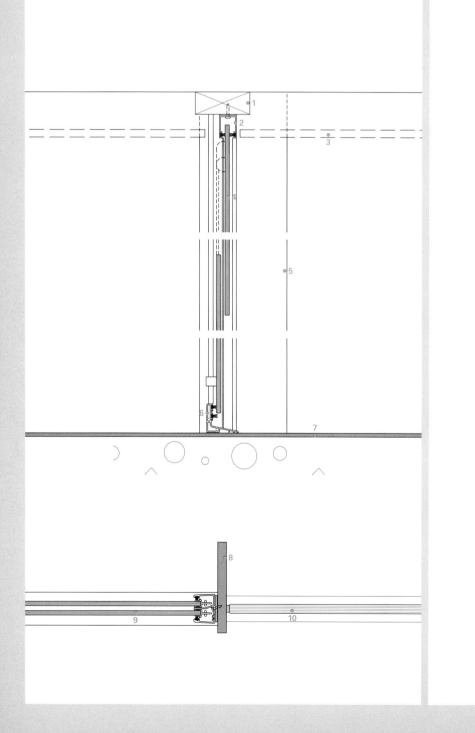

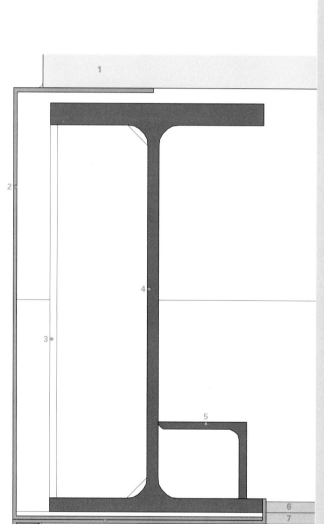

3.123
**Window Section Detail
1:10**

Avanti Architects
Long View [35]

1 Brickwork weepholes above and below window opening, flashing from structural timber wall at head to angle across cavity to weepholes
2 Flashing
3 150 mm (6 inch) insulation between studding
4 Vapour control layer
5 12.5 mm (1/2 inch) plasterboard on 50 x 40 mm (2 x 1 5/8 inch) battens
6 Air gap built into brickwork
7 Compriband between brick and window
8 Mastic seal between timber frame and window
9 150 x 50 mm (6 x 2 inch) timber stud frame
10 Window fixed with Schuco bracket
11 12.5 mm (1/2 inch) plasterboard reveal
12 Double glazed aluminium window
13 Aluminium coping
14 Window board
15 Moulded brick

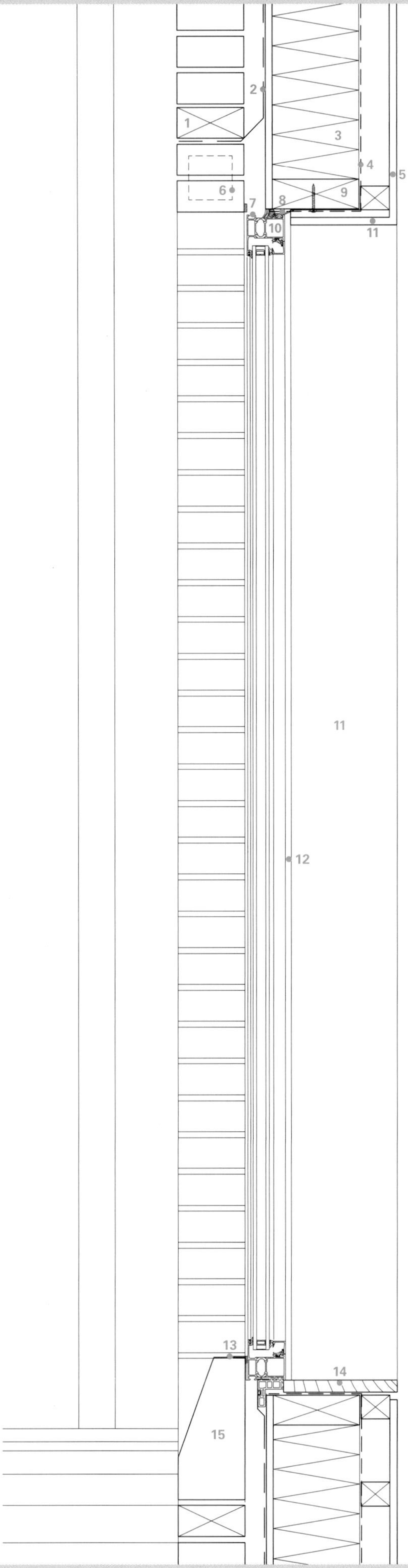

3.124
Fixed Window Jamb Detail 1:5

The Miller Hull Partnership
Chuckanut Drive Residence [31]

1 Metal cladding
2 12 mm (1/2 inch) plywood
3 Silicone bead sealant
4 Frameless double glazed clear glass window panel comprised of 6 mm (1/4 inch) glass, 12 mm (1/2 inch) air space and 6 mm (1/4 inch) glass
5 Metal siding batten
6 Z-clip to anchor glazing framing
7 Silicone bead sealant
8 Framing 'ripped' to 125 mm (5 inch) depth
9 12 mm (1/2 inch) painted medium density fibreboard removable jamb fixed by countersunk screws
10 Metal edging to protect corner of wall board
11 Insulation
12 12 mm (1/2 inch) gypsum wall board

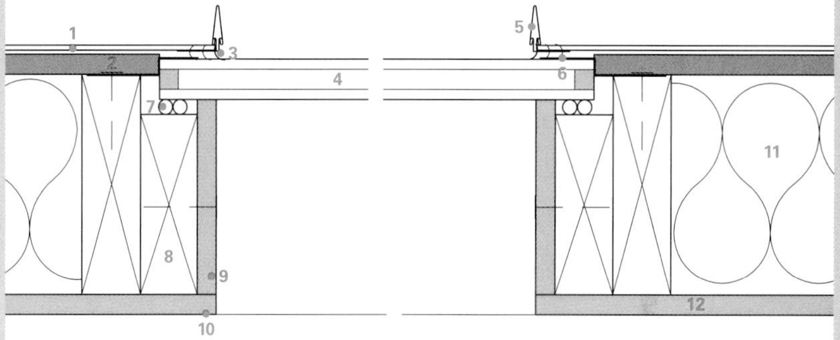

3.125
Window Plan Detail 1:10

Shuhei Endo Architect Institute
Rooftecture S [27]

1 Internal wall of galvalume steel
2 Stainless steel reveal
3 100 x 100 mm (4 x 4 inch) steel beam
4 100 x 100 mm (4 x 4 inch) square hollow section column
5 88 mm (3 1/2 inch) steel hollow section
6 125 x 90 x 7 mm (5 x 3 1/2 x 1/4 inch) hot dip zinc-aluminium alloy coated steel angle
7 Hot dip zinc-aluminium alloy coated steel sheet
8 Double glazed fixed window with 6 mm (1/4 inch) air gaps

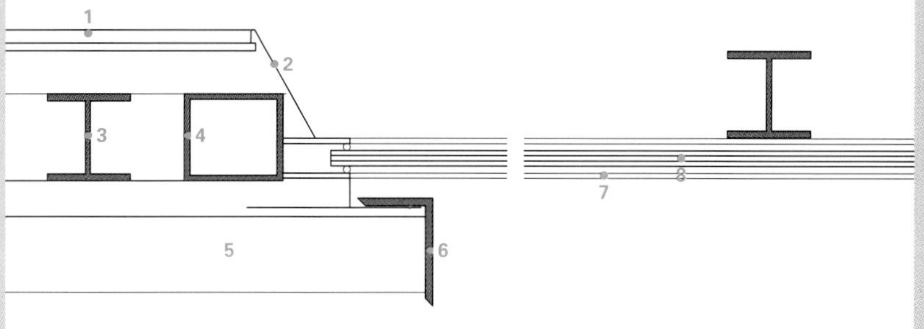

3.126
Window Jamb Detail
1:10

Hampson Williams
Glass and Timber
Houses [33]

1 Canadian western
  red cedar cladding
2 Battens not
  continuous
3 Euroform Versapanel
4 Visqueen 500 vapour
  barrier
5 25 mm (1 inch)
  taper-edged
  plasterboard taped
  and skimmed
  comprised of two
  12.5 mm (1/2 inch)
  thick layers
6 50 x 50 mm (2 x 2
  inch) powder-coated
  aluminium angle
  glazing support
  carriage
7 37 mm (1 1/2 inch)
  argon-filled
  toughened and
  laminated offset
  double glazed unit
8 Compressible seal
9 Mastic seal
10 Douglas fir subframe
11 Bitutape seal
12 Kingspan insulation
13 Vapour control layer
14 25 mm (1 inch)
  taper-edged
  plasterboard taped
  and skimmed
  comprised of two
  12.5 mm (1/2 inch)
  thick layers

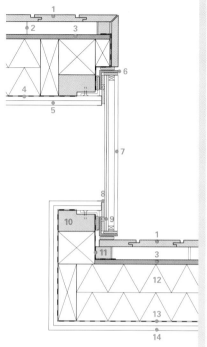

3.127
Window Detail 1:10

Hampson Williams
Glass and Timber
Houses [33]

1 25 mm (1 inch)
  taper-edged
  plasterboard, taped
  and skimmed,
  comprised of two
  12.5 mm (1/2 inch)
  thick layers
2 Vapour control layer
3 150 x 50 mm (6 x 2
  inch) tanalised
  softwood structural
  timber sections
4 150 mm (6 inch)
  thermal insulation
  comprised of two 75
  mm (3 inch) thick
  layers
5 100 x 85 mm (4 x 3 1/3
  inch) tanalised
  softwood structural
  timber section
6 Douglas Fir subframe
7 43 x 43 mm (1 7/10 x
  1 7/10 inch) larch
  vertical closing
  counter battens
8 12 mm (1/2 inch)
  cementitous
  exterior-grade lining
  panel
9 18 mm (7/10 inch)
  tongue and groove
  Canadian western
  red cedar cladding
  impregnated with
  non-com exterior fire
  retardant

10 50 x 50 mm (2 x 2
  inch) powder-coated
  aluminium angle
  glazing support
  carriage
11 Compressible seal
12 37 mm (1 1/2 inch)
  thick argon-filled
  toughened and
  laminated fixed
  double glazed unit
13 18 mm (7/10 inch)
  tongue and groove
  Canadian western
  red cedar cladding
  impregnated with
  non-com exterior fire
  retardant
14 160 x 22 mm (6 1/3 x
  9/10 inch) exterior-
  grade marine
  plywood fascia and
  sill condition

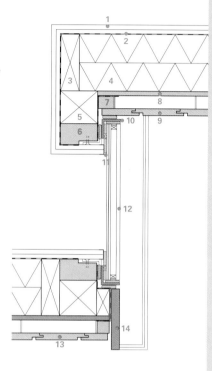

3.128
Window Detail 1:10

Hampson Williams
Glass and Timber
Houses [33]

1 25 mm (1 inch) taper
  edged plasterboard,
  taped and skimmed,
  comprised of two
  12.5 mm (1/2 inch)
  thick layers
2 Bitutape seal
3 Douglas fir sub frame
4 150 x 50 mm (6 x 2
  inch) tanalised
  softwood structural
  timber sections
5 18 mm (7/10 inch)
  tongue and groove
  Canadian western
  red cedar cladding
  impregnated with
  non-com exterior fire
  retardant
6 127 x 22 mm (5 x 9/10
  inch) exterior-grade
  marine plywood
  fascia and sill
  condition
7 50 x 50 mm (2 x 2
  inch) powder-coated
  aluminium angle
8 37 mm (1 1/2 inch)
  thick argon-filled
  toughened and
  laminated fixed
  double glazed unit

9 Marine plywood sill
10 25 mm (1 inch)
  taper-edged
  plasterboard, taped
  and skimmed,
  comprised of two
  12.5 mm (1/2 inch)
  thick layers
11 Compressible seal
12 12 mm (1/2 inch)
  cementitous exterior
  grade lining panel
13 18 mm (7/10 inch)
  tongue and groove
  Canadian western
  red cedar cladding
  impregnated with
  non-com exterior fire
  retardant
14 160 x 22 mm (6 1/3 x
  9/10 inch) exterior-
  grade marine
  plywood fascia and
  sill condition

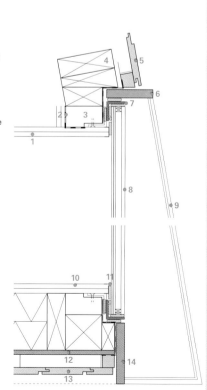

3.129
Corner Window Detail
1:10

Hampson Williams
Glass and Timber
Houses [33]

1 25 mm (1 inch)
  taper-edged
  plasterboard, taped
  and skimmed,
  comprised of two
  12.5 mm (1/2 inch)
  thick layers
2 150 mm (6 inch)
  thermal insulation
  comprised of two 75
  mm (3 inch) thick
  layers
3 12 mm (1/2 inch) thick
  cementitous
  exterior-grade lining
  panel
4 18 mm (7/10 inch)
  tongue and groove
  Canadian western
  red cedar cladding
  impregnated with
  non-com exterior fire
  retardant
5 34 x 34 mm (1 1/3 x
  1 1/3 inch) vertical
  closing larch counter
  battens
6 127 x 22 mm (5 x 9/10
  inch) exterior-grade

marine plywood
fascia and sill
condition
7 50 x 50 mm (2 x 2
  inch) powder-coated
  aluminium angle
8 Douglas fir sub frame
9 37 mm (1 1/2 inch)
  argon-filled
  toughened and
  laminated fixed
  double glazed unit
10 Marine plywood sill
11 25 mm (1 inch) taper
  edged plasterboard,
  taped and skimmed,
  comprised of two
  12.5 mm (1/2 inch)
  thick layers
12 12 mm (1/2 inch)
  cementitous
  exterior-grade lining
  panel
13 18 mm (7/10 inch)
  tongue and groove
  Canadian western
  red cedar cladding
  impregnated with
  non-com exterior fire
  retardant
14 160 x 22 mm (6 1/3 x
  9/10 inch) exterior-
  grade marine
  plywood fascia and
  sill condition

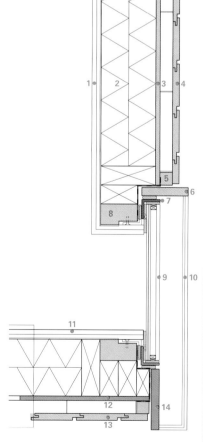

3.130
Window Detail 1:10

Tham & Videgård
Arkitekter
Archipelago House [40]

1 23 x 95 mm (9/10 x
  33/4 inch) tongue and
  groove timber with
  rough sawn face
2 45 mm (13/4 inch)
  Rockwool insulation
3 150mm (6 inch)
  Rockwool insulation
4 45 x 45 mm (13/4 x
  13/4 inch) battens
5 Plywood screwed at
  200 mm (8 inch)
  centres to 45 x 45
  mm (13/4 x 13/4 inch)
  and 22 x 22 mm (9/10
  x 9/10 inch) battens
6 150 x 45 mm (6 x 13/4
  inch) timber stud
  frame
7 Brushed timber

lining to window
head, reveals and sill
8 Black silicone
  permanently elastic
  sealing material
9 Aluminium window
  frame
10 Insulated double
   glazing

3.131
Window Detail 1:10

Touraine Richmond
Architects
One Window House [27]

1 Solid core timber
  door
2 15 mm (5/8 inch)
  drywall with corner
  J-bead
3 12 mm (1/2 inch)
  drywall
4 152 x 152 mm (6 x 6
  inch) timber jamb
  framing
5 Sliding glass door

6 12 mm (1/2 inch)
  oriented strand
  board sheathing
7 20 mm (7/8 inch)
  corrugated
  galvanized metal
  cladding

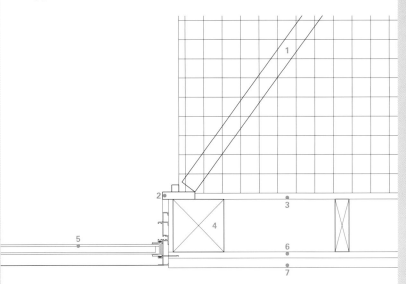

3.132
**Double Hung Shutters
to Window Detail
1:10**

Tzannes Associates
Parsley Bay Residence
[21]

1 Render and plaster
  set wall edges
2 Timber faced jamb to
  counterweights
3 Timber framed
  double hung window
4 Packing
5 Double hung
  counterweights

6 Flashing
7 Timber bead
8 Double hung timber
  louvre shutters
9 Timber sill below

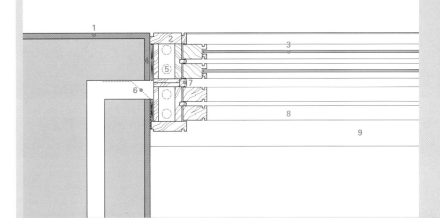

3.133
Window Plan Detail 1:10

TNA Architects
Stage House [28]

1 Urethane foam spray
  insulation
2 102 x 120 mm (4 x
  4³/4 inch) timber stud
  frame
3 12 mm (¹/2 inch)
  insulating fibre board
  with emulsion paint
  finish
4 Sealant
5 Double glazing
  comprised of 8 mm
  (¹/3 inch) glass, 12
  mm (¹/2 inch) air gap
  and 8 mm (¹/3 inch)
  glass
6 Sealant
7 Steel window frame
8 210 x 105 mm (8¹/4 x
  4¹/8 inch) timber
  frame
9 Rigid foam insulation
10 Galvanized coloured
   sheet-steel cladding

3.134
Window Plan Detail 1:5

TNA Architects
Stage House [28]

1 9.5 mm (¹/3 inch)
  plasterboard with
  acrylic insulating
  paint finish
2 Galvanized coloured
  sheet-steel exterior
  cladding
3 Sheet steel window
  support
4 Steel window frame
5 Steel angle
6 Steel frame to
  window shutter
7 Galvanized coloured
  sheet-steel backing
  to window shutter
8 Galvanized coloured
  sheet steel to
  window shutter
9 Wire mesh insect
  screen
10 Galvanized coloured
   sheet steel to
   window reveal
11 Galvanized coloured
   sheet-steel window
   sill
12 12.5 mm (¹/2 inch)
   plasterboard wall
   lining with acrylic
   emulsion paint finish
13 Timber framing
14 20 mm (³/4 inch)
   plywood
   substructure
15 Galvanized coloured
   sheet-steel exterior
   cladding

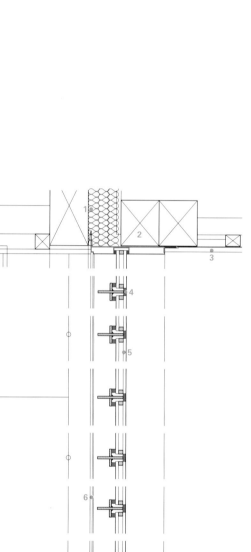

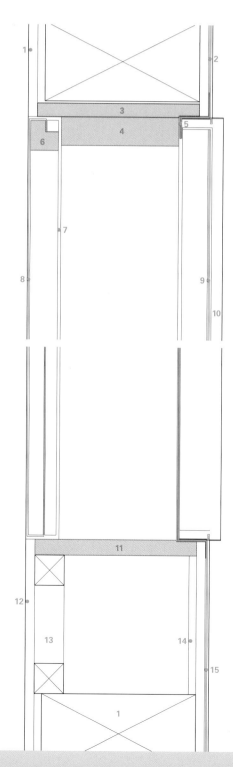

3.135
First Floor Window Detail 1:10

Agence Michel Tortel
Mikado House [08]

1 Argon-filled double glazing with Planitherm film
2 Sliding, coated aluminium frame
3 Prefabricated flush window flashing
4 Internal window framing in 18 mm (3/4 inch) plasterboard and coated aluminium
5 18 mm (3/4 inch) plasterboard lining
6 Internal insulation
7 Concrete wall and floor slab
8 External waterproofing
9 Floating, heating screed in polished concrete

3.136
Window Detail 1:20

Tonkin Zulaikha Greer
Hastings Parade House [26]

1 Zinc flashing
2 150 x 75 mm (6 x 3 inch) parallel flange channel
3 Painted compressed fibre cement
4 13 mm (1/2 inch) plasterboard ceiling fixed to firring channels
5 Fixed glazing
6 Outline of zinc flashing
7 89 x 89 x 5 mm (3 1/2 x 3 1/2 x 1/4 inch) square hollow section column fixed to column behind. Aluminium cover on inside and outside to match window frames
8 Outline of box gutter
9 Sashless double hung window
10 Outline of downpipe
11 Outline of zinc spreader
12 Zinc floor sheeting fixed to plywood underlayer
13 Timber rafters

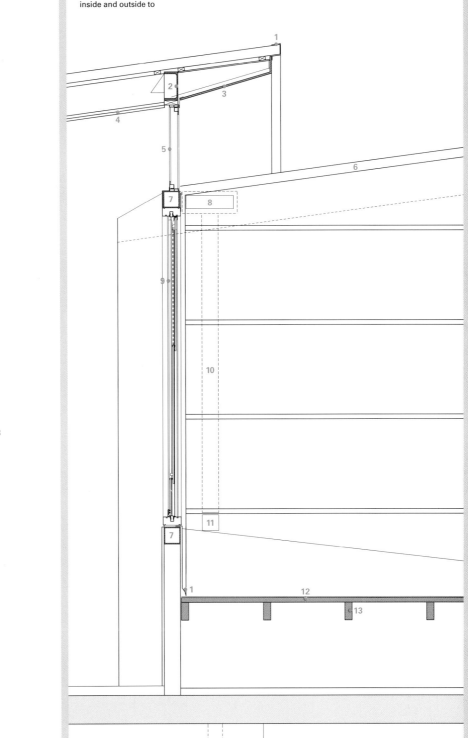

3.137
Sliding Window Detail at Living Room 1:10

Alison Brooks Architects
Herringbone Houses
[33]

1 Double glazing unit
2 18 mm (3/4 inch) medium density fibreboard window sill painted to match walls
3 12.5 mm (1/2 inch) plasterboard with 2.5 mm (1/10 inch) skim coat
4 1 mm (1/36 inch) vapour control layer
5 6 mm (1/4 inch) thin coat render system
6 50 mm (2 inch) rigid insulation
7 3 mm (1/8 inch) Tyvek building paper
8 18 mm (3/4 inch) plywood
9 100 x 70 mm (4 x 2 3/4 inch) timber studs
10 15 x 40 mm (3/5 x 15/8 inch) aluminium angle skirting
11 Hardwood timber flooring
12 65 mm (21/2 inch) underfloor heating
13 30 mm (11/5 inch) rigid insulation
14 150 mm (6 inch) thick hollow core concrete plank system
15 Waterproof membrane
16 8 mm (3/10 inch) galvanized plate to perimeter of gravel gully to retain external ground finish
17 Limestone gravel gully
18 Natural ground

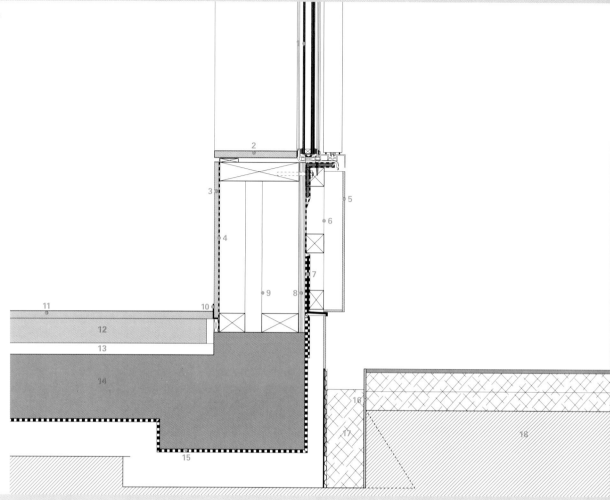

3.138
Window Plan Detail 1:5

Glas Architects
The Nail Houses [23]

1 215 mm (8 1/2 inch) Celcon medium-dense concrete party-wall block
2 Thistle plaster hardwall undercoat and thistle finish
3 Two layers of 12.5 mm (1/2 inch) plasterboard with thistle finish to reduce sound flanking transmission
4 Intumescent seal
5 Insulation
6 85 x 50 mm (33/8 x 2 inch) tanalised treated timber battens
7 Internal timber component of composite timber and aluminium window unit
8 Compriband seal
9 40 x 50 mm (15/8 x 2 inch) tanalised treated timber battens
10 25 mm (1 inch) pre-finished marine grade plywood cladding panel fixed to battens
11 Windproof vapour barrier
12 100 mm (4 inch) Rockwool insulation slab
13 Polyester powder-coated aluminium pressed flashing to match window frames
14 24 mm (1 inch) double glazed unit in polyester powder-coated aluminium frame

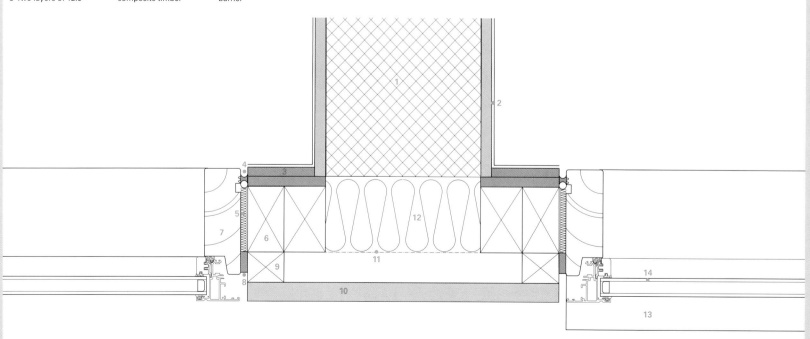

3.139
Bay Window Sill Detail
1:20

MacGabhann Architects
Tuath Na Mara [14]

1 Powder-coated
  aluminium window
  with double glazing
2 Anthrazinc window
  sill
3 Steel frame structure
4 Concrete sill beam
5 Anthrazinc standing
  seam cladding
6 62 x 12 mm (2^1/2 x ^{1}/2
  inch) softwood
  skirting
7 Smooth plaster wall
  finish
8 Solid oak board floor
  fixed to 50 x 75 mm
  (2 x 3 inch) timber
  battens with 40 mm
  (1^5/8 inch) high
  density insulation

9 Spray foam
  insulation
10 175 mm (7 inch)
  concrete slab
11 80 mm (3^1/8 inch)
  Kingspan insulation
12 Layers of well
  compacted hardcore
13 100 mm (4 inch)
  block wall
14 60 mm (2^3/8 inch)
  Kingspan insulation
15 215 mm (8^1/2 inch)
  block wall
16 Reinforced concrete
  footing

3.140
Den Window Section
Detail 1:10

Johnston Marklee &
Associates
Hill House [22]

1 Waterproofing
  membrane
2 15 mm (^{5}/8 inch)
  plywood substrate
3 Timber firring
  members at 610 mm
  (24 inch) centres
4 Timber nailer
5 Universal steel beam
6 Joist hanger
7 50 x 254 mm (2 x 10
  inch) timber joists
8 15 mm (^{5}/8 inch)
  gypsum board
9 Timber framing
10 15 mm (^{5}/8 inch)
  plywood substrate
11 Metal reveal for drip
  stop
12 50 x 100 mm (2 x 4
  inch) firring at 400
  mm (16 inch) centres
13 Timber framing
14 Corner bead
15 Curtain track
16 Aluminium window
  frame
17 Double glazed
  window
18 Window sill
19 75 x 75 x 10 mm (3 x
  3 x ^{3}/8 inch) steel
  square hollow
  section
20 Timber packer
21 Ripped 50 x 100 mm
  (2 x 4 inch) timber
  bearers at 300 mm
  (12 inch) centres

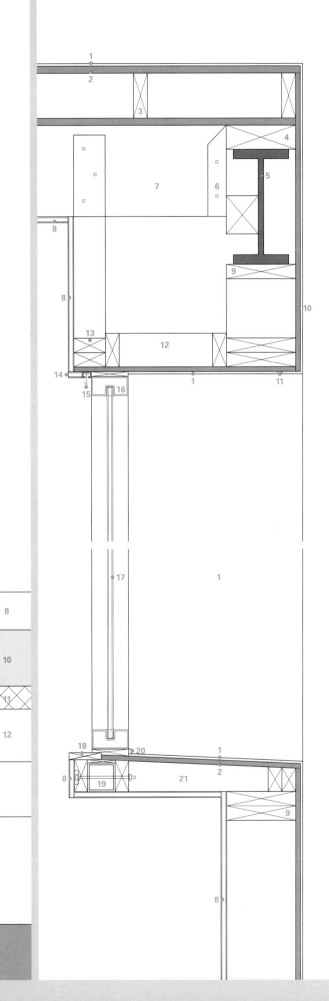

4.001

4.001
Sliding Door and Timber
Screen Detail 1:10

Tzannes Associates
Parsley Bay Residence
[21]

1 Copper capping on
   marine ply substrate
2 Ballast
3 Membrane
4 18 mm (3/4 inch)
   marine grade

plywood
5 Framing to suit
   minimum 1:100 fall
6 Insulation
7 Horizontal tongue
   and groove cladding
8 100 x 10 mm (4 x 3/8
   inch) galvanized mild
   steel plate, screw
   fixed to timber
   bearer
9 200 x 65 mm (8 x 2 1/2
   inch) parallel flange
   channel

10 Sliding screen/door
   tracks fixed to timber
   blocking
11 Timber framed
   sliding doors with 19
   mm (3/4 inch) timber
   louvres at 30° incline
12 Timber framed
   glazed sliding door
13 Column beyond
14 Brass channel sliding
   screens and doors
   set in sill
15 Timber hardwood sill

16 Timber threshold
17 Stainless steel angle
18 Timber fascia
19 Timber structure
20 Timber deck with
   caulked sealed joints
21 Cover plates to guide
   slipway, shown
   dotted
22 Slipway
23 Timber framed
   structure
24 Packing under
   slipway as required

to obtain falls
25 Line of rock shelf

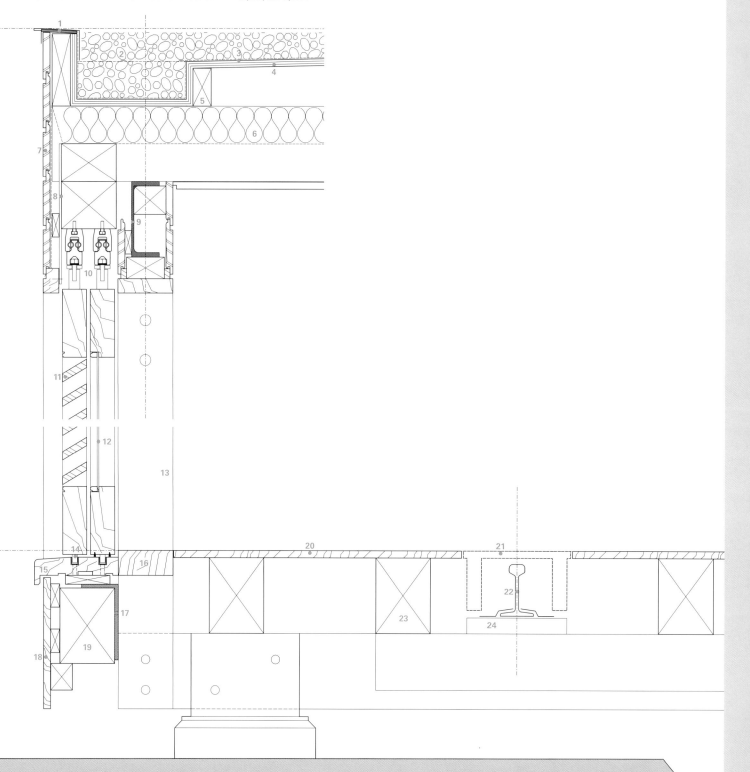

4.002
Sliding Glass Door
Section Detail 1:5

Lee + Mundwiler
Architects
The Coconut House [12]

1 Hardwood floor
2 18 mm (7/10 inch) plywood floor sheeting
3 Structural timber beam
4 Phenolic-resin wood veneer panels
5 Weather resistant barrier, vapour permeable building paper
6 Timber framing
7 Sliding and folding door top track
8 24 gauge metal flashing
9 12.5 mm (1/2 inch) plasterboard ceiling
10 Timber casing
11 Aluminium folding and sliding french door
12 Line of steel post shown dotted
13 Double glazed folding and sliding door
14 Sliding and folding door bottom track
15 Plywood subfloor
16 Hardwood floor
17 Reinforced concrete floor slab
18 Metal threshold
19 Timber decking with size, elevation and direction to match hardwood floor
20 Metal threshold and drip edge
21 Timber deck sleepers to provide slope

4.003
Pantry Door Detail 1:5

Lee + Mundwiler
Architects
The Coconut House [12]

1 Timber blocking between ceiling joists
2 Silicone caulking
3 Fixed glass hardware
4 15 mm (5/8 inch) drywall ceiling
5 Fixed glass clamp hardware
6 12.5 mm (1/2 inch) clear glass
7 Fixed glass recessed bottom track
8 Hardwood timber floor
9 18 mm (7/10 inch) plywood floor sheeting
10 Rough stair face
11 12.5 mm (1/2 inch) finished wood face to stair
12 Air gap
13 15 mm (5/8 inch) drywall patch finish
14 Timber beam assembly
15 Batt insulation
16 Bolt connection to timber beams
17 Fixed glass hardware
18 Glass sliding door rollers
19 Glass sliding door top track
20 Sliding panel with 12.5 mm (1/2 inch) glass
21 Fixed panel with 12.5 mm (1/2 inch) glass
22 Glass sliding door bottom track
23 Concrete slab

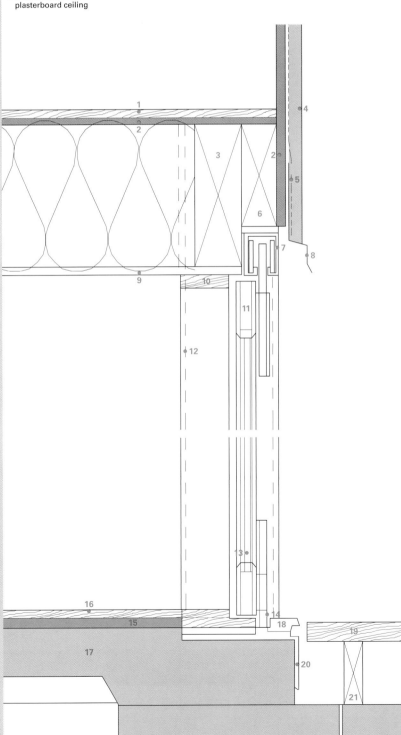

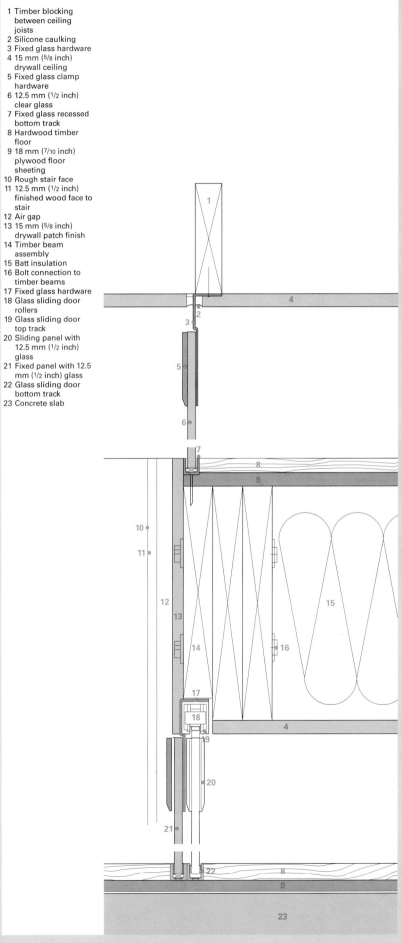

4.004
Door Plan Detail 1:10

Boyd Cody Architects
Richmond Place House
[22]

1 Solid oak edging
   piece
2 Panel splayed at end
   to accommodate
   stainless steel hinge
   with veneer strip
   cover

3 18 mm (7/10 inch)
   white oak veneered
   panel applied to front
   of door
4 18 mm (7/10 inch)
   white oak veneered
   panel applied to back
   of door
5 Timber trim piece
6 Timber door frame
7 Timber wall framing
8 18 mm (7/10 inch)
   veneered plywood
   internal wall lining

9 Insulation
10 Plasterboard wall
   lining with paint
   finish

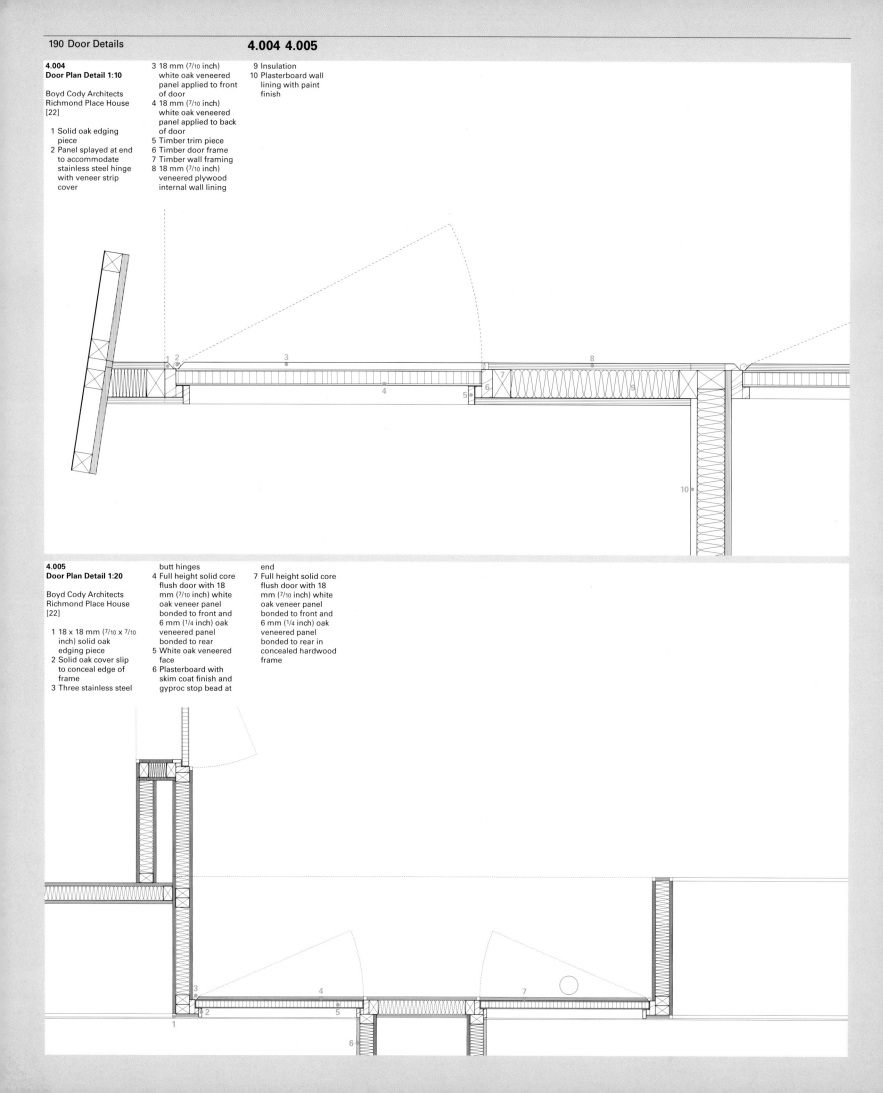

4.005
Door Plan Detail 1:20

Boyd Cody Architects
Richmond Place House
[22]

1 18 x 18 mm (7/10 x 7/10
   inch) solid oak
   edging piece
2 Solid oak cover slip
   to conceal edge of
   frame
3 Three stainless steel

butt hinges
4 Full height solid core
   flush door with 18
   mm (7/10 inch) white
   oak veneer panel
   bonded to front and
   6 mm (1/4 inch) oak
   veneered panel
   bonded to rear
5 White oak veneered
   face
6 Plasterboard with
   skim coat finish and
   gyproc stop bead at

end
7 Full height solid core
   flush door with 18
   mm (7/10 inch) white
   oak veneer panel
   bonded to front and
   6 mm (1/4 inch) oak
   veneered panel
   bonded to rear in
   concealed hardwood
   frame

4.006
Door Head and Sill
Detail 1:10

Cassion Castle
Architects
Twofold House [12]

1 12 mm (1/2 inch) foil
  backed gypsum
  plasterboard with 3
  mm (1/8 inch) plaster
  skim coat
2 200 x 200 mm (8 x 8
  inch) rolled steel joist
3 50 mm (2 inch)
  mineral wool
  insulation
4 Intermittent steel
  brackets welded on
  to rolled steel joist at
  800 mm (32 inch)
  centres
5 18 mm (7/10 inch)
  waterproof plywood
6 Architectural
  fluorescent lighting

fixture
7 29 mm (11/8 inch)
  double glazed unit
  comprised of 6 mm
  (1/4 inch) Pilkington-K
  glass, 16 mm (5/8
  inch) argon-filled
  spacer and 7 mm (1/4
  inch) Georgian wired
  glass
8 4 mm (1/6 inch)
  anodized aluminium
  sheet
9 60 x 60 mm (23/8 x
  23/8 inch) anodized
  aluminium angle
10 12 mm (1/2 inch)
  security glazing tape
  and sealant
11 55 mm (21/8 inch)
  solid door with
  midnight hue
  anti-flypost paint
  medium finish
12 Brush draught-
  proofing
13 80 mm (31/8 inch)

power floated
  concrete screed with
  underfloor heating
14 80 mm (31/8 inch)
  rigid insulation
15 1.6 mm (1/24 inch)
  polythene damp
  proof membrane
16 200 mm (8 inch)
  reinforced concrete
  slab

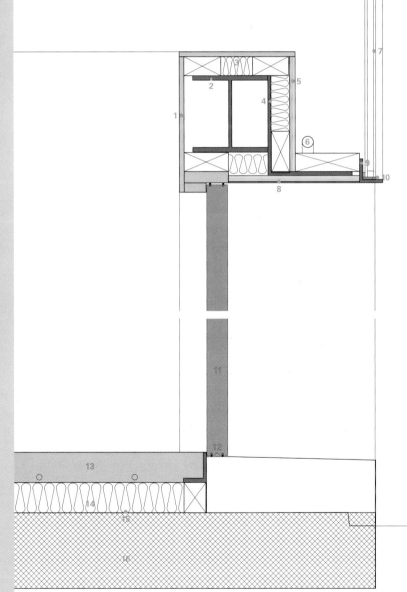

4.007
Door Jamb Detail 1:10

Cassion Castle
Architects
Twofold House [12]

1 15 mm (5/8 inch)
  Fireline plasterboard
2 3 mm (1/8 inch)
  plaster skim coat
3 3 mm (1/8 inch)
  galvanized stop bead
  overlapped with
  scrim tape
4 45 mm (17/8 inch)
  thick solid fire door
  with polyurethane

spray finish
5 Draught excluding
  intumescent strip
6 80 mm (11/8 inch)
  rigid insulation

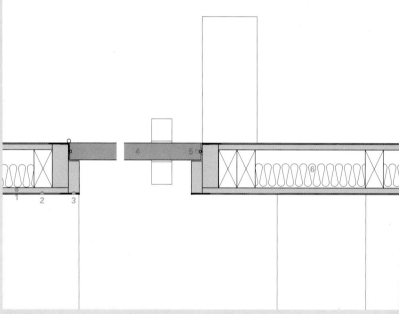

4.008
Door Jamb Detail 1:10

Cassion Castle
Architects
Twofold House [12]

1 20 mm (3/4 inch) sand
  and cement render
  on breather
  membrane. Corner
  and stop beads used
  at corners and edges
  of render
2 75 mm (3 inch)
  diameter concealed
  rainwater downpipe
3 5 x 5 mm (1/5 x 1/5

inch) Sealmaster
  draught proofing
4 Hardwood timber
  sliding door and
  frame
5 12 mm (1/2 inch)
  security glazing tape
6 17 x 5 mm (11/16 x 1/5
  inch) Sealmaster
  draught proofing
7 Anodized aluminium
  angle
8 12 mm (1/2 inch)
  security glazing tape
9 28 mm (11/8 inch)
  double glazed unit
  comprised of 6 mm
  (1/4 inch) Pilkington-K

toughened glass, 16
  mm (5/8 inch)
  argon-filled spacer
  and 6 mm (1/4 inch)
  Pilkington Optifloat
  toughened glass
10 80 mm (31/8 inch)
  rigid insulation
11 12 mm (1/2 inch) foil
  backed gypsum
  plasterboard with 3
  mm (1/8 inch) plaster
  skim coat

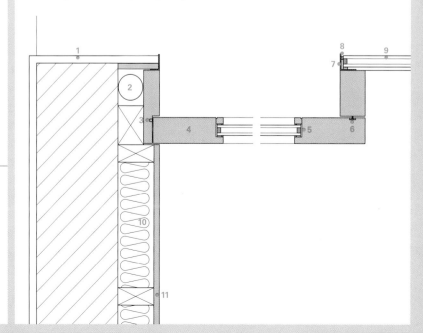

4.009
Balcony Doors Detail
1:20

Pezo von Ellrichshausen
Architects
Poli House [09]

1 150 mm (6 inch)
  reinforced concrete
  wall
2 25 x 100 mm (1 x 4
  inch) recycled pine
  board cladding
3 30 mm (1¹/₅ inch)
  timber rail for shutter
4 Black electro-painted
  aluminium frame
5 25 x 100 mm (1 x 4
  inch) recycled pine
  board shutter
6 Double glazed
  balcony door
7 30 mm (1¹/₅ inch)
  mortar bed
8 30 mm (1¹/₅ inch)
  mortar bed

9 140 mm (5¹/₂ inch)
  reinforced concrete
  slab
10 100 mm (4 inch)
  gravel bed
11 60 mm (2³/₈ inch)
  consolidated soil
  layer
12 Reinforced concrete
  wall
13 5 mm (¹/₅ inch)
  sealing layer

4.010
Security Door Section
Detail 1:25

Koffi & Diabaté
Architectes
Villa Talon [28]

1 20 mm (³/₄ inch)
  concrete column
  with lacquered finish
2 Tinted glass fixed
  panel (green colour)
3 Roller shutter
4 Steel C-section beam
  frame
5 Fixed tinted glass
  panel (dark blue
  colour)
6 Fixed tinted glass
  panel (dark blue
  colour)
7 Roller shutter guide
  rail
8 Openable glass panel
  in timber frame
9 Terracotta tile

external cladding
10 Terracotta tile
  external cladding
11 Terracotta tile
  external cladding

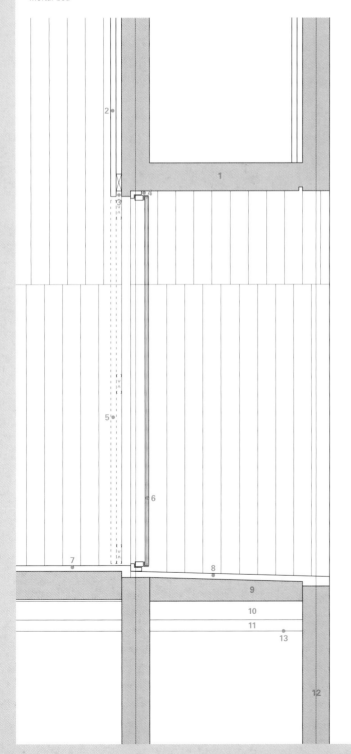

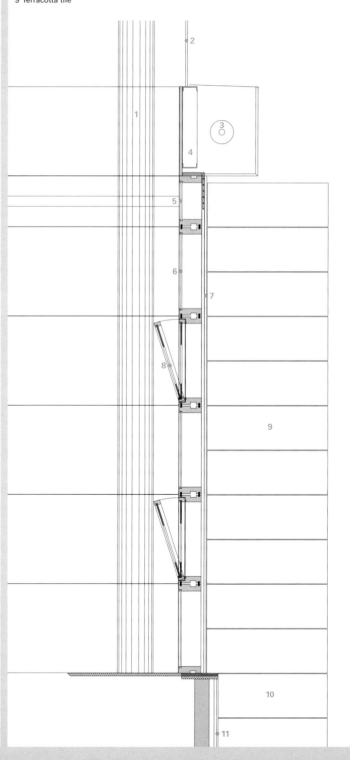

4.011
Sliding Door Detail 1:5

Arjaan de Feyter
Zoersel House [29]

1 140 x 140 mm (5¹/₂ x 5¹/₂ inch) steel column
2 Line of horizontal beam
3 Line of cross beam
4 Powder-coated folded aluminium profile with mosquito net
5 Powder-coated aluminium double glazed sliding door
6 Double glazed fixed window unit
7 50 x 120 mm (2 x 4³/₄ inch) powder-coated aluminium mullion with insulation infill
8 Line of casing to support beam
9 Brush draught excluder

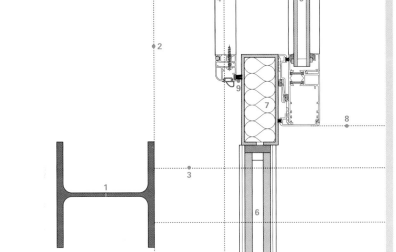

4.012
Entrance Door Plan and Elevation Detail 1:50

Koffi & Diabaté
Architectes
Villa Talon [28]

1 Timber door frame
2 Fixed tinted-glass panel
3 Fixed tinted-glass panel
4 Openable tinted-glass panel
5 Timber door panel
6 Timber door frame
7 Door handle
8 Travertine clad stair treads and risers
9 Terracotta tile external cladding

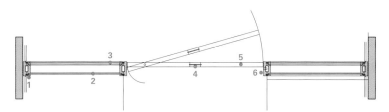

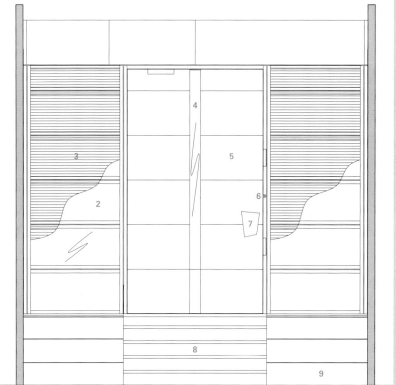

4.013
Sliding Door Detail 1:5

Arjaan de Feyter
Zoersel House [29]

1 Double glazed fixed window unit with 10 mm (³/₈ inch) glass, 15 mm (⁵/₈ inch) air space and 10 mm (³/₈ inch) glass
2 Line of horizontal beam
3 Powder-coated aluminium double glazed door with 6 mm (¹/₄ inch) glass, 15 mm (⁵/₈ inch) air space and 6 mm (¹/₄ inch) glass
4 Structural joint with silicone weatherproof building sealant
5 50 x 50 mm (2 x 2 inch) powder-coated aluminium angle
6 Line of cross beam
7 140 x 140 mm (5¹/₂ x 5¹/₂ inch) steel column

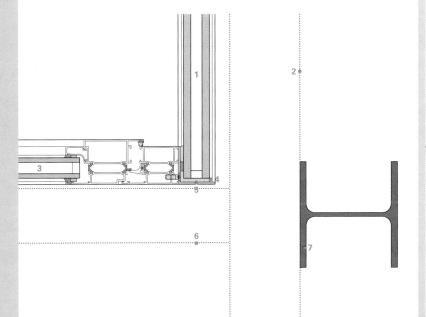

4.014
Sliding Door Plan Detail
1:10

WPA
Weese Young Residence
[28]

1 Corrugated
  zincalume on timber
  battens on
  waterproof
  membrane on
  plywood
2 Corner flashing
3 Aluminium sliding
  glass door
4 Painted square
  hollow section
  column
5 Lite-ply wall and
  door panel
6 Solid poplar trim and
  door panel
7 Steel tube frame
8 Recess for sliding
  door
9 Timber stud framing
  to form recess

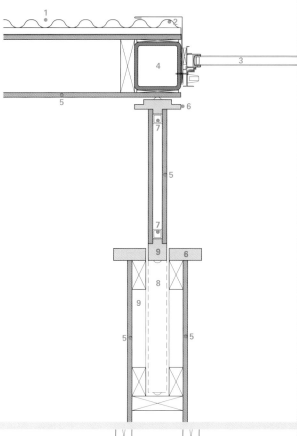

4.015
Sliding Door Section
Detail 1:10

WPA
Weese Young Residence
[28]

1 Timber framing to
  form recess for
  sliding assembly
2 Roller hardware
3 Solid Poplar head of
  door panel
4 Lite-ply ceiling and
  door lining
5 Steel tube frame
6 Solid poplar door
  pull for sliding door
7 Sliding door track
8 Vertical grain pine on
  plywood subfloor

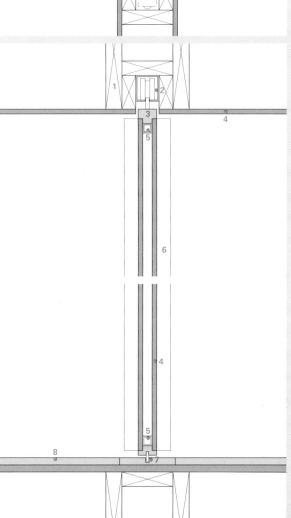

4.016
Glass Sliding Door
Section Detail 1:10

WPA
Weese Young Residence
[28]

1 Recycled rubber tiles
2 Waterproof
  membrane on
  plywood
3 Engineered timber
  joist
4 Insulation
5 Lite-ply ceiling lining
6 Painted exterior
  grade plywood
7 Cedar boards
8 Painted rectangular
  hollow section beam
9 Aluminium fixed
  window
10 Painted square
  hollow section
  transom
11 Aluminium-framed
  sliding glass door
12 Vertical grain pine on
  plywood subfloor
13 Timber joist
14 Ipe floorboards
15 Two timber joists
  bolted to edge beam
  to support boards
16 Painted rectangular
  hollow section
  column

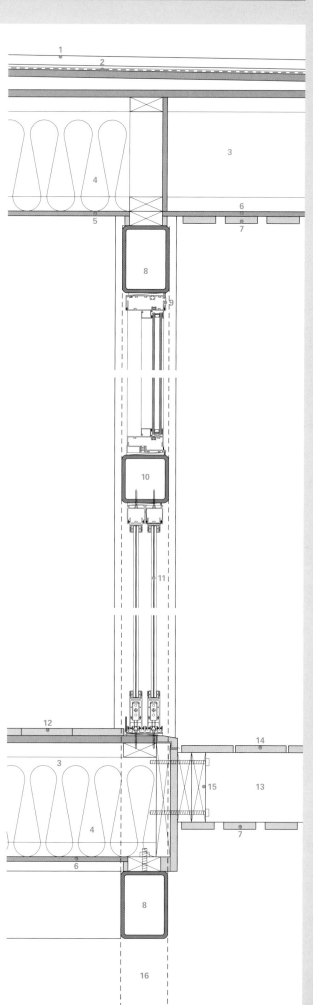

4.017
External Sliding Door
Section Detail 1:5

Paulo David with Luz
Ramalho
Casa Funchal [16]

1 Waterproof paint
2 Concrete screed with
waterproof paint
3 Seal of silicone
beads under sill
4 Door sill of local
black rock
5 Aluminium window
frame

6 Plaster finish
7 Concrete wall
8 Neoprene wedge
9 25 x 25 mm (1 x 1
inch) timber batten
10 Hardwood trim to
batten
11 Sliding door track
assembly
12 6 mm (1/4 inch) birch
veneered sheathing
13 Hardwood framing at
top and bottom of
door
14 Aluminium sliding
door track
15 12 mm (1/2 inch)
medium density

fibreboard to reveals
16 Polyurethane floor
with protective layer

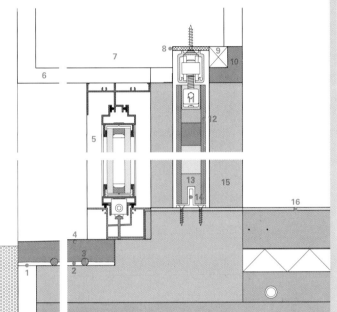

4.018
External Sliding Door
Plan Detail 1:5

Paulo David with Luz
Ramalho
Casa Funchal [16]

1 Hardwood door jamb
2 Door lock
3 Aluminium door
handle
4 Vertical hardwood
frame in door core
5 Hardwood edging
6 12 mm (1/2 inch)
medium density
fibreboard with

adhesive strip
7 30 x 30 mm (11/4 x
11/5 inch) square
hollow section steel
tube framing
8 15 mm (5/8 inch)
hardwood skirting
9 Aluminium window
frame
10 Concrete wall
11 Plaster finish
12 Double glazed
window

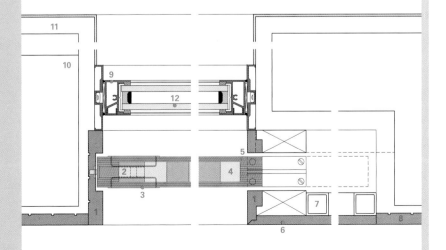

4.019
Patio Sliding Door Detail
1:10

Bercy Chen Studio
Riverview Gardens [38]

1 25 mm (1 inch)
double glazed sliding
glass door
2 Metal joist
3 25 mm (1 inch)
double glazed sliding
glass door
4 25 mm (1 inch)
double glazed sliding
glass door
5 20 mm (3/4 inch)
Indian sandstone
exterior flooring
6 Drip profile
7 Sliding door frame
8 20 mm (3/4 inch)
Indian sandstone
interior flooring
9 28 mm (11/10 inch)
plywood subfloor
10 Batt insulation
11 Structural timber
joist
12 16 mm (5/8 inch)
gyprock ceiling

4.020
Glazed Door Detail 1:10

MELD Architecture with
Vicky Thornton
House in Tarn et
Garonne [34]

1 Bespoke double
   glazed oak framed
   doors
2 Lime render finish to
   concrete blockwork
3 Expanded
   polystyrene full-fill
   cavity insulation
4 200 mm (8 inch)
   load-bearing
   concrete blockwork
5 Expanded
   polystyrene full-fill
   cavity insulation
6 300 mm (6 inch)
   limestone rubble
7 Top hung sliding
   shutter in laminated
   pine boarding with
   galvanized cladding
8 Concrete paving
   slabs
9 Mixed pebbles to
   drainage channel

4.021
Door Jamb Detail 1:10

MELD Architecture with
Vicky Thornton
House in Tarn et
Garonne [34]

1 14 mm (5/8 inch)
   oriented strand
   board on timber
   studs with mineral
   wool insulation
   between
2 Solid core flush
   timber door with
   eggshell paint finish
   and stainless steel
   ironmongery
3 Softwood timber
   frame
4 Softwood door jamb
5 Oriented strand
   board on timber
   studs

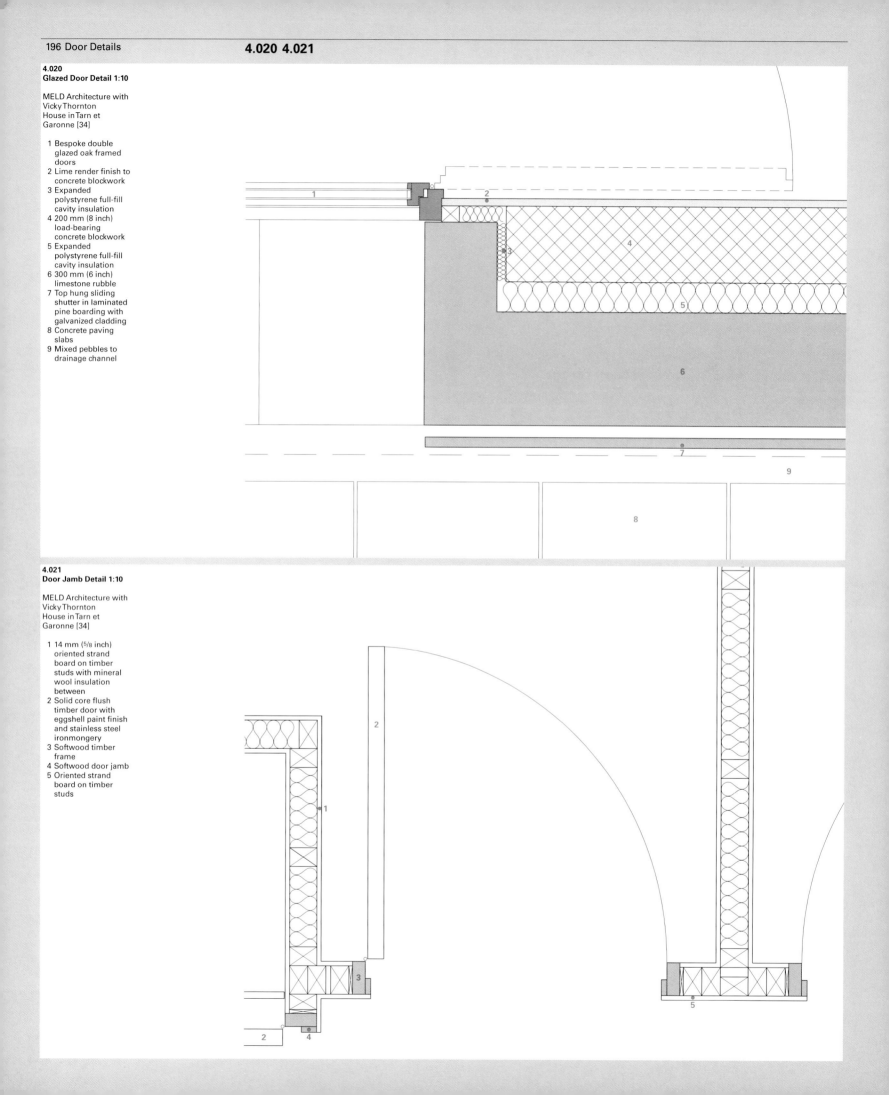

4.022
Front Door Detail 1:10

Rowan Opat Architects
Courtyard House [38]

1 Solid door core
2 Door style beyond
3 Paintable putty
4 Box with artwork to
  be fixed behind glass
5 6 mm (1/4 inch) fixed
  glass

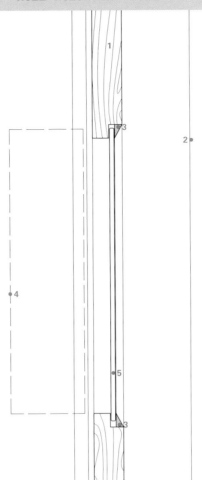

4.023
**Door and Window Detail
1:5**

Rowan Opat Architects
Somers Courtyard
House [38]

1 Indigenous
  hardwood timber
  deck, radial sawn,
  shown beyond
2 Silicone bead
3 Timber mullion cover
  plate with paint finish
4 Timber mullion with
  paint finish
5 Sashless double

hung glazing unit
  timber cover with
  paint finish
6 Sashless double
  hung window frame
7 Double glazing
8 Board and batten
  radial sawn timber
  cladding with paint
  finish
9 Structural steel post
  with paint finish
10 Timber door jamb
11 Stainless steel towel
   rail

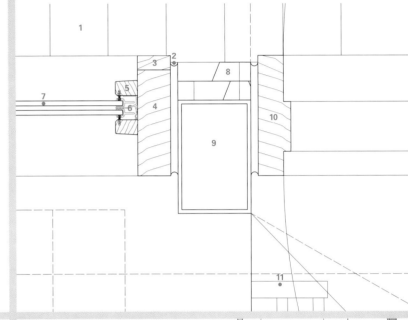

4.024
**Sliding Door Detail at
Living Room 1:10**

Lahz Nimmo Architects
Casuarina Ultimate
Beach House [31]

1 Anodized aluminium
  louvre blades with
  matching clips.
  Louvre unit angled
  eight degrees off
  vertical
2 Profiled dressed
  hardwood sill
3 Painted medium
  density fibreboard
  lining fixed to packer
4 Folded Colorbond
  flashing lapped over
  membrane
5 Butynol membrane
  roof on plywood
  substrate
6 Timber blocking
7 Medium density
  fibreboard returned
  into window reveal
8 Aluminium sliding
  door on recessed
  head and sill track
9 Flush finish door and
  ceiling track
10 Polished timber
   floorboards
   continued into reveal
11 Floor finish and door
   track finished flush
12 Timber decking with
   boards running in
   the same direction as
   floorboards
13 Timber floor joists

4.025
Sliding Door Detail 1:10

Lahz Nimmo Architects
Casuarina Ultimate
Beach House [31]

1 13 mm (1/2 inch)
  plasterboard
2 Roller blind head box
  and bracket fixed to
  timber structure.
  Hem bar to finish
  flush with bulkhead
3 Removable 20 mm
  (3/4 inch) thick
  hardwood panel
  fixed with stainless
  steel allen key
  screws for servicing
  blind and door track
4 Aluminium door
  head channel fixed to
  timber beam with
  track concealed
  within bulkhead
5 Sliding door track to
  timber batten door
6 120 x 20 mm (43/4 x
  3/4 inch) recycled
  blue gum hardwood
  boards shiplapped
  with joints secret
  nailed and stain
  finished
7 Building paper
8 Ensure flush finish
  across opening
9 Sliding glazed door
10 Sliding glazed door
   and batten door to
   slide into cavity
   recess
11 Timber battens
   beyond
12 20 mm (3/4 inch)
   dressed hardwood
   trim to reveal
13 Weather seal to both
   sides of vertical
   members of timber
   door

14 Limestone pavers to
   floor
15 Track to aluminium
   sliding door to finish
   flush with tiles
16 Waterproof
   membrane on 50
   mm (2 inch) sand bed
17 Recessed sliding
   door channel
18 Limestone threshold
   with 15 mm (5/8 inch)
   overhang
19 25 mm (1 inch) set
   down slab at
   openings
20 Steel trowel trim coat
   finish to exposed
   face of concrete
21 Concrete paver on
   sand bed

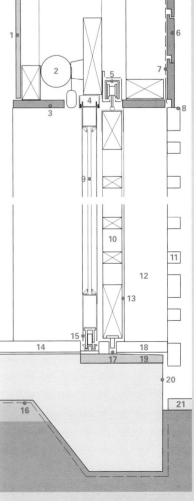

4.026
Door Jamb Detail 1:5

Stephenson Bell
Architects
House 780 [18]

1 Single skin of 12 mm
 (1/2 inch)
 plasterboard on dabs
2 100 mm (4 inch)
 blockwork wall
3 Medium density
 fibreboard lining
 painted black
4 Recessed acoustic
 door seal integrated
 into sliding door

system
5 Door ironmongery
6 Plasterboard stop
 bead
7 Plasterboard high
 strength corner bead
8 Sliding door
9 Two layers of 12 mm
 (1/2 inch)
 plasterboard
10 25 mm (1 inch)
 minimum insulation
11 Recessed acoustic
 door seal integrated
 into sliding door
 system

4.027
Door Head Detail 1:2

Stephenson Bell
Architects
House 780 [18]

1 Concrete lintel
2 100 x 40 mm (4 x 15/8
 inch) softwood
 packer
3 Two layers 12 mm
 (1/2 inch)
 plasterboard on
 metal firring system
4 Plasterboard stop
 bead
5 Painted hardwood

packer with finished
face
6 Recessed acoustic
 door seal and
 draught excluder
7 54 mm (21/8 inch)
 flush timber door

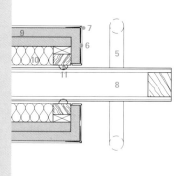

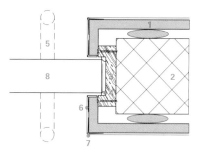

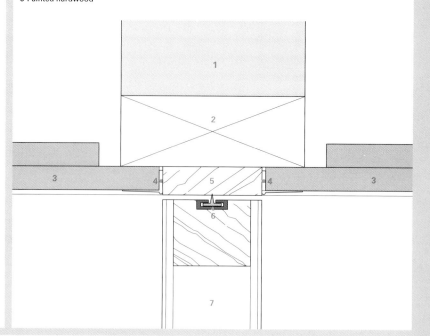

4.028
Triple Track Sliding Door Detail 1:10

Tzannes Associates
Parsley Bay Residence
[21]

1 Flawless glass
 balustrade
2 Stainless steel
 balustrade channel
3 Stone paving support
 beamers with clear

drainage paths to
 spitter location
4 Membrane
5 Render coat to
 concrete
6 Stainless steel
 framing to door head
7 Sliding louvred
 shutters
8 Sliding glazed doors
9 Stone sill with brass
 door guides and
 brush seals
10 Brass angle

11 Stone flooring
12 Screed
13 Concrete slab
14 Sliding shutter and
 door tracks fixed at
 head to timber
 packers

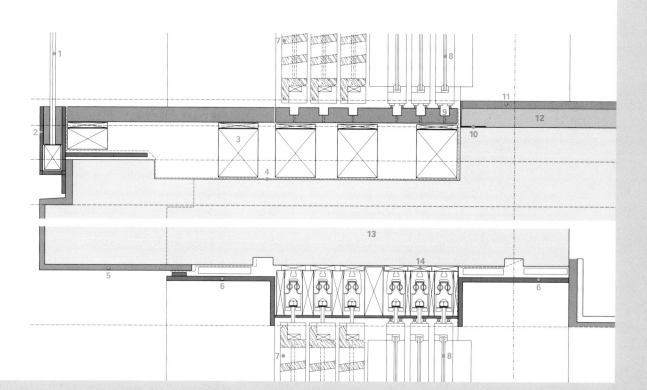

4.029
Triple Track Sliding Door Detail 1:10

Tzannes Associates
Parsley Bay Residence
[21]

1 Line of wall finish beyond
2 Slot diffuser
3 Removable timber door head
4 Timber packers to sliding track
5 Reinforced concrete first floor slab
6 Packing and infill strip between door tracks at height to suit door seals
7 Timber trim
8 Dowel spine beyond, shown dotted
9 Sliding louvred shutters
10 Sliding glazed doors
11 Stone flooring
12 Screed
13 Stone sill with brass channel guide tracks and drainage holes
14 Stone surface
15 Screed
16 Concrete slab laid to fall
17 Door beyond
18 Render finish to concrete

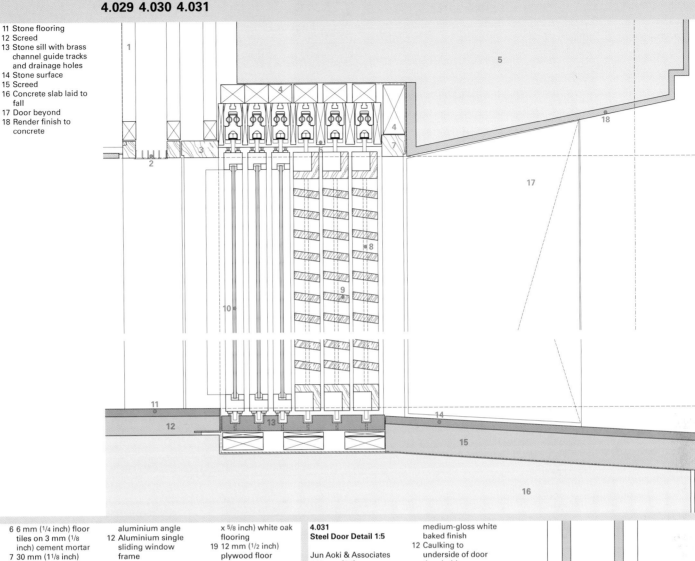

4.030
Sliding Door Detail 1:5

Jun Aoki & Associates
J House [24]

1 Double glazed window of 6 mm (1/4 inch) glass, 6 mm (1/4 inch) air gap and 8 mm (1/3 inch) glass
2 Aluminium sliding door frame
3 Waterproof seal
4 Mortar finish on metal lath
5 Lysine sprayed mortar render
6 6 mm (1/4 inch) floor tiles on 3 mm (1/8 inch) cement mortar
7 30 mm (11/8 inch) mortar bed
8 4 mm (1/6 inch) waterproof fibre reinforced plastic membrane over 6 mm (1/4 inch) calcium silicate board
9 9 mm (1/3 inch) plywood
10 60 x 27 mm (23/8 x 1 inch) cedar stud frame
11 20 x 40 x 2 mm (3/4 x 15/8 x 1/12 inch)
aluminium angle
12 Aluminium single sliding window frame
13 Accordion storage system for insect screen
14 2 mm (1/12 inch) polyvinyl chloride floor tiles
15 12 mm (1/2 inch) plywood floor substrate
16 9.5 mm (3/8 inch) spruce edging
17 White acrylic emulsion paint finish
18 150 x 15 mm thick (6
x 5/8 inch) white oak flooring
19 12 mm (1/2 inch) plywood floor substrate
20 12 mm (1/2 inch) structural plywood
21 100 mm (4 inch) glasswool insulation
22 100 x 40 mm (4 x 15/8 inch) timber floor joist

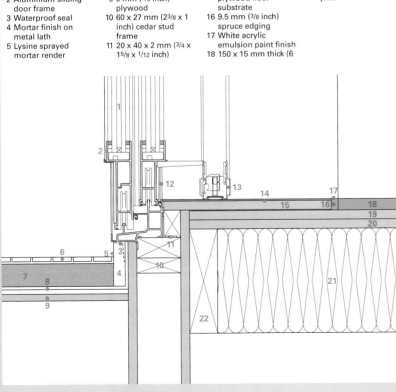

4.031
Steel Door Detail 1:5

Jun Aoki & Associates
J House [24]

1 Lysine spray on mortar render
2 12 mm (1/2 inch) structural plywood
3 Mortar finish on metal lath
4 90 x 60 mm (31/2 x 23/8 inch) timber stud frame
5 Waterproof seal
6 Welded steel sections to form door head
7 2.3 mm (1/10 inch) shaped steel plate with medium gloss white baked finish
8 Airtight rubber seal
9 Flush bolt to door assembly
10 Steel flush door with gloss-white baked finish
11 2.3 mm (1/10 inch) steel plate door threshold with
medium-gloss white baked finish
12 Caulking to underside of door threshold
13 Trowelled mortar to required thickness
14 2.3 mm (1/10 inch) shaped steel plate bottom frame
15 Concrete screw
16 Laminated lumber
17 Caulking
18 Waterproof acrylic resin coating
19 Backing rod of round bar and polyethylene foam
20 65 mm to 50 mm (21/2 to 2 inch) earth, raked to fall as required for drainage
21 Reinforced concrete floor slab

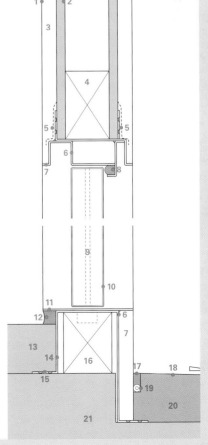

4.032
Kitchen Sliding Door
Detail 1:10

Studio Bednarski
Hesmondhalgh House
[33]

1 18 mm (3/4 inch)
   weather bonded and
   proofed plywood
2 Pre-patinated copper
   capping and facing
3 Extra layer of
   capping sheet at
   border
4 30 to 40 mm (11/5 to
   15/8 inch) size pebble
   border
5 Drainage trim
6 Sedum blanket
7 Drainage mat
8 Underlayer
9 90 mm (31/2 inch)
   insulation
10 500 gauge vapour
   barrier

11 18 mm (3/4 inch)
   weather bonded and
   proofed plywood
12 Treated softwood
   firrings laid to a
   minimum fall of 1:80
13 150 x 50 mm (6 x 2
   inch) softwood joists
   at 400 mm (16 inch)
   centres
14 Two layers of 12.5
   mm (1/2 inch)
   gypsum fireline
   board with a 2 mm
   (1/12 inch) skim coat
15 152 x 152 x 37 mm (6
   x 6 x 11/2 inch)
   universal channel
16 25 mm (1 inch)
   weather bonded and
   proofed plywood
   fascia
17 Pre-patinated copper
   fascia and drip
18 Sliding door gear in
   timber surround
19 Double glazed

   hardwood sliding
   door
20 Sliding door track
21 Timber floor
22 Cement screed
   topping with
   integrated underfloor
   heating
23 Insulation
24 Tanking
25 Reinforced concrete
   ground slab
26 Hardwood threshold
27 1200 x 600 mm (48 x
   24 inch) raised
   paving slabs with 10
   mm (3/8 inch) gaps
28 Paving slab support
29 Drainage

4.033
Sliding Door Detail 1:10

Studio Bednarski
Hesmondhalgh House
[33]

1 Garden stairs
2 100 x 75 mm (4 x 3
   inch) and 75 x 50 mm
   (3 x 2 inch) hardwood
   mullion
3 Fixed double glazed
   window
4 100 x 50 mm (4 x 2
   inch) mild steel
   rectangular hollow
   section steel column
5 Timber sill
6 100 x 50 mm (4 x 2
   inch) timber stud
7 Hardwood glazed
   sliding door
8 Sliding door track
9 Hardwood frame
10 Vertical damp proof
   course

11 Render
12 100 mm (4 inch)
   dense blockwork
13 Insulated cavity
   closer
14 75 mm (3 inch)
   full-fill insulation
15 11 mm (3/8 inch)
   gypsum thistle
   hardwall plaster with
   skim coat

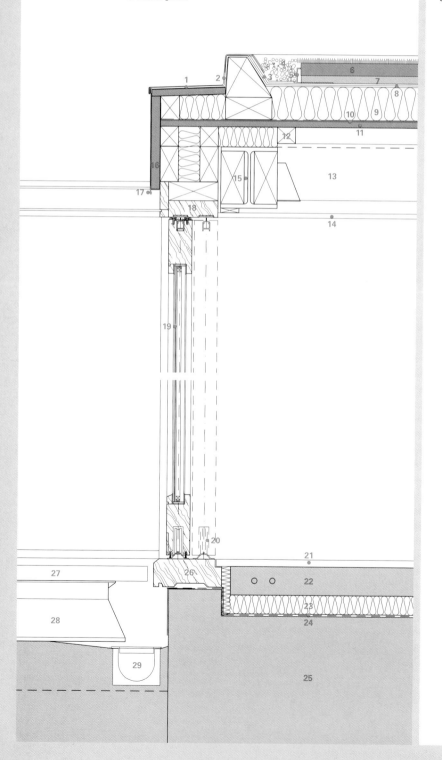

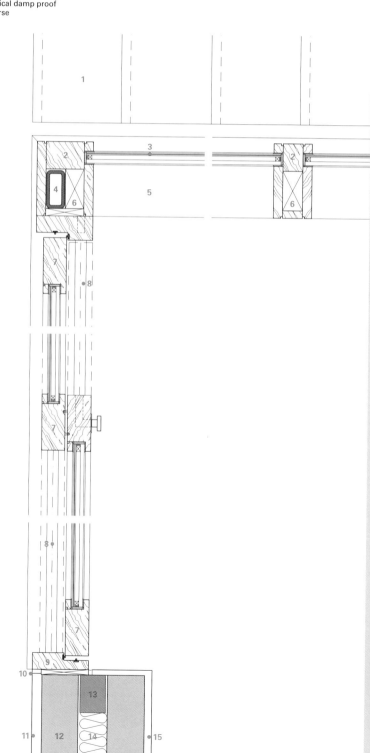

4.034
Sliding Door Detail 1:5

Avanti Architects
Long View [35]

1 Two layers of 12.5
   mm (1/2 inch)
   plasterboard
2 Vapour control layer
3 150 x 50 mm (6 x 2
   inch) timber stud
4 90 x 60 mm (3 1/2 x
   2 3/8 inch) vertical
   battens
5 Breather membrane
6 12 mm (1/2 inch)
   plywood bracing

7 50 x 75 mm (2 x 3
   inch) horizontal
   counter battens
8 160 x 160 mm (6 1/4 x
   6 1/4 inch) steel
   column with
   insulation infill
9 90 x 60 mm (3 1/2 x
   2 3/8 inch) vertical
   battens
10 65 x 22 mm (2 1/2 x 7/8
   inch) tongue and
   groove
   weatherboards
   secret fixed vertically
   to horizontal
   counter-battens
11 Insect mesh

12 3 mm (1/8 inch)
   folded polyester
   powder-coated
   aluminium flashing
   to jamb
13 150 x 25 mm (6 x 1
   inch) timber stud
14 Aluminium angle
15 Timber packer
16 Silicone fill
17 Aluminium window
   frame
18 Double glazing
19 Strip drain

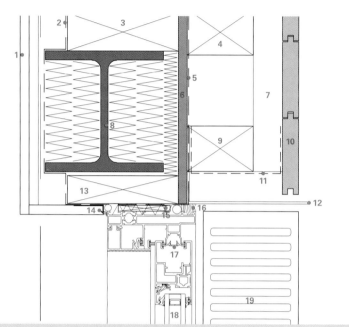

4.035
**Sliding Door and Screen
Detail 1:5**

Barclay & Crousse
Architecture
Casa O [08]

1 Reinforced concrete
   header beam
2 Galvanized steel
   track for timber sun
   screens
3 Sliding sun screen
   comprised of cedar
   battens attached to
   timber framing
4 40 x 126 mm (1 5/8 x 5

inch) cedar frame to
sun screen
5 Aluminium tracks for
   tempered glass
   screens

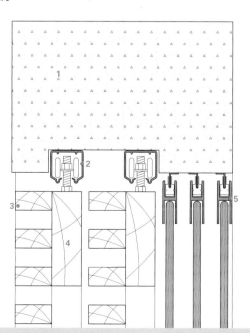

4.036
**Overhead Door Detail
1:33**

Barton Myers Associates
Bekins Residence [25]

1 Roofing membrane
2 Gypsum roof board
3 Rigid insulation
4 Galvanized steel deck
5 Neoprene closure
   with galvanized
   metal insert
6 Galvanized steel
   gutter
7 Overhead door
   torsion springs
8 Steel I-beam
9 Aluminium door top
   rail
10 Aluminium door
   track
11 Steel column
12 Glazing
13 Structural concrete
   slab
14 Moisture barrier
15 Continuous void
   form
16 Grade beam
17 Concrete caisson
   beyond

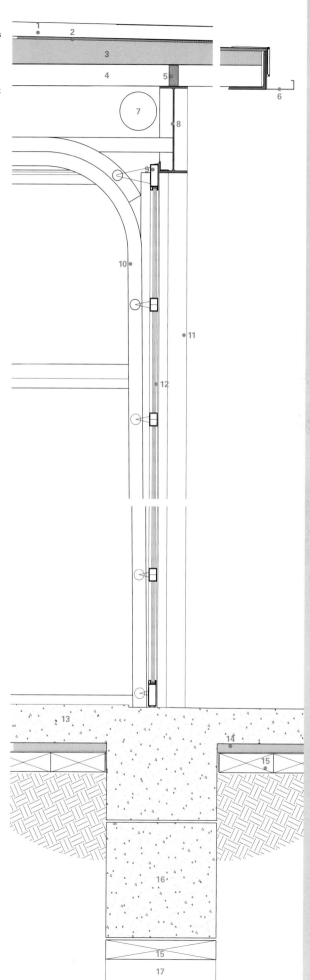

4.037
Door Detail 1:10

A-Piste Arkkitehdit
Villa O [39]

1 Fine plaster wall
 finish
2 130 mm (5 1/8 inch)
 facade masonry
3 30 mm (1 1/4 inch)
 ventilated cavity
4 25 mm (1 inch)
 weathershield
5 125 mm (5 inch)
 mineral wool
 insulation
6 Silicone seal
7 250 x 80 mm (10 x
 3 1/8 inch)
 laminated
 timber window
 frames
8 Triple glazing
 comprised of 6 mm
 (1/4 inch), 4 mm (1/8
 inch) and 6 mm (1/4
 inch) glass panes
9 Double glazed
 double doors
10 Double glazing
 comprised of two 6
 mm (1/4 inch) glass
 panes
11 33 x 90 mm (1 1/4 x
 3 1/2 inch) aspen
 boarding, finger
 jointed and untreated
12 9 mm (3/8 inch)
 veneered plywood
 weathershield
13 20 x 97 mm (3/4 x 3 7/8
 inch) battens and
 counter battens
 providing ventilation
14 50 mm (2 inch)
 mineral wool
 insulation between
 48 x 172 mm (1 7/8 x
 6 3/4 inch) timber
 studs
15 197 x 48 mm (7 3/4 x
 1 9/10 inch) timber

supporting frame
16 25 mm (1 inch) sawn
 wood fibreboard
 weathershield
17 250 x 80 mm (10 x
 3 1/8 inch) laminated
 timber door frames
18 13 mm (1/2 inch)
 plasterboard
19 9 mm (3/8 inch)
 veneered plywood
20 Vapour barrier
21 200 mm (8 inch)
 mineral wool
 insulation between
 48 x 197 mm (1 7/8 x
 7 3/4 inch) timber
 studs

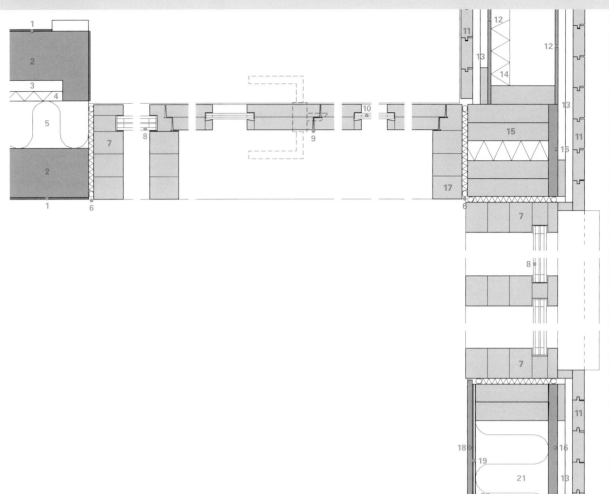

4.038
Sliding and Pivot Door
Detail 1:20

McBride Charles Ryan
The Dome House [21]

1 White melamine
 joinery unit
2 45 x 90 mm (1 3/4 x
 3 1/2 inch) timber stud
3 White melamine
 joinery unit
4 Medium density
 fibreboard lining
 with selected timber
 veneer finish to
 match kitchen joinery
5 Square hollow
 section steel column
6 Painted plasterboard
 and stud wall
7 Semi-solid door
8 35 mm (1 1/3 inch)
 painted medium
 density fibreboard
 door jamb

9 Edge of step
10 Cavity slider door
 with rebate at base to
 accommodate stair
11 Square hollow
 section steel column
12 Insulation and
 sarking
13 Aluminium framed
 glazing

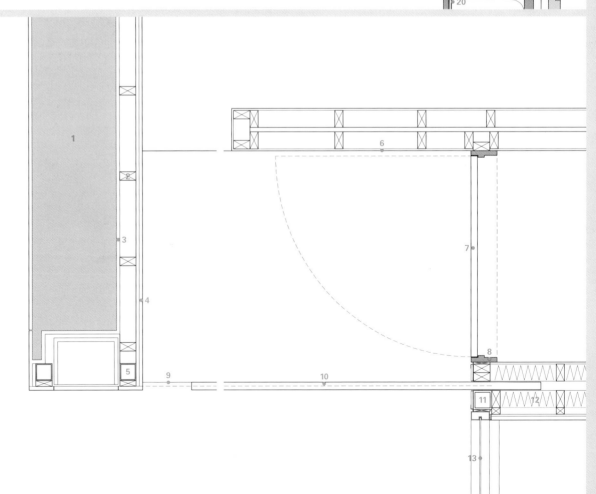

4.039
Entrance Door Plan
Detail 1:10

Blank Studio
Xeros Residence [29]

1 20 gauge metal
  fascia cladding on
  self-healing
  waterproof
  membrane on 12.5
  mm (1/2 inch) exterior
  plywood
2 Batt insulation
3 Glazed door
4 Light gauge metal
  U-framing

5 16 gauge, cold-rolled
  steel plate sheet on
  12.5 mm (1/2 inch)
  plywood sheathing
6 Open position of
  door
7 Concealed
  rectangular hollow
  section steel tube
  door frame
8 Timber blocking
9 50 mm (2 inch) steel
  floor grating below

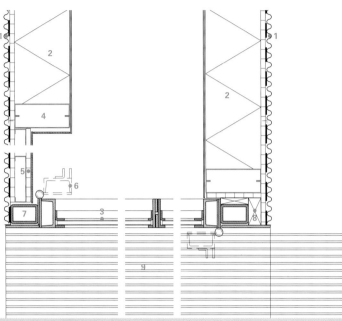

4.040
Balcony Door Head
Detail 1:10

Blank Studio
Xeros Residence [29]

1 Exposed steel beam
  beyond
2 Metal flashing on
  wood slope strip on
  5 mm (1/5 inch) steel
  plate
3 Membrane roof
  system with rock
  ballast to match site
4 Timber blocking
5 12.5 mm (1/2 inch)

plywood roof
sheathing on sloping
battens
6 20 gauge metal
  fascia cladding on
  self-healing
  waterproof
  membrane on 12.5
  mm (1/2 inch) exterior
  plywood
7 200 mm (8 inch) steel
  I-beam
8 Wood block at steel
  web to support joist
  hangers
9 Batt insulation
10 Hawa Junior patch
  fittings and caps with

12.5 mm (1/2 inch)
coloured laminated
glass door
11 Light gauge steel hat
  channels and hanger
  wire for ceiling
  support
12 12.5 mm plaster (1/2
  inch) on 12.5 mm (1/2
  inch) cement board
  on suspended ceiling
  hangers

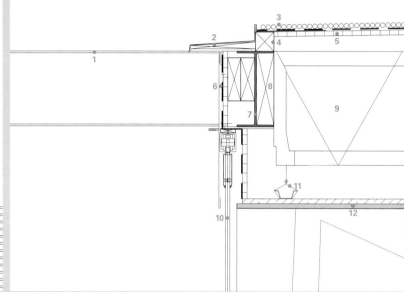

4.041
Entrance Door Head
Detail 1:10

Blank Studio
Xeros Residence [29]

1 Embedded site
  gravel in 37 mm (11/2
  inch) foam roof
  system
2 12.5 mm (1/2 inch)
  plywood roof
  sheathing on sloping
  battens
3 Batt insulation
4 Light gauge steel hat
  channels and hanger

wire for ceiling
support
5 Timber framing
6 Doubled timber
  framing at door head
7 Wax-sealed skim coat
  plaster on 12.5 mm
  (1/2 inch) gypsum
  board
8 Glazed door
9 Wax-sealed skim coat
  plaster on 12.5 mm
  (1/2 inch) exterior
  cement board

4.042
Door Jamb Detail 1:5

Go Hasegawa
Associates
Forest House [34]

1 12 mm (1/2 inch)
  structural plywood
  and 5.5 mm (1/4 inch)
  plywood with oil
  stain clear lacquer
  finish
2 30 mm (11/4 inch)
  Japanese linden
  plywood interior
  door with urethane
  paint finish
3 5.5 mm (1/4 inch)
  plywood with oil
  stain clear lacquer
  finish
4 45 x 105 mm (13/4 x
  41/8 inch) timber stud
5 12 mm (1/2 inch)
  structural plywood
  and 9 mm (3/8 inch)
  insulating fibreboard
  with urethane paint
  finish
6 100 mm (4 inch) red
  cedar exterior door
  frame with urethane
  paint finish
7 56 mm (21/4 inch) red
  cedar exterior door
  with urethane paint
  finish

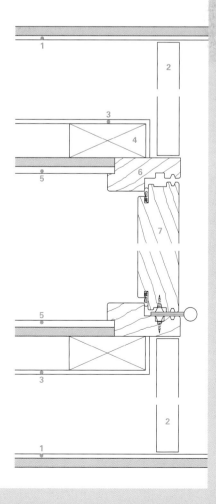

4.043
Door Jamb Detail 1:2.5

Tony Fretton Architects
The Courtyard House
[13]

1 Line of skirting
2 Wall finishes (varies according to particular door)
3 Wall finishes (varies according to particular door)
4 One part of hardwood timber door frame
5 Rebated intumescent seals to back of frame
6 Lever door furniture
7 Variable length hardwood timber stop
8 Connecting tongue to align both parts of two-part timber

frame
9 One part of hardwood timber door frame
10 Rebated intumescent seals to door lipping (for fire doors only)
11 Typical door leaf with plywood facing and hardwood lippings
12 Wall (construction and thickness varies according to particular detail)

4.044
Sliding Door Detail 1:5

Tony Fretton Architects
The Courtyard House
[13]

1 Plaster skim coat finish
2 Two layers of 12.5 mm (1/2 inch) plasterboard
3 100 mm (4 inch) Rockwool insulation fitted between studs
4 150 x 50 mm (6 x 2 inch) softwood framing
5 100 x 50 mm (4 x 2 inch) softwood stud frame
6 Softwood blocking
7 25 x 25 mm (1 x 1 inch) plasterboard edge trim
8 Sliding door track recessed into

bulkhead and fixed to softwood framing
9 Solid core door blank
10 Dotted line denotes line of wall beyond
11 Floor guide for sliding door track fixed to timber floor
12 30 mm (1 1/4 inch) timber floor continued under door to meet stainless steel plate at edge of glass floor
13 10 mm (3/8 inch) shadow gap around base of wall and pier
14 Fire-rated walk-on double glazed floor unit with screen printed carborundum anti-slip finish
15 Frame to fire-rated walk-on double glazed floor unit
16 Gap between double

glazed unit and edge frame
17 Stainless steel plate at edge of glass floor
18 Mild steel edge frame to double glazed units
19 Fire-rated walk-on double glazed floor unit with screen printed carborundum anti-slip finish
20 Mild steel edge frame to double glazed units
21 22 mm (4/5 inch) plywood floating floor deck laid on resilient acoustic flooring system
22 Universal steel beam
23 Steel angle
24 200 x 50 mm (8 x 2 inch) softwood floor joists
25 Steel connecting plate welded

between flanges of steel beam

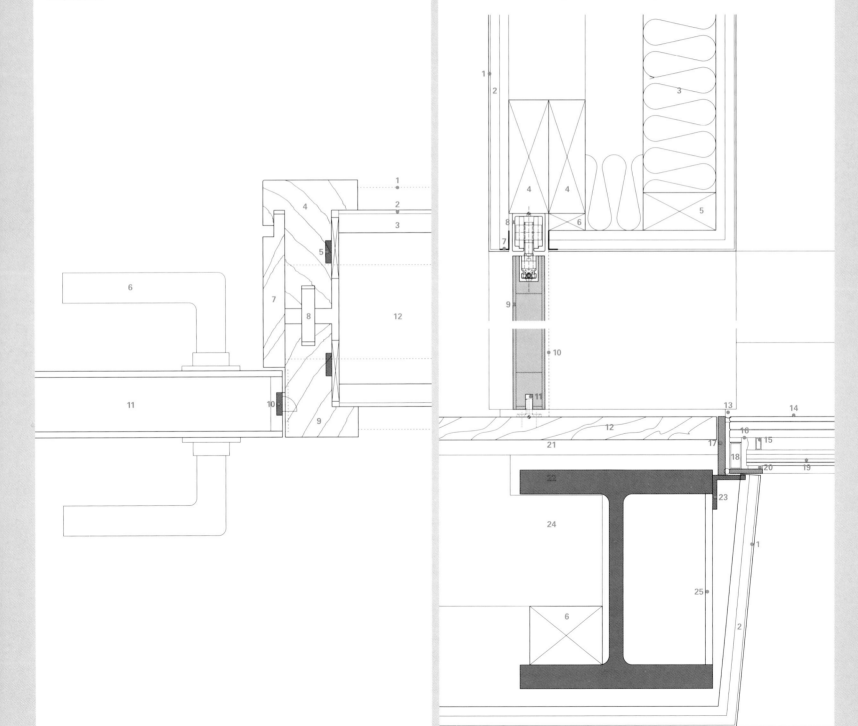

4.045
Exterior Glass Door
Detail 1:5

BmasC Arquitectos
Mayo House [20]

1 Fibre cement sheet
 exterior cladding
2 60 x 20 mm (2³/₈ x ³/₄
 inch) timber batten
3 Building paper
4 15 mm (⁵/₈ inch)
 exterior plywood
 sheathing
5 140 x 40 mm (5¹/₂ x
 1⁵/₈ inch) timber stud
6 Batt insulation on all
 exterior walls
7 130 x 130 mm (5¹/₈ x
 5¹/₈ inch) square
 hollow section steel
 column
8 Timber blocking as
 required
9 Waterproof
 membrane

10 12 mm (¹/₂ inch)
 gypsum board
11 Timber reveal lining
12 Aluminium door
 frame
13 Line of skirting
14 Double glazed
 exterior sliding glass
 door
15 130 x 50 mm (5¹/₈ x 2
 inch) rectangular
 hollow section steel
 column
16 12 mm (¹/₂ inch)
 plywood sheathing
 to rectangular hollow
 section

4.046
Sliding Door and
Window Detail 1:10

TNA Architects
Stage House [28]

1 Galvanized coloured
 steel-sheet roofing
2 Sealant
3 12 mm (¹/₂ inch) steel
 tension rod
4 Vapour permeable
 waterproof
 membrane
5 Urethane foam spray
 insulation
6 330 x 120 mm (13 x
 4³/₄ inch) timber
 header beam
7 Support for roller
 blind
8 Roller blind
9 12.5 mm (¹/₂ inch)
 insulating fibreboard
 with emulsion paint
 finish

10 Bent steel plate to
 window head
11 Double glazing
 comprised of 8 mm
 (¹/₃ inch) glass, 12
 mm (¹/₂ inch) air gap
 and 8 mm (¹/₃ inch)
 glass
12 6 mm (¹/₄ inch)
 Japanese linden
 plywood
13 120 x 135 mm (4³/₄ x
 5¹/₃ inch) timber
 beam
14 6 mm (¹/₄ inch)
 Japanese linden
 plywood ceiling
15 150 x 90 mm (6 x 3¹/₂
 inch) steel L-angle
16 Bent steel plate sill
17 Sealant
18 Flashing
19 Wire insect screen
20 Double glazing
 comprised of 8 mm
 (¹/₃ inch) glass, 12
 mm (¹/₂ inch) air gap

and 8 mm (¹/₃ inch)
 glass
21 Double glazing
 comprised of 8 mm
 (¹/₃ inch) glass, 12
 mm (¹/₂ inch) air gap
 and 8 mm (¹/₃ inch)
 glass

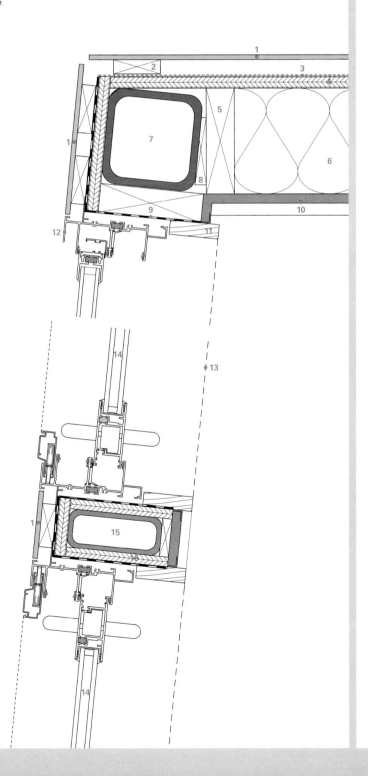

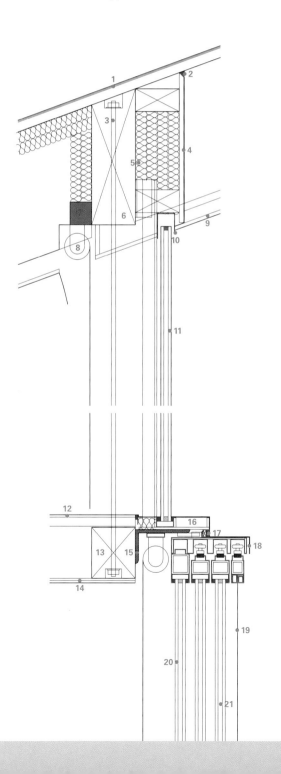

4.047
Sliding Door Head Detail
1:5

Barton Myers Associates
Bekins Residence [25]

1 Glazing
2 Aluminium mullion
3 Steel angle
4 Galvanized steel
  flashing
5 Steel beam
6 Glazing
7 Sliding glass door
8 Insect screen
9 Exterior

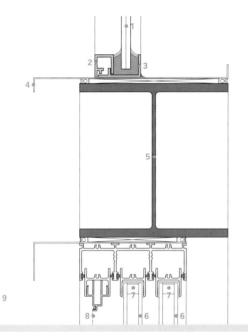

4.048
Pocket Door Head Detail
1:5

Bates Masi + Architects
Noyack Creek Residence
[37]

1 Rough sawn 25 x 200
  mm (1 x 8 inch)
  tongue and groove
  centre-matched flush
  jointed western red
  cedar siding
2 Batt insulation
3 12 mm (1/2 inch)
  painted gypsum
  board ceiling
4 Angle bead as plaster
  stop
5 140 x 40 mm (51/2 x
  15/8 inch) timber stud
6 Sliding door track
7 Timber blocking as
  required to form
  recess
8 Space for shims
9 70 x 20 mm (23/4 x 3/4
  inch) door head
  lining to match
  skirting
10 45 mm (13/4 inch)
  solid core door
11 Line of door jamb
12 Line of skirting
13 Sliding door guide
14 Flooring over 20 mm
  (3/4 inch) plywood
  substrate
15 Building felt
16 20 mm (3/4 inch)
  plywood subfloor,
  glued and nailed

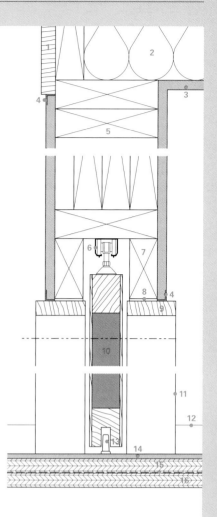

4.049
Marble Sliding Door
Detail 1:20 and
Cruciform Column Detail
1:5

Powerhouse Company
Villa 1 [15]

1 Aluminium structure
  to connect the two
  parts of the door
2 Wheels for sliding
  door
3 Sliding door
  structure from 50
  mm (2 inch)
  sandwich panel
  either side of steel
  I-section with
  aluminium frame
  and styrofoam filling,
  boarded with 2mm
  (1/16 inch) aluminium
4 20 mm (3/4 inch) thick
  Ultralite marble
  veneer panels glued
  to exterior face of
  door
5 16 mm (5/8 inch)
  green marble
  cladding panels on 4
  mm (1/6 inch)
  honeycomb panels
6 50 mm (2 inch) door
  sandwich panel with
  aluminium finish
7 Timber door frame
8 Rubber strip
9 Draught brush
  mounted on steel
  profile
10 Glazing of 10 mm (3/8
  inch), 15 mm (5/8
  inch) and 8 mm (3/8
  inch) glass panels
11 320 x 320 mm (123/4
  x 123/4 inch) steel
  column
12 Rubber cladding

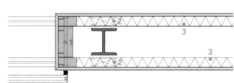

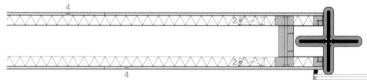

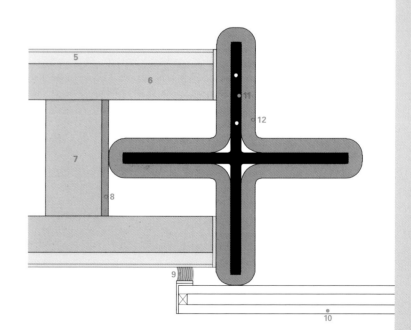

4.050
Door Section Detail 1:20

de Blacam and Meagher
Architects
Morna Valley Residence
[20]

1 12.5 mm (1/2 inch)
  plasterboard
  skimmed and painted
2 Timber framing
3 Painted hardwood
  door frame
4 Painted hardwood
  door leaf
5 600 x 400 x 20 mm
  (24 x 16 x 3/4 inch)
  white Ibiza marble
  tile
6 20 mm (3/4 inch) sand
  and cement bedding
  mortar
7 80 mm (31/8 inch)
  screed with
  underfloor heating
  system
8 Extruded polystyrene
  insulation
9 Structural screed
10 Reinforced concrete
11 Terracotta arch panel

4.051
**Entrance Door Detail
1:10**

Peter Stutchbury
Architecture
Avalon House [29]

1 0.48 mm (1/36 inch)
  Colorbond roof
  sheeting
2 Sarking under roof
  sheeting
3 200 x 75 mm (8 x 3
  inch) galvanized steel
  channel
4 200 mm (8 inch)
  galvanized universal
  beam
5 10 mm (2/5 inch)
  galvanized steel cleat
6 10 mm (2/5 inch)
  galvanized steel cleat
7 Polyester/wool
  insulation
8 40 x 5 mm (15/8 x 1/5
  inch) galvanized steel
  glazing bar welded to
  underside of channel
9 9 mm (3/8 inch)
  plywood ceiling
  panels fixed to firring
  channels at spacing
  to suit panel size
10 Saw-cut plywood for
  3 mm (1/8 inch)
  aluminium flat bar
  set flush with
  plywood at junction
  with panels
11 6 mm (1/4 inch) clear
  glazing
12 Galvanized steel
  flat-sheet cladding
13 100 x 45 mm (4 x 13/4
  inch) hardwood
  decking boards
14 200 mm (8 inch)
  galvanized universal
  steel beam with
  connection cleats
15 200 mm (8 inch)
  galvanized universal
  steel bearer with
  connection cleats
16 25 mm (1 inch)
  hardwood tongue
  and groove
  floorboards
17 18 mm (7/10 inch)
  structural plywood
  fixed to floor purlins
18 200 mm (8 inch)
  galvanized steel floor
  purlins
19 Firring channels
  spaced to suit
  plywood ceiling
  panels
20 90 x 45 mm (31/2 x
  13/4 inch) timber
  studs
21 Painted plasterboard
  wall lining
22 Polyester and wool
  insulation

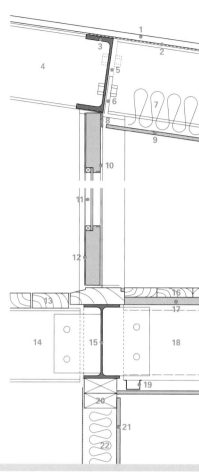

4.052
**Sliding Doors to Terrace
Detail 1:20**

Saunders Architecture
Villa Storingavika [40]

1 Fixed window
2 9 mm (1/3 inch)
  gyprock boarding
3 50 x 150 mm (2 x 6
  inch) timber posts
4 Spruce overlap
  cladding, stained
  black
5 13 mm (1/2 inch)
  waterproof gyprock
  boarding
6 13 mm (1/2 inch)
  waterproof gyprock
  boarding
7 Spruce overlap
  cladding, stained
  black
8 13 mm (1/2 inch)
  waterproof gyprock
  boarding
9 Spruce overlap
  cladding, stained
  black
10 Laminated timber
  post
11 9 mm (1/3 inch)
  gyprock boarding
12 Glass sliding door
13 Timber door jamb
14 Terrace boards,
  stained black
15 50 x 50 mm (2 x 2
  inch) timber battens
16 50 x 150 mm (2 x 6
  inch) timber posts

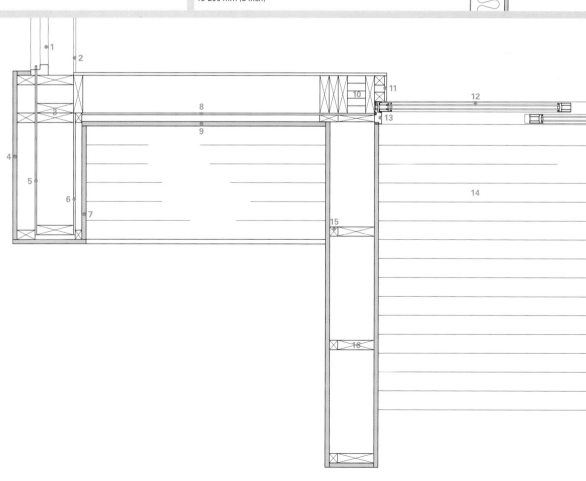

4.053
Door Plan Detail 1:10

Haddow Partnership
Higher Farm [17]

1 102mm (4 inch)
  facing brickwork
2 50mm (2 inch) cavity
  insulation
3 125mm (5 inch)
  blockwork wall
4 12.5 mm (1/2 inch)
  internal plaster
5 10 mm (3/8 inch)
  shadow gap
6 125 x 125 mm (5 x 5
  inch) square hollow

section steel column
7 44 mm (13/4 inch)
  door frame
8 Door lining
9 210 mm (81/4 inch)
  blockwork wall

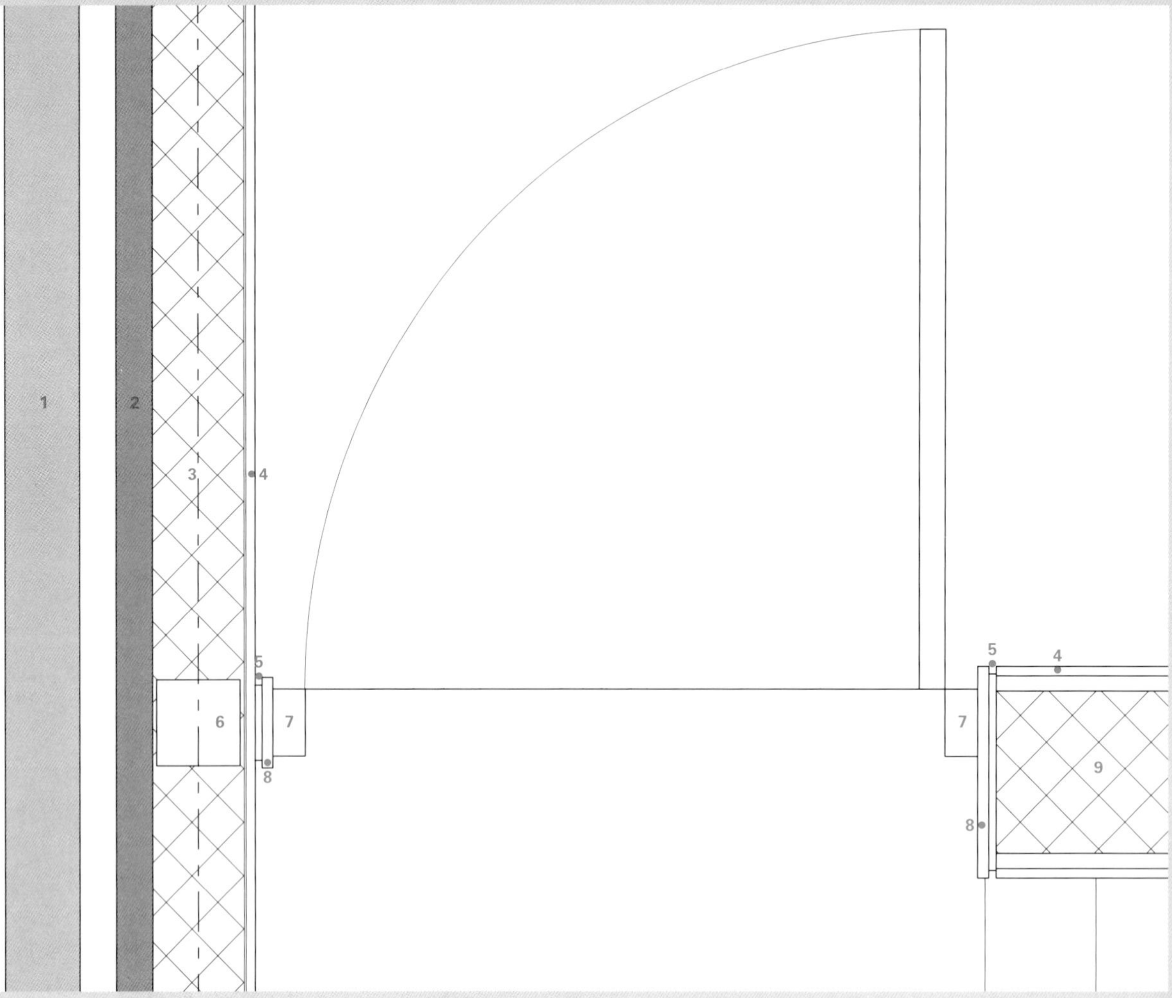

4.054
Entrance Door Plan
Detail 1:5

Barclay & Crousse
Architecture
Casa O [08]

1 Stucco and paint
  finish to external
  concrete wall
2 Stainless steel frame
  to fixed glazed
  window
3 10 mm (2/5 inch) thick
  tempered glass
4 Stainless steel door
  frame

5 Painted medium
  density fibreboard
  door panel
6 Stainless steel door
  frame
7 Stainless steel door
  handle
8 Stainless steel door
  pull
9 Medium density
  fibreboard panel with
  dovetail joint,
  finished with blue
  paint
10 Stainless steel door
  frame

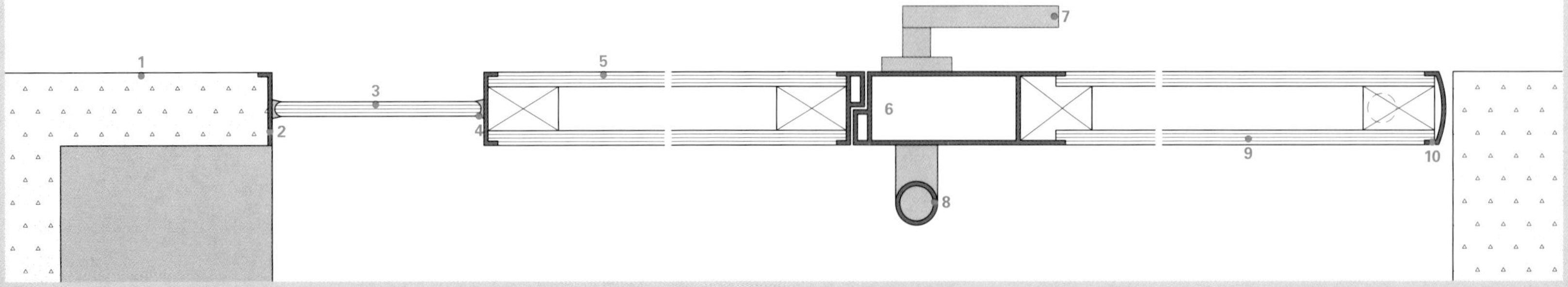

4.055
**Entry Hall Glass Door
Section Detail 1:5**

Javier Artadi Arquitecto
Las Arenas Beach House
[19]

1 Stainless steel
self-tapping screws
with plastic
blockhead
2 Aluminium top rail
for sliding door
3 10 mm (3/8 inch)
tempered clear glass
4 Circular aluminium
door handle

5 Brush seal
6 Aluminium coloured
silicone
7 Aluminium locking
mechanism
8 Aluminium lower rail
for sliding door
9 Stainless steel
self-tapping screws
with plastic
blockhead

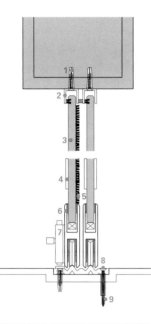

4.056
**Living Room Glass Door
Plan Detail 1:5**

Javier Artadi Arquitectos
Las Arenas Beach House
[19]

1 Silicone seal
2 Aluminium lower rail
for sliding door
3 10 mm (3/8 inch)
tempered clear glass
4 Aluminium socle for
fixed glass
5 Aluminium profile
door frame
6 Aluminium coloured

silicone
7 Aluminium profile
door frame
8 Brush seal

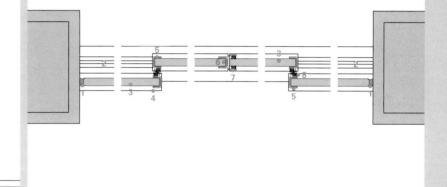

4.057
**Living Room Glass Door
Section Detail 1:5**

Javier Artadi Arquitectos
Las Arenas Beach House
[19]

1 Stainless steel
self-tapping screws
with plastic
blockhead
2 Aluminium frame for
fixed glass
3 Aluminium top rail
for sliding door
4 Aluminium coloured
silicone

5 10 mm (3/8 inch)
tempered clear glass
6 Circular aluminium
door handle
7 Socle for sliding door
with pulley and latch
8 Brush seal
9 Aluminium socle for
fixed glass
10 Aluminium lower rail
for sliding door

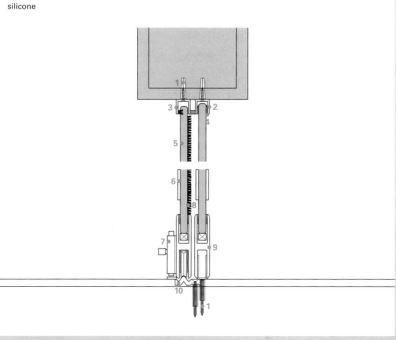

4.058
Timber Gate Detail 1:5

Designworkshop: SA
Igoda View House [24]

1 50 x 75 mm (2 x 3
inch) galvanized mild
steel unequal leg
angle
2 Roller guide fixing
bolt
3 Roller guides
4 75 mm (3 inch)
galvanized mild steel
bar
5 Roller guide fixing
bolt

6 Hardwood timber
slats equally spaced
along height of door
7 Bottom rollers
8 Timber wedge the
length of the sliding
screen to be added
onto the door
9 5 mm (1/5 inch)
stainless steel plate
10 Electro-galvanized
recessed brass track
for sliding screen
11 50 x 50 (2 x 2 inch)
galvanized mild steel
equal leg angle
12 50 mm (2 inch)
screed flooring

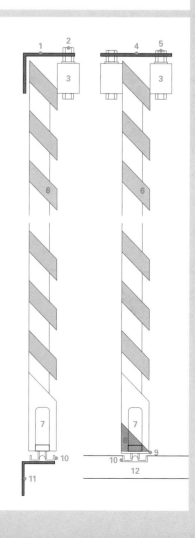

4.059
Sliding Door Detail 1:5

Kallos Turin
Casa Zorzal [10]

1 Schuco aluminium framed lift and slide door
2 15 mm (5/8 inch) laminated glass
3 Schuco aluminium framed pocketing insect screen
4 Aluminium glazing frame
5 5 mm (1/5 inch) stainless steel corner bead
6 Pebble layer
7 100 x 100 mm (4 x 4 inch) grille
8 40 mm (15/8 inch) diameter PVC pipe
9 Cement screed
10 Reinforced concrete foundation beam
11 45 mm (13/4 inch) pigmented cement screed
12 Underfloor heating
13 25 mm (1 inch) polystyrene insulation
14 Waterproof mortar
15 Reinforced concrete slab
16 Ballast layer of gravel
17 Subsoil

4.060
Sliding Glazed Door Detail 1:10

Alphaville
Hall House 1 [07]

1 Fair-faced concrete roof with osmosis liquid waterproofing paint finish and fair-faced concrete ceiling
2 25 x 25 x 2 mm (1 x 1 x 1/12 inch) aluminium C-channel sash
3 80 x 50mm (31/8 x 2 inch) timber frame with emulsion paint finish
4 50 mm (2 inch) urethane foam insulation
5 Emulsion paint finish on 9.5 mm (3/8 inch) plasterboard fixed to
70 x 30 mm (23/4 x 11/5 inch) timber substrate framing with 50 mm (2 inch) urethane foam
6 Double glazing comprised of two layers of 3 mm (1/8 inch) float glass separated by 6 mm (1/4 inch) air space
7 100 x 30 mm (4 x 11/5 inch) timber facade rail
8 Folding screen door
9 Japanese hemlock frame with urethane paint finish to interior and 1 mm (1/24 inch) aluminium plate to exterior
10 Double glazing unit comprised of 5 mm (1/5 inch) tempered laminated glass, 6 mm (1/4 inch) air space and 5 mm (1/5
inch) frosted glass
11 Terrace
12 Bedroom
13 600 x 600 x 10 mm (24 x 24 x 3/8 inch) floor tiles on 20mm (3/4 inch) mortar underbed
14 Fair-faced concrete floor with water repellent paint finish

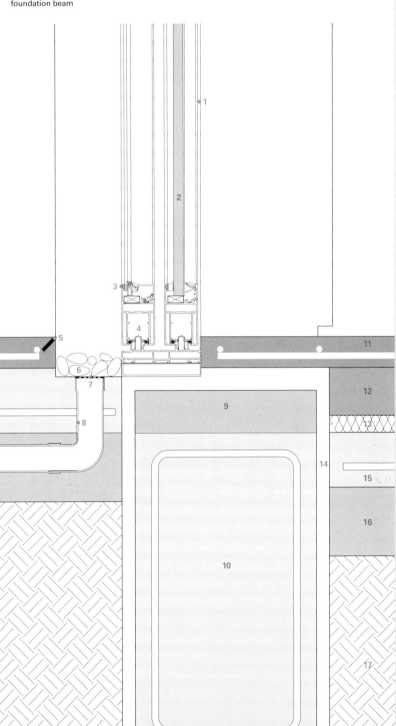

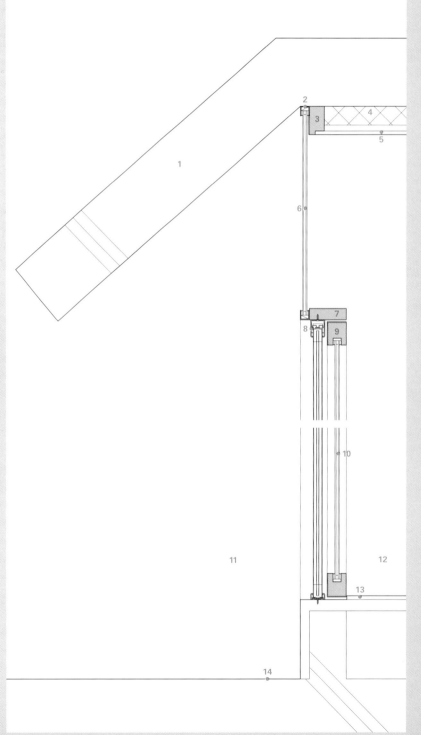

4.061
**Lift-and-Slide Head and
Sill Detail at Pocket
Door 1:7.5**

The Miller Hull
Partnership
Chuckanut Drive
Residence [31]

1 Plywood roof
  sheathing
2 25 x 100 mm (1 x 4
  inch) skip sheathing
  with clear sealer
3 200 x 75 mm (8 x 3
  inch) exposed roof
  joist
4 30 mm (1¼ inch)
  timber trim
5 Sealant with backer
  rod
6 Flashing
7 12 mm (½ inch) trim
8 Timber window jamb
9 Aluminium-clad
  timber window
  frame
10 Aluminium window
   jamb
11 Timber window sill
12 Metal cover, colour
   to match window
13 Four 200 x 50 mm (8
   x 2 inch) timber
   bearers to form
   beam
14 Douglas fir trim
15 Sealant with backer
   rod
16 Header track
17 Double glazed
   lift-and-slide door
18 Rolling hardware
19 Recessed track
20 Porcelain floor tiles
21 Thin-set mortar bed
   for floor tiles

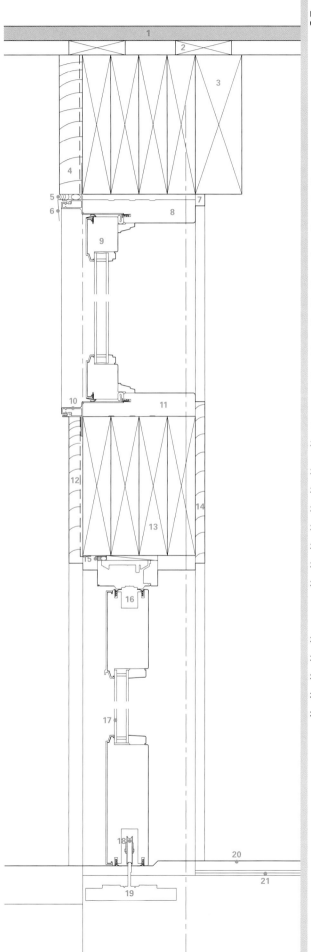

4.062
**Inward Opening Glass
Door Detail 1:10**

Hawkes Architecture
Crossway [16]

1 Unweathered zinc
2 Waterproof plywood
3 Chamfered treated
  timber fillet
4 Unweathered zinc
5 Waterproof plywood
6 Black rubber EPDM
  (ethylene propylene
  dieme monomer)
  waterproofing
7 Waterproof plywood
8 Joist
9 Panelvent
  vapour-permeable
  sheathing board
10 Wood fibre web infill
   insulation
11 Internorm Edition
   Passiv timber framed
   window
12 Plasterboard fixed on
   Dupont Energain
   thermal mass board
13 Toughened glass
   argon-filled triple
   glazing
14 Aluminium capping
   to all windows
15 Insulated aluminium
   spandrel panel
16 Isonat flax and
   lambswool acoustic
   insulation
17 Isonat flax and
   lambswool acoustic
   insulation
18 Aluminium and
   polyurethane
   insulation capping to
   all timber framed
   windows
19 Painted timber
   skirting board
20 Crushed glass bottle
   and resin polished
   flooring
21 Internorm door
   threshold
22 External stone
   paving
23 Crushed bottle Eco
   sand
24 Kaycel Super-plus
   Graphite insulation
25 Kaycel Super-plus
   Graphite insulation
26 Reinforced concrete
   slab
27 Visqueen
   Ecomembrane damp
   proof membrane
   bonded to bituthene
   self-adhesive damp
   proof membrane
28 Kaycel Super-plus
   Graphite insulation
29 Kaycel Super-plus
   Graphite insulation
30 Warmcell recycled
   newspaper insulation
31 Tyvek Enercor wall
   membrane
32 Ventilation zone

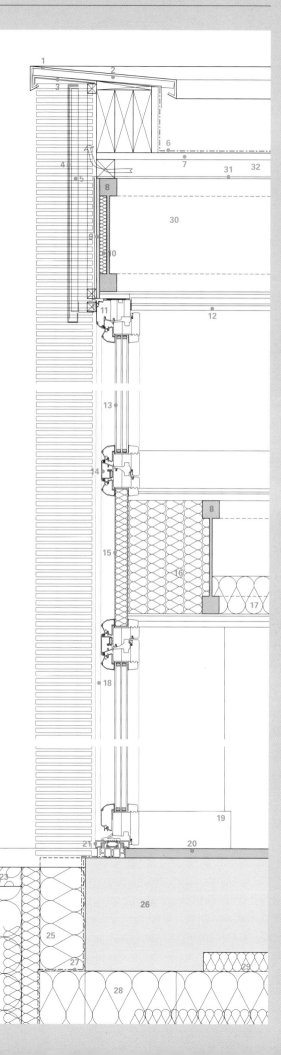

4.063
Sliding Doors to Deck
Head and Sill Detail 1:5

Marsh Cashman
Koolloos Architects
Maroubra House [36]

1 Recess to take retractable fabric blinds – recess lined with paint finished plasterboard
2 Steel beam
3 Damp proof membrane
4 Anodized aluminium angle
5 Timber packing as required
6 Flashing, neatly trimmed around ceiling edge
7 Insulation
8 Waterproof sarking lining
9 Carbon fibre

composite ceiling lining with paint finish
10 Anodized aluminium framed bi-fold doors
11 Hardwood timber floorboards
12 Hardwood timber boards on timber battens
13 Anodized aluminium sill
14 Packing as required
15 Anodized aluminium sub-sill
16 75 x 75 x 10 mm (3 x 3 x 3/8 inch) neoprene pads
17 High performance waterproof membrane
18 Carbon fibre composite sheet roofing
19 Timber battens
20 190 x 120 mm (7 1/2 x 4 3/4 inch) steel beam

21 220 x 40 mm (8 2/3 x 1 5/8 inch) timber joist

4.064
Sliding Door Detail 1:10

Architectus
North Shore House [36]

1 90 mm (3 1/2 inch) wide timber to form upstand
2 40 mm (1 3/5 inch) timber fillet
3 20 mm minimum to 30 mm maximum (3/4 to 1 1/5 inch) pebbled roof laid level over filter textile
4 15 mm (5/8 inch) drainage cell over waterproof membrane
5 18 mm (7/10 inch) construction ply screw fixed on 50 mm (2 inch) timber firrings, over 200 mm (8 inch) purlins at 600 mm (24 inch) centres

6 40 x 3 mm (1 3/5 x 1/8 inch) aluminium to terminate membrane
7 240 x 45 mm (9 1/2 x 1 3/4 inch) laminated timber fascia board, bottom edge chamfered to form drip
8 100 x 50 mm (4 x 2 inch) timber structure
9 100 x 20 mm (4 x 3/4 inch) dressed timber
10 Greenstuf insulation
11 Hoop pine plywood veneer over 50 x 50 mm (2 x 2 inch) battens at 400 mm (16 inch) centres
12 43 x 45 mm (1 5/8 x 1 3/4 inch) dressed timber
13 75 x 20 mm (3 x 3/4 inch) dressed jamb liner
14 Safety glazing in anodized aluminium section

15 Stainless steel capping to glulam timber beam
16 Painted parallel flange channel frame bolt fixed to glulam timber beam
17 Waterproof membrane over 12 mm (1/2 inch) construction ply
18 50 x 75 x 65 mm thick (2 x 3 x 2 1/2 inch) anodized aluminium gutter to fall 15 mm (5/8 inch) to outlet
19 450 x 90 mm (18 x 3 1/2 inch) glulam beam
20 Safety glazing in anodized aluminium section with bottom track set flush with decking
21 Roller blind
22 76 mm (3 inch) diameter circular

hollow section column
23 100 x 25 mm (4 x 1 inch) Lawson cypress duckboards on timber firrings packed off membrane with 10 x 50 x 50 mm (3/8 x 2 x 2 inch) long packers
24 Membrane on construction plywood, screw fixed at 600mm (24 inch) centres
25 5 mm (1/5 inch) steel angle fixed with M10 coachscrews at 400 mm (16 inch) centres
26 Joists at 400 mm (16 inch) maximum centres
27 Tylok nail plate top and bottom to each nogging
28 Noggings at 1200 mm (48 inch) centres

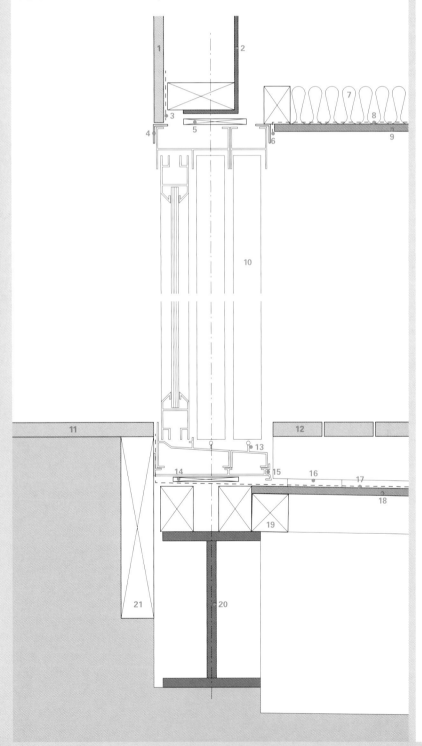

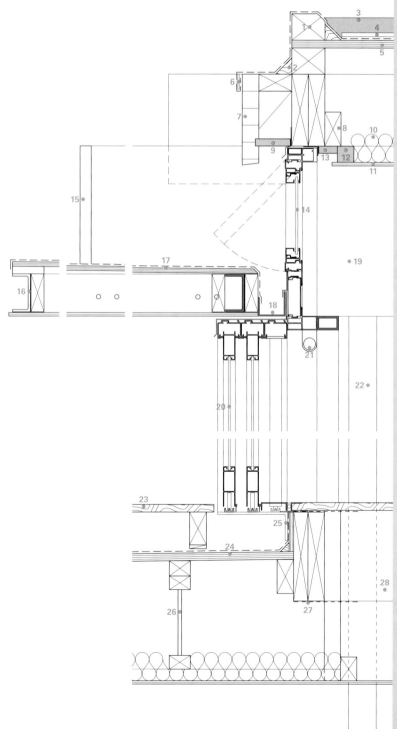

4.065
Door Head Detail 1:5

Morphogenesis
N85 Residence [08]

1 Interior wall panel with premium plastic emulsion
2 12 mm (1/2 inch) plasterboard
3 Reinforced concrete beam
4 Fastener
5 40 x 40 mm (1⅝ x 1⅝ inch) rough sawn timber
6 Mild steel frame

7 Teak beading
8 Teak frame with polyurethane varnish
9 6 x 6 mm (1/4 x 1/4 inch) shadow gap in false ceiling at wall junction
10 Exterior cladding with premium plastic emulsion paint finish
11 Teak frame with polyurethane varnish
12 Veneer with polyurethane varnish
13 12 mm (1/2 inch) waterproof base plywood
14 Hardwood internal

frame
15 4 mm (1/8 inch) groove with varnish on base plywood to match the veneer cladding

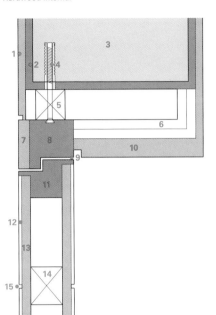

4.067
Sliding Door Detail 1:10

Room 11
Kingston House [34]

1 Hardwood blocking
2 Sliding door track
3 Plaster stopping angle
4 Hardwood timber nogging supports between rafters at 450 mm (18 inch) centres. Notch supports to allow track to sit flush with plasterboard

5 50 mm (2 inch) insulation
6 170 x 40 mm (6¾ x 1⅝ inch) timber rafters
7 Hollow core door
8 Line of skirting board beyond
9 Monoclad sheet metal roof sheeting laid to fall to two degree pitch
10 Reflective backed sarking and building paper
11 Timber batten
12 Timber counter batten

13 140 mm (5½ inch) reinforced concrete floor slab
14 Aluminium suspended ceiling system
15 Aluminium firring channel and 10 mm (2/5 inch) plasterboard ceiling

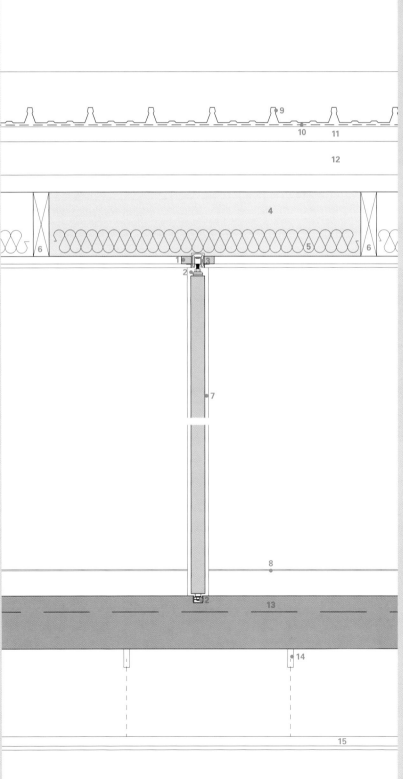

4.066
Door Jamb Detail 1:5

Peter L. Gluck and Partners, Architects
Inverted Guest House [26]

1 Corrugated copper cladding
2 Gypsum wall board
3 Batt insulation
4 Gypsum wall board
5 Timber blocking
6 Insulated glass unit
7 Silicone joint
8 38 x 38 x 4 mm (1½ x 1½ x 1/8 inch)

anodized aluminium angle
9 38 x 25 x 4 mm (1½ x 1 x 1/8 inch) anodized aluminium angle
10 Batt insulation
11 150 x 150 mm (6 x 6 inch) square hollow section steel posts
12 50 x 100 mm (2 x 4 inch) timber stud
13 Copper sub-flashing
14 Gasketed bronze screw
15 Corrugated copper cladding
16 Moisture barrier

17 Rubber bulb gasket
18 Copper lap flashing
19 Steel tube integral to insulated steel framed garage door
20 Insulated steel framed garage door

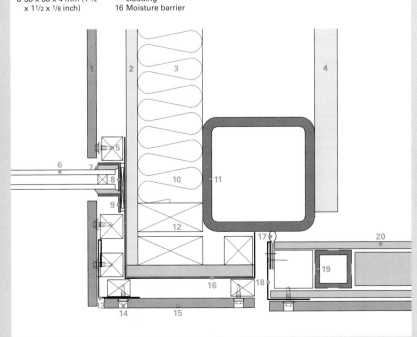

4.068
Front Door Elevation Detail 1:50

Keith Williams Architects
The Long House [23]

1 White laminated glazing
2 London stock brick
3 25 mm (1 inch) external-grade medium density fibreboard panel with edges sealed
4 Insulated render system
5 Structural opening shown dotted
6 Pre-formed zinc clad panel
7 54 mm (2¹/8 inch) solid core door, pivoted with rebated long edges and external-grade medium density fibreboard cladding
8 Entry system
9 50 x 250 mm (2 x 10 inch) letterbox opening in zinc panel with 75 x 300 mm (3 x 12 inch) opening in blockwork leaf behind

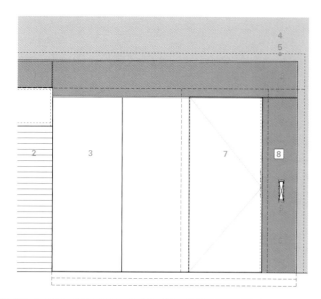

4.069
External Door Head and Base Detail 1:10

Keith Williams Architects
The Long House [23]

1 Insulated render system
2 Two coats of Toughseal painted on face of concrete
3 Zinc cladding panel
4 Two coats of Toughseal painted on face of concrete, battens and over edge of medium density fibreboard soffit
5 Hardwood door frame with paint finish
6 One layer of 12.5 mm (¹/2 inch) wall board with painted plaster skim finish
7 54 mm (2¹/8 inch) external door leaf with perimeter hardwood batten and external-grade medium density fibreboard cover panel
8 Brush type weather seal recessed into door edges
9 20 mm (³/4 inch) honed and sealed limestone on thin bed of adhesive
10 Waterproof plywood subfloor glued and screwed at 150 mm (6 inch) centres
11 Resin backfill to drainage unit
12 Brickslot drain with asymmetrical angle slot set flush with floor finishes
13 External stone setts and pavement finish, set to fall away from building

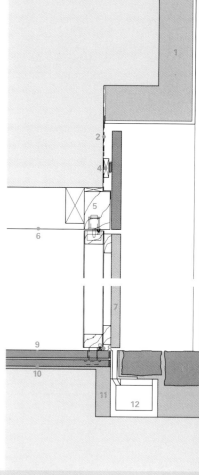

4.070
Door Jamb Detail 1:10

Keith Williams Architects
The Long House [23]

1 13 mm (¹/2 inch) white plaster finish
2 Expanded mesh to cover joint in blockwork
3 Ruberoid insulated cavity closer with damp proof course tucked behind door frame
4 Hardwood door frame with painted finish
5 Painted external-grade medium density fibreboard cladding panel
6 Pivot strap set into bottom of door
7 Standard 54 mm (2¹/10 inch) external door leaf with perimeter hardwood batten and external-grade medium density fibreboard cover panel
8 Medium density fibreboard door panel and carcass with spray paint finish
9 25 mm (1 inch) insulation
10 Vertical letterbox opening formed in zinc cassette panel with sprayed external grade medium density fibreboard lining through to joinery unit
11 Zinc cladding panel
12 Damp proof membrane
13 140 mm (5¹/2 inch) blockwork
14 Mastic bead
15 Insulated render system

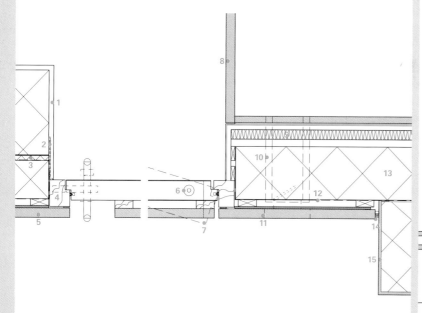

4.071
Sliding Door Detail 1:5

Western Design Architects
The Moat House [20]

1 Dense concrete blockwork
2 100 x 100 mm (4 x 4 inch) square hollow section column
3 12.5 mm (¹/2 inch) thick plaster
4 Aluminium angle cover strip with foam insulation behind
5 Double glazed sliding door
6 Powder-coated aluminium curtain walling
7 Powder-coated thermally broken aluminium window frame with 6 mm (¹/4 inch) thick self-cleaning high performance clear glass outer pane, 12 mm (¹/2 inch) argon-filled cavity, 6 mm (¹/4 inch) thick low-emissivity coated glass inner pane for thermal control

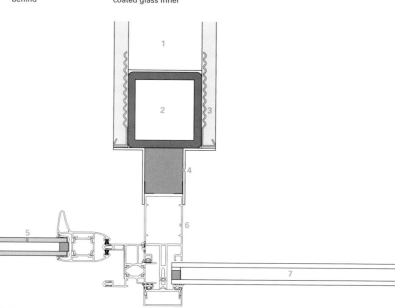

4.072
Entry Door Plan Detail
1:10

Bercy Chen Studio
Riverview Gardens [38]

1 6 mm (1/4 inch) steel
   plate
2 8 mm (1/3 inch)
   polygal on 50 x 100
   mm (2 x 4 inch)
   timber stud framing
3 25 mm (1 inch)
   insulated glass
4 10 mm (3/8 inch) steel
   work surface support
5 Butyl tape seals
   between polygal and
   steel end plate
6 50 x 50 mm (2 x 2
   inch) steel tube with
   6 mm (1/4 inch) steel
   plate end cap
7 8 mm (1/3 inch)
   polygal door panel
8 Heavy duty door
   hinge
9 8 mm (1/3 inch)
   polygal wall lining
10 Two layers bubble
   wrap

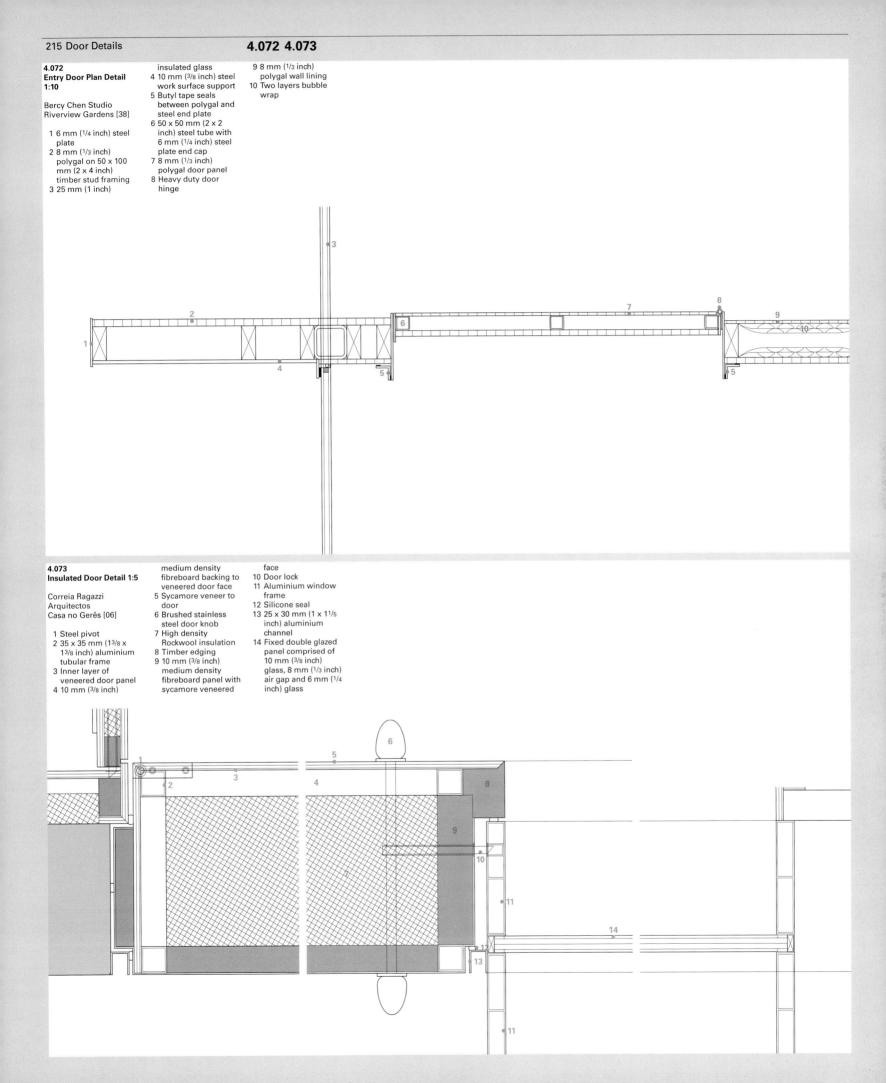

4.073
Insulated Door Detail 1:5

Correia Ragazzi
Arquitectos
Casa no Gerês [06]

1 Steel pivot
2 35 x 35 mm (1 3/8 x
   1 3/8 inch) aluminium
   tubular frame
3 Inner layer of
   veneered door panel
4 10 mm (3/8 inch)
   medium density
   fibreboard backing to
   veneered door face
5 Sycamore veneer to
   door
6 Brushed stainless
   steel door knob
7 High density
   Rockwool insulation
8 Timber edging
9 10 mm (3/8 inch)
   medium density
   fibreboard panel with
   sycamore veneered
   face
10 Door lock
11 Aluminium window
   frame
12 Silicone seal
13 25 x 30 mm (1 x 1 1/5
   inch) aluminium
   channel
14 Fixed double glazed
   panel comprised of
   10 mm (3/8 inch)
   glass, 8 mm (1/3 inch)
   air gap and 6 mm (1/4
   inch) glass

4.074
Door Plan Detail 1:10

diederendirrix
Villa PPML [21]

1 External layer of 6 mm (1/4 inch) boarding
2 Internal layer of 6 mm (1/4 inch) boarding
3 Timber wall framing
4 40 mm (1 3/5 inch) solid plywood door
5 Two layers of 6 mm (1/4 inch) boarding on solid door
6 Cast lime and sandstone block interior dividing wall
7 Stucco wall finish
8 Hinge for glass door
9 Door floor spring for glass door
10 Glass door
11 Fixed glass panel

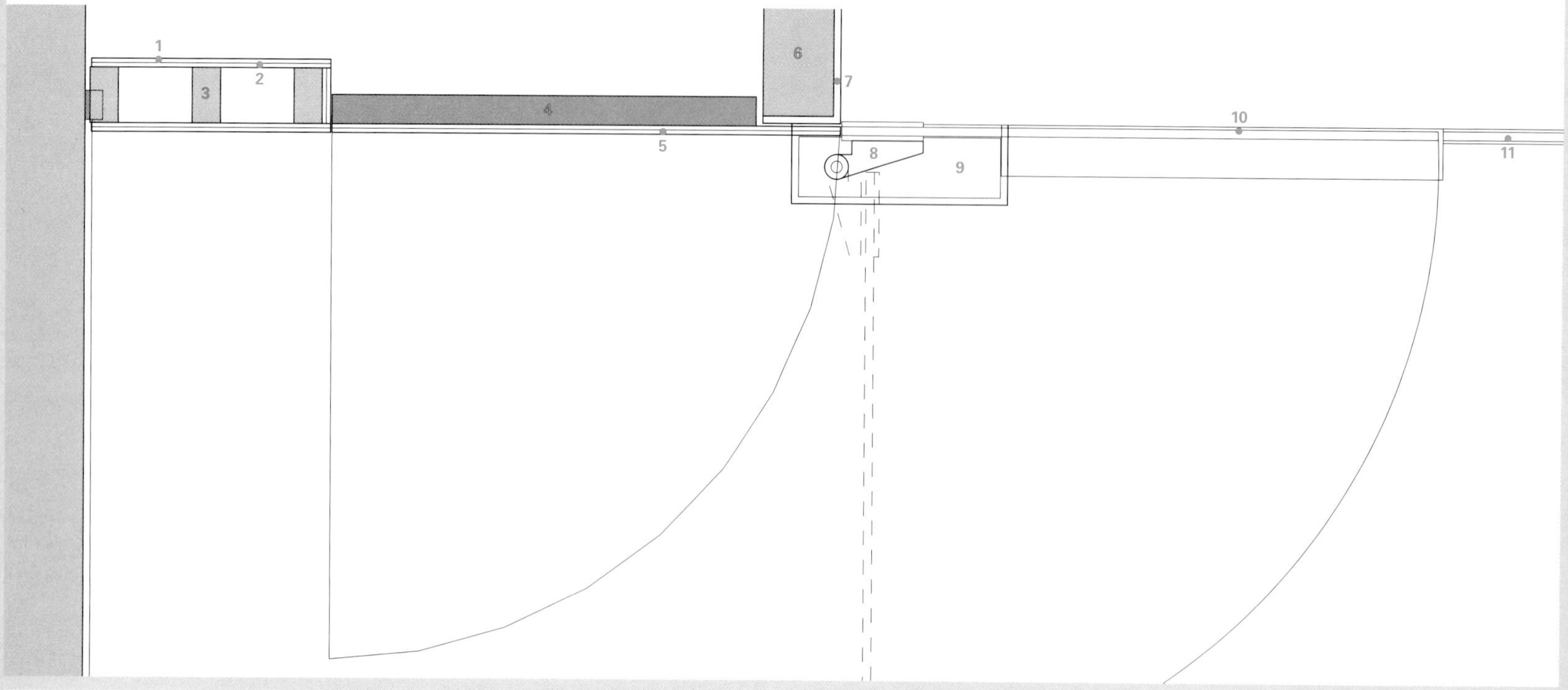

4.075
Four-Track Cavity Sliding Door Detail 1:10

Jackson Clements Burrows Architects
Edward River House [32]

1 180 mm (7 1/8 inch) pre-cast concrete panel to ground floor
2 180 mm (7 1/8 inch) pre-cast concrete panel
3 Recessed brass sliding door guide channels
4 70 x 20 mm (2 3/4 x 3/4 inch) spotted gum timber decking
5 100 x 40 mm (4 x 1 5/8 inch) cedar sliding door frame
6 13 mm (1/2 inch) internal plasterboard wall lining
7 100 x 40 mm (4 x 1 5/8 inch) cedar sliding door with 10 mm (3/8 inch) fixed float glass
8 100 x 40 mm (4 x 1 5/8 inch) cedar sliding door with fly-wire
9 90 x 40 mm (3 1/2 x 1 5/8 inch) pine stud frame
10 Insulation fill between studs
11 18 mm (3/4 inch) joinery carcass

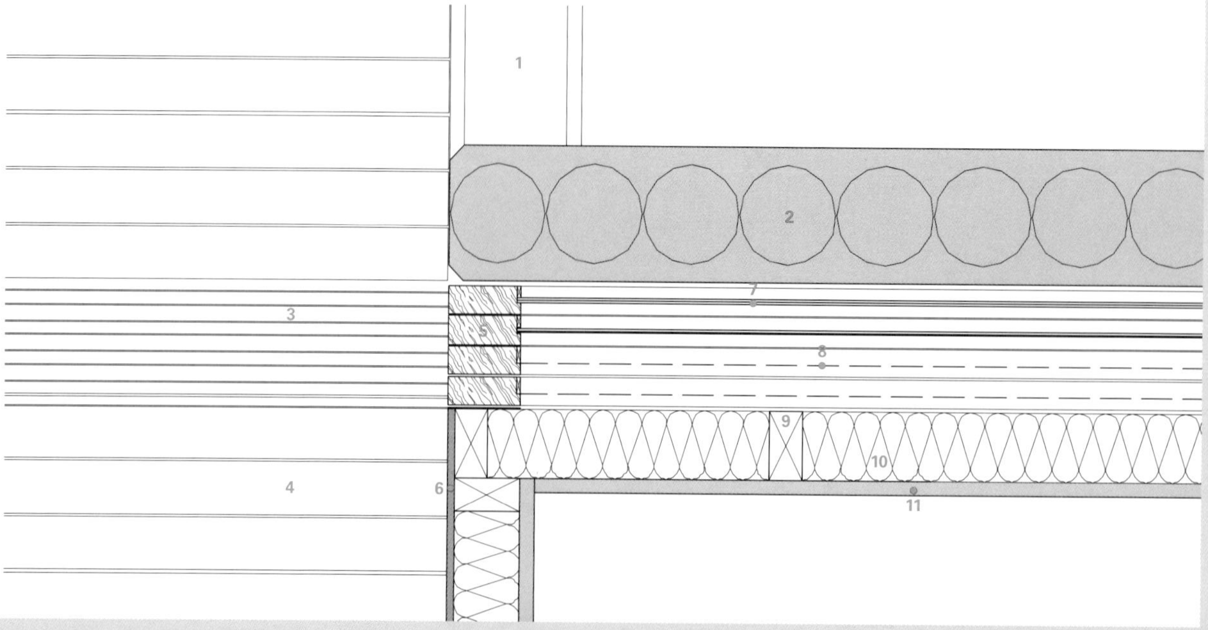

4.076
Porch Door Section
Detail 1:10

Jun Igarashi Architects
Rectangle of Light [37]

1 9.5 mm (3/8 inch)
solid conifer plywood
weatherboarding on
battens with
decay-resistant paint
finish
2 12.5 mm (1/2 inch)
plasterboard with
vinyl polyethylene
film
3 100 mm (4 inch)
glass wool insulation
4 Waterproof paper
5 12 mm (1/2 inch)
insulation board
6 Plaster edge bead
7 Dewatering drain
8 Galvanized and
aluminium coated
steel sheet turned-up

at edge under
cladding
9 Membrane
waterproofing on 24
mm (1 inch)
structural plywood
10 Steel sheet casting
surface
11 100 x 100 mm (4 x 4
inch) timber framing
12 Steel sheet casting
surface
13 Upper component of
door sash
14 Lower component of
door sash
15 Sealant
16 Timber door
17 12.5 mm (1/2 inch)
plasterboard with
vinyl cloth
18 9.5 mm (3/8 inch)
solid conifer plywood
weatherboarding on
battens with
decay-resistant paint
finish

19 Galvanized and
aluminium coated
steel sheet flashing
bent into shape
20 Concrete
21 Styrofoam insulation
22 Protective mortar
layer
23 Finished ground
level

4.077
Sliding Door Detail
at Living Room 1:10

Steven Holl Architects
Swiss Embassy
Residence [14]

1 Steel tube beyond
for channel glass
support
2 Motorized sunshade
3 Silicone seal and
backer rod
4 Fabric wrapped
hembar
5 Top-hinged in-swing
aluminium window
6 Stainless steel side
guide wire
7 Weatherboard
8 Curtain wall support,
welded and bolted to
substructure
9 Channel glass
perimeter frame
assembly

10 Line of steel strut
welded to vertical
substructure
11 Timber floor
12 Glazing bead
13 Waterproof
membrane
14 Two steel angles for
window support
15 50 mm (2 inch) rigid
insulation
16 Anchor bolts
17 Steel plate anchored
to concrete slab
18 Channel glass
19 Two layers 15 mm
(5/8 inch) gypsum
wall board
20 Corner bead
21 Fixed glazing
aluminium frame
22 Caulking on backer
rod
23 Perimeter radiator
24 Waterproof
membrane
25 Intermittent

steel tube
26 Insect screen
27 6 mm (1/4 inch) steel
plate
28 Concrete parapet
29 75 mm (3 inch)
pavers
30 Trench drain

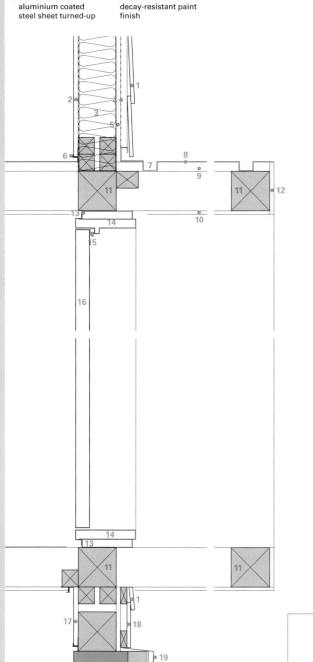

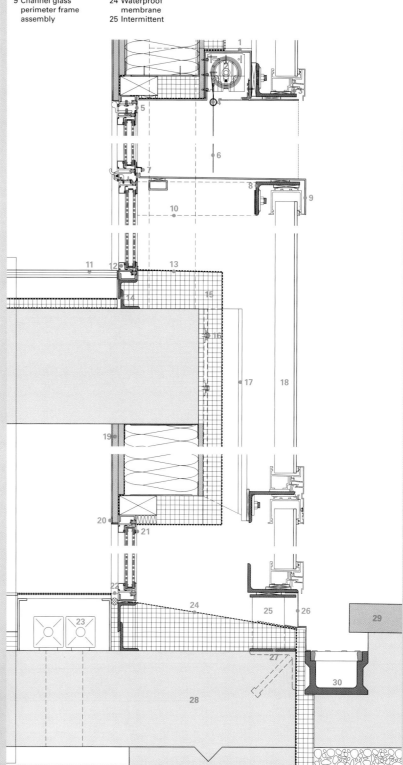

4.078
Sliding Door Threshold
Detail 1:5

Stephenson Bell
Architects
House 780 [18]

1 Double glazing unit
2 Powder–coated
aluminium glazing
system
3 Powder–coated
aluminium flashing
4 110 x 45 mm (4³/₈ x
1³/₄ inch)
preservative treated
softwood packer
5 Limestone sill on
galvanized mild steel
angle
6 Black granite bonded
to blockwork and
insulation
7 50 mm (2 inch)
external limestone
8 Insulation
9 Coursing block
cantilevered out to
support limestone sill
and close cavity
10 Liquid membrane
dressed over damp
proof course with
minimum lap of 75
mm (3 inch), up and
over packer and
down 150 mm (6
inch) face of

blockwork
11 Concrete screed
12 Underfloor heating
with insulation
13 Damp proof
membrane turned up
along face of
concrete
14 Perimeter insulation
to prevent cold
bridge
15 Damp proof
membrane
16 Insulation through
floor construction
17 Weak mix concrete
fill to terminate 225
mm (8⁴/₅ inch) below
damp proof course
level
18 100 mm (4 inch)
blockwork

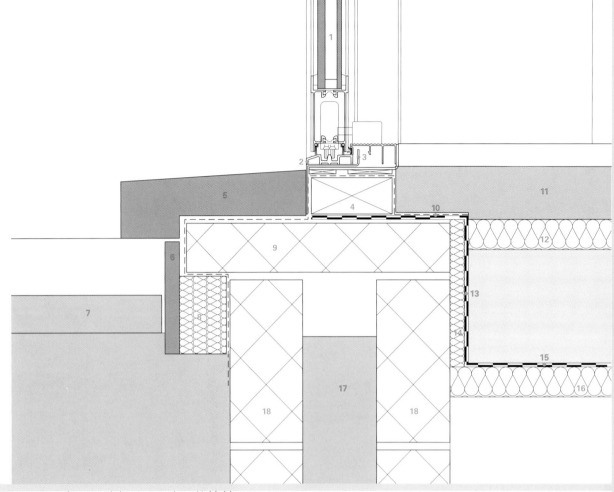

4.079
Sliding Door Detail 1:5

TNA Architects
Stage House [28]

1 Floor of 6 mm (¹/₄
inch) Japanese
linden plywood
2 12 mm (¹/₂ inch) steel
rod
3 Bent steel plate
4 Double glazing
comprised of 8 mm
(¹/₃ inch) glass, 12
mm (¹/₂ inch) air gap
and 8 mm (¹/₃ inch)
glass
5 Bent steel plate
6 Sealant
7 Flashing
8 150 x 90 mm (6 x 3¹/₂
inch) steel L-angle
9 120 x 135 mm (4³/₄ x
5³/₁₀ inch) timber
beam
10 Roller blind
11 Fixed steel frame to
full height double
glazed window
12 Steel frame to sliding
double glazed door
13 Steel frame to sliding
double glazed door
14 Double glazing
comprised of 8 mm
(¹/₃ inch) glass, 12
mm (¹/₂ inch) air
gap and 8 mm

(¹/₃ inch) glass
15 Ceiling of 6 mm (¹/₄
inch) Japanese
linden plywood
16 20 mm (³/₄ inch) ulin
timber board
17 20 mm (³/₄ inch) ulin
timber board to
terrace
18 45 x 60 mm (1³/₄ x
2³/₈ inch) timber floor
joists at 955 mm
(37³/₅ inch) centres
19 Concrete floor
structure
20 Fixed steel frame to
full height double
glazed window
21 Rail support for
sliding glass doors
22 Ground level sill

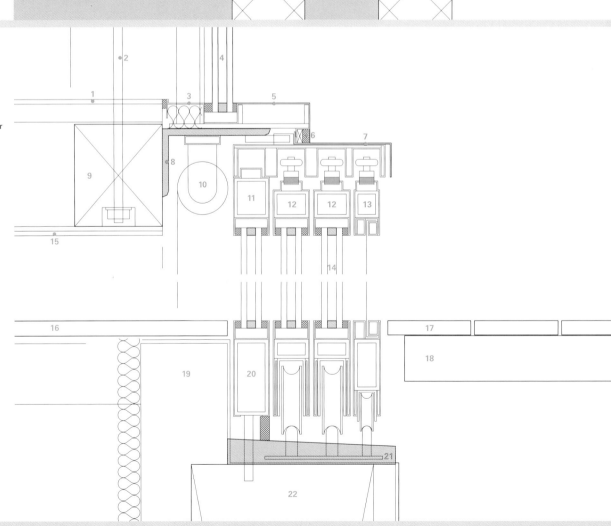

4.080
Security Door Plan
Detail 1:5

Koffi & Diabaté
Architectes
Villa Talon [28]

1 Cement render wall finish
2 Cement blockwork wall
3 Bolt connection between door frame
  and wall
4 Plywood door frame
5 Timber door frame
6 Screw fixing
7 Steel L-section
8 Timber door frame
9 Concealed sunken head screw fixing
10 50 x 30 mm (2 x 1 1/5 inch) steel rectangular hollow section
11 30 mm (1 1/5 inch) veneered plywood
12 5 mm (1/5 inch) steel sheet door reinforcement
13 Door hinge
14 Steel square section to hold door frame in place
15 Screw fixing

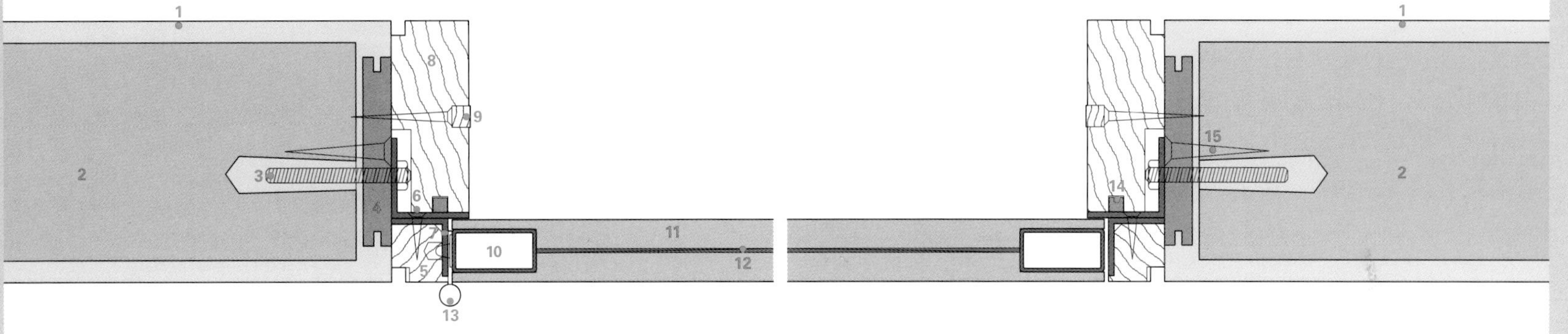

4.081
Sliding Door Head Detail
1:10

Safdie Rabines
Architects
Artist Bridge Studio [30]

1 350 x 150 mm (14 x 6 inch) glulam beam
2 Galvanized metal counter flashing with continuous sealant
3 Galvanized metal flashing
4 Formed metal drip
5 Sheet metal parapet capping sloped by firring to drain to roof side
6 Gasketed fasteners
7 Timber parapet framing
8 Built-up roof membrane
9 150 x 40 mm (6 x 1 5/8 inch) timber roof joist
10 Three 225 x 40 mm (9 x 1 5/8 inch) timber headers
11 Structural plywood roof sheathing
12 240 x 40 mm (9 1/2 x 1 5/8 inch) timber joist
13 Insulation
14 Roll-down shade screen
15 Recessed sliding door track
16 15 mm (5/8 inch) gypsum board ceiling
17 Double glazed aluminium framed sliding doors

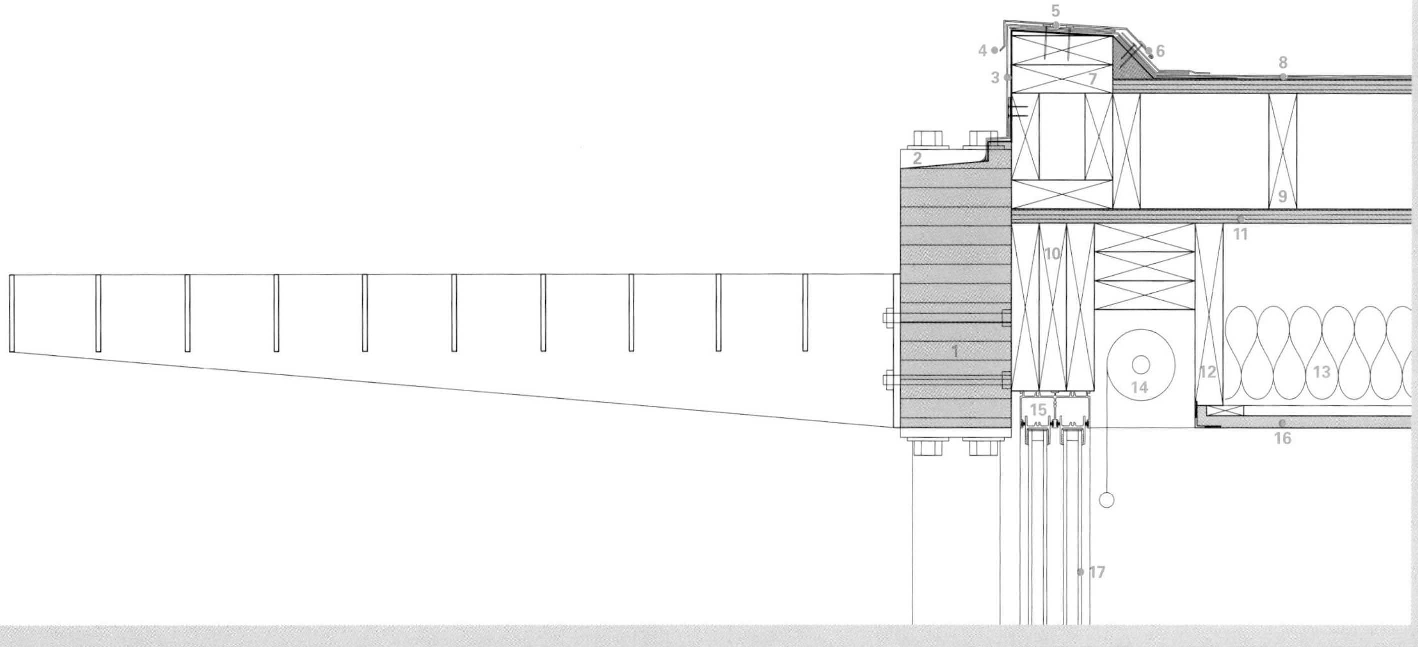

4.082
Sliding Glass Door
Detail 1:10

EZZO
Leça House [35]

1 40 x 40 mm (1⁵/8 x 1⁵/8 inch) stainless steel profile
2 Open timber frame painted with polyurethane paint
3 Open timber frame painted with polyurethane paint
4 40 x 50 mm (1⁵/8 x 2 inch) timber profile

on battens painted with polyurethane paint
5 Vertical timber fixing structure
6 Double glazing unit
7 Timber profile
8 Treated pine flooring
9 Open timber frame with paint finish
10 Open timber frame with paint finish
11 100 mm (4 inch) mineral wall insulation
12 40 mm (1⁵/8 inch) polystyrene thermal insulation

13 200 mm (8 inch) stainless steel structure
14 Drywall lining

4.083
Sliding Door Section
Detail 1:5

Mount Fuji Architects Studio
Rainy Sunny House [11]

1 5 mm (1/5 inch) float glass
2 25 x 16 mm (1x ⁵/8 inch) flat steel bar
3 190 x 19 mm (7¹/2 x ³/4 inch) flat steel bar
4 21 x 8 mm (⁷/8 x ³/8 inch) flat steel bar
5 2.3 mm (1/8 inch) steel plate
6 15 x 2 mm (⁵/8 x ¹/12 inch) flat steel bar
7 Window screen
8 15 x 4 mm (⁵/8 x 1/8 inch) stainless steel flat bar
9 Australian cypress herringbone flooring
10 24 x 2 mm (1 x ¹/12

inch) stainless steel flat bar
11 2 mm (¹/12 inch) stainless plate sill
12 Reinforced concrete floor slab
13 Hardwood herringbone parquet flooring

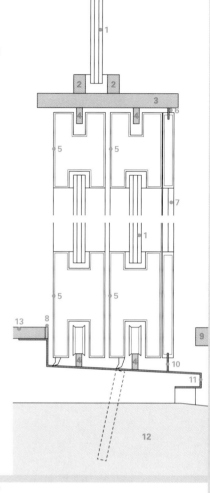

4.084
External Door Jamb
Detail 1:5

David Nossiter Architects
Kitsbury Road House [13]

1 12.5 mm (1/2 inch) plasterboard with vapour barrier
2 50 mm (2 inch) insulation
3 25 x 25 mm (1 x 1 inch) timber battens to hold insulation in place

4 100 x 50 mm (4 x 2 inch) timber studs
5 100 x 100 mm (4 x 4 inch) square hollow steel section
6 Silicone sealant
7 Vapour barrier
8 Insulation
9 18 mm (³/4 inch) weather bonded and proofed plywood with metal cover flashing
10 Thermally broken aluminium window
11 Double glazed openable window from 4 mm (1/8 inch)

low-E toughened glass with 20 mm (³/4 inch) argon-filled gas cavity

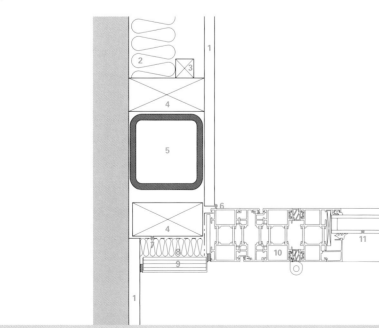

4.085
Sliding Door Sill Detail
1:10

Safdie Rabines Architects
Artist Bridge Studio [30]

1 Double glazed sliding doors
2 Sliding door track flush with hardwood floor
3 Prefinished metal door pan with continuous sealant
4 350 x 150 mm (14 x 6 inch) glulam beam

5 225 x 35 mm (9 x 1³/8 inch) timber joist
6 Hardwood floor
7 Plywood floor sheathing
8 Insulation
9 Two layers of gypsum board
10 22 mm (⁷/8 inch) plaster over metal lath
11 Glulam beam connection plate to concrete footing

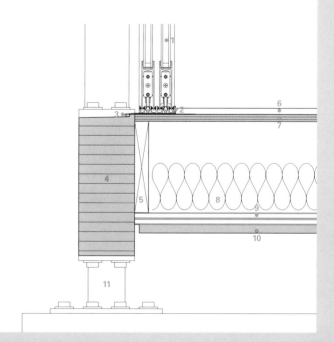

4.086
External Door Detail 1:10

ODOS Architects
House in Wicklow [18]

1 12.5 mm (1/2 inch) plasterboard internal partition skimmed and painted on 215 x 50 mm (81/2 x 2 inch) treated softwood studs at 400 mm (16 inch) with softwood noggings at 800 mm (32 inch) centres vertically
2 12.5 mm (1/2 inch) plasterboard internal partition skimmed and painted on 215 x 50 mm (81/2 x 2 inch) treated softwood studs at 400 mm (16 inch) with softwood noggings at 800 mm (32 inch) centres vertically
3 Rockwool acoustic insulation
4 Treated hardwood timber frames
5 Treated hardwood timber studs
6 Recessed treated hardwood timber frame
7 Full height, clear, double glazed fixed door unit comprised of 8 mm (1/3 inch) toughened glass outer pane, 12 mm (1/2 inch) air gap and 8 mm (1/3 inch) clear toughened inner pane in a recessed treated hardwood timber frame
8 Recessed brush seals
9 22 mm (9/10 inch) full height treated hardwood timber cladding panels secret fixed to structure behind
10 Full height insulated timber door with stainless steel drips top and bottom, made of secret-fixed, treated hardwood timber cladding with 13 mm (1/2 inch) marine grade plywood on treated softwood timber carcassing. Insulation in core with a vapour control layer internally and a damp proof course externally
11 Insulation core with vapour control layer and damp proof course
12 Full height double glazed clear fixed window unit
13 12.5 mm (1/2 inch) plasterboard, skimmed and painted
14 Treated softwood timber studs
15 Damp proof course
16 Compressible neoprene seal
17 Anodized aluminium drip to sill
18 Silicone-based paint finish to external walls on cement-based mineral render
19 Shadow gap
20 Finish to be 150 mm (6 inch) fair-faced power floated reinforced white concrete to match stairs and 35 mm (13/8 inch) wide flat stainless steel handrail fixed with stainless steel brackets

4.087
**Sliding Glass Door
Detail 1:10**

Vittorio Longheu
Casa C [16]

1 30 mm (11/4 inch) natural stone flooring
2 Concrete laying bed
3 60 mm (23/8 inch) concrete bed for laying underfloor heating
4 Fine concrete layer of Foamcem for laying of water and electrical services
5 Aluminium hanger for suspended plasterboard ceiling
6 Aluminium C-section
7 3 mm (1/8 inch) plexiglas sheet
8 Plasterboard false ceiling
9 Steel flat bar
10 20 mm (3/4 inch) Eraclit panel
11 Continuous lines of neon lamps
12 Roller blind
13 Two layers of 25 mm (1/2 inch) plasterboard
14 Steel angle
15 Sliding rail for window
16 Brush seal to roller blind
17 Flyscreen guides
18 Glazed window unit
19 Aluminium profile

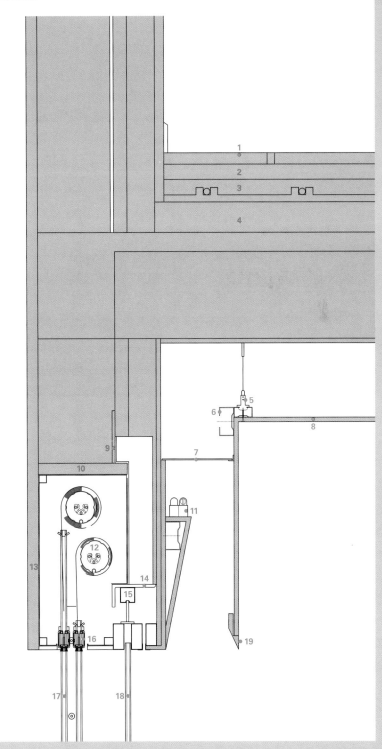

4.088
Door Detail 1:20

Tonkin Zulaikha Greer
Hastings Parade House
[26]

1 Existing wall with
   render
2 Car stacker engine
3 Car stacker engine
   cover plate
4 200 x 200 x 13 mm
   (7⁵/₈ x 7⁵/₈ x ¹/₂ inch)
   galvanized mild steel
   angle fixed to
   existing wall to
   support roller door
5 Timber fence
6 Linear drain
7 Car stacker elevating
   platform
8 Roller door with
   automatic opener
9 Car stacker elevating
   rack
10 150 x 150 x 10 mm (6

x 6 x ³/₈ inch)
galvanized mild steel
angle fixed to
existing wall to
support roller door
11 Existing masonry
   wall with render
12 Timber fence

4.089
Garage Door Detail 1:10

Agence Michel Tortel
Mikado House [08]

1 140 mm (5¹/₂ inch)
   horizontal steel
   I-beam to take
   bending under wind
   load
2 Epoxy-coated
   profiled aluminium
   capping
3 Curtain walling with
   aluminium spine,
   double glazing and
   planitherm film
4 Water collection
   grille
5 Gutter
6 Waterproofing
   complex
7 External polished
   concrete slab
8 Internal floating
   polished concrete

floor screed
9 Insulation and
   underfloor heating
10 Concrete slab
11 Garage roller shutter
   door

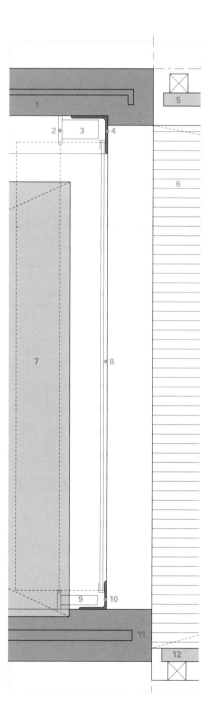

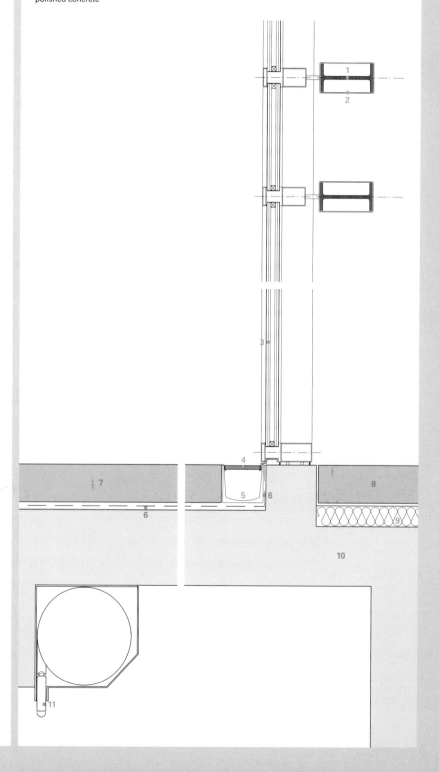

4.090
Sliding Doors to Terrace
Detail 1:20

Saunders Architecture
Villa Storingavika [40]

1 Fixed window
2 Edge of terrace
3 Timber door jamb
4 Locks and handle of
  sliding door
5 Two layers of
  insulating glass
6 Timber door jamb
7 9 mm (1/3 inch)
  gyprock boarding
8 Fixed window
9 13 mm (1/2 inch)
  waterproof gyprock
10 Canadian cedar
  cladding

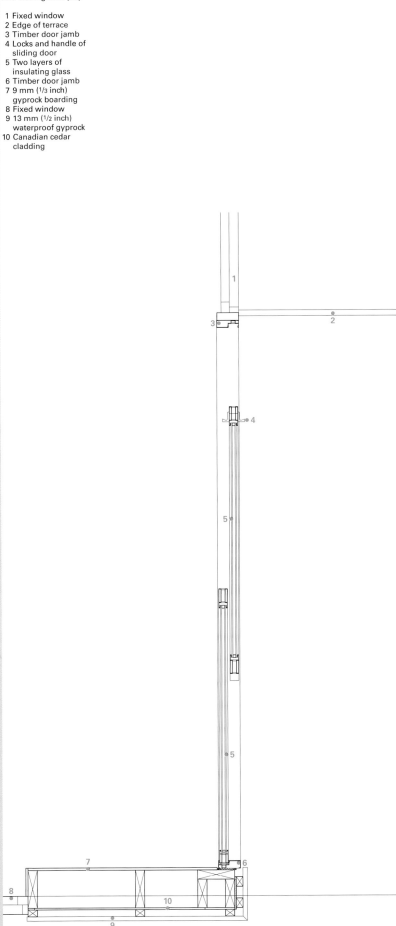

4.091
Sliding Glass Door
Detail 1:10

Johnston Marklee &
Associates
Hill House [22]

1 Timber framing
2 Firring as necessary
3 Timber header beam
4 Plywood substrate
5 Waterproof layer
6 Patch over angle and
  bolt head with 10
  mm (3/8 inch)
  gypsum wall board
  to provide smooth
  finish
7 200 x 150 x 8 mm (8
  x 6 x 7/16 inch) steel
  angle attached to
  beam or solid
  blocking
8 Timber packer
9 Aluminium frame to
  sliding doors
10 Metal reveal for drip
  stop
11 Sliding glass doors
12 63 x 38 x 4 mm (21/2
  x 11/2 x 3/16 inch) steel
  angle top and bottom
  rail
13 Steel tube post
  capped at exposed
  ends with steel plate
14 16 mm (5/8 inch)
  laminate safety glass
  mounted to top and
  bottom angles with
  frameless pin
  connections
15 Stainless steel lock
  hook connection for
  wire mesh
  attachment at top
  and bottom rail
16 Aluminium frame to
  sliding doors
17 Aluminium threshold
18 Steel tube sleeve
  imbedded in
  concrete floor for
  tube-post connection
19 Poured concrete on
  corrugated metal
  decking
20 Poured concrete sill
21 25 mm (1 inch)
  extruded aluminium
  reveal
22 Top flange of steel
  beam
23 Steel beam
24 Rigid insulation
  extended to
  underside of
  concrete deck
25 Waterproof layer
26 Plywood substrate
27 Firring strips
28 Concrete wall
29 Bottom flange of
  steel beam
30 Timber nailer bolt
  fixed to bottom
  flange of steel beam
31 Timber firring at 610
  mm (24 inch) centres
32 16 mm (5/8 inch)
  gypsum board

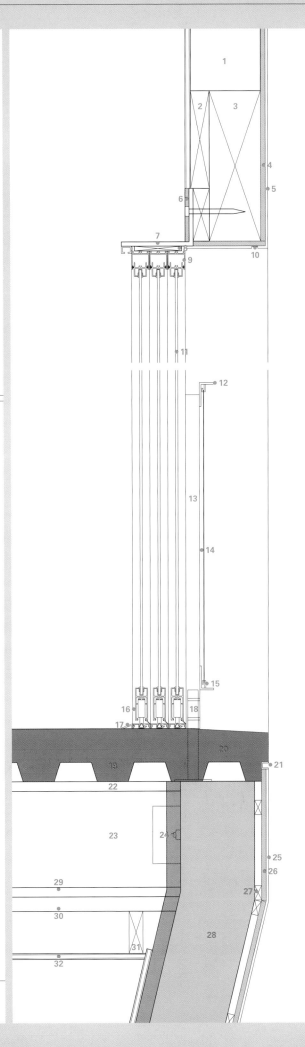

4.092
Internal Door Plan Detail
1:10

de Blacam and Meagher
Architects
Morna Valley Residence
[20]

1 12.5 mm (1/2 inch)
  plasterboard,
  skimmed and painted
2 Painted hardwood
  door frame
3 Painted hardwood
  door leaf
4 Terracotta blocks
5 Shadow gap

4.093
Door Jamb Detail 1:10

Frank Harmon Architect
Low Country Residence
[26]

1 45 mm (1 3/4 inch)
  solid core door
2 Wire pull and
  deadbolt
3 150 x 165 mm (6 x
  6 1/2 inch) steel
  column
4 Four 50 x 100 mm (2
  x 4 inch) vertical
  studs bolted together
5 Fixed double glazed

window
6 Storefront glazing
  frame
7 Door jamb
8 Metal closure
  element
9 Fixed double glazed
  window
10 Wire mesh insect
  screen

4.094
Door Detail 1:10

Charles Pictet
Architectes
Villa Frontenex [10]

1 Reinforced concrete
  wall
2 30 mm (1 1/5 inch)
  insulation
3 Timber window
  frame
4 Double glazing

comprised of 8 mm
(1/3 inch) laminated
and tempered glass
5 Timber door frame
6 Internal face of
  timber door
7 Invisible hinge
8 120 mm (4 3/4 inch)
  insulation
9 25 mm (1 inch)
  plasterboard

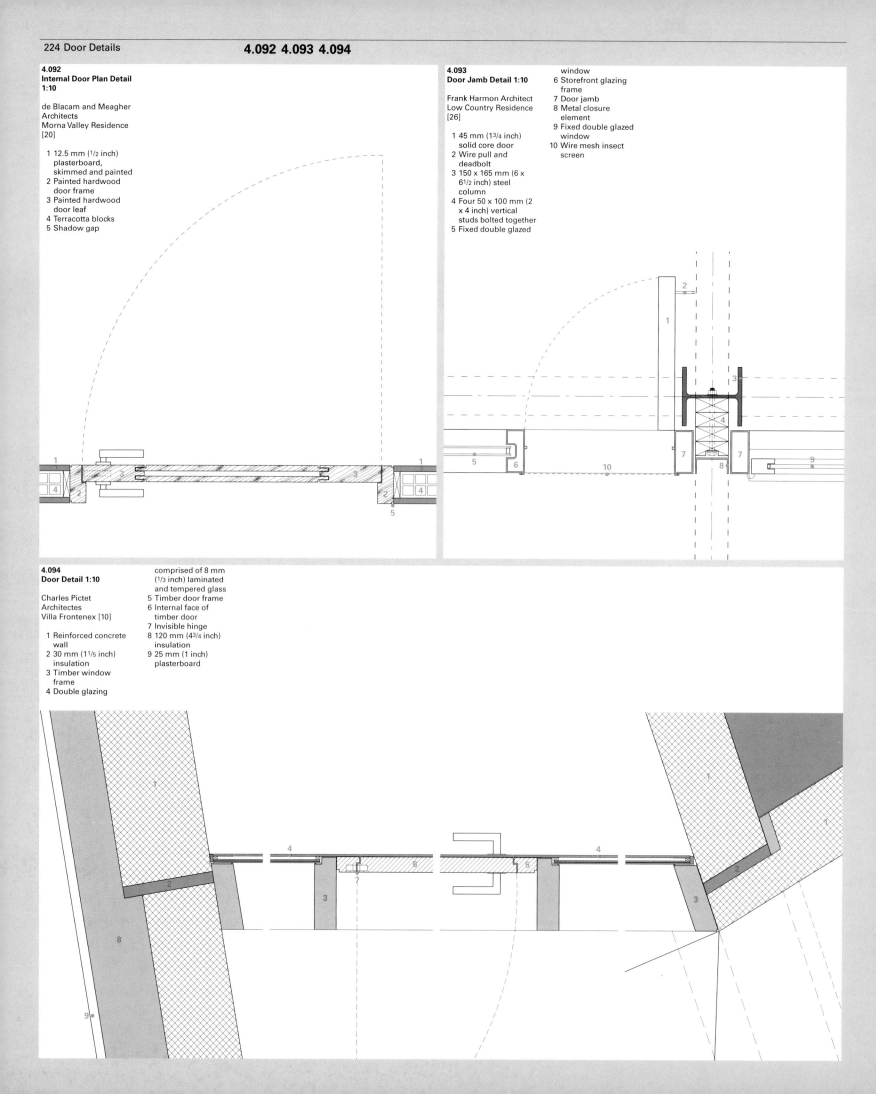

4.095
Overhead Door Detail
1:7.5

Barton Myers Associates
Bekins Residence [25]

1 Door torsion springs
2 Steel angle
3 Rubber weather
  gasket
4 Aluminium door top
  rail
5 75 mm (3 inch)

door tracks
6 Glass
7 Steel column beyond

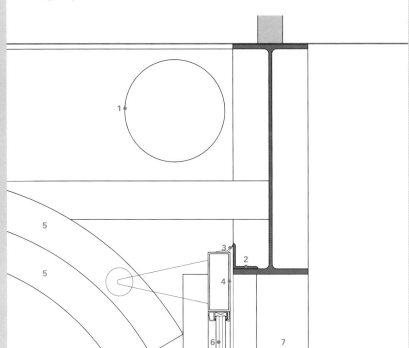

4.096
Overhead Door Sill
Detail 1:5

Barton Myers Associates
Bekins Residence [25]

1 Steel column beyond
2 Glazing
3 Galvanized steel door
  track
4 Anodized aluminium
  door rail
5 Rubber weather seal

6 Concrete slab
7 Exterior
8 Interior

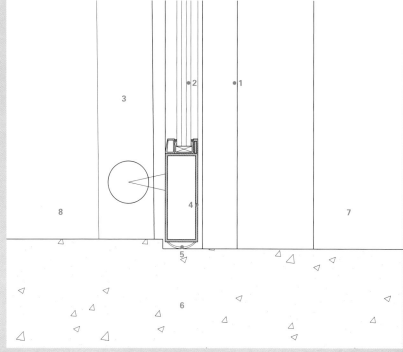

4.097
Sliding Glass Door Sill
Detail 1:4

Barton Myers Associates
Bekins Residence [25]

1 Insect screen
2 Glazing
3 Sliding glass door
4 Sheet metal door
  pan
5 Finished concrete
  floor

6 Galvanized steel
  flashing
7 Structural concrete
  slab
8 Exterior
9 Interior

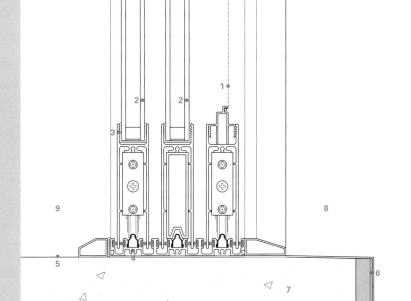

4.098
Door Detail 1:10

Peter L. Gluck and
Partners, Architects
Inverted Guest House
[26]

1 Corrugated copper
  cladding
2 Nylon lift strap
3 Insulated steel
  framed garage door
4 Rectangular hollow

section steel frame
5 Knuckle hinge
6 Flashing at bi-fold
  joint
7 Plywood screwed to
  bi-fold door
8 Cedar siding
9 Jamb beyond

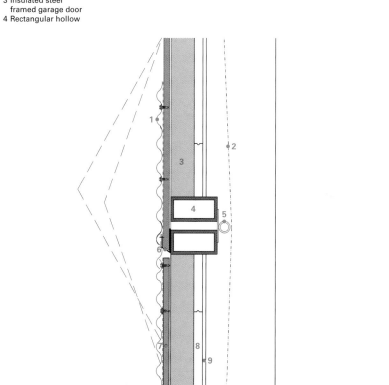

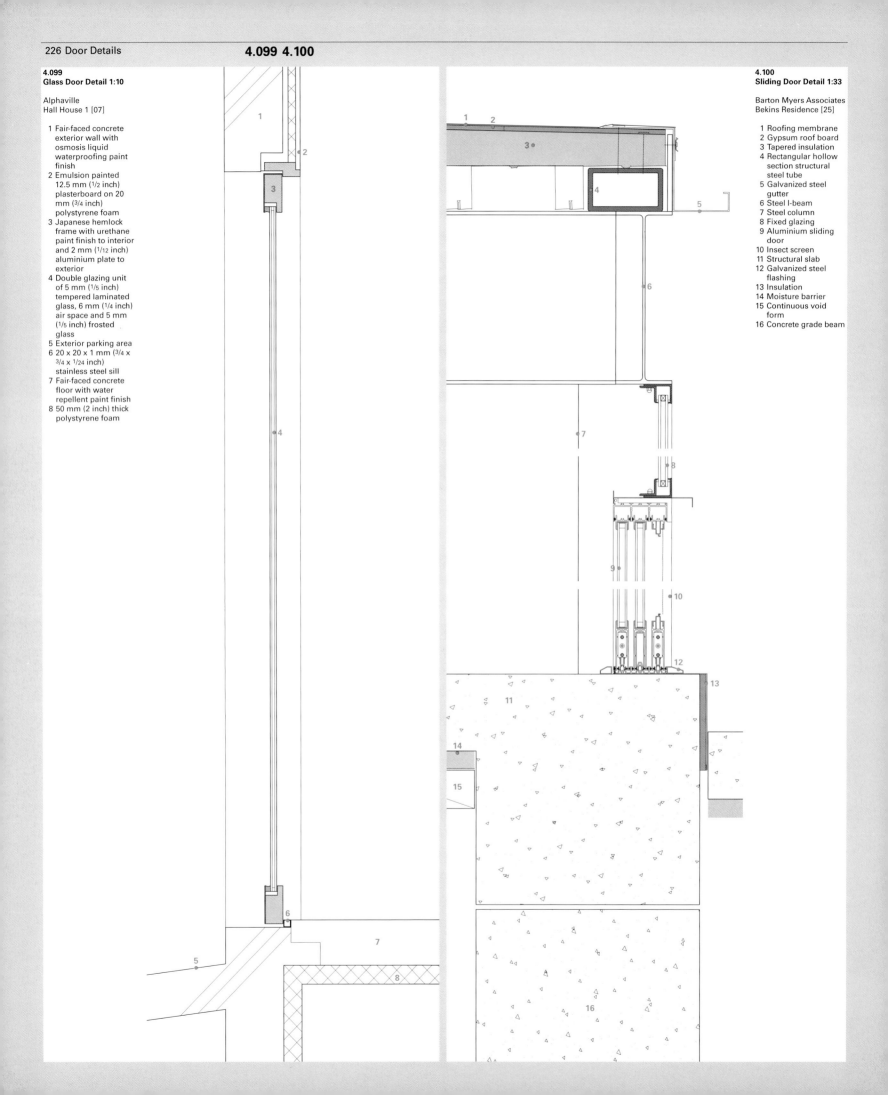

4.099
Glass Door Detail 1:10

Alphaville
Hall House 1 [07]

1 Fair-faced concrete
 exterior wall with
 osmosis liquid
 waterproofing paint
 finish
2 Emulsion painted
 12.5 mm (1/2 inch)
 plasterboard on 20
 mm (3/4 inch)
 polystyrene foam
3 Japanese hemlock
 frame with urethane
 paint finish to interior
 and 2 mm (1/12 inch)
 aluminium plate to
 exterior
4 Double glazing unit
 of 5 mm (1/5 inch)
 tempered laminated
 glass, 6 mm (1/4 inch)
 air space and 5 mm
 (1/5 inch) frosted
 glass
5 Exterior parking area
6 20 x 20 x 1 mm (3/4 x
 3/4 x 1/24 inch)
 stainless steel sill
7 Fair-faced concrete
 floor with water
 repellent paint finish
8 50 mm (2 inch) thick
 polystyrene foam

4.100
Sliding Door Detail 1:33

Barton Myers Associates
Bekins Residence [25]

 1 Roofing membrane
 2 Gypsum roof board
 3 Tapered insulation
 4 Rectangular hollow
 section structural
 steel tube
 5 Galvanized steel
 gutter
 6 Steel I-beam
 7 Steel column
 8 Fixed glazing
 9 Aluminium sliding
 door
10 Insect screen
11 Structural slab
12 Galvanized steel
 flashing
13 Insulation
14 Moisture barrier
15 Continuous void
 form
16 Concrete grade beam

**4.101
Entry Door Section
Detail 1:10**

Studio d'ARC Architects
Live / Work Studio II [19]

1 15 mm (5/8 inch) gypsum board
2 Vapour barrier
3 Batt insulation
4 50 x 150 mm (2 x 6 inch) timber blocking
5 Two 50 x 250 mm (2 x 10 inch) timber blocking
6 75 x 100 mm (3 x 4 inch) weathered steel angle
7 18 gauge weathered steel flashing
8 Aluminium reglet
9 Jamb and door to match wood species of windows, internal and external
10 100 x 75 x 8 mm (4 x 3 x 5/16 inch) weathered steel beyond
11 8 mm (5/16 inch) weathered steel plate
12 25 mm (1 inch) diameter hole in plate
13 Numbers cut into steel plate

**4.102
Rear Sliding Doors Head
and Sill Detail 1:5**

Marsh Cashman
Koolloos Architects
Maroubra House [36]

1 Aluminium blinds
2 Anodized aluminium framed fixed windows
3 Galvanized steel beam
4 Timber blocking as required
5 Flashing to match roof capping
6 Anodized aluminium angle
7 Anodized aluminium framed sliding doors
8 Selected timber floorboards on timber battens
9 Selected hardwood timber boards
10 Anodized aluminium sub-sill
11 Timber packing as required
12 185 x 35 mm (7 1/4 x 1 3/8 inch) timber joist
13 Waterproof membrane
14 Neoprene pads

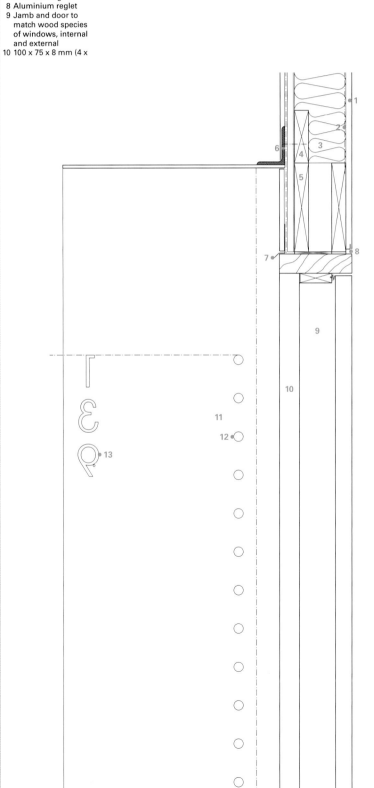

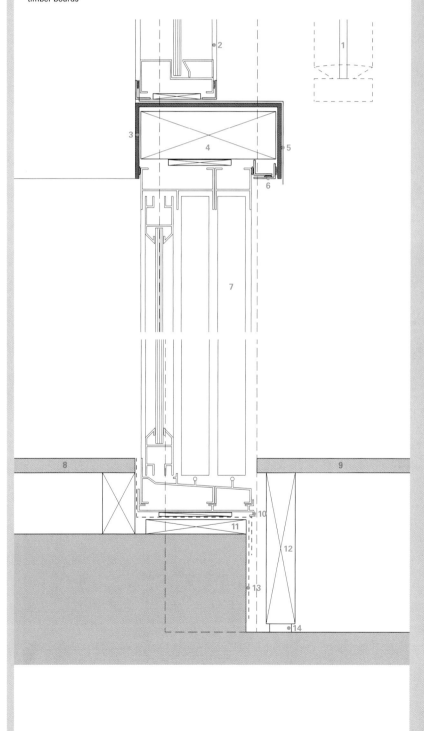

4.103
Interior Door Plan Detail
1:10

Marlon Blackwell
Architect
L-Stack House [35]

1 12 mm (1/2 inch)
 gypsum board
2 25 x 50 mm (1 x 2
 inch) painted poplar
 wood strip cladding
3 Blown cellulose
 insulation
4 50 x 100 mm (2 x 4
 inch) timber stud wall
 at 400 mm (16 inch)

centres
5 25 x 50 mm (1 x 2
 inch) painted poplar
 wood strip cladding
 over door
6 2100 x 45 mm (84 x
 13/4 inch) solid-core
 painted wood door

4.104
Interior Door Plan Detail
1:10

Marlon Blackwell
Architect
L-Stack House [35]

1 12 mm (1/2 inch)
 gypsum board
2 12 mm (1/2 inch)
 plywood sheathing
 for shear wall
3 50 x 100 mm (2 x 4
 inch) timber stud at
 400 mm (16 inch)
 centres
4 Blown cellulose

insulation
5 20 mm (3/4 inch)
 timber blocking
6 20 x 63 mm (3/4 x 21/2
 inch) painted poplar
 board trim
7 2100 x 45 mm (84 x
 13/4 inch) rift cut,
 white oak veneer
 solid-core door with
 clear finish

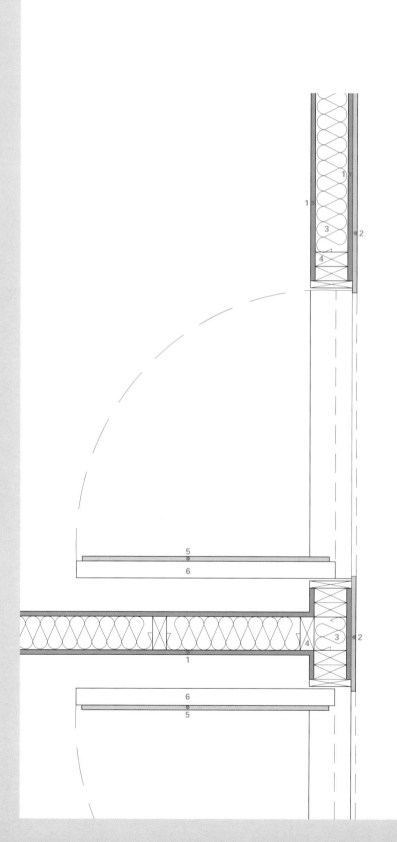

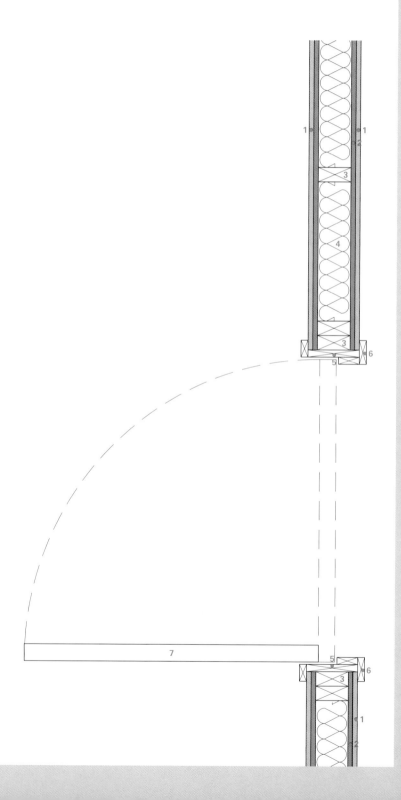

4.105
Glass Entry Door Jamb
1:10

Bercy Chen Studio
Peninsula House [36]

1 12.5mm (1/2 inch)
  sheetrock
2 Fry Reglet reveal
  moulding 12.5 mm
  (1/2 inch) depth 6 mm
  (1/4 inch) reveal width
3 19mm (3/4 inch)
  firring or sheathing
  as needed to flush
  sheetrock with jamb
4 30 x 140 mm (11/5 x

51/2 inch) solid milled
masa timber jamb
with edge gap for
siding lap
5 Solid blocking behind
  jamb
6 12.5 mm (1/2 inch)
  tempered clear glass
  door on central pivot
  hardware, sealed
  with self-adhesive
  weather stripping
7 Vertical 25 x 100 mm
  (1 x 4 inch) masa
  timber lap and gap
  siding, lap over jamb
  gap
8 12.5 mm (1/2 inch)

sheathing over
framing
9 Door sill
10 Patch lock
11 100 mm (4 inch)
  masa timber jamb
  notched to catch
  door
12 32 x 60 mm (11/4 x
  23/8 inch) masa
  timber block screwed
  to jamb-set glass
  before installing
  block
13 12.5 mm (1/2 inch)
  tempered clear glass
  with red interior
  plastic layer set

against exterior masa
timber block and
sealed with silicone
as needed
14 3 mm (1/8 inch) steel
  strike plate set into
  masa timber jamb
15 32 x 60 mm (11/4 x
  23/8 inch) Masa block
  screwed to jamb

4.106
Utility Closet Door
Detail 1:20

Ibarra Rosano Design
Architects
Winter Residence [23]

1 Full length
  aluminium channel
  door pulls
2 20 mm (3/4 inch) thick
  plywood closet doors
3 Blind corner hinge
4 50 x 100 mm (2 x 4
  inch) timber framed
  wall
5 20 mm (3/4 inch)

plywood wall panel
6 7 mm (1/4 inch)
  aluminium channel
  reveal

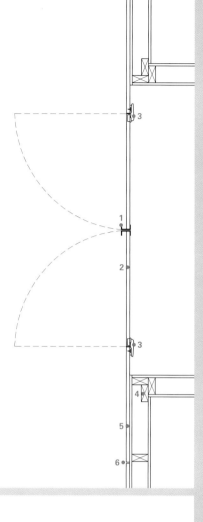

4.107
Door Head Detail 1:5

Boyd Cody Architects
Richmond Place House
[22]

1 150 mm (6 inch)
  Rockwool acoustic
  insulation
2 Timber beam
3 18 mm (7/10 inch)
  white oak veneered
  ceiling panel with
  hardwood frame
  concealed at head
4 Paint finish to door
  frame

5 Paint finish to
  internal face of
  solid-core door
6 18 mm (7/10 inch)
  veneered plywood
  internal wall lining
7 18 mm (7/10 inch)
  white oak veneered
  ceiling panel with
  hardwood frame
  concealed at head

4.108
Door Head Detail 1:5

Boyd Cody Architects
Richmond Place House
[22]

1 Insulation
2 Timber beam
3 Plasterboard with
  paint finish to ceiling
4 Paint finish to door
  frame
5 Oak veneered timber
  door reveal
6 6 mm (1/4 inch) white
  oak veneered panel
  to rear of door with

18 mm (7/10 inch) oak
veneered panel
bonded to front
7 18 mm (7/10 inch)
  white oak veneered
  ceiling panel with
  hardwood frame
  concealed at head

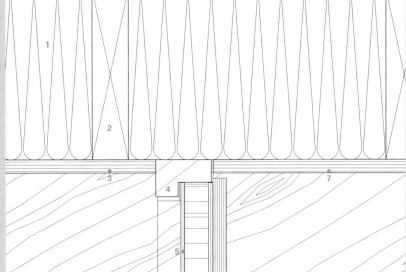

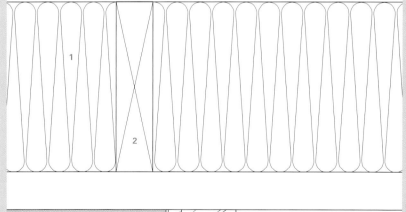

4.109
Entrance Door Detail
1:7.5

Kallos Turin
Casa Zorzal [10]

1 15 mm (3/8 inch)
   toughened glass
2 75 x 150 mm (3 x 6
   inch) lapacho
   hardwood panels
3 25 x 150 mm (1 x 6
   inch) lapacho

hardwood panels
4 Four Soss type
   concealed hinges
5 Horizontal hardwood
   structure
6 Finger door pull
7 Silicone seal

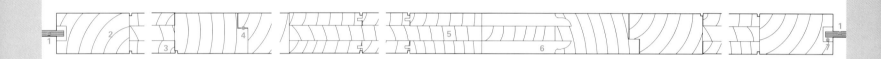

4.110
Door Plan Detail 1:10

Morphogenesis
N85 Residence [08]

1 Stainless steel
   hinges
2 Teak beading with
   polyurethane varnish
3 Teak frame with
   polyurethane varnish
4 Interlocking glazing
   clip
5 Silicone seal with
   backer rod
6 Glazing panel
7 25 x 60 mm (1 x 2 3/8
   inch) rectangular
   hollow section steel
   tube
8 Teak beading with
   polyurethane varnish
9 15 x 85 mm (3/5 x 3 1/3
   inch) teak beading
   with polyurethane
   varnish

10 12 mm (1/2 inch)
   waterproof base
   plywood
11 Timber veneer with
   polyurethane varnish
12 Hardwood handle
   with polyurethane
   varnish
13 Hardwood door with
   bowl-shaped
   sculptural cut-out
   with lacquer finish

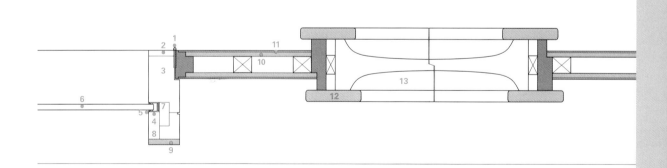

4.111
Door Jamb Detail 1:5

Architectus
North Shore House [36]

1 9.5 mm (3/8 inch)
 fibrous plaster lining
 finished into Beadex
 casing bead
2 Timber blocking
3 9.5 mm (3/8 inch)
 fibrous plaster lining
 finished into Beadex

casing bead
4 90 x 25 mm (3½ x 1
 inch) dressed pine,
 painted black
5 Split jamb
6 30 x 20 mm (1⅕ x 3/4
 inch) planted stop
7 Timber door
8 Door hinge

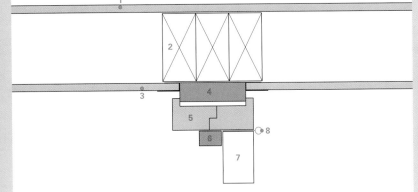

4.112
Entry Hall Glass Door
Plan Detail 1:5

Javier Artadi Arquitecto
Las Arenas Beach House
[19]

1 Brush seal
2 Socle for sliding door
 with pulley and latch
3 10 mm (3/8 inch)
 tempered clear glass
4 Aluminium profile

door frame
5 Brush seal
6 Aluminium lower rail
 for sliding door

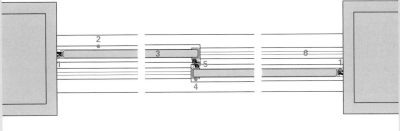

4.113
Door Detail 1:10

Glas Architects
The Nail Houses [23]

1 Plaster stop bead
2 44 mm (1¾ inch)
 timber hollow-core
 door
3 Standard size
 softwood door stop
4 25 x 132 mm (1 x 5¼
 inch) softwood

door jamb
5 100 x 30 mm (4 x 1⅕
 inch) timber stud
6 100 mm (4 inch)
 block wall
7 Plasterboard with
 skimmed plaster
 finish

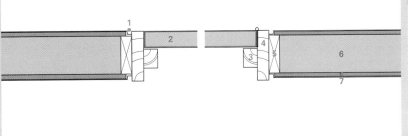

4.114
Door Detail 1:5

Tonkin Zulaikha Greer
Hastings Parade House
[26]

1 Solid timber door
 leaf
2 13 mm (1/2 inch)
 painted plasterboard
 fixed to 90 x 45 mm
 (3½ x 1¾ inch)
 timber studs

3 Timber door frame to
 match existing
 timber floor
4 Timber stud
5 75 x 75 mm (3 x 3
 inch) timber batten
 flush with door frame
 and matched with
 existing timber floor
6 Stair edge shown
 dotted
7 13 mm (1/2 inch)
 painted plasterboard
 fixed to 90 x 45 mm

(3½ x 1¾ inch)
timber studs

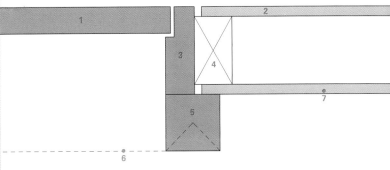

4.115
Sliding Door Detail 1:10

Studio Bednarski
Hesmondhalgh House
[33]

1 Recessed track
  radiators
2 Sliding door track
3 Hardwood glazed
  sliding door
4 Hardwood sill
5 Draught seal
6 Two layers 12.5 mm
  (^{1}/2 inch)
  plasterboard
7 Insulation
8 100 x 50 mm (4 x 2
  inch) timber stud
  frame
9 Acoustic separation
10 Hardwood framing
11 100 x 50 mm (4 x 2
  inch) mild steel
  rectangular hollow
  section steel column
12 Hardwood glazed
  door
13 Timber decking

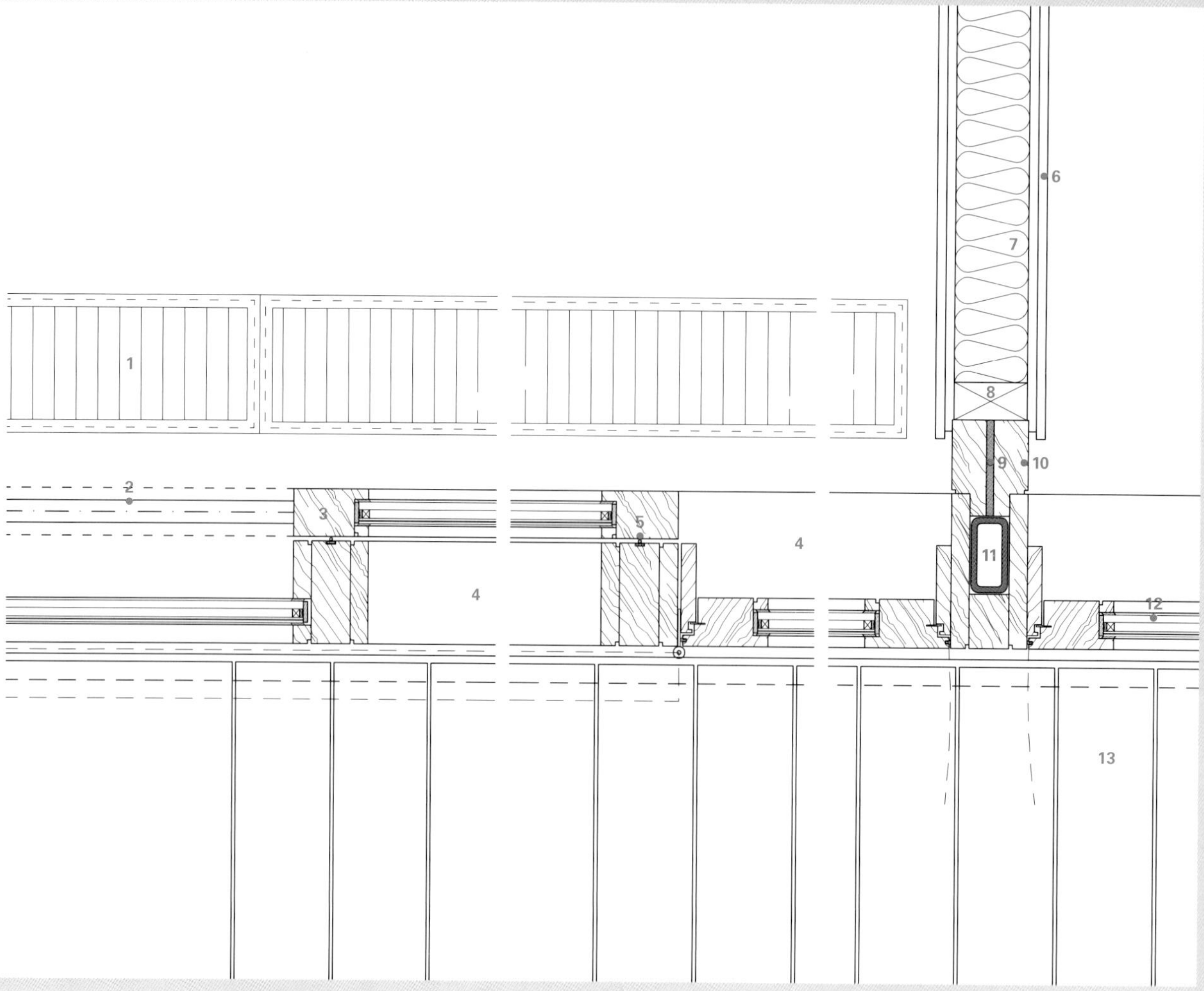

4.116
Porch Door Plan Detail
1:10

Jun Igarashi Architects
Rectangle of Light [37]

1 9.5 mm (^{3}/8 inch)
  solid conifer plywood
  weatherboarding
  with decay-resistant
  paint finish
2 Waterproof paper
3 12 mm (^{1}/2 inch)
  insulation board
4 100 mm (4 inch)
  glass wool insulation
5 9.5 mm (^{3}/8 inch)
  solid conifer plywood
  weatherboarding
  with decay-resistant
  paint finish
6 Letterbox
7 105 x 105 mm (4 x 4
  inch) timber stud
8 Porch
9 Polyethylene film
10 12.5 mm (^{1}/2 inch)
  plasterboard
11 Urethane injected
  insulation
12 9.5 mm (^{3}/8 inch)
  solid conifer plywood
13 Door frame
14 Natural-finish laurel
  stair treads

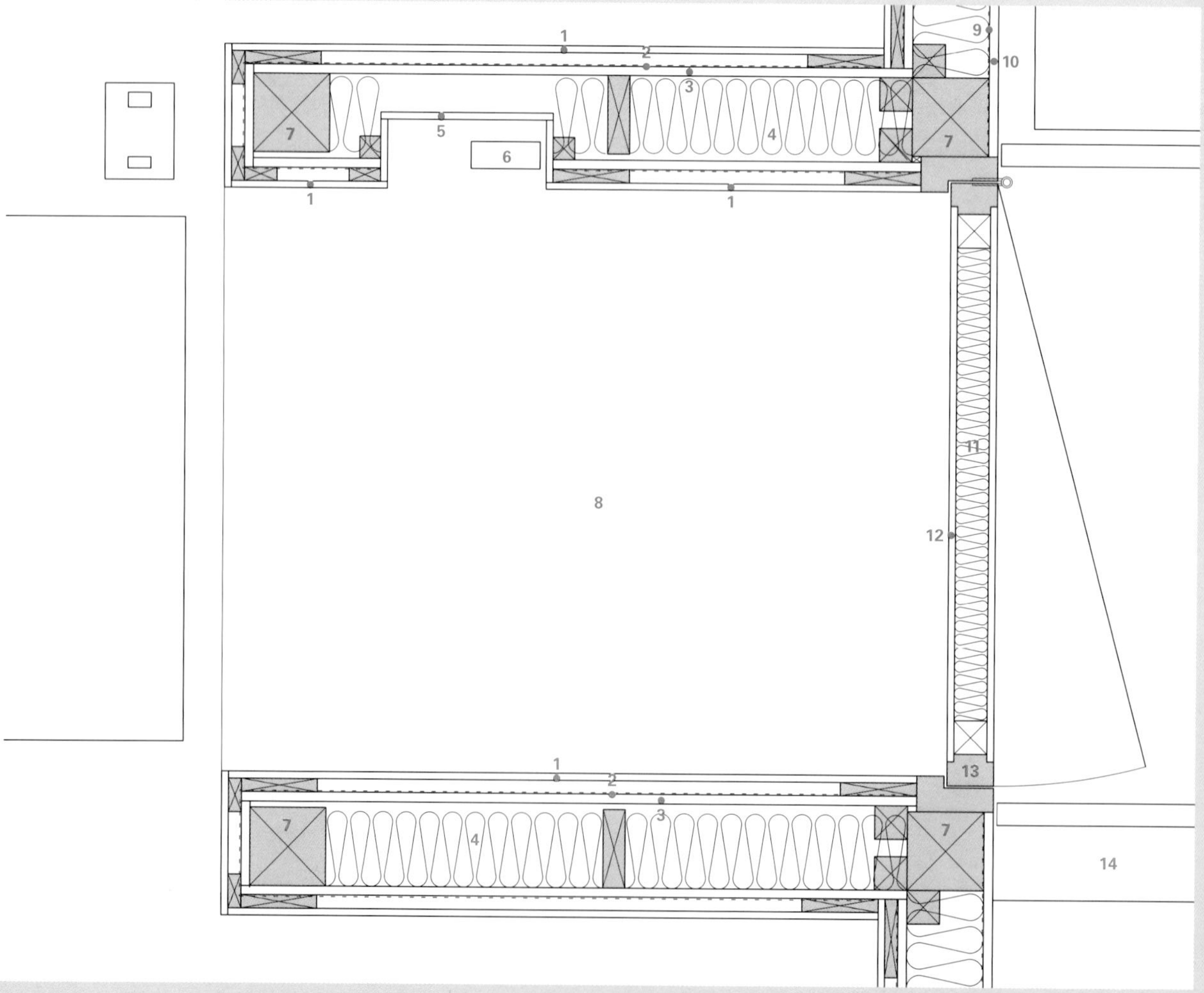

4.117
Door Head Detail 1:2

Stephenson Bell
Architects
House 780 [18]

1 Insulation
2 Two layers of 12 mm
 (1/2 inch)
 plasterboard
3 Metal stud to form
 framework at door
 head
4 Softwood packers,
 painted black
5 Sliding door gear
 and track
6 Recessed acoustic
 door seal
7 Medium density
 fibreboard lining
 painted black
8 Plasterboard high
 strength corner bead
9 Plasterboard stop
 bead
10 Flush timber sliding
 door

4.118
**Glass Entrance Door
Detail 1:10**

Agence Michel Tortel
Mikado House [08]

1 Itauba timber floor
2 Timber battens
3 Waterproofing
 membrane complex
4 External concrete
 slab to first floor
5 External waterproof
 coating
6 Fixed, coated
 aluminium frame to
 glazed door
7 Argon-filled double
 glazing with
 planitherm film
8 Floating, polished
 concrete floor screed
9 Internal insulation
 and underfloor
 heating
10 Ground floor
 reinforced concrete
 floor slab

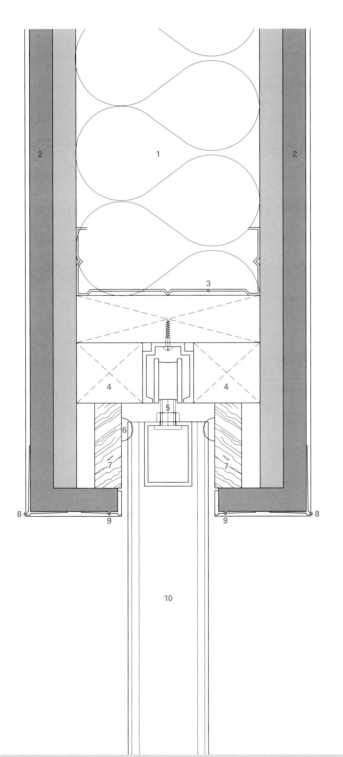

4.119
Entrance Door Plan
Detail 1:20

Barclay & Crousse
Architecture
Casa O [08]

1 460 x 915 mm (18 x
  36 inch) 'Sombra
  Tempora' Peruvian
  dark marble flooring
2 Medium density
  fibreboard door
  panel with dovetail
  joint and blue paint
  finish
3 Frameless tempered
  glass sliding partition
4 Medium density
  fibreboard fixed
  panel with dovetail
  joint and blue paint
  finish
5 10 mm (3/8 inch) fixed
  tempered glass panel

4.120
Entrance Door Elevation
1:20

Barclay & Crousse
Architecture
Casa O [08]

1 Medium density
  fibreboard fixed
  panel with dovetail
  joint and blue paint
  finish
2 Stainless steel frame
3 Stainless steel door
  pull
4 Medium density
  fibreboard door
  panel with dovetail
  joint and blue paint
  finish
5 Stucco and white
  paint finish to
  exterior door

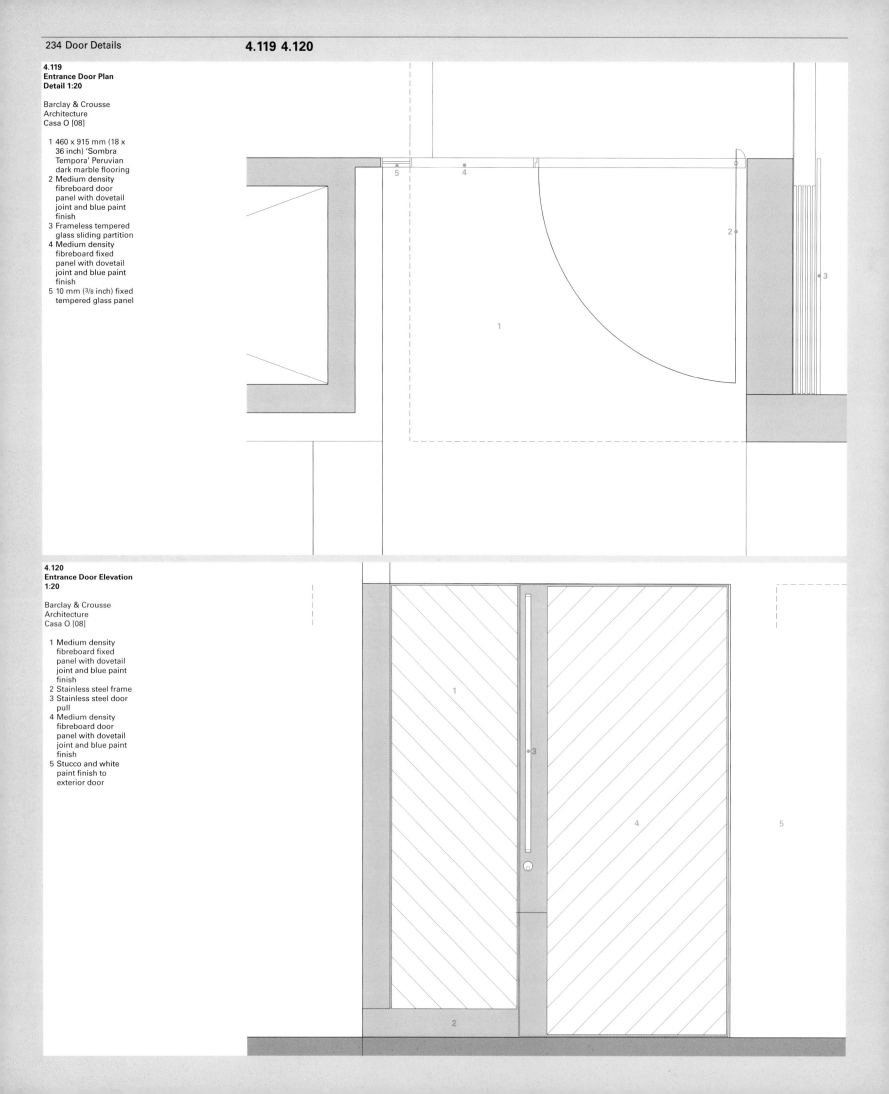

4.121
**Sliding Glass Door Plan
Detail 1:5**

Lee + Mundwiler
Architects
The Coconut House [12]

1 Exposed square
  hollow section steel
  column
2 Aluminium window
  assembly
3 Aluminium folding
  and sliding french
  door
4 Aluminium folding
  and sliding french
  door hardware
5 24 mm (1 inch)
  insulating low-E
  safety glass
6 38 x 88 mm (1¹/₂ x
  3¹/₂ inch) ironwood
  timber decking
7 Sliding and folding
  door bottom track

and threshold
8 15 mm (⁵/₈ inch)
  drywall lining
9 18 mm (⁷/₁₀ inch)
  plywood sheeting
10 Concealed steel post
11 18 mm (⁷/₁₀ inch)
  plywood shear wall
  sheeting
12 Air space
13 Phenolic resin
  treated timber
  veneer panels
14 Hardwood casing

4.122
**Sliding Glass Doors to
Pool Edge Detail 1:20**

Bercy Chen Studio
Peninsula House [36]

1 Steel beam with
  ceramic coating and
  painted finish
2 Sliding panel beyond
3 12.5 mm (¹/₂ inch)
  grey-tinted tempered
  glass submerged
  beneath surface of
  water
4 Reinforced
  cantilevered splash
  break
5 New foundation with
  12.5 mm (¹/₂ inch)
  travertine flooring on
  6mm (¹/₄ inch)
  thick-set mortar
6 Gunite pool shell
  with integral
  perimeter beam

7 Submerged ledge
8 Floor mounted glass
  guide
9 Radius edge as small
  as possible to pool
  ledge
10 304 mm (12 inch)
  deep sheet piling to
  create pool
  excavation

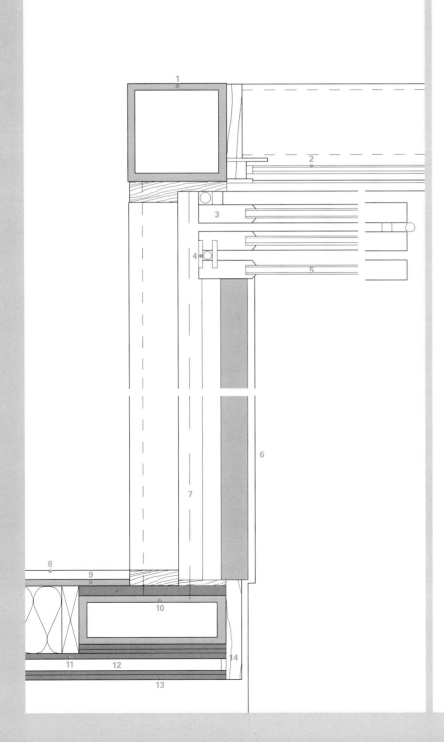

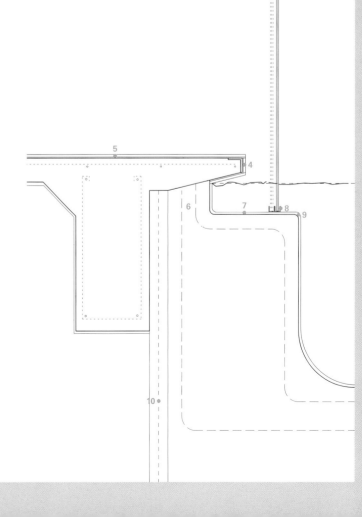

4.123
Casement Jamb Detail at Pocket Door 1:5

The Miller Hull Partnership
Chuckanut Drive
Residence [31]

1 25 x 150 mm (1 x 6 inch) tongue and groove cedar siding
2 12 mm (1/2 inch) gypsum wall board
3 Aluminium window jamb
4 Fixed aluminium clad timber window
5 Timber window jamb
6 Timber window jamb trim
7 12 mm (1/2 inch) clear tempered glass
8 Lift-and-slide door to pocket in front of fixed window
9 Shim space
10 Two 140 x 40 mm (51/2 x 15/8 inch) timber stud framing
11 Building paper
12 12 mm (1/2 inch) plywood sheathing
13 Weatherstripping to pocket door

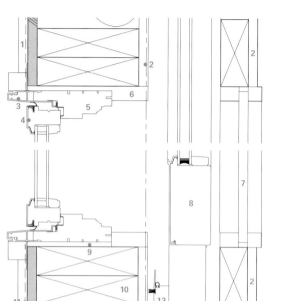

4.124
Lift-and-Slide Jamb Detail at Pocket Door 1:5

The Miller Hull Partnership
Chuckanut Drive
Residence [31]

1 Insulated glazing
2 Pocket door weatherstripping
3 Sheet metal corner flashing
4 25 x 150 mm (1 x 6 inch) tongue and groove cedar cladding
5 Building paper
6 Timber trim
7 12 mm (1/2 inch) plywood
8 140 x 140 mm (51/2 x 51/2 inch) timber bearer
9 Interlocking weatherstripping
10 Pocket door
11 Pocket door jamb
12 Removable timber trim
13 Pocket for lift-and-slide door
14 38 mm (11/2 inch) deep timber framing
15 12 mm (1/2 inch) gypsum board wall lining

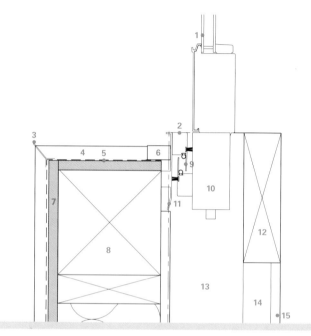

4.125
Garage Wall and Door Plan Detail 1:5

The Miller Hull Partnership
Chuckanut Drive
Residence [31]

1 Standing seam metal wall panel
2 12 mm (1/2 inch) gypsum board wall lining
3 12 mm (1/2 inch) gypsum board wall lining
4 Building paper
5 25 x 150 mm (1 x 6 inch) tongue and groove wood cedar) cladding
6 12 mm (1/2 inch) plywood
7 Cedar trim
8 Timber window jamb
9 Aluminium clad timber window
10 Window stop timber profile
11 Timber trim
12 Aluminium window mullion cover
13 Insulated glazing
14 50 x 150 mm (2 x 6 inch) timber framing with batt insulation
15 100 x 12 mm (4 x 1/2 inch) plywood spacer

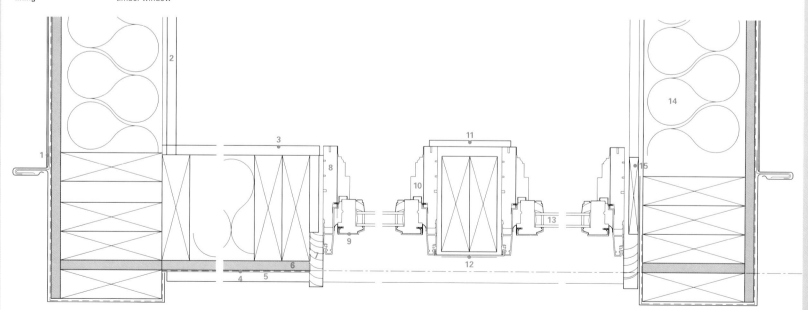

4.126
Sliding Door Section
Detail 1:5

Bates Masi + Architects
Noyack Creek Residence
[37]

1 Metal joist hanger
2 Insulation
3 Dotted line indicating
   holes drilled through
   beam for air
   conditioning return
   air duct
4 Continuous heating,
   ventilation and
   air-conditioning duct
5 Rough sawn 25 x 200
   mm (1 x 8 inch)
   tongue and groove
   centre matched flush
   jointed western red
   cedar siding
6 Angle to support
   grille
7 Sliding door track

and roller
8 20 mm (3/4 inch)
   siding
9 45 mm (13/4 inch)
   solid-core door
10 12 mm (1/2 inch)
   plywood sheathing
11 140 x 40 mm (51/2 x
   15/8 inch) timber stud
12 12 mm (1/2 inch)
   moisture proof
   gypsum board
   ceiling
13 Insulation
14 Flooring over 20 mm
   (3/4 inch) plywood
   substrate
15 Sliding door guide
16 25 mm (1 inch)
   timber flooring
17 Building felt
18 20 mm (3/4 inch)
   plywood subfloor,
   glued and nailed

4.127
Glazed Door Plan Detail
1:10

MELD Architecture with
Vicky Thornton
House in Tarn et
Garonne [34]

1 14 mm (5/8 inch)
   oriented strand
   board on timber
   studs with glasswool
   insulation between

2 125 mm (5 inch) wide
   board on untreated
   chestnut cladding
3 Bespoke double
   glazed oak framed
   doors
4 50 x 15 mm (2 x 5/8
   inch) painted steel
   flat section
   screw-fixed into
   timber studs
5 Untreated chestnut
   cladding
6 Zinc sill

7 Timber shutters of
   125 mm (5 inch) wide
   board on untreated
   chestnut cladding
   (running in line with
   wall cladding) on
   laminated pine
   backing board, with
   parliament hinges

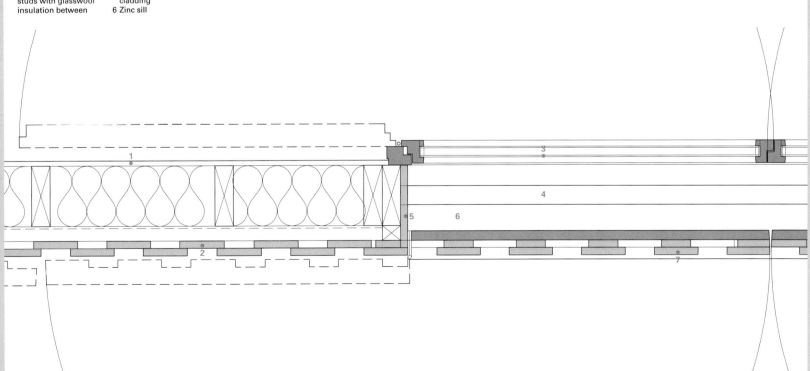

4.128
Sliding Door Detail 1:10

Avanti Architects
Long View [35]

1 Double glazed,
 aluminium framed,
 sliding glass door
2 Cavity sliding door
3 140 mm (5½ inch)
 diameter steel
 column
4 Folded aluminium
 profile reveal
5 Double glazed,
 aluminium framed,
 sliding glass door

6 Strip drain to length
 of terrace
7 Brick paving on
 external terrace

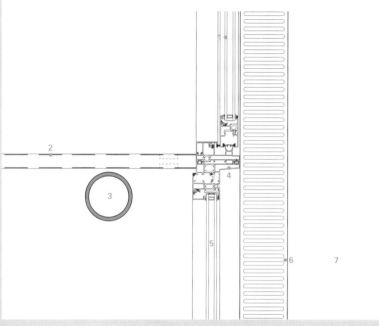

4.129
**Entrance Door Plan
Detail 1:5**

Paulo David with Luz
Ramalho
Casa Funchal [16]

1 8 mm (3/8 inch) birch
 veneer sheathing to
 door jamb
2 Hinge concealed for
 heavy doors
3 6.5 mm (1/4 inch)
 birch veneer to door
 front
4 9 mm (1/3 inch) birch
 veneer to door front

5 50 x 30 mm (2 x 1 1/5
 inch) rectangular
 hollow section
 steel tube framing
6 2 mm (1/12 inch) steel
 plate
7 Door handle
8 Door lock
9 Birch wood door
 jamb

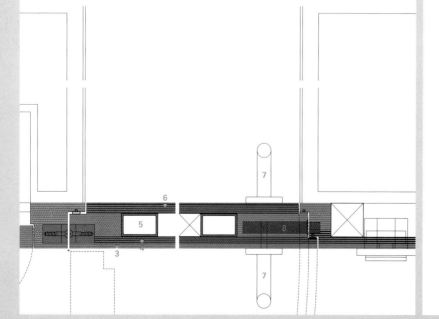

4.130
Door Detail 1:10

Scott Tallon Walker
Architects
Fastnet House [25]

1 Reinforced concrete
 roof slab
2 Face of C-profile stud
3 Mineral fibre acoustic
 insulation
4 Top of acoustic
 insulation
5 Ceiling hanger
6 Mineral fibre acoustic
 quilt insulation
7 Painted skim finish

to plasterboard
8 C-profile stud
9 Oak veneered
 medium density
 fibreboard panels
10 Mineral Rockwool
 and packing
11 Solid oak door
 frame
12 Oak beading to end
 of veneer panel
13 Oak veneered
 solid-core door
14 Timber corner
 framing

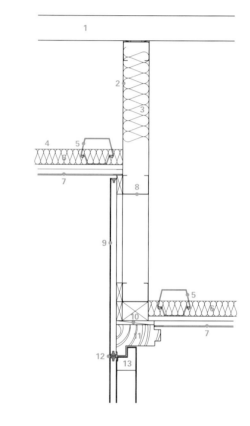

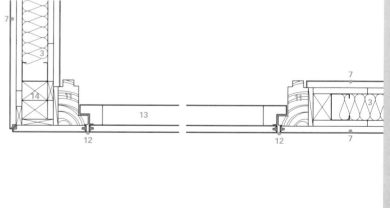

4.131
Sliding Door Detail 1:5

ARTEC Architekten
Holiday House [39]

1 Silicone fill
2 Timber door frame
3 Aluminium profile
4 Double glazing to
  door
5 M16 thread rod
6 Aluminium profile
7 Timber frame profile
8 22 mm (9/10 inch)
  parquet birch floor
9 Insulation
10 95 x 95 mm (3³/4 x

3³/4 inch) zinc coated
  steel bracket
11 108 mm (4¹/4 inch)
  solid timber structure

4.132
Door Detail 1:5

Scott Tallon Walker
Architects
Fastnet House [25]

1 Cedar timber
  cladding panel
2 Cedar timber
  cladding panel
3 Door jamb secret
  fixing
4 Square hollow
  section
5 Door knob
6 Mild steel plate
  welded to square

hollow section
7 Solid door frame in
  cedar
8 Thermally broken
  double glazed unit
9 Transom below
10 Solid cedar window
  frame
11 Solid cedar door
  frame
12 Weather seal
13 Insulation
14 Untreated cedar
  panels to pivot
  jointed door

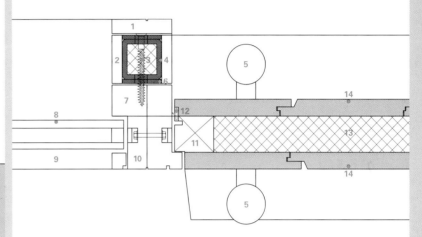

4.133
Pocket Door Detail 1:10

Public
Rattlesnake Creek
House [15]

1 Universal steel beam
2 Structural silicone
  seal
3 Glass partition
4 Structural steel
  sliding door track
  cover, mounted flush
  with top of cubicle
5 Timber hollow-core
  sliding door
6 10 mm (3/8 inch)

veneered plywood
7 Wood veneered
  plywood wall lining
8 20 mm (3/4 inch)
  plywood with fine
  wood veneer at both
  sides of wall and at
  ceiling
9 Sliding door guide
  track
10 Hardwood floor on
  50 x 50 mm (2 x 2
  inch) timber bearers
11 Concrete slab

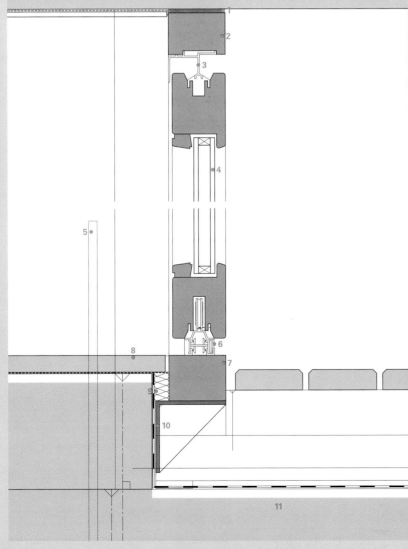

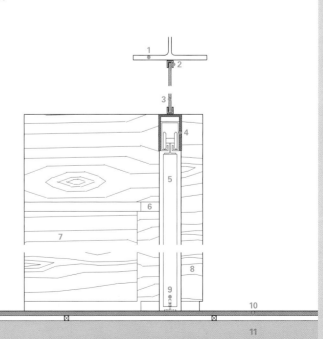

5.001
Trafficable Flat Roof
Detail 1:10

BmasC Arquitectos
Mayo House [20]

1 Filtering geotextile
   felt
2 High performance
   elastomer bitumen
   roof surface with
   polyester frame and
   auto-adhesive joints
3 10 mm (3/8 inch) sand
   and cement mortar
4 Mortar bed to create
   roof slope
5 Oxiasphalt vapour
   barrier
6 Asphalt primer
7 Galvanized grating
   for drain protection
8 Rigid extruded
   polystyrene panels
9 Polyester draining
   geotextile on

synthetic fabric
10 Sand and cement
   mortar
11 Stoneware flooring
   treated for externals
12 Double air-brick wall
13 Semi-resistant joist
   and small vault slab

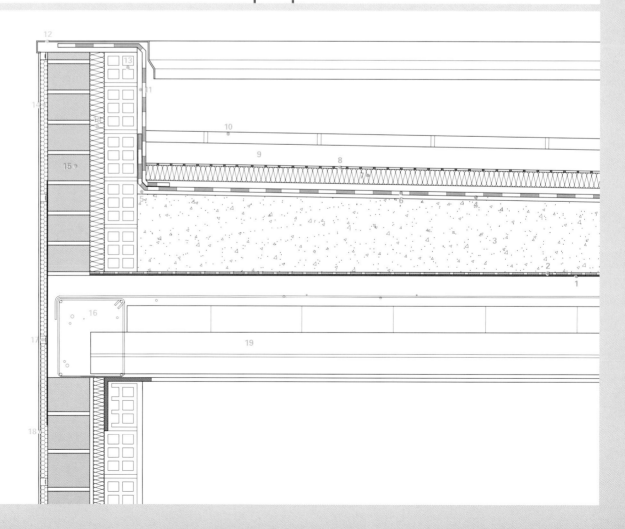

5.002
Trafficable Flat Roof and
Parapet Detail 1:10

BmasC Arquitectos
Mayo House [20]

1 Asphalt primer
2 Oxiasphalt vapour
   barrier
3 Arlita light arids
   mortar for slope
4 10 mm (3/8 inch) sand
   and cement mortar
5 Mortar angled at
   junction of mortar
   and double air-bricks
6 Filtering geotextile
   felt
7 Rigid extruded
   polystyrene panels
8 Polyester draining
   geotextile on
   synthetic fabric
9 Sand and cement
   mortar
10 Stoneware flooring

treated for exteriors
11 Insulation over water-
   repellent mortar
12 Folded galvanized
   and painted 2 mm
   (1/12 inch) steel
   culmination sheet
   with screw fixings
13 Double air-brick
14 Insulation
15 Perforated brick
16 Steel beam
17 Steel fixation
18 Steel sheet
19 Semi-resistant joist
   and small vault slab
   with 250 mm (10
   inch) overlapped
   fibreglass mesh on
   both sides of slab

5.003
Roof and Clerestory
Glazing Detail 1:10

Donovan Hill
Z House [24]

1 50mm (2 inch) layer of Nambuca River stones
2 Polyester geotextile fabric membrane
3 Extruded polystyrene insulation panel
4 Bitumen coated waterproof membrane
5 Concrete structural slab
6 Pre-cast concrete ceiling panels as permanent formwork
7 150 x 30 x 6 mm (6 x 1 1/8 x 1/4 inch) anodized aluminium angle
8 Silicone sealant and timber backing rod
9 9mm (3/8 inch) fixed toughened glass
10 Reinforced core-filled face brickwork
11 Hardwood timber beam
12 Fluorescent lighting
13 Aluminium flashing and waterproofing
14 Glasswool insulation batts
15 Solar reflective corrugated steel roof sheeting
16 Termite-proof pine top plate
17 9mm (3/8 inch) fibre cement sheeting
18 Hardwood timber top plate
19 Hardwood timber batten
20 Hardwood timber frame
21 Venusta planting on stainless steel cables

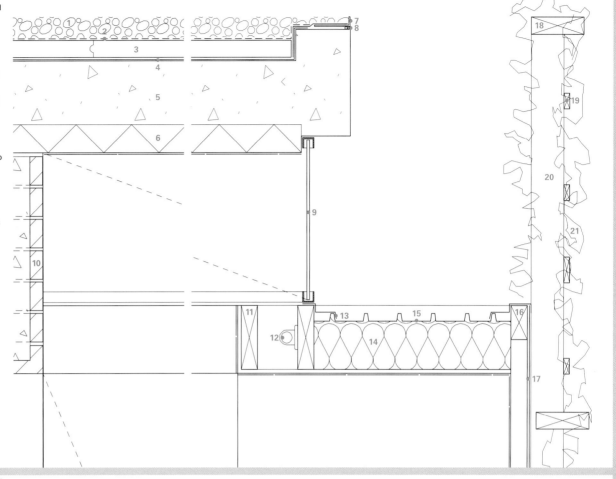

5.004
Roof Edge Detail 1:10

Donovan Hill
Z House [24]

1 Extruded polystyrene insulation panel
2 Bitumen coated waterproof membrane
3 Polyester geotextile fabric membrane
4 50mm (2 inch) layer of Nambucca River stones
5 150 x 30 x 6 mm (6 x 1 1/8 x 1/4 inch) anodized aluminium angle as waterproofing
6 Silicone sealant and timber backing rod
7 Concrete structural slab
8 Pre-cast concrete ceiling panels as permanent formwork
9 Reinforced core-filled face brickwork
10 Aluminium flashing and waterproofing
11 Dressed spotted gum hardwood timber top plate to underside of brickwork
12 70 x 45 mm (2 3/4 x 1 3/4 inch) dressed spotted gum hardwood batten
13 9 mm (3/8 inch) fixed toughened glass
14 Aluminium angle as door stop on packer
15 Dressed spotted gum hardwood timber fascia with clear finish
16 Bi-folding door hardware
17 9mm (3/8 inch) fixed toughened glass

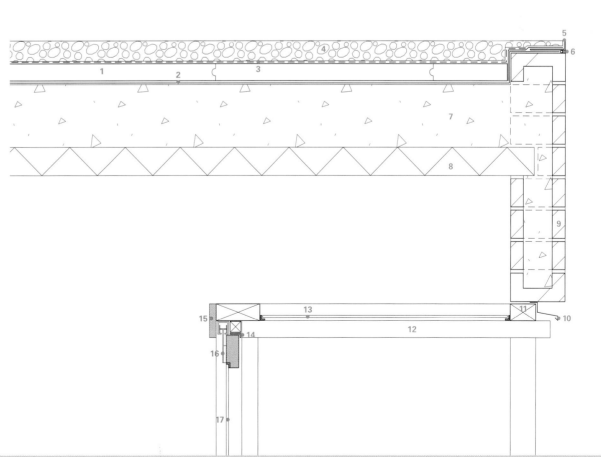

5.005
Roof Parapet Detail 1:10

A-Piste Arkkitehdit
Villa O [39]

1 Sheet copper parapet capping
2 Waterproof bituminous roof membrane
3 18 mm (7/10 inch) matchboard
4 25 mm (1 inch) sawn wood fibreboard weathershield
5 Ventilation space
6 33 x 90 mm (1 1/4 x 3 1/2 inch) aspen boarding, finger jointed and untreated
7 Two layers waterproof bituminous roof membrane
8 23 x 95 mm (7/8 x 3 3/4 inch) matchboard
9 150 x 150 mm (6 x 6 inch) battens and counter battens providing ventilation
10 30 mm (1 1/8 inch) weathershield
11 Two layers of 150 mm (6 inch) mineral wool insulation
12 72 mm (2 4/5 inch) mineral wool insulation
13 Vapour barrier
14 6 mm (1/4 inch) hardboard on 50 x 50 mm (2 x 2 inch) timber battens
15 20 mm (3/4 inch) aspen soffit lining on 25 x 50 mm (1 x 2 inch) timber battens
16 13 mm (1/2 inch) plasterboard
17 9 mm (1/3 inch) veneered plywood
18 51 x 260 mm (2 x 10 1/4 inch) timber
end joist
19 95 mm (3 3/4 inch) mineral wool insulation
20 250 x 80 mm (10 x 3 1/8 inch) laminated timber window frames
21 Triple glazing comprised of 6 mm (1/4 inch) glass, 4 mm (1/8 inch) air gap, 6 mm (1/4 inch) glass, 4 mm (1/8 inch) air gap and 6 mm (1/4 inch) glass

5.006
Stair Vestibule Roof Detail 1:10

Studio d'ARC Architects
Live / Work Studio II [19]

1 Roofing system
2 40 mm (1 1/2 inch) rigid insulation
3 22 gauge metal decking fixed to joists with 6 gauge 40 mm (1 5/8 inch) wood screws at 450 mm (18 inch) centres
4 Galvalume drip edge
5 Pressure-treated wood nailer
6 Galvalume drip edge fascia
7 20 mm (3/4 inch) exterior-grade plywood sheathing
8 15 mm (5/8 inch) gypsum board
9 50 x 250 mm (2 x 10 inch) timber joists at 400 mm (16 inch) centres
10 Corner trim
11 Batt insulation
12 15 mm (5/8 inch) gypsum board
13 Glazing system

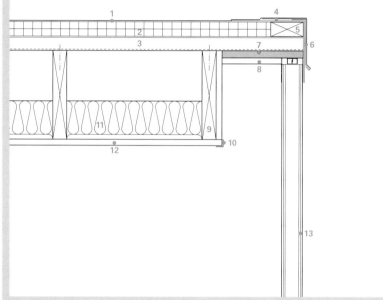

5.007
Roof and Gutter Detail 1:10

Studio d'ARC Architects
Live / Work Studio II [19]

1 Sedum soil mix
2 Green roof hemp-lined tray
3 Heavy duty geotextile fabric
4 Roofing system layer
5 Sealant layer
6 Two 50 x 100 mm (2 x 4 inch) pressure-treated wood nailers
7 Aluminium drip edge
8 Custom formed aluminium gutter
9 Sealant
10 100 mm (4 inch) diameter galvanized downspout
11 Two 50 x 150 mm (2 x 6 inch) timber studs
12 50 x 250 mm (2 x 10 inch) timber rim joist
13 Black asphalt shingle
14 Building felt
15 20 mm (3/4 inch) exterior-grade plywood sheathing
16 350 mm (14 inch) joists
17 Vapour barrier
18 15 mm (5/8 inch) gypsum board

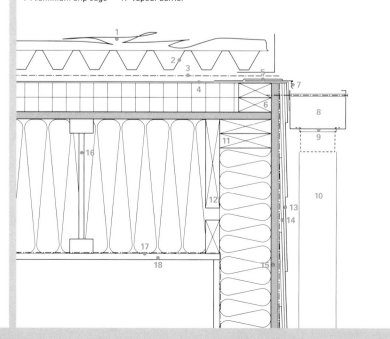

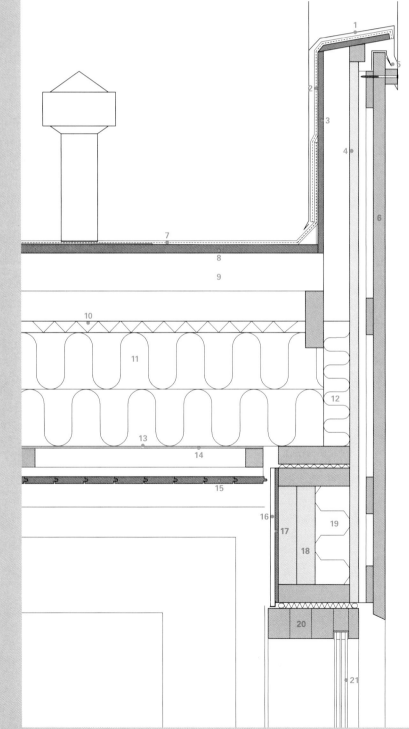

5.008
Roof Detail 1:10

Steffen Leisner, Ali Jeevanjee, Phillip Trigas
1+3=1 House [17]

1 Stainless steel cable guardrail
2 38 mm (1¹/₂ inch) diameter hot rolled steel pipe upright
3 600 x 600 x 50 mm (24 x 24 x 2 inch) concrete roof pavers
4 75 mm (3 inch) diameter hole saw-cut in paver
5 100 mm (4 inch) diameter adjustable pedestal to support roof pavers
6 Two layers of asphalt roofing felt
7 Upright baseplate for guardrail
8 Two layers of plywood roof sheathing
9 Timber blocking for guardrail upright
10 Air space
11 Rigid insulation
12 12 mm (¹/₂ inch) plywood
13 Laminated veneer lumber roof joist

5.009
Roof Detail 1:10

Steffen Leisner, Ali Jeevanjee, Phillip Trigas
1+3=1 House [17]

1 20 gauge corrugated galvanized metal roofing
2 Metal flashing
3 Two layers asphalt roofing felt
4 Plywood sheathing
5 Air space
6 Timber perimeter blocking
7 Rigid insulation
8 12 mm (¹/₂ inch) plywood roof decking
9 Laminated veneer lumber joist
10 Laminated veneer lumber edge piece
11 Cement plaster with smooth trowelled finish
12 Waterproofing layer
13 J-Mold sealant and backer rod
14 Gypsum wall board with paint finish
15 Timber wall framing
16 Batt insulation
17 Plywood wall sheathing

5.010
Roof Terrace Edge Detail 1:10

McBride Charles Ryan
The Dome House [21]

1 Copper sheeting on two layers of 8 mm (¹/₃ inch) plywood substrate with folder copper capping, silicone sealed at ends
2 150 x 45 mm (6 x 1³/₄ inch) laminated veneer lumber
3 9 mm (¹/₃ inch) compressed fibre cement sheet
4 Timber framing
5 Two layers 6 mm (¹/₄ inch) compressed fibre cement sheet, painted to match timber stain, caulking at cladding junctions
6 Custom shiplap profile timber cladding with vapour permeable sarking behind
7 Sarking

5.011
Roof and Ceiling Detail
1:20

de Blacam and Meagher
Architects
Morna Valley Residence
[20]

1 Concrete capping
  poured in-situ
2 Reinforcing bar
3 Hollow concrete
  block
4 Painted cement
  render
5 Extruded polystyrene
  insulation
6 450 x 250 mm (18 x
  10 inch) reinforced
  concrete beam
7 250 x 250 mm (10 x
  10 inch) reinforced
  concrete column
8 Terracotta arch panel
9 50 x 100 mm (2 x 4
  inch) pre-cast
  concrete beam
10 Reinforced concrete
  slab
11 Screed laid to fall
12 Rigid insulation
13 White marble gravel

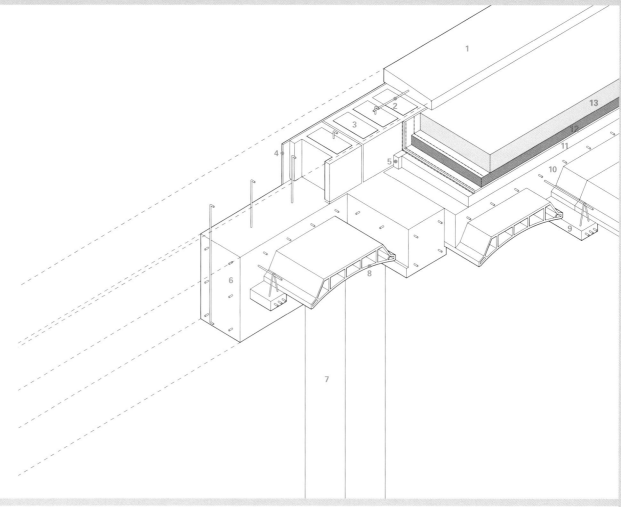

5.012
Roof Parapet Detail 1:10

de Blacam and Meagher
Architects
Morna Valley Residence
[20]

1 Concrete capping
2 Sand and cement
  render
3 White marble gravel
4 Geotextile
  membrane
5 Extruded polystyrene
  insulation
6 Bitumen membrane
7 Extruded polystyrene
  insulation
8 Screed laid to falls
9 Reinforced concrete
  beam
10 Terracotta arch panel
11 50 x 100 mm (2 x 4
  inch) pre-cast
  concrete beam

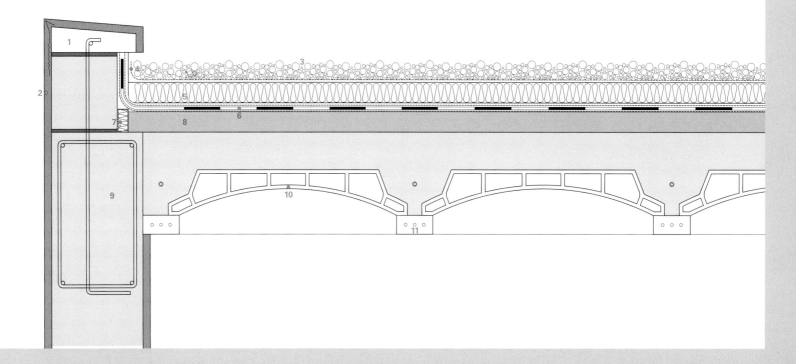

5.013
Gutter Detail at Parapet
Detail 1:10

Tony Fretton Architects
The Courtyard House
[13]

1 Dotted line indicating
 parapet beyond
2 150 x 75 mm (6 x 3
 inch) purpose made
 perforated stainless
 steel retaining angle
3 Loose laid river
 washed pebbles
4 Built-up bitumen
 sheet warm-roof
 construction
5 100 mm (4 inch)
 insulation
6 Anodized
 aluminium-finish
 purpose made gutter
 fascia
7 Stainless steel drip
8 Purpose made
 aluminium gutter
 and outlet spouts
9 Torch-on vapour
 control layer as part
 of warm roof
 construction
10 25 mm (1 inch)
 plywood decking
11 200 x 50 mm (8 x 2
 inch) softwood joists
12 450 x 150 mm (18 x 6
 inch) universal beam
13 Fixing plates to steel
 column beyond
14 175 x 75 mm (7 x 3
 inch) softwood
 blocking
15 Fixing plates to steel
 column beyond
16 Plasterboard lining
 on 35 x 35 mm (1³/8 x
 1³/8 inch) battens
17 Timber joists
18 Galvanized joist
 hanger

19 Anodized aluminium
 coping
20 Existing parapet wall
21 45 x 45 mm (1³/4 x
 1³/4 inch) softwood
 framing
22 18 mm (³/4 inch)
 plywood
23 140 x 45 mm (5¹/2 x
 1³/4 inch) timber wall
 plate
24 Internal plaster finish
25 140 mm (5¹/2 inch)
 blockwork
26 Brick tie channel with
 channel ties
27 Tapered insulation to
 form gutter of
 built-up bitumen
 sheet roofing
28 Torch-on vapour
 control layer dressed
 up behind insulation
 at gutter edge

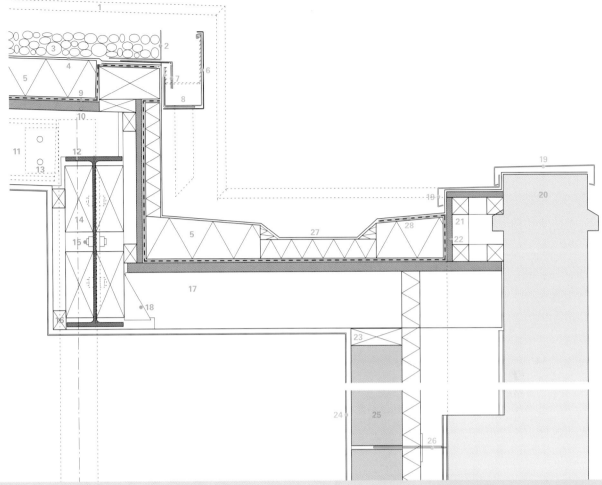

5.014
Gutter Detail 1:10

Tony Fretton Architects
The Courtyard House
[13]

1 Fixed double glazed
 roof light
2 Guide channel to
 motorized blind
3 Rod mechanism to
 blind
4 Motorized fabric
 blackout blind
5 Aluminium blind box
6 Compressible foam
 sealant strip
7 Softwood framing to
 form roof light
 upstand
8 Powder-coated
 aluminium frame to
 roof light
9 Lead wrapped timber
 roll beyond
10 Lead roof covering
 on building paper
11 19 mm (³/4 inch)
 plywood on 50 x 50
 mm (2 x 2 inch)
 softwood battens to
 create 50 mm (2 inch)
 ventilated void
12 Two layers of 12.5
 mm (¹/2 inch)
 plasterboard lining
 with integral vapour
 control layer
13 Breather membrane
14 Prefabricated eaves
 fitting, incorporating
 insect mesh
15 Insulation
16 175 x 50 mm (7 x 2
 inch) softwood
 timber rafters
17 Hanger for
 double-grid
 metal-framed
 suspended ceiling
 system

18 200 x 100 mm (8 x 4
 inch) rectangular
 hollow section with
 plate fixings to roof
 joists
19 Metal section with
 suspended
 plasterboard ceiling
 lining
20 Stone coping
21 Gutter lining
 membrane lapped up
 wall and dressed
 beneath coping
22 50 x 50 mm (2 x 2
 inch) angle fillet
 bedded in hot
 bitumen
23 20 mm (³/4 inch) rigid
 insulation
24 Waterproof bonded
 plywood box gutter
 with 19 mm (³/4 inch)
 base and 15 mm (⁵/8
 inch) sides on 75 x 50
 mm (3 x 2 inch)
 softwood bearers
25 Damp proof
 membrane between
 wall and plywood
 gutter
26 Top of existing
 brickwork wall raised
27 Brick-tie channel with
 channel ties
28 50 mm (2 inch) rigid
 insulation
29 140 mm (5¹/2 inch)
 blockwork wall
30 Plaster finish

5.015
Roof Detail 1:20

Hamiltons
Holmewood House [17]

1 Powder-coated steel hollow section profile
2 Laminated etched glass canopy panel
3 Powder-coated steel support bracket for canopy
4 Steel support angle for fascia
5 Anodized aluminium fascia panel
6 Concrete nib wall at end of facade
7 Support bracket
8 Support bracket
9 Anodized aluminium soffit panel
10 Waterproofing membrane
11 Anodized aluminium external louvres to plantroom
12 215 mm (8 1/2 inch) blockwork wall with paint skin
13 Anodized aluminium internal louvres to plantroom
14 Insulation
15 Powder-coated coping panel
16 Powder-coated steel post for rail and fall-arrest system
17 Gravel strip
18 Grass on topsoil green roof system
19 Drainage membrane and root barrier
20 120 mm (4 3/4 inch) insulation
21 Waterproofing system
22 Curved structural concrete roof with polystyrene void formers
23 Curved concrete soffit
24 Wet plaster coat

5.016
Roof Detail 1:20

Hamiltons
Holmewood House [17]

1 Joint line between coping panels
2 Powder-coated aluminium coping panels
3 Steel support angle for fascia
4 Waterproofing membrane
5 Powder-coated steel profile
6 Powder-coated steel profile
7 Laminated etched glass panel
8 Powder-coated steel support bracket for canopy
9 Insulation
10 Anodized aluminium fascia panel
11 Motor drive for pop-out and sliding door
12 Anodized aluminium soffit panel with slots for door pins
13 Full height glazed pop-out and sliding door
14 Roller blinds
15 Structural concrete roof upstand
16 Structural concrete soffit
17 Wet plaster coat to ceiling
18 Anodized aluminium ventilation grille and cornice panel
19 Powder-coated steel post for rail and fall-arrest system
20 Gravel strip
21 Grass on topsoil green roof system
22 Drainage membrane and root barrier
23 120 mm (4 3/4 inch) insulation
24 Hot-applied waterproofing system
25 Structural concrete roof with polystyrene void formers

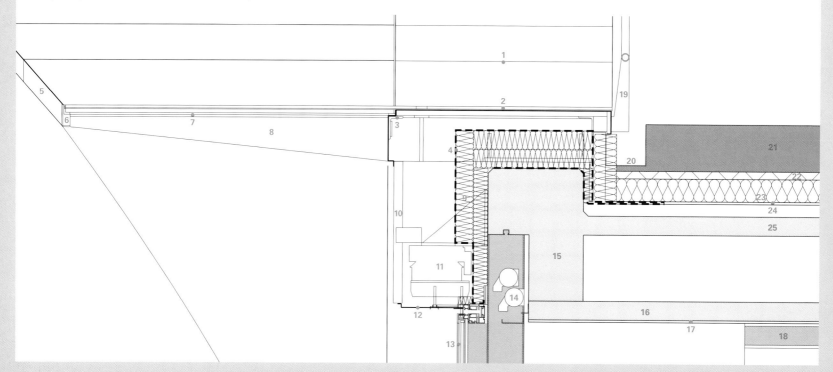

5.017
Roof Detail 1:20

Hamiltons
Holmewood House [17]

1 Powder-coated steel
post for rail and
fall-arrest system
2 Elevation of coping
3 Powder-coated
aluminium coping
panel
4 Support brackets

5 Insulation
6 Waterproofing
membrane
7 120 mm (4³/₄ inch)
insulation
8 Cavity wall
comprised of
external skin of
blockwork with paint
finish
9 Ivy zone
10 Elevation of cladding
panel at opposite
end of facade

11 Structural concrete
roof upstand
12 Structural concrete
soffit
13 Blockwork cavity wall
internal skin of 215
mm (8¹/₂ inch)
blockwork
14 Wet plaster coat
15 Grass on topsoil
green roof system
16 Drainage membrane
and root barrier
17 120 mm (4³/₄ inch)

insulation
18 Hot-applied
waterproofing
system
19 Make-up zone for
concrete pitch at roof
apex
20 Structural concrete
roof with polystyrene
void formers
21 Fixing for support
bracket
22 Support bracket for
coping

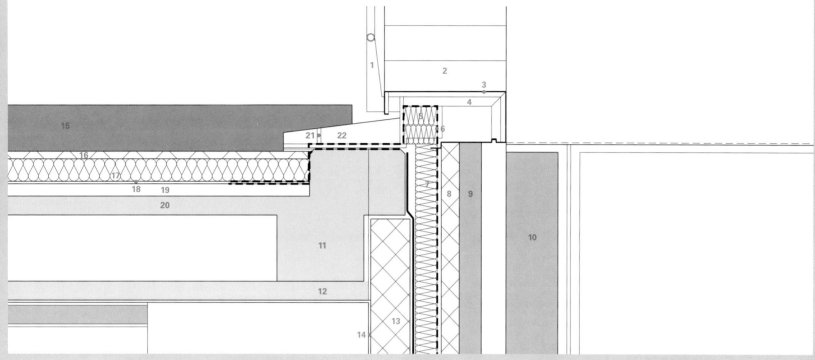

5.018
Roof Edge and Gutter
Detail 1:10

O'Donnell + Tuomey
Architects
The Sleeping Giant –
Killiney House [09]

1 100 mm (4 inch)
concrete screed
capping, trowelled
smooth
2 Damp proof
membrane
3 4 mm (1/6 inch)
Paralon base layer
with 3 mm (1/8 inch)

polyester reinforced
membrane
4 110 mm (4³/8 inch)
insulation
5 Vapour barrier
comprised of 1.2 mm
(1/25 inch) foil and
thermostatic primer
6 50 mm (2 inch)
insulation
7 Top of concrete
screed capping to be
same angle as roof
slab
8 Gutter upstand to be
watertight concrete
9 Roof, gutter edge and
top to be

sandblasted, cleaned
and sealed
10 In-situ reinforced
concrete slab
11 Fair-faced soffit to be
sandblasted, cleaned
and sealed
12 Stainless steel
plaster stop
13 Damp proof course
14 Angle of roof slab
varies
15 Stepped damp proof
course

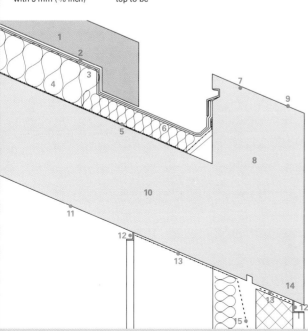

5.019
Roof Edge and Gutter
Detail 1:10

O'Donnell + Tuomey
Architects
The Sleeping Giant –
Killiney House [09]

1 100 mm (4 inch)
concrete screed
capping with
trowelled finish
2 Damp proof
membrane
3 4 mm (1/6 inch)
Paralon base layer
with 3 mm (1/8 inch)

polyester reinforced
membrane
4 110 mm (4³/8 inch)
insulation
5 Vapour barrier from
1.2 mm foil and
thermostatic primer
6 50 mm (2 inch)
insulation
7 Hot dip galvanized
preformed flashing
fixed into groove cast
in concrete
8 Top to be same angle
as roof slab
9 Gutter upstand to be
watertight concrete
10 Roof, gutter edge and

top to be sandblasted
cleaned and sealed
11 Fair-faced soffit to be
sandblasted, cleaned
and sealed
12 Anti capillary groove
in locations of
windows
13 Sealant
14 Transparent sealant
15 Damp proof course
under timber packer
16 Double glazed fixed
window

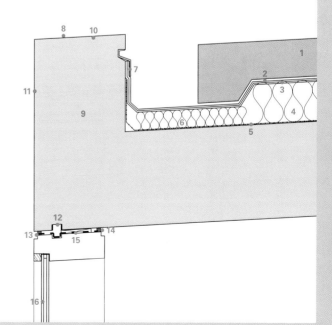

5.020
Roof and Gutter Detail
1:10

Innovarchi
Gold Coast House [12]

1 Zincalume metal
  deck roofing
2 Insulation
3 Stainless steel gutter
4 Zincalume fascia
5 Painted fibre cement
  cladding

6 Ventilation breather
  membrane
7 Pine timber truss
8 Painted plasterboard
  ceiling
9 Fixed full height
  laminated glass
10 Painted steel mullion
11 Painted steel
  structure
12 Painted zincalume
  downpipe

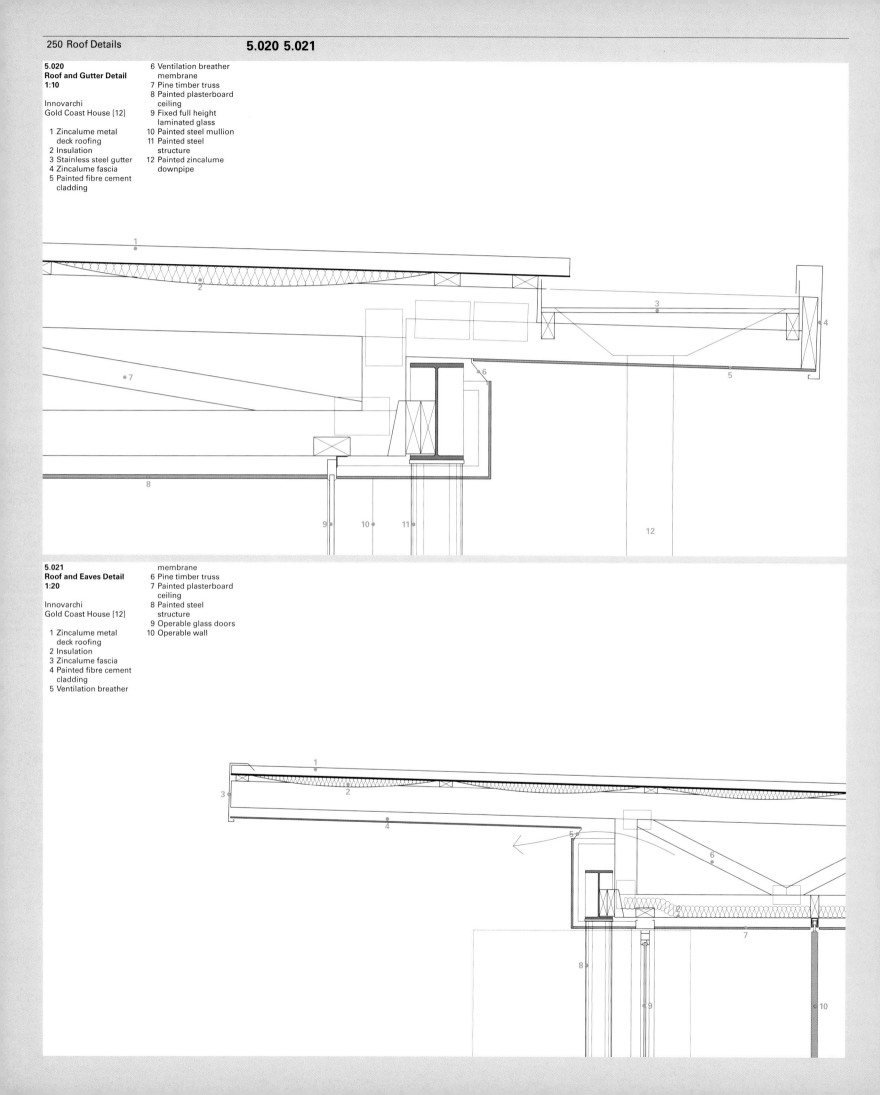

5.021
Roof and Eaves Detail
1:20

Innovarchi
Gold Coast House [12]

1 Zincalume metal
  deck roofing
2 Insulation
3 Zincalume fascia
4 Painted fibre cement
  cladding
5 Ventilation breather

membrane
6 Pine timber truss
7 Painted plasterboard
  ceiling
8 Painted steel
  structure
9 Operable glass doors
10 Operable wall

5.022
Terrace Roof Overhang
Detail 1:10

Kallos Turin
Casa Zorzal [10]

1 Sheet metal
   protection
2 Ballast layer of gravel
3 5 mm (1/5 inch)
   aluminium foil
   waterproof
   membrane
4 Levelling layer
5 Concrete filling to
   form 1:50 slope
6 25 mm (1 inch)
   polystyrene
   insulation
7 Vapour barrier
8 Tarquini integrated
   plaster
9 Waterproof mortar
10 Reinforced concrete
   slab
11 Schuco aluminium
   window
12 15 mm (5/8 inch)
   laminated glass
13 Electric roller blind
   concealed in pocket
14 3 mm (1/8 inch)
   plaster skim coat
   with paint finish

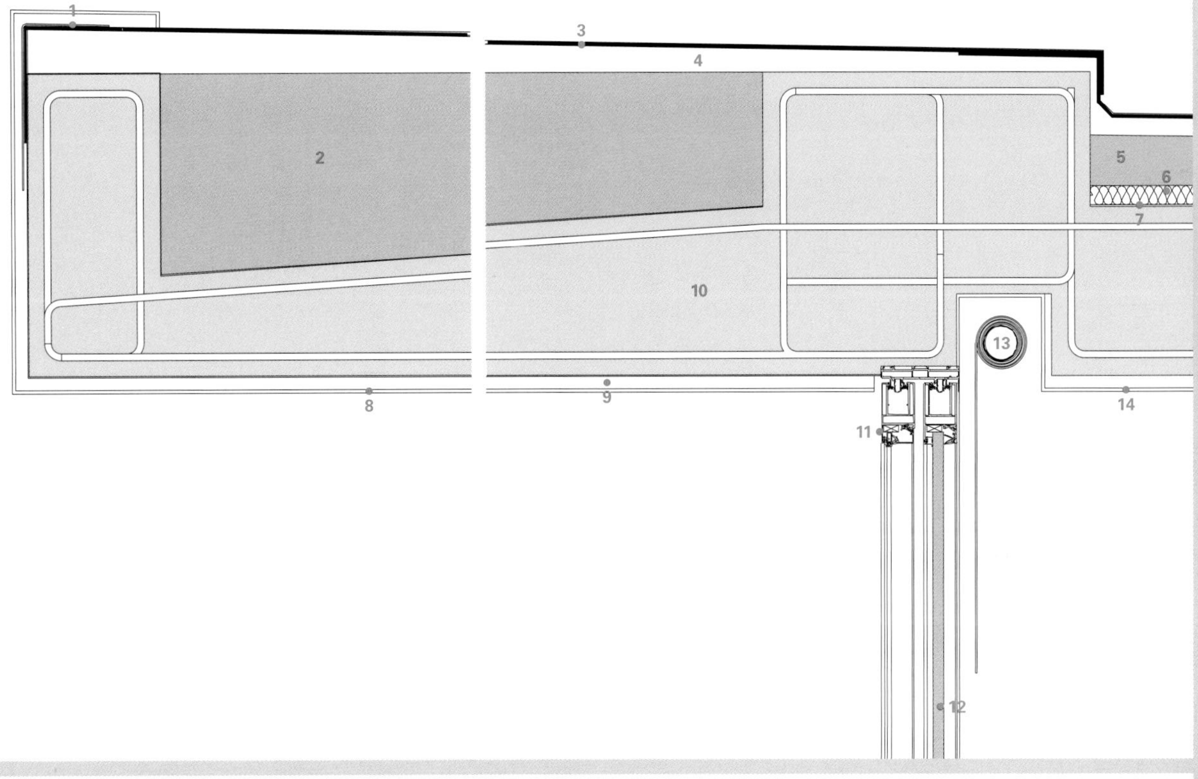

5.023
Roof Parapet Detail 1:5

Kallos Turin
Casa Zorzal [10]

1 Tarquini integrated
   plaster
2 Waterproof mortar
3 Brick wall
4 Cavity
5 25 mm (1 inch)
   polystyrene
   insulation
6 5 mm (1/5 inch)
   aluminium foil
   waterproof
   membrane
7 Levelling layer
8 Concrete filling to
   form 1:50 slope
9 Vapour barrier
10 Reinforced concrete
   slab
11 Cement mortar
12 3 mm (1/8 inch)
   plaster skim coat
   with paint finish

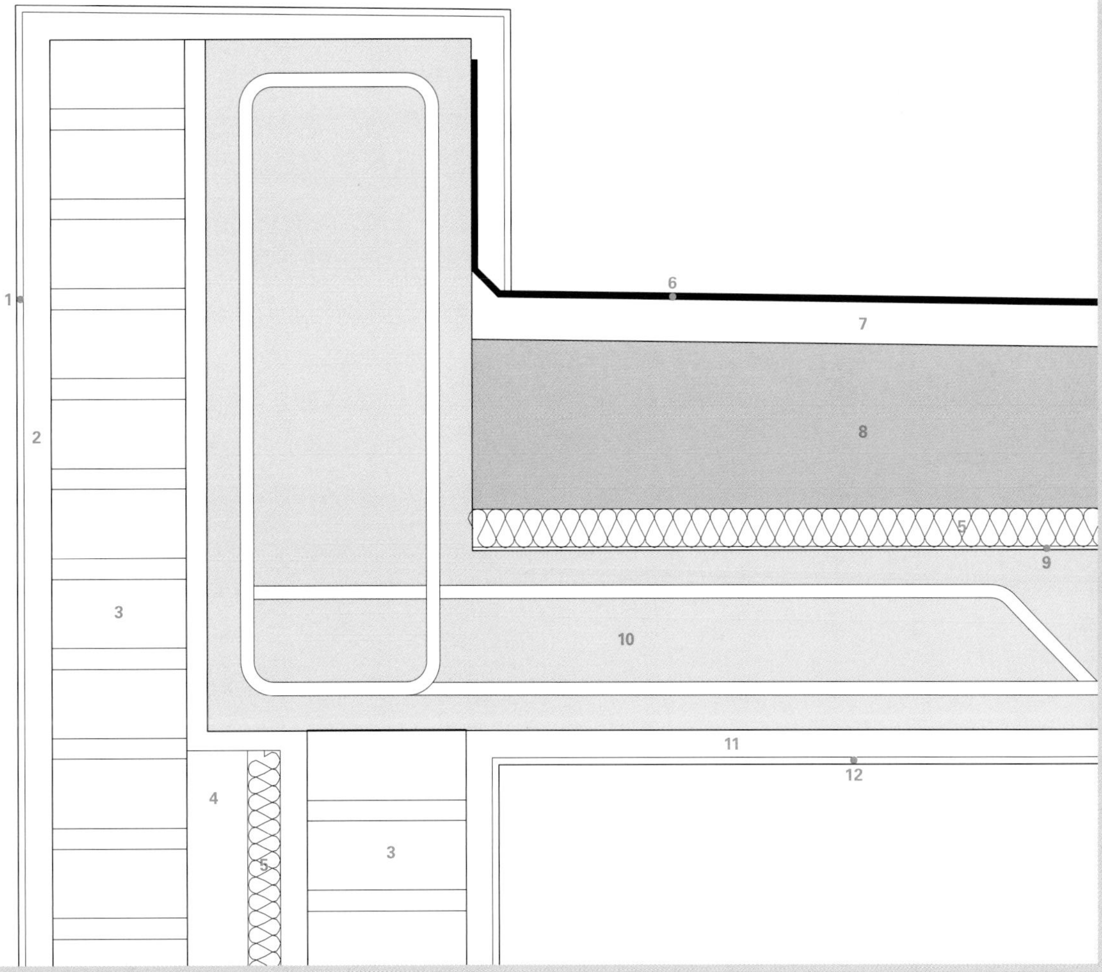

5.024
Roof Detail 1:20

Designworkshop: SA
Igoda View House [24]

1 Face brickwork with vertically brushed bagged finish (no sand added) to internal walls and where indicated on external elevations. Mortar to fully surround brick and be sponged flush with face when laid
2 375 micron stepped damp proof course with grano haunching where required above slab junction
3 230 x 595 mm (9 x 23¾ inch) reinforced concrete beam
4 Gutter formed with 18 mm (¾ inch) shutter board with fillets as necessary and waterproofed with one layer of 4 mm (⅙ inch) Derbigum membrane, fully bonded to primed surface by torch-on fusion, with 75 mm (3 inch) side laps and 100 mm (4 inch) end laps
5 Kliplok aluminium roof sheeting in continuous lengths fixed with aluminium concealed fixing clips with four 63 mm (2½ inch) annular galvanized nails. Stop ends to be formed at the apex and turned down at the eaves to form a drip
6 50 x 50 mm (2 x 2 inch) battens fixed through plywood to rafter below at 1200 mm (48 inch) centre
7 100 x 50 mm (4 x 2 inch) rafters at 400 mm (16 inch) centres
8 50 mm (2 inch) polystyrene insulation fixed between purlins
9 9 mm (⅜ inch) external-grade plywood fixed to rafters to form ceiling
10 1 mm (1/25 inch) mill finish aluminium coping bent to shape and embedded in bituminous compound, laid level and flat with butt joints – no bedding compound to be visible on brick face
11 340 mm (13⅖ inch) cavity wall to be made watertight by bagging and applying seal to outer face of inner skin
12 15 mm (⅗ inch) internal steel trowelled plaster, skimmed with cretestone for ultra smooth finish and primed and painted
13 340 x 170 mm (13⅖ x 6⁷/₁₀ inch) reinforced concrete lintel
14 Double glazing

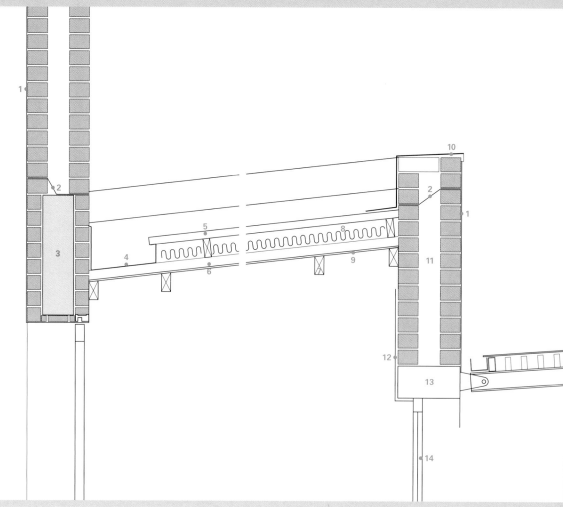

5.025
Steel Canopy Detail 1:20

Designworkshop: SA
Igoda View House [24]

1 Clear polycarbonate Kliplok roofing with minimum 200 mm (8 inch) overlap
2 30 mm (1⅕ inch) isoboard insulation
3 150 x 38 mm (6 x 1½ inch) timber beam
4 Gutter formed with 22 mm (⅞ inch) shutter board on waterproof membrane
5 Aluminium T-section to form coping proofing membrane
6 Face brickwork with vertically brushed bagged finish to internal walls
7 Brick infill between beams with plastered and bagged finish
8 Beam cut 30 mm (1⅕ inch) short for roof conduits
9 120 x 30 mm (4¾ x 1⅕ inch) wall plate
10 230 x 520 mm (9 x 20½ inch) reinforced concrete beam
11 Stainless steel support bracket
12 16 mm (⅝ inch) diameter stainless steel rod support hanger
13 230 x 595 mm (9 x 23⅖ inch) reinforced concrete beam
14 Stainless steel 'tuning fork' support plate built into concrete beam
15 2.5 mm (⅛ inch) continuous aluminium rainwater deflector plate
16 50 x 50 x 6 mm (2 x 2 x ¼ inch) mild steel angle to form glass support at ends
17 150 x 50 x 20 x 2 mm (6 x 2 x ¾ x 1/12 inch) channel with support cleats welded at intervals
18 Toughened plate glass in panels, silicone fixed to aluminium
19 60 x 6 mm (2⅜ x ¼ inch) mild steel flat bar to form top flange of structural T-support
20 6 mm (¼ inch) support cleat butt welded to centre line of main T support
21 30 mm (1⅕ inch) outside diameter stainless steel ferrule welded to support cleat
22 100 x 6 mm (4 x ¼ inch) mild steel flat bar to form web of structural T-support and shaped
23 32 x 50 mm (1¼ x 2 inch) hardwood grounds, rebated one side to conceal web
24 22 x 19 mm (⅞ x ¾ inch) Oregon pine slats at 19 mm (¾ inch) centres
25 60 x 60 x 6 mm (2⅜ x 2⅜ x ¼ inch) flat plate, welded to web to conceal end grain of timber
26 50 x 50 mm (2 x 2 inch) mild steel angle to form glass front end support

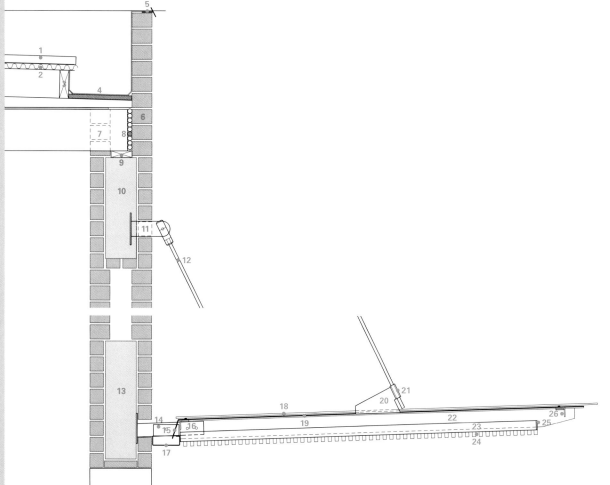

5.026
Roof Eaves and Gutter Detail 1:5

David Nossiter
Architects
Kitsbury Road House
[13]

1 Roof light with 26 mm (1 inch) thick insulating glass unit with a 5 degree fall
2 Roof light glazing
3 Roof light framing
4 12.5 mm (1/2 inch) moisture resistant plasterboard lining
5 18 mm (3/4 inch) weather proof plywood sheathing
6 Vapour barrier
7 Insulation
8 Single ply EPDM (ethylene propylene dieme monomer) roof membrane
9 Treated timber batten
10 Metal edge flashing with formed drip
11 Gutter bracket
12 127 x 102 mm (5 x 4 inch) aluminium gutter
13 152 x 152 mm (6 x 6 inch) steel beam
14 Treated timber blocking
15 10 mm (2/5 inch) steel plate welded to steel beam
16 Silicone sealant
17 Thermally broken aluminium window frame
18 Thermally broken double glazed window
19 Silicone sealant
20 Insulation
21 18 mm (3/4 inch) weatherproof plywood fascia and soffit
22 2 mm (1/12 inch) aluminium flashing to fascia and soffit
23 65 mm (21/2 inch) aluminium rainwater pipe

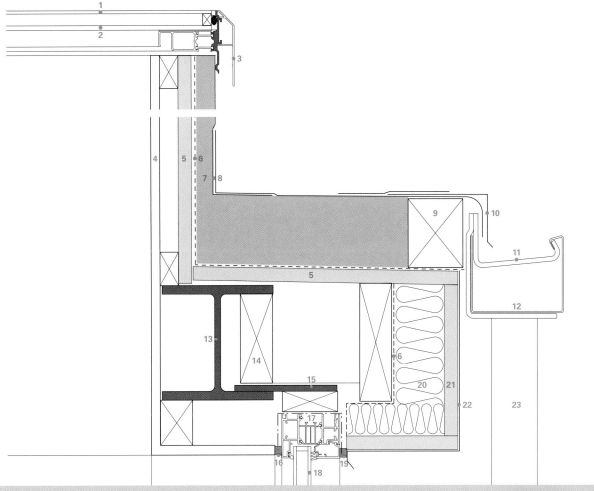

5.027
Roof and Skylight Detail 1:10

David Nossiter
Architects
Kitsbury Road House
[13]

1 EPDM (ethylene propylene dieme monomer) roofing membrane
2 Insulation
3 Vapour barrier
4 18 mm (3/4 inch) weather bonded and proofed plywood decking with staggered joints
5 Timber firrings to form minimum fall of 1:60
6 12.5 mm (1/2 inch) moisture resistant plasterboard lining
7 EPDM (ethylene propylene dieme monomer) roofing membrane
8 Roof light framing
9 Plaster stop bead
10 Roof light with 26 mm (1 inch) insulating glass unit with a 5 degree fall
11 Render to masonry wall
12 Metal flashing with formed drip
13 Metal flashing chased into wall and sealed
14 Treated timber joists
15 Masonry wall
16 Dimmable concealed light fitting
17 100 x 50 mm (4 x 2 inch) timber stud at 400 mm (16 inch) centres
18 Plasterboard with integral vapour barrier
19 60 mm (23/8) acoustic insulation batts

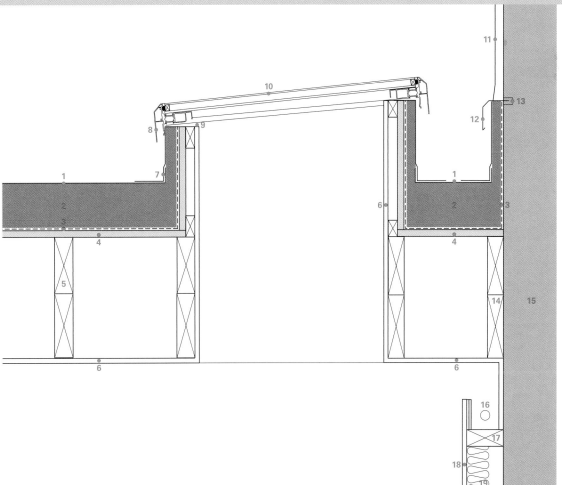

**5.028
Sliding Roof Over
Glasshouse Detail 1:10**

dRMM (de Rijke Marsh
Morgan Architects)
Sliding House [14]

1 Larch rainscreen
  cladding
2 Timber battens
3 Membrane
4 Full-fill insulation
  between timber
  studs
5 Oriented strand
  board sheathing with
  polycarbonate
  cladding
6 Nylon brush air seal
7 Double glazing units
8 Insulated corner
  glazing
9 Thermally broken
  aluminium curtain
  walling transom
10 Double glazing units
11 Closed position
12 Open position

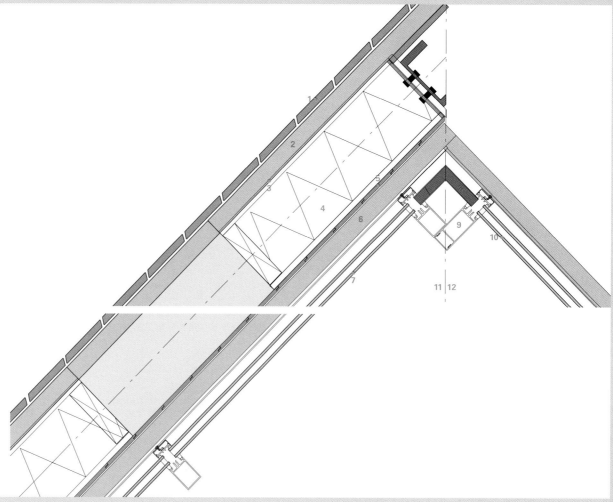

**5.029
Metal Roof Edge Detail
1:5**

The Miller Hull
Partnership
Chuckanut Drive
Residence [31]

1 Pre-finished rake
  flashing
2 Angle cleat fastened
  at 300 mm (12 inch)
  centres
3 Pop rivet and clip
4 Metal roof panels on
  self-adhered
  membrane
5 12 mm (1/2 inch)
  plywood placed with
  good side down and
  finished with clear
  sealant
6 Rigid insulation with
  electric box locations
  for light installation
  above timber decking
7 Exposed sheathing
  with clear sealant
8 Timber blocking
9 150 x 50 mm (6 x 2
  inch) timber stud
  framing with
  insulation infill
10 Exposed rafters
11 25 x 100 mm (1 x 4
  inch) skip sheathing
  with clear sealer
12 12 mm (1/2 inch)
  painted gypsum
  wallboard
13 Fibreglass batt
  insulation

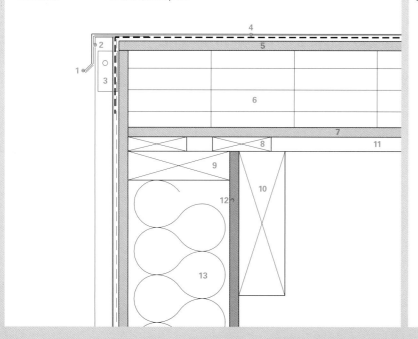

**5.030
Metal Roof Edge Detail
1:5**

The Miller Hull
Partnership
Chuckanut Drive
Residence [31]

1 Pre-finished rake
  flashing
2 Metal roof panels on
  self-adhered
  membrane
3 12 mm (1/2 inch)
  plywood
4 Rigid insulation
5 Angle cleat fastened
  at 300 mm (12 inch)
  centres
6 12 mm (1/2 inch)
  plywood placed
  good side down and
  finished with clear
  sealant
7 Exposed sheathing
  with clear sealant
8 25 x 100 mm (1 x 4
  inch) skip sheathing
  with clear sealant
9 Exposed rafters
10 16 gauge 187 x 90
  mm (7 3/8 x 3 1/2 inch)
  stainless steel end
  caps

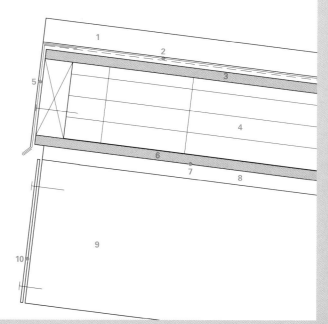

5.031
Roof Section Detail 1:10

Marsh Cashman
Koolloos Architects
Maroubra House [36]

1 Plasterboard lined
  handrail with paint
  finish
2 Aluminium framed
  fixed glazing
3 Timber sill to match
  cladding
4 Timber cladding
5 Selected medium
  density sheet
  cladding
6 Timber flooring
7 Insulation
8 Timber rafters
9 Timber beam
10 Timber battens
11 Insulation
12 25 mm (1 inch) thick
  Styrofoam insulation
13 Existing roof
  construction to be
  reused
14 New carbon fibre
  composite lining to
  existing eaves with
  paint finish
15 Continuous 10 x 10
  mm (3/8 x 3/8 inch)
  aluminium angle,
  flush with ceiling to
  form drip groove

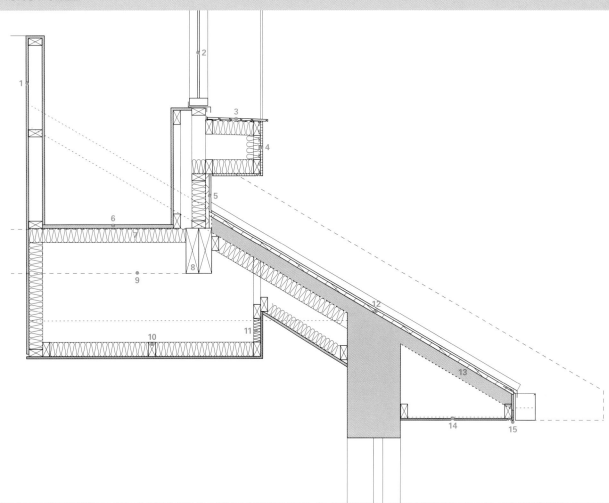

5.032
Roof Detail 1:5

Jun Aoki & Associates
J House [24]

1 2 mm (1/12 inch)
  aluminium coping
  screw fixed to firring
2 Waterproof
  membrane
3 Waterproof seal
4 6 mm (1/4 inch)
  calcium silicate
  board
5 Laminated timber
  framing
6 4 mm (1/6 inch)

waterproof fibre
reinforced plastic
cladding
7 6 mm (1/4 inch)
  calcium silicate
  board roofing
8 9 mm (3/8 inch) roof
  boards
9 12 mm (1/2 inch)
  structural plywood
  on vapour-proof
  sheet
10 Roof drain outlet
  with protective
  weather hood
11 6 mm (1/4 inch)
  calcium silicate
  board

12 100 mm (4 inch)
  glasswool insulation
13 180 x 40 mm (71/8 x
  15/8 inch) timber joist
14 Void
15 90 x 40 mm (31/2 x
  15/8 inch) timber
  bearer
16 60 mm (23/8 inch)
  PVC rainwater
  downpipe
17 12 mm (1/2 inch)
  structural plywood
18 Mortar finished and
  lysine sprayed
  cladding

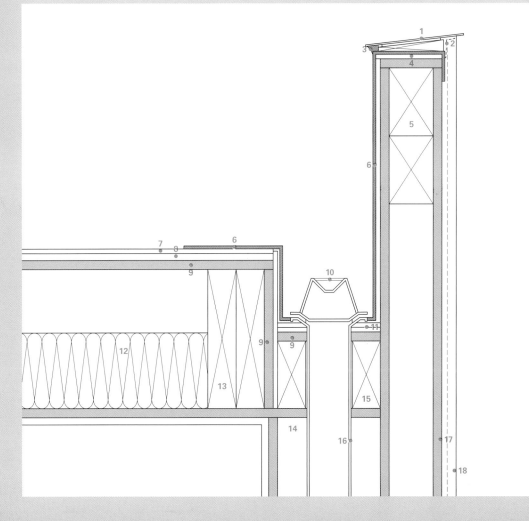

5.033
Roof Terrace Detail 1:10

Cassion Castle
Architects
Twofold House [12]

1 Hardwood timber decking cladding to all terrace surfaces
2 4 mm (3/16 inch) aluminium sheet capping
3 50 x 50 mm (2 x 2 inch) anodized aluminium angle
4 29 mm (11/8 inch) double glazed unit comprised of 6 mm (1/4 inch) Pilkington-K glass, 16 mm (5/8 inch) air space and 6 mm (1/4 inch) Georgian wired glass
5 18 mm (3/4 inch) waterproof ply
6 Ventilation doors open full width of terrace
7 Glass fibre rainwater tray
8 150 mm (6 inch) mineral wool insulation
9 15 mm (5/8 inch) Fireline plasterboard with 3 mm (1/8 inch) plaster skim coat
10 Roller solar shade
11 150 x 150 mm (6 x 6 inch) rolled steel joist
12 12 mm (1/2 inch) glazing security tape
13 50 x 50 mm (2 x 2 inch) anodized aluminium T-section

5.034
Roof Ridge Detail 1:5

Atelier Tekuto +
Masahiro Ikeda
Lucky Drops [13]

1 Galvanized, coloured steel sheet capping to roof
2 Backer rod and sealant
3 3 mm (1/8 inch) fibre-reinforced plastic plain board external sheeting
4 28 x 28 mm (11/8 x 11/8 inch) steel hollow square section with anti-corrosive finish
5 50 x 30 mm (2 x 11/5 inch) steel hollow rectangular section structure
6 100 x 36 mm (4 x 11/2 inch) square hollow section steel tube with insulation paint finish

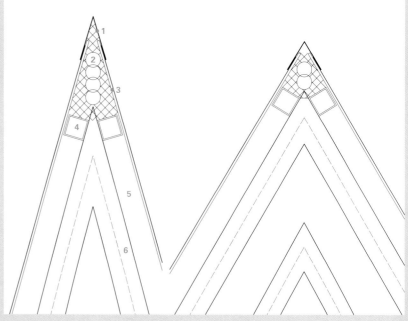

5.035
Flat Roof Detail 1:20

Keith Williams Architects
The Long House [23]

1 Aluminium parapet coping with secret fixing
2 100 mm (4 inch) self-coloured external insulated render system
3 Fixing angle for mastic asphalt roof covering
4 Pre-cast concrete paving slabs
5 Adjustable supports for paving slabs
6 100 mm (4 inch) styrofoam insulation system
7 Two coat polymer-modified asphalt roof covering
8 Screed laid to fall of 1:60 minimum along diagonal valleys
9 200 mm (8 inch) reinforced concrete slab
10 Reinforcing coat on mesh, skim coated and painted with two coats to smooth surface
11 Double glazed window unit
12 Natural white plastered blockwork
13 Ceiling lining with white natural plaster finish

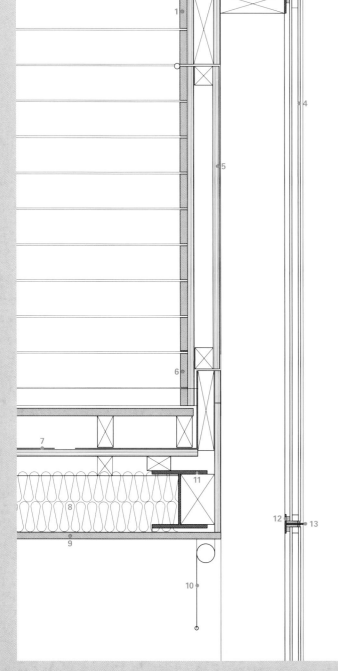

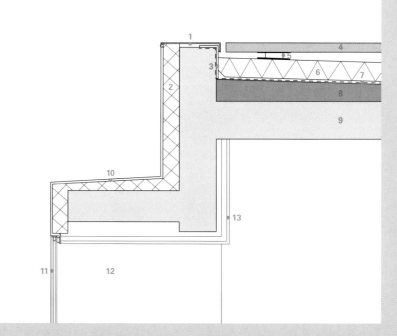

5.036
Roof and Skylight
Detail 1:10

Tham & Videgård
Arkitekter
Archipelago House [40]

1 Steel skylight
  structure
2 Glass plate
3 L-shaped steel profile
  glazing angle
4 Bolt to fix steel
  flange to concrete
5 Roofing membrane
6 Insulation
7 Reinforced concrete

8 Screed
9 Accentuated seal
  between roof and
  wall structures
10 Architectonic
   reinforced concrete
   wall

5.037
Awning Roof Detail 1:10

Thaler Thaler Architekten
Z House [40]

1 8 mm (1/3 inch) fibre
  cement sheeting
2 40 mm (13/5 inch)
  mineral wool
  insulation
3 140 mm (51/2 inch)
  thermal insulation
4 12.5 mm (1/2 inch)
  plasterboard on 40 x
  60 mm (13/5 x 23/8
  inch) timber battens
5 16 mm (2/3 inch)

oriented strand
board with vapour
barrier
6 Timber frame
7 Shadow line at base
  of plasterboard wall
  lining
8 13 mm (1/2 inch) oak
  parquet flooring
9 70 mm (23/4 inch)
  floated cement
  screed
10 Soft impact sound
   insulation
11 16 mm (2/3 inch)
   oriented strand
   board with vapour
   barrier

12 Laminated timber
   beam
13 Flashing
14 Waterproofing layer
15 Timber framing
16 8 mm (1/3 inch) fibre
   cement sheeting
17 8 mm (1/3 inch) fibre
   cement sheet soffit
   lining
18 Lighting fixture
19 Vapour barrier
20 12.5 mm (1/2 inch)
   plasterboard on open
   boarding
21 16 mm (2/3 inch)
   laminated timber to
   entrance door

22 Thermal insulation
   with vapour barrier
23 8 mm (1/3 inch) fibre
   cement sheeting

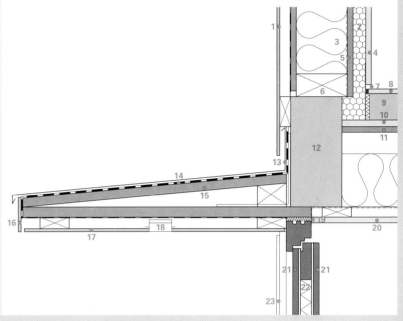

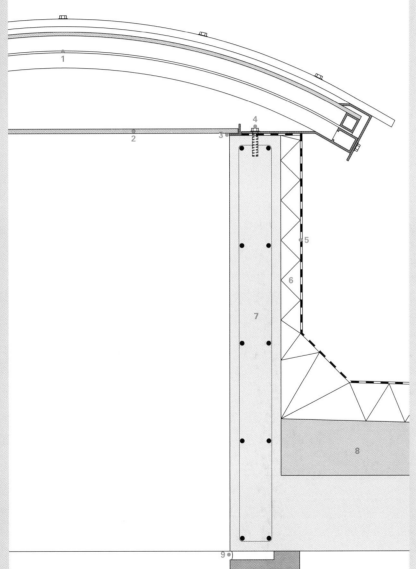

5.038
Roof Detail 1:10

Thaler Thaler Architekten
Z House [40]

1 Sheet aluminium
  covering
2 30 x 80 mm (11/5 x
  31/8 inch) timber
  battens
3 8 mm (1/3 inch) fibre
  cement sheeting
4 Sealant
5 Softwood door frame
  with paint finish
6 Softwood door frame
  with paint finish

7 Double glazed unit
8 50 mm (2 inch) gravel
  layer
9 Sealing layer
10 19 mm (3/4 inch)
   oriented strand
   board
11 50 mm (2 inch)
   ventilated cavity
12 16 mm (2/3 inch)
   oriented strand
   board
13 140 mm (51/2 inch)
   thermal insulation
   with vapour barrier
14 12.5 mm (1/2 inch)
   plasterboard on open
   boarding

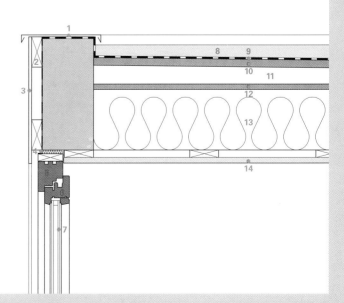

5.039
Steel and Concrete Roof Structure Section Detail 1:50

Ensamble Studio
Hemeroscopium House
[07]

1 2400 x 2400 x 1200 mm (94¹/₂ x 94¹/₂ x 47¹/₄ inch) granite block with hollows and drill holes for iron bars and connections
2 Pre-drilled holes for steel connection plate
3 Hollow section for steel connection plate
4 Pre-cast concrete beam

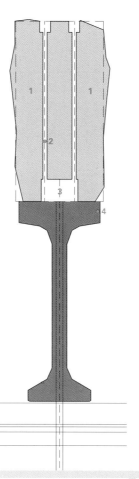

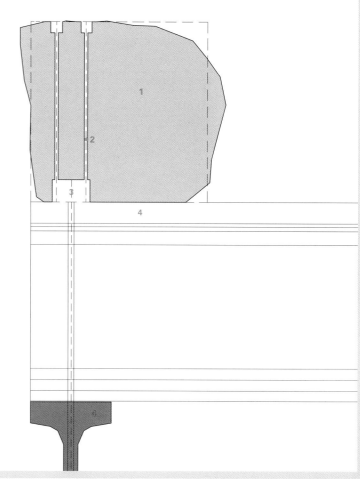

5.040
Steel and Concrete Roof Structure Plan Detail 1:50

Ensamble Studio
Hemeroscopium House
[07]

1 2400 x 2400 x 1200 mm (94¹/₂ x 94¹/₂ x 47¹/₄ inch) granite block with hollows and drill holes for iron bars and connections
2 Pre-drilled holes for steel connection plate
3 Steel connection plate
4 Pre-cast concrete beam

5.041
Roof Detail at Carport 1:10

Ibarra Rosano Design Architects
Winter Residence [23]

1 3 ply built-up roofing
2 Plywood sheathing
3 Flashing
4 50 x 200 x 5 mm (2 x 8 x ³/₁₆ inch) tubular steel section
5 12.5 mm (¹/₂ inch) weld plate
6 Steel fascia with drip edge extended 12.5 mm (¹/₂ inch) beyond bottom of gypsum wall board
7 Two 200 x 12.5 mm (8 x ¹/₂ inch) diameter anchor bolts
8 Solid grout CMU (concrete modular unit) bond beam
9 Two continuous reinforcing bars
10 Fry Reglet reveal
11 18 mm (⁵/₈ inch) gypsum wall board
12 'Hat' channels at 400 mm (16 inch) centres
13 200 mm (8 inch) CMU (concrete modular unit) wall with truss type horizontal reinforcing at 400 mm (16 inch) centres and bond beam at 1200 mm (47¹/₄ inch) centres
14 Stucco finish

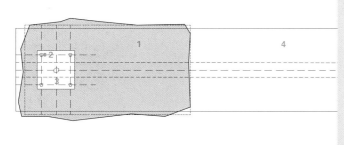

5.042
Roof Detail at Children's Wing 1:10

Ibarra Rosano Design Architects
Winter Residence [23]

1 Three ply built-up roof
2 Plywood sheathing
3 Flashing
4 Steel fascia with drip edge
5 12.5 mm (1/2 inch) plywood spacer/ nailer
6 Fry Reglet reveal
7 12.5 mm (1/2 inch) gypsum wall board
8 50 x 200 mm (2 x 8 inch) joist at 400 mm (16 inch) centres
9 Channel glass header frame
10 Channel glass
11 Batt insulation
12 12.5 mm (1/2 inch) aluminium soffit

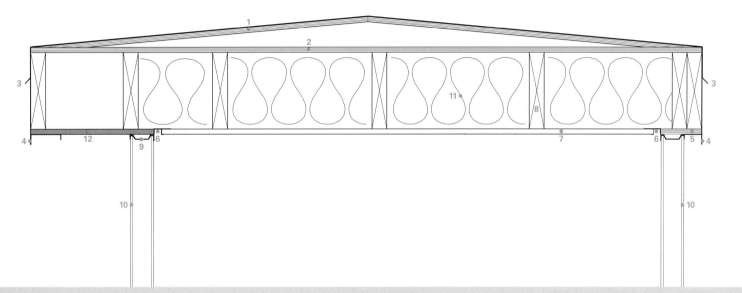

5.043
Roof and External Wall Detail 1:5

Kengo Kuma & Associates
Steel House [27]

1 Waterproof urethane roofing membrane
2 Mortar bed
3 3 mm (1/8 inch) hot dip galvanized vertical steel plate structure seen in elevation
4 50 mm (2 inch) thick hard urethane foam insulation
5 12 mm (1/2 inch) plywood
6 Steel joist
7 Timber battens
8 1.5 mm (1/16 inch) hot dip galvanized steel plate with insulating coating
9 35 mm (1/8 inch) hot dip galvanized steel plate roof structure
10 40 x 40 mm (1 5/8 x 1 5/8 inch) steel L-angle
11 75 x 75 mm (3 x 3 inch) steel angle
12 16 mm (2/3 inch) steel plate
13 20 mm (3/4 inch) hard urethane spray foam insulation
14 40 mm (1 5/8 inch) hollow polycarbonate sheeting to form Takiron 'Lume' wall system

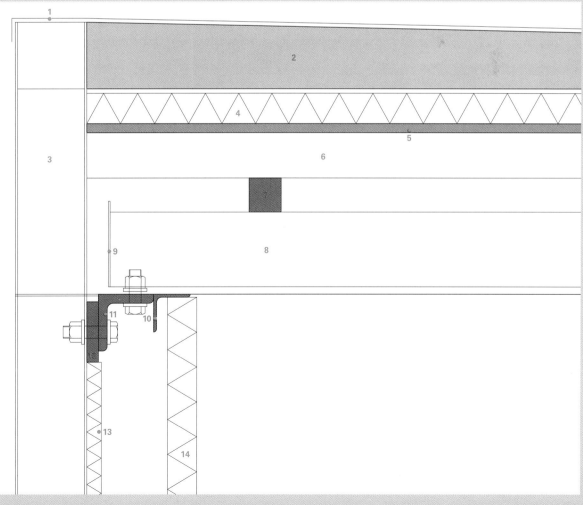

**5.044
Pool Room Roof Detail
1:20**

Keith Williams Architects
The Long House [23]

1 Clear laminated glass floor unit, double glazed with 16 mm (5/8 inch) air gap
2 20 mm (3/4 inch) limestone cladding supported on metal structure with mastic joints coloured to match stone
3 75 mm (3 inch) extruded polystyrene insulation adhered to reinforced concrete upstand
4 Waterproofing to upstand to overlap with mastic asphalt upstand
5 Reinforced concrete upstand
6 100 mm (4 inch) styrofoam insulation system
7 600 x 600 mm (24 x 24 inch) x 40 mm (15/8 inch) thick Batieg blue limestone paving slabs with 10 mm (3/8 inch) nominal gap
8 Two coat polymer-modified asphalt roof covering
9 Adjustable plastic supports for stone floor
10 Powder-coated double glazed aluminium sliding unit
11 20 mm (3/4 inch) oiled solid timber strip flooring, bonded to sand and cement screed with wood flooring adhesive
12 Grille for air handling

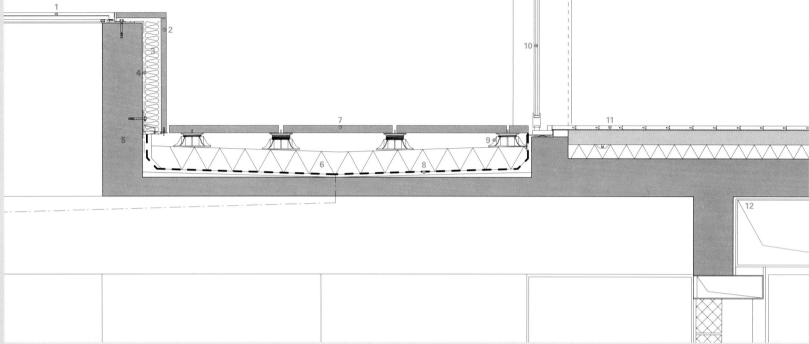

**5.045
Roof and Gutter Detail
1:20**

Lee + Mundwiler Architects
The Coconut House [12]

1 Formed ridge vent of 24 gauge galvanized steel screen opening
2 Timber ridge beam
3 Curb beyond
4 Line of 200 x 200 mm (8 x 8 inch) steel post
5 12.5 mm (1/2 inch) plywood sheathing
6 Building paper on roofing felt
7 Batt insulation
8 12.5 mm (1/2 inch) plywood sheathing
9 24 gauge galvanized steel roof and standing seam on building paper and roofing felt
10 Continuous timber blocking to support guttering
11 Timber rafters
12 15 mm (5/8 inch) drywall ceiling
13 Dotted line indicates 100 x 50 mm (4 x 2 inch) beam
14 Timber blocking between roof rafters
15 24 gauge galvanized steel continuous gutter connected to downspouts
16 100 mm (4 inch) overhang to form drip
17 Phenolic resin wood veneer panels
18 Timber top plate
19 12.5 mm (1/2 inch) plywood sheathing
20 Air space

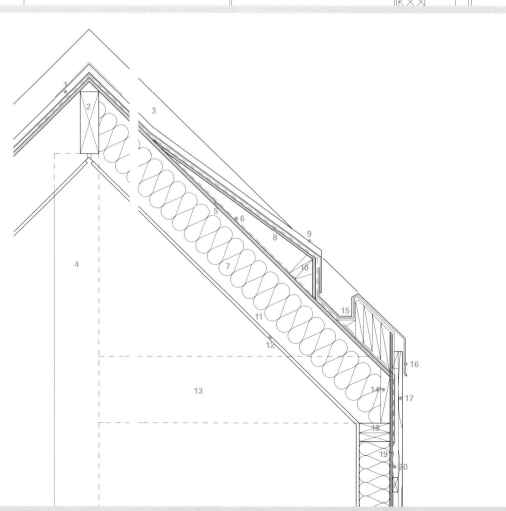

5.046
Roof and Skylight Detail
1:20

Matharoo Associates
Dilip Sanghvi Residence
[07]

1 PCS silicone skylight
bubble in 2mm ($^1/_{12}$
inch) sheet fitted to
concrete curbing
using brass screws
with neoprene
padding in between
2 Concrete curb
3 25 mm (1 inch) china
mosaic tiled roof
surface
4 Cement bed
5 250 mm ($9^4/_5$ inch)
thick vermiculite
6 250 mm ($9^4/_5$ inch)
ply finish reinforced
concrete slab with
bottom exposed and
top treated with a
layer of acrylic vinyl
7 Grating made from
10 mm ($^3/_8$ inch) mild
steel flats with 25
micron hard-
galvanized iron finish

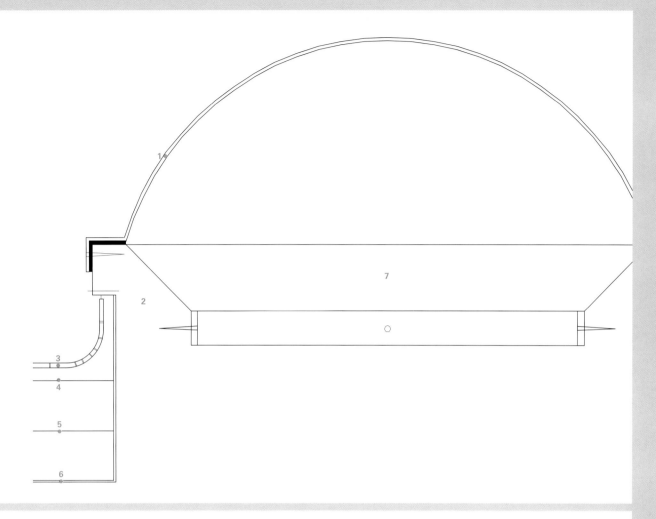

5.047
Roof Drainage Detail
1:20

Morphogenesis
N85 Residence [08]

1 Pre-cast concrete
coping
2 300 mm ($11^4/_5$ inch)
brick parapet
3 20 mm ($^3/_4$ inch) thick
external finish
4 450 x 450 mm (18 x
18 inch) Khurra
waterproofing
5 Brick batt insulation
with waterproofing
6 75 mm (3 inch) thick
insulation
7 Waterproofing coat
with cement plaster
over structural slab
8 Reinforced concrete
slab
9 PVC rainwater pipe

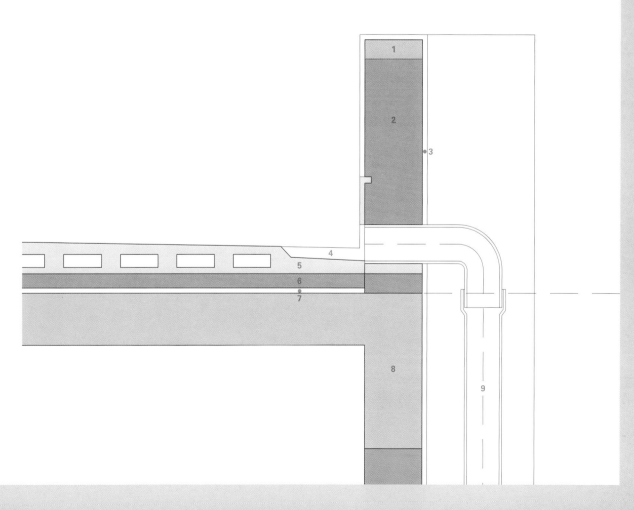

5.048
Garage Glass Roof
Detail 1:10

Peter L. Gluck and
Partners, Architects
Inverted Guest House
[26]

1 Insulated glass roof
   light
2 Structural silicone to
   aluminium angle
3 100 x 37 x 3 mm (4 x
   1 1/2 x 1/8 inch)
   aluminium angle
4 12 mm (1/2 inch)
   caulk joint
5 Fabric flashing
   lapping over channel
   to create
   condensation pan
6 Membrane flashing
   to form continuous
   seal
7 25 mm (1 inch) rigid
   insulation
8 Upstand from 25 mm
   (1 inch) rigid
   insulation and 12
   mm (1/2 inch) board
9 50 x 75 mm (2 x 3
   inch) aluminium
   channel
10 50 x 150 mm (2 x 6

inch) timber blocking
11 50 x 150 mm (2 x 6
   inch) timber blocking
12 20 mm (3/4 inch)
   plywood fastened to
   joint chords and
   upstand
13 Single ply EPDM
   (ethylene propylene
   dieme monomer)
   roof membrane
14 Continuous timber
   fillet
15 20 mm (3/4 inch)
   plywood finish hung
   on cleats
16 Batt insulation
17 Timber cleat to
   accept pre-
   assembled and
   pre-finished plywood
   frame
18 Plywood trim
   installed before
   skylight box
19 50 x 200 mm (2 x 8
   inch) timber framing
   between bar joists at
   skylight locations
   only
20 Bar joist beyond
21 Cedar planking
22 Continuous 50 x 100
   mm (2 x 4 inch)
   timber blocking

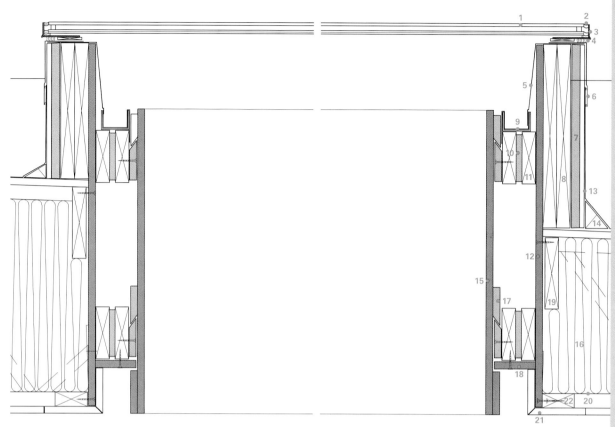

5.049
Roof and Gutter Detail
1:12.5

Simon Walker Architects
Dane House [06]

1 Standard Roadstone
   natural colour flat
   concrete roof tile
   with dyeing agents
   removed
2 35 x 25 mm (1 1/3 x 1
   inch) tanalised
   timber roofing
   counter battens
3 35 x 25 mm (1 1/3 x 1
   inch) tanalised
   timber roofing
   battens
4 Torch-on Paralon felt
   on 18 mm (7/10 inch)
   waterproof plywood
   roof deck
5 Ventilation space
6 Fibreglass quilt
   insulation
7 Treated timber roof
   joists shot-fixed to
   steel frame
8 Skim finish ceiling on
   12.5 mm (1/2 inch)
   plasterboard
9 White paint finish to
   350 x 175 x 46 mm

(13 3/4 x 6 4/5 x 1 4/5
inch) steel roof beam
with lower half left
exposed to room
10 Formed concrete
   aqueduct with lead
   lining to act as casing
   to 300 x 300 x 10 mm
   (11 4/5 x 11 4/5 x 2/5
   inch) universal angle
11 300 x 300 x 10 mm
   (11 4/5 x 11 4/5 x 2/5
   inch) universal angle
   from which to
   suspend sliding door
   gear
12 18 mm (7/10 inch)
   solid iroko housing
   to sliding track
13 Solid iroko guide
   track to sliding doors
14 Sliding door gear
   and track
15 Solid iroko sliding
   door unit
16 Laminated double
   glazed unit
   comprised of 8.4 mm
   (1/3 inch) glass, 12
   mm (1/2 inch) air gap
   and 8.4 mm (1/3 inch)
   glass

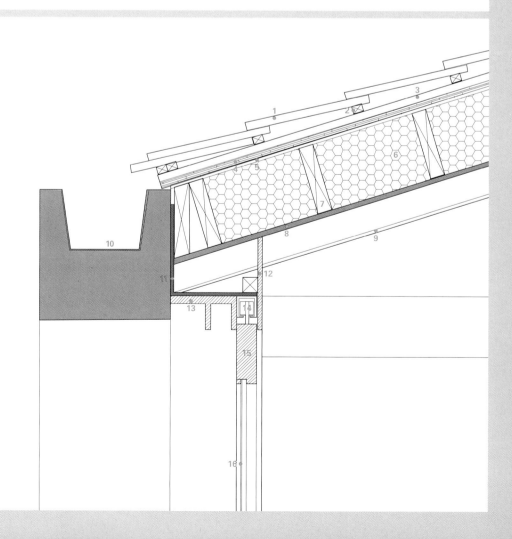

5.050
Roof Detail 1:10

Tham & Videgård
Arkitekter
Archipelago House [40]

1 Steel sheet gutter and covering
2 Waterproofing layer
3 22 x 120 mm (7/8 x 43/4 inch) pressure impregnated timber boards
4 Air cavity
5 45 x 220 mm (13/4 x 85/8 inch) black tinova beam with insulation between
6 90 x 270 mm (31/2 x 105/8 inch) laminated, brushed, black tinova beam
7 20 x 160 mm (3/4 x 61/4 inch) dovetailed timber boarding
8 45 x 220 mm (13/4 x 85/8 inch) timber beam
9 70 x 70 mm (23/4 x 23/4 inch) timber battens
10 90 x 205 mm (31/2 x 8 inch) window frame
11 Vapour barrier

12 23 x 95 mm (9/10 x 33/4 inch) dovetailed timber boards
13 Silent Gliss continuous curtain rail
14 Double glazing comprised of 6 mm (1/4 inch) glass, 15 mm (5/8 inch) air space and 6 mm (1/4 inch) glass

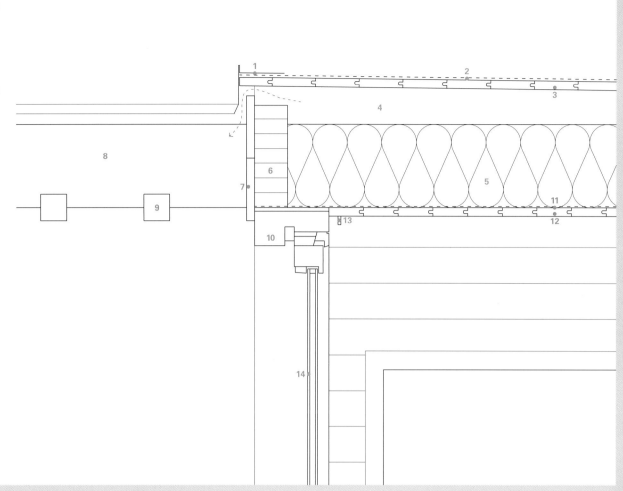

5.051
Roof Overhang Detail 1:10

Saunders Architecture
Villa Storingavika [40]

1 Black metal flashing
2 Timber blocking to create inward fall to top of parapet
3 Spruce overlap cladding, stained black

4 50 x 50 mm (2 x 2 inch) vertical battens
5 25 mm (1 inch) plywood as edge board
6 50 x 150 mm (2 x 6 inch) timber blocking
7 Waterproof membrane
8 Timber firring to create inward fall to roof
9 Timber strips, stained black to soffit

10 50 x 50 mm (2 x 2 inch) horizontal battens
11 13 mm (1/2 inch) waterproof gyprock boarding
12 Metal angle profile
13 Two 50 x 150 mm (2 x 6 inch) timber blocking to form top sill
14 9 mm (1/3 inch) gyprock boarding
15 250–350 mm

(94/5–133/4 inch) thick insulation
16 Structural roof decking
17 9 mm (1/3 inch) gyprock boarding

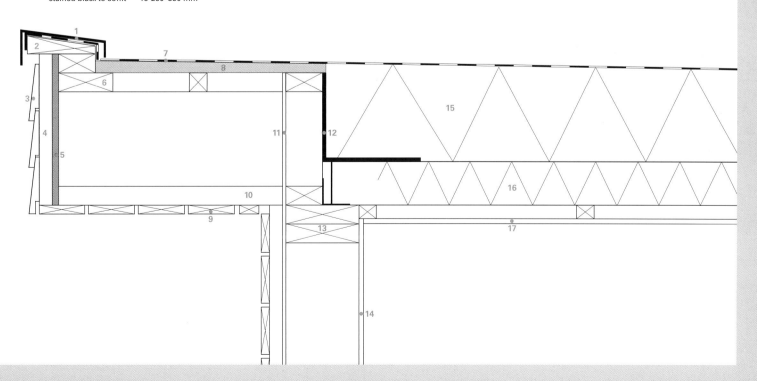

5.052
Glass Ceiling Detail 1:5

Go Hasegawa &
Associates
Forest House [34]

1 9 mm (3/8 inch)
 plasterboard to attic
 space ceiling with
 urethane paint finish
2 45 x 30 mm (13/4 x
 11/5 inch) firring
 strips
3 75 x 75 mm (3 x 3
 inch) knee brace at
 1820 mm (72 inch)
 centres with
 urethane paint finish
4 9 mm (3/8 inch)
 plywood ceiling with
 oil stain clear lacquer
 finish
5 3 mm + 3 mm (1/8 +
 1/8 inch) float glass
 ceiling
6 90 x 90 mm (31/2 x
 31/2 inch) beam with
urethane paint finish
7 12 mm (1/2 inch)
 structural plywood
 and 5.5 mm (1/4 inch)
 plywood with oil
 stain clear lacquer
 finish
8 Spruce window
 frame with oil stain
 clear lacquer

5.054
Roof Parapet Detail 1:10

Studio d'ARC Architects
Live / Work Studio II [19]

1 Galvalume cap
 flashing
2 Sealant with backer
 rod
3 Neighbouring
 structure
4 Solid 200 mm (8
 inch) concrete
 masonry unit
5 200 mm (8 inch)
 concrete masonry
 unit
6 Sealant
7 Aluminium counter
 flashing
8 Sedum soil mix
9 Green roof
 hemp-lined tray
10 Heavy duty
 geotextile fabric
11 Roofing system layer
12 75 mm (3 inch)
 sloped rigid
 insulation
13 20 mm (3/4 inch)
 exterior-grade
 plywood sheathing
14 50 x 250 mm (2 x 10
 inch) timber rim joist
15 20 mm (3/4 inch) Hilti
 bolt anchors at 600
 mm (24 inch) centres
16 Continuous grouted
 bond beam
17 Joist hanger
18 Plywood shim each
 side of joist
19 350 mm (14 inch)
 truss joist at 600 mm
 (24 inch) centres with
 batt insulation
20 15 mm (5/8 inch)
 gypsum board
21 Aluminium reglet

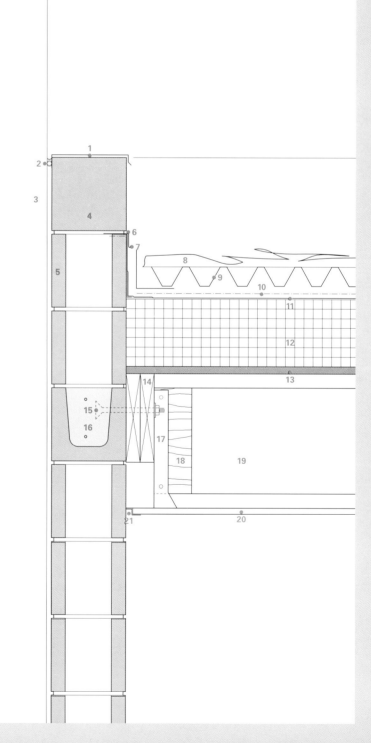

5.053
**Roof and Skylight Detail
1:5**

Jun Aoki & Associates
J House [24]

1 150 x 160 x 30 mm (6
 x 61/4 x 11/5 inch) red
 cedar deck treated
 with wood
 preservative
2 Cedar bearer
3 50 x 50 x 3 mm (2 x 2
x 1/8 inch) aluminium
 angle
4 Weatherproof mastic
 seal
5 8 mm (3/8 inch)
 tempered glass with
 shatter-proof film
6 Aluminium channel
 to take reinforced
 plastic
7 Seal
8 4 mm (1/6 inch)
 waterproof fibre
 reinforced plastic,
painted white
9 9 mm (3/8 inch) roof
 boards
10 Timber joists
11 24 mm (1 inch)
 plywood
12 8 mm (1/3 inch
 calcium silicate
 board, with acrylic
 emulsion white paint
 finish

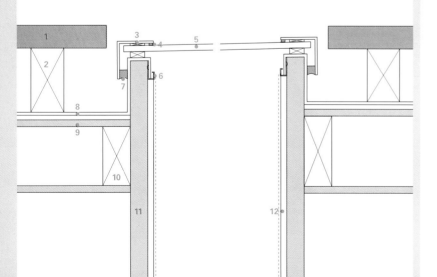

5.055
Box Gutter Detail 1:10

Troppo Architects
Buttfield Town House
[30]

1 120 x 45 mm (4³/4 x
  1³/4 inch) purlins,
  hanger-fixed to
  rafters
2 150 x 45 mm (6 x 1³/4
  inch) laminated
  veneer lumber
3 Galvanized
  perforated closing
4 Galvanized ridge
  flashing
5 150 x 50 mm (6 x 2
  inch) rectangular
  hollow section ridge
  beam
6 170 x 42 mm (6³/4 x
  1³/4 inch) hardwood
  handrail
7 Strut at 1200 mm (48
  inch) maximum

centres
8 Roller blind
9 Cleats fixed either
  side of beam by two
  M12 bolts
10 Insulation
11 Anodized aluminium
  window frame
12 Sub-sill to match
  aluminium frame
13 Hardwood decking
14 150 x 42 mm (6 x 1³/4
  inch) hardwood joist
  at maximum 450 mm
  (18 inch) centres
15 90 x 42 mm (3¹/2 x
  1³/4 inch) wallplate
  fixed to wall at 450
  mm (18 inch) centres
16 Galvanized flashing
17 12.5 mm (¹/2 inch)
  painted plasterboard
  interior wall lining
18 Galvanized box
  gutter on 12 mm (¹/2
  inch) marine-ply
  board

19 90 x 45 mm (3¹/2 x
  1³/4 inch) ladder
  frame at 450 mm (18
  inch) centres
20 45 x 45 mm (1³/4 x
  1³/4 inch) ladder
  frame at 450 mm (18
  inch) centres
21 Zincalume Miniorb
  U-trim
22 150 x 150 mm (6 x 6
  inch) rectangular
  hollow section rafter
23 Cleats fixed either
  side of rafter by two
  M12 bolts
24 230 x 75 mm (9 x 3
  mm (18 inch) centres
  channel beam
25 Plasterboard stop
  bead

5.056
**Roof and Gutter Detail
1:10**

Chenchow Little
Architects
Freshwater House [32]

1 Sheet metal roofing
  with seam upstand
2 Flashing
3 Plywood to form
  gutter structure
4 Timber packing
5 Insulation
6 Vapour barrier
7 150 x 50 mm (6 x 2
  inch) timber purlins

at 600 mm (23²/3
inch) centres
8 180 mm (7¹/10 inch)
  steel parallel flange
  channel
9 Suspended
  plasterboard ceiling
  system, paint
  finished
10 Gutter
11 Compressed fibre
  cement sheeting
12 Timber packing
13 50 mm (2 inch)
  insulation
14 Timber packing

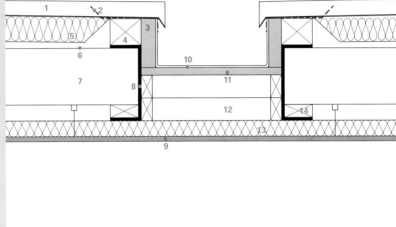

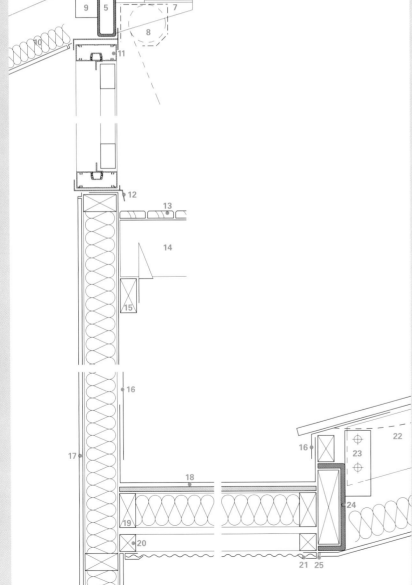

5.057
**Roof Overhang Detail
1:10**

Peter Stutchbury
Architecture
Avalon House [29]

1 0.48 mm (¹/36 inch)
  Colorbond roof
  sheeting
2 Sarking under roof
  sheeting
3 200 x 75 mm (8 x 3
  inch) galvanized steel
  channel
4 200 mm (8 inch)
  galvanized universal
  beam
5 10 mm (²/5 inch)
  galvanized steel cleat
  welded to roof beam
6 Polyester wool
  insulation
7 40 x 5 mm (1⁵/8 x ¹/5
  inch) galvanized steel
  glazing bar welded to
  underside of channel
8 9 mm (³/8 inch)
  plywood ceiling
  panels fixed to firring
  channels at spacing
  to suit panel size
9 150 x 100 x 5 mm (6 x
  4 x ¹/5 inch)
  galvanized
  rectangular hollow
  section steel column
10 40 x 5 mm (1⁵/8 x ¹/5
  inch) galvanized steel
  glazing bar welded to
  side of column
11 Awning window
  constructed from 40
  x 40 x 5 mm (1⁵/8 x
  1⁵/8 x ¹/5 inch)
  galvanized steel
  angle frame with
  clear glazed infill
12 40 x 5 mm (1⁵/8 x ¹/5
  inch) galvanized steel
  glazing bar welded to

topside of window
sill
13 Rondo shadowline
14 125 x 75 x 6 mm (5 x
  3 x ¹/4 inch)
  galvanized steel
  angle window sill
15 Sarking behind
  cladding shown
  dotted
16 Galvanized steel flat
  sheet cladding on
  timber studs with
  overlap of 150 mm (6
  inch) with joints
  sealed with silicone
  bead
17 Plasterboard wall
  lining
18 Polyester/wool batt
  insulation

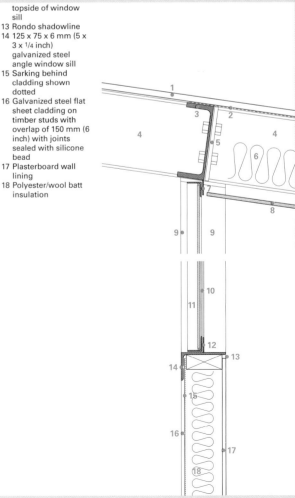

5.058
Roof Detail 1:5

Frank Harmon Architect
Low Country Residence
[26]

1 25 mm (1 inch) thick
plywood decking
2 50 x 150 mm (2 x 6
inch) timber roof joist
3 50 x 150 mm (2 x 6
inch) tongue and
groove ceiling and
soffit lining
4 25 x 76 mm (1 x 3
inch) timber trim
5 Timber nailer and
packer
6 Storefront glazing
frame
7 Double glazing unit
8 Steel column

5.059
Roof Parapet Detail 1:10

Boyd Cody Architects
Richmond Place House
[22]

1 Brick coping oriented
flat side upwards and
tilted down by 5 mm
($^1/_5$ inch) to the rear
2 Canted brick coping
on Paralon
membrane bonded
onto slate cavity
closer
3 Paralon roof
membrane bonded
to slate and dressed
over and bonded to
upstand
4 50 x 50 mm (2 x 2
inch) treated
softwood fillet
5 50 mm (2 inch) layer
of selected lava
chippings
6 Roof comprised of
proprietary mineral
finished membrane
on 3 mm ($^3/_{16}$ inch)
underlay, flame
bonded to 120 mm
($4^3/_4$ inch) insulation
on 12 mm ($^1/_2$ inch)
fibreboard on
bitumen boards, 3
mm ($^3/_{16}$ inch)
glass-reinforced
vapour control layer
flame bonded to 18
mm ($^7/_{10}$ inch) ply
deck, and firring
pieces on 150 x 44
mm (6 x $1^3/_4$ inch)
timber joists at 300
mm (12 inch) centres
7 Stepped damp proof
course dressed
under slate, stepped
down and across
cavity into brick outer
leaf with weep holes
at 400 mm (16 inch)
centres
8 Treated softwood
firring pieces
9 100 mm (4 inch) brick
outer leaf in stretcher
bond
10 175 x 44 mm (7 x $1^3/_4$
inch) timber joists at
300 mm (12 inch)
centres
11 203 x 203 mm (8 x 8
inch) steel beam
12 Rigid insulation
packed into steel
beam
13 12.5 mm ($^1/_2$ inch)
plasterboard ceiling
14 Plywood packer

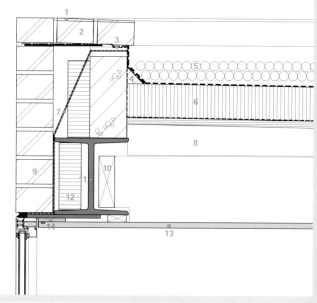

5.060
Roof Edge Detail 1:10

Cassion Castle
Architects
Twofold House [12]

1 Glass fibre roof
nosing
2 20 mm ($^3/_4$ inch) sand
and cement render
on breather
membrane
3 Glass fibre roof finish
4 18 mm ($^7/_{10}$ inch)
waterproof plywood
5 200 mm (8 inch)
blockwork
6 Zinc joist hangers
7 200 mm (8 inch) rigid
insulation between
joists
8 80 mm ($3^1/_8$ inch)
rigid insulation
9 12 mm ($^1/_2$ inch)
gypsum plasterboard
with 3 mm ($^3/_{16}$ inch)
plaster skim coat
10 12 mm ($^1/_2$ inch)
plasterboard with 25
mm (1 inch) rigid
insulation backing
and 3 mm ($^1/_8$ inch)
skim
11 50 x 250 mm (2 x 10
inch) timber joists
12 Firrings laid at 1:80
fall
13 50 mm (2 inch)
continuous
ventilation between
joists below firring
14 Upstand for skylight

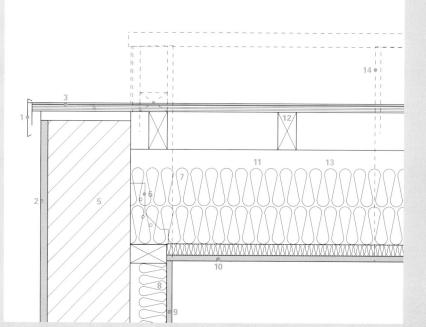

5.061
Gutter Detail 1:2

John Onken Architects
Dolphin Cottage [32]

1 Roof slates
2 Pre-formed zinc
coping snapped
down over cleats and
continuously
crimped to gutter
section
3 Cleats fixed at 400
mm (16 inch) centres
4 42 x 140 mm (1 3/4 x
5 1/2 inch)
Thermowood
capping rail fixed
over treated
softwood grounds
5 Line of zinc flashing
beyond
6 25 mm (1 inch)
diameter aluminium
overflow tube cut
and welded to top

edge of stop end of
gutter to terminate
below zinc flashing
7 12 mm (1/2 inch)
plywood wall
sheathing
8 Timber blocking
between joists
9 Zinc gutter formed
in-situ, tacked and
crimped at coping
and laid over
underlayment
10 21 mm (7/8 inch)
Thermowood
cladding board
11 85 x 45 mm (3 3/8 x
1 3/4 inch) treated
softwood continuous
plate at top of
battens
12 76 mm (3 inch)
diameter downpipe
welded to underside
of gutter and
concealed behind
cladding

5.062
Roof Parapet Detail 1:10

Stephenson Bell
Architects
House 780 [18]

1 Pre-cast white
concrete coping with
stainless steel
pressed metal
flashing fixed to
upstand with
single-ply roof
membrane
supported on render
reinforcing coat on
render carrier board
2 Stainless steel drip
3 100 x 100 mm (4 x 4
inch) galvanized mild
steel angle bolted to
blockwork wall to
support pre-cast
concrete coping
4 Insulation turned up
perimeter of parapet

wall with single-ply
membrane
5 130 mm (5 1/8 inch)
insulated render
system mechanically
fixed to blockwork
6 15 mm (5/8 inch)
drainage cavity
between insulation
and blockwork
7 50 mm (2 inch)
ballast on filter layer
on 130 mm (5 1/8 inch)
insulation on
single-ply membrane
8 Concrete screed
9 Pre-cast concrete
roof unit with
minimum fall of 1:80
10 50 mm (2 inch)
insulation
11 100 mm (4 inch)
blockwork
12 UPVC (unplasticized
polyvinyl chloride)
holding track and
shims

13 12 mm (1/2 inch)
plasterboard and
plaster skim coat
14 Metal firring ceiling
system with
plasterboard and
skim finish
15 Damp proof course
cavity tray and weep
holes
16 40 mm (1 5/8 inch)
insulation with
waterproof render
system
17 200 x 130 mm (8 x
5 1/8 inch) steel beam
as insulated lintel
18 Plasterboard and
skim to form recess
19 Extruded aluminium
trim
20 Recess for motorized
blind track
21 Extruded aluminium
trim
22 Timber packer with
damp proof course

taped to front face
and dressed into
glazing frame
23 Render stop bead
24 Sealant with backing
rod
25 PVC bead angle
26 Powder-coated
aluminium glazing
system
27 Double glazing unit

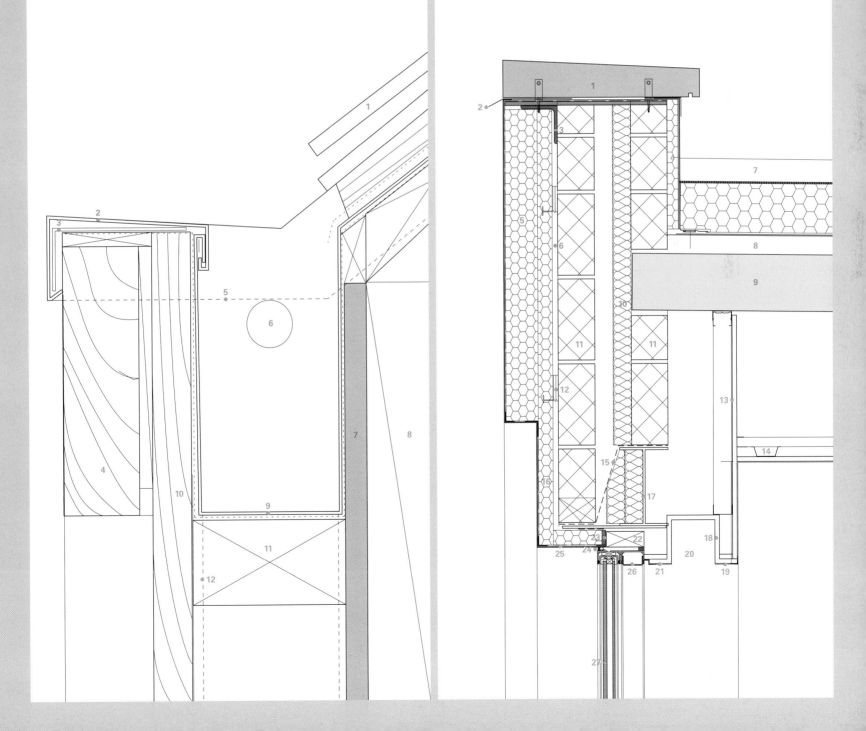

5.063
Roof and Skylight Detail
1:10

Studio Bednarski
Hesmondhalgh House
[33]

1 Metal roof decking over waterproof membrane and timber structure
2 Stainless steel glazing frame
3 Silicone glazing sealant with polyethylene backing rod
4 Timber packer
5 100 x 50 mm (4 x 2 inch) mild steel rectangular hollow section steel beam
6 Painted plasterboard ceiling lining
7 Recessed lighting track
8 Double glazed roof light unit
9 Metal gutter support
10 Copper gutter brackets at 700 mm (28 inch) centres
11 Ventilation gap with insect screen
12 Pre-patinated copper box gutter
13 Folded end to copper cladding with drip profile lapped over
14 Pre-patinated copper cladding
15 Breather membrane
16 18 mm (3/4 inch) weather bonded and proofed plywood sheathing
17 Insulation
18 Painted plasterboard wall lining
19 25 mm (1 inch) void for services
20 12 mm (1/2 inch) plywood sheathing
21 100 gauge vapour control layer

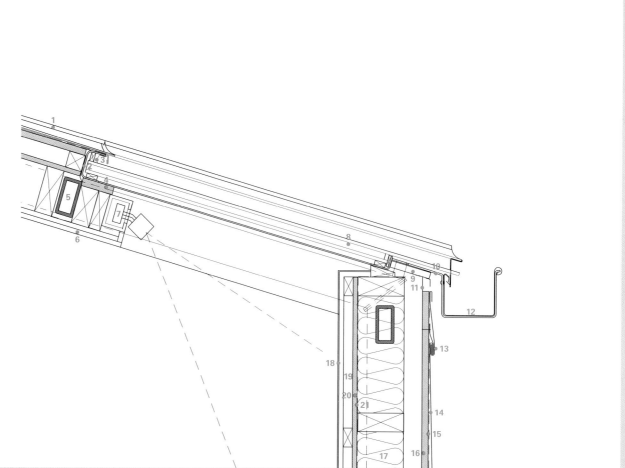

5.064
Roof and Clerestory
Window Detail 1:10

MacGabhann Architects
Tuath na Mara [14]

1 Anthrazinc standing seam cladding
2 Separating layer
3 19 mm (3/4 inch) weather bonded and proofed external plywood sheeting
4 50 x 50 mm (2 x 2 inch) timber battens
5 225 x 44 mm (9 x 13/4 inch) timber joists at 400 mm (16 inch) centres
6 220 mm (9 inch) Kingspan Thermapitch insulation
7 Vapour barrier
8 12.5 mm (1/2 inch) plasterboard lining
9 50 x 50 mm (2 x 2 inch) timber battens
10 203 x 133 mm (8 x 51/4 inch) universal beam
11 Valley gutter
12 Powder-coated aluminium framed roof light
13 Anthrazinc clad window reveal
14 Powder-coated aluminium glazing
15 250 x 20 mm (10 x 3/4 inch) solid red deal boards at head and sill
16 Anthrazinc standing seam cladding
17 Separating layer
18 19 mm (3/4 inch) weather bonded and proofed external plywood sheeting
19 35 x 50 mm (13/8 x 2 inch) timber battens
20 Proprietary sill cavity closer
21 215 mm (81/2 inch) blockwork wall
22 60 mm (23/8 inch) Kingspan insulation
23 100 mm (4 inch) blockwork wall

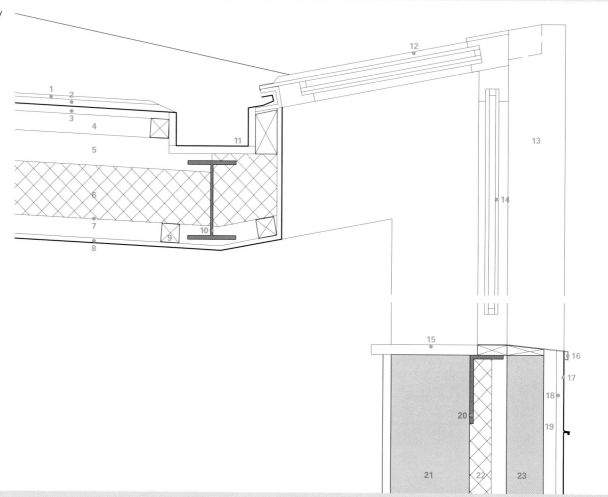

5.065
Living Room Roof Detail
1:10

MacGabhann Architects
Tuath na Mara [14]

1 Anthrazinc standing
 seam cladding
2 Separating layer
3 19 mm (3/4 inch)
 weather bonded and
 proofed external
 plywood sheeting
4 35 x 50 mm (13/8 x 2
 inch) timber battens
5 254 x 146 x 37 mm
 (10 x 53/4 x 11/2 inch)
 universal beam
6 Double glazed
 aluminium curtain
 walling system
7 50 x 50 mm (2 x 2
 inch) timber battens
8 225 x 44 mm (9 x 13/4
 inch) timber joists at
 400 mm (16 inch)
 centres
9 150 mm (6 inch)
 Kingspan
 Thermapitch
 insulation
10 Vapour barrier
11 Timber batten
 sub-construction
12 12.5 mm (1/2 inch)
 plasterboard lining
13 Timber packers
14 Steel universal beam

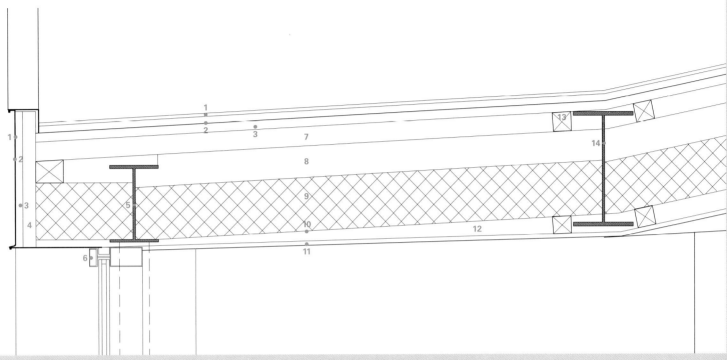

5.066
Roof Detail 1:10

Boyd Cody Architects
Richmond Place House
[22]

1 Continuous slate
 cavity closer to head
 of cavity with
 continuous damp
 proof course under
 and dressed up
 behind
2 40 mm (13/5 inch)
 clear ventilated
 cavity between outer
 and inner leaves
3 100 mm (4 inch) brick
 outer leaf laid in
 stretcher bond
4 Stepped damp proof
 course dressed
 under slate and
 stepped down and
 across cavity into
 brick outer leaf
5 25 mm (1 inch)
 thermal break
 between steel and
 brickwork
6 Weep holes at 450
 mm (18 inch) centres
7 50 mm (2 inch) layer
 of selected lava
 chippings
8 Roof comprised of
 proprietary mineral
 finished membrane
 on 3 mm (3/16 inch)
 underlay, flame
 bonded to 120 mm
 (43/4 inch) insulation
 on 12 mm (1/2 inch)
 fibreboard on
 bitumen boards, 3
 mm (3/16 inch)
 glass-reinforced
 vapour control layer
 flame bonded to 18
 mm (7/10 inch) ply
 deck, firring pieces
on 150 x 44 mm (6 x
 13/4 inch) timber
 joists at 300 mm (12
 inch) centres
9 150 mm (6 inch) steel
 beam beyond
10 150 x 44 mm (6 x 13/4
 inch) timber joists at
 400 mm (16 inch)
 centres
11 Underfloor heating
 between joists, with
 plywood flooring to
 sit tight to top of
 heating trays
12 200 x 44 mm (8 x 13/4
 inch) softwood joists
 at 300 mm (12 inch)
 centres supported on
 galvanized steel
 hangers
13 150 mm (6 inch)
 Rockwool acoustic
 insulation
14 203 x 203 mm (8 x 8
 inch) steel beam
15 150 x150 mm (6 x 6
 inch) steel box
 section
16 Natural fluorescent
 strip lighting

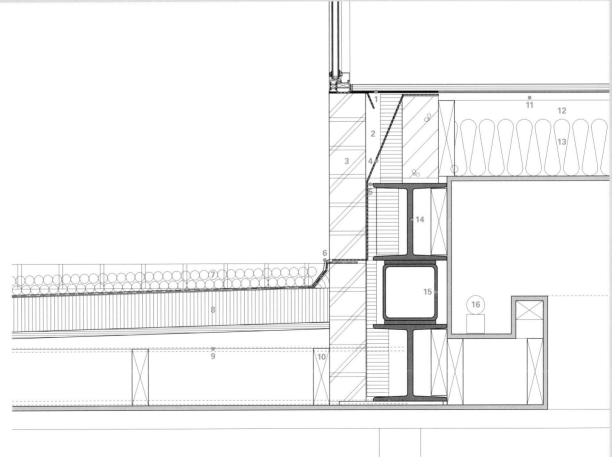

5.067
Roof Detail 1:10

Go Hasegawa &
Associates
Forest House [34]

1 Narrow-pitch
galvanized
aluminium coated
corrugated sheet on
10 x 30 mm (3/8 x 11/5
inch) firring strips at
455 mm (181/4 inch)

centres on asphalt
roofing on 12 mm (1/2
inch) structural
plywood and 100
mm (4 inch) heat
insulating material
2 90 x 180 mm (31/2 x 7
inch) beam
3 89 x 19 mm (31/2 x 3/4
inch) ipe guard rail
with oil stain clear
lacquer finish
4 60 x 30 mm (23/8 x
11/5 inch) steel pole

at 910 mm (361/2
inch) centres coated
with zinc and oil
paint finish
5 89 x 19 mm (31/2 x 3/4
inch) ipe floor with
oil stain clear lacquer
finish
6 90 x 45 mm (31/2 x
13/4 inch) ipe floor
joist at 455 mm (181/4
inch) centres with oil
stain clear lacquer
7 90 x 75 mm (31/2 x 3

inch) steel angle at
910 mm (361/2 inch)
centres coated with
zinc and oil paint
finish
8 90 x 90 x 6 mm (31/2
x 31/2 x 1/4 inch) steel
plate, for stumble
prevention, coated
with zinc and oil
paint finish
9 12 mm (1/2 inch) bolt
10 9 mm (3/8 inch)
plasterboard to attic

space ceiling with
urethane paint finish
11 9 mm (3/8 inch)
plywood ceiling with
oil stain clear lacquer
12 120 x 150 mm (43/4 x
6 inch) timber beam

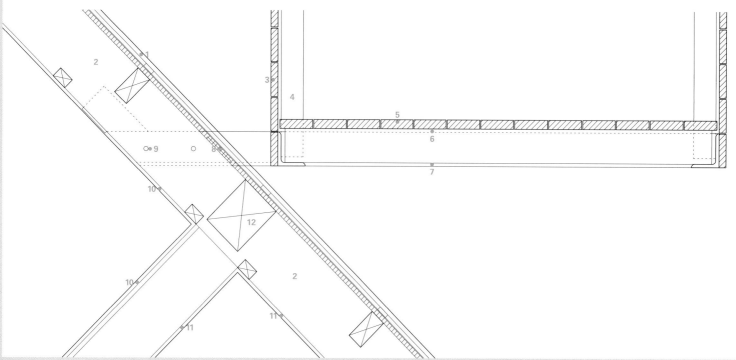

5.068
**Ceiling and Roof Detail
1:5**

Kotaro Ide / ARTechnic
Architects
Shell House [09]

1 Sealant
2 Steel bracket
3 Glazing stop
4 Sealant
5 Steel bracket
6 Air space

7 Glazing stop
8 Steel bracket
9 Synthetic resin with
vermiculite material
spray finish
10 Hard urethane foam
11 Exposed concrete
penetrative sealer
finish
12 Double glazing
13 Double glazing
14 Glazing stop
15 Sealant
16 Glazing stop

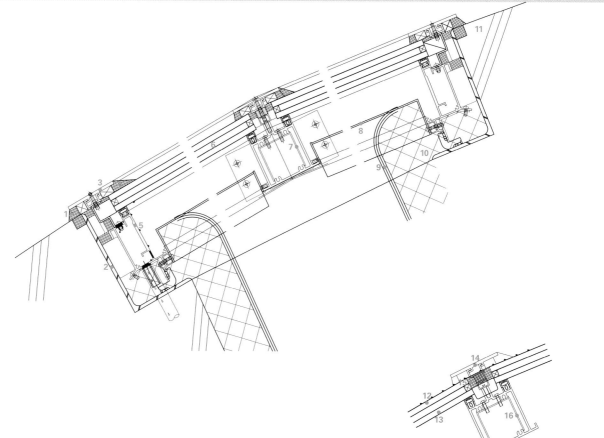

5.069
Roof Parapet Detail 1:10

Stam Architecten
Two Apartments [10]

1 Aluminium profile to
   form drip
2 Insulation
3 Air cavity
4 Architectonic
   reinforced concrete
5 Roofing membrane
6 Brickwork
7 Screed
8 Reinforced concrete
9 L-shaped steel profile
   to window head
10 Column beyond

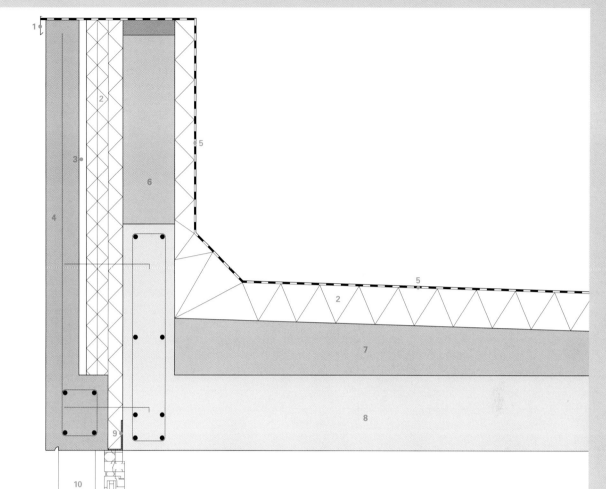

5.070
Roof Parapet Detail 1:10

Touraine Richmond
Architects
One Window House [27]

1 Galvanized metal
   coping
2 Walnut stained
   plywood sheathing
   with clear sealer
3 20 mm (7/8 inch)
   corrugated
galvanized metal roof
cladding
4 Batt insulation
5 Waterproof
   membrane
6 12.5 mm (1/2 inch)
   drywall lining
7 Double glazed
   skylight unit
8 19 mm (3/4 inch)
   oriented strand
   board sheathing
9 50 x 254 mm (2 x 10
   inch) timber framing
10 Batt insulation
11 12.5 mm (1/2 inch)
   drywall lining
12 15 mm (5/8 inch)
   drywall lining

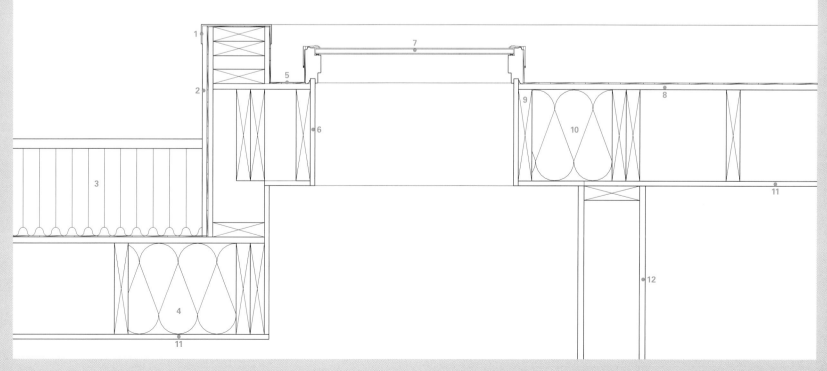

5.071
Vaulted Roof Detail 1:10

Terry Pawson Architects
The Tall House [38]

1 Planted roof system on 2 ply membrane on 12 mm (^{1}/$_2$ inch) plywood and 12 mm (^{1}/$_2$ inch) weather- and-boil proof plywood deck screwed to joists
2 50 mm (2 inch) clear air gap vented at both ends of vault
3 120 x 80 x 8 mm (4^3/$_4$

x 3^1/$_8$ x ^{1}/$_3$ inch) curved rectangular hollow section
4 175 x 50 mm (6^5/$_8$ x 2 inch) softwood joists
5 100 mm (4 inch) insulation
6 10 mm (^{3}/$_8$ inch) Glasrock plasterboard to underside of joists
7 Gravel filling for gutter
8 100 x 50 x 3 mm (4 x 2 x ^{1}/$_8$ inch) mild steel plate painted to match main steel colour

9 Steel glazing angle screwed to hardwood packer, painted to match main steel colour
10 200 x 100 x 4 mm (8 x 4 x ^{1}/$_6$ inch) mild steel angle bolted with countersunk bolts through timber packer to main steel
11 Softwood packer as required
12 Double glazed sealed window unit comprised of 10 mm (^{2}/$_5$ inch) outer glass pane, 12 mm (^{1}/$_2$

inch) air gap and 6 mm (^{1}/$_4$ inch) inner glass pane, silicone bonded into frame
13 Line of structural steel column beyond
14 Window sill board
15 140 x 70 mm (5^1/$_2$ x 2^3/$_4$ inch) steel channel
16 Fair-faced brick wall
17 80 mm (3^1/$_8$ inch) insulation
18 100 mm (4 inch) blockwork

5.072
Roof Overhang Detail 1:10

Marlon Blackwell
Architect
L-Stack House [35]

1 Modified bitumen roofing over 15 mm (^{5}/$_8$ inch) plywood sheathing
2 Pre-finished painted sheet metal flashing
3 Treated timber blocking
4 19 mm (^{3}/$_4$ inch) fir plywood sheathing

5 25 x 150 mm (1 x 6 inch) Brazilian redwood tongue and groove fascia board
6 300 mm (11^7/$_8$ inch) roof joists at 600 mm (24 inch) centres
7 Steel portal frame
8 Soy-based spray foam insulation at roof and floor
9 Painted gypsum board ceiling on 50 x 100 mm (2 x 4 inch) timber blocking
10 Gypsum-board lined recess for roller blind
11 Aluminium-framed

fixed glass storefront window
12 50 x 100 mm (2 x 4 inch) treated wood blocking
13 12 mm (^{1}/$_2$ inch) thick cement board
14 Window reveal of painted cementitious board

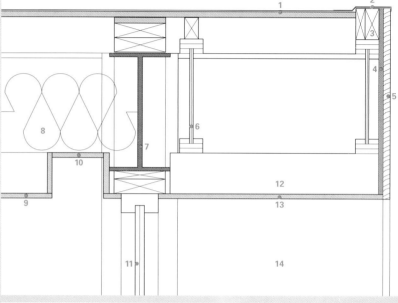

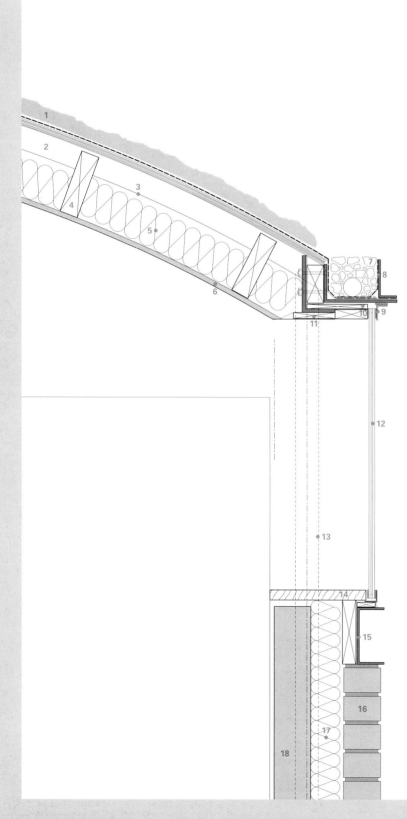

5.073
Roof Edge Detail 1:33

OFIS Arhitekti
Alpine Hut [39]

1 Aluminium sheet
2 Flashing
3 200 x 200 mm (8 x 8 inch) timber beam with water drainage
4 120 x 160 mm (4^3/$_4$ x 6^3/$_{10}$ inch) timber rafter
5 Joist
6 100 mm (4 inch) insulation
7 200 x 200 mm (8 x 8

inch) reinforced concrete
8 20 mm (^{7}/$_8$ inch) timber cladding on thermal insulation
9 200 mm (8 inch) clay brick wall with 100 mm (4 inch) thermal insulation with external timber cladding
10 Timber construction
11 Timber beam
12 200 x 200 mm (8 x 8 inch) larch pillar

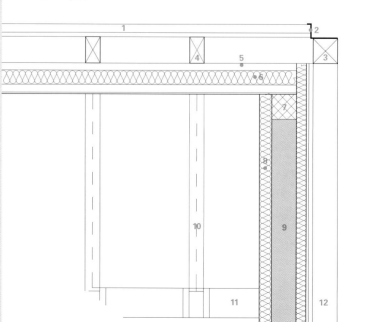

5.074
Roof Pitch Detail 1:33

OFIS Arhitekti
Alpine Hut [39]

1 Eternit tiles roof
  covering
2 50 x 40 mm (2 x 1⁵/₈
  inch) timber structure
3 Ventilated cavity,
  rainproof foil on
  wooden panels on
  160 x 120 mm (6³/₁₀ x
  4³/₄ inch) timber
  rafter
4 80 mm (3¹/₈ inch)
  insulation

5 Plasterboard lining
6 250 x 200 mm (10 x 8
  inch) ridge beam
7 Vertical timber truss
  component
8 250 x 200 mm (10 x 8
  inch) ridge beam

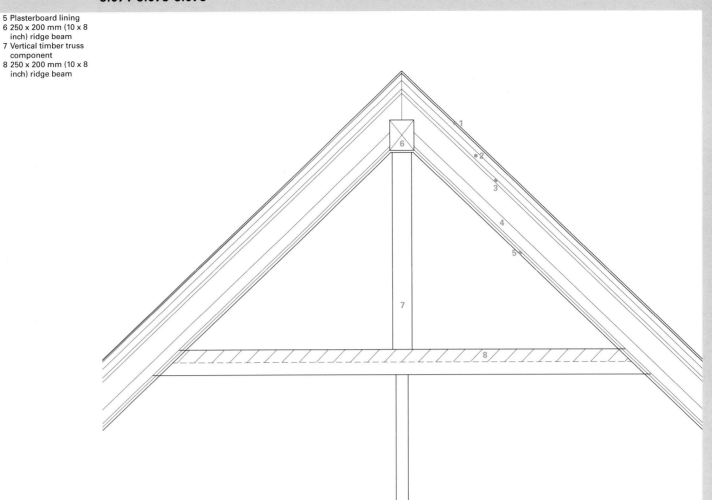

5.075
Roof Eaves Detail 1:33

OFIS Arhitekti
Alpine Hut [39]

1 Eternit tiles roof
  covering
2 50 x 40 mm (2 x 1⁵/₈
  inch) timber structure
3 Ventilated cavity,
  rainproof foil on
  wooden panels on
  160 x 120 mm (6³/₁₀ x
  4³/₄ inch) timber
  rafter
4 7 mm (¹/₄ inch) larch
  strip as soffit

5 150 x 150 mm (6 x 6
  inch) timber bearer
6 200 x 200 mm (8 x 8
  inch) reinforced
  concrete
7 Timber cladding on
  50 mm (2 inch)
  thermal insulation
8 200 mm (8 inch) clay
  brick wall
9 100 mm (4 inch)
  insulation with
  plaster render and 7
  mm (1/4 inch) larch
  strip
10 Hidden water
  drainage
11 100 x 175 mm (4 x

6⁷/₈ inch) timber
  bearer
12 200 x 200 mm (8 x 8
  inch) larch pillar
13 Oiled and brushed
  oak parquet flooring
14 180 mm (7¹/₁₀ inch)
  reinforced concrete
  plate
15 Larch window frame

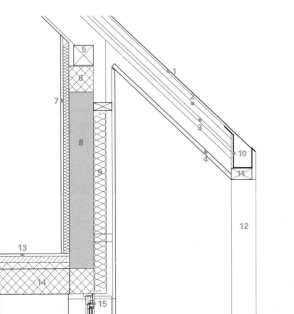

5.076
Roof Edge Detail 1:20

Marsh Cashman
Koolloos Architects
Maroubra House [36]

1 Folded seam
  Colorbond steel
  roofing
2 Top Hat section at
  450 mm (18 inch)
  centres
3 New aluminium
  purlins
4 Selected medium
  density sheet
  cladding

5 25 mm (1 inch)
  styrofoam insulation
6 Waterproof
  membrane
7 Insulation on
  waterproof sarking
  lining
8 New aluminium
  purlins
9 New steel roof beam
10 Insulation
11 Plasterboard lining to
  ceiling and walls
12 Timber cladding
13 Insulation

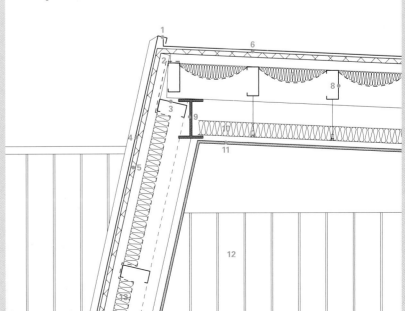

5.077
**Roof and Ceiling Detail
1:5**

Glas Architects
The Nail Houses [23]

1 Powder-coated
  aluminium flashing
  and capping to
  parapet
2 Metal clip
3 Timber battens for
  fixing metal clip
4 Vapour barrier
  lapped over parapet
5 Insulated cavity
  closer
6 80 x 50 mm (3 1/8 x 2
  inch) timber frame
7 Single ply polymeric
  membrane fully
  adhered to 25 mm (1
  inch) insulation
8 Single ply roof
  membrane fully
  adhered to insulation

9 18 mm (3/4 inch)
  weather bonded and
  proofed plywood on
  timber firrings
10 Timber firring laid at
  1:60 fall
11 18 mm (3/4 inch)
  weather bonded and
  proofed plywood
12 End of joist wrapped
  in damp proof
  membrane
13 440 x 102.5 x 102.5
  mm (17 1/2 x 4 x 4
  inch) polished Medici
  block, Bellini colour,
  to front elevation
14 100 mm (4 inch)
  Rockwool cavity slab
  insulation
15 225 x 50 mm (9 x 2
  inch) timber roof joist
16 12.5 mm (1/2 inch)
  plasterboard,
  skimmed and painted
17 15 mm (5/8 inch)
  plaster, skimmed and

painted
18 100 mm (4 inch)
  medium dense block

5.078
Roof Detail 1:10

O'Donnell + Tuomey
Architects
The Sleeping Giant –
Killiney House [09]

1 0.8 gauge flashing
2 175 x 25 mm (6 7/8 x 1
  inch) softwood
  packing
3 25 mm (1 inch)
  waterproof bonded
  plywood with vapour
  barrier and polyester
  fleece insulation
4 Trocal membrane
  with metal upstand
5 19 mm (3/4 inch)
  waterproof bonded
  plywood base for
  gutter lining
6 Softwood firrings to
  allow ventilation
7 Two 50 x 200 mm (2
  x 8 inch) timber

edge joists
8 100 mm (4 inch)
  insulation
9 Vapour barrier
10 18 mm (3/4 inch) iroko
  boarding
11 195 x 70 mm (7 3/4 x
  2 3/4 inch) iroko frame
12 Double glazing
13 38 mm (1 1/2 inch)
  iroko window board/
  desktop notched into
  frame
14 Iroko sill fixed to
  outer leaf or to steel
  angle
15 Glazing bead
16 Lead flashing under
  window frame and
  dressed into render
17 Steel angle acting as
  cavity closer

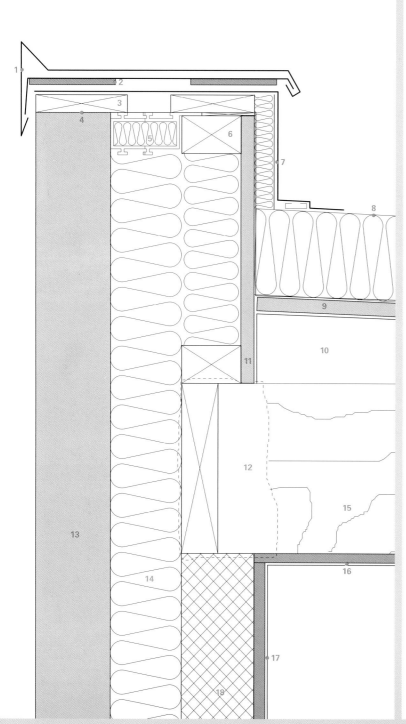

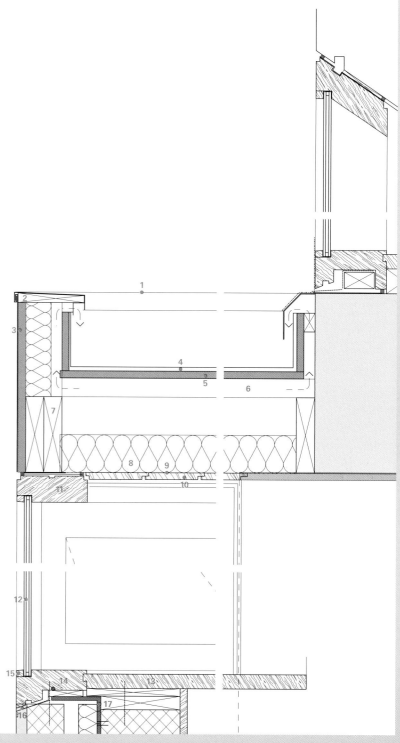

5.079
Roof Detail 1:10

Frank Harmon Architect
Low Country Residence
[26]

1 Modified bitumen
   roof
2 Metal flashing
3 140 mm (5 1/2 inch)
   tapered insulation
4 20 mm (3/4 inch)
   plywood
5 50 x 100 mm (2 x 4
   inch) timber packer
6 40 mm (1 1/2 inch)
   tongue and groove

timber deck
7 200 x 50 mm (8 x 2
   inch) steel parallel
   flange channel
8 150 x 100 mm (6 x 4
   inch) steel purlin
9 Steel beam

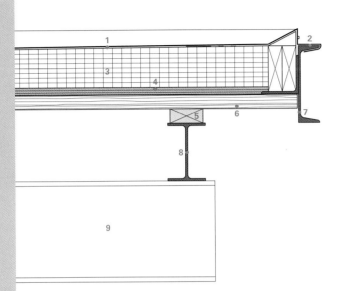

5.080
Roof Detail 1:20

Designworkshop: SA
Igoda View House [24]

1 Proprietary
   aluminium 'T' to
   form coping and
   flash off waterproof
   membrane
2 Face brickwork with
   vertically brushed
   bagged finish to
   internal walls
3 Kliplok clear
   polycarbonate
   covering with

minimum 200 mm (8
inch) overlap
4 150 x 50 mm (6 x 2
   inch) grounds to be
   tapered and fixed
   above every third
   beam
5 50 x 27 mm (2 x 1
   inch) Oregon pine
   sanded and painted
   slats
6 Beam cut 30 mm
   (1 1/5 inch) short for
   roof conduits
7 Brick infill between
   beams with plastered
   and bagged finish
8 120 x 30 mm (4 3/4 x

1 1/5 inch) copper
chrome arsenate-
treated wall plate
9 230 x 595 mm (9 x
   23 2/5 inch) reinforced
   concrete beam
10 15 mm (3/5 inch)
   internal steel
   trowelled plaster,
   skimmed with
   cretestone for ultra
   smooth finish and
   primed and painted
11 150 x 38 mm (6 x 1 1/2
   inch) fixed with
   brackets to tapered
   grounds
12 220 x 70 mm (8 3/4 x

2 3/4 inch) rough sawn
sand-blasted
reclaimed Oregon
pine beams
13 Gutter formed with
   22 mm (7/8 inch)
   shutter board with
   fillets on 4 mm (1/6
   inch) waterproof
   membrane fully
   bonded to primed
   surface
14 Derbigum roof
   membrane pressed
   continuously up
   inner face of outer
   skin

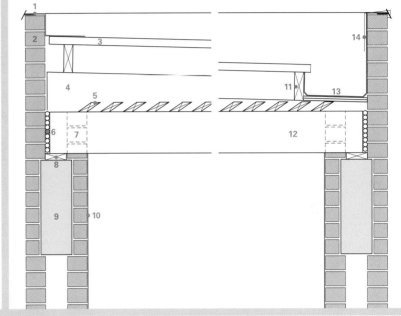

5.081
Roof Detail 1:10

Room 11
Kingston House [34]

1 Colorbond steel
   flashing, 10 mm (3/8
   inch) cover over
   plywood
2 Kliplok Colorbond
   steel profile roofing
3 170 x 43 mm (6 3/4 x
   1 3/4 inch) timber
   rafters at 900 mm (36
   inch) centres,
   attached to parallel
   flange channel via

170 x 100 x 10 mm
(6 3/4 x 4 x 3/8 inch)
cleat welded to
parallel flange
channel
4 8 mm (3/8 inch) steel
   cap to 90 x 90 mm
   (3 1/2 x 3 1/2 inch)
   square hollow
   section
5 150 x 75 mm (6 x 3
   inch) parallel flange
   channel attached to
   90 x 90 mm (3 1/2 x
   3 1/2 inch) square
   hollow section
6 12 mm (1/2 inch)
   smooth stained Boral

Evolution plywood
over timber battens
7 10 mm (3/8 inch)
   plasterboard on 30
   mm (1 1/5 inch) firring
   channels with bulk
   insulation
8 Aluminium glazing
   frame with double
   glazed unit

5.082
**Roof and Gutter Detail
1:10**

Public
Rattlesnake Creek
House [15]

1 Sheet metal capping
2 Timber fascia board
3 Sheet metal cleat
4 Sheet metal box
   gutter
5 6 mm (1/4 inch) thick
   steel channel
6 Fold down double
   standing seam at
   flashing at low point
   of roof
7 Metal roof sheeting
   with standing seams
8 Roofing membrane
9 20 mm (3/4 inch)
   plywood
10 Profile closure steel
   angle at end of
   decking
11 Corrugated metal
   decking roof
   structure
12 Steel beam

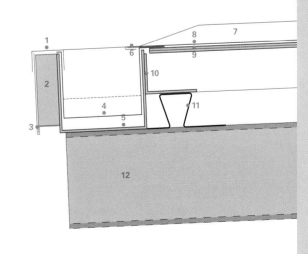

5.083 5.084

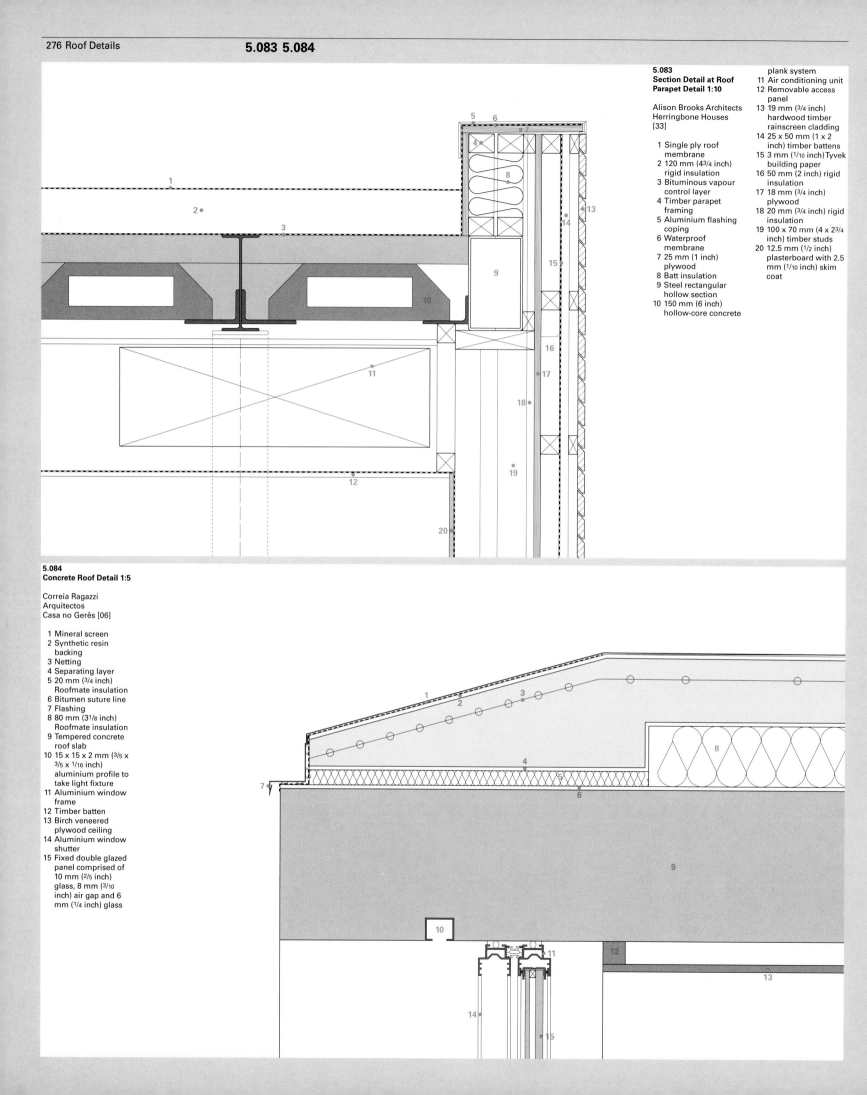

5.083
Section Detail at Roof Parapet Detail 1:10

Alison Brooks Architects
Herringbone Houses
[33]

1 Single ply roof membrane
2 120 mm (4³/4 inch) rigid insulation
3 Bituminous vapour control layer
4 Timber parapet framing
5 Aluminium flashing coping
6 Waterproof membrane
7 25 mm (1 inch) plywood
8 Batt insulation
9 Steel rectangular hollow section
10 150 mm (6 inch) hollow-core concrete plank system
11 Air conditioning unit
12 Removable access panel
13 19 mm (³/4 inch) hardwood timber rainscreen cladding
14 25 x 50 mm (1 x 2 inch) timber battens
15 3 mm (¹/10 inch) Tyvek building paper
16 50 mm (2 inch) rigid insulation
17 18 mm (³/4 inch) plywood
18 20 mm (³/4 inch) rigid insulation
19 100 x 70 mm (4 x 2³/4 inch) timber studs
20 12.5 mm (¹/2 inch) plasterboard with 2.5 mm (¹/10 inch) skim coat

5.084
Concrete Roof Detail 1:5

Correia Ragazzi
Arquitectos
Casa no Gerês [06]

1 Mineral screen
2 Synthetic resin backing
3 Netting
4 Separating layer
5 20 mm (³/4 inch) Roofmate insulation
6 Bitumen suture line
7 Flashing
8 80 mm (3¹/8 inch) Roofmate insulation
9 Tempered concrete roof slab
10 15 x 15 x 2 mm (³/5 x ³/5 x ¹/16 inch) aluminium profile to take light fixture
11 Aluminium window frame
12 Timber batten
13 Birch veneered plywood ceiling
14 Aluminium window shutter
15 Fixed double glazed panel comprised of 10 mm (²/5 inch) glass, 8 mm (³/10 inch) air gap and 6 mm (¹/4 inch) glass

5.085
Roof Overhang Detail 1:10

diederendirrix
Villa PPML [21]

1 Ballast tile
2 Insulation
3 High quality pressure-resilient insulation
4 Cast in-situ reinforced concrete

roof
5 Void in roofing for concealing base of steel frame
6 Gypsum board ceiling
7 115 mm (4½ inch) diameter steel column
8 EPDM (ethylene propylene dieme monomer) roofing
9 Water resistant plywood protection

strip
10 Insulation
11 Window sub frame
12 67 x 139 mm (2²/₃ x 5½ inch) timber window frame
13 Insulated double glazing
14 Timber beam
15 25 mm (1 inch) water resistant plywood boarding
16 Steel awning framing with continuous steel

strips and torque bulkheads
17 46 x 121 mm (1⁴/₅ x 4³/₄ inch) timber beam
18 Fibre reinforced cementitious boards on framework
19 Stucco soffit lining
20 EPDM (ethylene propylene dieme monomer) roofing membrane
21 Roof edge

construction from 12 mm (½ inch) water resilient plywood
22 Roof edge timber framework
23 Roof edge timber framework
24 Steel awning framing with continuous steel strips and torque bulkheads
25 Timber beam for mounting sun screens

26 450 x 10 mm (17⁷/₁₀ x ²/₅ inch) galvanized and painted steel flat bar
27 Electric motor for sun screens
28 Adjustable sun screen

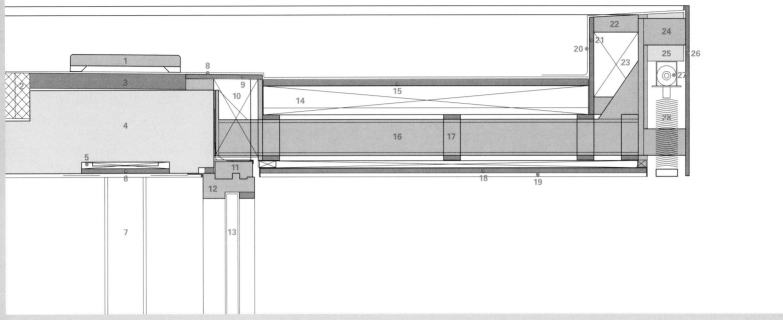

5.086
Roof Detail 1:10

Hampson Williams
Glass and Timber
Houses [33]

1 37 mm (1½ inch) thick Argon filled toughened and laminated double glazed unit
2 50 x 50 mm (2 x 2 inch) powder-coated aluminium angle glazing support carriage
3 100 x 50 mm (4 x 2 inch) Douglas Fir sub-frame
4 Bonded aluminium flashing
5 150 x 50 mm (6 x 2 inch) tanalised softwood framing
6 Vapour control layer
7 13 mm (½ inch) cementitous exterior-grade lining panel
8 17 x 125 mm (⁵/₈ x 5 inch) Canadian western red cedar cladding
9 Multi-layer thermal insulation
10 River pebble border
11 Extensive sedum roof blanket
12 241 x 89 mm (9½ x 3½ inch) glulam beam

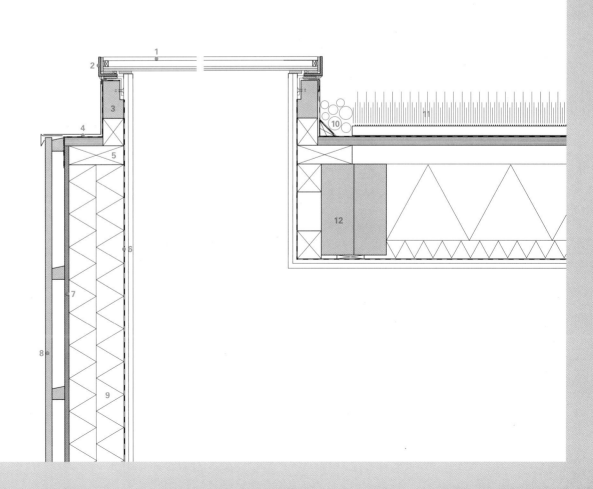

5.087
Roof Edge Detail 1:10

Charles Pictet
Architectes
Villa Frontenex [10]

1 Layer of pebbles
2 2 x 80 mm ($1/16$ x $3 1/8$ inch) insulation
3 Reinforced concrete wall
4 30 mm ($1 1/5$ inch) insulation
5 Plasterboard
6 Insulation
7 Fixed steel glazing system
8 Sliding steel glazing system
9 Double glazing comprised of 8 mm ($1/3$ inch) laminated and tempered glass

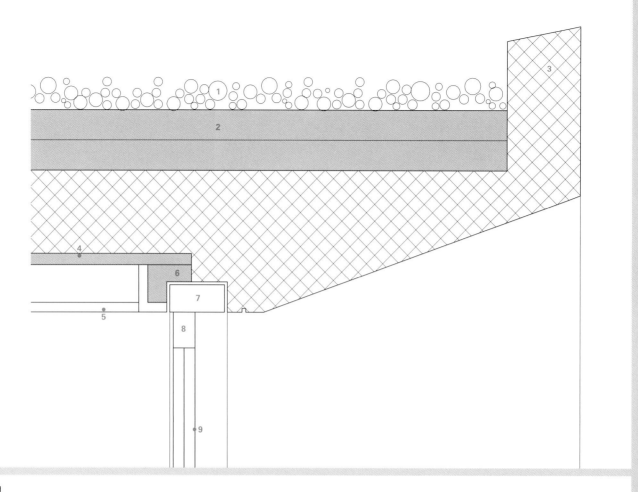

5.088
Roof Edge Detail 1:5

Terry Pawson Architects
The Tall House [38]

1 3 mm ($1/8$ inch) stainless steel plate used as cover trim to end of roof
2 Two ply membrane
3 12 mm ($1/2$ inch) curved plywood
4 Softwood battens
5 10 mm ($3/8$ inch) masterboard with continuous air vent in soffit at both ends of vaulted roof, minimum 25 mm (1 inch) wide with insect mesh
6 15 mm ($3/5$ inch) compressed insulation board
7 12 mm ($1/2$ inch) plywood
8 10 mm ($3/8$ inch) masterboard with continuous air vent in soffit at both ends of vaulted roof, minimum 25 mm (1 inch) wide with insect mesh
9 Breather membrane
10 6 mm ($1/4$ inch) masterboard on 20 mm ($3/4$ inch) battens on breather paper on 12 mm ($1/2$ inch) plywood with 100 x 50 mm (4 x 2 inch) softwood frame with Rockwool insulation, vapour barrier and 12 mm ($1/2$ inch) plasterboard internal lining
11 12 mm ($1/2$ inch) plywood
12 15 mm ($3/5$ inch) compressed insulation board
13 90 x 90 mm ($3 1/2$ x $3 1/2$ inch) curved structural steel
14 Softwood nogging
15 125 mm (5 inch) mineral wool insulation
16 Planted roof system on two ply membrane, on curved 12 mm ($1/2$ inch) plywood panels screwed to joist
17 Minimum 50 mm (2 inch) air gap and continuous 125 mm (5 inch) Rockwool insulation with vapour barrier and 9 mm ($3/8$ inch) plasterboard ceiling
18 9 mm ($3/8$ inch) curved plasterboard ceiling

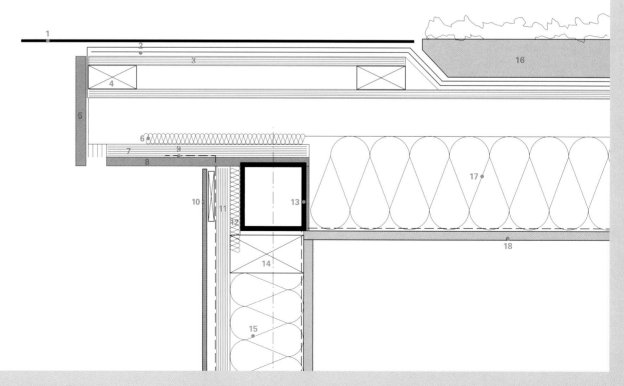

5.089
Roof Overhang Detail
1:10

Avanti Architects
Long View [35]

1 Formed galvanized steel capping
2 Zinc sheets on underlay over two layers of 12 mm (1/2 inch) plywood, glued and screwed
3 6 mm (1/4 inch) taped and glued Trespa board
4 25 mm (1 inch) air gap with insect mesh
5 Polyester powder-coated aluminium flashing profile
6 Waterproof membrane
7 220 x 220 mm (83/4 x 83/4 inch) steel beam with insulation infill either side of web
8 Air gap with insect mesh
9 75 x 50 mm (3 x 2 inch) battens at 400 mm (16 inch) centres, void retained for ventilation
10 Waterproof membrane
11 50 mm (2 inch) insulation between Masonite beams
12 Vapour barrier
13 65 x 22 mm (23/8 x 7/8 inch) tongue and groove weather boards secret fixed vertically to horizontal counter battens
14 Breather membrane
15 12 mm (1/2 inch) weather bonded and

proofed plywood bracing
16 Ventilation conduit
17 160 x 160 mm (61/4 x 61/4 inch) steel column shown dotted
18 12.5 mm (1/2 inch) plasterboard, taped and skimmed, fixed to 75 x 50 mm (3 x 2 inch) battens
19 Vapour control layer fixed over timber studs and horizontal counter battens
20 Adjustable conduit cover
21 150 mm (6 inch) insulation
22 75 x 50 mm (3 x 2 inch) timber batten

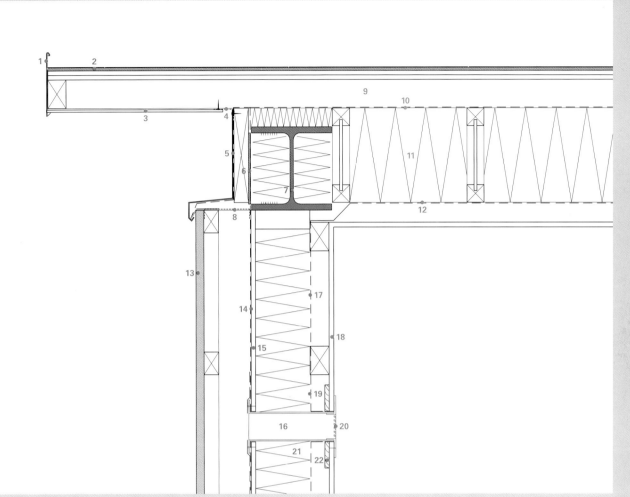

5.090
Eaves Detail 1:10

Lahz Nimmo Architects
Casuarina Ultimate Beach House [31]

1 Corrugated metal sheeting with Colorbond finish
2 Welded cleat connection to screw fixed fascia purlin
3 Profiled timber outrigger intermediate support shown dotted
4 Roof beam with bottom flange removed, bolt-fixed to welded plate connector
5 20 mm (3/4 inch) thick hardwood trim with clear stain finish
6 6 mm (1/4 inch) compressed fibre cement sheet with paint finish
7 Steel cleat welded to end of steel U-beam rafter
8 End of steel U-beam rafter
9 Eaves beam
10 Rotary hoop pine veneer to ceiling on 12 mm (1/2 inch) external grade plywood
11 Insulation
12 Timber roof purlins
13 Ceiling battens fixed off spacers to roof purlins
14 Rotary hoop pine veneer to ceiling on 13 mm (1/2 inch) plywood fixed to ceiling battens with countersunk stainless steel allen head screws
15 Anodized aluminium louvre blades with matching clips, with louvre unit angled eight degrees off vertical

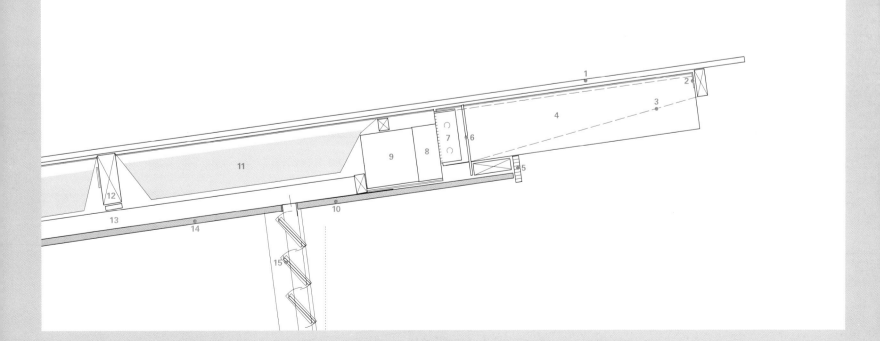

5.091
Skylight Detail 1:2

Paulo David with Luz
Ramalho
Casa Funchal [16]

1 Flashing to roof edge
2 Zinc capping to
  edges of skylight
3 50 x 50 mm (2 x 2
  inch) steel angle
4 Clear silicone seal
  resistant to
ultraviolet radiation
5 Exterior section of
  double glazed
  skylight
6 Interior section of
  double glazed
  skylight
7 Support pad
8 Fine cement wall
  finish
9 Concrete wall
10 Two layers of
  waterproof
  membrane

5.092
**Roof and Parapet Detail
1:10**

Architectus
North Shore House [36]

1 3 mm (1/8 inch)
  aluminium cap
  flashing
2 75 x 25 mm (3 x 1
  inch) batten with 6
  mm (1/4 inch) rebates
3 Henderson
  galvanized steel track
  and rollers, bolted
  into 40 x 40 x 5 mm
  (13/8 x 13/8 x 1/5 inch)
  mild steel angle
  welded to frame
4 90 x 45 mm (31/2 x
  13/4 inch) timber
  plate
5 90 x 45 mm (31/2 x
  13/4 inch) noggings at
  600 mm (24 inch)
  centres
6 25 x 25 x 3 mm (1 x 1
  x 1/8 inch) galvanized
  steel rectangular
  hollow section frame
  at 600 mm (24 inch)
  centres
7 12 mm (1/2 inch)
  Lawson cypress ply
  veneer cladding over
  breather building
  paper
8 Stainless steel
  downpipe
9 4 mm (1/6 inch)
  perforated
  aluminium flat bar
  fixed to folded angle
  to conceal end of
  drainage cell
10 40 x 3 mm (13/8 x
  1/8 inch) aluminium
  bar to terminate
  membrane
11 290 x 45 mm (112/5 x
  13/4 inch) laminated
fascia board with
bottom edge
chamfered to form
drip
12 Bituminous
  membrane over 18
  mm (7/10 inch)
  construction ply
  screw-fixed over
  framing
13 Gravel on roof finish
  over filter textile
14 15 mm (3/8 inch)
  Atlantis drainage cell
  over waterproof
  membrane
15 18 mm (7/10 inch)
  staggered layout
  construction ply,
  screw fixed on 50
  mm (2 inch) wide
  timber firrings for
  roof fall, over 200
  mm (8 inch) purlins
  at 600 mm (24 inch)
  centres
16 Greenstuf insulation
17 405 x 90 mm (16 x
  31/2 inch) glulam
  beam
18 25 mm (1 inch)
  timber fillet
19 90 x 45 mm (31/2 x
  13/4 inch) dressed
  pine continuous
  plate
20 140 x 45 mm (51/2 x
  13/4 inch) timber
  noggings
21 9 mm (1/3 inch) hoop
  pine plywood soffit
  lining

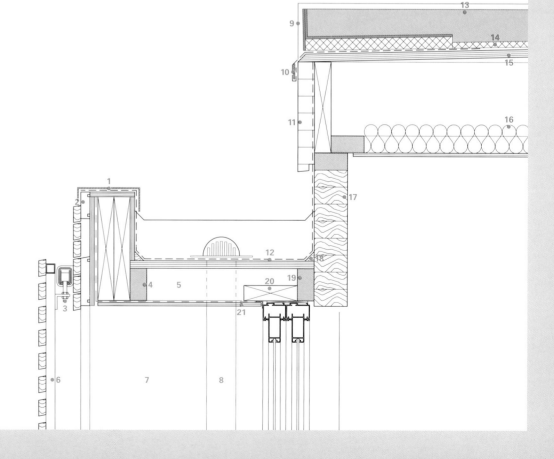

5.093
Roof Detail 1:20

Tonkin Zulaikha Greer
Hastings Parade House
[26]

1 13 mm (1/2 inch)
  plasterboard ceiling
  fixed to firring
  channels
2 150 x 45 mm (6 x 1 3/4
  inch) laminated
  veneer lumber

rafters at 450 mm (18
  inch) centres
3 Zinc roof sheeting
  fixed to timber
  battens
4 Zinc flashing
5 Painted compressed
  fibre cement
6 150 x 75 mm (6 x 3
  inch) parallel flange
  channel
7 Roller blind fixed to
  rafters in bedrooms.
  Rafters to have

cut-out to hide blind
  fitting
8 Louvred glass
  window
9 150 x 75 mm (6 x 3
  inch) parallel flange
  channel
10 300 x 120 mm (12 x
  4 3/4 inch) zinc box
  gutter
11 370 x 19 mm (15 x 3/4
  inch) plywood
  sheeting fixed to
  pre-formed channels

to support gutter
12 150 x 75 mm (6 x 3
  inch) parallel flange
  channel
13 Steel cleat

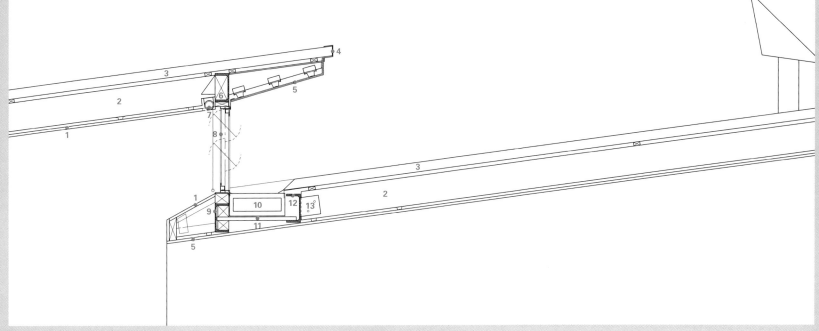

5.094
Planted Roof Detail 1:5

EZZO
Leça House [35]

1 Concrete slab
2 Colourless tempered
  glass
3 Transparent silicone
  seal
4 50 x 45 mm (2 x 1 3/4
  inch) stainless steel
  angle
5 Stainless steel bar
6 Rainwater drainage
  channel
7 40 mm (1 3/8 inch)
  polystyrene thermal
  insulation
8 Concrete support
9 Reinforced concrete
  slab
10 170 mm (6 3/4 inch)
  concrete slab
11 Planting
12 100 mm (4 inch)

black earth
13 Plaster
14 Anti-root membrane
15 PVC screen
16 Painted solid timber
  frame
17 30 x 40 mm (1 1/5 x
  1 5/8 inch) stainless
  steel L-profile
18 Silicone filled joint
19 Fixed double glazed
  window

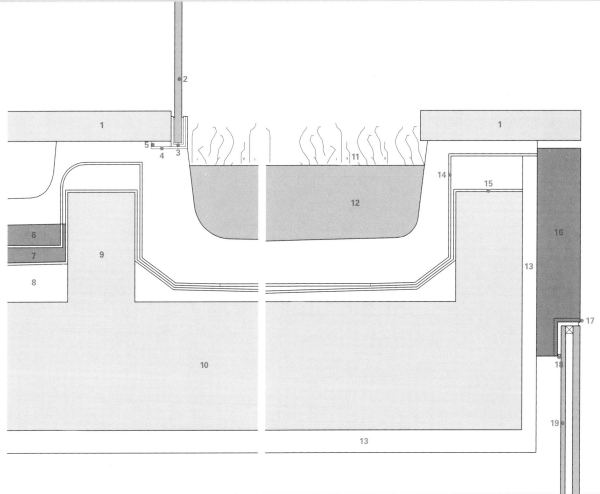

5.095
Roof Detail 1:5

Hampson Williams
Glass and Timber
Houses [33]

1 Roof planted with
vegetation including
sedums, herbs and
grasses
2 Multi-layered
extensive soil
3 Filter fleece
4 Drainage and
reservoir board
5 Sarnafil roof
membrane
6 22 mm (7/8 inch)
marine waterproof
plywood decking
7 Ventilation zone on
50 x 50 mm (2 x 2
inch) tanalised
timber battens
8 241 mm (9 1/2 inch)
deep joists

9 Two layers of 100
mm (4 inch)
Kingspan insulation
10 50 mm (2 inch)
Kingspan insulation
11 Vapour control layer
12 12.5 mm (1/2 inch)
taper edged
plasterboard, jointed
and skimmed

5.096
Roof Parapet Detail 1:20

Hertl Architekten
Krammer House [19]

1 Aluminium parapet
capping
2 60 mm (2 3/8 inch)
granulate material on
EPDM (ethylene
propylene dieme
monomer)
membrane
3 Eternit clapboard
cladding
4 Inclined timber
wedge for drainage
5 Foil layer
6 300 mm (12 inch)
timber beams with
insulation in between
7 15 mm (5/8 inch)
gypsum plasterboard
8 15 mm (5/8 inch)
oriented strand
board

9 Vapour barrier
10 Insulation glass of
two layers of
toughened safety
floatglass
11 Glass reinforced
plastic U-profile
12 Drip profile
embedded in glass
reinforced plastic
window sill
13 Glass fibre reinforced
plastic channel and
EPDM (ethylene
propylene dieme
monomer)
membrane
14 22 mm (7/8 inch)
oriented strand
board
15 15 mm (3/5 inch)
oriented strand
board
16 Ventilation slot
17 50 mm (2 inch)
Gravek
18 Foil layer

19 300 mm (12 inch)
timber beams with
insulation in between
20 15 mm (5/8 inch)
oriented strand
board
21 Vapour barrier
22 15 mm (5/8 inch)
gypsum plasterboard
23 Cement ligated
flakeboard
24 Timber beam

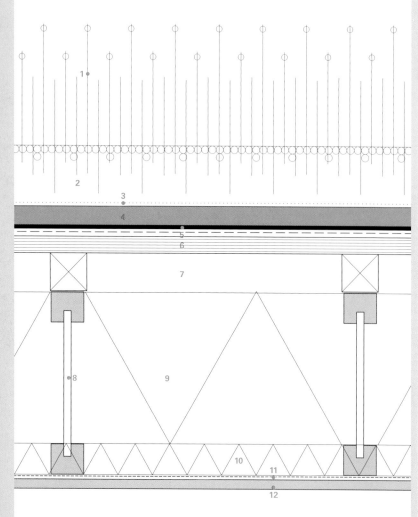

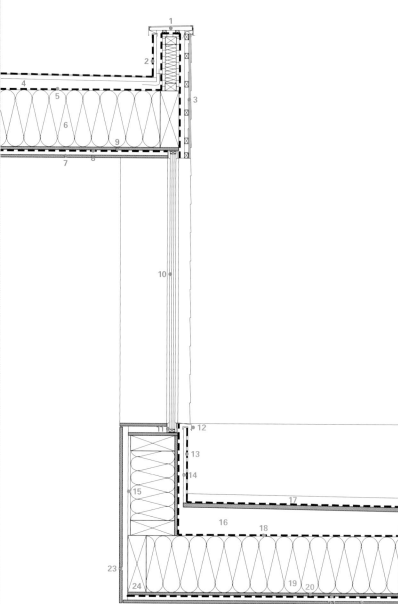

5.097
Box Gutter Detail 1:20

McBride Charles Ryan
The Dome House [21]

1 Copper sheeting on
   two layers of 8 mm
   ($1/3$ inch) plywood
   substrate
2 Copper sheet folded
   over
3 Copper counter-
   flashing

4 Timber rafter
5 Insulation
6 Metal mesh
7 Fibre cement sheet
8 Copper counter-
   flashing
9 Insulation
10 Copper capping on
   cleat
11 Face brickwork
12 Copper box gutter on
   plywood support
13 Box gutter on
   plywood support

14 Acoustic insulation
15 10 mm ($2/5$ inch)
   plasterboard

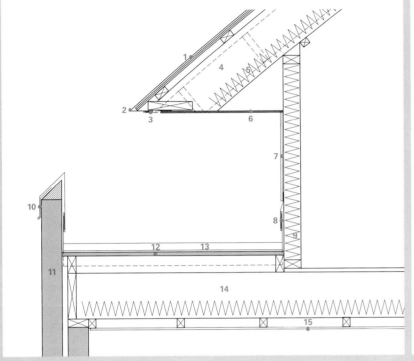

5.098
Terrace Roof Detail 1:10

Blank Studio
Xeros Residence [29]

1 4 mm ($1/6$ inch)
   unfinished steel plate
   fastened to steel
   flange
2 22 gauge hemmed
   Paint-lok fascia with
   continuous clips
3 Membrane roof

system with rock
ballast to match site
4 275 x 22 mm (11 x $7/8$
   inch) framing and
   hangers
5 Steel beam
6 20 gauge metal
   fascia cladding on
   self-healing
   waterproof
   membrane on 12.5
   mm ($1/2$ inch) exterior
   plywood
7 12.5 mm ($1/2$ inch)

plaster on 12.5 mm
($1/2$ inch) cement
board on suspended
ceiling hangers
8 Stretched wire mesh
   shade screen
9 Steel edge beam
   beyond
10 12.5 mm ($1/2$ inch)
   plaster on 12.5 mm
   ($1/2$ inch) cement
   board on suspended
   ceiling hangers

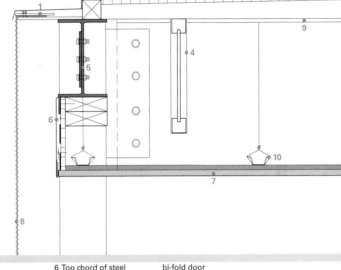

5.099
**Gutter Detail at Stepped
Roof Detail 1:10**

Tony Fretton Architects
The Courtyard House
[13]

1 Dotted line indicating
   parapet beyond
2 150 x 75 mm (6 x 3
   inch) purpose made
   perforated stainless
   steel retaining angle
3 Loose laid
   river-washed pebbles
4 Built-up bitumen
   sheet warm-roof

construction
5 100 mm (4 inch)
   insulation
6 Anodized aluminium
   finish purpose made
   gutter fascia
7 Stainless steel drip
8 Purpose made
   aluminium gutter
   and outlet spouts
9 Torch-on vapour
   control layer as part
   of warm-roof
   construction
10 25 mm (1 inch)
   plywood decking
11 200 x 50 mm (8 x 2
   inch) softwood joists

12 450 x 150 mm (18 x 6
   inch) universal beam
13 Galvanized joist
   hanger
14 175 x 75 mm (7 x 3
   inch) softwood
   blocking
15 Fixing plates to steel
   column beyond
16 Plasterboard lining
   on 35 x 35 mm ($13/8$ x
   $13/8$ inch) battens
17 Timber joists
18 Universal channel
   between steel posts
   shown dotted

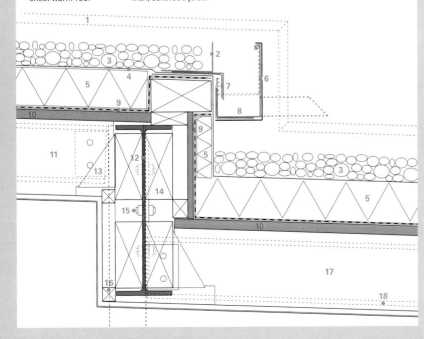

5.100
Roof Parapet Detail 1:10

Peter L. Gluck and
Partners, Architects
Inverted Guest House
[26]

1 Copper roof flashing
2 Single ply EPDM
   (ethylene propylene
   dieme monomer)
   roof membrane
3 Plywood roofing
   substrate
4 Steel beam
5 Continuous timber
   blocking

6 Top chord of steel
   truss
7 Continuous timber
   blocking
8 152 x 152 x 10 mm (6
   x 6 x $3/8$ inch) clip
   angle
9 Copper flashing
10 Steel tube integral to
   insulated steel
   framed garage door
11 Two 200 x 40 mm (8
   x $15/8$ inch) timber
   blocking
12 Corrugated copper
   cladding
13 Moisture barrier
14 Plywood attached to

bi-fold door
15 Insulated steel
   framed garage door
16 Nylon pull strap
17 Painted timber fascia
18 Continuous timber
   blocking
19 Bottom chord of steel
   truss
20 Bottom chord truss
   extension

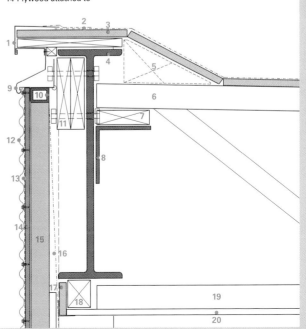

5.101
Skylight Detail 1:10

Skene Catling de la Peña
Architects
The Dairy House [31]

1 Double glazed unit
2 Aluminium trim
3 Steel plate
4 Lead cover to gutter
5 Firring pieces with
 insulation between
6 18 mm (3/4 inch)

plywood formed
 gutter
7 Existing steel column
8 Timber packing
9 12.5 mm (1/2 inch)
 plywood sheathing
10 Roofing felt
11 25 x 35 mm (1 x 13/8
 inch) timber battens
12 Waterproof layer
13 Natural slate tiles
14 200 mm (8 inch)
 rafters with
 insulation between

15 12.5 mm (1/2 inch)
 plasterboard with
 vapour barrier
16 25 mm (1 inch)
 chipboard flooring
17 Two 200 x 50 mm (8
 x 2 inch) timber joists
 supporting rafters
18 12.5 mm (1/2 inch)
 plasterboard,
 skimmed and painted

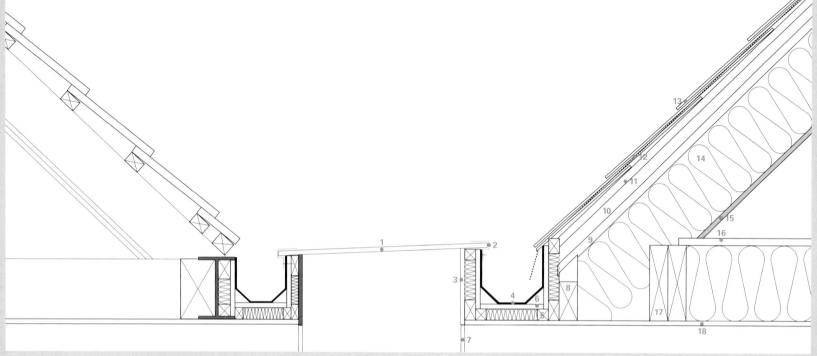

5.102
**Roof and Parapet Detail
1:10**

Glas Architects
The Nail Houses [23]

1 Powder-coated
 aluminium flashing
 as capping to
 upstand
2 440 x 100 x 107.5 mm
 (171/2 x 4 x 41/4 inch)
 Forticrete splitface
 block, pewter colour
 to rear elevation
3 Timber battens for
 fixing of metal clip
4 Insulated cavity
 closer
5 100 mm (4 inch)
 Rockwool cavity slab
 insulation
6 Single ply polymeric
 membrane fully
 adhered to 25 mm (1
 inch) insulation
7 Concrete blockwork
 to inside leaf of
 cavity wall parapet
8 Single ply polymeric
 membrane fully
 adhered to 25 mm (1
 inch) insulation
9 Single ply roof
 membrane fully
 adhered to insulation
10 Damp proof
 membrane
11 Weep hole
12 Timber firring at 1:60
 fall
13 Tanalised treated
 timber batten with
 top cut at an angle
 for drainage
14 15 mm (5/8 inch)
 pre-finished marine
 grade plywood
15 Single ply roof
 membrane fully
 adhered to 18 mm

(3/4 inch) weather
 bonded and proofed
 plywood
16 100 x 50 mm (4 x 2
 inch) tanalised
 treated timber
 structure
17 100 mm (4 inch)
 cavity slab insulation
18 Roof membrane
 lapped over timber
 fillet
19 Single ply roof
 membrane fully
 adhered to insulation
20 110 mm (43/8 inch)
 insulation
21 Vapour barrier
22 18 mm (3/4 inch)
 weather bonded and
 proofed plywood
23 150 x 50 mm (6 x 2
 inch) timber ceiling
 joists with timber
 firrings to fall
24 Insulation
25 Metal drip edge
26 Compriband seal
27 24 mm (1 inch)
 double glazed
 window unit in
 polyester
 powder-coated
 aluminium frame
28 Timber battens fixed
 to underside of joists
29 15 mm (5/8 inch)
 pre-finished marine
 grade plywood
30 15 mm (5/8 inch)
 pre-finished marine
 grade plywood to
 sides

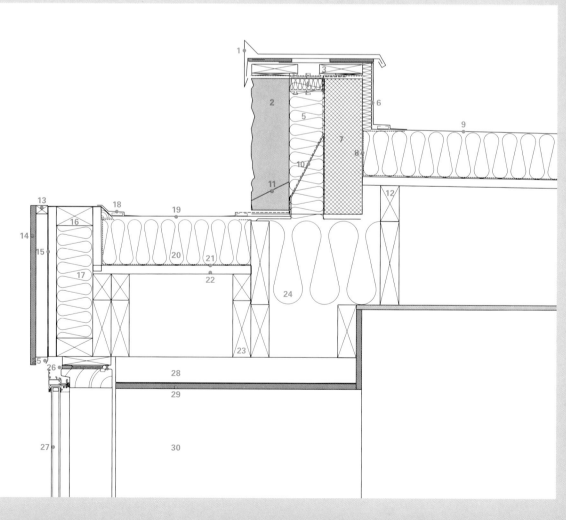

5.103
Roof Detail 1:20

Pierre Minassian
Architecte
Biscuit House [11]

1 Planting
2 Formed stainless
  steel edge to contain
  roof planting
3 Lava stones
4 Insulation
5 Concrete roof slab
6 Suspended plaster
  ceiling
7 Isowool insulation
8 Aluminium profile

edge capping
9 Rail with wheels for
  sliding Iroko shutter
10 Silicone seal
11 Stainless steel angle
12 Stainless steel cable
13 Iroko wood slats
14 Steel column
15 Double glazed fixed
  window

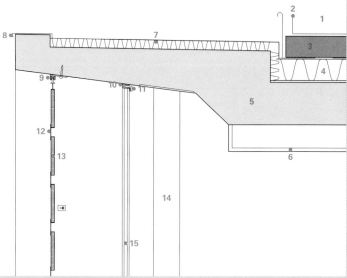

5.105
Roof Parapet Detail 1:10

ODOS Architects
House in Wicklow [18]

1 Profiled metal drip
2 Fire-rated 4.8kg
  granular surfaced
  polyester reinforced
  APP-modified
  bitumen high
  performance
  membrane, fully
  torch bonded
3 Packing timbers
4 Vapour barrier
5 18 mm (7/10 inch)

marine grade
plywood
6 Structural steel beam
7 Silicone based paint
  finish to external
  walls on cement-
  based mineral render
  on insulation system
8 Compressible
  neoprene seal
9 Recessed hardwood
  timber frame
10 Full height, clear
  double glazed fixed
  unit comprised of 8
  mm (1/3 inch)
  toughened glass
  outer pane, 12 mm

(1/2 inch) air gap
and 8 mm (1/3 inch)
clear toughened
inner pane in a
recessed treated
hardwood timber
frame with all joints
between glass panes
silicone-sealed and
bonded
11 Heavy draped curtain
  system comprised of
  extruded aluminium
  curtain track recessed
  in ceiling, to run
  length of full height
  glazing
12 12.5 mm (1/2 inch)

plasterboard,
skimmed and painted

5.104
**Roof and Gutter Detail
1:5**

Rowan Opat Architects
Courtyard
House [38]

1 Steel roof beam
2 Sheet metal roof
  cladding with
  zincalume finish
3 Insulation
4 Steel valley-gutter
  beam
5 Folded steel valley
  gutter sheet
6 Marine grade ply

gutter board
7 Steel framed gutter
  support
8 Steel valley-gutter
  beam
9 Laminated timber
  rafters
10 Painted plasterboard
  internal lining

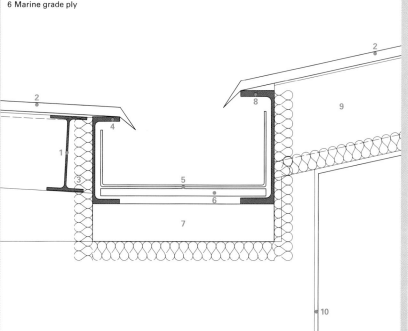

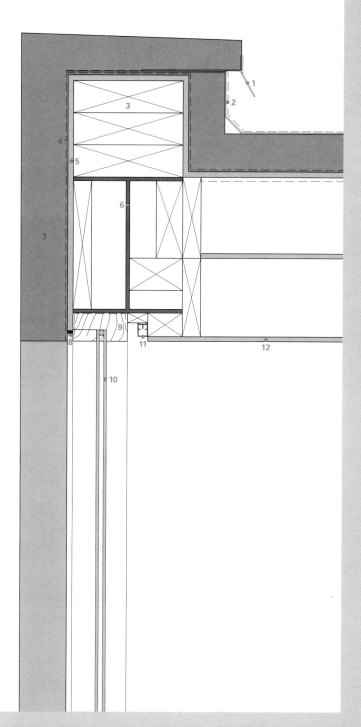

5.106
Roof and Skylight Detail 1:20

Vittorio Longheu
Casa C [16]

1 Aluminium capping with formed drips
2 Concrete string course
3 20 mm (3/4 inch) external render
4 200 mm (8 inch) brick wall
5 20 mm (3/4 inch) plaster
6 Reinforced concrete

and glass block
7 20 mm (3/4 inch) external render
8 Flashing
9 Flooring on bearers
10 Waterproof layer
11 Two layers 60 mm (2 3/8 inch) insulating board
12 Insulating layer
13 Concrete bed for defining 50 mm (2 inch) slope
14 40 mm (1 3/8 inch) concrete capping
15 Tile-lintel floor
16 10 mm (3/8 inch) plaster

17 3 mm (1/8 inch) plexiglas sheet
18 Lines of neon lamps
19 30 mm (1 1/4 inch) external render
20 10 mm (3/8 inch) render coat
21 40 mm (1 3/8 inch) polystyrene insulating board
22 80 mm (3 1/8 inch) brick

5.107
Eaves Detail 1:20

Bercy Chen Studio
Peninsula House [36]

1 Standing seam copper roof
2 Roofing felt over insulation and firring
3 37 mm (1 1/2 inch) rigid insulation between firring comprised of one layer of 25 mm (1 inch) rigid insulation and one layer of 12.5 mm (1/2 inch) rigid

foam with radiant barrier face up
4 50 x 100 mm (2 x 4 inch) firring strips at 450 mm (18 inch) centres with firring as needed to level out existing roof
5 75 x 50 x 6 mm (3 x 2 x 1/4 inch) steel angle attached through copper to sheathing, sealed as needed
6 New timber framing to eaves
7 Continuous copper sheet broken at eaves edge to form

soffit
8 Continuous 75 x 6 mm (3 x 1/4 inch) steel plate attached to sheathing to keep clean line at copper edge
9 Copper soffit sealed to retain colour
10 Timber headers
11 112 x 12.5 mm (4 2/5 x 1/2 inch) solar shade housing with access panel in soffit to allow access to full length of shade
12 12.5 mm (1/2 inch) steel plate bearing

seat welded to beam
13 Sheetrock turned down in front of blocking
14 25 mm (1 inch) insulated, tinted, low-E glass
15 Steel column beyond
16 Rigid insulation sprayed between existing rafters
17 14 mm (5/8 inch) sheetrock over existing ceiling joists

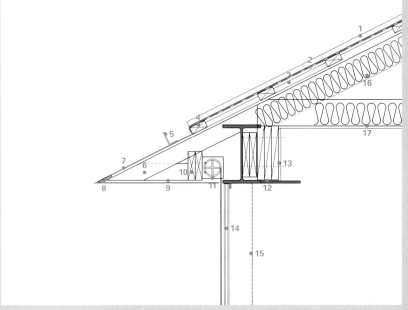

5.108
Skylight Detail 1:20

Pezo von Ellrichshausen Architects
Poli House [09]

1 Skylight double glazing
2 Black electro-painted aluminium frame
3 30 mm (1 1/4 inch) mortar bed with water repellent coating
4 160 to 120 mm (6 1/4 to 4 3/4 inch) insulating concrete

laid to falls
5 5 mm (1/5 inch) bituminous sealing layer
6 140 mm (5 1/2 inch) reinforced concrete slab
7 25 x 100 mm (1 x 4 inch) pine boards
8 25 x 100 mm (1 x 4 inch) pine boards painted white
9 Reinforced concrete, painted white

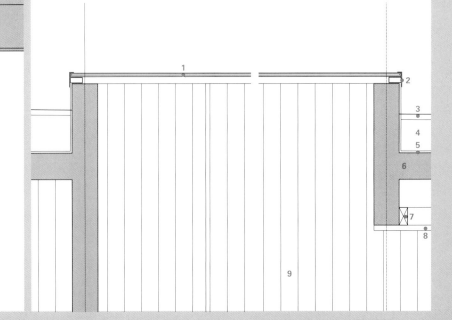

5.109
Roof, Gutter and Guardrail Detail 1:10

WPA
Weese Young Residence [28]

1 Galvanized steel handrail with stainless steel cables
2 Painted rectangular hollow section column
3 Recycled rubber tile flooring
4 Waterproof membrane on two layers of plywood
5 Engineered timber joist
6 Bent steel gutter
7 Cap flashing
8 Painted exterior-grade plywood
9 Cedar boards to ceiling
10 Timber blocking
11 Painted rectangular hollow section beam
12 Flashing

5.110
Roof and Gutter Detail 1:5

Powerhouse Company
Villa 1 [15]

1 Waterproof membrane
2 100 mm (4 inch) insulation laid to fall
3 Mastic wood
4 Aluminium capping
5 80 mm (3¹/₈ inch) drainage grille
6 18 mm (³/₄ inch) multiplex boarding
7 60 mm (2³/₈ inch) diameter drain pipe
8 Timber packer
9 Welded steel strip to attach roof edge construction
10 200 x 190 mm (8 x 7¹/₂ inch) steel beam
11 18 mm (³/₄ inch) waterproof bonded plywood multiplex boarding
12 400 x 800 x 20 mm (16 x 32 x ³/₄ inch) travertine panels glued to multiplex boarding
13 100 x 40 mm (4 x 1⁵/₈ inch) timber rail
14 80 mm (3¹/₈ inch) insulation
15 100 mm (4 inch) beam
16 18 mm (³/₄ inch) cementitious boarding
17 12 mm (¹/₂ inch) cementitious boarding

attached between 100 mm (4 inch) packer

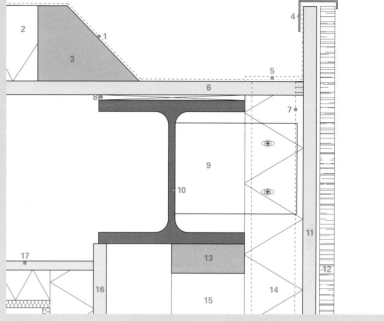

5.111
Roof Parapet Detail 1:10

Safdie Rabines Architects
Artist Bridge Studio [30]

1 Sheet metal parapet capping sloped by firring to drain to roof side
2 Formed metal drip
3 Galvanized metal flashing
4 100 x 50 mm (4 x 2 inch) timber studs to form parapet
5 Galvanized metal counter flashing with continuous sealant
6 350 x 150 mm (14 x 6 inch) glulam beam
7 Base flashing
8 Timber angle fillet
9 Built-up roof membrane
10 Two layers of 20 mm (³/₄ inch) structural plywood sheathing
11 240 x 40 mm (9¹/₂ x 1⁵/₈ inch) timber joist
12 Insulation
13 15 mm (⁵/₈ inch) gypsum board ceiling
14 140 x 40 mm (5¹/₂ x 1⁵/₈ inch) timber stud
15 Trespa high performance exterior cladding panels
16 Building paper
17 Structural plywood sheathing
18 Insulation
19 15 mm (⁵/₈ inch) gypsum wall board

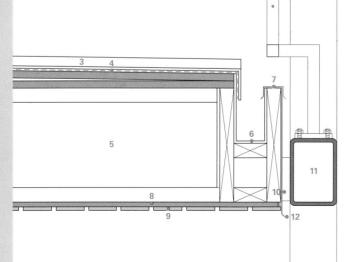

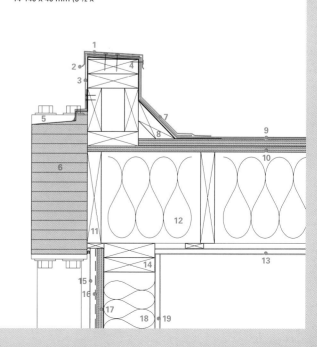

5.112
Roof Detail 1:10

ARTEC Architekten
Holiday House [39]

1 Sarnafil glued on 22 mm (7/8 inch) timber planking and ventilation gap, two 100 mm (4 inch) rigid insulation layers on 108 mm (41/4 inch) solid wood board, moisture barrier and 6.5 mm (1/4 inch) birch plywood lining
2 180 x 200 mm (7 x 8 inch) timber bearer
3 Two 100 mm (4 inch) rigid insulation layers
4 Zinc plate, seamed eaves gutter
5 150 x 80 mm (6 x 31/8 inch) timber bearer
6 300 x 30 mm (12 x 11/5 inch) larch fascia board
7 Insect screen
8 Moisture barrier
9 530 mm (21 inch) threaded rod, glued in construction timber
10 12 mm (1/2 inch) on 200 mm (8 inch) construction timber and insulation, and with 12 mm (1/2 inch) oriented strand board and 9 mm (3/8 inch) birch plywood board
11 Polyurethane foam
12 Furnishing band
13 120 x 50 mm (43/4 x 2 inch) scantling

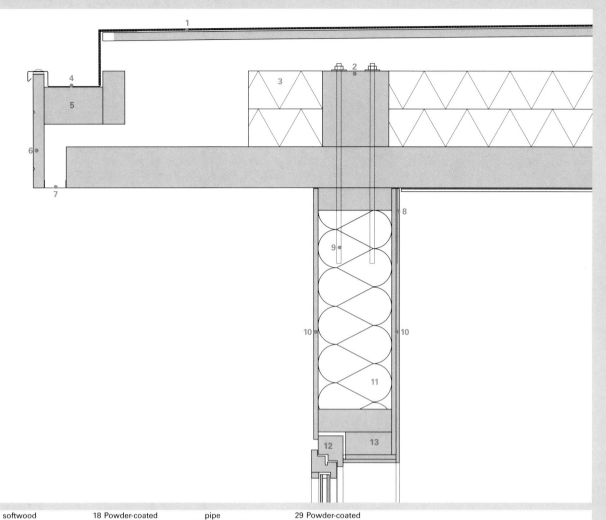

5.113
Eaves Detail 1:10

Haddow Partnership
Higher Farm [17]

1 Single ply membrane
2 100mm (4 inch) insulation
3 Three layers of 6 mm (1/4 inch) plywood
4 100 x 75 (4 x 3 inch) treated softwood trimmer
5 50mm (2 inch) insulation
6 200 x 50mm (8 x 2 inch) treated softwood
7 Waterproof plywood
8 Single ply membrane welded to rainwater outlet
9 Aluminium grate
10 Pressed aluminium flashing
11 200 x 50 mm (8 x 2 inch) treated softwood
12 Single ply membrane pressed trim
13 Treated softwood fillet
14 Treated softwood fillet
15 Proprietary fixing
16 150 x 75 mm (6 x 3 inch) preformed channel eaves beam
17 Powder-coated pressed aluminium fascia sheet
18 Powder-coated pressed aluminium trim
19 100 x 18 mm (4 x 3/4 inch) heat treated Scandinavian pine tongue and groove boarding
20 25 x 38 mm (1 inch x 11/2 inch) treated softwood counter battens
21 Powder-coated aluminium rainwater pipe
22 102.5 mm (4 inch) facing brickwork
23 175 mm (7 inch) insulation
24 203 x 133 mm (8 x 51/4 inch) universal beam
25 50 mm (2 inch) insulation
26 125mm (5 inch) blockwork
27 Damp proof course
28 Insulated lintel
29 Powder-coated aluminium window frame
30 12.5 mm (1/2 inch) internal plaster
31 Powder-coated aluminium window frame

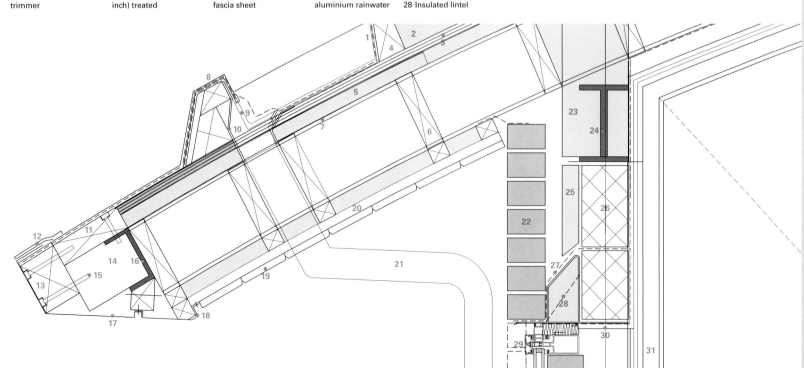

5.114
Roof Parapet and
Skylight Detail 1:10

John Onken Architects
Dolphin Cottage [32]

1 Double glazed
pyramid roof light in
polyester
powder-coated
aluminium framing
over lead flashing
2 Lead flashing

3 200 mm (8 inch) wide
pebble edging
4 Curb formed in 50 x
100 mm (2 x 4 inch)
treated softwood
5 Double timber
trimmers
6 Turf/sedum roof
planting on
proprietary
growing-medium
slabs with filter fabric
and root barrier
sheet below

7 Flat single ply
membrane adhered
over 100 mm (4 inch)
polyurethane
insulation
8 Roof decking laid to
fall
9 Roof joists
10 Plasterboard ceiling
11 Pre-weathered zinc
snap-down coping
over treated
softwood grounds
12 Top timber rail

13 Blockwork wall
14 Vertical timber
cladding
15 Wall ties
16 Breather membrane
17 Full-fill cavity
insulation

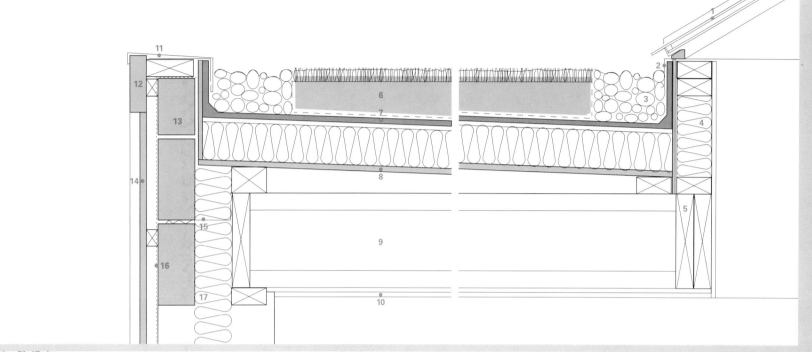

5.115
Roof Detail 1:10

Robert Seymour &
Associates
The Riverhouse [22]

1 Polyester
powder-coated
sealed double glazed
roof light
2 100 x 50 mm (4 x 2
inch) galvanized and
sprayed parallel
flange channel
beyond
3 75 x 75 mm (3 x 3
inch) rolled steel
angle
4 230 x 75 mm (9 x 3
inch) galvanized and
sprayed parallel
flange channel with
50 mm (2 inch) mild
steel flat upstand
notched around
parallel flange
channel
5 10 mm (3/8 inch) thick
painted medium
density fibreboard on
50 x 50 mm (2 x 2
inch) softwood
studding with
insulation
6 150 x 90 mm (6 x 31/2
inch) rolled steel
angle welded to
parallel flange
channel
7 Painted softwood sill
8 125 x 65 mm (5 x 21/2
inch) parallel flange
channel with mild
steel flat upstand
beyond
9 Membrane dressed
up front of blockwork
to underside of
parallel flange
channel
10 Single ply roof

membrane on fleece
lining, mechanically
fixed on insulation,
minimum 100 mm (4
inch) thick, cut to fall,
on vapour control
layer on 18 mm (3/4
inch) waterproof
plywood deck
11 150 x 50 mm (6 x 2
inch) timber joists
fixed to joist hangers
12 12.5 mm (1/2 inch)
plasterboard with
skim plaster finish
13 100 mm (4 inch)
blockwork
14 60 mm (23/8 inch)
insulation in 100 mm
(4 inch) cavity
15 StoRend flex coat
silicone through
colour render system
comprising 5 mm (1/4
inch) silicone outer
finish with 15 mm (5/8
inch) base coat on
mesh, applied
directly to blockwork
externally and
internally

5.116
Roof Detail 1:10

Room 11
Kingston House [34]

1 12 mm (1/2 inch) toughened glass
2 Glazing tape
3 10 mm (3/8 inch) Colorbond steel flashing
4 Kliplok Colorbond steel profile roofing
5 90 x 45 mm (3 1/2 x 1 3/4 inch) hardwood timber stud frame
6 170 x 43 mm (6 3/4 x 1 3/4 inch) timber rafters at 900 mm (36 inch) centres
7 10 mm (3/8 inch) plasterboard ceiling on 30 mm (1 1/5 inch) aluminium firring channels with 50 mm (2 inch) bulk insulation
8 12 mm (1/2 inch) smooth stained Boral Evolution plywood over timber battens, bulk insulation and building paper
9 20 x 50 mm (3/4 x 2 inch) hardwood timber batten

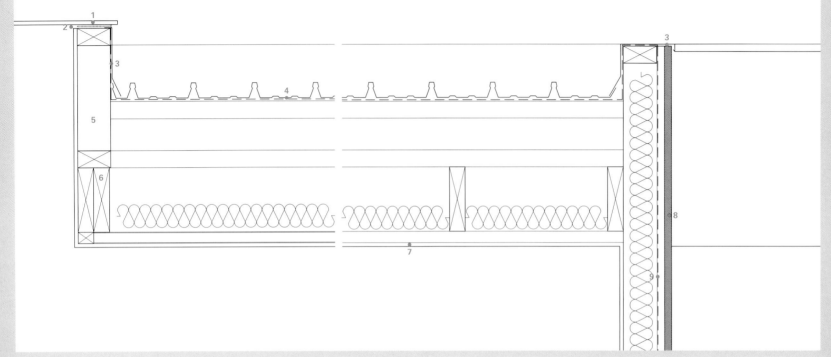

5.117
Flat Roof Overhang
Detail 1:10

Troppo Architects
Buttfield Town House [30]

1 120 x 45 mm (4 3/4 x 1 3/4 inch) purlins at 900 mm (36 inch) centres
2 6 mm (1/4 inch) cleat fixed to rafter with two M10 bolts
3 150 x 45 mm (6 x 1 3/4 inch) parallel flange channel taper cut to profile
4 Galvanized corrugated roofing
5 Galvanized barge trim
6 150 x 50 mm (6 x 2 inch) rectangular hollow section rafter
7 Fixing block
8 Ceiling firring channel system
9 Galvanized flashing
10 Sisalation
11 300 x 45 mm (12 x 1 3/4 inch) laminated veneer lumber edge joist
12 200 x 45 mm (8 x 1 3/4 inch) laminated veneer lumber joist at 450 mm (18 inch) centres
13 Galvanized Custom Orb cladding
14 Acoustic insulation
15 Pine packer
16 Folded galvanized bottom flashing

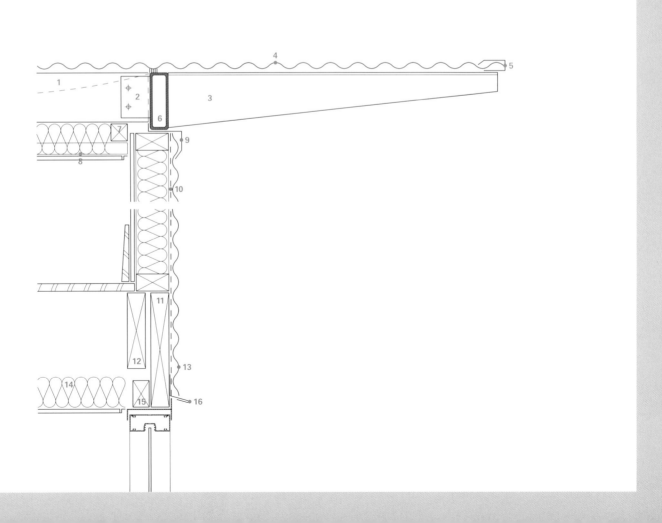

5.118
Roof Overhang Detail
1:10

Troppo Architects
Buttfield Town House
[30]

1 Galvanized ridge trim with drip
2 75 x 75 mm (3 x 3 inch) angle fascia purlin to rafter end
3 150 x 50 mm (6 x 2 inch) rectangular hollow section rafter taper cut to profile
4 Corrugated profile sealing strip
5 Sisalation
6 6 mm (1/4 inch) fillet welded to rectangular hollow section
7 Galvanized perforated ventilation strip
8 Cleat to both sides of rafter fixed by two M12 bolts
9 150 x 100 mm (6 x 4 inch) rectangular hollow section ridge beam
10 Silicone seal
11 Timber packing as required
12 Galvanized apron flashing
13 6 mm (1/4 inch) flat bar welded to rafter
14 230 x 75 mm (9 x 3 inch) parallel flange channel beam
15 150 x 50 mm (6 x 2 inch) rectangular hollow section rafter
16 Metal section firring channels
17 Cleat welded to beam and bolted to rectangular hollow section rafter
18 Galvanized flashing
19 150 x 42 mm (6 x 1 5/8 inch) fascia beam
20 Galvanized half-round gutter with brackets at 1000 mm (40 inch) centres
21 Solar panels and supporting purlins
22 125 x 75 mm (5 x 3 inch) rectangular hollow section outrigger to ridge beam with tapered cut to profile
23 150 x 100 mm (6 x 4 inch) rectangular hollow section ridge beam
24 Glazing frame
25 Fixed glazing

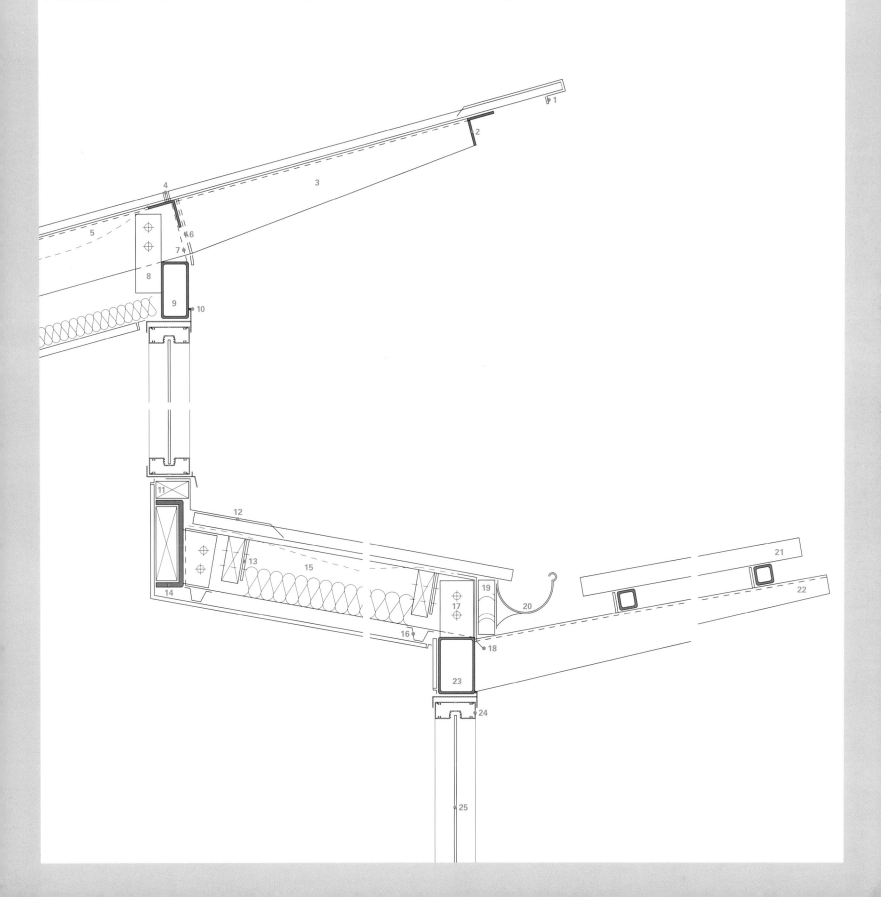

5.119
Gutter Detail 1:10

Skene Catling de la Peña
Architects
The Dairy House [31]

1 Natural slate roof
   tiles
2 Waterproof layer
3 25 x 35 mm (1 x 1³/₈
   inch) timber battens
4 Existing roof deck
5 200 mm (8 inch)

rafters with
insulation in between
6 12.5 mm (¹/₂ inch)
   plasterboard with
   vapour barrier
7 Two 200 x 50 mm (8
   x 2 inch) timber joists
   supporting rafters
8 Firring pieces with
   insulation between
9 Lead cover to gutter
10 18 mm (³/₄ inch)
   plywood formed
   gutter

11 Timber fillet to form
   gutter corner

5.120
Roof Edge and Gutter
Detail 1:10

Agence Michel Tortel
Mikado House [08]

1 Profiled steel roof
2 Mineral wool
   insulation
3 120 mm (4³/₄ inch)
   steel I-beams
4 Galvanized steel
   gutter

5 270 mm (10⁵/₈ inch)
   steel I-section edge
   beam
6 Epoxy-coated steel
   plate cladding
7 Modified slender 300
   mm (12 inch) I-beam
8 18 mm (³/₄ inch)
   plasterboard with
   water repellent finish

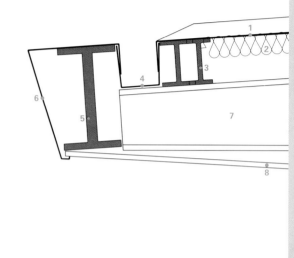

5.121
Roof Parapet Detail 1:10

Tonkin Zulaikha Greer
Hastings Parade House
[26]

1 19 x 66 mm (³/₄ x 2³/₅
   inch) hardwood
   timber decking
   continued to cover
   glass balustrade
   support and concrete
   upturn
2 85 x 30 mm (3¹/₃ x
   1¹/₅ inch) hardwood
   joists at 450 mm
   (17⁷/₁₀ inch) centres

spanning from
bearer to bearer
3 150 mm (6 inch)
   reinforced concrete
   slab with fall
4 13 mm (¹/₂ inch)
   plasterboard ceiling
   fixed to firring
   channels with paint
   finish
5 Glass balustrade
   fixed in 8 mm (³/₁₀
   inch) fabricated steel
   plate supporter with
   galvanized finish
   fixed to concrete
   upturn
6 Mild steel galvanized

angle fixed to
concrete upturn to
support joists
7 19 x 66 mm (³/₄ x 2³/₅
   inch) hardwood
   timber decking
8 Concrete upturn
   beam with fall
   spanning to end
   walls
9 Concealed gutter
   shown dotted
10 50 mm (2 inch)
   diameter zincalume
   spitter
11 100 mm (4 inch)
   diameter half-round
   zincalume gutter

12 Timber framed
   glazed door

5.122
Gutter Detail 1:10

Western Design
Architects
The Moat House [20]

1 Single ply roof
   covering dressed
   over 25 mm (1 inch)
   exterior-quality
   plywood to form
   back gutter. Gutter to
   discharge into
   rainwater pipe via
   rainwater chute
   through parapet wall
2 100 mm (4 inch) thick

insulation
3 25 mm (1 inch)
   exterior-quality
   plywood
4 Void
5 100 mm (4 inch)
   insulation
6 100 mm (4 inch)
   insulation to
   underside of back
   gutter
7 50 x 150 mm (2 x 6
   inch) timber roof
   joists at 400 mm (16
   inch) centres
8 Polyester
   powder-coated
   pressed aluminium

coping coloured to
match render
9 Single ply roof
   covering dressed
   over parapet wall
10 Cavity closer
11 100 mm (4 inch)
   glass fibre quilt
   between treated
   timber frame
12 50 mm (2 inch) cavity
   insulation
13 50 x 100 mm (2 x 4
   inch) treated timber
   frame
14 Treated timber
   battens at 400 mm
   (16 inch) centres

15 20 mm (³/₄ inch)
   polymer reinforced
   through colour
   render

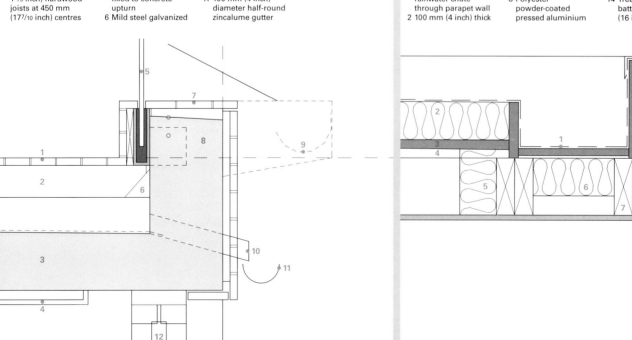

5.123
Roof and Skylight Detail 1:10

Tzannes Associates
Parsley Bay Residence
[21]

1 Aluminium framed roof light
2 Separating membrane below aluminium frame
3 Steel flats
4 Copper flashing
5 Concrete
6 Plasterboard on firring channels
7 Drip groove
8 Slip joint
9 Timber packer
10 Plasterboard stop bead
11 Light fitting
12 Gravel
13 Insulation
14 Render coat
15 Membrane
16 Flashing
17 Panelling on split battens
18 Timber trim

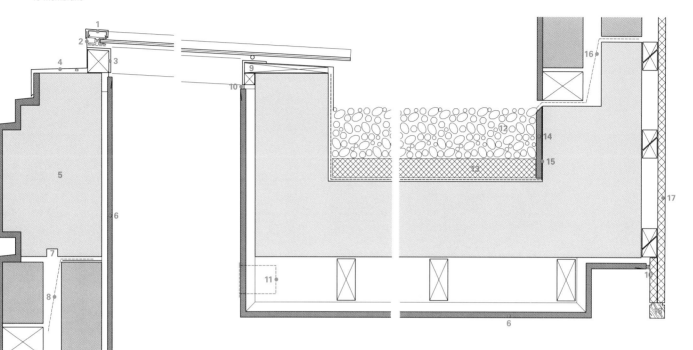

5.124
Roof Parapet Detail 1:10

Western Design Architects
The Moat House [20]

1 Polyester powder-coated pressed aluminium coping coloured to match render
2 Single ply roof covering dressed over parapet wall
3 25 mm (1 inch) exterior quality plywood
4 20 mm (3/4 inch) polymer reinforced through colour render on stainless steel Renderlath mesh
5 Treated timber grounds shot fired on to steel
6 50 x 200 mm (2 x 8 inch) batten between universal beams
7 178 x 102 mm (7 x 4 inch) universal beam
8 Colour coordinating unplasticized polyvinyl chloride movement bead
9 20 mm (3/4 inch) polymer reinforced through colour render
10 Renderlath panel
11 Treated timber battens
12 White soffit ventilators at 900 mm (36 inch) centres
13 Powder-coated pressed aluminium flashing and drip
14 Powder-coated thermally broken aluminium window frame with 6 mm (1/4 inch) self-cleaning high performance clear glass outer pane, 12 mm (1/2 inch) argon-filled cavity, 6 mm (1/4 inch) low-emissivity, coated glass inner pane for thermal control
15 Powder-coated thermally broken aluminium curtain walling
16 25 mm (1 inch) insulation to the ceiling perimeter
17 200 x 90 mm (8 x 31/2 inch) parallel flange channel
18 100 mm (4 inch) roof insulation
19 Vapour control layer
20 Minimum 20 mm (3/4 inch) – maximum 65 mm (21/2 inch) treated timber firring pieces
21 100 mm (4 inch) thick insulation
22 200 mm (8 inch) roof joist at 400 mm (16 inch) centres
23 12.5 mm (1/2 inch) plasterboard with skim finish

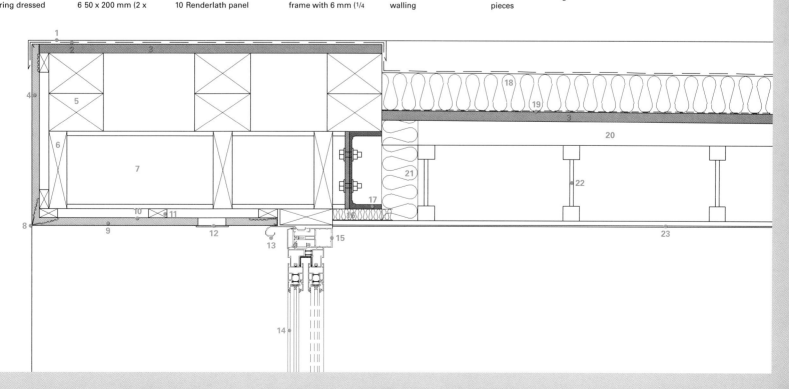

5.125
Roof Edge and Gutter Detail 1:10

EZZO
Leça House [35]

1 40 x 50 mm (1⅝ x 2 inch) timber profile on battens painted with polyurethane paint
2 Corrugated waterproof board
3 30 x 40 mm (1⅕ x 1⅝ inch) waterproof timber
4 20 mm (¾ inch) medium density fibreboard
5 100 mm (4 inch) mineral wall insulation with Kraft on one side
6 Zinc rainwater gutter
7 70 mm (2¾ inch) timber board painted with polyurethane paint
8 Air gap
9 12 mm (½ inch) plasterboard
10 Timber profile
11 Open timber frame painted with polyurethane paint

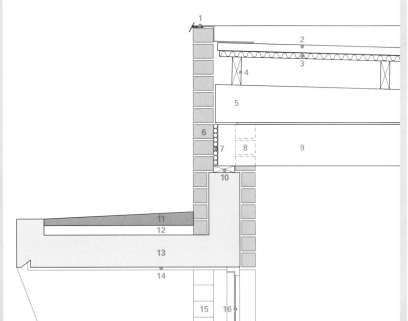

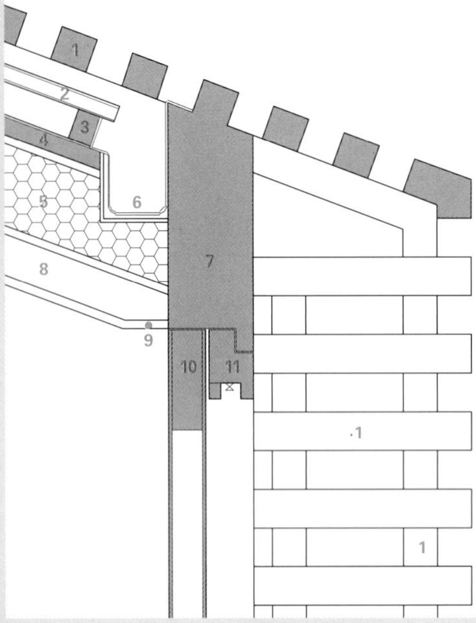

5.126
Flat Roof Detail 1:10

EZZO
Leça House [35]

1 40 x 50 mm (1⅝ x 2 inch) timber profile on battens painted with polyurethane paint
2 Corrugated waterproof board
3 300 gauge geotextile layer
4 30 x 40 mm (1⅕ x 1⅝ inch) waterproof timber
5 20 mm (⅜ inch) waterproof medium density fibreboard
6 100 mm (4 inch) mineral wall insulation
7 Drywall lining
8 110 mm (4⅜ inch) brick wall skin
9 PVC screen
10 40 mm (1⅝ inch) thermal insulation
11 Sanded plaster
12 12 mm (½ inch) plasterboard

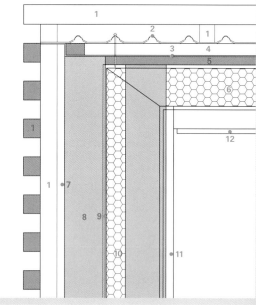

5.127
Roof Detail 1:20

Designworkshop: SA
Igoda View House [24]

1 Aluminium T-section to form coping and flash-off waterproofing membrane
2 Modek clear polycarbonate Kliplok roofing with minimum 200 mm (8 inch) overlap
3 30 mm (1⅕ inch) Isoboard insulation
4 150 x 38 mm (6 x 1½ inch) timber purlins fixed to tapered grounds with brackets
5 150 x 50 mm (6 x 2 inch) tapered grounds fixed above every third beam
6 Face brickwork with vertically brushed bagged finish to internal walls
7 Beam cut 30 mm (1⅕ inch) short for roof conduits
8 Brick infill between beams plastered/bagged according to schedule
9 220 x 70 mm (9 x 2¾ inch) rough sawn, sandblasted, reclaimed Oregon pine beams
10 120 x 30 mm (4¾ x 1⅕ inch) treated wall plate
11 Lightweight screed
12 50 mm (2 inch) screed laid to fall
13 Reinforced concrete slab with smooth off shutter finish to exposed faces
14 Off shutter concrete soffit with 15 mm (⅝ inch) internal steel trowelled plaster, skimmed with cretestone for ultra smooth finish and primed and painted
15 Face brickwork with vertically brushed bagged finish to internal walls
16 Proprietary powder-coated aluminium framed glass door

5.128
Roof Detail 1:10

Steffen Leisner, Ali Jeevanjee, Phillip Trigas
1+3=1 House [17]

1 Stainless steel cable guardrail
2 600 x 600 x 50 mm (24 x 24 x 2 inch) concrete roof pavers
3 Sheet metal flashing
4 Timber perimeter blocking
5 100 mm (4 inch) diameter adjustable pedestal
6 Two layers of asphalt roofing felt
7 Timber blocking
8 Two layers of plywood roof sheathing
9 Rigid insulation
10 Air space
11 12 mm (½ inch) plywood
12 Laminated veneer lumber edge piece
13 Laminated veneer lumber joist
14 Cement plaster with smooth trowel finish
15 Batt insulation
16 Gypsum wallboard
17 Plywood sheathing
18 Waterproofing layer

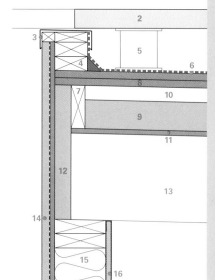

5.129 5.130

5.129
Roof Parapet Detail 1:10

Hawkes Architecture
Crossway [16]

1 Unweathered zinc
  parapet capping
2 Waterproof plywood
3 Chamfered treated
  timber fillet
4 Treated softwood
  upstand
5 Lambs red brick with
  lime mortar using
  crushed bottle sand
6 Tyvek Enercor wall
  membrane
7 Waterproof plywood
8 Black rubber EPDM
  (ethylene propylene
  dieme monomer)
  waterproofing
9 Treated softwood
  battens forming
  ventilation zone
10 Warmcell recycled

newspaper insulation
11 Plywood sheathing
  board
12 Plasterboard fixed on
  Dupont Energain
  thermal mass board
13 Plasterboard fixed on
  Dupont Energain
  thermal mass board
14 Panelvent
  vapour-permeable
  sheathing board
15 Tyvek Enercor wall
  membrane

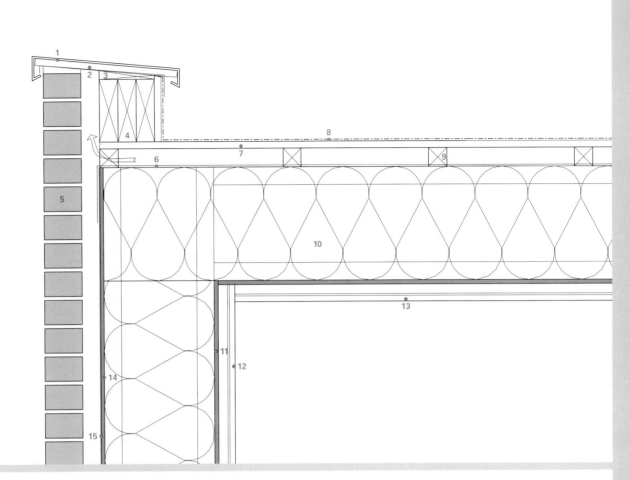

5.130
Roof Lighting Detail 1:5

Kallos Turin
Casa Zorzal [10]

1 5 mm (1/5 inch)
  aluminium foil
  waterproof
  membrane
2 Levelling layer
3 Concrete filling to
  form 1:50 slope
4 25 mm (1 inch)
  polystyrene
  insulation
5 Vapour barrier
6 3 mm (1/8 inch)

plaster skim coat
  with paint finish
7 Cement mortar
8 Reinforced concrete
  slab
9 Concealed
  incandescent strip
  lighting
10 115 mm (41/2 inch)
  brick wall

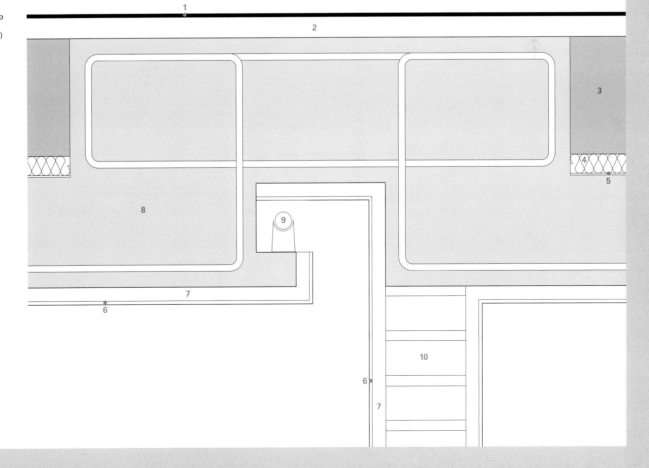

5.131
Eaves Detail 1:10

Skene Catling de la Peña
Architects
The Dairy House [31]

1 Natural slate roof
   tiles
2 Waterproof layer
3 25 x 35 mm (1 x 1³/₈
   inch) timber battens
4 Existing roof deck
5 200 mm (8 inch)

rafters with
insulation
in-between
6 12.5 mm (¹/₂ inch)
   plasterboard with
   vapour barrier
7 Timber wall plate
8 Painted timber fascia
9 Insulation
10 Local oak
11 Expanding foam filler
12 Laminated glass
   block
13 Neoprene gasket

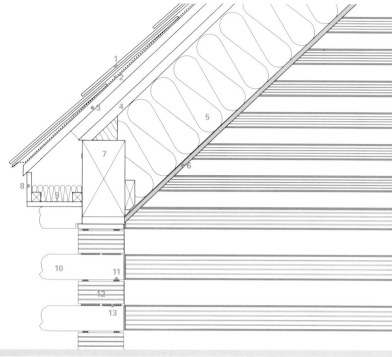

5.132
Roof Ridge Detail 1:10

Skene Catling de la Peña
Architects
The Dairy House [31]

1 Lead ridge capping
2 Timber ridge
3 Natural slate tiles
4 Waterproof layer
5 25 x 35 mm (1 x 1³/₈
   inch) timber battens
6 Existing deck

7 200 mm (8 inch)
   rafters with
   insulation between
8 12.5 mm (¹/₂ inch)
   plasterboard with
   vapour barrier

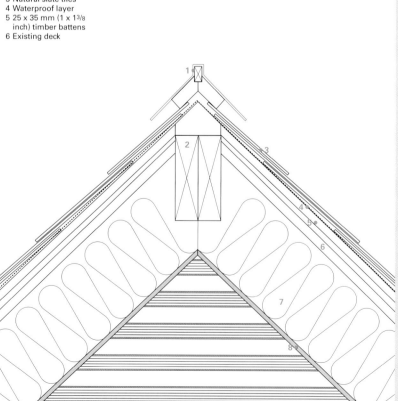

5.133
Roof Parapet Detail 1:5

Paulo David with Luz
Ramalho
Casa Funchal [16]

1 Black volcanic pebble
2 Geotextile blanket
3 Two layers of 40 mm
   (1⁵/₈ inch) insulation
4 Two layers of
   waterproof
   membrane

5 Concrete screed
6 Concrete roof slab
7 Zinc capping to
   parapet wall
8 Concrete extended
   from inner layer to
   cover block wall
9 Roof drainage pipe
10 150 mm (6 inch)
   concrete block wall
11 Monomass render
   system to external
   wall
12 30 mm (1¹/₈ inch)

insulation
13 Air cavity
14 Fine plaster lining to
   concrete block wall

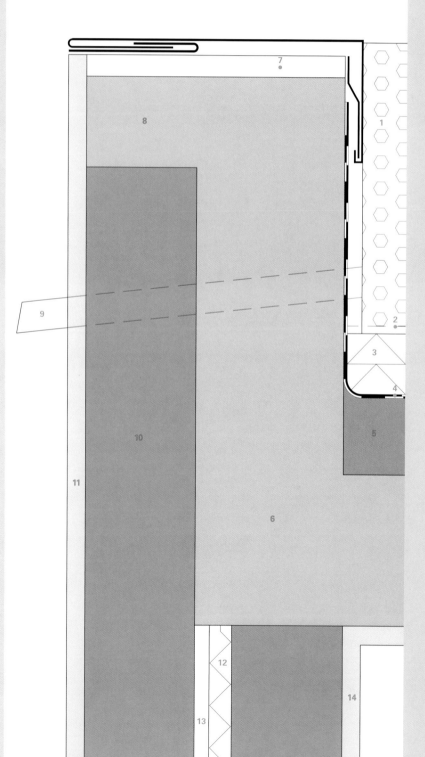

5.134
Roof Detail 1:10

Alphaville
Hall House 1 [07]

1 Fair-faced concrete roof with osmosis liquid waterproofing paint finish
2 50mm (2inch) urethane foam insulation
3 Emulsion paint finish on 9.5 mm (3/8 inch) plasterboard fixed to 70 x 30 mm (23/4 x 11/5 inch) timber

substrate framing
4 Construction joint sealed with resin mortar
5 Fair-faced concrete exterior wall with osmosis liquid waterproofing paint finish
6 Emulsion painted 12.5 mm (1/2 inch) plasterboard on 20 mm (3/4 inch) polystyrene foam

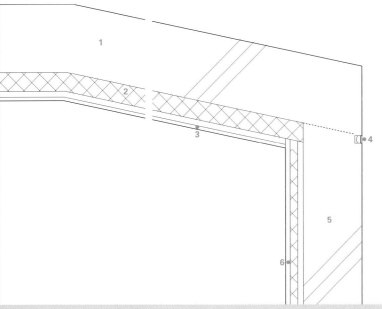

5.135
Roof Parapet Detail 1:10

Boyd Cody Architects
Richmond Place House [22]

1 Brick coping to be oriented flat side upwards and tilted down by 5 mm (1/5 inch) to the rear
2 Canted brick coping on Paralon NT bonded onto slate cavity closer
3 Paralon roof membrane bonded

to slate and dressed over and bonded to upstand. Roof membrane carried under slate and dressed over stepped damp proof course
4 50 x 50 mm (2 x 2 inch) treated softwood fillet
5 50 mm (2 inch) layer of selected lava chippings
6 Roof comprised of proprietary mineral finished membrane on 3 mm (3/16 inch) underlay, flame

bonded to 120 mm (43/4 inch) insulation on 12 mm (1/2 inch) fibreboard on bitumen boards, 3 mm (3/16 inch) glass-reinforced vapour control layer, flame bonded to 18 mm (7/10 inch) ply deck, and firring pieces on 150 x 44 mm (6 x 13/4 inch) timber joists at 300 mm (12 inch) centres
7 Stepped damp proof course dressed under slate, stepped

down and across cavity into brick outer leaf with weep holes at 400 mm (16 inch) centres
8 Treated softwood firring pieces to fall of minimum 1:40
9 100 mm (4 inch) brick outer leaf in stretcher bond
10 175 x 44 mm (7 x 13/4 inch) timber joists at 300 mm (12 inch) centres
11 12.5 mm (1/2 inch) thick plasterboard ceiling

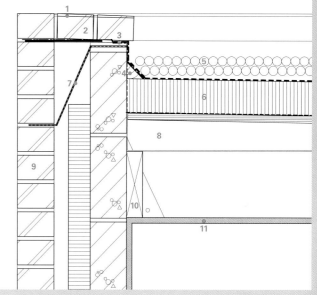

5.136
Terrace Roof Detail 1:10

de Blacam and Meagher Architects
Morna Valley Residence [20]

1 Concrete capping
2 Sand and cement render
3 White marble gravel
4 Geotextile membrane
5 Extruded polystyrene insulation
6 Bitumen membrane
7 Extruded polystyrene

insulation
8 Screed laid to falls
9 Reinforced concrete beam
10 Reinforced concrete beam supporting terracotta arch panel
11 Reinforced concrete column

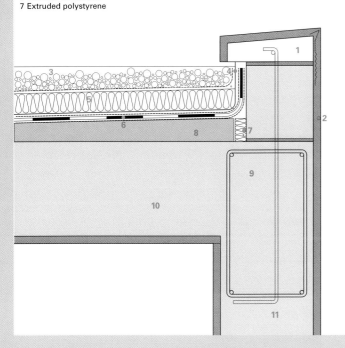

5.137
Roof Overhang Detail 1:10

Troppo Architects
Buttfield Town House [30]

1 Sub-sill to match window frame
2 Plaster edge stop to form shadow gap
3 10 mm (3/8 inch) plasterboard
4 142 x 19 mm (55/8 x 3/4 inch) skirting board with clear finish

5 Carpet floor finish
6 Folded galvanized bottom flashing
7 Concrete slab
8 6 mm (1/4 inch) continuous drip to underside of slab

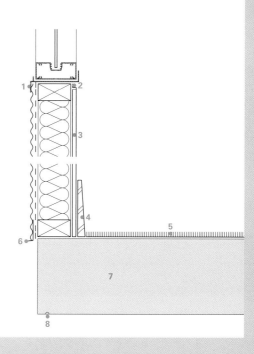

5.138
Roof Parapet Detail 1:10

Cassion Castle
Architects
Twofold House [12]

1 Hardwood timber
   decking cladding to
   all terrace surfaces
2 Vapour barrier
3 18 mm (7/10 inch)
   waterproof plywood
4 2 mm (1/12 inch) lead
   flashing
5 200 mm (8 inch)
   blockwork
6 18 mm (7/10 inch)
   waterproof plywood
7 50 mm (2 inch)
   ventilation above
   insulation and joists
8 Concealed rainwater
   pipe
9 Hardwood timber
   decking
10 Glass fibre

rainwater tray
11 Firring to give
   rainwater tray fall of
   1:90
12 150 mm (6 inch)
   mineral wool
   insulation
13 15 mm (5/8 inch)
   Fireline plasterboard
   with 3 mm (1/8 inch)
   plaster skim coat

5.139
Roof Deck Balustrade
Detail 1:20

Marsh Cashman
Koolloos Architects
Maroubra House [36]

1 Solid timber handrail
   to match cladding
2 Waterproof sarking
   lining
3 Timber cladding
4 New hardwood
   timber decking
5 High performance
   waterproof
   membrane
6 Spacer joist on 75 x
   75 x 10 mm (3 x 3 x
   3/8 inch) neoprene
   pads
7 Insulation on
   waterproof sarking
   lining
8 Timber joist
9 Medium density

roof cladding
10 25 mm (1 inch)
   styrofoam insulation
11 Existing masonry
   wall
12 Existing ceiling
   construction

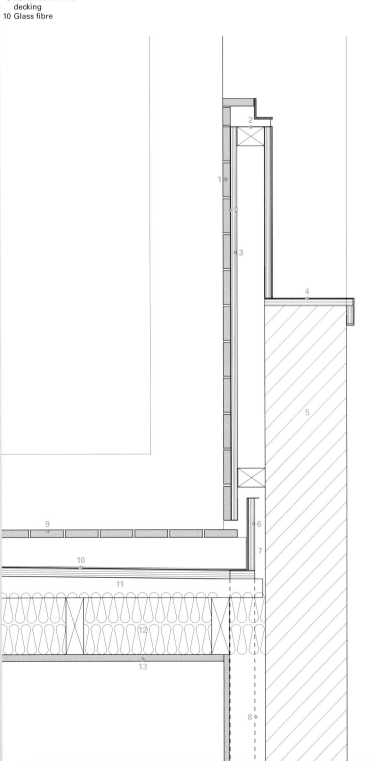

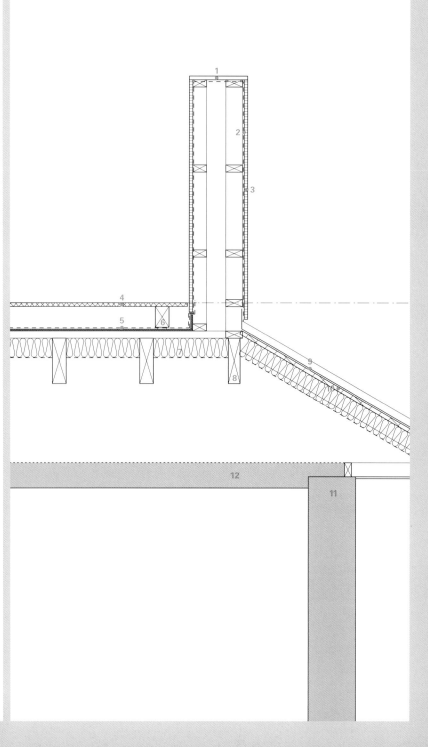

5.140
Zinc Roof and Skylight
Detail 1:20

Keith Williams Architects
The Long House [23]

1 Fixed double glazed
   roof light system
2 Pre-patinated zinc
   cladding and
   standing seam to
   roof
3 Foam glass
   insulation substrate
   with serrated clip
   fixings over
   bituminous primer
4 Exposed fair-faced
   concrete finish
5 Zinc lined gutter
6 Folded zinc coping
   over rendered
   parapet
7 100 mm (4 inch)
   insulated render
   cladding

8 10 mm (3/8 inch)
   calcium silicate
   board substrate
9 Recessed light fitting
10 Render to insulation
   at soffit and reveal
11 Powder-coated
   double glazed
   aluminium sliding
   unit

5.141
Roof and Elevator Shaft
Detail 1:20

Morphogenesis
N85 Residence [08]

1 Top of parapet
2 10 x 10 mm (3/8 x 3/8
   inch) aluminium drip
   groove
3 Aluminium louvres
   with bird screen
4 Brick batt insulation
   with waterproofing
5 Inverted reinforced
   concrete beam
6 75 mm (3 inch)
   insulation
7 Waterproofing coat
   with cement plaster
   over concrete
   structural slab
8 Mild steel post
9 12 mm (1/2 inch)
   diameter mild steel
   hollow section

10 Pre-cast concrete
   coping
11 Concrete structural
   beam
12 Cement screed with
   maximum slope of
   1:100
13 Waterproof priming
   coat with cement
   plaster over
   structural slab
14 Lift shaft

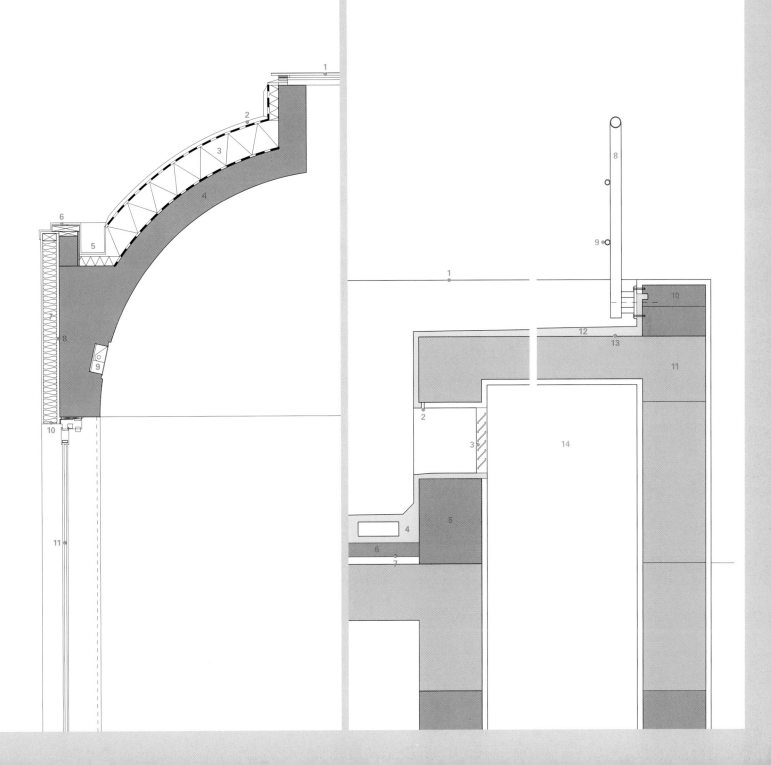

5.142
Gutter Detail 1:10

ARTEC Architekten
Holiday House [39]

1 60 x 80–120 mm (2¹/₃ x 3¹/₈–4³/₄ inch) timber beam sized to facilitate slope for water run off
2 Zinc coated metal eaves gutter
3 Timber gutter support
4 Timber packing
5 300 x 30 mm (11⁴/₅ x 1¹/₅ inch) larch faced

plywood fascia
6 Metal plate stiffener
7 Timber nailer
8 Insect mesh
9 Stainless steel tension cable

5.143
Roof Edge Detail 1:10

Public
Rattlesnake Creek
House [15]

1 Fold-down double standing seam at flashing at high point of roof
2 Roofing membrane
3 20 mm (3/4 inch) plywood
4 Timber beam creating insulation cavity
5 Timber edge beam

6 Timber fascia board
7 Corrugated metal decking
8 Sheet metal flashing with folded profile at bottom edge
9 Steel beam

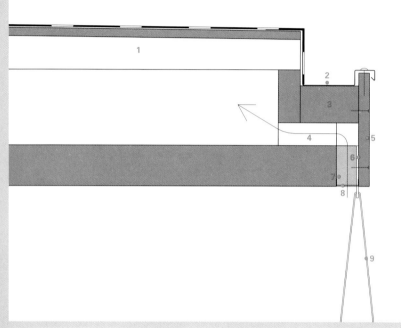

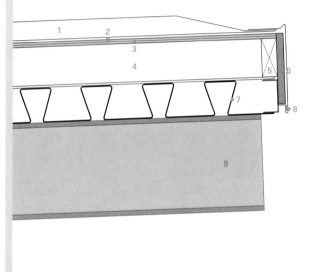

5.144
Roof Detail 1:7.5

Simon Walker Architects
Dane House [06]

1 Natural colour standard Roadstone flat concrete roof tile with dyeing agents removed
2 Natural colour standard Roadstone flat concrete roof tile with dyeing agents removed
3 35 x 25 mm (1¹/₃ x ¹/₂ inch) tanalised

timber roofing counter battens
4 Sand-and-cement pointing
5 100 x 50 x 6 mm (4 x 2 x ¹/₄ inch) cold rolled stainless steel box frame
6 Mill finish aluminium square capping section
7 Backing plate with neoprene gaskets
8 35 x 25 mm (1¹/₃ x ¹/₂ inch) tanalised timber roofing battens
9 Torch-on Paralon felt

on 18 mm (7/10 inch) waterproof plywood roof deck
10 225 x 50 mm (8⁴/₅ x 2 inch) treated timber joists, shot-fixed to steel
11 Skim finish ceiling on 12.5 mm (¹/₂ inch) plasterboard
12 Line of ceiling corner upstand seen in elevation
13 White painted finish 350 x 175 x 46 mm (13³/₄ x 6⁹/₁₀ x 1⁴/₅ inch) universal steel roof beam with lower

half left exposed to room

5.145
Roof Detail 1:10

Tham & Videgård
Arkitekter
Archipelago House [40]

1 Steel sheet, gutter and covering with black drop apron
2 Waterproofing layer
3 22 x 120 mm (7/8 x 4³/₄ inch) pressure impregnated timber boards
4 45 x 95 mm (1³/₄ x 3³/₄ inch) timber beam

5 45 x 220 mm (1³/₄ x 8⁵/₈ inch) timber beam
6 20 x 160 mm (3/4 x 6³/₁₀ inch) timber boarding
7 Dovetailed timber boards to ceiling
8 Polythene sheet vapour barrier
9 Shower curtain rail
10 Window frame
11 Insulated double glazing

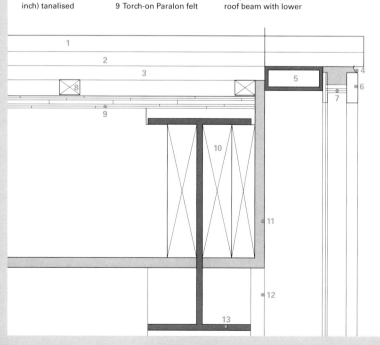

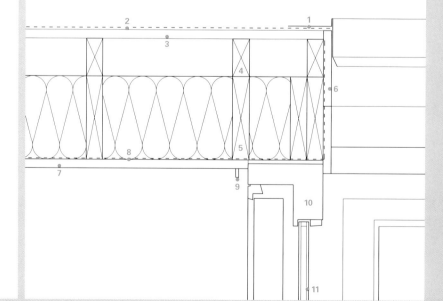

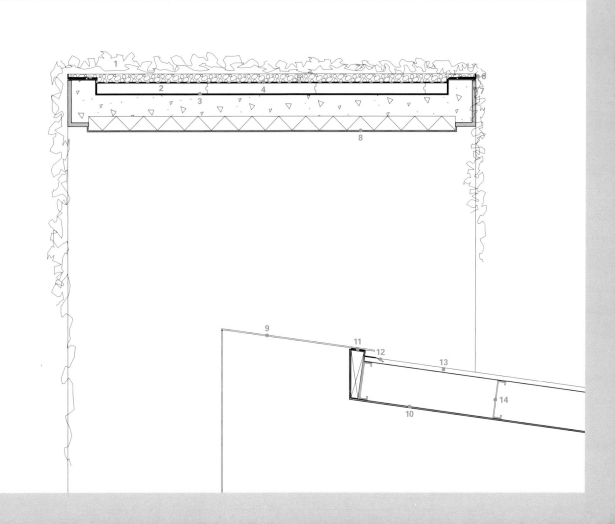

5.146
Roof and Parapet Detail 1:10

Architectus
North Shore House [36]

1 Line of upstand behind
2 Continuous edge section of 30 mm (1¹/₅ inch) drainage cell, spot glued to membrane
3 250 x 50 mm (10 x 2 inch) timber trimmer rafter
4 Membrane lapped behind fascia to underside of ply roof
5 200 mm (8 inch) purlins at 600 mm (24 inch) centres
6 Dressed battens painted black
7 405 x 90 mm (16 x 3¹/₂) glulam beam
8 25 mm (1 inch) timber fillet
9 3 mm (¹/₈ inch) anodized aluminium capping, inside clipped and outer face screw-fixed at 300 mm (12 inch)

centres into batten through inseal strip
10 75 x 25 mm (3 x 2 inch) batten with 6 mm (¹/₄ inch) rebates
11 12 mm (¹/₂ inch) Ecoply cladding over breather type building paper
12 Thermal insulation to cavity
13 9 mm (¹/₃ inch) hoop pine plywood lining screw fixed to framing at 80 mm (3¹/₈ inch) centres to the full perimeter
14 9.5 mm (¹/₃ inch) fibrous plaster wall lining
15 50 x 25 mm (2 x 1 inch) shaped Lawson cypress rainscreen battens over insect mesh on 75 x 25 (3 x 1 inch) vertical timber battens at 400 mm (15³/₄ inch) centres maximum

5.147
Roof Detail 1:20

Donovan Hill
Z House [24]

1 Vanusta planting grown from ground on stainless steel cables
2 Extruded polystyrene insulation panel
3 Bitumen coated waterproof membrane
4 Polyester geotextile fabric membrane
5 20 mm (³/₄ inch) deep layer of Nambuca river stones
6 150 x 30 x 6 mm (6 x 1¹/₈ x ¹/₄ inch) anodized aluminium angle
7 Flexible polymer render
8 20 x 20 mm (³/₄ x ³/₄

inch) blue mosaic tile ceiling
9 9 mm (³/₈ inch) toughened glass
10 Chalk USA paint on square set plasterboard
11 Glazing tape and structural silicone sealant
12 Aluminium flashing as waterproofing
13 Solar reflective corrugated steel roof sheeting
14 Roll formed steel C-channel purlin

5.148
Canopy Detail 1:20

Designworkshop: SA
Igoda View House [24]

1 Toughened
  plate-glass
  silicone-fixed to
  aluminium
2 50 x 50 x 6 mm (2 x 2
  x 1/4 inch) mild steel
  angle to form glass
  end support with
  ends shaped to suit
  structural T-profile.
  Angles screw fixed
  with countersunk

fixings to gussets
which are welded to
T-section
3 100 x 6 mm (4 x 1/4
  inch) mild steel flat
  bar to form web of
  structural T-support
4 32 x 50 mm (1 1/4 x 2
  inch) hardwood
  timber grounds, one
  side rebated to
  conceal web.
  Grounds fixed
  through web at
  maximum 400 mm
  (16 inch) centres
5 22 x 19 mm (7/8 x 3/4
  inch) Oregon pine

slats at 19 mm (3/4
inch) centres
screwed and plugged
to timber grounds
with brass screws
6 2 mm (1/12 inch) mild
  steel flat plate bent to
  form gutter and
  sitting on flat plates
  welded to parallel
  flange channels
7 130 x 50 x 6 mm (6 x
  2 x 1/4 inch) mild steel
  box welded between
  parallel flange
  channels
8 50 x 100 mm (2 x 4
  inch) parallel flange

channels to form
main central rib
9 Double-sided tape
  and silicone as fixing
10 60 x 60 x 6 mm (2 3/8
   x 2 3/8 x 1/4 inch) flat
   plate slotted and
   welded to web to
   conceal end grain of
   timber grounds

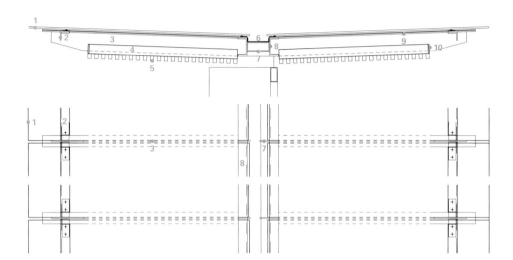

5.149
Roof and Clerestory
Window Detail 1:10

John Onken Architects
Dolphin Cottage [32]

1 Roofing slates
  pinned over treated
  softwood tile battens
  screwed down over
  counter battens
2 200 mm (8 inch)
  fibreglass batt
  insulation between
  joists with breather
  foil membrane above
  200 mm (8 inch) deep
  truss-joist rafters at
  600 mm (24 inch)
  centres
3 12 mm (1/2 inch)
  foil-backed painted
  plasterboard
  screwed to underside
  of rafters
4 Edge of pressed zinc
  guttering to form
  trim to cladding
5 Zinc drip flashing
6 Zinc cover trim
7 21 x 90 mm (7/8 x 3 1/2
  inch) vertical stained
  Thermowood
  returning into stair

window niche
8 Double glazed
  fixed-frame window
9 18 mm (3/4 inch)
  tongue and groove
  chipboard decking
  screwed to joists
10 Truss-joist timber
   floor and ceiling
   structure
11 12 mm (1/2 inch)
   plasterboard,
   skimmed, painted
   and screw fixed

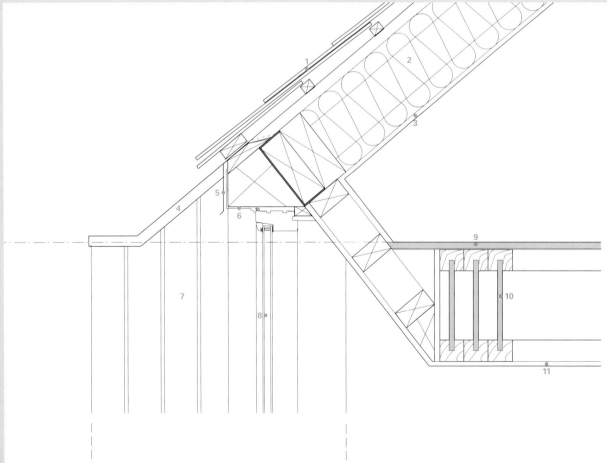

5.150
Skylight Detail 1:10

Tony Fretton Architects
The Courtyard House
[13]

1 Powder-coated
  aluminium frame to
  roof light
2 Compressible foam
  sealant strip
3 Fixed roof light
4 Motorized fabric
  blackout blind
5 Lead roof covering
6 19 mm (3/4 inch)
  plywood
7 Insulation
8 175 x 50 mm (7 x 2
  inch) softwood
  timber rafters
9 Two layers of 12.5
  mm (1/2 inch)
  plasterboard lining
  with integral vapour
  control layer
10 Hanger for double-
  grid metal-framed
  suspended ceiling
  system
11 Metal section firring
  with suspended
  plasterboard ceiling
  lining
12 Steel roof structure

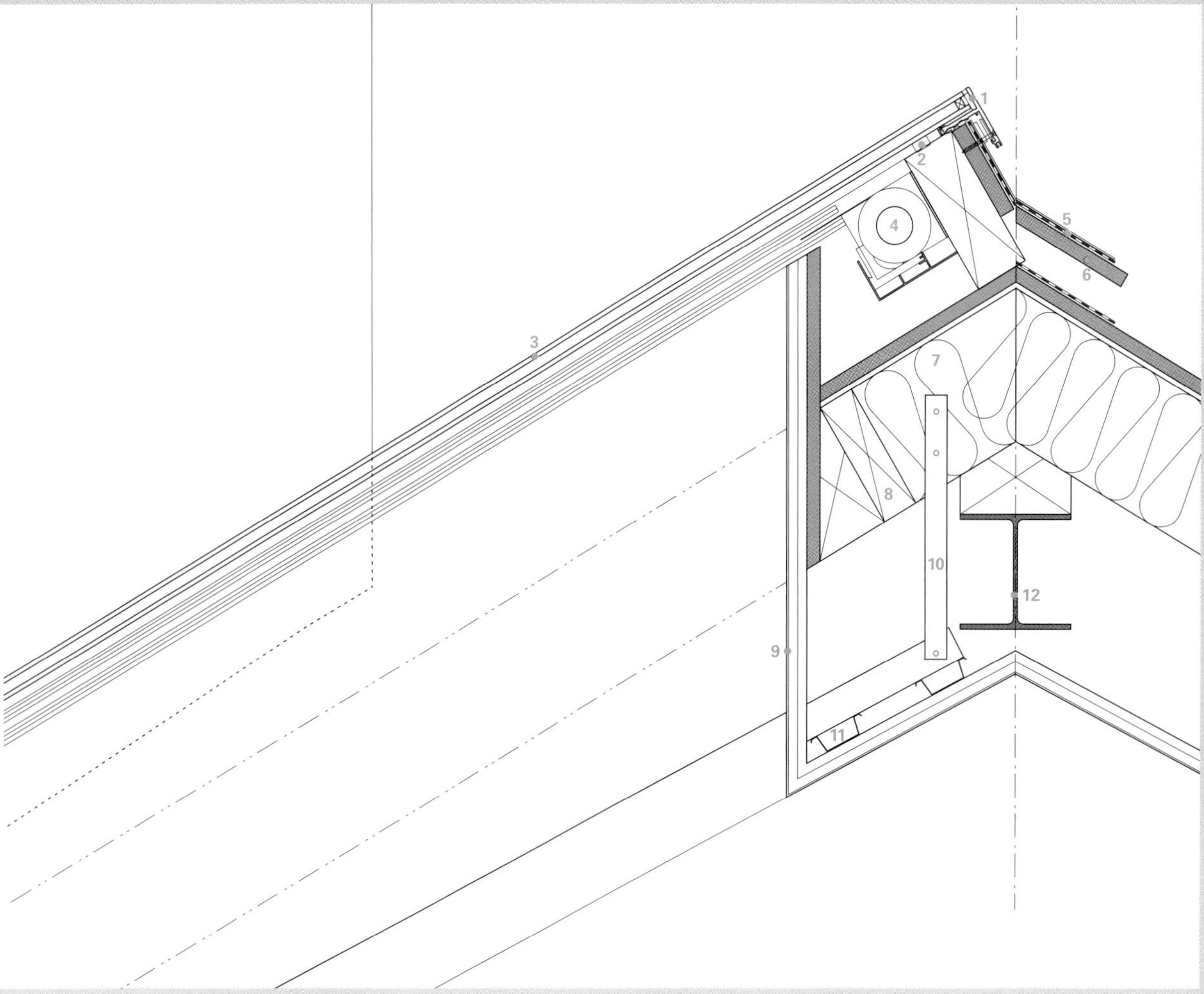

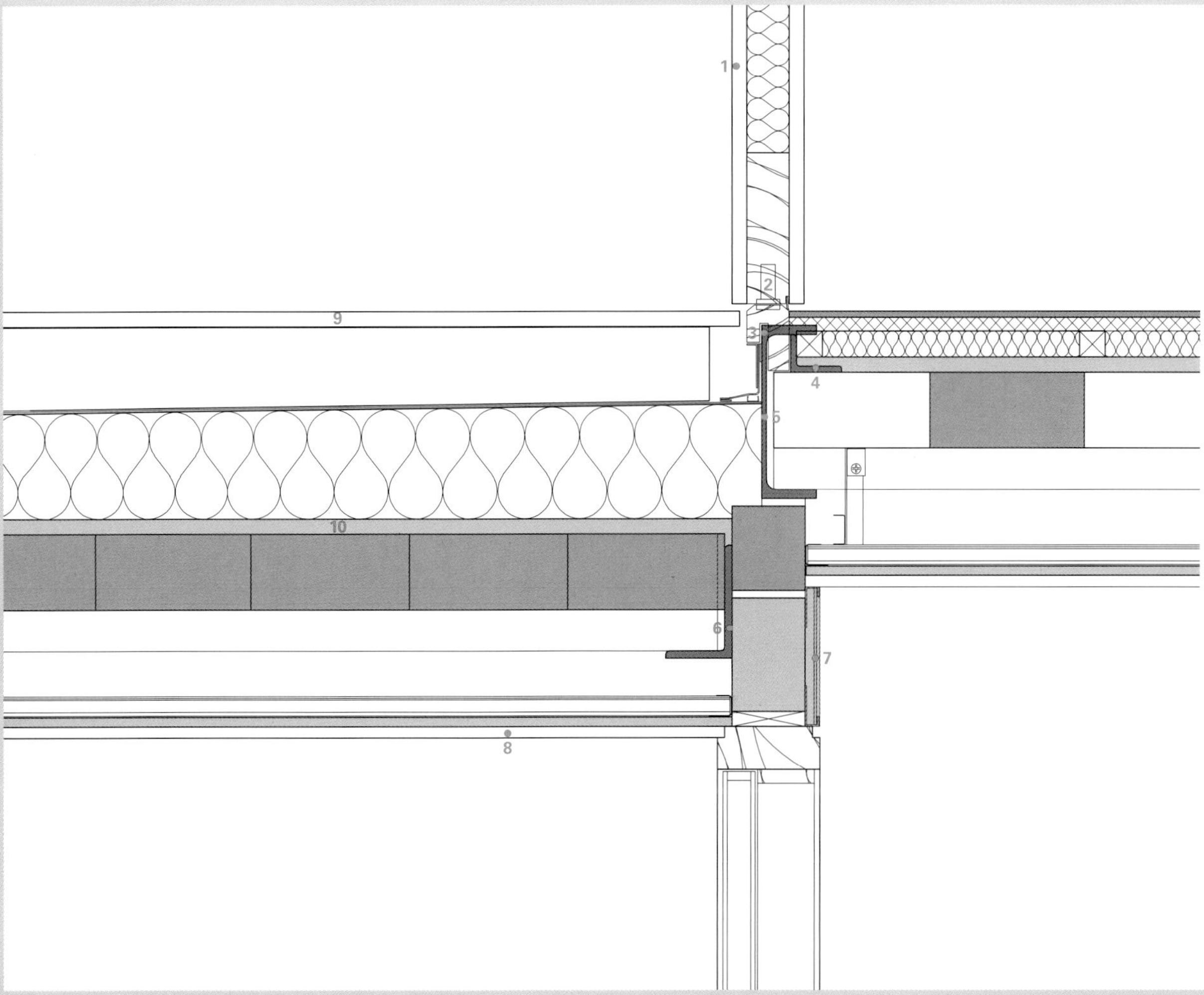

5.151
**Entrance Canopy Detail
1:10**

Robert Seymour &
Associates
The Riverhouse [22]

1 20 mm (3/4 inch)
  vertical tongue and
  groove boarding
  fixed both sides of
  timber framing for
  door
2 58 x 90 mm (21/4 x
  31/2 inch) hardwood
  threshold with pivot
  door gear in
  threshold and
  bottom edge of door
3 15 x 12 mm (5/8 x 1/2
  inch) rebate in
  threshold for parallel
  flange channel
  vertical leg and
  waterproof
  membrane from
  terrace
4 70 x 50 x 8 mm (23/4
  x 2 x 3/8 inch) rolled
  steel angle
5 230 x 90 mm (9 x 31/2
  inch) parallel flange
  channel with rolled
  steel angle to
  support end
6 150 x 90 mm (6 x 31/2
  inch) rolled steel
  angle to support end
  of beam and block
  terrace pre-cast
  concrete unit
7 20 mm (3/4 inch)
  StoRend flex coat on
  pre-cast concrete
  lintel
8 Shadow gap beyond
9 25 mm (1 inch) ipe
  decking on timber
  firring spacers on
  EPDM (ethylene
  propylene dieme
  monomer)
  membrane fastened
  to insulation cut to
  fall
10 20 mm (3/4 inch) resin
  levelling screed on
  pre-cast concrete
  beam and block units

5.152
Roof Parapet Detail 1:20

Vittorio Longheu
Casa C [16]

1 Aluminium capping
  with formed drips
2 Concrete string
  course
3 30 mm (1¼ inch)
  external render
4 200 mm (8 inch) brick
  wall
5 20 mm (¾ inch)
  plaster
6 Trafficable tiled roof
  surface

7 50 mm (2 inch) thick
  mortar laying bed
8 Waterproof layer
9 Two layers of 60 mm
  (2⅜ inch) insulating
  board
10 Insulating layer
11 Concrete bed for
   defining 50 mm (2
   inch) slope
12 40 mm (1⅗ inch)
   concrete capping
13 Concrete roof
   structure
14 10 mm (⅜ inch)
   plaster
15 100 mm (4 inch)
   diameter PVC

downpipe
16 Plasterboard false
   ceiling
17 Two layers of 12 mm
   (½ inch)
   plasterboard

5.153
Glass Ceiling Detail 1:5

Go Hasegawa &
Associates
Forest House [34]

1 75 x 75 mm (3 x 3
  inch) knee brace at
  1820 mm (72 inch)
  centres with
  urethane paint finish
2 9 mm (⅜ inch)
  plywood ceiling with
  oil stain clear lacquer
  finish
3 White urethane sheet
  back-up material

4 3 mm + 3 mm (⅛ +
  ⅛ inch) float glass
  ceiling
5 6.5 mm (¼ inch)
  white urethane sheet
  back-up material
6 40 x 2 mm (1⅝ x 1/12
  inch) aluminium flat
  bar bead
7 24 x 10 mm (1 x ⅜
  inch) bead base
8 9 mm (⅜ inch)
  plywood window for
  maintenance with oil
  stain clear lacquer
  finish

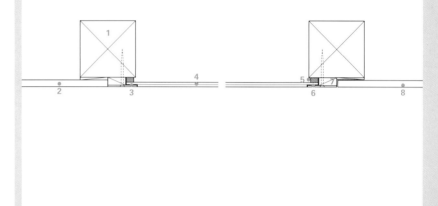

5.154
Roof Detail 1:10

Thaler Thaler Architekten
Z House [40]

1 Sheet aluminium
  covering
2 Sealing layer
3 16 mm (⅔ inch)
  oriented strand
  board
4 Laminated timber
  structure

5 30 x 80 mm (1⅕ x
  3⅛ inch) timber
  battens
6 Laminated timber
  structure
7 Aluminium window
  frame
8 Double glazing unit
9 50 mm (2 inch) gravel
  layer
10 Sealing layer
11 19 mm (¾ inch)
   oriented strand
   board

12 50 mm (2 inch)
   ventilated cavity
13 Vapour barrier
14 140 mm (5½ inch)
   thermal insulation
15 12.5 mm (½ inch)
   plasterboard on open
   boarding

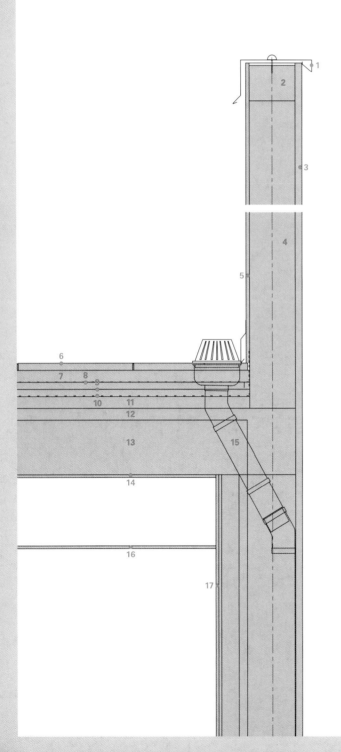

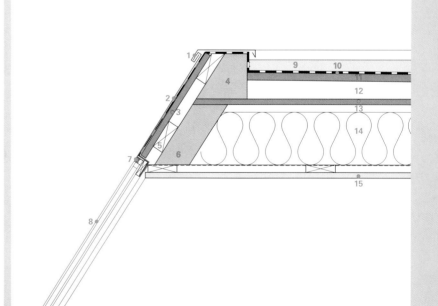

5.155
Canopy Roof Detail 1:10

Avanti Architects
Long View [35]

1 Double glazed aluminium clerestory window
2 Moisture resistant 15 mm (5/8 inch) medium density fibreboard
3 Timber framing
4 Aluminium sill
5 Mineral wool insulation
6 Moisture resistant 15 mm (5/8 inch) medium density fibreboard
7 Vapour control barrier
8 Single ply roof membrane, fully adhered to weather bonded and proofed board
9 200 x 100 mm (8 x 4 inch) rectangular hollow section steel
10 Aluminium channel for venetian blind
11 Double glazing to sliding glass door
12 Sliding door frame
13 12 mm (1/2 inch) Knauf high density board
14 Timber joist
15 Single ply roof membrane fully adhered to weather bonded and proofed board
16 200 x 100 mm (8 x 4 inch) rectangular hollow section shown dotted
17 Single ply roof membrane fully adhered to 18 mm (3/4 inch) weather bonded and proofed plywood, laid to falls on softwood firrings
18 Sarnametal roof edge trim
19 3 mm (1/8 inch) gauge polyester powder-coated aluminium channel to collect rainwater
20 150 x 75 x 12 mm (6 x 3 x 1/2 inch) angle
21 150 x 75 x 12 mm (6 x 3 x 1/2 inch) angle fascia plate

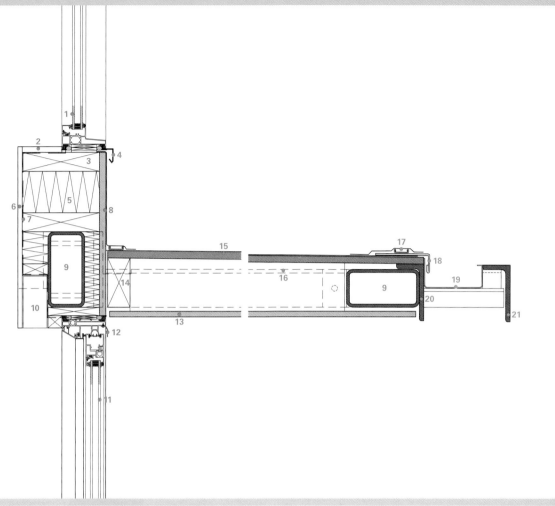

5.156
Canopy Roof Detail 1:10

Avanti Architects
Long View [35]

1 3 mm (1/10 inch) polyester powder-coated aluminium coping section
2 Timber framing
3 Single ply roofing membrane
4 Mineral wool insulation
5 Single ply roofing membrane
6 200 x 50 mm (8 x 2 inch) engineered timber joist
7 Ipe timber floorboards
8 12 mm (1/2 inch) high density board, skimmed and painted
9 100 x 100 mm (2 x 2 inch) rolled steel
10 Sarnametal roof edge trim
11 150 x 75 x 12 mm (6 x 3 x 1/2 inch) angle
12 Galvanized steel plate louvre
13 Single ply roof membrane fully adhered to 18 mm (3/4 inch) weather bonded and proofed plywood laid to falls
14 200 x 100 mm (8 x 4 inch) rectangular hollow section
15 12 mm (1/2 inch) high density board, skimmed and painted
16 3 mm (1/8 inch) gauge polyester powder-coated aluminium channel to collect rainwater
17 Steel gutter support brackets at equal

angles at 600 mm (23 2/3 inch) centres

centres
18 150 x 75 x 12 mm (6 x 3 x 1/2 inch) angle fascia plate

on softwood firrings

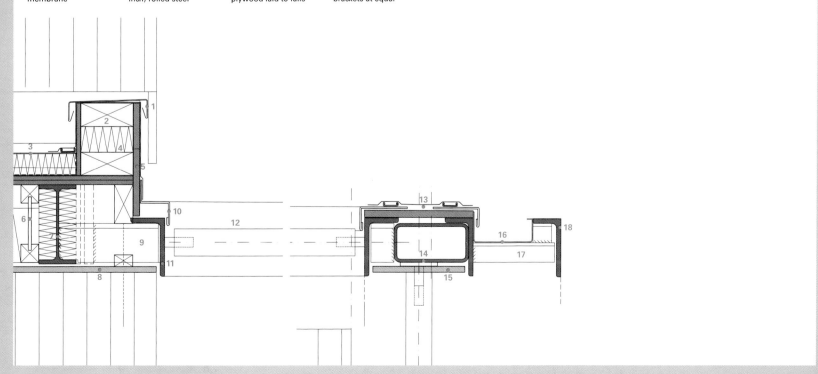

5.157
Skylight Detail 1:10

Powerhouse Company
Villa 1 [15]

1 Board insulation
2 100 mm (4 inch) rigid
  insulation
3 20 mm ($^3/4$ inch)
  stuccoed
  plasterboard
4 12.5 mm ($^1/2$ inch)
  plasterboard ceiling

lining
5 120 mm ($4^3/4$ inch)
  sandline brickwork
  column
6 12 mm ($^1/2$ inch)
  plasterboard with
  stucco finish
7 8 mm ($^5/16$ inch)
  aluminium profile to
  support and close
  skylight
8 Aluminium angle
9 10 mm ($^3/8$ inch) thick
  transparent plastic

skylight
10 Roof formed by
  EPDM (ethylene
  propylene dieme
  monomer)
  membrane, 30 mm
  ($1^1/5$ inch) board
  insulation, 100 mm (4
  inch) board
  insulation, triple
  layer of 18 mm ($^7/10$
  inch) plywood
  panels, 70 x 200 mm
  ($2^3/4$ x 8 inch) timber

rafter and 80 mm
($3^1/8$ inch) board
insulation, and
timber frame with 50
x 30 mm (2 x $1^1/5$
inch) beams and
false ceiling from 20
mm ($^3/4$ inch)
plasterboard

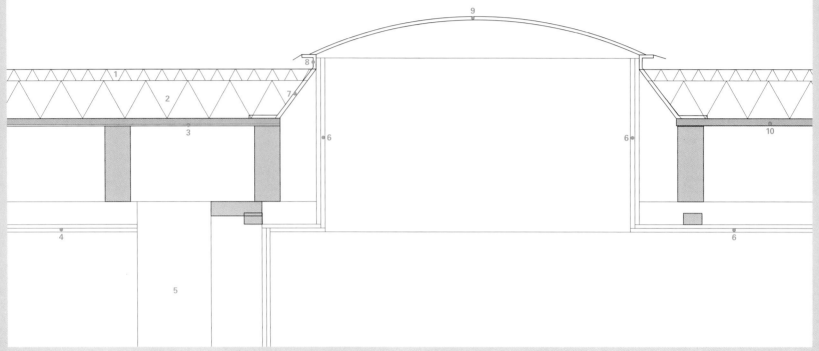

5.158
**Roof and Skylight Detail
1:10**

Powerhouse Company
Villa 1 [15]

1 Glass roof comprised
  of 4 mm ($^1/8$ inch)
  toughened glass, 10
  mm ($^2/5$ inch) cavity
  and two layers of 4
  mm ($^1/8$ inch)
  laminated safety

glass, glued into
aluminium channel
section
2 Verotec panels with
  roofing membrane
  over
3 18 mm ($^7/10$ inch)
  waterproof multiplex
  board
4 140 x 70 mm ($5^1/2$ x
  $2^3/4$ inch) timber
  bearer support frame
5 Universal steel beam
6 180 x 67 mm (7 x $2^2/3$

inch) timber post
7 12 mm ($^1/2$ inch) fibre
  cement board
8 Thermal insulation
  from 90 mm ($3^1/2$
  inch) polystyrene
9 800 x 800 mm ($31^1/2$
  x $31^1/2$ inch)
  travertine tiles fixed
  with adhesive to
  waterproof multiplex
  board
10 Gutter lining
11 Timber fillet piece

12 Roof formed by
  EPDM (ethylene
  propylene dieme
  monomer)
  membrane, 30 mm
  ($1^1/5$ inch) board
  insulation, 100 mm
  (4 inch) board
  insulation, triple
  layer of 18 mm ($^7/10$
  inch) plywood
  panels, 70 x 200 mm
  ($2^3/4$ x 8 inch) timber
  rafter and 80 mm

($3^1/8$ inch) board
insulation, and
timber frame with 50
x 30 mm (2 x $1^1/5$
inch) beams and
false ceiling from 20
mm ($^3/4$ inch)
plasterboard
13 Steel structure
14 Timber infill
  structure attached to
  roof edge
15 18 mm ($^3/4$ inch)
  multiplex boarding

16 Stucco finish on
  Verotec panels
17 Timber window
  frame
18 Stucco finish on
  verotec panels
19 Fixed glazed panel
  comprised of two
  layers of 12 mm ($^1/2$
  inch) float glass
20 Vierendeel bookshelf

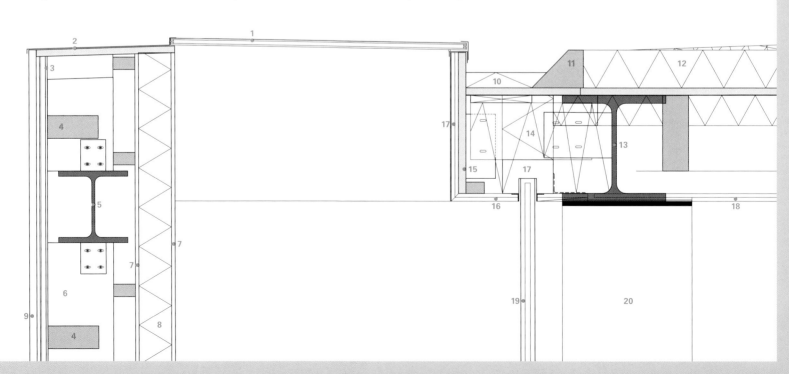

5.159
Roof Parapet Detail 1:10

Public
Rattlesnake Creek
House [15]

1 Fold-down double
 standing seam at
 flashing at high point
 of roof
2 Waterproof
 membrane
3 20 mm (3/4 inch)
 plywood
4 Rigid insulation
5 Flashing to roof edge
6 50 x 100 mm (2 x 4
 inch) timber edge
 beam
7 Timber fascia board
8 Corrugated metal
 decking
9 Silicone seal
10 Steel beam beyond
11 Double glazed fixed
 window
12 Rigid insulation
13 Line of storefront
 glazing system
 beyond
14 Roofing termination
 profile
15 Roofing membrane
16 Timber fillet piece
17 Poured concrete wall
18 Rigid insulation
19 50 x 100 mm (2 x 4
 inch) timber blocking
20 Corrugated metal
 decking
21 12.5 mm (1/2 inch)
 steel plate bolted to
 concrete with 20 mm
 (3/4 inch) anchor bolts
22 Steel beam welded
 to plate

5.160
Roof Edge Detail 1:5

Ensamble Studio
Hemeroscopium House
[07]

1 Waterproofing with
 PVC membrane
2 5 mm (1/5 inch) thick
 steel plate covering
3 8–14 mm (1/3–1/2 inch)
 thick crushed granite
 rock gravel bed
4 Geotextile fabric
5 30 mm (11/5 inch)
 extruded polystyrene
 foam insulation
6 Geotextile fabric
7 Concrete mass
 reinforcement
8 5 mm (1/5 inch) steel
 plate
9 60 mm (21/3 inch)
 square steel hollow
 section
10 5 mm (1/5 inch) thick
 steel plate covering
11 Waterproofing with
 PVC membrane
12 Pre-cast concrete
 beam

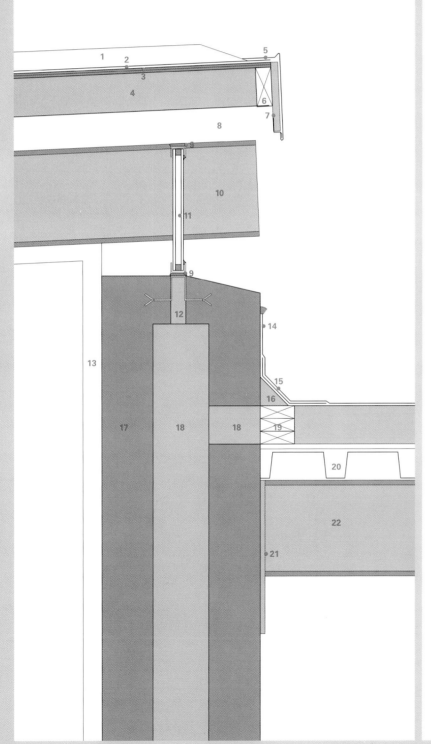

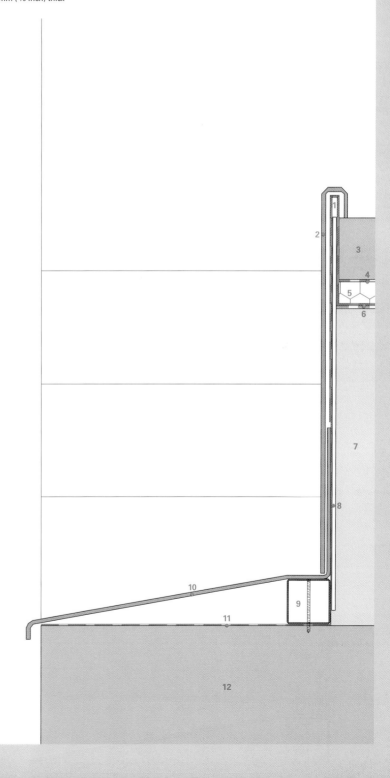

6.001
Staircase Detail 1:10

Troppo Architects
Buttfield Town House
[30]

1 60 mm (2³/₈ inch)
   diameter steel
   column
2 170 x 75 mm (6³/₄ x 3
   inch) mild steel angle
   profile cut to stringer
3 19 x 19 mm (³/₄ x ³/₄
   inch) hardwood
   trimmer to match
   stair treads
4 Landing timber to
   match stair treads
5 180 x 75 mm (7¹/₈ x 3
   inch) parallel flange
   channel stringer
6 10 mm (³/₈ inch) cleat
   to stringer and
   column
7 180 x 75 mm (7¹/₈ x 3
   inch) parallel flange
   channel to end of
   stringer with mitre
   weld
8 75 x 10 mm (3 x ³/₈
   inch) cleat to parallel
   flange channel fixed
   to underside of
   landing
9 Landing beyond
10 Galvanized Miniorb
   U-trim
11 89 mm (3¹/₂ inch)
   square hollow
   section in wall line
12 10 mm (³/₈ inch) cleat
   angle to meet square
   hollow section
   column
13 10 mm (³/₈ inch) base
   plate anchor bolted
   to blockwork wall
14 Plaster and paint to
   internal face of
   blockwork wall

6.002
Staircase Detail 1:10

Troppo Architects
Buttfield Town House
[30]

1 32 mm (1¹/₄ inch)
   hardwood tread with
   3 mm (¹/₈ inch) arris
   to top edges
2 150 x 75 mm (6 x 3
   inch) mild steel angle
   welded to stringer
3 180 x 75 mm (6³/₄ x 3
   inch) parallel flange
   channel stringer
4 89 mm (3¹/₂ inch)
   square hollow
   section in wall line
5 90 mm (3¹/₂ inch)
   studwork as false
   wall for cavity slider
6 50 mm (2 inch)
   diameter Tasmanian
   oak handrail
7 Stainless steel
   bracket screw-fixed
   to steel column
8 60 mm (2³/₈ inch)
   diameter central
   steel column
9 Glazing in anodized
   aluminium channel
10 10 mm (³/₈ inch) cleat
   to column and
   stringer

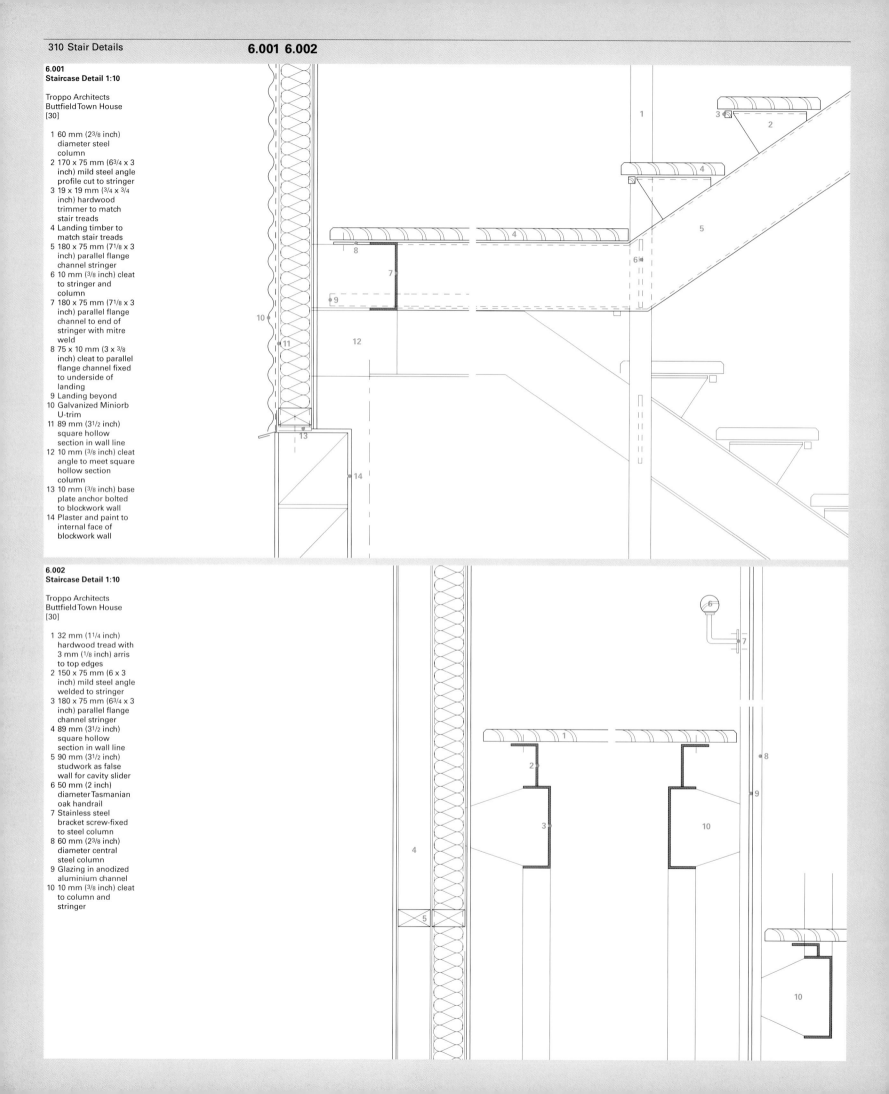

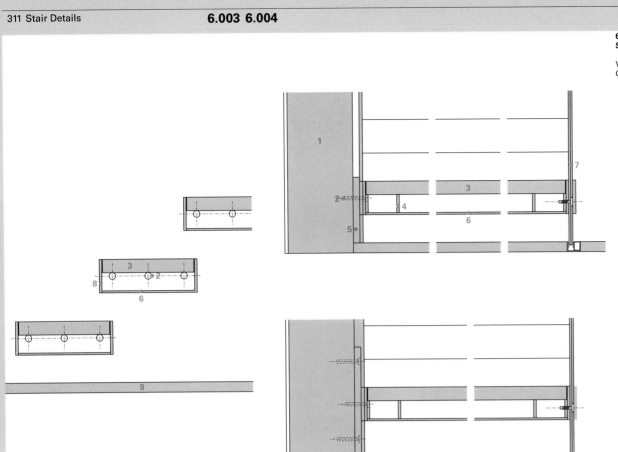

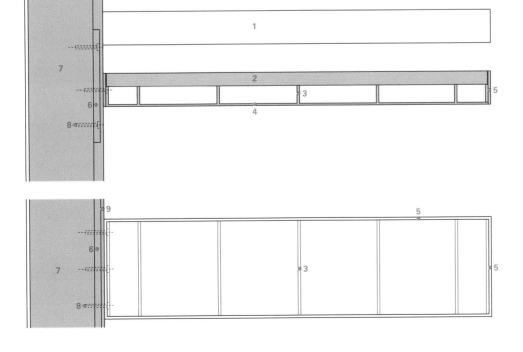

6.005
**Stone Staircase Detail
1:10**

Tony Fretton Architects
The Courtyard House
[13]

1 Continuous stainless
steel skirting
2 Line of pocket to take
stair structure in
reinforced concrete
wall
3 Cantilevered stone
staircase. Treads to
have square seating
to be built into recess
in reinforced
concrete wall
4 Line of pocket to take
stair structure in
reinforced concrete
wall
5 Solid stone set into
floor depth
6 Stone landing

7 Adhesive bedding to
stone flooring
8 75 mm (3 inch)
floating screed with
underfloor heating
9 75 mm (3 inch)
insulation and
separating layer
10 Stone wall lining
11 140 mm (5 1/2 inch)
blockwork wall
12 50 mm (2 inch) cavity
wall insulation
13 Cavity drain
waterproofing to
concrete retaining
wall
14 Stainless steel
skirting
15 Stone flooring
16 Adhesive bedding to
stone flooring
17 75 mm (3 inch)
floating screed with
underfloor heating
18 50 mm (2 inch)
insulation and

separating layer
19 Cavity drain
waterproofing to new
ground slab
20 Concrete slab

6.006
**Stair and Balustrade
Detail 1:10**

Tony Fretton Architects
The Courtyard House
[13]

1 Structural glass
balustrade with 100 x
50 mm (4 x 2 inch)
rectangular polished
stainless steel
capping
2 30 mm (1 1/4 inch)
timber floor
3 50 x 45 mm (2 x 1 3/4
inch) softwood
bearers
4 Brushed stainless
steel clamping plate
5 Continuous stainless
steel skirting down
stair
6 Concrete floor slab
7 Inner brushed
stainless steel plate

to balustrade support
system
8 Packing at edge of
concrete to suit
alignment of metal
clamp fixing for glass
balustrade
9 100 x 50 mm (4 x 2
inch) stud framing
10 Suspended ceiling
11 Timber studwork
partition to rear of
built-in cupboards
with skim plaster
coat finish to all faces
except under stair
where boards are to
be taped and jointed
12 Hardwood staircase
with concealed
timber stringer and
medium density
fibreboard infill
lining beneath treads
and risers to improve
sound deadening
13 Stepped hardwood

gutter at edge of
staircase following
line of rear of treads
and risers with 30
mm (1 1/5 inch) recess
14 200 x 50 mm (8 x 2
inch) timber bearers
15 18 mm (3/4 inch)
plywood lining to
underside of
concealed string with
12.5 mm (1/2 inch)
plasterboard lining
under, taped and
jointed as finished
face
16 10 mm (3/8 inch)
shadow gap
following line of
stepped gutter
formed by using
gypsum edge reveal
17 75 x 50 mm (3 x 2
inch) softwood
framing

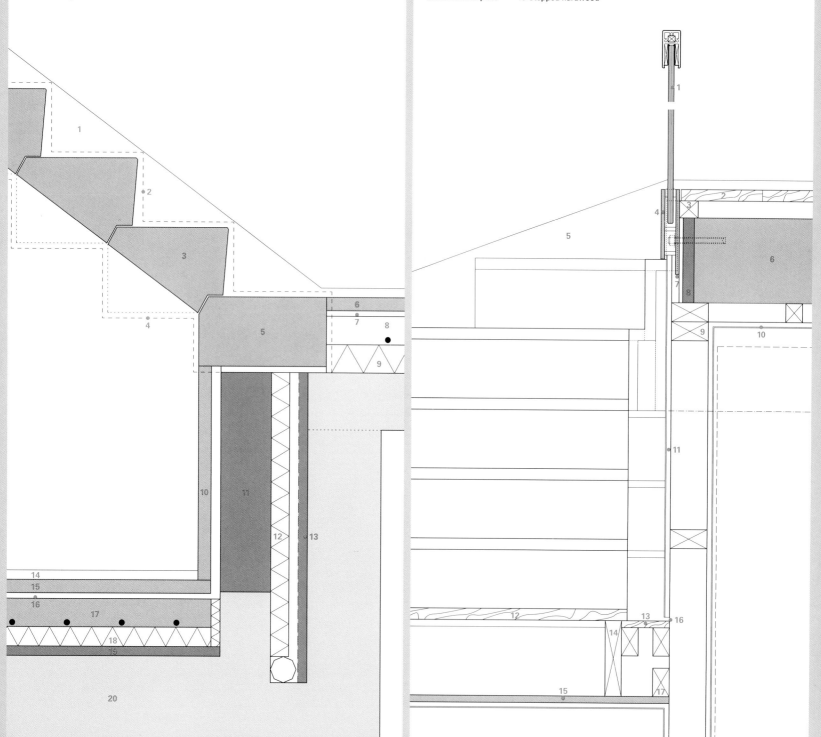

6.007
Stair With Concealed Lighting Detail 1:20

Kallos Turin
Casa Zorzal [10]

1 Reinforced concrete structure
2 Sand and cement mortar
3 4 mm (1/6 inch) microcement
4 Brick wall
5 Waterproof mortar
6 3 mm (1/8 inch) plaster skim coat with paint finish
7 Concealed LED light
8 Ballast layer of gravel
9 Subsoil

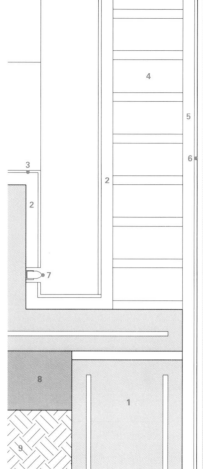

6.008
Interior Stair Detail 1:10

Kallos Turin
Casa Zorzal [10]

1 5 x 20 mm (1/5 x 3/4 inch) stainless steel flat section
2 4 mm (1/6 inch) microcement cementitious covering
3 Sand and cement mortar
4 Reinforced concrete structure
5 Ballast layer of gravel
6 Subsoil

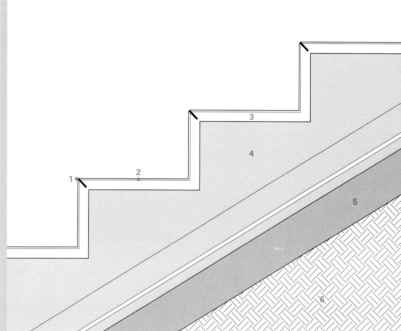

6.009
Stair Tread Cross Section Detail 1:5

Skene Catling de la Peña Architects
The Dairy House [31]

1 12.5 mm (1/2 inch) plasterboard
2 10 mm (3/8 inch) plaster
3 20 mm (3/4 inch) square hollow section upright with welded threaded bolt
4 35 mm (13/8 inch) oak tread
5 Expamet plaster bead and shadow gap trimmed where it engages with treads and risers

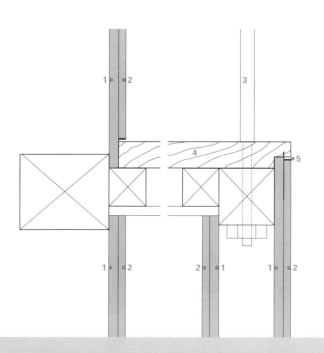

6.010
Stair Tread Horizontal Section Detail 1:5

Skene Catling de la Peña Architects
The Dairy House [31]

1 12.5 mm (1/2 inch) plasterboard
2 10 mm (3/8 inch) plaster
3 Expamet plaster bead and shadow gap trimmed where it engages with tread and riser
4 20 mm (3/4 inch) oak riser

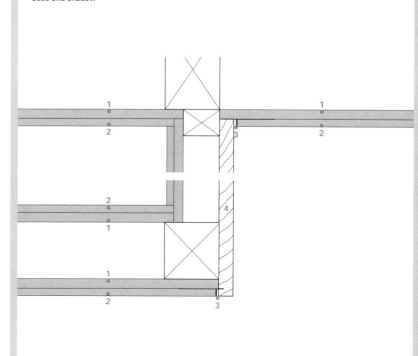

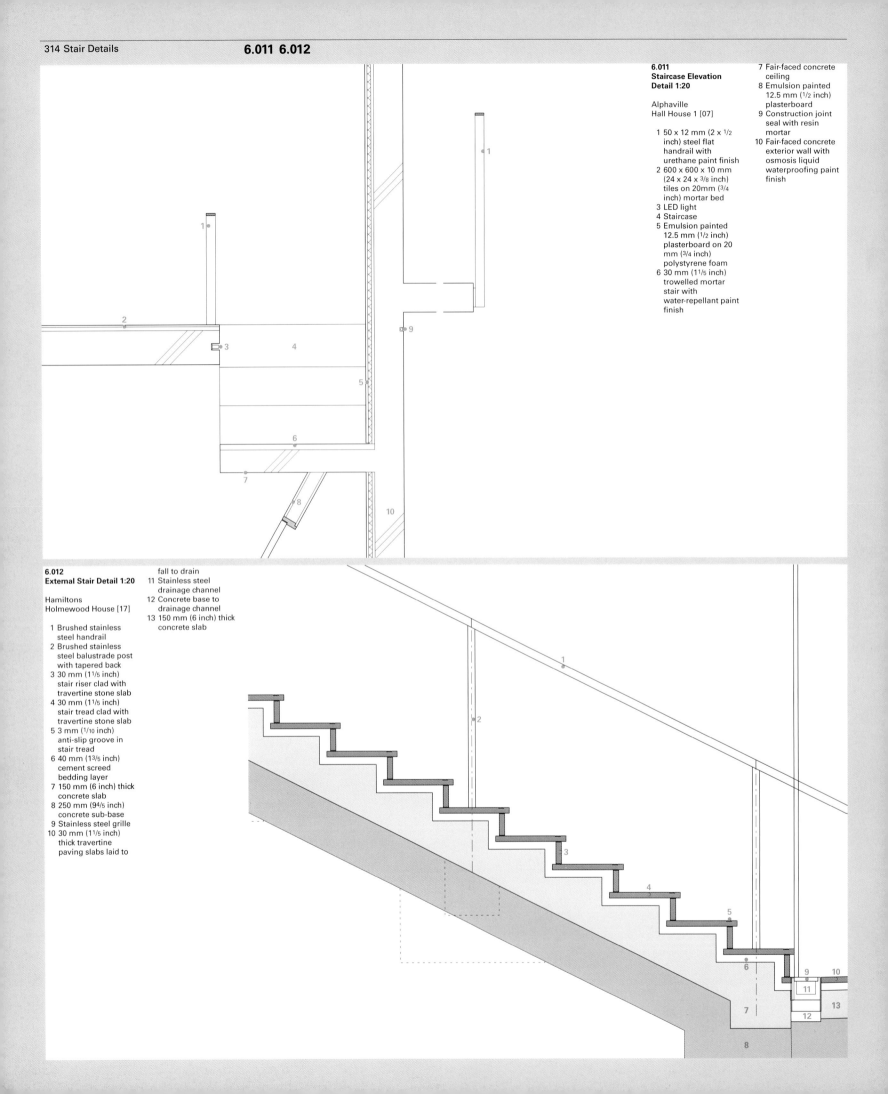

6.011
Staircase Elevation
Detail 1:20

Alphaville
Hall House 1 [07]

1 50 x 12 mm (2 x 1/2 inch) steel flat handrail with urethane paint finish
2 600 x 600 x 10 mm (24 x 24 x 3/8 inch) tiles on 20mm (3/4 inch) mortar bed
3 LED light
4 Staircase
5 Emulsion painted 12.5 mm (1/2 inch) plasterboard on 20 mm (3/4 inch) polystyrene foam
6 30 mm (1 1/5 inch) trowelled mortar stair with water-repellant paint finish

7 Fair-faced concrete ceiling
8 Emulsion painted 12.5 mm (1/2 inch) plasterboard
9 Construction joint seal with resin mortar
10 Fair-faced concrete exterior wall with osmosis liquid waterproofing paint finish

6.012
External Stair Detail 1:20

Hamiltons
Holmewood House [17]

1 Brushed stainless steel handrail
2 Brushed stainless steel balustrade post with tapered back
3 30 mm (1 1/5 inch) stair riser clad with travertine stone slab
4 30 mm (1 1/5 inch) stair tread clad with travertine stone slab
5 3 mm (1/10 inch) anti-slip groove in stair tread
6 40 mm (1 3/5 inch) cement screed bedding layer
7 150 mm (6 inch) thick concrete slab
8 250 mm (9 4/5 inch) concrete sub-base
9 Stainless steel grille
10 30 mm (1 1/5 inch) thick travertine paving slabs laid to

fall to drain
11 Stainless steel drainage channel
12 Concrete base to drainage channel
13 150 mm (6 inch) thick concrete slab

6.013
Stair and Handrail Detail
1:20

Morphogenesis
N85 Residence [08]

1 4 mm (1/8 inch)
   veneer laminated on
   12 mm (1/2 inch)
   board fixed to mild
   steel framework
   supported on
   reinforced concrete
2 40 mm (15/8 inch)
   diameter stainless
   steel handrail
3 12 mm (1/2 inch) thick
   tempered glass
4 Polished coffee-pearl
   marble slab flooring
5 Formed reinforced
   concrete slab for
   staircase
6 Polished coffee-pearl
   marble rise
7 20 mm (3/4 inch)

polished coffee pearl
marble tread
8 Premium plastic
   emulsion paint finish
   to underside of stair
9 75 mm (3 inch) high
   polished coffee-pearl
   skirting
10 Two-way spider
   fitting with flush
   countersunk
   connectors

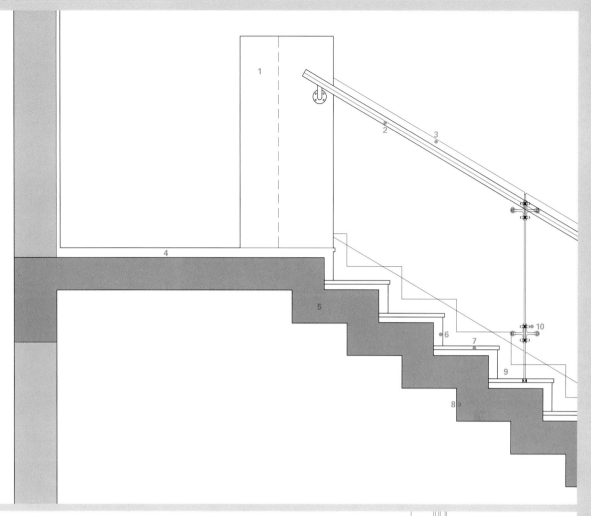

6.014
Stair Detail 1:20

Scott Tallon Walker
Architects
Fastnet House [25]

1 Limestone tiling
2 Sand-cement screed
3 Reinforced concrete
   floor slab
4 Timber framing to
   support ceiling
5 Painted skim coat on
   plasterboard
6 Mild steel angle
7 Mild steel plate
   welded to parallel
   flange channel
8 Stainless steel
   clamping disk
9 Laminated and
   toughened glazed
   balustrade
10 Solid oak handrail at
   landing level
11 Solid oak handrail to
   stair flight
12 Laminated and
   toughened glazed
   balustrade

13 Oak clad stair tread
   with glued and
   pinned mitred joints
14 Glazed balustrade in
   background
15 Rectangular hollow
   section bolted to side
   wall
16 Cedar mullion in
   background
17 Thermally broken
   double glazed unit
18 Solid cedar window
   frame
19 Strip insulation
20 Gravel drain
21 Concrete cobble
   paving
22 Sand bedding
23 Reinforced concrete
   roof slab
24 Insulation
25 Timber framing to
   support ceiling
26 Painted skim coat on
   plasterboard
27 Bolted connections
   to support stair tread

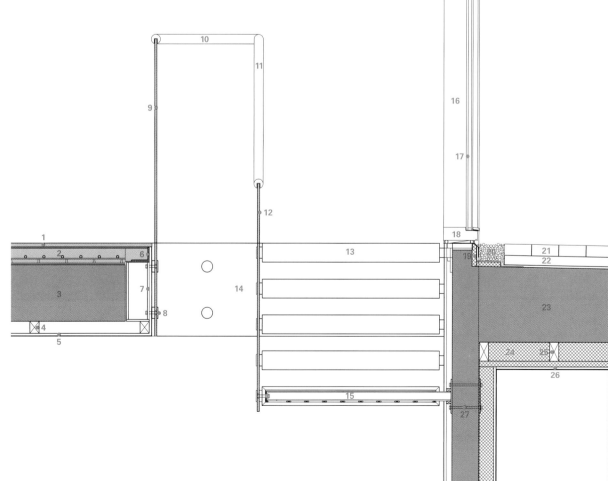

6.015
Stair Detail 1:20

Atelier Tekuto +
Masahiro Ikeda
Lucky Drops [13]

1 6 x 38 mm (1/4 x 1 1/2 inch) steel handrail beyond shown dotted
2 Steel structure to stair landing
3 28 x 28 mm (1 1/5 x 1 1/5 inch) steel box column with oil paint finish
4 40 x 40 mm (1 5/8 x 1 5/8 inch) steel angle with oil paint finish
5 6 mm (1/4 inch) thick steel stair tread
6 6 mm (1/4 inch) thick steel stair riser
7 Steel bar stringer reinforcing
8 I-section steel column
9 60 x 19 mm (2 1/3 x 3/4 inch) steel floor beam
10 Tile floor finish
11 Insulation
12 12 mm (1/2 inch) steel plate permanent structure

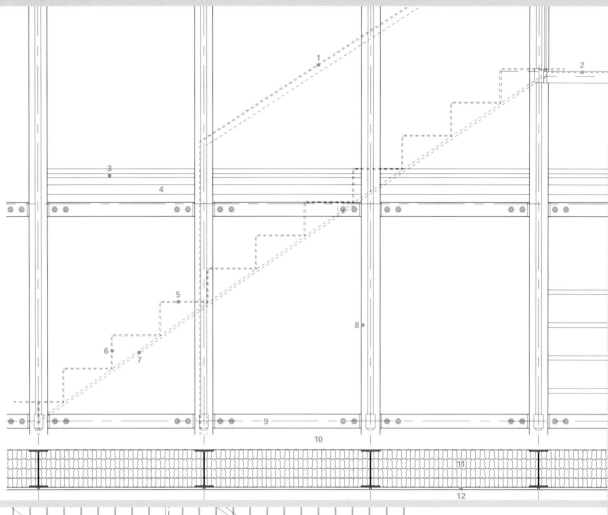

6.016
Stair Elevation Detail 1:20

Bates Masi + Architects
Noyack Creek Residence [37]

1 3 mm (1/8 inch) stainless steel cables equally spaced
2 Aluminium window frame
3 Handrail
4 Handrail fixing bracket
5 Timber tread
6 Timber riser
7 Cable rail surface mount
8 50 x 300 mm (2 x 12 inch) stair stringer
9 Access door to storage under stairs
10 Wall seams to align with floor seams
11 Cabinet in foreground
12 Transition of flooring under cabinetry
13 Timber floor joists

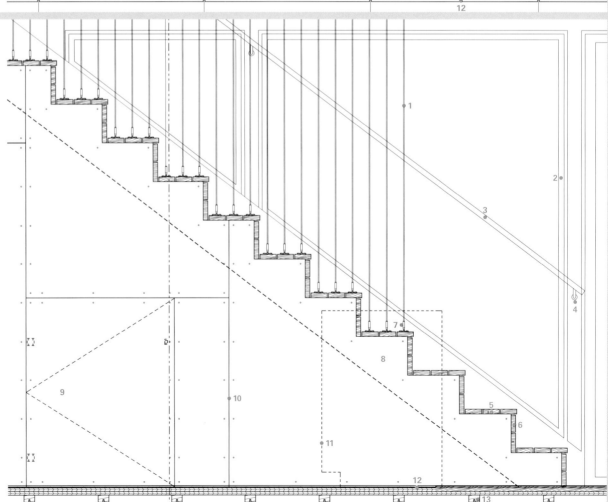

6.017
Balustrade Detail at Second Floor Stair Landing 1:10

Alison Brooks Architects
Herringbone Houses [33]

1 Aluminium roof light system
2 20 mm (3/4 inch) rigid insulation
3 Timber stud attached to metal framing system
4 Timber stair treads and risers
5 12.5 mm (1/2 inch) plasterboard with 2.5 mm (1/10 inch) skim coat
6 Steel I-beam
7 Steel angle
8 20 mm (3/4 inch) hardwood veneer
9 Glass balustrade
10 20 mm (3/4 inch) hardwood flooring on 65 mm (2 1/2 inch) battens with underfloor heating system
11 20 mm (3/4 inch) hardwood veneer to stair stringer
12 30 mm (1 1/8 inch) Rockwool insulation
13 Steel I-beam
14 Steel angle
15 150 mm (6 inch) pre-cast beam plank

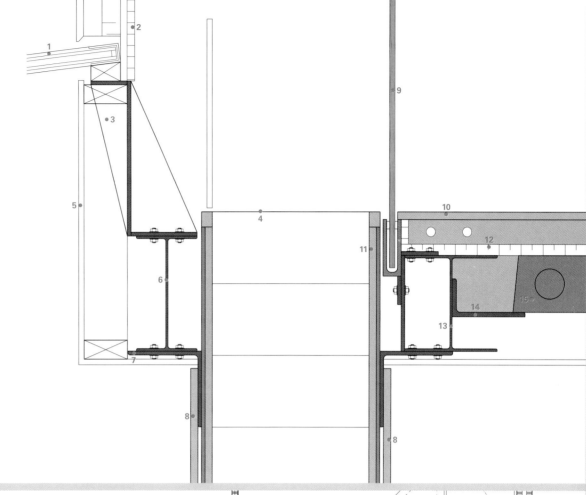

6.018
Stair Section Detail 1:50

diederendirrix
Villa PPML [21]

1 Plywood construction finished with stained 10 mm (2/5 inch) beech veneer
2 50 x 280 mm (2 x 11 inch) stained beech stair treads
3 Flooring of cement screed with trowelled finish
4 Stair platform from stained beech veneered plywood
5 Stained beech veneered plywood stair riser
6 Flooring of cement screed with trowelled finish
7 Cast lime and sandstone blocks with stucco finish
8 Flooring of cement screed with trowelled finish
9 Steel structure to anchor stair structure
10 Reinforced concrete floor slab

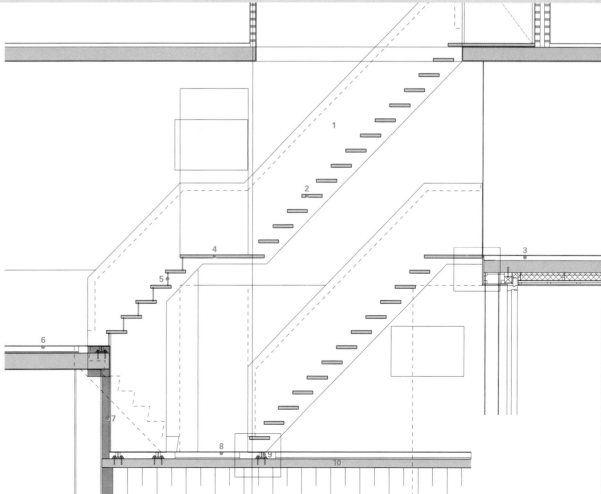

6.019
Internal Stair Detail 1:10

A-Piste Arkkitehdit
Villa O [39]

1 15 mm (5/8 inch)
  Siberian larch
  flooring, brushed
  and wax oiled
2 22 mm (7/8 inch)
  chipboard
3 Two layers
  comprised of 100 +
  150 mm (4 + 6 inch)
  impact-sound
  insulation
4 45 x 260 mm (13/4 x
  101/4 inch) end joists
5 30 mm (11/5 inch)
  weathershield
6 9 mm (1/3 inch)
  veneered plywood
7 40 mm (15/8 inch)
  Siberian larch solid
  wood tread
8 40 mm (15/8 inch)
  Siberian larch solid
  timber stair riser
9 150 mm (6 inch)
  impact-sound
  insulation
10 13 mm (1/2 inch)
  plasterboard lining
11 Fine plaster wall
  finish
12 130 mm (51/8 inch)
  facade masonry
13 30 mm (11/5 inch)
  ventilated cavity
14 25 mm (1 inch)
  weathershield
15 125 mm (5 inch)
  mineral wool
  insulation
16 Triple glazing of 6
  mm (1/4 inch), 4 mm
  (1/8 inch) and 6 mm
  (1/4 inch) glass panes

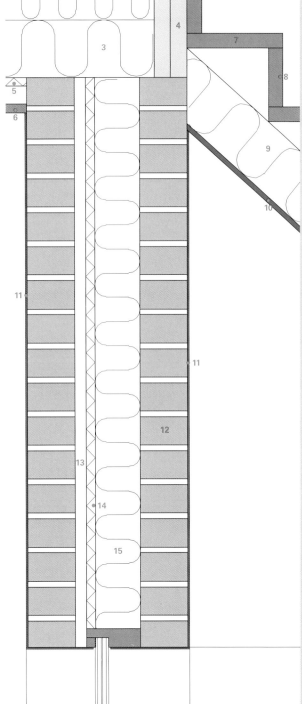

6.020
Stair Tread Detail 1:10

Western Design
Architects
The Moat House [20]

1 Oak hardwood
  facings with all secret
  joints glued
2 Stainless steel strip
  insert
3 Softwood core
4 75 x 150 mm (3 x 6
  inch) rolled steel
  angle cantilevered
  from steel stringer in
  wall

5 Ten 75 mm (3 inch)
  long stainless steel
  countersunk wood
  screws at 250 mm (10
  inch) centres

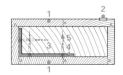
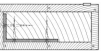

6.021
Stair Tread and
Balustrade Detail 1:2

Western Design
Architects
The Moat House [20]

1 20 mm (3/4 inch) thick
  laminated glass
  partition
2 Stainless steel single
  point glass fixing
3 Plastic spacer and
  sacrificial edge
4 30 mm (11/8 inch)
  stainless steel spacer
5 M10 40 mm (15/8

inch) long stainless
  steel threaded insert
  bolted to steel plate
6 Steel plate welded to
  end of angle to take
  M10 bolt
7 75 x 150 mm (3 x 6
  inch) rolled steel
  angle
8 Softwood core
9 Oak hardwood facing

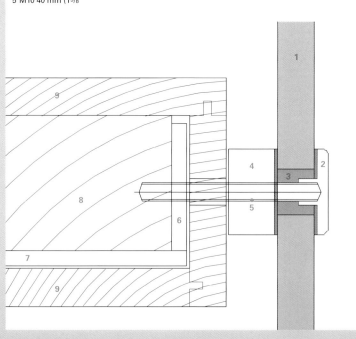

6.022
Concrete and Timber
Stair Detail 1:10

Agence Michel Tortel
Mikado House [08]

1 12 x 50 mm (1/2 x 2
  inch) steel flats as
  balustrade with
  perforated plate infill
2 Internal insulation
3 External
  waterproofing
4 18 mm (3/4 inch)
  plasterboard
  partition
5 Itauba timber

cladding to stair
6 Floating heated floor
  screed in polished
  concrete
7 Concrete floor slab
  and stair

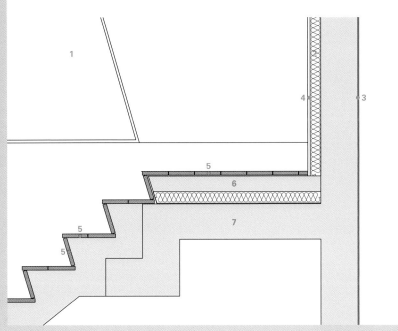

6.023
Steel and Timber Stair
Detail 1:10

Agence Michel Tortel
Mikado House [08]

1 210 mm (81/4 inch)
  diameter central
  steel post
2 Fabricated steel step
  in 8 mm (3/8 inch) and
  5 mm (1/5 inch) plate
3 Itauba timber infill
4 12 x 50 mm (1/2 x 2
  inch) steel flats as
  balustrade with
  perforated plate infill

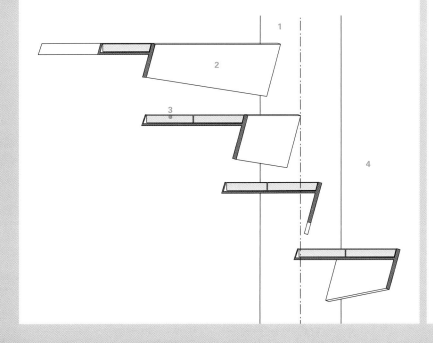

6.024
Circular Stair Detail 1:50

Haddow Partnership
Higher Farm [17]

1 Aluminium window
  with timber external
  lining
2 50 mm (2 inch) stone
  landing at floor level
3 40 mm (11/2 inch)
  diameter polished
  curving steel handrail
4 50 mm (2 inch) stone
  tread
5 125 x 100 mm (5 x 4
  inch) circular stone
  interlocking tread
  ends forming stair
  spine
6 100 mm (4 inch)
  circular angled
  external deck support
7 30 mm (11/5 inch)
  stone floor tile on 60
  mm (23/8 inch) screed

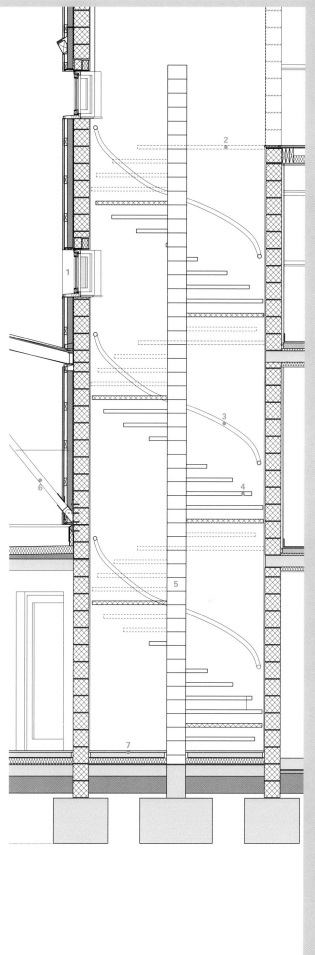

6.025
Stair Balustrade Detail
1:10

Hampson Williams
Glass and Timber
Houses [33]

1 260 x 60 mm (10$1/4$ x
  2$3/8$ inch) Douglas fir
  balustrade
2 65 mm (2$1/4$ inch)
  solid Douglas fir stair
  tread
3 150 x 90 x 10 mm (6 x
  3$1/2$ x $3/8$ inch) angle
  mounting brackets,
  200 mm (8 inch)
  long, rebated into
  face of stair upright,
  fixed with five screws
  and epoxy adhesive
  fixed to top of beam
  with three
  self-drilling and
  self-tapping screws
4 Continuous 90 x 10

mm (3$1/2$ x $3/8$ inch)
bearer plate rebated
to top of floor beam
and fixed with
screws at 125 mm (5
inch) staggered
centres
5 Three self-drilling/
  self-tapping screws
  and 20 x 5 mm ($3/4$ x
  $1/5$ inch) outstand bar
  stitch welded to
  bottom of angle
6 Continuous 60 x 30 x
  5 mm (2$3/8$ x 1$1/5$ x $1/5$
  inch) angle, rebated
  to face of floor beam
  and fixed with
  screws at 125 mm (5
  inch) centres
7 Paired 241 x 89 mm
  (9$1/2$ x 3$1/2$ inch) floor
  edge beams

6.026
Stair Balustrade Detail
1:10

Hampson Williams
Glass and Timber
Houses [33]

1 260 x 60 mm (10$1/4$ x
  2$3/8$ inch) Douglas fir
  balustrade
2 200 x 90 x 10 mm (7
  $7/8$ x 3$1/2$ x $3/8$ inch)
  angle mounting
  brackets, 200 mm (8
  inch) long, fixed to
  face of stair upright,
  fixed with five screws
  and epoxy
  adhesive-fixed to top
  of beam with three
  self-drilling/
  self-tapping screws
3 180 x 90 mm (7 x 3$1/2$
  inch) parallel flange
  channel mounting
  rail stitch welded to

225 x 6 mm (9 x $1/4$
inch) mild steel plate
fixed through to
timber beam with
mild steel bolts at
300 mm (6 inch)
staggered centres
4 Three self-drilling/
  self-tapping screws
  and 50 x 6 mm (2 x
  $1/4$ inch) outstand bar
  stitch welded to
  bottom of angle
5 Additional screw
  fixings top and
  bottom at 300 mm
  (12 inch) centres
6 Paired 241 x 89 mm
  (9$1/2$ x 3$1/2$ inch) edge
  beams
7 200 mm (8 inch)
  Douglas fir stair riser

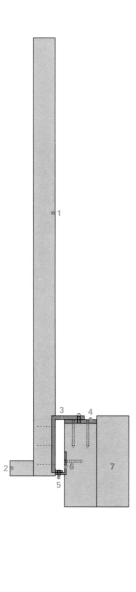

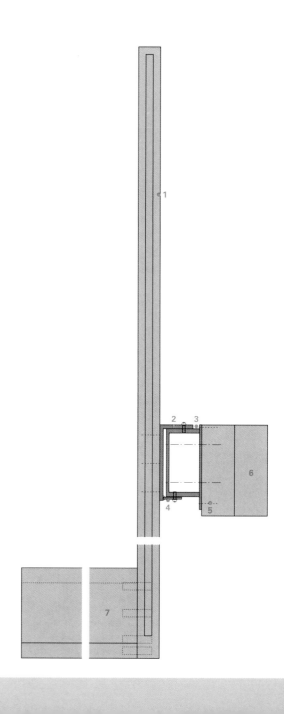

6.027
**Stair Balustrade Detail
1:10**

Hampson Williams
Glass and Timber
Houses [33]

1 Typical balustrade
  end section
2 Typical balustrade
  mid section
3 16 mm (5/8 inch)
  laminated toughened
  glass balustrade
  panel set with high
  modulus silicone into
  31 x 25 x 3 mm (11/5
  x 1 x 1/8 inch)
  aluminium channel
  screw-fixed to timber
  at 150 mm (6 inch)
  centres with 10 mm
  (3/8 inch) embedment
  of glass to permit
  'shuffle glazing'
4 Aluminium channel

screw-fixed to timber
at 150 mm (6 inch)
centres
5 Blind rebate with 40
  x 20 mm (13/5 x 3/4
  inch) tongue and
  groove board glued
  to one side and glass
  panel able to slide
  into the other
6 260 x 60 mm (101/4 x
  23/8 inch) Douglas fir
  balustrade
7 Floor structure
8 Douglas fir stair tread
9 Six 20 mm (3/4 inch)
  diameter adhesive-
  bonded timber
  dowels per unit

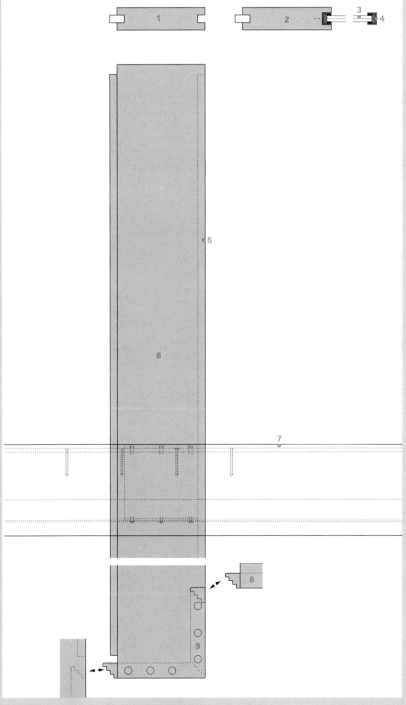

6.028
Concrete Stair Detail 1:5

Paulo David with Luz
Ramalho
Casa Funchal [16]

1 15 mm (5/8 inch)
  hardwood tread and
  risers
2 Concrete screed
3 Reinforced concrete
  base
4 Polyurethane floor
  with protective layer
5 Stuccoed plaster
  surface

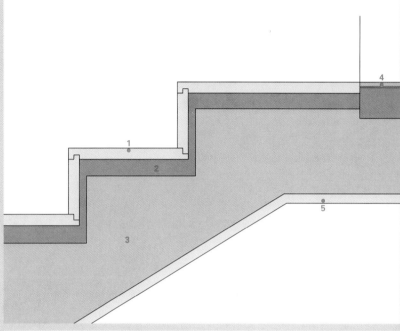

6.029
Stair Detail 1:5

Peter L. Gluck and
Partners, Architects
Inverted Guest House
[26]

1 Solid Parallam
  timber blocking
2 Gypsum wall board
3 50 x 50 mm (2 x 2
  inch) cedar girt
4 Corrugated copper
  cladding
5 10 mm (3/8 inch) steel
  plate tread/landing
6 Steel spacer

7 160 x 65 mm (61/3 x
  21/2 inch) rectangular
  hollow section steel
  stringer
8 95 x 95 mm (33/4 x
  33/4 inch) steel clip
  angle
9 Lag bolt

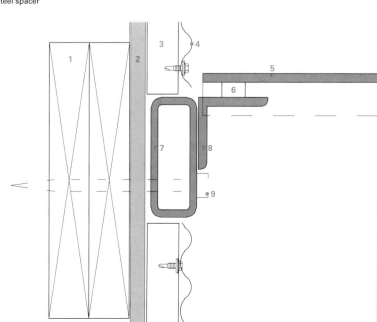

6.030
Staircase Detail 1:10

Javier Artadi Arquitecto
Las Arenas Beach House
[19]

1 Wall plastered, filled
 and painted with
 Spray Tech in stucco
2 Timber cover plug
3 Mahogany stair
 treads
4 Washed and brushed

terrazzo risers,
 continuous under
 timber treads
5 Terrazzo treads and
 risers
6 Expansion bolt to
 anchor treads to
 concrete
7 Reinforced concrete

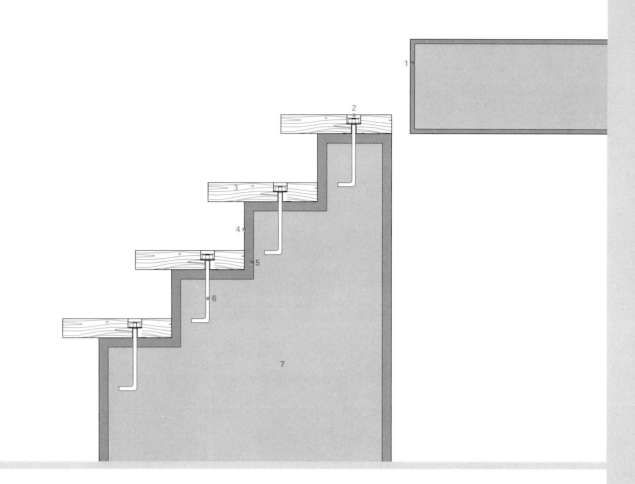

6.031
Stair Detail 1:10

Koffi & Diabaté
Architectes
Villa Talon [28]

1 50 mm (2 inch)
 diameter stainless
 steel handrail
2 50 mm (2 inch)
 diameter junction
 section to stainless
 steel handrail

3 15 mm (^{3}/5 inch)
 diameter
 intermediate rail
4 10 x 50 mm (^{2}/5 x 2
 inch) stainless steel
 rectangular section
5 Poured concrete stair
6 Steel disc handrail
 support bolted to
 concrete
7 Travertine stair tread
8 Travertine stair riser

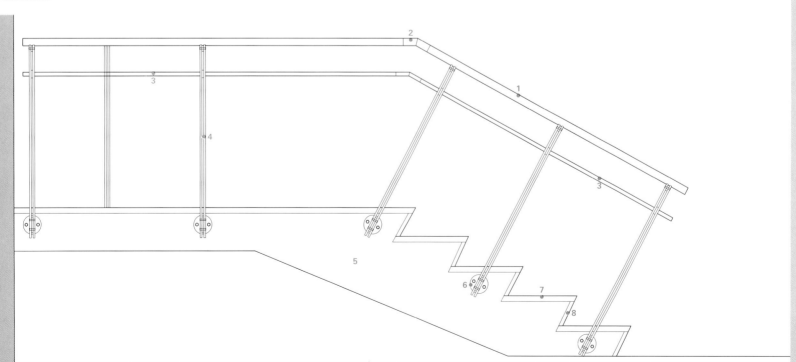

6.032
Stair Section Detail 1:10

Marlon Blackwell
Architect
L-Stack House [35]

1 25 mm (1 inch)
external diameter
painted steel handrail
2 20 x 10 mm (3/4 x 3/8
inch) flat steel plate
at intermediate rails
3 12 x 6 mm (1/2 x 1/4
inch) steel connector
welded to connect
vertical support to
handrail

4 25 x 12 mm (1 x 1/2
inch) flat steel plate
as vertical support
5 20 mm (3/4 inch)
plywood tongue and
groove subfloor
6 Two 350 mm (14
inch) laminated
veneer lumber joists
7 Soy-based spray
foam insulation
8 Five ply waterproof
exterior-grade
plywood substrate
with self-
waterproofing
membrane
9 25 x 150 mm (1 x 6

inch) Brazilian teak
tongue and groove
strips to form tread
over 50 x 300 mm (2
x 12 inch) timber sub-
tread
10 Angle bracket welded
to steel stringer on
both sides of
staircase to support
50 x 300 mm (2 x 12
inch) timber
sub-tread
11 25 x 150 mm (1 x 6
inch) Brazilian teak
riser to match tread
finish
12 10 x 220 mm (2/5 x

8 2/3 inch) painted
steel stringers
spaced 1050 mm (42
inch) apart to provide
clearance for tread
width
13 50 x 100 mm (2 x 4
inch) treated wood
blocking
14 20 mm (3/4 inch)
plywood substrate
15 Lapped seams to
black zinc cladding
16 45 mm (13/4 inch)
Brazilian redwood
rainscreen

6.033
Stair Detail 1:5

John Onken Architects
Dolphin Cottage [32]

1 Two layers of 22 mm
(7/8 inch) timber
treads and risers
recessed to take mild
steel frame
2 20 x 50 mm (7/8 x 2
inch) fully welded
mild steel frame
fabricated into
stepped profile for
concealment in stair
treads and risers

3 Two countersunk
bolts per tread, filled
and plugged to fix
bottom layer to steel
frame
4 Four countersunk
screws per tread to
join two layers of
tread together. Screw
heads to be filled
5 Identical assembly
for risers

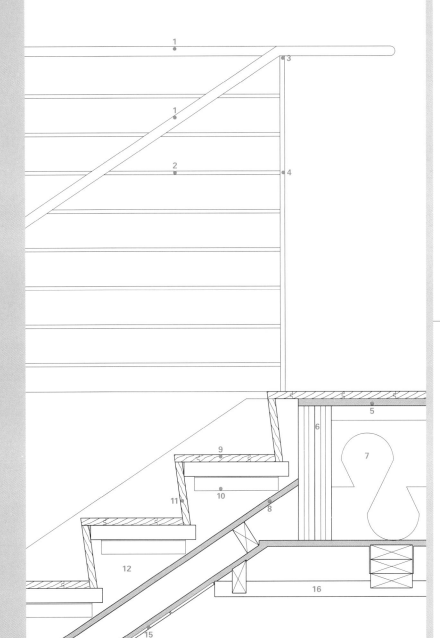

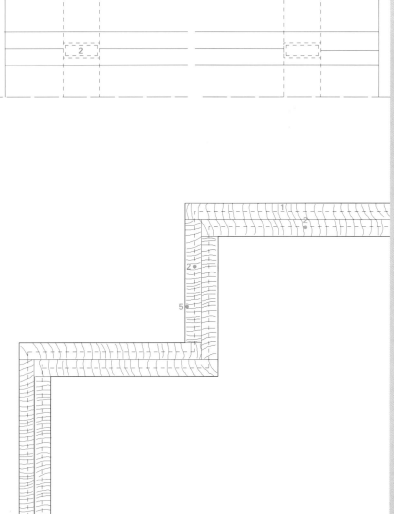

6.034
Staircase Detail 1:5

Go Hasegawa &
Associates
Forest House [34]

1 30 mm (1 1/4 inch)
 Japanese linden
 plywood with
 urethane paint finish
2 12.5 mm (1/2 inch)
 plasterboard to slope
 of attic space with

urethane paint finish
3 90 x 150 mm (3 1/2 x 6
 inch) knee brace (and
 ceiling firring
 material) at 910 mm
 (36 inch) centres
4 9 mm (3/8 inch)
 plywood ceiling with
 oil stain clear lacquer

6.035
Stair Detail 1:5

Jun Aoki & Associates
J House [24]

1 30 mm (1 1/8 inch)
 laminated plywood
 treads and risers
2 12 mm (1/2 inch)
 plywood
3 90 x 40 mm (3 1/2 x
 1 5/8 inch) timber
 joists at 270 mm

(10 3/4 inch) centres
4 3 x 5 mm (1/8 x 1/5
 inch) non-slip rubber
 plate
5 12.5 mm (1/2 inch)
 plasterboard with
 acrylic emulsion
 paint finish
6 30 mm (1 1/8 inch)
 laminated stringer to
 stair

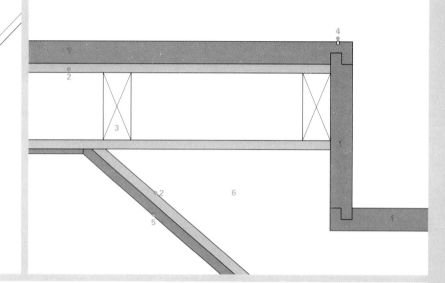

6.036
Stair Detail 1:50

Hawkes Architecture
Crossway [16]

1 Painted timber
 skirting board
2 Clay tile timbrel
 vaulted arch beyond
3 Recycled blockwork
 fireplace used as
 thermal mass heat
 store
4 Kaycel Super-plus
 Graphite insulation
5 Kaycel Super-plus
 Graphite insulation
6 Reinforced concrete
 slab
7 Crushed glass bottle
 and resin polished
 flooring
8 Clay tile timbrel
 vaulted staircase
9 Kerto ply stair treads
10 Flax rope balustrade

11 Recycled timber
 handrail on metal
 supports made from
 scaffold tubing
12 Painted plasterboard
13 Black rubber EPDM
 (ethylene propylene
 dieme monomer)
 waterproofing
14 Strip of internal
 English cedar
 weatherboarding
 from entrance hall

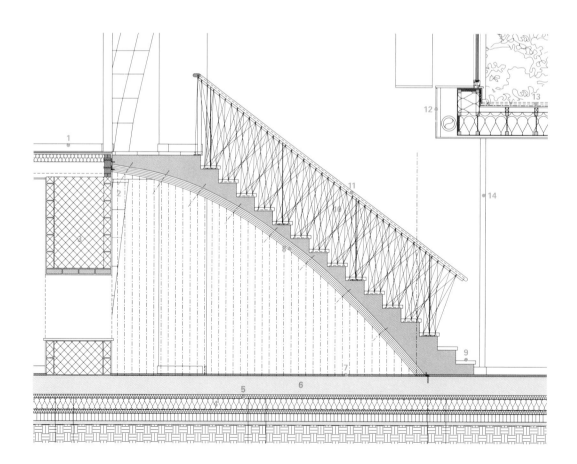

6.037
Stair Landing
Elevation Detail 1:20

Jun Igarashi Architects
Rectangle of Light [37]

1 Timber frame
2 2 mm (1/16 inch) tile
  on 24 mm (1 inch)
  structural plywood
3 12.5 mm (1/2 inch)
  plasterboard with
  vinyl cloth finish

4 2 mm (1/16 inch) tile
  on 24 mm (1 inch)
  structural plywood
5 Open entrance area
6 Timber door
7 12.5 mm (1/2 inch)
  plasterboard with
  vinyl cloth finish
8 40 mm (13/5 inch)
  thick, natural finish,
  spotted laurel treads
9 Wall with vinyl cloth
  finish
10 40 mm (13/5 inch)

thick, natural finish,
spotted laurel floor
finish
11 Void

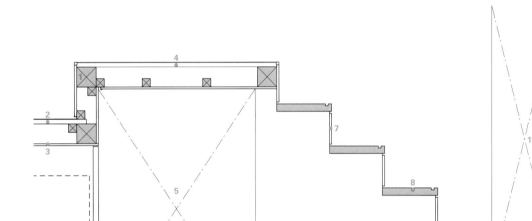

6.038
Terrace Stair Detail 1:20

Kotaro Ide / ARTechnic
Architects
Shell House [09]

1 Ulin hardwood
  flooring
2 Plywood flooring
  substrate
3 Timber terrace
  structure
4 Ulin hardwood

louvres to form stair
risers
5 Steel column head
  fixed to timber
  structure
6 Steel column
7 Concrete footing

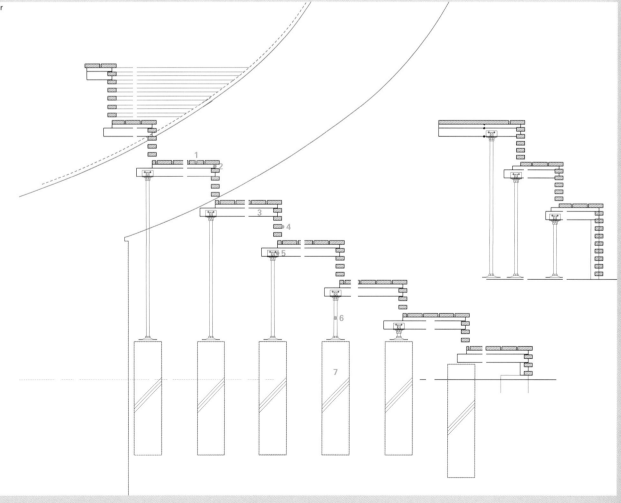

6.039
Stair Section Detail 1:20

EZZO
Leça House [35]

1 30 mm (1¼ inch) diameter painted steel tube handrail
2 200 mm (8 inch) pine tread
3 30 mm (1¼ inch) treated pine stringer
4 20 mm (¾ inch) painted medium density fibreboard
5 22 mm (⅞ inch) treated pine wood

flooring
6 Underfloor radiant heating
7 Extruded polystyrene thermal insulation
8 PVC sheet
9 30 mm (1¼ inch) sand and cement screed
10 Concrete layer on gravel base
11 30 mm (1¼ inch) treated pine floorboards

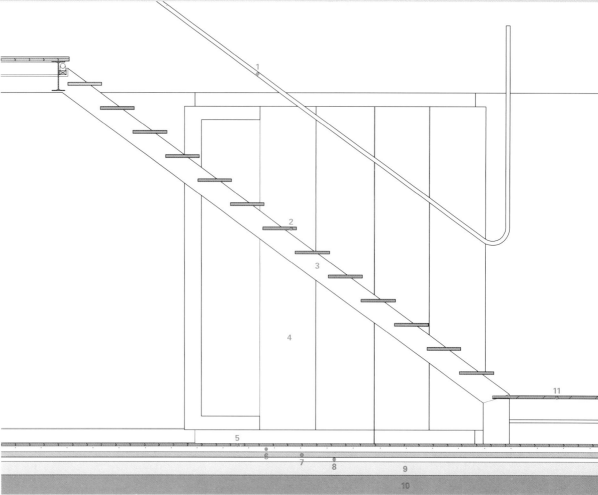

6.040
Internal Stair Detail 1:50

Room 11
Kingston House [34]

1 70 x 10 mm (2¾ x ⅖ inch) steel flat bar painted gloss white
2 70 x 10 mm (2¾ x ⅖ inch) steel flat bar painted gloss white
3 Stainless steel wire infill
4 70 x 10 mm (2¾ x ⅖ inch) steel flat bar painted gloss white
5 40 mm (1⅗ inch)

Tasmanian oak timber stair treads
6 40 mm (1⅗ inch) Tasmanian oak timber stair risers
7 40 mm (1⅗ inch) Tasmanian oak stringer shaped to tread profile
8 90 mm (3½ inch) timber stud wall
9 22 x 90 mm (⅞ x 3½ inch) tongue and groove Tasmanian oak timber flooring

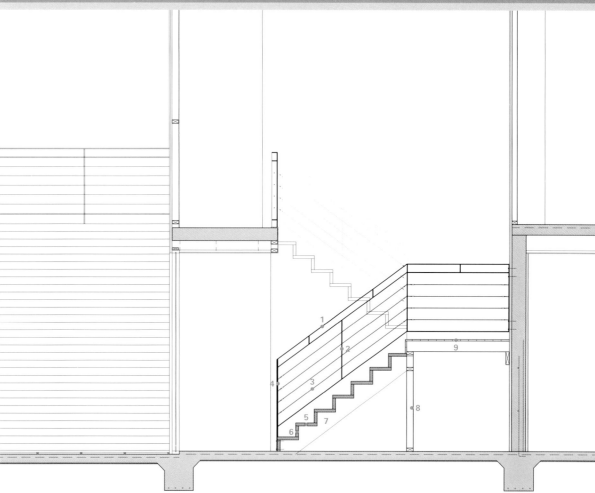

6.041
Stair Section Detail 1:20

Pierre Minassian
Architecte
Biscuit House [11]

1 20 mm (3/4 inch)
  laminated glass
  balustrade
2 Rectangular hollow
  steel support cross
  beam
3 Stainless steel
  handrail
4 Stainless steel
  balustrade
5 Stainless steel

suspension cable
6 Stainless steel cable
7 Steel flat treads
8 Stair stringer
9 Concrete floor slab

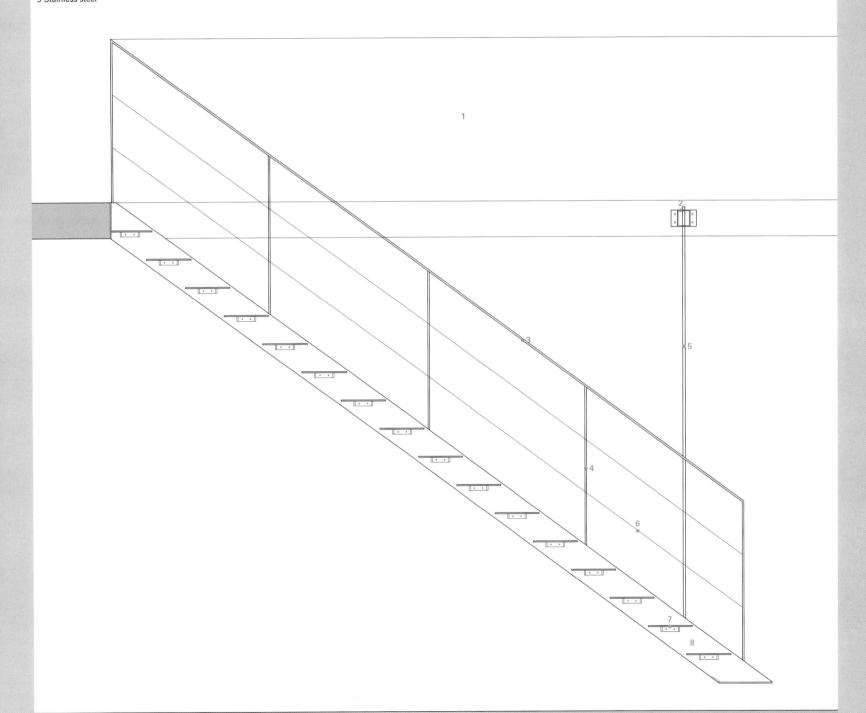

6.042 6.043

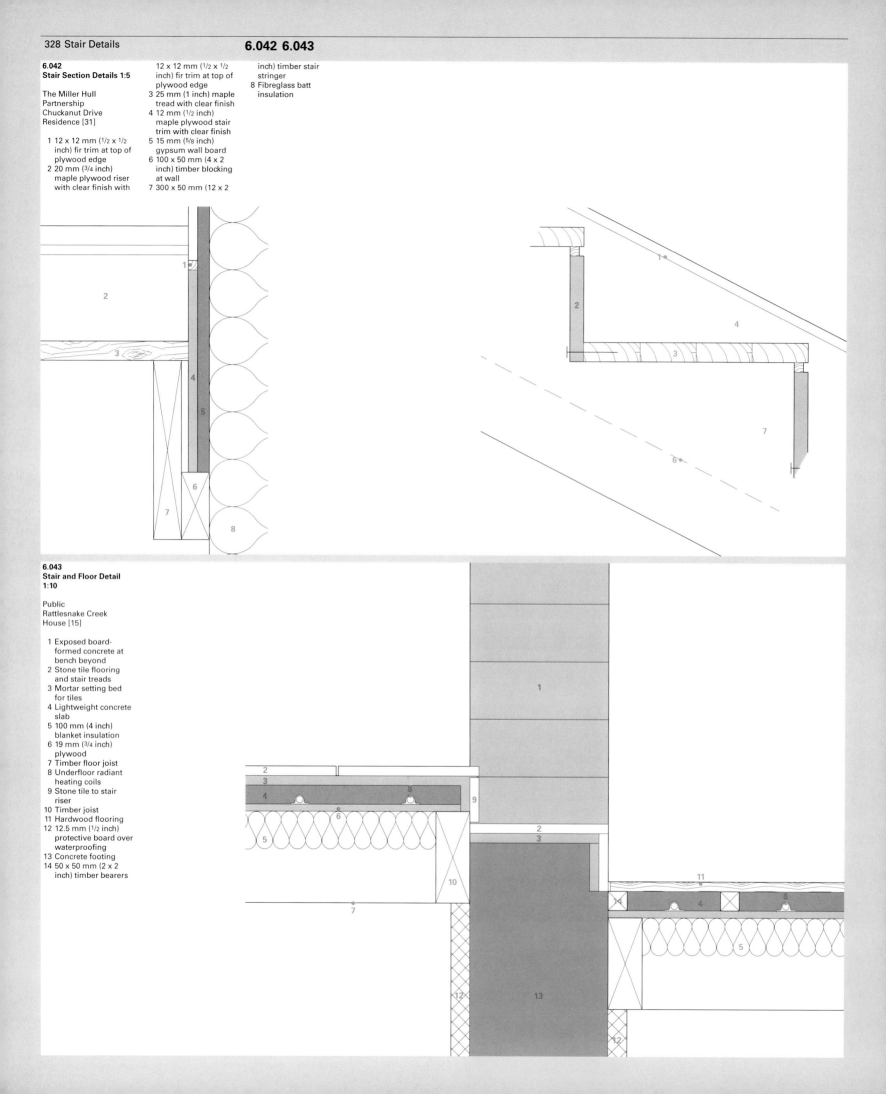

6.042
Stair Section Details 1:5

The Miller Hull
Partnership
Chuckanut Drive
Residence [31]

1 12 x 12 mm (1/2 x 1/2
inch) fir trim at top of
plywood edge
2 20 mm (3/4 inch)
maple plywood riser
with clear finish with
12 x 12 mm (1/2 x 1/2
inch) fir trim at top of
plywood edge
3 25 mm (1 inch) maple
tread with clear finish
4 12 mm (1/2 inch)
maple plywood stair
trim with clear finish
5 15 mm (5/8 inch)
gypsum wall board
6 100 x 50 mm (4 x 2
inch) timber blocking
at wall
7 300 x 50 mm (12 x 2
inch) timber stair
stringer
8 Fibreglass batt
insulation

6.043
**Stair and Floor Detail
1:10**

Public
Rattlesnake Creek
House [15]

1 Exposed board-
formed concrete at
bench beyond
2 Stone tile flooring
and stair treads
3 Mortar setting bed
for tiles
4 Lightweight concrete
slab
5 100 mm (4 inch)
blanket insulation
6 19 mm (3/4 inch)
plywood
7 Timber floor joist
8 Underfloor radiant
heating coils
9 Stone tile to stair
riser
10 Timber joist
11 Hardwood flooring
12 12.5 mm (1/2 inch)
protective board over
waterproofing
13 Concrete footing
14 50 x 50 mm (2 x 2
inch) timber bearers

6.044
Staircase Plan Detail
1:10

Welsh + Major
Pitt Street House [37]

1 Original winding
  stair treads below
2 Remnant of existing
  baluster
3 25 mm (1 inch) dowel
  at 140 mm (5½ inch)
  centres
4 100 x 15 mm (4 x ⅝
  inch) painted ply
  crossrail
5 100 x 15 mm (4 x ⅝
  inch) painted ply
  stanchion shown
  dotted

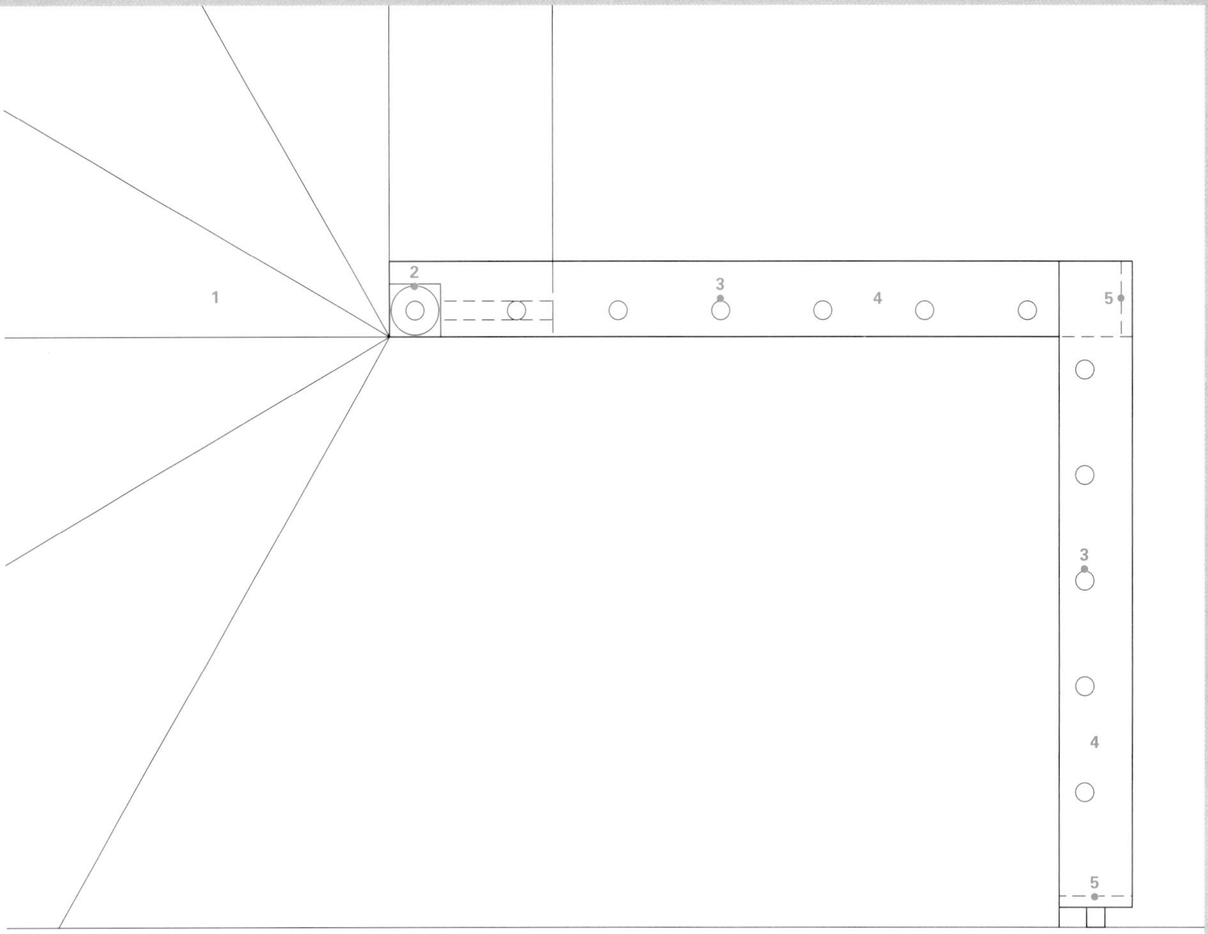

6.045
Staircase Balustrade
Detail 1:10

Welsh + Major
Pitt Street House [37]

1 Remnant baluster
2 25 mm (1 inch) dowel
  at 140 mm (5½ inch)
  centres
3 100 x 15 mm (4 x ⅝
  inch) ply crossrail
4 100 x 15 mm (4 x ⅝
  inch) ply stanchion
  shown dotted

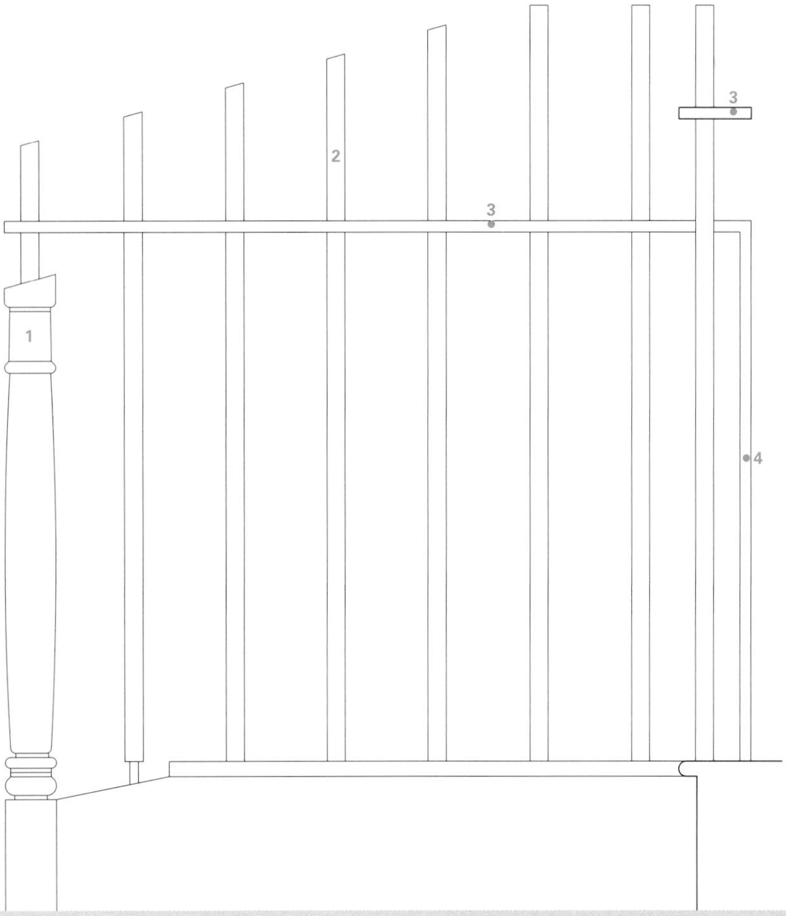

6.046
**Exterior Stair Section
Detail 1:25**

Bates Masi + Architects
Noyack Creek Residence
[37]

1 Double glazed
   aluminium framed
   sliding door
2 Timber decking as
   floor and stair treads
   with 6mm ($1/4$ inch)
   space between
   boards
3 Double timber floor
   bearer

4 Timber decking as
   risers with 6mm ($1/4$
   inch) space between
   boards
5 Timber decking as
   treads with 6mm ($1/4$
   inch) space between
   boards
6 50 x 300 mm (2 x 12
   inch) timber stringer
7 Skirting board
   material and finish to
   match base
8 Heating, ventilation
   and air-conditioning
   duct register
9 20 mm ($3/4$ inch)
   plywood subfloor

10 Engineered wood
   fibre I-profile floor
   joist
11 Insulation

6.047
**Staircase Detail at
Second Floor Stair
Landing 1:10**

Alison Brooks Architects
Herringbone Houses
[33]

1 40 mm ($13/5$ inch)
   solid oak stair tread
2 40 mm ($13/5$ inch)
   solid oak stair riser
3 Harwood beech
   veneered plywood
   stair stringer
4 40 x 50 mm ($13/5$ x 2
   inch) suspended

solid oak riser
5 20 mm ($3/4$ inch)
   hardwood flooring
6 65 mm ($21/2$ inch)
   battens with 30 mm
   ($11/5$ inch) Rockwool
   insulation and
   underfloor heating
   system
7 12.5 mm ($1/2$ inch)
   plasterboard with 2.5
   mm ($1/10$ inch) skim
   coat
8 Steel angle
9 150 mm (6 inch)
   pre-cast beam plank
10 Steel I-beam
11 12.5 mm ($1/2$ inch)

plasterboard with 2.5
mm ($1/10$ inch) skim
coat to ceiling

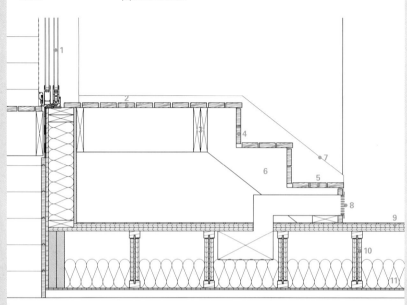

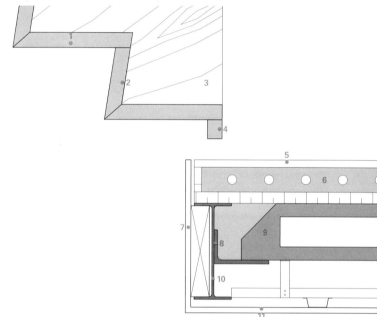

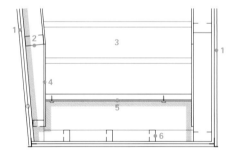

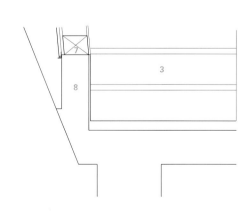

6.048
**Staircase Plan and
Section Detail 1:20**

Shuhei Endo Architect
Institute
Rooftecture S [27]

1 30 mm ($11/5$ inch)
   foamed urethane
   sheet-waterproofing
2 60 x 30 mm ($23/8$ x
   $11/5$ inch) steel
   channel
3 30 mm ($11/5$ inch)
   glulam laminated
   timber stair tread
4 Bamboo cladding to
   stringer
5 Oil paint finish to
   risers
6 60 x 30 mm ($23/8$ x
   $11/5$ inch) steel
   channel
7 Timber framing
8 Concrete wall
   structure

9 Concealed wall
   structure shown
   dotted
10 Bamboo cladding to
   stringer
11 9 mm ($1/3$ inch)
   plywood with oil
   stain finish
12 43 mm ($12/3$ inch)
   diameter stainless
   steel hand rail
13 340 mm ($131/3$ inch)
   diameter circular
   steel column

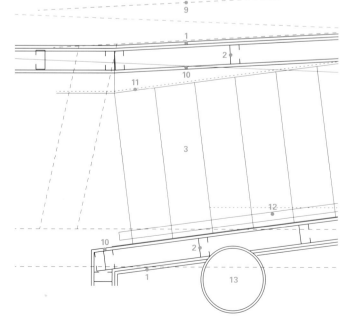

6.049
**Typical Stair Tread and
Riser Detail 1:10**

Architectus
North Shore House [36]

1 300 x 50 mm (12 x 2
 inch) dressed solid
 timber treads and
 risers, rebated and
 screw-fixed to 150 x
 50 x 6 mm (6 x 2 x 1/4
 inch) cleat welded off
 stringer with two
 countersunk
 hexagonal-head
 wood screws

2 Dressed solid timber
 risers
3 Bolt fixing
4 Stringer of two 200 x
 10 mm (8 x 3/8 inch)
 steel flats with 12
 mm (1 inch)
 toughened glass
 balustrade bolted
 between plates at
 350 mm (14 inch)
 centres with
 countersunk bolt
 fixings and dome
 nuts

6.050
Terrace Stair Detail 1:10

Studio d'ARC Architects
Live / Work Studio II [19]

1 38 x 254 mm (11/2 x
 10 inch) solid maple
 stair tread
2 44 x 6 mm (13/4 x 1/4
 inch) welded steel
 bar
3 20 mm (3/4 inch)
 tongue and groove
 maple flooring
4 20 mm (3/4 inch)
 plywood subfloor
5 160 x 160 mm (61/4 x

 61/4 inch) rolled steel
 beam
6 20 mm (3/4 inch)
 diameter bolts
7 8 mm (5/16 inch) steel
 plate
8 320 x 40 mm (13 x
 15/8 inch) timber
 nailer
9 12.5 mm (1/2 inch)
 gypsum board
10 Aluminium reglet
11 350 mm (14 inch)
 truss joist at 600 mm
 (24 inch) centres
12 12 mm (1/2 inch)
 plywood ceiling,
 sanded and finished

6.051
Stair Detail 1:20

WPA
Weese Young Residence
[28]

1 Polycarbonate panel
2 Timber handrail
3 Plywood wall lining
4 Vertical grain pine
 stair treads
5 Timber cross beam
6 Timber stair stringer
7 Lite-ply wall and
 ceiling lining
8 Poplar base and
 skirting
9 Vertical grain pine on
 plywood subfloor
10 Painted rectangular
 hollow section beam
11 Engineered timber
 joist

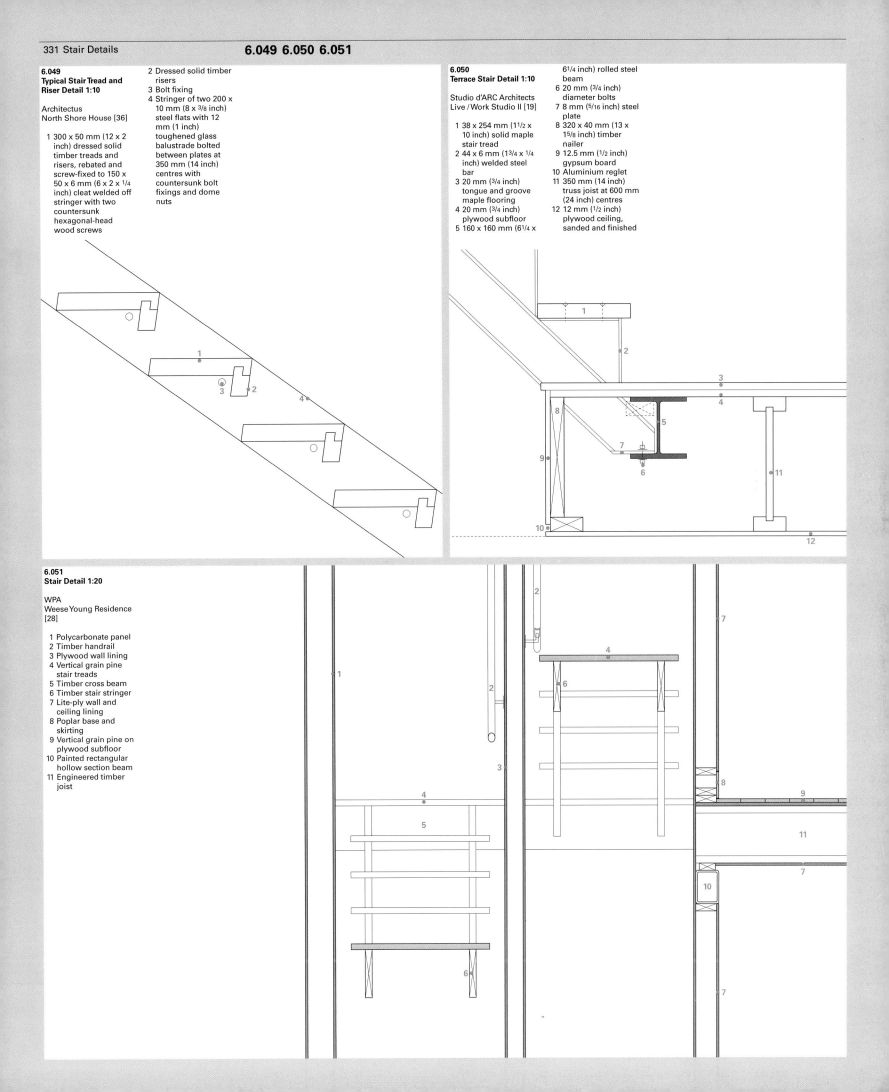

6.052
Stair Section Detail 1:20

McBride Charles Ryan
The Dome House [21]

1 Aluminium handrail
  and fixing plate
  behind
2 Stringer continues as
  skirting to stairway
  landing, stringers
  with rebated treads
  and risers

3 Continuous carpet to
  treads and risers
4 32 mm (1 1/4 inch)
  medium density
  fibreboard treads
  with 20 mm (3/4 inch)
  radius bullnose
5 18 mm (7/10 inch)
  medium density
  fibreboard risers
6 Cut stringer and
  continue above tread
  only
7 Timber framing

8 10 mm (2/5 inch)
  plasterboard

6.053
Stair Section Detail 1:10

Steffen Leisner, Ali
Jeevanjee, Phillip Trigas
1+3=1 House [17]

1 20 mm (3/4 inch)
  plywood with 'A' face
  exposed and with oil
  based semi-gloss
  finish
2 Timber stair framing
3 Sawn lumber stair

stringer
4 Sound attenuating
  batt insulation
5 20 mm (3/4 inch)
  plywood with 'A' face
  exposed
6 Two layers of
  gypsum wall board
  with paint finish to
  underside of stair

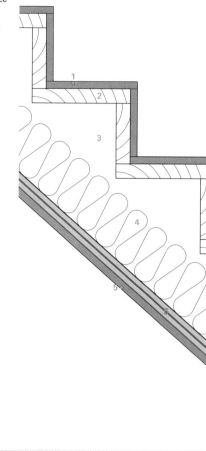

6.054
Staircase and
Balustrade Detail 1:5

Terry Pawson Architects
The Tall House [38]

1 44 x 20 mm (1 3/4 x 3/4
  inch) brushed mild
  steel balustrade with
  waxed finish and
  with no protruding
  fixings on steelwork
2 12 mm (1/2 inch) riven

slate tile on thin bed
  of adhesive
3 In-situ concrete stair
  structure
4 Collar on socket to
  prevent epoxy resin
  loss to surface of
  concrete
5 Threaded stainless
  steel socket fixed into
  concrete using epoxy
  resin to receive bolt
6 Threaded bolt with 6
  mm (1/4 inch)

diameter hole for
  locating pin
7 6 mm (1/4 inch)
  stainless steel
  locating pin fixed
  into M12 bolt
  through body of
  balustrade

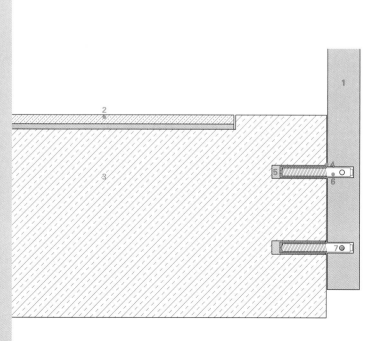

6.055
Staircase Detail 1:10

Touraine Richmond
Architects
One Window House [27]

1 Timber stringer
2 19 mm (3/4 inch)
  sanded and stained
  oriented strand
  board-finished stair
  treads and risers
3 100 x 200 mm (4 x 8

inch) parallel strand
  lumber framing
4 Parallel strand
  lumber riser framing
5 Sheet metal lining
6 Sheet metal lining

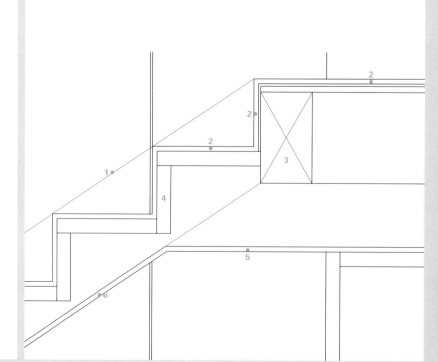

6.056
Staircase Section Detail
1:20

Shuhei Endo Architect
Institute
Rooftecture S [27]

1 43 mm (1³/₄ inch)
  diameter stainless
  steel handrail
2 Expanded metal floor
3 15 mm (³/₅ inch) thick
  timber floorboards

with clear urethane
  paint finish
4 100 x 60 mm (4 x 2³/₈
  inch) timber floor
  joist
5 250 x 125 mm (9⁴/₅ x
  5 inch) steel beam
6 Steel connector plate
  with bolt fixings
7 Folded steel plate
  risers painted with
  rustproof oil paint
8 Urethane foam
  insulation

9 30 mm (1¹/₅ inch) oak
  glued laminated
  timber tread
10 60 x 30 mm (2³/₈ x
  1¹/₅ inch) galvanized
  steel C-profile
  framing
11 Waterproof
  galvanized steel
  sheet
12 Steel stringer with
  rustproof oil paint
  finish
13 Concrete floor with

trowelled finish
14 Concrete screed
15 Reinforced concrete
  floor slab
16 Bolted connection
  between steel stair
  structure and
  concrete floor slab

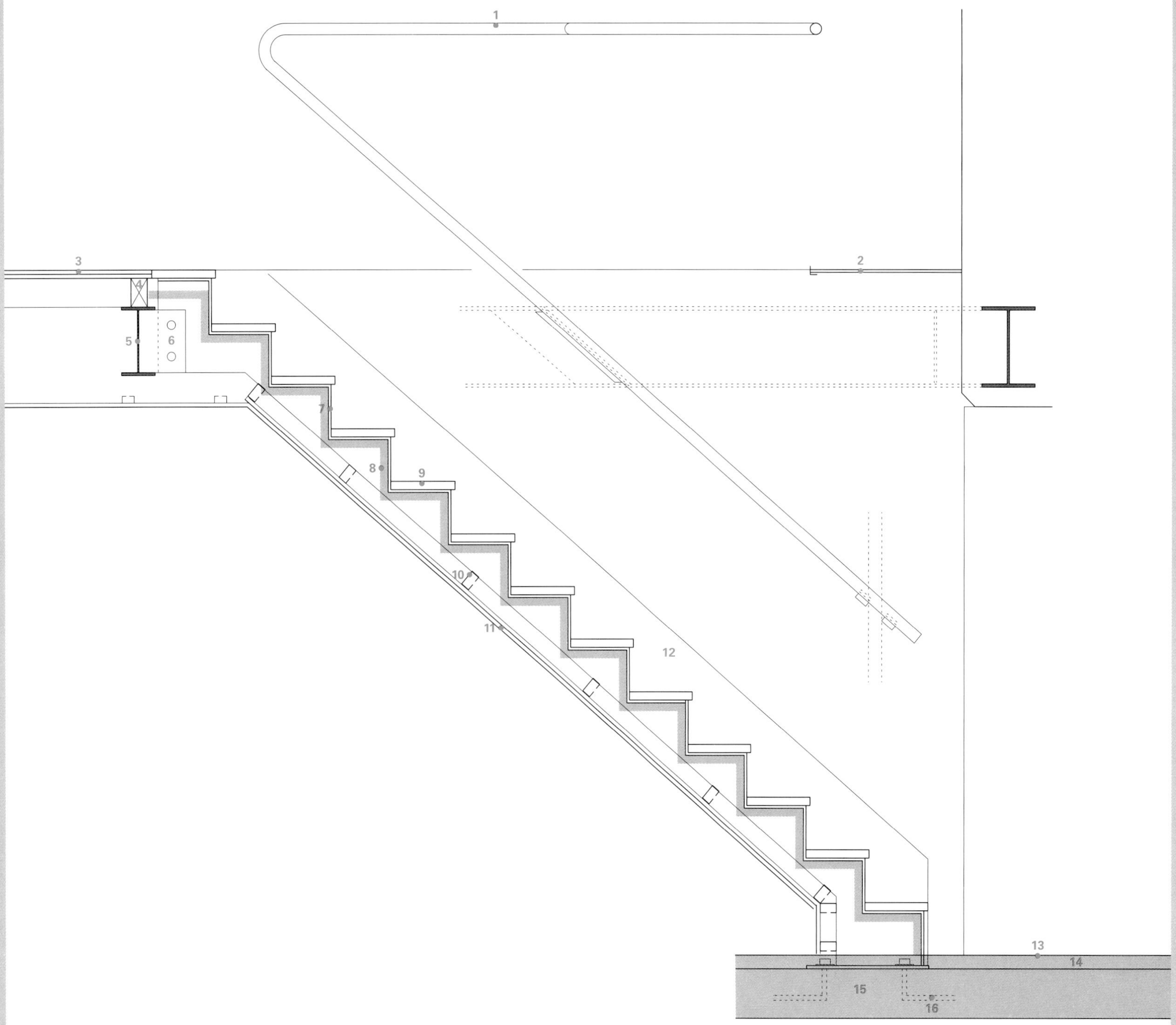

6.057
Staircase Detail 1:10

MELD Architecture with
Vicky Thornton
House in Tarn et
Garonne [34]

1 30 mm (1¼ inch)
  solid oak tread with 5
  mm (1/5 inch) rebate
2 Softwood frame
3 20 mm (3/4 inch) oak
  riser
4 Concealed softwood
  stringer

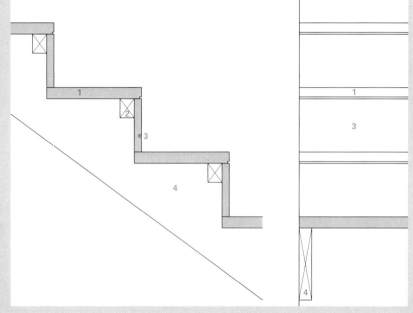

6.058
**Staircase Elevation
Detail 1:20**

Kotaro Ide / ARTechnic
Architects
Shell House [09]

1 Ulin hardwood stair
  tread
2 Ulin hardwood tread
  edge notched into
  main part of tread
3 Timber batten for
  louvred riser
  assembly
4 Ulin hardwood
  louvred stair risers
5 Paint finish to
  concrete understair
  surface
6 Vertical timber
  louvred riser support
7 Ulin hardwood
  timber flooring
8 Plywood flooring
  substrate

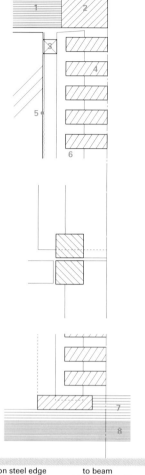

6.059
**Concrete Stair Detail
1:20**

Rowan Opat Architects
Courtyard House [38]

1 Polished, reinforced,
  suspended coloured
  concrete slab with
  paint finish
2 Reinforced concrete
  steps with rough
  sawn timber blocks
  over
3 Polished, reinforced,
  suspended coloured
  concrete slab with
  paint finish
4 Polished, reinforced,
  suspended coloured
  concrete floor slab
  with paint finish
5 Brick piers
6 Reinforced concrete
  footing
7 Subfloor area

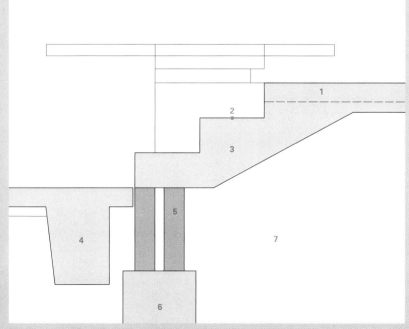

6.060
Steel Stair Detail 1:10

Peter Stutchbury
Architecture
Avalon House [29]

1 10 mm (3/8 inch)
  galvanized steel rod
  between stair treads
2 200 x 10 mm (8 x 3/8
  inch) galvanized steel
  plate stringer
3 40 x 40 x 5 mm (15/8
  x 15/8 x 1/5 inch)
  galvanized steel
  angle tread supports
  bolted to steel plate
4 Two 125 x 40 mm (5
  x 15/8 inch) hardwood
  treads
5 Plywood facing to
  rectangular hollow
  section steel edge
  beam
6 140 x 40 mm (51/2 x
  15/8 inch) hardwood
  tread with 20mm (3/4
  inch) nosing
  overhang to match
  stair treads
7 Two M20 threaded
  studs welded to
  stringer and bolted
  to rectangular hollow
stringer
section steel edge
beam
8 100 x 200 mm (4 x 8
  inch) rectangular
  hollow section steel
  edge beam
9 100 x 25 mm (4 x 1
  inch) hardwood
  flooring
10 20 mm (3/4 inch)
  plywood layer
11 200 mm (8 inch)
  galvanized universal
  steel beam
12 Timber blocking to
  plywood junction
  painted black
13 Firring channels fixed
to beam
14 Plywood ceiling

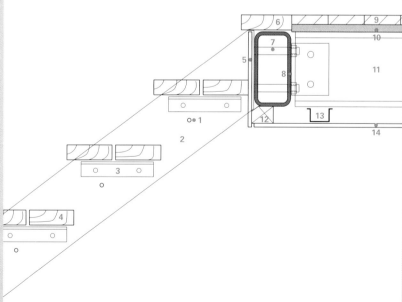

6.061
Glass Balustrade Detail
1:10

Pierre Minassian
Architecte
Biscuit House [11]

1 20 mm (3/4 inch)
   laminated glass
   balustrade
2 Neoprene seal
3 10 mm (3/8 inch)
   stainless steel fascia
   plate
4 Square steel hollow
   section
5 Concrete floor

6 Steel stair structure
7 Steel stair stringer

6.062
Stair Elevation Detail
1:20

Pierre Minassian
Architecte
Biscuit House [11]

1 20 mm (3/4 inch)
   laminated glass
   balustrade
2 Timber capping
3 Rectangular hollow
   steel support cross
   beam
4 Concrete slab
5 Neoprene seal
6 Suspended plaster

ceiling
7 Stainless steel
   suspension cable
8 Stainless steel
   handrail
9 Steel flat treads
10 Painted plasterboard
   wall lining
11 Insulation
12 Concrete wall

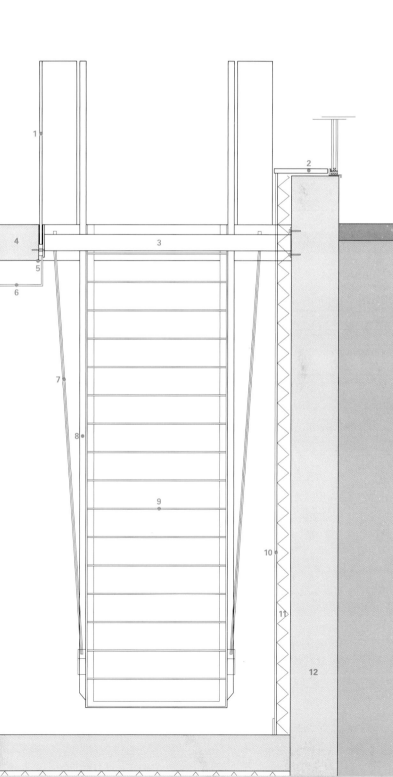

6.063
Stair Section Detail 1:20

Arjaan de Feyter
Zoersel House [29]

1 60 x 160 mm (2³/8 x
  6¹/4 inch) steel stair
  stringer welded to
  landing support steel
2 Steel flat to support
  tread, welded to
  stringer
3 Solid oak stair treads
  with dark stain
4 Stair treads
  bolt-fixed to steel
  supports

6.064
Stair Elevation Detail
1:20

EZZO
Leça House [35]

1 40 x 50 mm (1⁵/8 x 2
  inch) timber profile
  on battens painted
  with polyurethane
  paint
2 110 mm (4³/8 inch)
  brick wall
3 Reinforced concrete
4 30 mm (1¹/4 inch)
  diameter painted
  steel tube handrail
5 15 mm (⁵/8 inch)
  diameter painted
  steel tube for
  handrail wall fixing
6 Double layer of 12
  mm (¹/2 inch) thick
  plasterboard
7 200 mm (8 inch) pine
  tread

8 200 mm (8 inch) pine
  stringer
9 22 mm (⁷/8 inch)
  treated pine wood
  flooring
10 Underfloor radiant
   heating
11 Extruded polystyrene
   thermal insulation
12 PVC sheet
13 30 mm (1¹/4 inch)
   sand and cement
   screed
14 Concrete layer on
   gravel base

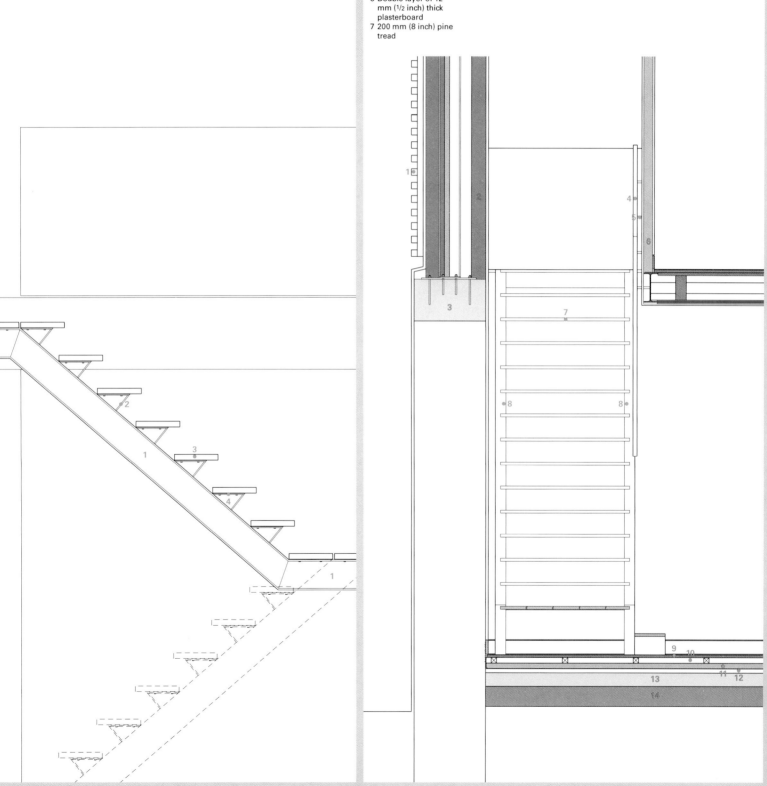

6.065
Stair Section Detail 1:20

Bercy Chen Studio
Riverview Gardens [38]

1 Batt insulation
2 Steel beam
3 50 x 300 mm (2 x 12 inch) stringer
4 20 mm (3/4 inch) stone treads and risers on 12 mm (1/2 inch) plywood
5 15 mm (5/8 inch) gypsum ceiling
6 Steel cross-bracing
7 25 mm (1 inch) double glazed, frosted fixed window
8 20 mm (3/4 inch) stone on 30 mm (1 1/5 inch) plywood
9 6 mm (1/4 inch) painted Hardiplank panels
10 6 mm (1/4 inch) steel

plate welded to beam flange
11 Aluminium angle reveal at edge

6.066
Stair Railing Detail 1:20

Ibarra Rosano Design Architects
Winter Residence [23]

1 25 x 25 mm (1 x 1 inch) tube steel, ends aligned with face of first and last riser and painted to match existing steel of house
2 Drill and epoxy into existing wall
3 Existing CMU (concrete masonry unit) wall
4 Stucco over 25 mm (1 inch) foam insulation
5 Concrete stair with 150 mm (6 inch) risers and 300 mm (12 inch) treads

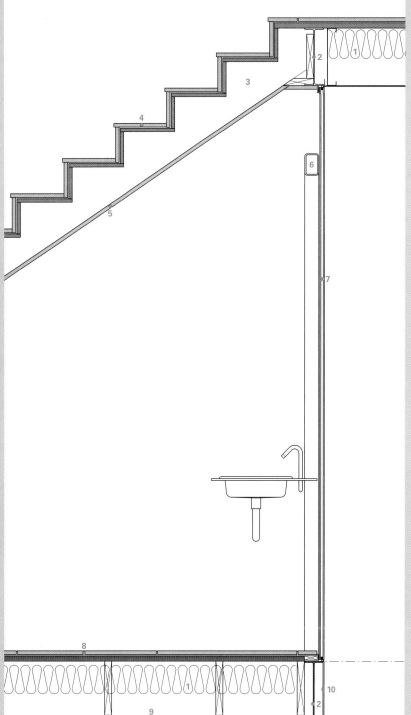

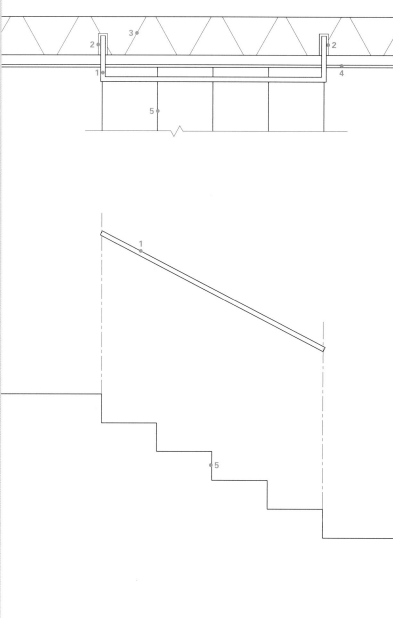

6.067
Timber Stair Detail 1:20

Lee + Mundwiler
Architects
The Coconut House [12]

1 20 mm (3/4 inch)
 hardwood risers
2 20 mm (3/4 inch)
 hardwood treads
3 Mitred edge
4 15 mm (5/8 inch)
 gypsum wall board
5 Timber stringer
6 20 mm (3/4 inch)
 plywood to risers
 and treads

7 Concrete slab
8 20 mm (3/4 inch)
 plywood under
 hardwood floor and
 over concrete slab

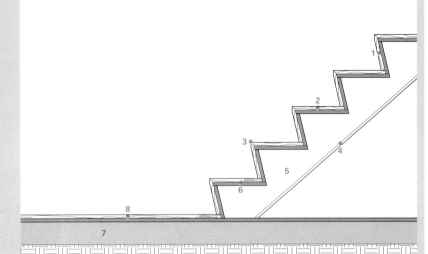

6.068
**Concrete Stair Detail
1:10**

The Miller Hull
Partnership
Chuckanut Drive
Residence [31]

1 25 mm (1 inch)
 timber floor on
 sleeper
2 Concrete tread
 poured separately
3 Porcelain tile floor
 finish
4 Vapour barrier

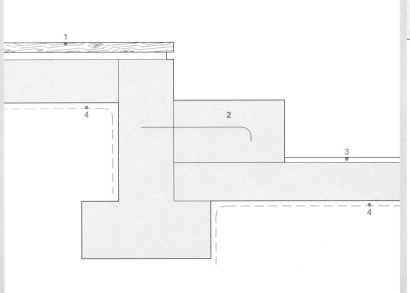

6.069
Stair Detail 1:20

Designworkshop: SA
Igoda View House [24]

1 50 x 50 x 10 mm (2 x
 2 x 3/8 inch) mild steel
 T-section handrail
 welded to stanchions
2 50 x 50 mm (2 x 2
 inch) mild steel
 stanchions welded to
 top of square hollow
 section to support
 handrail
3 12 mm (1/2 inch) mild
 steel pin connector

epoxy-fixed to
concrete side walls to
stabilize stair
4 50 x 50 x 5 mm (2 x 2
 x 1/5 inch) square
 hollow section mild
 steel stringer welded
 to connector plate at
 ground and first floor
 plate with welds
 ground down for
 flush finish
5 100 x 160 x 4 mm (4 x
 6 1/4 x 1/6 inch) mild
 steel flat plate
 welded between
 stringers to form
 support to treads

6 940 x 280 x 50 mm
 (37 x 11 1/8 x 2 inch)
 timber stair tread
 routed below to suit
 base plate and cover
 plate fixings

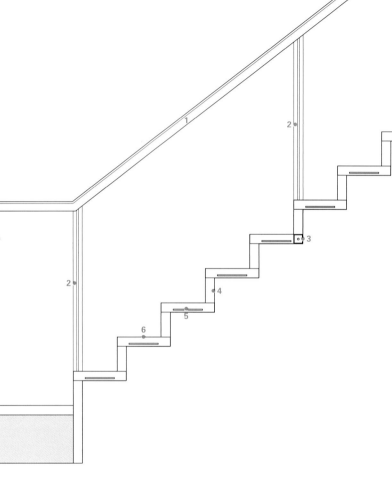

6.070
Stair Section Detail 1:50

Keith Williams Architects
The Long House [23]

1 Timber stud wall
 balustrade faced in
 skimmed
 plasterboard with
 sealed natural white
 plaster finish
2 Sealed natural white
 plaster finish to wall
 and ceiling areas
3 140 mm (5 1/2 inch)
 blockwork
4 20 mm (3/4 inch) oiled

oak hardwood floor
finish, secret fixed on
18 mm (7/10 inch)
flooring grade
chipboard
5 Skimmed
 plasterboard
 suspended ceiling
 with sealed natural
 white plaster finish
6 15 mm (3/5 inch) oiled
 oak strip finish to
 wall cladding,
 concealed fixing to
 battens
7 175 mm (6 9/10 inch)
 structural concrete
 wall

8 300 x 155 mm (11 4/5 x
 6 1/10 inch) honed and
 sealed Pietro Lauro
 limestone blocks on
 adhesive bedding
9 175 mm (6 9/10 inch)
 reinforced concrete
 stair
10 20 mm (3/4 inch) oiled
 oak hardwood floor
 finish, secret fixed on
 18 mm (7/10 inch)
 flooring grade
 chipboard
11 Sand-cement screed
 to the required level

6.071
Stair Plan Detail 1:50

Keith Williams Architects
The Long House [23]

1 Sealed natural white
 plaster finish to wall
 and ceiling areas
2 15 mm (3/5 inch) oiled
 oak strip finish to
 wall cladding,
 concealed fixing to
 battens
3 140 mm (5 1/2 inch)
 blockwork
4 Sealed natural white
 plaster finish to wall

and ceiling areas
5 300 x 155 mm (11 4/5 x
 6 1/10 inch) honed and
 sealed Pietro Lauro
 limestone blocks on
 adhesive bedding
6 50 x 15 mm (2 x 5/8
 inch) satin stainless
 steel flat bar
 handrail, all wall
 plates secret fixed
 behind surfaces
7 175 mm (6 9/10 inch)
 structural concrete
 wall
8 20 mm (3/4 inch) oiled
 oak strip cladding to
 sloping surface

9 Fire-rated frameless
 self-closing pivot
 door on floor spring
10 20 mm (3/4 inch) solid
 hardwood strip finish
 to stair treads and
 risers with 15 x 10
 mm (3/5 x 2/5 inch)
 deep rebated shadow
 gap detail to
 horizontal sides of
 tread and vertical
 sides of riser
11 Sliding door

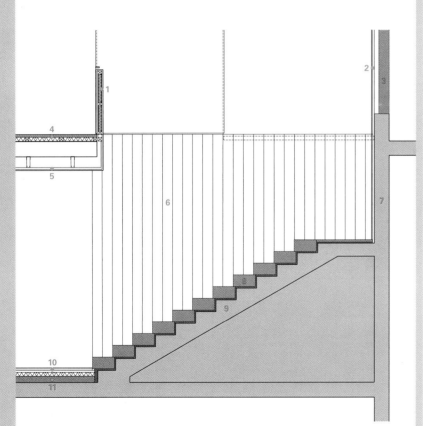

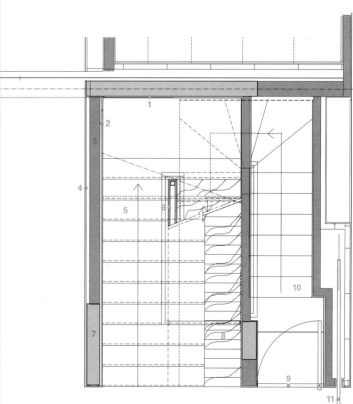

7.001
Letterbox Section Detail
1:20

McBride Charles Ryan
The Dome House [21]

1 Copper sheeting on two layers of 8 mm (1/3 inch) plywood substrate, roof battens and timber box beam
2 Profile cut level at edges
3 Roof batten
4 Folded translucent perspex lighting

5 Light fitting
6 Stainless steel screw fix with spacer behind
7 Dry stacked rocks behind steel reinforcement bars at 400 mm (16 inch) grid, with bars continued through centre of 140 mm (5 1/2 inch) reinforced blockwork
8 Steel reinforcing bars
9 Stainless steel letterbox
10 140 mm (5 1/2 inch)

cover
reinforced concrete blockwork
11 Timber box beam
12 Selected pavers on cement screed with aluminium angle to all paving edges
13 Concrete slab and strip footing
14 Slotted agricultural drain with stones

7.002
Front Fence Detail 1:10

Bercy Chen Studio
Peninsula House [36]

1 Steel plate with connector tab
2 25 x 101 mm (1 x 4 inch) fencing notched to receive steel and copper tabs
3 Steel plate fence upright
4 Copper fence board spacer
5 Concrete on grade
6 Steel plate

bottom rail
7 Fence post embedded in concrete footing
8 229 mm (9 inch) concrete footing

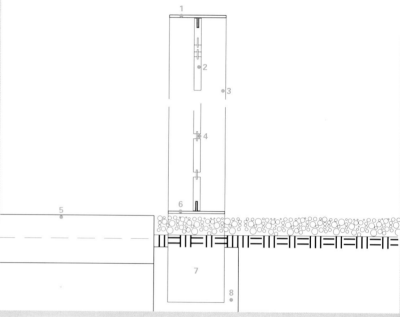

7.003
Boat Dock Bench Detail
1:20

Bercy Chen Studio
Peninsula House [36]

1 Protruding leg of steel angle finished to a point
2 300 mm (12 inch) wide massaranduba slat seat back trimmed in 3 mm (1/8 inch) steel plate
3 Notched steel plate surround at bracket
4 Steel angle seat bracket welded to vertical support with slats attached to angle
5 3 x 50 mm (1/8 x 2 inch) steel plate surround
6 Steel angle scissor support

7 25 x 101 mm (1 x 4 inch) massaranduba decking
8 50 x 152 mm (2 x 6 inch) pressure treated blocking to steel beam
9 Steel beam welded to steel piles
10 50 x 254 mm (2 x 10 inch) pressure treated ledger to steel beam
11 Joist hanger
12 Protruding leg of steel angle and straight angle leg
13 Reinforcing steel angle welded to plate dock skirt
14 Pressure-treated timber joists
15 15.2 metre (50 foot) deep steel piles driven to bedrock

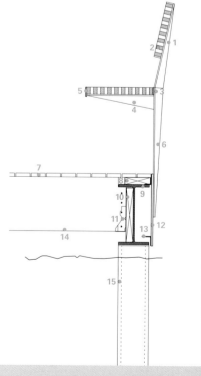

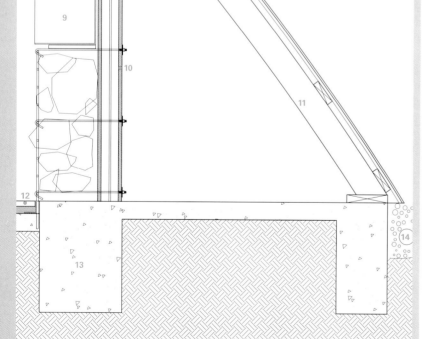

7.004
Interior Floor and Pool
Detail 1:10

Javier Artadi Arquitecto
Las Arenas Beach House
[19]

1 Wall plastered, filled
  and painted
2 Concrete side and
  steps finished in
  water resistant paint
3 Maximum level of
  water in pool
4 Reinforced concrete

7.005
Pool Detail 1:50

Ibarra Rosano Design
Architects
Winter Residence [23]

1 Gunite sprayed
  concrete mix with
  terrazzo finish
2 Pre-cast gunite piers
3 250 x 250 mm (10 x
  10 inch) glass tiles
4 100 mm (4 inch)
  cantilevered concrete
  slab bridge
5 100 mm (4 inch) pool
  deck
6 Concrete pool
  perimeter curb
7 Waterline

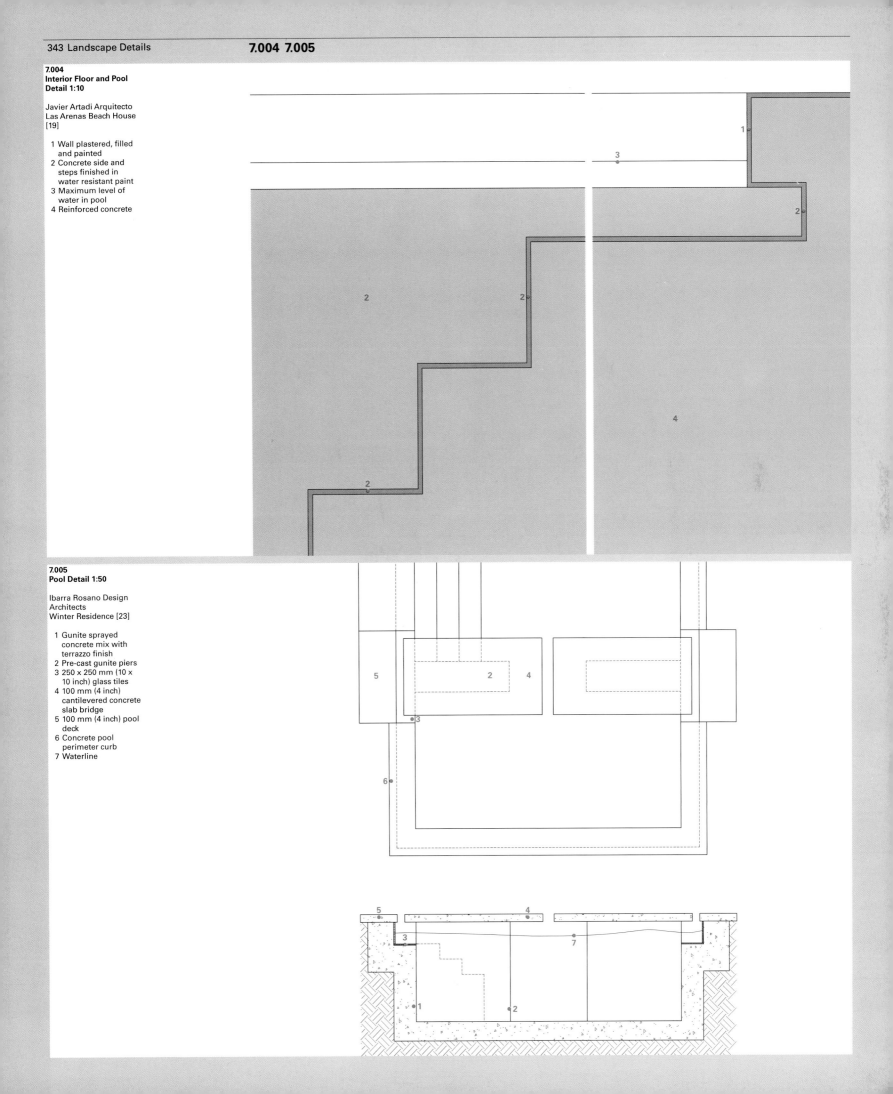

7.006
Pool Bench at Concealed
Return Detail 1:20

Bercy Chen Studio
Peninsula House [36]

1 Metal studs
2 63 mm (2 1/2 inch)
  concrete over metal
  deck attached to
  joists below
3 Travertine flooring
  on concrete laid to
  fall for drainage
4 Timber blocking to
  attach joists
5 50 x 50 mm (2 x 2
  inch) edge angle
  welded to steel beam
6 Travertine tiles held
  away from edge to
  allow for drainage
7 Travertine tile to pool
  edge upright
8 Tiled coping sloped
  to drain in direction
  of pool
9 Bond beam
10 Travertine tile to
   upper part of pool
   lining
11 Pool bench
   comprised of
   monolithic gunite
   over equipment void
   space
12 Void space under
   bench
13 Custom perforated
   stainless steel grate
   attached to hinge
   anchored into pool
   shell
14 12 x 355 mm (1/2 x 14
   inch) stainless steel
   manhole cover and
   sealing ring with
   heavy duty gasket
   and locking
   mechanism

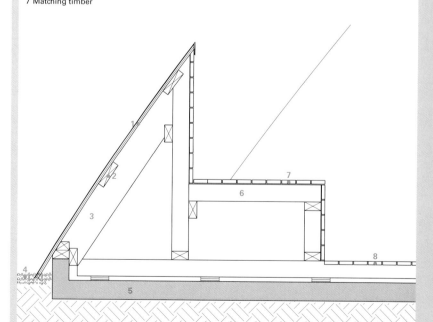

7.007
External Decking Detail
1:10

David Nossiter
Architects
Kitsbury Road House
[13]

1 63 mm (2 1/2 inch)
  aluminium rainwater
  pipe
2 Profiled and treated
  timber decking
  minimum 10 mm (4
  inch) width with 7
  mm (1/4 inch) gap
  between boards,

decking on 100 x 50
mm (4 x 2 inch)
battens at 450 mm
(18 inch) centres
3 Uni-shim suspended
  floor system on
  spacer feet
4 Geotextile
  membrane
5 Gravel topping on
  well compacted
  hardcore
6 Pre-cast concrete
  drainage channel on
  concrete bed with
  minimum 150 mm (6
  inch) clear depth

7.008
External Wall with
Built-in Seat
Detail 1:20

McBride Charles Ryan
The Dome House [21]

1 Copper cladding on
  plywood substrate
2 Timber battens
3 Timber framing
4 Selected stones
5 Concrete slab
6 90 x 45 mm (3 1/2 x
  1 3/4 inch) pine deck
  framing
7 Matching timber

decking to seat and
back of bench
8 Timber decking
  supported by timber
  joists on graded
  paving slab

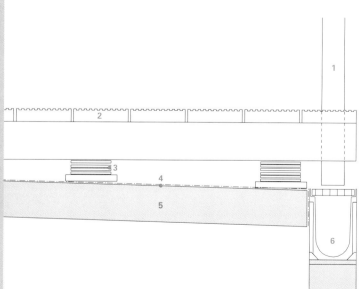

7.009
Concealed Lighting Detail 1:5

Jun Aoki & Associates
J House [24]

1 7.5 mm (5/16 inch) cement board fixed to timber stud wall
2 Permeable vapour waterproof membrane
3 17 mm (5/8 inch) metal lath
4 Lysine sprayed mortar render
5 40 x 20 mm (15/8 x 3/4 inch) aluminium angle
6 Mixture of half red soil and half black earth
7 180 x 75 mm (7 x 3 inch) steel channel
8 Fluorescent light fitting
9 100 x 100 mm (4 x 4 inch) steel mesh reinforcement
10 60 mm (23/8 inch) reinforced concrete floor slab
11 Earth
12 60 x 60 mm (23/8 x 23/8 inch) structural steel column

7.010
Pond and Paving Detail 1:10

Architectus
North Shore House [36]

1 End paver bedded in flexible epoxy grout
2 Concrete haunch cast against 6 mm (1/4 inch) fibre cement board over tanking, with edge strip of membrane adhered to deck waterproofing and sealed into channel
3 600 x 600 x 40 mm (24 x 24 x 15/8 inch) terrazzo concrete paving slabs bedded on 30 mm (11/5 inch) minimum free-draining sand on filter textile
4 15 mm (5/8 inch) drainage cell over waterproof membrane
5 Hyvol rebated channel set into concrete haunch on compacted fill. Channel to discharge into pond
6 9 mm (3/8 inch) hoop pine ply lining to ceiling over 35 x 50 mm (13/8 x 2 inch) battens at 400 mm (16 inch) centres and 35 mm (13/8 inch) extruded polystyrene insulation board to cavity
7 Pond
8 12 mm (1/2 inch) plaster with waterproof additive
9 125 mm (5 inch) thick concrete slab
10 Line of existing ground level
11 Backfill
12 Geonet drainage cell with filter fabric over
13 240 mm (91/2 inch) wide insulated masonry Hotblocs

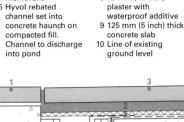

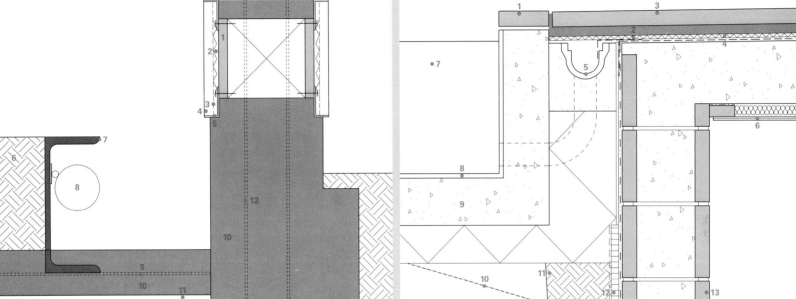

7.011
Letterbox Plan Detail 1:20

McBride Charles Ryan
The Dome House [21]

1 Copper cladding on plywood substrate
2 Timber rafters and battens above
3 Selected stone tiles on cement mortar, aluminium angles to return edges
4 Dry stacked rocks behind steel reinforcement bars at 400 mm (16 inch) grid with bars continued through centre of 140 mm (51/2 inch) reinforced blockwork
5 Steel reinforcing bars

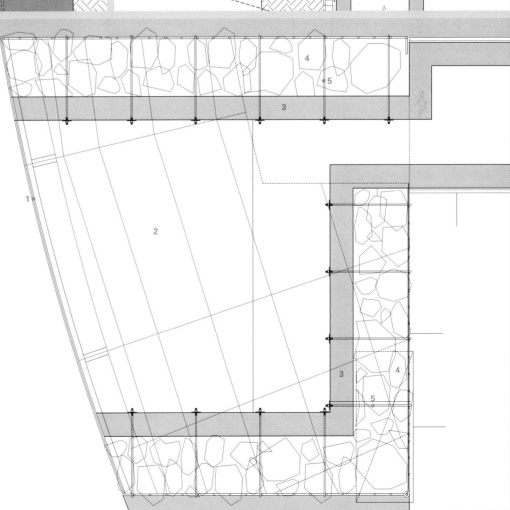

7.012
Pool Section Detail 1:10

John Onken Architects
Dolphin Cottage [32]

1 Water pump in
 inspection chamber
 with cover
2 White, smooth,
 self-coloured render
 over expanded metal
 mesh
3 Removable panel for
 access to reservoir
4 Stone capping to
 match flooring
5 100 x 50 mm (4 x 2
 inch) lintels over
 opening
6 8 mm (3/8 inch)
 shadow gap
7 Preformed 5 mm (1/5
 inch) stainless steel
 water feature
 including water
 holding chamber and
 drip spout, welded at
 edges to form single
 continuous piece
8 Stone facing to
 match floor tiles, to
 finish above water
 level
9 2 mm (1/12 inch) butyl
 pond liner laid over
 50 mm (2 inch)
 screed to lap up
 behind stone facing
10 Sand-cement screed
 to inside faces of
 pond
11 Filter to water pipe to
 pump
12 Sand-cement
 levelling screed
13 Concrete slab
14 100 mm (4 inch)
 blockwork with
 reinforcement bars
 on concrete footings
15 24 mm (1 inch) white,
 smooth, self-
 coloured render

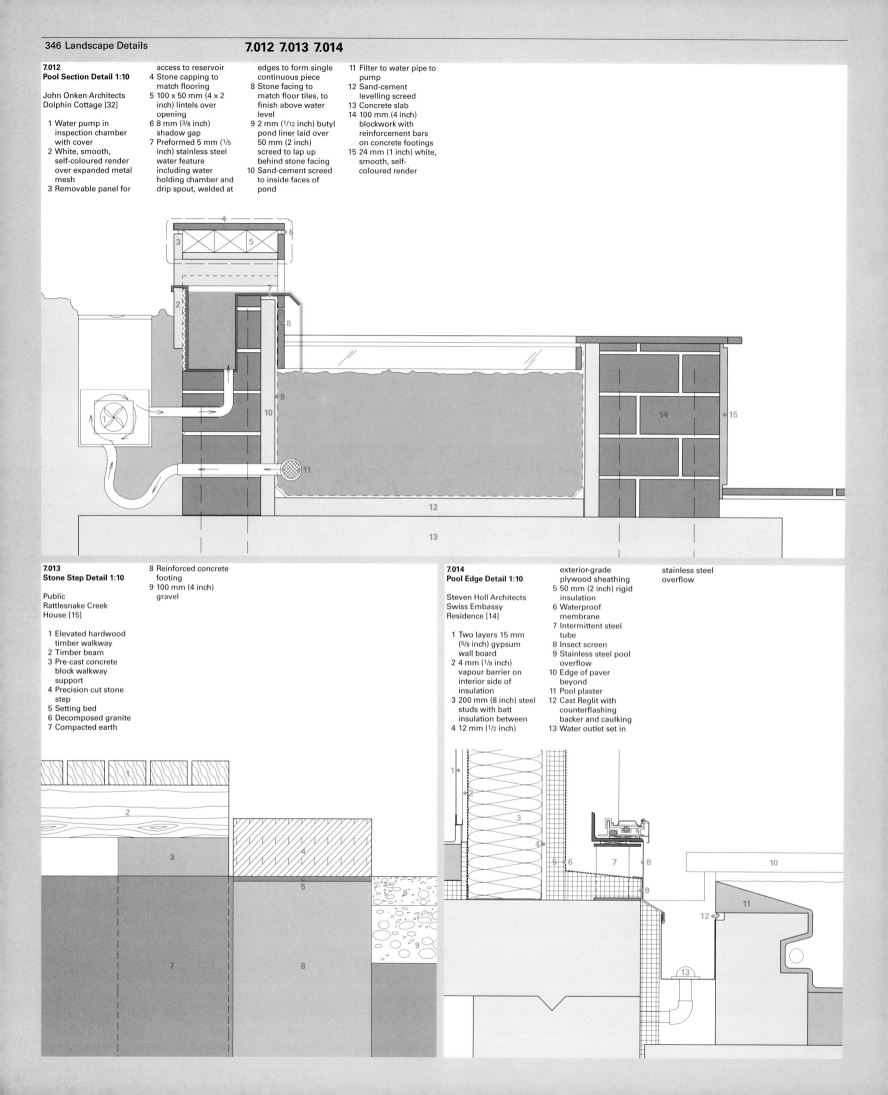

7.013
Stone Step Detail 1:10

Public
Rattlesnake Creek
House [15]

1 Elevated hardwood
 timber walkway
2 Timber beam
3 Pre-cast concrete
 block walkway
 support
4 Precision cut stone
 step
5 Setting bed
6 Decomposed granite
7 Compacted earth
8 Reinforced concrete
 footing
9 100 mm (4 inch)
 gravel

7.014
Pool Edge Detail 1:10

Steven Holl Architects
Swiss Embassy
Residence [14]

1 Two layers 15 mm
 (5/8 inch) gypsum
 wall board
2 4 mm (1/8 inch)
 vapour barrier on
 interior side of
 insulation
3 200 mm (8 inch) steel
 studs with batt
 insulation between
4 12 mm (1/2 inch)
 exterior-grade
 plywood sheathing
5 50 mm (2 inch) rigid
 insulation
6 Waterproof
 membrane
7 Intermittent steel
 tube
8 Insect screen
9 Stainless steel pool
 overflow
10 Edge of paver
 beyond
11 Pool plaster
12 Cast Reglit with
 counterflashing
 backer and caulking
13 Water outlet set in
 stainless steel
 overflow

7.015
Pond Detail 1:10

Chenchow Little
Architects
Freshwater House [32]

1 Aluminium sliding
   doors with
   aluminium section
   isolated from
   incompatible metals
2 Tiled floor
3 Mortar tiling bed
4 Aluminium door
   track and sub-sill
5 Stainless steel grate
6 Integrated drain
7 Membrane
8 Flexible joint
9 Wet edge to pond
   edge
10 Concrete slab and
   beam
11 Stainless steel pond
12 Water level not to
   exceed 300 mm (12
   inch) in depth
13 Geotextile fabric
14 Drainage cell
15 Suspended ceiling
   system
16 13 mm (1/2 inch)
   plasterboard ceiling
   with painted finish

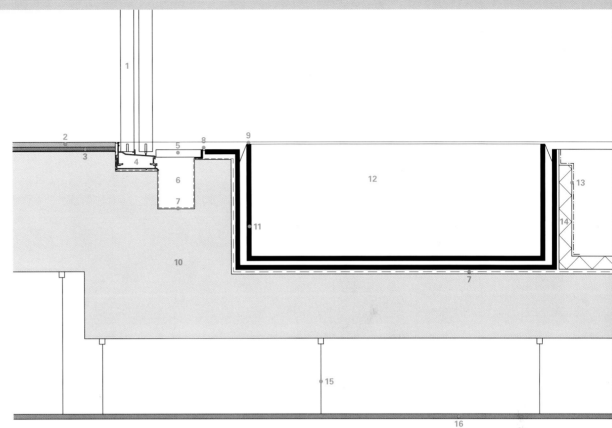

7.016
Pool Stair Detail 1:20

Hamiltons
Holmewood House [17]

1 30 mm (1 1/5 inch)
   thick limestone floor
   paving
2 100 mm (4 inch) thick
   limestone pool edge
   slab
3 Skimmer channel
   formed in concrete
   with waterproof
   lining and render
   finish
4 Carved limestone
   pool steps
5 Raising mechanism
   for pool steps
   comprised of steel
   cage with buoyancy
   tank
6 30 mm (1 1/5 inch)
   swimming pool
   render
7 Polystyrene void
   former
8 100 mm (4 inch) pool
   wall insulation
9 Drainage membrane
10 Structural concrete
   slab and tanking
11 Steel frame to allow
   pool steps to lock
   into position
12 Rendered pool floor
   finish
13 Concrete slab for
   pool

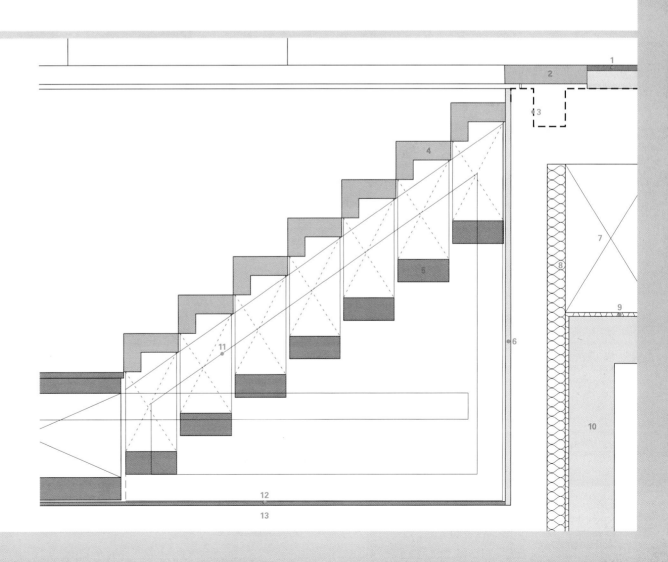

A-Piste Arkkitehdit
Villa O [39]
Year of Completion: 2007
Project Team: Jenni Hölttä, Jussi Murole
Structural Engineer: Insinööritoimisto Kimmo Kaitila
Mechanical Engineer: Lähiputkiyhtiöt
Electrical Engineer: Jama-asennus
Main Contractor: Ari Lehto

Agence Michel Tortel
Mikado House [08]
Year of Completion: 2005
Project Team: Michel Tortel
Client: Michel Tortel
Structural Engineer: CICM steel structure

Alison Brooks Architects
Herringbone Houses [33]
Year of Completion: 2006
Project Team: Alison Brooks, Michael Woodford,
Juan Francisco Rodriquez, James Taylor
Client: Alex Wingate
Structural Engineer: Price & Myers
Services Engineer: Peter Deer & Associates
Quantity Surveyor: Carruth Marshall Partnership
Main Contractor: Unimead Ltd (Phase 1),
Kaymac Construction (Phase 2)

Alphaville
Hall House 1 [07]
Year of Completion: 2006
Project Team: Kentaro Takeguchi, Asako Yamamoto
Structural Engineer: Yoshiki Mondo

Architectus
North Shore House [36]
Year of Completion: 2003
Project Team: Patrick Clifford, Malcolm Bowes, Michael
Thomson, Carsten Auer, James Mooney, Prue Fea,
Stephen Bird, Lance Adolph, Sean Kirton, John Lambert,
Juliet Pope, Rachael Rush, Raymond Soh
Structural Engineer: Thorne Dwyer Structures
Quantity Surveyor: Page Kirkland NZ
Landscape Architect: Rod Barnett

Arjaan de Feyter
Zoersel House [29]
Year of Completion: 2007
Project Team: Arjaan de Feyter

ARTEC Architekten
Holiday House [39]
Year of Completion: 2005
Project Team: Bettina Götz, Richard Manahl, Ronald
Mikolics, Helmut Lackner, Julia Beer, Lena Schacherer,
Burkhard Schelischansky
Client: Dr. Renate Balic-Benzing and Emin Balic
Structural Engineer: Peter Bauer
Services Engineer: Christian Koppensteiner Engineers
Main Contractor: Oberwart Schwarz

Atelier Tekuto + Masahiro Ikeda
Lucky Drops [13]
Year of Completion: 2005
Project Team: Shinji Haraguchi, Miki Amano
Structural Engineer: Masahiro Ikeda
Main Contractor: Kikushima Construction

Avanti Architects
Long View [35]
Year of Completion: 2006
Project Team: John Allan, Fiona Lamb, Michael Goy
Structural Engineer: Elliott Wood Partnership
Services Engineer: Martin Thomas Associates
Quantity Surveyor: Stace
Main Contractor: BWE Bauwerkserhaltung

Barclay & Crousse Architecture
Casa O [08]
Year of Completion: 2007
Project Team: Sandra Barclay, Jean Pierre Crousse,
Vhal del Solar, Martha Montalvo
Structural Engineer: Antonio Blanco Ingeniería
Electrical Engineer: Diaz Lui Ingeniería
Mechanical Engineer: Manuel Chamorro Ingeniería
Main Contractor: Eduardo Flores

Barton Myers Associates
Bekins Residence [25]
Year of Completion: 2008
Project Team: Barton Myers, Thomas Schneider, Yianna
Bouyioukou, Kengo Nozu, Heather Waters, Peter Wilson,
John Wyka
Structural Engineer: Stephen Perlof Consulting
Services Engineer: AGME
Electrical Engineer: JMPE
Civil Engineer: Penfield & Smith
Landscape Architect: Arcadia Studios
Main Contractor: Peck Homes

Bates Masi + Architects
Noyack Creek Residence [37]
Year of Completion: 2009
Project Team: Paul Masi
Client: Eric Rasmussen
Structural Engineer: Steven L. Maresca
Environmental Consultant: En-Consultants
Surveyor: Squires, Holden, Weisenbacher & Smith

Bercy Chen Studio
Peninsula House [36]
Year of Completion: 2008
Project Team: Thomas Bercy, Calvin Chen
Structural Engineer: Jerry Garcia Structures
Project Manager: Thomas Tornbjerg
Site Superintendent: Bryan Dixon

Bercy Chen Studio
Riverview Gardens [38]
Year of Completion: 2005
Project Team: Thomas Bercy, Calvin Chen
Structural Engineer: Jerry Garcia Structures
Lighting Consultant: Guenter Recht

Blank Studio
Xeros Residence [29]
Year of Completion: 2006
Project Team: Matthew Trzebiatowski
Client: Matthew and Lisa Trzebiatowski
Structural Engineer: BDA Engineers
Services Engineer: Kunka Engineering
Landscape Design: DBLD
Soil Engineer: Fugro South

BmasC Arquitectos
Mayo House [20]
Year of Completion: 2003
Client: Jose Luis Mayo, Charo Peiró
Structural Engineer: Jacinto de la Riva Gómez

Boyd Cody Architects
Richmond Place House [22]
Year of Completion: 2005
Client: Mark Harty
Structural Engineer: John Casey
Main Contractor: Joe O'Reilly Ridgeside Developments

Cassion Castle Architects
Twofold House [12]
Year of Completion: 2008
Project Team: Cassion Castle, Carl Turner, Alicja
Borkowska, Antonia Bromhead, Sean MacMahon,
Anna Tenow
Structural Engineer: Wright Consultancy Group /
Lucas Associates

Quantity Surveyor: Boyden & Co.
Main Contractor: Cassion Castle Architects

Charles Pictet Architecte
Villa in Frontenex [10]
Year of Completion: 2006
Project Team: Charles Pictet, Philippe Le Roy
Structural Engineer: Jean Regad

Chenchow Little Architects
Freshwater House [32]
Year of Completion: 2008
Project Team: Tony Chenchow, Stephanie Little,
Janice Chenchow, Jenni Dang, Angela Rowson
Client: Stefan and Janelle Williams
Structural Engineer: Benvenuti S.C.
Hydraulic Consultant: TJ Taylor Consultants
Main Contractor: Tecorp Constructions

Correia Ragazzi Arquitectos
Casa no Gerês [06]
Year of Completion: 2006
Project Team: Graça Correia, Roberto Ragazzi,
Ana Neto Vieira, Susana Silva, Telmo Gomes,
Katharina Wiederman, Pedro Gama
Client: João Telmo Monteiro, P. Ferreira
Structural Engineer: GOP
Electrical Engineer: Raul Serafim & Associados
Main Contractor: Almeidas & Magalhães

David Nossiter Architects
Kitsbury Road House [13]
Year of Completion: 2008
Client: Steve Lancefield and Louise Richardson
Structural Engineer: Hardman Structural Engineers
Main Contractor: B & T Contractors

de Blacam & Meagher Architects
Morna Valley Residence [20]
Year of Completion: 2007
Project Team: John Meagher, John Flood
Structural Engineer: Pere Roig Riera
Quantity Surveyor: de Blacam Meagher and Pander
Projects
Project Manager: Pander Projects
Main Contractor: Construcciones Collado Ballesteros

Designworkshop: SA
Igoda View House [24]
Year of Completion: 2006
Client: Diamond Igoda View
Structural Engineer: Arup
Services Engineer: Taylor & Associates Trust
Quantity Surveyor: MMPA Quantity Surveyors
Civil Engineer: Sonnekus & Toerien
Environmentalist: Carter Environmental
Landscape Architect: African Environmental Design
Main Contractor: PBC Projects

diederendirrix
Villa PPML [21]
Year of Completion: 2004
Project Team: Bert Dirrix, Karel van Eijken, Iwan
Westerveen, Marc Verhoef, Joris van der Linden
Client: Mr. P. Post and Mrs. M. van der Linden
Structural Engineer: Ingenieursbureau van de Laar
Services Engineer: Nelissen Ingenieursbureau
Landscape Architect: Buro Lubbers
Landschapsarchitectuur & Stedelijk Ontwerp
Main Contractor: Driessen Bouwbedrijf

Donovan Hill
Z House [24]
Year of Completion: 2008
Project Team: Timothy Hill, James Davidson, Michael
Hogg, Paul Jones, Anna O'Gorman, Robert Myszkowski,
Martin Arroyo, Peter Harding
Client: Stephen Zarb

Structural Engineer: TFA Project Group
Hydraulics Engineer: Steve Paul & Partners
Landscape Contractor: Steven Clegg Design
Main Contractor: James Trowse Constructions

dRMM (de Rijke Marsh Morgan Architects)
Sliding House [14]
Year of Completion: 2009
Project Team: Alex de Rijke, Joana Pestana Lages
Goncalves, Michael Spooner
Structural Engineer: Michael Hadi Associates &
Rutger Snoek
Mechanical Engineer: DJW Consulting
Electrical Engineer: Robert Hart Electrical Engineering

Ensamble Studio
Hemeroscopium House [07]
Year of Completion: 2008
Project Team: Antón García- Abril, Elena Pérez, Débora
Mesa, Marina Otero, Ricardo Sanz, Jorge Consuegra
Client: Hemeroscopium
Quantity Surveyor: Javier Cuesta
Main Contractor: Materia Inorgánica

EZZO
Leça House [35]
Year of Completion: 2008
Project Team: César Machado Moreira
Client: Filipe Holtreman Roquette
Structural Engineer: José Pedro Rocha
Services Engineer: José Pedro Rocha, SEPN
Quantity Surveyor: 10
Main Contractor: Albopiges LDA

Frank Harmon Architect
Low Country Residence [26]
Year of Completion: 2005
Project Team: Frank Harmon, Erin Sterling
Structural Engineer: 4SE Structural Engineers
Landscape Architect: Judy Harmon
Geotechnical Engineers: S+ME Geotechnical

Glas Architects
The Nail Houses [23]
Year of Completion: 2006
Project Team: Nazar Sayigh, Ed Francis, Parag Sharma
Client: Mr A. Nail
Structural Engineer: Structure Workshop
Planning Consultant: Andy Rogers

Go Hasegawa & Associates
Forest House [34]
Year of Completion: 2006
Project Team: Go Hasegawa
Structural Engineer: Kanebako Structural Engineers

Haddow Partnership
Higher Farm [17]
Year of Completion: 2008
Project Team: Robin Haddow
Client: Dr. A. Pitcher and Dr. J. Maconochie
Structural Engineer: Stephen Penfold Associates
Quantity Surveyor: Chris Newman Associates
Main Contractor: Herbert H. Drew & Sons

Hamiltons
Holmewood House [17]
Year of Completion: 2008
Project Team: Robin Partington, Niall Monaghan,
Gudrun Spitzer, Tobias Fieding-Crawley, Tim O'Rourke,
Andrew Purvis, Douglas Black
Structural Engineer: Expedition Engineering
Services Engineer: Curona Design
Quantity Surveyor: Wheeler Group
Lighting Consultant: Speirs Majors Associates
Landscape Architects: Machin Bates
Acoustics Consultant: Sandy Brown Associates
Main Contractor: John O'Neill and Partners

Hampson Williams
Glass and Timber Houses [33]
Year of Completion: 2007
Project Team: Martin Williams, Christopher Hampson,
Andrew Wood
Client: Bill and Sarah Bradley
Structural Engineer: Built
Environmental Consultants: ENG design

Hawkes Architecture
Crossway [16]
Year of Completion: 2009
Project Team: Richard Hawkes
Client: Richard and Sophie Hawkes
Structural Engineer: Scott Wilson
Services Engineer: Weald Technical Services
Sustainability Advisers: Carbon Free Group
Main Contractor: Ecolibrium Solutions

Hertl Architekten
Krammer Haus [19]
Year of Completion: 2006
Project Team: Gernot Hertl, Lothar Bauer, Astrid Meyer,
Kerstin Steininger
Client: Werner Krammer
Structural Engineer: Zeller Ingenieure

Ibarra Rosano Design Architects
Winter Residence [23]
Year of Completion: 2005
Project Team: Luis Ibarra and Teresa Rosano
Client: Jerry and Desi Winter
Structural Engineer: Oasis Engineering
Landscaping: Ibarra Landscapes
Main Contractor: Repp Design + Construction

Innovarchi
Gold Coast House [12]
Year of Completion: 2003
Project Team: Stephanie Smith, Ken McBryde, Ben
Duckworth, Jad Silvester, Guilietta Biraghi, Torben Kjaer
Client: Prudence Bowen-Lennon and Richard Lennon
Structural Engineer: Bligh Tanner
Glazing Consultant: Hyder Consulting
Main Contractor: Rick Hering

Jackson Clements Burrows Architects
Edward River House [32]
Year of Completion: 2006
Project Team: Jon Clements, Graham Burrows, Tim
Jackson, Ben Pitman
Structural Engineer: Adams Consulting Engineers
Main Contractor: Tim Nolan Constructions

Javier Artadi Arquitecto
Las Arenas Beach House [19]
Year of Completion: 2004
Project Team: Javier Artadi, Oscar Luyo, Ivan Navas
Structural Engineer: Jorge Indacochea
Electrical Engineer: Roberto Mayorga
Services Engineer: Angel Dall'Orto
Main Contractor: Justo Olivera

John Onken Architects
Dolphin Cottage [32]
Year of Completion: 2005
Project Team: John Onken, Gemma White, Jan Hoeffken
Structural Engineer: Tari Willis Associates
Project Manager: Richard Newnham
Main Contractor: John Peck Construction Limited

Johnston Marklee & Associates
Hill House [22]
Year of Completion: 2004
Project Team: Mark Lee, Sharon Johnston, Jeff Adams,
Mark Rea Baker, Diego Arraigada, Brennan Buck,
Michelle Cintron, Daveed Kapoor, Anne Rosenberg,
Anton Schneider

Client: Chan Luu
Structural Engineer: William Koh & Associates
Lighting Consultant: Dan Weinreber
Landscape Architect: Lush Life LA
Main Contractor: Hinerfeld-Ward

Jun Aoki & Associates
J House [24]
Year of Completion: 2007
Project Team: Jun Aoki, Masayuki Oishi
Structural Engineer: Kanebako Structural Engineers
Main Contractor: Eiger

Jun Igarashi Architects
Rectangle of Light [37]
Year of Completion: 2007
Structural Engineer: Daisuke Hasegawa & Partners
Main Contractor: OOOKA Industry

Kallos Turin
Casa Zorzal [10]
Year of Completion: 2008
Project Team: Stephania Kallos, Abigail Turin, Jose Luis
Ravenna, Matt Diamond, Alex Martin
Local Architects: Alvaro Perez, Vicky Alberti
Client: Obsidian Ltd UK
Structural Engineer: Alfredo Fernandez
Services Engineer: ISTEC Ingeniería
Main Contractor: Baubeta

Keith Williams Architects
The Long House [23]
Year of Completion: 2007
Project Team: Keith Williams, Richard Brown, David
Russell, Sandra Denicke, Carl Trenfield, James Davies
Structural Engineer: Techniker
Planning Consultant: Turley Associates
Quantity Surveyor: Michael F. Edwards & Associates
Main Contractor: Durkan Pudelek Limited

Kengo Kuma & Associates
Steel House [27]
Year of Completion: 2007
Structural Engineer: Ejiri Structural Engineers
Main Contractor: Eiger

Koffi & Diabaté Architectes
Villa Talon [28]
Year of Completion: 2007
Project Team: Guillaume Koffi, Issa Diabaté,
Lassina Traoré
Client: Mr. and Mrs. Talon
Structural Engineer: Boniface Mévo
Quantity Surveyor: Guillaume Djié

Kotaro Ide / ARTechnic architects
Shell House [09]
Year of Completion: 2008
Project Team: Moriyuki Fujihara, Ruri Mitsuyasu, Takashi
Mototani, Kenyu Fujii, Manami Ide
Client: Mr. Kunimoto
Structural Engineer: NAO
Electrical Engineer: EPS
Mechanical Engineer: TNA
Main Contractor: GIKAKU

Lahz Nimmo Architects
Casuarina Ultimate Beach House [31]
Year of Completion: 2001
Project Team: Annabel Lahz, Andrew Nimmo,
Peter Titmuss, Tim Horton, Marcus Trimble
Client: Don O'Rorke
Structural Engineer: Salmon McKeague Partnership
Hydraulic Consultant: James Design
Landscape Consultant: Alan Grant Landscape
Project Manager: Hutchinson Builders
Main Contractor: Hutchinson Builders

Lee + Mundwiler Architects
The Coconut House [12]
Year of Completion: 2005
Project Team: Stephan Mundwiler, Cara Lee, Hiroyuki Watanabe, Danielle Lockareff
Client: Brenda Bergman
Structural Engineer: CTW Engineers
Mechanical Engineer: Solargy Inc
Main Contractor: Niagara Construction

McBride Charles Ryan
The Dome House [21]
Year of Completion: 2005
Project Team: Rob McBride, Debbie-Lyn Ryan, Jamie McCutcheon, Lisa Cummings, Fang Cheah, Adam Pustola, Drew Williamson, Matt Borg
Client: Heather Ryan
Structural Engineer: P.J. Yttrup & Associates
Services Engineer: Scheme Group Consulting Engineers
Quantity Surveyor: Westbay Consulting Services
Main Contractor: Smart & Cain Construction

MacGabhann Architects
Tuath na Mara [14]
Year of Completion: 2007
Project Team: Tarla MacGabhann, Antoin MacGabhann, Niels Merschbrock, Barry Maguire
Client: Colm Campbell and Christine Maggs

Marlon Blackwell Architect
L-Stack House [35]
Year of Completion: 2006
Project Team: Marlon Blackwell, Meryati Johari Blackwell, Chris Baribeau, Matt Griffith, Michael Pope, Jorge Ribera
Client: Marlon and Meryati Johari Blackwell
Structural Engineer: Joe Looney
Landscape Designer: Stuart Fulbright
Lighting Designer: John Rogers Lighting Design

Marsh Cashman Koolloos Architects
Maroubra House [36]
Year of Completion: 2006
Project Team: Mark Cashman, Steve Koolloos, Michael Bucherer, Daniel Reinhardt
Structural Engineer: Simpson Design Associates
Services Engineer: John Amey & Associates
Quantity Surveyor: QS Plus
Main Contractor: DLR Enterprises

Matharoo Associates
Dilip Sanghvi Residence [07]
Year of Completion: 2007
Project Team: Gurjit Singh Matharoo, Dilip Revar, Chandan Suravarapu, Harita Salvi
Client: Dilip Sanghvi
Structural Engineer: Matharoo Associates
Mechanical Engineer: Vraj Sanitation
Services Consultant: Pankaj Dharkar & Associates
Electrical Consultant: Jhaveri Associates
Landscape Architect: Vagish Naganur
Main Contractor: RIVA Constructions & Consultancy

MELD Architecture with Vicky Thornton
House in Tarn et Garonne [34]
Year of Completion: 2008
Project Team: Vicky Thornton, Jef Smith
Structural Engineer: Arup
Main Contractor: Arpose le Grand

Morphogenesis
N85 Residence [08]
Year of Completion: 2007
Project Team: Sonali Rastogi, Vijay Dahiya, Shubra Dahiya, Sachi Gupta
Structural Engineer: Optimal
Electrical Engineer: Spectral
Landscape Architect: Morphogenesis
Main Contractor: Bhayana Builders, Vadehra Builders

Mount Fuji Architects Studio
Rainy Sunny House [11]
Year of Completion: 2008
Project Team: Masahiro Harada
Structural Engineer: Jun Sato

O'Donnell + Tuomey Architects
The Sleeping Giant – Killiney House [09]
Year of Completion: 2007
Project Team: Sheila O'Donnell, John Tuomey, Triona Stack, Susie Carson, Jitka Leonard, My Lundblad, Elizabeth Burns

ODOS Architects
House in Wicklow [18]
Year of Completion: 2008
Project Team: David O'Shea, Darrell O'Donoghue, Leighann Heron
Structural Engineer: Cora Engineers

OFIS Arhitekti
Alpine Hut [39]
Year of Completion: 2008
Project Team: Rok Oman, Spela Videcnik, Tomaz Gregoric, Andrej Gregoric, Anna Breda
Structural Engineer: Projecta
Main Contractor: P-Grad

Paulo David with Luz Ramalho
Casa Funchal [16]
Year of Completion: 2006
Project Team: Paulo David with Luz Ramalho
Structural Engineer: Mário Rui
Services Engineer: Fernando Sousa Pereira, Marco Coelho

Peter L. Gluck and Partners, Architects
Inverted Guest House [26]
Year of Completion: 2004
Project Team: Peter L. Gluck, Jennifer Bloom, Natalie Wigginton, Thomas Zoli
Structural Engineer: Silman Associates
Mechanical Engineer: Simon Rodkin

Peter Stutchbury Architecture
Avalon House [29]
Year of Completion: 2007
Project Team: Peter Stutchbury, Marika Jarv, Rachel Hudson
Structural Engineer: Simon May + Associates
Main Contractor: Builtform

Pezo von Ellrichshausen Architects
Poli House [09]
Year of Completion: 2005
Project Team: Mauricio Pezo, Sofía von Ellrichshausen
Client: Eduardo Meissner, Rosmarie Prim
Structural Engineer: Cecilia Poblete
Main Contractor: PvE

Pierre Minassian Architecte
Biscuit House [11]
Year of Completion: 2005
Project Team: Pierre Minassian
Structural Engineer: Syner Engeniere

Powerhouse Company
Villa 1 [15]
Year of Completion: 2008
Project Team: Nanne de Ru, Charles Bessard, Alexander Sverdlov, Nolly Vos, Wouter Hermanns, Bjørn Andreassen, Joe Matthiessen, Charles Bessard, Anne Luetkenhues
Structural Engineer: BREED ID
Lighting Consultant: LS2 and BEDA electro
Interior Contractor: Smeulders IG
Main Contractor: Valleibouw BV Veenendaal

Public
Rattlesnake Creek House [15]
Year of Completion: 2004
Project Team: James Brown, James Gates, Ruediger Thierhof, Steve Rosenstein, Mike Paluso, Scott Bennet
Client: Matt and Marian Maxwell
Structural Engineer: Eclipse Engineering
Services Engineer: Haynal and Company
Quantity Surveyor: Professional Consultants
Main Contractor: Nick Peschel

Robert Seymour & Associates
The Riverhouse [22]
Year of Completion: 2008
Project Team: Robert Seymour, Paul Crier, Colin Tierney, Nigel Holt, Gill Kuruber, Valerie Cornet, Mark Russell
Structural Engineer: Chris Wright Associates
Services Engineer: DCL Scott Wilson
Quantity Surveyor: Davis Langdon
Lighting Consultant: John Cullen Lighting
Main Contractor: Midas Construction

Room 11
Kingston House [34]
Year of Completion: 2006
Project Team: Aaron Roberts, Thomas Bailey
Structural Engineer: Aldanmark Engineers

Rowan Opat Architects
Courtyard House [38]
Year of Completion: 2007
Project Team: Jon Henzel, Nathan Marshall, Rowan Opat
Structural Engineer: J.V. Consulting Engineers
Sustainability Consultant: Ark Resources
Main Contractor: P.J. & O.R. Oldenburger

Safdie Rabines Architects
Artist Bridge Studio [30]
Year of Completion: 2006
Project Team: Taal Safdie, Ricardo Rabines, Charles Crawford
Client: Eleanor and David Antin
Structural Engineer: Burkett and Wong Engineers
Landscape Architect: Leslie Ryan
Lighting Consultant: Safdie Rabines Architects
Main Contractor: Cavanaugh Construction

Saunders Architecture
Villa Storingavika [40]
Year of Completion: 2007
Project Team: Todd Saunders
Client: Jan Sem Olsen, Eli Bakka, Sem Olsen
Structural Engineer: Node AS
Services Engineer: Node AS
Quantity Surveyor: Saunders Architecture
Main Contractor: Hannisdal & Søviknes

Scott Tallon Walker Architects
Fastnet House [25]
Year of Completion: 2005
Project Team: Dr. Ronald Tallon, Niall Scott, Karl Burton, Eric Trillo
Client: Greg and Anne Coughlan
Structural Engineer: Walsh and Goodfellow
Services Engineer: D & K Partnership
Quantity Surveyor: KMCS
Planning and Landscape Consultants: Cunnane Stratton Reynolds

Shuhei Endo Architect Institute
Rooftecture S [27]
Year of Completion: 2005
Project Team: Shuhei Endo, Atsuo Miyatake
Client: Ryosuke and Yasuko Uenishi
Structural Engineer: Design-Structure Laboratory

Simon Walker Architects
Dane House [06]
Year of Completion: 2003
Project Team: Simon Walker, Philip Browne, Fergal White, Miriam Delaney
Structural Engineer: E. G. Pettit & Co.
Landscape Consultants: Toby Hild, James O'Shea
Quantity Surveyor: Jim Scannell & Co.

Skene Catling de la Peña Architects
The Dairy House [31]
Year of Completion: 2006
Project Team: Charlotte Skene Catling, Jaime de la Peña, José Duran, Sam Chisholm, Tania Moreira David, Cecilia Susca, Tatiana Vela Jara
Client: Niall Hobhouse
Structural Engineer: Anthony Ward Partnership
Services Engineer: Downie Consultants
Landscape Consultant: Niall Hobhouse
Lighting Consultant: Claire Spellman
General Contractor: Paul Longpré

Stam Architecten
Two Apartments [10]
Year of Completion: 2004
Project Team: Coby Manders, Jo Van Roey
Client: Mr Verbuyst
Structural Engineer: Pyramid & Co

Steffen Leisner, Ali Jeevanjee, Phillip Trigas
1+3=1 House [17]
Year of Completion: 2006
Project Team: Steffen Leisner, Ali Jeevanjee, Phillip Trigas
Structural Engineer: Inc. & Associates, Inc
Main Contractor: CALASIA Construction

Stephenson Bell Architects
House 780 [18]
Year of Completion: 2006
Project Team: Roger Stephenson, Jeffrey Bell, Andrew Edmunds
Structural Engineer: R&D Engineering
Mechanical and Electrical Engineer: JRB Environmental Design
Quantity Surveyor: The Vinden Partnership
Main Contractor: Planetree Properties

Steven Holl Architects
Swiss Embassy Residence [14]
Year of Completion: 2006
Project Team: Steven Holl, Tim Bade, Stephen O'Dell, Olaf Schmidt, Arnault Biou, Peter Englaender, Annette Goderbauer, Li Hu, Irene Vogt, Mimi Kueh, Justin Rüssli, Andreas Gervasi, Phillip Röösli, Rafael Schnyder, Urs Zuercher
Local Architect: Rüssli Architekten
Client: Swiss Federal Office for Buildings and Logistics
Structural Engineer: A. F. & J. Steffen Consulting Engineers, Robert Silman Associates
Mechanical Engineer: B2E Consulting Engineers, B+B Energietechnik
Landscape Architect: Robert Gissinger
Interior Designer: ZedNetwork Hannes Wettstein
Main Contractor: James G. Davis Construction

Studio Bednarski
Hesmondhalgh House [33]
Year of Completion: 2007
Project Team: Cezary Bednarski
Client: Ivo Hesmondhalgh and Ann-Mari Beatty
Structural Engineer: Techniker
Services Engineer: MEC Bird Associates
Quantity Surveyor: Stuart & Duffy
Main Contractor: Diamond Construction

Studio d'ARC Architects
Live / Work Studio II [19]
Year of Completion: 2008
Project Team: Gerard Damiani, Debbie Battistone, Edward Parker
Client: Gerard Damiani & Debbie Battistone
Structural Engineer: The Kachele Group
Services Engineer: Meucci Engineering
Landscape Architect: LaQuatra Bonci Associates
Main Contractor: Smith Construction

Terry Pawson Architects
The Tall House [38]
Year of Completion: 2002
Project Team: Terry Pawson, Sean Albuquerque, Jeremy Browne, Gustav Ader, Ruth Edwards
Client: Terry & Gilly Pawson
Structural Engineer: Barton Engineers

Thaler Thaler Architekten
Z House [40]
Year of Completion: 2005
Project Team: Norbert Thaler, Ursina Thaler-Brunner
Client: Zajic Family
Main Contractor: Holzbau Themessl, Baufirma Lenz

Tham & Videgård Arkitekter
Archipelago House [40]
Year of Completion: 2006
Project Team: Bolle Tham and Martin Videgård Hansson, Lukas Thiel
Structural Engineer: Konkret
Main Contractor: NTK Bygg

The Miller Hull Partnership
Chuckanut Drive Residence [31]
Year of Completion: 2008
Structural Engineer: Perbix Bykonen
Main Contractor: Emerald Builders

TNA Architects
Stage House [28]
Year of Completion: 2007
Project Team: Makoto Takei, Chie Nabeshima
Structural Engineer: ASA
Lighting Consultant: Masahide Kakudate Lighting Architect & Associates
Main Contractor: Niitsu Gumi

Tonkin Zulaikha Greer
Hastings Parade House [26]
Year of Completion: 2007
Project Team: Tim Greer, Bettina Siegmund, Helen Hughes
Structural Engineer: Simpson Design Associates
Quantity Surveyor: QS Plus

Tony Fretton Architects
The Courtyard House [13]
Year of Completion: 2008
Project Team: Tony Fretton, Jim McKinney, Sandy Rendel, Nina Lundvall, Don Matheson, Michael Lee, Simon Jones, Martin Nassen, Don Matheson, Piram Banpabutr, Max Lacey
Structural Engineer: Dewhurst Macfarlane and Partners
Services Engineer: Mendick Waring
Quantity Surveyor: Davis Langdon
Landscape Architect: Schoenaich Landscape Architects
Lighting Designer: Isometrix
Main Contractor: R.J. Parry

Touraine Richmond Architects
One Window House [27]
Year of Completion: 2006
Project Team: Deborah Richmond, Olivier Touraine
Client: Deborah Richmond and Olivier Touraine
Structural Engineer: Gilsanz Murray Steficek
Main Contractor: Brown Oswaldsson Builders

Troppo Architects
Buttfield Town House [30]
Year of Completion: 2006
Project Team: Phil Harris, Cary Duffield, Jamie Gill, Hugh Wilkinson
Client: Ian & Barbara Buttfield
Structural Engineer: Combe Pearson Reynolds
Services Engineer: David Winch & Co.
Landscape Architect: Oxigen

Tzannes Associates
Parsley Bay Residence [21]
Year of Completion: 2006
Project Team: Phillip Rossington, Alec Tzannes, Bruce Chadlowe, Nadia Zhao, Emma Webster
Structural Engineer: Sinclair Knight Mertz
Electrical Engineer: Haron Robson
Hydraulic Engineer: Whipps Wood Consulting
Mechanical Engineer: Nappin & Partners
Quantity Surveyor: Donald Bayley & Associates
Main Contractor: Infinity Constructions

Vittorio Longheu
Casa C [16]
Year of Completion: 2004
Project Team: Vittorio Longheu, Paolo De Biasi, Francesco Durante, Elisabetta Roman, Roberto Bona, Ugo Rossi
Structural Engineer: Archingegne, Silea
Main Contractor: Cengio costruzioni

WPA
Weese Young Residence [28]
Year of Completion: 2007
Project Team: Anthony Pellecchia, Tony Goins
Client: Shirley Weese and Donald Young
Structural Engineer: Gregory P. Luth & Associates

Waro Kishi + K. Associates Architects
Hakata House [18]
Year of Completion: 2008
Project Team: Waro Kishi
Structural Engineer: Sadatosi Onimaru, Yoshiki Mondo

Welsh + Major
Pitt Street House [37]
Year of Completion: 2008
Project Team: David Welsh, Christine Major, Tim Sutherland, Shu Fun Kwan, Philip Duffy
Client: Malcolm Robinson and Sarah Ferguson
Structural Engineer: Simpson Design Associates
Heritage Consultants: Tropman and Tropman Architects, B Cubed Sustainability

Western Design Architects
The Moat House [20]
Year of Completion: 2007
Project Team: Phil Easton, Matthew Haley, Steven Lawrence
Client: Mr. & Mrs. Taylor
Structural Engineer: RQ5 Structural Consultancy
Services Engineer: Kensa Engineering

Page / Architect / Photo Credit

6 Simon Walker Architects / © Sue Barr / VIEW
Correia Ragazzi Arquitectos / © Juan Rodriguez
7 Alphaville / © Edmund Sumner/VIEW
Matharoo Associates / © Dinesh Mehta
Ensamble Studio / Courtesy Ensamble Studio
8 Agence Michel Tortel / © Arnaud Rinuccini
Morphogenesis / © Edmund Sumner/VIEW
Barclay & Crousse Architecture / © Jean Pierre
Crousse
9 Pezo von Ellrichshausen Architects / © Cristobal
Palma Photography
Kotaro Ide/ARTechnic architects / © Hiroyasu
Sakaguchi
O'Donnell + Tuomey Architects / © Dennis Gilbert /
VIEW
10 Stam Architecten / © Toon Grobet
Kallos Turin / © Dennis Gilbert / VIEW
Charles Pictet Architecte / © Francesca Giovanelli
11 Mount Fuji Architects Studio / © Ryota Atarashi
Pierre Minassian Architect / © Erick Saillet
12 Lee + Mundwiler Architects / © Juergen Nogai + ©
Julius Shulman
Innovarchi / © Jon Linkins
Cassion Castle Architects / © Keith Collie
13 David Nossiter Architects / © Steve Lancefield
Tony Fretton Architects / © Helene Binet
Atelier Tekuto + Masahiro Ikeda / © Makoto Yoshida
14 Steven Holl Architects / © Andy Ryan
dRMM (de Rijke Marsh Morgan Architects) / © Alex
de Rijke
MacGabhann Architects / © Dennis Gilbert / VIEW
15 Powerhouse Company / © Jeroen Musch
Public / © David Harrison/Harrison Photographic
16 Vittorio Longheu / Courtesy Vittorio Longheu
Architects
Hawkes Architecture / © James Brittain/VIEW
Paulo David with Luz Ramalho / © Leonardo Finotti
17 Haddow Partnership / © SelfBuild and Design
Magazine
Steffen Leisner, Ali Jeevanjee, Phillip Trigas / ©
Christopher Culliton
Hamiltons / © Will Pryce
18 Stephenson Bell Architects / © Daniel Hopkinson
Waro Kishi, K-Associates Architects / © Hiroshi
Ueda
ODOS Architects / © Ros Kavanagh
19 Hertl Architekten / © Paul Ott
Javier Artadi Arquitecto / © Alexander Kornhuber
Studio d'ARC Architects / © Ed Massery
Photography, Inc
20 BmasC / © Angel Baltanas
Western Design Architects / © Peter Booton
de Blacam and Meagher Architects / © Peter Cook /
VIEW
21 McBride Charles Ryan / © John Gollings
Tzannes Associates / © John Gollings
diederendirrix / © Constantin Meyer
22 Boyd Cody Architects / © Paul Tierney
Robert Seymour & Associates / Courtesy Robert
Seymour & Associates Ltd
22 Johnston Marklee & Associates / © Eric
Staudenmaier + © Julius Shulman
23 Keith Williams Architects / © Helene Binet
Glas Architects / © Hufton&Crow /
VIEW
Ibarra Rosano Design Architects / © Bill Timmerman
24 Donovan Hill / © Jon Linkins
Designworkshop:SA / © Dennis Gilbert / VIEW
Jun Aoki & Associates / © Daici Ano / FWD Inc.
25 Barton Myers Associates / © Ciro Coelho
Scott Tallon Walker Architects / © Dennis Gilbert /
VIEW
26 Tonkin Zulaikha Greer / © Michael Nicholson
Peter L. Gluck and Partners, Architects / © Paul
Warchol Photography
Frank Harmon Architect / © Richard Leo Johnson/
AtlanticArchives, Inc.

27 Touraine Richmond Architects / © Benny Chan
Shuhei Endo Architect Institute / © Edmund
Sumner / VIEW
Kengo Kuma & Associates / © Edmund Sumner /
VIEW
28 TNA Architects / © Edmund Sumner / VIEW
Koffi & Diabaté Architectes / © James Brittain / VIEW
WPA / © Langdon Clay
29 Blank Studio / © Bill Timmerman
Aarjan de Feyter / © Toon Grobet
Peter Stutchbury Architecture / © Michael Nicholson
30 Safdie Rabines Architects / © Undine Pröhl
Troppo Architects / © Randy Larcombe
31 Lahz Nimmo Architects / © Brett Boardman
Photography
Skene Catling de la Peña Architects / © James
Morris
The Miller Hull Partnership / © Benjamin
Benschneider
32 John Onken Architects / © Edmund
Sumner/VIEW
Jackson Clements Burrows Architects / © Jon
Clements
Chenchow Little Architects / © John Gollings
33 Hampson Williams / © Timothy Soar
Alison Brooks Architects / © Cristobal Palma
Photography
Studio Bednarski / © Jasiek & Cezary M. Bedarski
34 MELD Architecture / © Tim Crocker / www.
timcrocker.co.uk
Go Hasegawa & Associates / © Shinkenchiku-sha
Room 11 / © Jasmin Latona
35 EZZO / Mariana Themudo / JFF
Avanti Architects / © Nick Kane
Marlon Blackwell Architect / © Timothy Hursley
36 Marsh Cashman Koolloos Architects / © Shannon
McGrath
Architectus / © Patrick Reynolds Photography Ltd
Bercy Chen Studio / Ryan Michael
Welsh + Major / © Brett Boardman Photography
37 Bates Masi + Architects / Courtesy Bates Masi
Architects
Jun Igarashi Architects / Courtesy Jun Igarashi
Architects Inc.
38 Bercy Chen Studio / Ryan Michael
Rowan Opat Architects / © Peter Bennetts
Terry Pawson Architects / © Richard Bryant/
arcaid.co.uk
39 OFIS Arhitekti / © Tomaz Gregoric
ARTEC Architekten / Courtesy Artec Architekten
A-Piste Arkkitehdit / © Rauno Träskelin
40 Thaler Thaler Architekten / © Rupert Steiner
Tham & Videgård Arkitekter / © Åke E:son Lindman
Saunders Architecture / © Michael Perlmutter
Architectural Photography

All architectural drawings are supplied courtesy of the
architects

Acknowledgments

Thanks above all to the architects who submitted
material for this book. Special thanks to Hamish Muir,
for the superb design, to Sophia Gibb for her
indomitable dedication in researching the pictures and
to Mr. Laurence King for waiting patiently for this book
to come to fruition. Sincere thanks also to Philip Cooper
and Gaynor Sermon at Laurence King, to Justin Fletcher
for editing the drawings, to Vic Brand for his technical
expertise and for wrangling with the drawings, to Vimbai
Shire for her perseverance and patient research and to
Emily Asquith for taking on the proof reading challenge.
And finally, special thanks to Sharon Francis, Bill Dowzer
and Phoebe Francis-Dowzer.

About the CD

The attached CD can be read on both Windows and
Macintosh computers. All the material on the CD is
copyright protected and is for private use only. All
drawings in the book and on the CD were specially
created for this publication and are based on the
architects' original designs.

The CD includes files for all of the drawings included in
the book. The drawings for each building are contained
in a numbered folder. They are supplied in two versions:
the files with the suffix '.eps' are 'vector' Illustrator EPS
files but can be opened using other graphics programs
such as Photoshop; all the files with the suffix '.dwg' are
generic CAD format files and can be opened in a variety
of CAD programs.

Each file is numbered according to its location in the
book: the first number refers to the chapter (1 for Walls,
2 for Floors, etc.); the second number refers to the
location of the detail within the chapter, and the final
number refers to the scale. Hence, '01_001_10.eps'
would be the eps version of the first drawing in the first
chapter and has a scale of 1:10.

The generic '.dwg' file format does not support 'solid fill'
utilized by many architectural CAD programs. All the
information is embedded within the file and can be
reinstated within supporting CAD programs. Select the
polygon required and change the 'Attributes' to 'Solid',
and the colour information can be automatically
retrieved. To reinstate the 'Walls'; select all objects
within the 'Walls' layer/class and amend their 'Attributes'
to 'Solid'.